THE PAPERS OF
BENJAMIN FRANKLIN

SPONSORED BY

*The American Philosophical Society
and Yale University*

Benjamin Franklin. Mezzotint by Edward Fisher after Mason Chamberlain

THE PAPERS OF

Benjamin Franklin

VOLUME 10   *January 1, 1762, through December 31, 1763*

LEONARD W. LABAREE, *Editor*

Helen C. Boatfield, Helene H. Fineman, and

James H. Hutson, Assistant Editors

New Haven and London YALE UNIVERSITY PRESS, 1966

Designed by Alvin Eisenman and Walter Howe,
and printed in the United States of America
at The Lakeside Press,
R. R. Donnelley & Sons Company, Chicago, Illinois,
and Crawfordsville, Indiana.

Library of Congress catalogue number: 59–12697

51023

Contents

CONTENTS

CONTENTS

CONTENTS

List of Illustrations

Benjamin Franklin. Mezzotint by Edward Fisher after
Mason Chamberlain   *Frontispiece*

Shortly before Franklin left London for Philadelphia in 1762 his Virginia friend Philip Ludwell asked him to sit for a portrait by a painter of Ludwell's choosing. The artist was Mason Chamberlain (d. 1787), "a solid sort of limner with a reputation for accurate likenesses." The original of this portrait is now in the possession of Wharton Sinkler of Philadelphia. Later in 1762 or during the next year, an Irishborn engraver and "competent craftsman," Edward Fisher (1730–1785), made a mezzotint. This print competed for popularity with the one James McArdell had engraved in 1761 from the Benjamin Wilson portrait (above, IX, frontispiece) and seems to have attained greater success. Even before seeing it, William Franklin ordered a hundred of the prints, in part at least as a commercial venture, and in 1764 his father sent eighteen to New England for distribution as gifts to friends and relatives. Franklin to William Franklin, April 20, 1771; to Jonathan Williams, Feb. 24, 1764 (both in APS); and to Ezra Stiles, June 19, 1764 (Yale Univ. Lib.). The bells supported on wires, at which Franklin is looking, represent those he installed in his home in September 1752 to signal the presence of electricity in the atmosphere. He wrote Deborah in 1758 that, if they frightened her, she could prevent their ringing by connecting the bells with a piece of wire "and that will conduct the lightning without ringing or snapping, but silently." Above, V, 69–71; VIII, 94. Charles Coleman Sellers, *Benjamin Franklin in Portraiture* (New Haven and London, 1962), pp. 56–60, 218–21. Reproduced by courtesy of the Yale University Library.

Lord Charles Cavendish's Electrical Experiment   43

The conditions under which glass might become permeable to electricity had become a matter of interest to experimenters and had occasioned a good deal of discussion among them (e.g., above, IV, 25–34, 426; VI, 98; IX, 240, 243 n, 283–4). In quoting to Ebenezer Kinnersley a report of the experiment devised by Lord Charles Cavendish, Franklin apparently included a sketch of the apparatus used. The original sketch has not survived, but an engraved version, reproduced here, appears with the printed text of Franklin's letter to Kinnersley in *Experiments and Observations on Electricity* (London, 1769), facing p. 403.

Map of De Fonte's Purported Discoveries   86

To support and explain his defense of the validity of Bartholomew de Fonte's alleged water-borne journey across Canada in 1640, Franklin enclosed to Pringle a marked copy of a map which Thomas Jefferys had adapted from Joseph-Nicholas Delisle and had included in his 1761 translation of Gerhard F. Müller's *Voyages from Asia to America, For Completing the Discoveries of the North West Coast of America.* Franklin drew "two crooked red Lines" on the map as a correction to show where he believed "the strait Ronquillo" ought to have been placed to connect "L. De Fonte or Mishinipi" with Hudson Bay. These lines can be seen to the west of the "H" of the lettering "Hudsons Bay." The map is attached to the last page of the letter to Pringle, now in the deCoppet Collection of the Princeton University Library, and is reproduced here by courtesy of the Library.

Sketch of a Device for Skeining Worsted   109

This drawing appears on the third page of the draft of a letter to Mary Stevenson along with memoranda of people to see and things to be bought before Franklin left London for Philadelphia. It is clear that the sketch has nothing to do with the subject matter of the letter or, so far as can be determined, with the purpose of any of the errands he planned to perform at that time. Nothing has been found among his other papers to explain the device or to indicate when he used this blank part of a sheet of paper to make the sketch. It is reproduced here simply as an addition to the other documentation of Franklin's wide-ranging interest in the practical arts of his time, and with the hope that some reader of this volume will be able to establish its particular significance. Reproduced by courtesy of the Library of Congress.

Franklin's Glass Armonica   121

In describing his new musical instrument to Beccaria in 1762 Franklin seems to have sent as illustration only a sketch of one of the glass hemispheres, but no picture of the complete armonica. Ten years later, however, when Jacques Barbeu Dubourg was preparing a French edition of Franklin's works, the inventor sent the editor, Dec. 8, 1772, a somewhat fuller explanation of some details of the construction and added that he was having an engraving made and hoped to send it soon. Dubourg included it in *Oeuvres de M. Franklin, Docteur ès Loix*

Contributors to Volume 10

The ownership of each manuscript, or the location of the particular copy used by the editors of each contemporary pamphlet or similar printed work, is indicated where the document appears in the text. The sponsors and editors are deeply grateful to the following institutions and individuals for permission to print in the present volume manuscripts or other materials which they own:

INSTITUTIONS

American Philosophical Society
Assay Office, Birmingham, England
British Museum
Columbia University Library
Dartmouth College Library
Franklin Institute of the State of Pennsylvania
Harvard College Library
Historical Society of Pennsylvania
Henry E. Huntington Library and Art Gallery
Universitätsbibliothek, Leipzig
Library Company of Philadelphia
Library of Congress
The London Hospital
Maine Historical Society
Massachusetts Historical Society
Morristown National Historical Park
New Haven Colony Historical Society

New Jersey Historical Society
New-York Historical Society
New York Public Library
University Archives, Oxford University
University of Pennsylvania Library
Trustees of the University of Pennsylvania
Department of Records, Recorder of Deeds, Philadelphia
Pierpont Morgan Library
Princeton University Library
Redwood Library and Athenaeum, Newport
Royal Archives, Windsor Castle
The Royal Society, London
Royal Society of Arts
Royal Society of Edinburgh
Rutgers University Library
Scottish Record Office
Westchester (Pennsylvania) State Teachers College
Yale University Library

INDIVIDUALS

Miss Mary A. Benjamin, New York City
Mrs. Daniel Buckley, Broadaxe, Pennsylvania

Henry N. Haiken, New York City
Mrs. George S. Maywood, Garden City, New York

Method of Textual Reproduction

An extended statement of the principles of selection, arrangement, form of presentation, and method of textual reproduction observed in this edition appears in the Introduction to the first volume, pp. xxxiv-xlvii. A condensation and revision of the portion relating to the method of reproducing the texts follows here.

Printed Material:

In general Franklin's writings printed under his direction should be regarded as his ultimate intention and should therefore be reproduced without change, except as modern typography requires. In fact, however, newspapers and pamphlets were often set by two or more journeymen with different notions of spelling, capitalization, and punctuation. Although the resulting inconsistencies and errors did not represent Franklin's intentions, they are not eliminated by the editors. Again, in cases where Franklin's writings were printed by another, they were sometimes carelessly or willfully revised without his consent. He once complained, for example, that an English printer had so corrected and excised one of his papers "that it can neither scratch nor bite. It seems only to paw and mumble."[1] What was thus printed was obviously not what Franklin wrote, but, in the absence of his manuscript, the editors have no alternative but to reprint it as it stands. Still other Franklin letters are known only in nineteenth-century printings, vigorously edited by William Temple Franklin, Duane, or Sparks. Here, too, the editors follow the texts as printed, only noting obvious misreadings.

In reproducing printed materials, the following general rules are observed:

1. The place and date of composition of letters are set at the top, regardless of their location in the original printing.

2. Proper nouns, including personal names, which were often printed in italics, are set in roman, except when the original was italicized for emphasis.

---

1. BF to William Franklin, Jan. 9, 1768.

3. Prefaces and other long passages, though italicized in the original, are set in roman. Long italicized quotations are set in roman within quotation marks.

4. Words in full capitals are set in small capitals, with initial letters in full capitals if required by Franklin's normal usage.

5. All signatures are set in capitals and small capitals.

6. Obvious typographical errors are silently corrected. An omitted parenthesis or quotation mark, for example, is inserted when the other of the pair was printed.

7. Every sentence is closed with a period or other appropriate mark of punctuation (usually a question mark).

8. Longhand insertions in the blanks of printed forms are set in italics, with space before and after.

Manuscript Material:

a. *Letters* are presented in the following form:

1. The place and date of composition are set at the top, regardless of their location in the original.

2. The complimentary close is set continuously with the text.

3. Addresses, endorsements, and docketing are so labeled and printed at the end of the letter.

b. *Spelling* of the original is retained. When, however, it is so abnormal as to obscure meaning, the correct form is supplied in brackets or footnote, as: "yf [wife]."

c. *Capitalization* has been retained as written, except that every sentence is made to begin with a capital. When there is doubt whether a letter is a capital, it is printed as like letters are in the same manuscript, or, that guide failing, as modern usage directs.

d. Words underlined once in the manuscript are printed in *italics;* words underlined twice or written in large letters or full capitals are printed in SMALL CAPITALS.

e. *Punctuation* has been retained as in the original, except:

1. Every sentence ends with a period or other appropriate mark (usually a question mark), unless it is not clear where the sentence ends, when the original punctuation (or lack of it) is preserved.

2. Dashes used in place of commas, semicolons, colons, or periods are replaced by the appropriate marks; and when a sentence ends with both a dash and a period, the dash is omitted.

3. Commas scattered meaninglessly through a manuscript are eliminated.

4. When a mark of punctuation is not clear or can be read as one of two marks, modern usage is followed.[2]

5. Some documents, especially those of a legal character, lack all punctuation. This is supplied with restraint, and the fact indicated in a footnote. In some other, inadequately punctuated documents, it is silently added when needed for clarity, as in a long series of names.

f. *Contractions and abbreviations* in general are expanded except in proper names. The ampersand is rendered as "and," except in the names of business firms, in the form "&c.," and in a few other cases. Letters represented by the thorn or tilde are printed. The tailed "p" is spelled out as per, pre, or pro. Symbols of weights, measures, and monetary values follow modern usage, as: £34. Superscript letters are lowered. Abbreviations in current use are retained, as: Col., Dr., N.Y., i.e.

g. *Omitted or illegible words or letters* are treated as follows:

1. If not more than four letters are missing, they are silently supplied when there is no doubt what they should be.

2. The omission of more than four letters or one or more words is supplied conjecturally within brackets. The addition of a question mark within the brackets indicates uncertainty as to the conjecture.

3. Other omissions are shown as follows: [*illegible*], [*torn*], [*remainder missing*], or the like.

4. Missing or illegible digits are indicated by suspension points in brackets, the number of points corresponding to the estimated number of missing figures.

5. Blanks spaces are left as blanks.

2. The typescripts from which these papers are printed have been made from photocopies of the manuscripts, and marks of punctuation are sometimes blurred or lost in photography. It has often been impossible to consult the originals in these cases.

h. *Author's additions and corrections:*

1. Interlineations and brief marginal notes are brought into the text without comment. Longer notes are brought into the text with the notation [*in the margin*].

2. Author's footnotes are printed at the bottom of the appropriate pages between the text and any editorial footnotes.

3. Canceled words and phrases are in general omitted without notice; if significant, they are printed in footnotes. The canceled passages of important documents, such as drafts of treaties, are brought into the text enclosed in angle brackets *before* the words substituted.

4. When alternative words and phrases have been inserted in a manuscript but the original remains uncanceled, the alternatives are given in brackets, preceded by explanatory words in italics, as: "it is [*written above:* may be] true."

5. Variant readings of several versions are noted if important.

Abbreviations and Short Titles

Acts Privy Coun., Col.	W. L. Grant and James Munro, eds., *Acts of the Privy Council of England, Colonial Series, 1613–1783* (6 vols., London, 1908–12).
ADS	Autograph document signed.[1]
ALS	Autograph letter signed.
APS	American Philosophical Society.
Autobiog. (APS-Yale edit.)	Leonard W. Labaree, Ralph L. Ketcham, Helen C. Boatfield, Helene H. Fineman, eds., *The Autobiography of Benjamin Franklin* (New Haven, 1964).
BF	Benjamin Franklin
Bigelow, *Works*	John Bigelow, ed., *The Complete Works of Benjamin Franklin* . . . (10 vols., N.Y., 1887–88).
Board of Trade Journal	*Journal of the Commissioners for Trade and Plantations . . . April 1704 to . . . May 1782* (14 vols., London, 1920–38).
Cohen, *BF's Experiments*	I. Bernard Cohen, ed., *Benjamin Franklin's Experiments. A New Edition of Franklin's Experiments and Observations on Electricity* (Cambridge, Mass., 1941).
Colden Paps.	*The Letters and Papers of Cadwallader Colden.* New-York Historical Society *Collections* for 1917–23, 1934, 1935.
DAB	*Dictionary of American Biography.*
Darlington, *Memorials*	William Darlington, *Memorials of John Bartram and Humphrey Marshall* (Phila., 1849).
Dexter, *Biog. Sketches*	Franklin B. Dexter, *Biographical Sketches of the Graduates of Yale College* . . . (6 vols., N.Y. and New Haven, 1885–1912).
DF	Deborah Franklin

1. For definitions of this and other kinds of manuscripts, see above, I, xliv-xlvii.

DNB	*Dictionary of National Biography.*
DS	Document signed.
Duane, *Works*	William Duane, ed., *The Works of Dr. Benjamin Franklin . . .* (6 vols., Phila., 1808–18). Title varies in the several volumes.
Evans	Charles Evans, *American Bibliography* (14 vols., Chicago and Worcester, Mass., 1903–59). Surviving imprints are reproduced in full in microprint in Clifford K. Shipton, ed., *Early American Imprints, 1639–1800* (microprint, Worcester, Mass.).
Exper. and Obser.	*Experiments and Observations on Electricity, made at Philadelphia in America, by Mr. Benjamin Franklin, . . .* (London, 1751). Revised and enlarged editions were published in 1754, 1760, 1769, and 1774 with slightly varying titles. In each case the edition cited will be indicated, e.g., *Exper. and Obser.*, 1751 edit.
Gipson, *British Empire*	Lawrence H. Gipson, *The British Empire before the American Revolution* (12 vols., to date: Vols. 1–3, Caldwell, Idaho, 1936; Vols. 4–12, N.Y., 1939–65; Vols. 1–3, revised edit., N.Y., 1958–60).
Lib. Co. Phila.	Library Company of Philadelphia.
LS	Letter signed.
Montgomery, *Hist. Univ. Pa.*	Thomas H. Montgomery, *A History of the University of Pennsylvania from Its Foundation to A.D. 1770* (Phila., 1900).
MS, MSS	Manuscript, manuscripts.
Namier and Brooke, *House of Commons*	Sir Lewis Namier and John Brooke, *The History of Parliament. The House of Commons 1754–1790* (3 vols., London and N.Y., 1964).
N.J. Arch.	William A. Whitehead and others, eds., *Archives of the State of New Jersey* (2 series, Newark and elsewhere, 1880–).

	Editors, subtitles, and places of publication vary.
N.Y. Col. Docs.	E. B. O'Callaghan, ed., *Documents relative to the Colonial History of the State of New York* (15 vols., Albany, 1853–87).
Pa. Arch.	Samuel Hazard and others, eds., *Pennsylvania Archives* (9 series, Phila. and Harrisburg, 1852–1935).
Pa. Col. Recs.	*Minutes of the Provincial Council of Pennsylvania* . . . (16 vols., Phila., 1838–53). Title changes with Volume 11 to *Supreme Executive Council.*
Pa. Gaz.	*The Pennsylvania Gazette.*
Pa. Jour.	*The Pennsylvania Journal.*
Phil. Trans.	The Royal Society, *Philosophical Transactions.*
PMHB	*Pennsylvania Magazine of History and Biography.*
Sibley's Harvard Graduates	John L. Sibley, *Biographical Sketches of Graduates of Harvard University* (Cambridge, Mass., 1873–). Continued from Volume 4 by Clifford K. Shipton.
Smyth, *Writings*	Albert H. Smyth, ed., *The Writings of Benjamin Franklin* . . . (10 vols., N.Y., 1905–07).
Sparks, *Works*	Jared Sparks, ed., *The Works of Benjamin Franklin* . . . (10 vols., Boston, 1836–40).
Statutes at Large, Pa.	*The Statutes at Large of Pennsylvania from 1682 to 1801, Compiled under the Authority of the Act of May 19, 1887* . . . (Vols. 2–16, [Harrisburg], 1896–1911). Volume 1 was never published.
Van Doren, *Franklin*	Carl Van Doren, *Benjamin Franklin* (N.Y., 1938).
Van Doren, *Franklin-Mecom*	Carl Van Doren, ed., *The Letters of Benjamin Franklin & Jane Mecom* (Memoirs of the American Philosophical Society, XXVII, Princeton, 1950).

Van Doren and Boyd, *Indian Treaties*	Carl Van Doren and Julian P. Boyd, eds., *Indian Treaties Printed by Benjamin Franklin 1736–1762* (Phila., 1938).
Votes	*Votes and Proceedings of the House of Representatives of the Province of Pennsylvania, Met at Philadelphia . . . 1750, and continued by Adjournments* (Phila., 1751–). Each annual collection of the journals of separate sittings is designated by the year for which that House was elected, e.g., *Votes,* 1750–51.
WF	William Franklin
WTF, *Memoirs*	William Temple Franklin, ed., *Memoirs of the Life and Writings of Benjamin Franklin, LL.D., F.R.S., &c. . . .* (3 vols., 4to, London, 1817–18).

Genealogical references. An editorial reference to one of Benjamin Franklin's relatives may be accompanied by a citation of the symbol assigned to that person in the genealogical tables and charts in volume I of this work, pp. xlix-lxxvii, as, for example: Thomas Franklin (A.5.2.1), Benjamin Mecom (C.17.3), or Benjamin Franklin Bache (D.3.1). These symbols begin with the letter A, B, C, or D. Similarly, a reference to one of Deborah Franklin's relatives may be accompanied by a symbol beginning with the letter E or F, as, for example, John Tiler (E.1.1.2), or Mary Leacock Hall (F.2.2.3). Such persons may be further identified by reference to the charts of the White and Cash families printed in VIII, 139–42.

Chronology

January 1, 1762, through December 31, 1763

1762

February 12: BF's broker sells the last of the stock in which he had invested Pennsylvania's share of the parliamentary grant. The net loss is a little less than £4000 sterling.

April 30: Oxford University confers on BF the honorary degree of Doctor of Civil Law; WF receives the degree of Master of Arts at the same ceremony.

July 13: BF sends Beccaria a detailed description of his recently invented musical instrument, the armonica, which attains great popularity in the following years.

August 8–10: BF leaves London for Portsmouth to embark.

August 23 or 24: BF sails from Portsmouth on board the *Carolina* under convoy of H.M.S. *Scarborough;* stops at Madeira for three days en route.

September 4: WF marries Elizabeth Downes at St. George's Church, Hanover Square.

September 9: WF commissioned governor of New Jersey.

November 1: BF arrives in Philadelphia.

November 3: Preliminary treaty of peace between Great Britain and France and Spain signed at Fontainebleau.

November 20: WF and wife sail from Portsmouth for America.

1763

January 11: The day after the Assembly convenes BF, who had been reelected in October, qualifies as a member.

February 10: Definitive treaty of peace between Great Britain and France and Spain signed at Paris; Portuguese ambassador accedes the same day.

February 19: WF and wife arrive in Philadelphia after a stormy voyage; because of ice in Delaware Bay they travel overland from Lewes, Delaware.

xxviii

February 23–March 3: BF accompanies his son to New Jersey where WF assumes office as governor.

March 16: BF receives £2214 10s. 7d. in payment of services as agent in England since 1757.

March 31: BF receives from the speaker the formal thanks of the Assembly for his services as agent.

April 6: BF makes first payment to builder for a new house to be erected on his Market St. land.

April 17?–May 16?: BF on a trip to Virginia on post-office business; his new associate, John Foxcroft, returns to Philadelphia with him.

May 9: Pontiac attacks British fort at Detroit, launching the Indian uprising; hostilities spread to western Pennsylvania before the end of May.

June 7–November 5: BF and Foxcroft, accompanied by Sarah Franklin, on an extended journey through New Jersey, New York, and New England, inspecting post offices. They travel as far as Portsmouth, N.H., between which town and Boston BF suffers the second of two falls, dislocating his shoulder and forcing a long stay in Boston for recovery. For detailed itinerary, see below, pp. 277–9.

November 8: BF meets for the first time with other provincial commissioners to sign pay orders for defense, he having been named to this position by a Supply Act passed October 22, during his absence.

December 14: A body of armed men (the "Paxton Boys") attacks a village of friendly Indians on Conestoga Manor in Lancaster County, killing and scalping the six Indians they find there.

December 27: The surviving fourteen Indians of the village, having been removed to the town of Lancaster and placed in the workhouse for safety, are again attacked and all are massacred.

THE PAPERS OF
BENJAMIN FRANKLIN

VOLUME 10

January 1, 1762, through December 31, 1763

From Sargent Aufrere & Co.[1]

ALS and copy: Historical Society of Pennsylvania

I.N.[2]

Dear sir,   Mincing Lane 8 Jany 1762.

Mr. Barclay is not come to Town yet, and it is uncertain whether we may be able to confer with him, and give you the result time enough for your writing by this packet, we will therefore take our own Resolution, and undertake to pay, ourselves, what part of the Colony's drafts on you (by means of the deficiency of the Stock) you shall not have wherewithall to discharge[3]—there needs no more than the reason of the Thing to justifye it, you'll be so kind to explain our Motives for doing it, and to let the Assembly know it was your advice to us, which we think Ourselves obliged to conform to: We make no doubt but that Mr. Barclay will readily concur with us when the Business is imparted to him.[4]

You'll be pleased to give us notice in due time of all the necessary particulars of such bills as you may refer to us for Payment. We return you the Letters you favour'd us with the Perusal of, much obliged to you for the friendly Offices that gave occasion to the mention of us in Them.[5] We think ourselves much honour'd by the

1. John Sargent and George Aufrere (above, IX, 359 n) had been appointed, along with John and David Barclay (above, IX, 190–1 n), by an act of the Pa. Assembly, Sept. 26, 1761, to receive the province's share of the parliamentary grant for the campaign of 1759 and to deposit it in the Bank of England. *Statutes at Large, Pa.*, VI, 114–18. It is not certain which of the Barclays is referred to in the first paragraph below.

2. This letter and nearly all those which follow relating to the parliamentary grant for the campaign of 1758 bear these initials, showing that they ultimately found their way into Isaac Norris' files. The "I.N." will not hereafter be explained in each instance.

3. For the Assembly's order to the trustees of the Provincial Loan Office to draw on BF for the province's share of the parliamentary grant for 1758, see above, IX, 358. For BF's sale of stocks, in which he had invested the grant, to pay the trustees' drafts, see above, IX, 392, and below, p. 34.

4. BF had proposed that Sargent Aufrere and the Barclays use the parliamentary grant for 1759 to pay the drafts which the proceeds from his sales of stock could not cover. The Barclays, at Thomas Penn's direction, refused to join the scheme. See below, pp. 4, 7–8.

5. BF's letters, in which he apparently recommended that the Assembly appoint Sargent Aufrere to receive the parliamentary grant for 1759 have not been found. Possibly also, letters from the Assembly committee or trustees of the Loan Office (not found) approving his suggestion.

3

Colonys Employ of us and shall be glad on any Occasion to shew our true Zeal for its Interests. The Act of Assembly[6] as it may be of some use to us, we take the Liberty of keeping, till we have the pleasure of seeing you next, which we hope will be soon. We remain with perfect Regard, Dear sir, Your most obedient Servants

SARGENT AUFRERE & CO.

directed. To Benja Franklin Esqr In Craven Street—Strand.

Endorsed: London Janry. 8. 1762 John Sargent & Compa. to Benja Franklin

To Sargent Aufrere & Co.

Two copies: Historical Society of Pennsylvania

To Messrs. Sargent & Aufrere,   Craven Street, Janry. 8. 1762

Gentlemen,

The very obliging manner in which you have undertaken to support the Credit of the Province Drafts, demands my thankful Acknowledgments in Behalf of the Province, which I beg you to accept.[7] Your doing it so readily and chearfully at my Instance I esteem a particular Obligation on myself. I shall not fail explaining your Motives in this Transaction to the Assembly as you desire. There can be no doubt of its being a right Measure that must be approved of. It appears by the Speaker's Letter,[8] that the Assembly order'd the Drawing on the Expectations, then general, that a Peace would be concluded and of Consequence the Value of their Stocks enhanced by the Time the Bills would arrive here. They thought, that by drawing for the original Sum only, they should be a good deal within bounds. It has happened otherwise, and there must be a considerable Deficiency. If the overdrawn Bills were to go back protested, there would be a Disappointment to the Merchants who purchas'd the Bills, which the Interest could not compensate:[9] The

6. The act of Sept. 26, 1761, mentioned in the first note to this letter.

7. See the letter immediately above for many of the matters mentioned here.

8. Norris' letter of Sept. 30, 1761; see above, IX, 357–62.

9. The trustees of the Loan Office stipulated that if their bills upon BF were not paid at thirty days sight, interest at "Six Pounds per Centum per Annum" was to be paid on the face value of each bill "from the Expiration of the said

4

Publick would have that Interest to pay, added to the Loss; and the Credit of their future Drafts would be impaired, and so probably not fetch so good a Price as otherwise they might do. I will give you in due time the Notice you desire of all the necessary Particulars relating to the Bills to be referr'd to you for Payment. The Act of Assembly I shall [have] no Occasion for: It may be of Use to you; be pleas'd to keep it. I am, with the greatest Esteem, Gentlemen, Your most obedient Servant   B. FRANKLIN

To Charles Norris and Thomas Leech[1]

ALS and copy: Historical Society of Pennsylvania

Gentlemen   London, Jany. 9. 1762
   When your Drafts upon me first came to hand, the Form appearing new to me and very particular,[2] containing as I thought an Alternative at my Choice to pay the Money in 30 Days or in 12 Months, I accepted some of them with the long Day, expecting that a Letter from you would explain your Intention in that Form; but receiving no Line on the Subject, and being soon inform'd that the Bill was merely a Copy of that us'd by the northern Governments,[3] I concluded, for Reasons which I have mention'd to the Speaker,[4] to retract that Acceptance and pay in 30 Days. I have accordingly now accepted near £22,000 and can assure you that altho' the Sale of the Province Stocks will not produce a Sum equal to what you have probably drawn for, yet all the Trustees Bills will be duly honoured and punctually paid.[5] I am, with the

---

Thirty Days, until paid." But no interest was to be paid after a year had elapsed. See above, IX, 372–3.
   1. Norris and Leech, mentioned frequently in earlier volumes, were trustees of the Pa. Loan Office.
   2. For one of the trustees' bills on BF, see above, IX, 372–3.
   3. That is, New England.
   4. None of BF's letters written about this time to Isaac Norris have been found.
   5. BF was forced to revise this optimistic statement in his letter of January 14; see below, p. 8. The trustees drew on BF for £25,000 sterling. The sale of stock netted only £21,936 10s., sterling, however, and Sargent Aufrere made up the difference from "their private Fortunes." 8 Pa. Arch., VI, 5341, 5365; below, pp. 34 n, 36.

greatest Respect and Deference for yourselves and the other Trustees Gentlemen Your most obedient humble Servant B FRANKLIN

Messrs. Norris and Leech

Endorsed: London Janry 9th 1762 Benjamin Franklin To Chas Norris and Thos Leech

To Edward Penington[6]   ALS: Massachusetts Historical Society

Sir,   London, Jan. 9. 1762

I receiv'd your Favour of Oct. 21[7]. with one enclos'd for Mr. Penn,[8] which I have deliver'd to him. I doubt he will not know of this Opportunity time enough to write to you, and therefore I may say for him that he appear'd well-pleas'd with your Letter, and dispos'd to follow your Advice of not selling the Mannor.[9] The Opinion that has been long expected on his Case[1] is not yet given, but will now very soon. I am now preparing to return, and propose taking Passage in the first Man of War that goes to any Part of North America in the ensuing Spring or Summer. It will be a Pleasure to me to meet with you in the Assembly, as I see by the Papers you are chosen for our County.[2] I am, Sir, Your most obedient humble Servant   B FRANKLIN

Mr Pennington

Addressed: To / Mr Edwd. Pennington / Mercht / Philadelphia / Free / B Franklin

Endorsed: Jany 9th. 1762 B Franklin

6. On Edward Penington (1726–1796), Philadelphia merchant, who was acting as adviser and agent in Pa. for his relative Springett Penn, see above, IX, 315 n.

7. Not found.

8. Springett Penn (1739–1766), the only male descendant in the senior line of William Penn, founder of Pa.; above, IX, 260–1.

9. Springettsbury Manor, in York Co., Pa., which belonged to young Springett Penn and which Thomas Penn wanted to buy; see the document cited in the first footnote to this letter.

1. Probably a reference to Springett Penn's claims to the proprietorship of Pa.

2. Penington was elected to the Assembly from Philadelphia Co., Oct. 1, 1761; *Pa. Gaz.* and *Pa. Jour.*, Oct. 8, 1761.

From George Aufrere

Two copies: Historical Society of Pennsylvania

To B. Franklin, Esqr.

Dear Sir,   Mincing Lane, 9th Janry. 1762

I have seen Mr. Barclay this Morning who concurs with our House in the Resolution we had taken to pay such of the Province Bills as the Cash in your Hands falls short of discharging.[3] The Method of doing this, will be for you to suffer them to be noted for Non-acceptance, and to direct the Holders of them to us when the 30 Days are run out from the Day of Presentation. We shall then in Conjunction with Messrs. Barclays pay them for Account of the Drawers under the Notarial Act of Honour usual in such Cases. As I hear there is a fresh Arrival to day from Philadelphia which may probably bring over the Remainder of the Bills I thought it necessary to apprize you of the Mode proposed by us for compleating this Transaction, and I am, with sincere Regard, Dear Sir, Your most faithful humble Servant   GEO. AUFRERE

From Sargent Aufrere & Co.

Two copies: Historical Society of Pennsylvania

To B. Franklin Esqr.   London 13th. Janry. 1762

Dear Sir

Mr. Barclay[4] having been with us to day in consequence of his waiting on the Proprietor of Pensylvania for the Exemplification of the Bill,[5] in order to take the necessary Steps for receiving the Colony's Money from the Treasury, hath acquainted us, that upon mentioning to him our Intention of joining to take up such Bills as you were not provided with the means of payment of, as expressed in our Letter of the 9th. Instant,[6] he utterly disapprov'd the same,

3. See the first document in this volume.

4. Probably John, rather than David, Barclay, as it was John who signed with George Aufrere as agents of Pa. in correspondence with the Treasury about the grant for 1760, June 25, 1762. *Pa. Col. Recs.*, IX, 50.

5. The Pa. act of Sept. 26, 1761, appointing the Barclays, Sargent, and Aufrere to receive the province's share of the parliamentary grants for 1759 and for subsequent years; see above, IX, 359 n.

6. See above, p. 3.

and assigned such Reasons that Messrs. Barclays could in no wise concur in that Measure, namely that his Governor[7] should never consent to our Reimbursement out of the Money we were to receive.[8] We find ourselves incapacitated from doing what we wished to do, and must leave it to your Prudence to take such Measures as you think most proper upon the occasion, assuring you there is nothing in our Power we would not willingly have done to remedy the Inconveniencies that may arise from the Return of the Bills, and that we are always with a perfect Regard, Dear Sir, Your most obedient humble Servants   SARGENT AUFRERE & CO.

To Thomas Leech and Charles Norris

ALS and copy: Historical Society of Pennsylvania

I.N.

Gentlemen,   London, Jany. 14, 1762

Notwithstanding what I wrote to you of the 9th Inst,[9] that all your Bills would be paid, which I was warranted to do by the Letter from Messrs. Sargent & Aufrere that I enclos'd to the Speaker, and another from the same wherein they inform'd me Messrs. Barclay had agreed thereto,[1] I have now the Mortification to acquaint you, that the last named Gentlemen have since been prevail'd on by the Proprietor to retract their Engagement, and in consequence the former, as you will see by the Copies of Letters that I send you annex'd.[2] I have now accepted all that I can venture to accept till the remaining Stocks are sold,[3] and indeed no more have yet been offer'd me. They are from No. 1. to No. 138 inclusive, except the following which have not yet appear'd, viz. No. 4, 24, 36, 43, 44,

7. James Hamilton.
8. For BF's suggestion that the Barclays and Sargent Aufrere pay the bills which his stock sales could not cover and reimburse themselves from the parliamentary grant for 1759, see above, p. 4. In 1761 Penn had taken legal steps at the Treasury to prevent payment to BF of the colony's share of later parliamentary grants. T. Penn to Hamilton, Jan. 9, June 13, 1761, Penn Papers, Hist. Soc. Pa.
9. See above, p. 5.
1. For Sargent Aufrere letters of Jan. 8 and 9, 1762, see above, pp. 3, 7.
2. See the letter immediately above.
3. For the sale of this stock, see below, p. 34.

50, 66, 68, 69, 70, 81, 92, 93, 95, 96, 121, 125, 126, 127. These, or most of them, must I believe be return'd. I now hope to be with you pretty early in the Summer, when I shall render a particular Account of this Transaction. In the mean time, I am, with great Regard, Gentlemen, Your most obedient Servant,   B FRANKLIN

Messrs. Leech and Norris

To Sargent Aufrere & Co.

Two copies: Historical Society of Pennsylvania

To Messrs. Sargent & Aufrere

Gentlemen,   London Jany. 14, 1762

I beg Pardon for giving you any farther Trouble relating to the Colony Drafts. It is only to request you would be assured yourselves, and do me the Favour to inform Messrs. Barclays, that I had not the least Intention to subject you and them to the precarious Pleasure of the Proprietor or his Governor, for your Reimbursement, when I requested your Honouring those Drafts.[4] I knew very well that it did not depend upon the Governor. The Drawers[5] must in the Nature of Things have been accountable to you. They actually keep the Money for which they sold the Bills in their own Hands, for their own Security, till they are advis'd of the Payment here, and to enable them to make good any possible Deficiency. They have accordingly allow'd themselves in the Drafts, a proper Time for that Purpose.[6] I did not mean to propose that any Part of the Money appropriated by the new Law[7] should be apply'd to make good any Deficiency in the old one; for I knew that could not be legally done without an Act. But I thought no Inconvenience could arise from borrowing a Part of the second

4. For BF's proposal that the Barclays and Sargent Aufrere & Co. pay the drafts his sales of stock could not cover and reimburse themselves from the province's share of the parliamentary grant for 1759, see above, p. 4. For Thomas Penn's opposition to this scheme, see above, p. 7.

5. The trustees of the Pa. Loan Office.

6. For one of the trustees' bills on BF, see above, IX, 372–3.

7. The Pa. act of Sept. 26, 1761, appointing the Barclays, Sargent, and Aufrere to receive Pa.'s share of the parliamentary grant for 1759; see above, IX, 359 n.

9

Grant to pay off the overdrawn Bills, and replacing it with the Money that must have been sent you by the Drawers, as soon as they could hear of your Transaction in their favour; especially as an Expence and Loss would thereby be sav'd to the Province, Disappointment to the Purchasers of the Bills prevented, and the Credit of the Publick Drafts supported to their future Advantage; while the Money borrowed for this purpose must otherwise for the Time lie quite dead and useless. Finding it impossible at this Time, to borrow Money of private Persons for their Payment, I have concluded, tho' with much Regret, to let the overdrawn Bills take their Course.[8] With the greatest Regard, I am Gentlemen, your most obedient humble Servant   B. FRANKLIN

From James Brown[9]   ALS: Historical Society of Pennsylvania

I.N.

Benj. Franklin Esqr.   Lombardstreet 14th Jany 1762
   This is to acquaint you that in consequence of your directions Mr. Shervell has Sold £5000 of the 3 Per Cents. at 65¾ that is without the Dividend 64¼[1]—he is attending the Sale of the remainder and as any thing is done in it will keep you advis'd. I am for Father and Self most Respectfully Yours   JAS. BROWN

Addressed: To | Benj. Franklin Esqr. | In Craven Street | In the Strand

8. In the second copy this final sentence and the complimentary close appear to be in BF's hand. The first part of this sentence reads somewhat differently: "Upon the whole, finding it impossible at this Time to borrow Money for the Payment," etc.

9. James Brown (above, IX, 218 n), a partner in his father's banking firm of Henton Brown & Son, was managing the sale of the stock BF had purchased with Pa.'s share of the parliamentary grant for 1758; he was being assisted by his broker, Mr. E. Shervell; see above, IX, 392.

1. Shervell made this sale on Jan. 12, 1762; see below, p. 34.

From Sargent Aufrere & Co.

To B. Franklin, Esqr;

Dear Sir,   Mincing Lane 15th Janry. 1762

We have this Morning receiv'd your two Letters, that of the 8th. Instant, which you had intended to favour us with sooner, and this of the 14th. Instant,[2] in which to be sure what you say regarding the Colony Drafts, of the Regret you shall feel to let any of them go back, and the very evident Service that will be done the Colony, by preventing it, is so clear and unanswerable, that we can't help feeling an equal Concern upon the Occasion with yourself, and will therefore out of Respect to you (though we cannot do it out of the Money we are to receive for the Colony,) resolve to pay them out of our own, and that without accepting any Security other than that which we know we have in your Character, of your good Offices with the Colony, to obtain our Reimbursement, as soon as possible,[3] as it really never was so inconvenient for us to do any Thing of this kind, as it is at present, from various Circumstances that you can't be a Stranger to. We have done you the Justice to explain to Mr. Barclay the Reasons on which you applyed to us, and invited him to join in this Advance for the Colony, but he seems to think it too delicate a Thing for him to meddle in, and declines it. We shall always shew ourselves, Dear Sir, Your assured Friends and humble Servants,   SARGENT AUFRERE & CO.

To Sargent Aufrere & Co.

To Messrs. Sargent & Aufrere.

Gentlemen,   Craven Street Janry, 16, 1762

Knowing as I do the present great Scarcity and Value of Money here, and the many profitable Uses it may be put to at this Time, I

2. See above, pp. 4–5, 9–10.

3. See below, pp. 12–13, for BF's letter to the trustees of the Loan Office, requesting speedy reimbursement of this generous and public-spirited firm.

4. The copy from which this letter is printed is marked "No. 7" and is the last of a series of copies on a single set of papers which is endorsed: "London Janry 8. 9 13 14 15 1762 Copies of Letters between B Franklin and Messrs.

cannot but esteem your Undertaking to pay those Bills out of your own Cash, a Proceeding extreamly generous towards the Province; as well as particularly obliging to me.[5] I shall not omit to express fully, my Sentiments of it to our Friends there by the first Opportunity, and doubt not but an adequate Remittance will immediately be made to Reimburse you, with their best Acknowledgments.[6] In the mean time be pleased to accept of mine, with the sincerest Wishes for your Prosperity. I am, Gentlemen, Your most obedient humble Servant   B. FRANKLIN

To the Trustees of the Loan Office

ALS and copy:[7] Historical Society of Pennsylvania

I.N.

Gentlemen,   London, Jany: 16. 1762

In mine of the 14th. Instant,[8] which I sent away by the same Night's Post, in hopes it would reach the Pacquet at Falmouth, I inform'd you, that I had been disappointed in my Expectations of the remaining Bills being paid by Messrs. Sargent, Aufrere and the Barclays. But this Day, in answer of my last to them,[9] of which I sent you a Copy, I receiv'd the following Letter,[1] whereby the two first nam'd Gentlemen do alone undertake to pay them for your Honour. I have had occasion, of late, to see so much of the Scarcity of Money, and the Demand for it here, that I hope they will as soon as possible be reimburs'd, the Interest being now by no means a Compensation for the Advance they make.[2] I have

---

Sargent & Co." It includes all the letters of this description printed above. The top corner of the first page carries the initials "I.N."

5. See immediately above.
6. See immediately below.
7. The ALS is followed on the same sheet by copies in BF's hand of Sargent Aufrere's letter of January 15 and his reply of the 16th. The copy of the present letter is on the same sheet with copies of BF's letters to Norris and Leech of January 9 and 14, and is endorsed: "London Janry 9 14 16 1762 Benja Franklin to the Trustees the L Office."
8. See above, pp. 8–9.
9. See above, pp. 9–10.
1. See above, p. 11.
2. Isaac Norris laid this letter before the Assembly on May 6, 1762. The same day the House directed that its thanks be presented to Sargent and

before acquainted you what Bills I had accepted, and what Numbers, between No. 1, and No. 138 inclusive, had not yet appear'd. Those, when they do appear, I shall refer to Messrs. Sargent & Aufrere for Payment. And when the Stocks are all Sold, which will probably be next Week, I shall make up the Account, and what Province Money remains in my Hands, if any, I shall apply to take up Bills as far as it will go; but I doubt there will be very little. The Amount of what I have accepted is £22,150.—from this you can judge pretty nearly what Sum will be necessary to remit Messrs. Sargent & Aufrere in order to their Re-imbursement. I am, with great Regard, Gentlemen, Your most obedient Servant

B FRANKLIN

Trustees of the Loan-Office

Addressed: To / Cha. Norris Esqr / Philadelphia / Postage Paid 1 s / via New York / per Packet

Endorsed: London Jany 16. 1762 B Franklin To Norris and Leech with a Letter from John Sargent abt paying the Bills and BFs Answer

To Sir Alexander Dick

ALS: New York Public Library; copy (incomplete): [3] Scottish Record Office

Dear Sir,   London, Jan. 21. 1762
    It gives me Pleasure to learn, by yours of Nov. 12. that my young Friend Mr. Morgan has render'd himself agreable to you, and that your Health and Eyes were much better.[4]

Aufrere and ordered the trustees of the Loan Office to reimburse immediately "all and every Sum" which these men had advanced "with Interest accruing." 8 *Pa. Arch.*, VI, 5341. On May 18 the trustees sent Sargent and Aufrere a bill for £2500, which they received on July 9, 1762, and which covered, with a small sum to spare, the money they had advanced to pay the bills drawn on BF. See below, pp. 113–14, 134–5.

    3. The second MS, described at the top as "Copy of part of a Letter" from BF to Dick, with the date, begins at the second paragraph of the ALS and omits the final two paragraphs, the complimentary close, and the signature. It is endorsed "Copy Letter from Dr. Franklin about his Chimney Machines. 21 January 1762."

    4. Dick's letter of November 12 not found; it probably acknowledged

I sent some time since to Mr. Dalrymple[5] one of my Machines for your Chimney, who readily paid the Smith's Bill for the same. But now, on discoursing with some Gentlemen from Edinburgh, I am in doubt whether it is what you intended and expected. If not, pray let me know, that I may endeavour to procure for you the Thing that you desire.

However, let me tell you, that after more than 20 Years Experience of my own Contrivances and those of others, for the Warming of Rooms, and much Thought on the Subject, I am of Opinion, that This, all Circumstances considered, is by far the best for common Use. You will judge of it, when I have explain'd the Manner of Fixing it up, and its Operation.[6]

It is a thin Iron Plate sliding in a grooved Frame of Iron. The Opening of your Chimney I suppose is wider than this Plate with its Frame is long, and deeper than it is wide: In which Case, your Mason is to contract the Opening, by raising within it two Jambs of Brickwork about 3 Feet high, and at such a Distance from each other, that the Frame and Plate being laid on them may rest firmly, and be fix'd by additional Brickwork above upon the Jambs, and across from Jamb to Jamb over the Frame, so as to close the Opening above the Frame. This new Brickwork may be fac'd with Dutch Tiles, Stone or Marble at your Pleasure. This Work is to be plac'd so far back in the Chimney, that when the Plate is close thrust in, the Chimney is quite stopt up, so as to prevent all Passage of Air up or down. Then when you make a Fire, the Plate is to be drawn out so far only as to admit a Passage for all the Smoke; which will be one, two, or three Inches, at different Times, according to the Coldness of the Weather, and the Strength of Draft in your Chimney. If at any time, you would have the Fire speedily blown up, the Plate is to be drawn out as far as the Hinge, and let down so as to hang perpendicular, which enlarging the Passage above the Fire,

---

a letter from BF of about Oct. 21, 1761, also not found, introducing the young medical student John Morgan; see above, IX, 373–7.

5. Not identified.

6. BF repeats here much of what he had written James Bowdoin, Dec. 2, 1758 (above, VIII, 194–6) about his "Sliding Plate" or damper to control the velocity of smoke and heated air passing up a chimney. Indication that the plate was to be hinged so that part could be let down to cover much of the fireplace opening is an addition to the description he had given Bowdoin.

and contracting it before, produces the Effect by occasioning a stronger Current of Air where it is required for the purpose.[7]

The Principles of this Construction are these. Chimney Funnels are made much larger than is necessary for Conveying the Smoke. In a large Funnel, a great Quantity of Air is continually ascending out of the Room, which must be supply'd thro' the Crevices of Doors, Windows, Floors, Wainscots, &c. This occasions a continual Current of cold Air from the extream Parts of the Room to the Chimney, which presses the Air warm'd by the direct Rays of the Fire into the Chimney, and carries it off, thereby preventing its diffusing itself to warm the Room. By contracting the Funnel with this Plate, the Draft of Air up the Chimney is greatly lessen'd, and the Introduction of cold Air thro' the Crevices to supply its Place is proportionably lessen'd. Hence the Room is more uniformly warm'd, and with less Fire; and the Current of cold Air towards the Chimney being lessen'd, it becomes much more comfortable Sitting before the Fire.

That the Draft of cold Air into the Room is lessen'd by this Plate maybe demonstrated by several easy Experiments. When you have a lively Fire burning, and the Plate as far in as it will bear to be without Stopping the Smoak, set the Door open about ½ an Inch, and hold your Hand against the Crevice; you will then feel the cool Air coming in, but slowly and weakly compar'd with what you will feel, if, while your Hand continues so plac'd, another Person suddenly draws out the Plate. The stronger Pressure of the outward Air into the Room, will, when the Plate is drawn out, push the Door more strongly; and being shut, the Rushing of the Air thro' Crevices makes a louder Noise.

Since I first us'd this Contrivance in the Chimneys of my Lodging here, many Hundreds have been set up in Imitation of it, in and about this City, and they have afforded general Satisfaction. Simplicity, Cheapness, and Easy Execution, have all contributed

7. A similar though sometimes dangerous method of inducing temporarily a strong draft in a fireplace, somewhat more common in Great Britain than in the United States, is to open out and hold a newspaper across the upper part of the fireplace opening. Constriction of the incoming air to the lowest segment of the opening increases the draft through the coals or wood and promotes more active burning of a sluggish fire. Perhaps BF knew of this method and characteristically developed an apparatus to achieve the same result more easily and safely.

to recommend it. Then it is no Obstruction to the Sweeping of the Chimney, is attended with no ill Smells, and in summer serves the Purpose of a Chimney-Board, by closing the Chimney entirely.

It has indeed been mistaken by some, as intended for the Cure of Smoaky Chimneys. But that is not to be expected from it, except in two Cases, viz. where the Chimney smokes because the Opening is too large; or where the Room is so tight and the Funnel so big, that all the Crevices together do not admit Air enough to supply the Draft: In these Cases it is of Service. But Chimneys often Smoke from other Causes, and must have other Remedies.

Possibly where a Chimney smokes from Wind sometimes blowing down, it may also be of some Service, the Push of the heated Air upwards being stronger in its narrow Passage. But in this Case I have had no Opportunity of seeing it try'd.

If you are desirous of obtaining still more Heat in your Room from the same Fire, I would recommend lining your Jambs with coving Plates of polish'd Brass. They throw a vast deal of Heat into the Room by Reflection. I have done my Parlour Chimney in that Manner with very good Effect. The Plates are thin, and the Expence of the two, but about twenty-five Shillings.

Please to acquaint your Friend Dr. Hope,[8] that I am about returning to America this Summer, and will send him free of Charge for Postage in America, any Letters containing Leaves of Plants or small Parcels of Seeds that shall be committed to my Care by any of his or your medical Friends there.

My Son joins in best Wishes for you and your Children. Our Compliments to the eldest, who proves an excellent Secretary for you. Be so good as to present our cordial Regards to Lord Kaims when you see him. I shall write to him shortly, being much in his Debt. With the greatest Esteem, I am, Dear Sir, Your most obedient humble Servant   B FRANKLIN

Sir Alexr. Dick

8. John Hope (1725–1786), physician and botanist, professor of botany at the University of Edinburgh, 1761, and superintendent of the botanical garden. He was associated with Dick in the cultivation of Tartarian rhubarb. Correspondence with John Bartram, developing out of this contact with BF, is printed in Darlington, *Memorials*, pp. 432–6.

To David Hume

AL (incomplete): Royal Society of Edinburgh; printed in full in *Essays and Observations, Physical and Literary*. *Read before the Philosophical Society in Edinburgh, and published by them*, III (Edinburgh, 1771), 129–41.[9]

Dear Sir,   London, [Jany.][1] 21. 1762

In Compliance with my Lord Marishall's Request,[2] communicated to me by you when I last had the Pleasure of seeing you,[3] I now send you what at present appears to me to be the shortest and simplest Method of securing Buildings, &c. from the Mischiefs of Lightning.

Prepare a Steel Rod 5 or 6 Feet long, half an Inch thick at its biggest End, and tapering to a sharp Point, which Point should be gilt to prevent its rusting. Let the big End of the Rod have a strong Eye or Ring of half an Inch Diameter: Fix this Rod upright to the Chimney or highest Part of the Building, by means of Staples, so as it may be kept steady. Let the pointed End be upwards, and rise three or four Feet above the Chimney or Building that the Rod is fix'd to. Drive into the Ground an Iron Rod of about an Inch Di-

9. Only the two pages of the first leaf of the MS survive; the remainder of the letter and the remarks that follow are supplied from the printed text.

1. In the MS an ink blot obscures the (obviously abbreviated) month; "January" is spelled out in the printed version. Someone at a later time apparently tried to overwrite what is left of the month in the MS to make it seem that BF had originally written "Augt" but this emendation was certainly in error. See the endorsement below and the footnote thereto. The MS clearly gives the day of the month as "21," but the printed letter gives it as "24." Sparks (*Works*, VI, 214), Bigelow (*Works*, III, 156), and Smyth (*Writings*, IV, 127), all follow the dating of the 1771 printed text.

2. George Keith, 10th Earl Marischal (1693?–1778), served as a young officer with Marlborough but joined the Old Pretender in 1715. Attainted and his estates forfeited, he lived in Spain for some years and then settled in Prussia, where his brother was a field marshal in Frederick II's army. The earl served as Prussian ambassador to France, 1751–52, and to Spain, 1759–60, and as governor of the principality of Neuchâtel, 1754–65. He was given a British pardon, 1759, and was allowed to return to Great Britain in 1760–61, receiving compensation for his forfeited estates. He met David Hume and they became warm friends. He returned to his post in Neuchâtel in 1762 and later settled in Potsdam. *DNB;* Edith E. Cuthell, *The Scottish Friend of Frederic the Great: The Last Earl Marischall* (2 vols., London, 1915).

3. Hume had been in London in 1761 arranging with Strahan for the publication of the last volumes of his *History of England*.

ameter, and ten or twelve feet long, that has also an Eye or Ring, in its upper End. It is best that this Rod should be at some Distance from the Foundation of the Building, not nearer than ten feet if your Ground will allow so much. Then take as much Length of Iron Rod, of about half an Inch Diameter, as will reach from the Eye in the Rod above to that in the Rod below; and fasten it securely to those Rods, by passing its Ends thro' the Rings, and bending those Ends round till they likewise form Rings. This Length of Rod may either be in one or several Pieces. If in several, let the Ends of the Pieces be also well hooked to each other. Then close and cover every Joint with Lead, which is easily done by making a small Bag of strong Paper round the Joint, tying it close below, and then pouring in the melted Lead. It being of Use in these Junctures, that there should be a considerable Quantity of metalline Contact between Piece and Piece: For if they were only hook'd together, and so touch'd each other but in Points, the Lightning in passing thro' them might melt and break them where they join. The Lead will also prevent the Weakening of the Joints by Rust. To prevent the Shaking of this Rod by the Wind, you may secure it by a few Staples to the Building till it comes down within ten feet of the Ground, and thence carry it off to your Ground Rod; near to which should be planted a Post, to support the Iron Conductor above the Heads of People walking under it. If the Building be large and long, as 100 feet or upwards, it may not be amiss to erect a pointed Rod at each End, and form a Communication by an Iron Rod between them. If there be a Well near the House, so that you can by such a Rod form a Communication from your Top Rod to the Water, it is rather better to do so than to use the Ground Rod above-mentioned. It may also be proper to paint the Iron, to render it more durable, by preserving it better from Rust.

A Building thus guarded, will not be damaged by Lightning, nor any Person or Thing therein kill'd, hurt or set on fire. For either the Explosion will be prevented by the Operation of the Point, or, if not prevented, then the whole Quantity of Lightning exploding near the House, whether passing from the Cloud to the Earth or from the Earth to the Cloud, will be convey'd in the Rods. And though the Iron be crook'd round the Corners of the Building, or make ever so many Turns between the upper and lower Rod, the Lightning will follow it, and be guided by it without affecting the Building.

I omit the Philosophical Reasonings and Experiments on which this Practice is founded; for they are many, and would make a Book. They are besides already known to most of the Learned throughout Europe. In the North-American British Colonies, many Houses have been, since the Year 1752, guarded on these Principles. Three Facts only have come to my Knowledge of the Effects of Lightning[4] on such houses,[5] which I shall here give you.

The first was some years since, on the house of Mr. Raven, at John's Island, near Charlestown, South Carolina.[6] As the size of a conductor sufficient for conveying the lightning could only be discovered by experience, this gentleman has used small brass wire to connect the upper and lower rods. It went down on the outside of his chimney, which stood at the end of the house. Within the chimney stood, leaning against the back, a musket or gun. The lightning passed in the wire, small as it was, except where furnished with a better conductor by the gun-barrel, between the top of which and the wire it made a very small hole through the wall, and in that place, and all above it, melted and separated the wire. If I mistake not, (for I write this from memory only), some hurt to the lower part of the gun-stock, and a few bricks of the hearth broken up, was all the damage done at this house: And this being ascribed to the smallness of the wire, which occasioned the lightning to deviate into the gun-barrel, larger conductors were afterwards more generally used.

The second was the house of Mr. William Mayne of the same Province.[7] He hath provided a conductor from the top to the bottom of his chimney composed of iron rods of near half an inch diameter, linked together by hooks, turned at their ends, the lowest joint being in the ground about three feet deep, close to the founda-

4. The MS original breaks off here.
5. In printing this letter Sparks, Bigelow, and Smyth omit everything from this point to the final sentence. Sparks announced his omission by a footnote citing the pages in another volume of his edition in which the incidents described here were recounted; Smyth similarly cited the appropriate pages of *Exper. and Obser.*, 1769 edit.; Bigelow jumped directly from "on such houses" to the final sentence of the letter with no indication that he had skipped more than 1200 words of the text.
6. For BF's source of information on this incident, see below, pp. 50, 53–5.
7. For Maine's extended account of his experience and BF's remarks on it, see below, pp. 54–9.

tion of his chimney; and the highest about six inches above the top, terminating in three brass wires, with silver points. The lightning passed in this canal, melted and dissipated the brass wires with their points, melted and burst the joints of the rods, so as to unhook and separate them; but did no damage to the chimney, except near the foundation, where some bricks were torn out, and some bricks of the hearth within forced up; the earth also for eight or nine inches round the rod was furrowed and torn up. This small damage appeared to be occasioned by the ground-rod's not entering the earth deep enough, and being placed too near the foundation of the chimney: Four persons were in the house, and one within a few feet of the chimney. They were stunned with the noise, which was extremely great; but otherwise received no hurt.

The third instance, I lately received an account of from Mr. Kinnersley, an ingenious electrician of Philadelphia, which I shall give you in his own words, from his letter to me, dated March 21. 1761.[8] "We had four houses in this city, and a vessel at one of the wharfs, struck and damaged by lightning last summer; one of the houses was struck twice in the same storm. But I have the pleasure to inform you, that our method of preventing such terrible disasters has, by a fact which like to have escaped our knowledge, given a very convincing proof of its great utility, and is now in higher repute with us than ever.

"Hearing a few days ago, that Mr. William West merchant in this city, suspected that the lightning, in one of the thunderstorms last summer, had passed through the iron conductor which he had provided for the security of his house, I waited on him to inquire what ground he might have for such a suspicion. Mr. West informed me, that his family and neighbours were all stunned with a very terrible explosion, and that the flash and crack were seen and heard at the same instant; whence he concluded that the lightning must have been very near; and as no house in the neighbourhood had suffered by it, that it must have passed through his conductor. Mr. White, his clerk, told me, that he was sitting at the time by a window about two feet distant from the conductor, leaning against the brick-wall, with which it was in contact, and that

8. What follows is an extended extract from Kinnersley's letter; see above, IX, 282–93.

he felt a smart sensation like an electric shock in that part of his body which touched the wall. Mr. West farther informed me, that a person of undoubted veracity assured him, that being in a door of an opposite house on the other side of the street, he saw the lightning diffused over the pavement, which was then very wet with rain, to the distance of two or three yards from the foot of the conductor: And that another person of very good credit told him, that he, being a very few doors off, on the other side of the street, saw the lightning above, darting in such direction, that it appeared to him to be directly over that pointed rod.

"Upon receiving this information, and being desirous of farther satisfaction, there being no traces of the lightning to be discovered in the conductor, as far as we could examine it below, I proposed to Mr. West our going to the top of the house to examine the painted [pointed] rod; assuring him, that if the lightning had passed through it, the point must have been melted: And, to our great satisfaction, found it so. This iron rod extended in height about 9 feet and an half above a stack of chimneys to which it was fixed; it was somewhat more than half an inch diameter in the thickest part, and tapering to the upper end. The conductor, from the lower end of it to the earth, consisted of square iron nail rods, not much above a quarter of an inch thick, connected together by interlinking joints. It extended down the cedar roof to the eaves, and from thence down the wall of the house, four stories and a half, to the pavement, in Water-street, being fastened to the wall in several places by small iron hooks. The lower end was fixed to a ring in the top of an iron stake that was down about 4 or 5 feet into the ground. The above mentioned iron rod had a hole in the top of it, about two inches deep, wherein was inserted a brass-wire about two lines thick, and, when first put there, about ten inches long, terminating in a very acute point; but now its whole length is no more than seven inches and a half, and the top very blunt. Some of the metal appears to be missing, the slenderest part of the wire being, as I suspect, consumed into smoke. But some of it, where the wire was a little thicker, being only melted by the lightning, sunk down while in a fluid state, and formed a rough irregular cap, lower on one side than the other, round the upper end of what remained, and became intimately united therewith.

"This was all the damage that Mr. West sustained by a terrible

21

stroke of lightning. A most convincing proof of the great utility of this method of preventing its dreadful effects.

"Mr. West was so good as to make me a present of the melted wire, which I keep as a great curiosity, and long for the pleasure of shewing it to you.[9] And now, Sir, I most heartily congratulate you on the pleasure you must have in finding your great and well grounded expectations so far fulfilled," &c. Thus far Mr. Kinnersly.

You will observe, Sir, that the size or thickness of the conductor I direct, is much greater than this of Mr. West's, which nevertheless proved effectual; but, the quantity of lightning discharged in some strokes being probably much greater, I prefer a larger conductor as the safer. If I have not been explicit enough in my directions, I shall, on the least intimation, endeavour to supply the defect. I am, &c.

D. Hume Esqr

MS *endorsed:* Dr. Franklin 21 Augt. 1762[1]

[Added at the end of the printed letter:]

Report on Dr. Franklin's Method of securing Buildings, &c. from the Mischiefs of Lightning, by Professor Russel.[2]

The Doctor's description of his method is the neatest and most distinct imaginable. No body can be at a loss to put it in practice.

9. Here BF omitted two sentences of Kinnersley's letter in which he mentioned and explained the "Representation" of the damaged lightning rod which he was sending to BF; see the illustration, above, IX, facing p. 286.

1. This endorsement, in the margin of the second page of the MS, was almost certainly added much later, probably after the remaining pages of the letter had been lost. BF was still in England on August 21, 1762—at Portsmouth impatiently awaiting a favorable wind to set sail—but the date cannot be correct. Hume's letter of May 10 acknowledging receipt of this long communication and BF's reply of May 19 (see below, pp. 80, 82) make certain that he had written it substantially before May, and there seems no reason to doubt the January dating ascribed to it.

2. James Russell, an Edinburgh surgeon-apothecary, was appointed professor of natural philosophy at the University of Edinburgh in 1764. The title here is explained by the fact that this "Report" was not printed until 1771. Hume sent BF a summary of these remarks in his letter of May 10, 1762, cited above, and BF commented on them in his reply of May 19.

Two remarks only have occurred to me, which I shall lay before the society. One is, That when a building, proposed to be guarded in this manner, is partly covered with lead, or has the water conveyed from the roof to the ground in leaden pipes; the lead, so far as it goes, may easily be made to supply the place of the iron conductor. This would be done by conducting the iron rods from the top to the nearest part of the lead, and there connecting the iron with the lead, by means of solder, in the same manner that the Doctor proposes that the iron-rods should be connected to each other; and then forming the connection between the ground-rod and that part of the lead which comes nearest to it, in the same manner. The other remark which I proposed to make is this: The Doctor directs, that when the conductor comes down within ten feet of the ground, it should thence be conveyed off from the building towards the ground-rod, and supported by a post above the heads of people walking under it. Now, I apprehend, it would be more convenient, and less operose, to carry this last part of the conductor a foot or two under ground.

From John Canton[3]

MS not found; reprinted from The Royal Society, *Philosophical Transactions*, LII (1761–62), 457–61.

Spital-Square, January 21, 1762.

Dear Sir,

Mr. Delaval, in his curious electrical experiments,[4] found that Portland stone, common tobacco-pipe,[5] &c. would readily con-

3. John Canton, electrical experimenter; see above, IV, 390 n. BF submitted this letter to be read at the Royal Society, February 4; see p. 30 below. It is recorded as having been read the same day.

4. On Edward Hussey Delaval, see above, VIII, 359–60 n. His experiments on the effect of changes in temperature upon the conductivity of various substances were reported in *Phil. Trans.*, LI (1759), 83–8; LII (1761–62), 353–6, and BF described some of them briefly to Kinnersley, July 28, 1759, above, VIII, 417.

5. Portland stone: a valuable building material quarried in the Isle of Portland. The term Portland cement, so called because it was thought to resemble the stone, does not seem to have appeared, at least by that name, before 1824.

duct the electrical fluid, when very hot, or when quite cold; but were non-conductors in an intermediate state. As no one, that I know of, has yet attempted to account for this, I shall submit the following solution to your judgment.

The stone, tobacco-pipe, wood, &c. I apprehend, conduct when cold, by the moisture they contain in that state; when their moisture is evaporated by heat, they become non-conductors; and when they are made very hot, the hot air at, or near their surfaces, will conduct, and the bodies appear to be conductors again.

To prove that hot air will conduct the electrical fluid, let the end of a poker, when red-hot, be brought, but for a moment, within three or four inches of a small electrified body, and its electrical power will be almost, if not entirely destroyed.

And if excited amber, &c. be held within an inch of the flame of a candle, it will lose its electricity before it has acquired a sensible degree of heat.*

That glass is a conductor in damp weather, on account of the moisture on its surface, is well known; as also, that warming it a

*I have observed also, that the Tourmalin,[6] Brazil Topaz, and Brazil Emerald, will give much stronger signs of electricity while cooling, after they have been held about a minute within two inches of an almost surrounding fire, where the air is a conductor, than they ever will after heating them in boiling water. And if both sides of either of those stones be equally heated, but in a less degree than will make the surrounding air a conductor, the electricity of each side, whether *plus* or *minus*, will continue so, all the time the stone is both heating and cooling; but will increase while it is heating, and decrease while it is cooling. Whereas, if the heat be sufficient to make the surrounding air conduct the electric fluid from the positive side of the stone to the negative side of it, while heating; the electricity of each side will increase, while the stone is cooling, and be contrary to what it was, while the stone was Heating. See the Philosophical Transactions, Vol. LI. p. 403 and 404.

OED. Tobacco-pipe: it seems clear from Delaval's reports and from the context later in this letter that Canton meant the common clay pipe used for smoking, not, as the term was occasionally used, for the variety of clay from which such pipes were made.

6. For experiments on the electrical properties of tourmalines by various scientists, including BF, see above, VIII, 393–6, 417.

little will render it a non-conductor; and that a great degree of heat will make it seem to be a conductor again. Now tobacco-pipe, wood, &c. will not only attract the moisture of the air to their surfaces, but will also absorb it; whence they are conductors in dry weather; and require more heat than glass, as well as a longer continuance in it, to render them non-conductors. It is re-markable, that tobacco-pipe, after it begins to cool, will become a conductor again, sooner than most other substances, and much sooner than wood. The cause of this appears to me, to be the tobacco-pipe's absorbing the moisture of the air faster than most other substances, and much faster than wood: for the surfaces of tobacco-pipe and wood being wetted, the surface of the wood will continue wet much longer than the surface of the tobacco-pipe.

That tobacco-pipe does not become a non-conductor by a par-ticular degree of heat, without evaporating its moisture, is evident, from the following experiments. If three or four inches of one end of a tobacco-pipe, of more than a foot in length, be made red-hot, without sensibly heating the other end; this pipe will prove a ready conductor, through the hot air surrounding one part of it, and the moisture contained in the other; although some part of it must have the degree of heat of a non-conductor. But if the whole pipe be made red-hot, and suffered to cool, till it has only superficial mois-ture enough to make it a good conductor; and then three or four inches of one end be again made red-hot, it will become a non-conductor. And if a nail be placed at, or near each end of a longish solid piece of any of the absorbent bodies above-mentioned, so that the point of each nail may be about half the thickness of the body, within its surface; this body, by heat, may be made a non-conductor externally, or superficially, while it remains a good con-ductor internally: for the electric fluid will pass readily from one nail to the other, through the middle of the body, when it will not pass on its surface; and even when the internal parts of the body are in an equal degree of heat with the external; as they must soon be, after it begins to cool. But if the same body be ex-posed, for a short time, to a greater degree of heat than before; or if it be kept longer in the same heat, it will become a non-conductor entirely.

In making the above experiments, I used the little electrometer, which I have described in the forty-eighth volume of the Philosophical Transactions, p. 783, and supported it by sealing-wax, or warm glass.

I well remember your acquainting me, that Mr. Delaval did not approve of the above manner of accounting for his experiment on tobacco-pipe, soon after you related it to him, which was some time last summer: but as it still appears satisfactory to me, not withstanding what that gentleman has lately offered against it,* your laying it before the Royal Society will oblige, Dear Sir, Your most obedient and most humble servant, JOHN CANTON.

P.S. Having formerly observed, that the friction between Mercury and Glass *in vacuo,* would not only produce the light of electricity, as in the luminous barometer, or within an evacuated glass ball, but would also electrify the glass on the outside; I immerged a piece of dry Glass in a basin of mercury, and found, that by taking it out, the Mercury was electrified *minus,* and the Glass electrified *plus,* to a considerable degree. I found also, that Amber, Sealing-wax, and Island Crystal,[8] when taken out of Mercury, were all electrified *positively.*† How does it then appear, that the electricity, which was observed upon rubbing the last mentioned substance, after it was taken out of Mercury surrounded by Ice, was owing to *cold,* and not to the *friction* between it and the Mercury, in taking it out? Island Crystal, when *warm,* is a non-conductor; and all non-conductors may be excited with proper rubbers.

*See a Letter from Mr. Delaval to Mr. Wilson, in the first part of the fifty-second volume of the Philosophical Transactions.[7]

†A small quantity of an *amalgama,* or mixture, of Mercury and Tin, with a very little Chalk or Whiting, being rubbed on the cushion of a globe, or on the oiled silk-rubber of a tube, will excite the globe or tube to great degree, with very little friction; especially if the rubbers be made more damp, or dry, as occasion may require.

7. *Phil. Trans.,* LII (1761–62), 353–6.
8. Iceland spar, a transparent variety of calcite, later used in demonstrating the polarization of light. *OED.*

From James Brown[9]   AL: Historical Society of Pennsylvania

I.N.   Lombardstreet 22d Jany 1762

Mr. Brown's compliments to Benj. Franklin Esqr. and acquaints him that he has sold Five Thousand Pounds more of the Annuities[1] Vizt.

$$£3000 \text{ at } 64\frac{1}{2}$$
$$\underline{2000 \text{ at } 64\frac{3}{8}}$$

which was all he could do—the price is now but 63¾ and therefore before he sold the remaining five thought it proper to acquaint him with it—and Mr. Brown desires Mr. Franklin will please to send him word per Bearer whether he shall finish it or postpone it for a day or two.

Addressed: To/Benj. Franklin Esqr./In Cravenstreet/In the Strand

To Lord Kames   ALS: Scottish Record Office

My dear Lord,   London, Janry. 27, 1762

I was encourag'd by your Favour of the 22d. of November,[2] to hope that the Beginning of the New Year would have brought me the Pleasure and Improvement I expect from the Perusal of your Elements of Criticism.[3] As yet I hear nothing of any Copies being come to London; and I grow a little impatient.

9. Comparison of the handwriting with the letter of January 14 indicates that the writer of this letter and that of February 2 below was James Brown, not his father, Henton.

1. Brown's broker, E. Shervell, sold this stock on January 15 and 16; see below, p. 34. For the sale of the remaining £5000 of stock, see *ibid.*

2. Not found.

3. Kames's *Elements of Criticism*, 3 vols., appears to have been published in January 1762. *The Scots Magazine,* XXIV (Jan. 1762), 21–26, describes it and reprints its dedication to the King, introduction, and table of contents. A very long review, in three installments, was printed in *The Critical Review: or, Annals of Literature,* XIII (London, 1762): (March) 205–22; (April) 285–303; (May) 365–79. By August BF had received the volumes and told Kames he was reserving them to read on the voyage home. See below, pp. 147–8.

I am now so much employ'd in Preparation for my Return to America, that tho' I may while I stay here find Time to read what I so much desire to read, I see I shall find none to write what you in so obliging a Manner urge me to write. When I am once again at home, I have reason to expect a good deal of Leisure, and purpose seizing the first Opportunity of compleating a Work which I flatter myself will be useful to many, and afford some Reputation to its Author.[4]

I am griev'd that you should live in a smoaky Room at Edinburgh, and that it is so difficult at this Distance to employ any Skill I may have in these Matters for your Relief. Perhaps I may be able to advise something after being inform'd of the following Particulars. Does the Chimney refuse constantly to carry Smoke, or is it only at particular Times? Is it in a calm Season, or only when Winds blow? If when Winds blow, what is its Situation? that is, What Point of the Compass does the Opening of the Chimney within your Room face towards, and what Winds chiefly affect it? Does the Smoke only come down in Puffs while the Wind blows, and at Times go well up, or does it constantly lag below and come continually into the Room more or less? Does it in calm Seasons smoke only when the Door is shut, and carry Smoke well up when a Door or Window is left open? What Distance is the Door from the Chimney, and how is it situated with respect to the Chimney? What is the Situation of your high Street in Edinburgh, with respect to the Compass? On which Side of the Street is the House you live in; and is the Room you speak of, in the Front or back Part of the House? Are there any Buildings near that are much higher than that you live in; and how are they situated with respect to it? What are the Dimensions of the Opening of your Chimney in the Room, and what the Dimensions of the Funnel? You will, I am afraid, hardly see a Reason for some of these Questions; and it would be too much for a Letter to explain them all properly. And after all perhaps I can give you no better Advice, than you might receive from a very ingenious Man you have with you, I mean Mr. Russel the Surgeon.[5] There are I think 5 or 6 different

---

4. BF's long-projected and repeatedly postponed project, *The Art of Virtue*. See above, IX, 104 n.

5. James Russell, surgeon-apothecary of Edinburgh. For BF's initial response to Kames's plea for advice about his smoky chimney, see above, IX, 376.

Cases of smoky Chimnies; all (except one) to be cured by different Means; and that one seems to me at present absolutely incurable. Chimneys in this Case, from what I remember of the Situation of Buildings in Edinburgh, I should fear you have more in proportion than any other Town in Britain. But Workmen, ignorant of Causes, are like Quacks, always tampering; applying the Remedy proper in one Case to another in which it is improper, as well as attempting the Cure of what from the Nature of Things is not to be cured.

My Son joins with me in the most cordial Congratulations to you and Lady Kaims on the Marriage of your Daughter so much to your Satisfaction, and with such a Prospect of Happiness to herself.[6] She was indeed a Favourite with us both. Pray intimate to her and to your Son in law that we sincerely wish them every kind of Felicity. Our Compliments likewise to your valuable Son.

I thank you for the kind Reception my young Friend Morgan[7] informs me you have been so good as to afford him. With the truest Esteem and Respect, I am, My dear Lord, Your Lordship's most obedient and most humble Servant   B FRANKLIN

P.S. Feb. 11. This Letter was to have gone with Mr. Alexander,[8] but miss'd that Opportunity.

Addressed: To / The Rt. Honble Lord Kaims / Edinburgh / per / J Bullock[9]

Endorsed: 1762 Jan. 27

6. In its issue for November 1761, *The Scots Magazine* (XXIII, 615) announced, without specific date, the marriage of "Patrick Heron, Esq; of Heron, to Miss Jeanie Home, only daughter of Henry Home of Kaims, Esq; one of the Lords of Session." Ten years later the marriage ended in divorce; see above, IX, 9 n. See the same note for the son, George Home, mentioned later in this paragraph.

7. John Morgan, medical student from Philadelphia; see above, IX, 374 n, 377.

8. Probably Robert Alexander, Edinburgh merchant; see above, VIII, 444–5 n.

9. Not identified.

From James Brown

AL: Historical Society of Pennsylvania

I.N.   Lombardstreet 2d Feby 1762
Mr. Brown's Compliments to B. Franklin Esqr. and acquaints
him he has sold the £5000—3 per Cents. to be transferr'd to morrow—to day being a Holliday, at 61⅞.[1]
Addressed: To / Benj. Franklin Esqr. / In Craven street / Strand

To Thomas Birch[2]

MS not found; reprinted from The Royal Society, *Philosophical Transactions,* LII (1761–62), p. 456.

Sir,   Craven-Street, Feb. 4, 1762.
Mr. Canton did me the favour to shew me the ingenious experiments he has described in the inclosed letter.[3] They succeeded
perfectly as he has related them; and I imagine, the communication of them must be agreeable to the curious in this branch of
natural knowledge. I am, Sir, with great respect, your most obedient and most humble servant,   B. FRANKLIN.

From Ezra Stiles

Letterbook copy: Yale University Library

Sir   Newport Feb. 5. 1762
Notwithstanding thro the Fate of War I suppose all my Letters
to you have been intercepted by the Enemy, I venture again to
write. You know Professor Winthrop to be a Gentleman of exel-
lent Abilities and Acquisitions in math[ematical] Learning.[4] And
persuade myself that you, Sir, who know his Merits, cannot but
think they would do honor to an Enrollment among the Fellows
of the Royal Society. If this should be your opinion, you will not
need Arguments to induce you to recommend him to this Honor.[5]

1. See below, p. 34.
2. Secretary of the Royal Society.
3. See above, pp. 23–6.
4. John Winthrop (1714–1779), Hollis professor of mathematics and
natural philosophy at Harvard since 1738.
5. BF did not act on this suggestion immediately upon receiving this letter,

To the inclosed (Lecture on Earthquakes and Relation Transit of Venus) I would have added his Lecture on Comets, but have them not by me.[6] His Writings are at least ingenious and shew him to be the most considerable for this kind of Learning in New England at present, and vastly superior to perhaps all the few who have received this Honor in N. Eng. before him—and tho not equal to some who have had the European Advantages, yet such as merits Distinction. If thro' your means he be introduced into that learned Body, you will have the pleasure of doing another good Act and friendly Office to your native Country, which will ever be affected with the respect paid to her progeny, and this perhaps may not a little contribute to transmitting your own Name with honor to distant Posterity, as a Patron of Literature and instrumental in deriving Rewards to learned Merit. If Mr. Winthrop was not a Man of Merit equal to it, I should not wish him distinguished with this Honor—as Learned Merit alone can possibly support the Dignity of the literary honors I see by the List of the Society that many Foreigners are received and I suppose those that have lived in America have been received in the same manner. We universally regret the Resignation of Mr. Pitt.[7] You can scarcly imagin how much it has dampt the public Confidance in the national Measures. I have the Honor to be with great Respect Dear sir Your obliged Friend and most humble Servant   EZRA STILES

Benj Franklin LLD. London

---

probably because of his own prospective departure from England. On June 27, 1765, however, he headed a list of five members who signed a paper nominating Winthrop to the Royal Society. Winthrop was duly elected, Feb. 20, 1766, and BF signed the bond for his contribution and paid his admission fee in November 1767. See above, VIII, 357.

6. *A Lecture on Earthquakes* (Boston, 1755) argued against the theory of a theological cause for earthquakes and the notion that lightning rods increased the danger of such disturbances. See above, VI, 404 n. His other writings mentioned here are *Relation of a Voyage from Boston to Newfoundland for the Observation of the Transit of Venus, June 6, 1761* (Boston, 1761), and *Two Lectures on Comets . . . 1759* (Boston, 1759). Stiles had preached a sermon on earthquakes in which he took the same position as Winthrop even before he had heard of the Harvard professor's pamphlet, but by 1771 he had changed his mind. Edmund S. Morgan, *The Gentle Puritan A Life of Ezra Stiles, 1727–1795* (New Haven and London, 1962), p. 170.

7. For Stiles's admiration for William Pitt, see above, IX, 403.

31

From Sir John Cust[8]

AL: American Philosophical Society

Teusday Morning Feb: 11th: [1762?][9]

Sir John Cust presents his Compliments to Mr. Franklyn and Mr. Franklyn Junior and hope for the favour of their Company to dinner tomorrow.

Sargent Aufrere & Co. to the Trustees of the Loan Office

ALS and copy:[1] Historical Society of Pennsylvania

I.N.   London, February 11, 1762

Messrs. Thos. Leech, Charles Norris, Mahlon Kirkbride, Francis Yarnall and James Wright, Trustees of the General Loan Office of Pensylvania

Gentlemen

We think it incumbent upon us to acquaint you that we have pursuant to the Powers given us by the Governor and Assembly of your Province jointly with Messrs. David Barclay Junior and Jno. Barclay[2] received the Sum of £   [3] which his Majesty hath allotted for the use of your Province for the Year 1759, the Fees and Expences of which, as they cannot be all settled yet, we must

8. Sir John Cust, 3d baronet (1718–1770), was M.P. for Grantham, 1743–1770, and speaker of the House of Commons from Nov. 3, 1761, to Jan. 19, 1770, five days before his death. Newcastle called him "a sort of plodding, ordinary man"; as a presiding officer he was diligent but neither particularly competent nor effective. *DNB*; Namier and Brooke, *House of Commons*, II, 290–1.

9. Cust must have erred in dating this note. The inclusion of BF's son in the invitation indicates the years 1758–62, during which time February 11 never fell on a Tuesday. The only year in which it did so fall during Cust's lifetime and when BF was in England was 1766, but WF was then in N.J. as governor and William Temple Franklin was still an infant. Cust was speaker of the House of Commons in 1762, and since there seem to have been no definite personal reasons for the invitation, it is placed here for want of a more likely date.

1. The copy (so marked) also bears the initials "I.N." and an address page with the names of the individual trustees of the Loan Office, but without indication of how it was sent to Philadelphia. The copy omits the postscript.

2. For the Pa. act of Sept. 26, 1761, empowering the Barclays and Sargent Aufrere & Co. to receive the province's share of the parliamentary grant for 1759 and for sebsequent years, see above, IX, 359 n.

3. Left blank in both versions of the MS; see the postscript.

defer sending you the particulars of untill the next Packet.[4] Whatever Bills you are pleased to draw in consequence hereof, you may be assured shall be duely honour'd. We are glad to have had an opportunity of shewing our Respect for the Colony and its Interests by assisting our Friend Mr. Benjamin Franklin in the Discharge of those Bills you had passed on him for the Money received last Year, which having been vested in the Stocks it falls short of. The Parties concerned in them are acquainted that We shall pay them for the Honour of the Drawers as they become due, and you may be assured of their being discharged accordingly.[5] We make no doubt of your speedy reimbursement, and are very much the Colony's, and Gentlemen Your most obedient humble Servants

SARGENT, AUFRERE & CO.

P.S. We cannot ascertain the Sum due to your Province as yet mislaid [sic] in the Treasury what we have received in one Warrant is £28545 from which the proportion due to the 3 lower Countrys must be deducted as well as the Fees and our Commission which perhaps you will be able to adjust.

Addressed: To Messrs. Thoms Leach, Chas Norris, / Mahlon Kirkbride, Frans Yarnall and / Jas Wright Trustees of the / General Loan Office of / Pensilvania / In Philadelphia / per Packet / QDC[6]

Endorsed: Londn Febr. 11th. 1762. Messrs. Sargent Aufrere & Co.

From E. Shervell
ALS: Historical Society of Pennsylvania

I.N.

Benj Franklin Esqr

Sir   12 feby. 1762

In consequence of Mr. Brown's order I have Enclosed the Account of Sales of the fifteen thousand Pounds 3 per Cents. which I hope will be agreable. Yours   E SHERVELL

4. Pa.'s share of the parliamentary grant for 1759 was £26,611 1s. 9d. After fees and commissions were deducted, the province received £26,302 17s. 9d. Sargent Aufrere to Charles Norris, July 8, 1762. Hist. Soc. Pa.
5. For the bills which Sargent Aufrere paid, see below, pp. 134–5.
6. Perhaps an abbreviation for *Quod Deus Conducat.*

33

Addressed: To / Benj Franklin Esqr / Craven street / in the Strand
Endorsed: from J. Brown Banker in Lombard Street. respecting the
Sale of Stocks.
Sales £15000 3 per Cts. No 7

[ENCLOSURE]
I.N.
sold for Benj. Franklin Esqr.
1762
Jan 12. £4000 Consd.[7] 3 per Cent. to W Morris at 64¼. Extra Divd

			£2570		
£1000. Do. to M Langdale	64¼.	642.10		
		3212.10		
Brokerage	6.5	£3206.5 [8]	
15 £3000. Do. to G Rutt	64½	1935 -	
16. £1000. Do. to T Greenwood	64⅜	643.15	
£ 300. Do. to B Forward	64⅜	193. 2.6	
£ 700. Do. to N Dawes	64⅜	450.12.6	
		3222.10	
Brokerage	6. 5	3216.5 [9]	
feb. 1. £3000. Do. to Jo Canco	61⅞	1856. 5	
£1800. Do. to W Gilbie	61⅞	1113.15	
£ 200. Do. to W Morris	61⅞	123.15	
		3093.15	
Brokerage	6. 5	3087.10	
per E SHERVELL		£9500:0.0 [1]	

7. Consolidated.
8. BF bought £5000 of this stock on May 5, 1761, at 87½, the cost (including brokerage fee) being £4381 5s. See above, IX, 313.
9. BF bought £10,000 of this stock, represented by these and the following blocks, between July 5 and Aug. 14, 1761, paying £8796 2s. 2d. (including brokerage fee and allowing for a discount for advance payment). See above, IX, 335.
1. These transactions completed the sales of stock BF had bought for Pa. Together with the sales of November and December 1761 (above, IX, 392), they show that BF received total net proceeds of £21,936 10s. Analysis of his accounts indicates that in November 1760 he had in hand as the Pa. share of the parliamentary grant for 1758 a total of £26,618 14s. 5d., after all fees and expenses were met and Delaware's share of the receipts and charges was

34

To the Trustees of the Loan Office

ALS and two duplicates: Historical Society of Pennsylvania; ALS: Yale University Library[2]

Gentlemen,   London, Feb. 13. 1762

Since mine of Jany. 14.[3] most of the Bills therein mentioned as not having then appear'd, have been presented, and I have accepted three more of them, viz. the Nos. 36, 50, and 121. which makes the whole Sum accepted by me £22,500. all of which is now paid except the three above mention'd Bills, which will also be paid in course. The others are noted, and when protested will be paid by Messrs. Sargent & Aufrere.[4]

A more unlucky Time could not have been pitch'd upon to draw Money out of the Stocks here, for it was in the midst of the Damp thrown upon them by the Breaking off the Negociations for Peace, the Resignation of Mr. Pitt, and the entring into a new War with Spain.[5] All imaginable Care and Pains was taken to sell our Stocks to the best Advantage, but it could only be done by degrees and

---

adjusted, and after allowance is made for a small error in his accounts. During the next nine months he had bought and paid for £30,000 face value of stocks at a total cost of £26,977 19s. 8d. (he apparently overinvested the principal to the extent of £359 5s. 3d.). The forced sales of stock in the late autumn and the winter of 1761–62 therefore resulted in a loss of £5041 9s. 8d. from his stock transactions. Meanwhile, however, he had received £1064 in interest on the stock, a form of income the fund would not have received had he left it on deposit in the Bank of England as originally proposed. The net loss on the entire transaction, therefore, appears to have been £3977 9s. 8d. "Account of Expences," pp. 54–5, 58, 59, 60, 61, 62, 63; *PMHB*, LV (1931), 127–8, 129, 130, 131, 132.

2. All four MSS are signed autographs and bear endorsements showing that they were sent to Philadelphia and received there, at least three of them by different ships. The one used here is the only one which contains the postscript and bears the names of four trustees of the Loan Office on the address page. The other two at Hist. Soc. Pa. (described above as "duplicates") carry the word "Copy" and the initials "I.N." in the upper left corner of the first page. They and the one in Yale Univ. Lib. have the names of only Charles Norris and Leech on their address pages.

3. See above, pp. 8–9.

4. See below, pp. 134–5.

5. The Anglo-French negotiations broke down during the late summer of 1761; Pitt resigned Oct. 5, 1761; Great Britain declared war on Spain, Jan. 4, 1762.

with Difficulty, there being sometimes no Buyers to be found. The whole Produce of the £15000 4 per Cents. was no more than

	£12,436. 10. 0[6]
and that of the £15000 3 per Cents. only	9,500. 0. 0[7]
In all £21,936. 10. 0	

as you will see by the Broker's Account of Sales inclos'd. However, as the Bills you have drawn will all be honoured and paid, no Disappointment will arise to the Trade of the Province and its Merchants, tho' perhaps, notwithstanding the good Price of Exchange receiv'd for the Bills beyond what they would have sold for when the Money was first vested in the Funds, there may still be some Loss to the Publick.[8] I am with great Respect, Gentlemen, Your most obedient humble Servant   B FRANKLIN

Enclos'd are Copies of my late Letters to you; and of the Letters between Messrs. Sargent & Aufrere and me relating to the Payment of the Bills.

Trustees of Gen. Loan Office

Addressed: To / Charles Norris / Thomas Leech / Mahlon Kirkbride / Francis Yarnal / Esqrs. / Trustees of the General Loan Office / Philadelphia

Endorsed: London Febry 13. 1762 Benjamin Franklin to the Trustees G L Office recd May 11th. 1762

6. See above, IX, 392.
7. See the document immediately above.
8. The trustees of the Loan Office, on the Assembly's recommendation, Sept. 25, 1761, sold the bills it drew on BF at "Seventy per Cent. Exchange, Pennsylvania Currency." 8 *Pa. Arch.*, VI, 5267. The exchange rate in Philadelphia when BF first began investing the parliamentary grant, Dec. 18–23, 1760, appears to have been 70 percent (it was 70 on Oct. 6, 1760, and on Feb. 9, 1761), so that, contrary to BF's belief, the province gained nothing on the exchange by waiting until October 1761 to draw on him. See above, IX, 235, 273.

To Ebenezer Kinnersley, with Associated Papers

MSS not found; reprinted from *Experiments and Observations on Electricity,* 1769 edition, pp. 397–425.[9]

When Franklin included this letter to Kinnersley in the 1769 edition of *Experiments and Observations on Electricity* he placed immediately after it two accounts of lightning strokes in South Carolina, which he had mentioned to Kinnersley, and his own remarks on the second of these incidents. Almost certainly the accounts had come to him in 1761 or early 1762 with a letter (not found) from some friend in South Carolina, probably Dr. John Lining. Although their dates would indicate that they should have appeared in the previous volume of this series, they are placed here, after the letter to Kinnersley, chiefly because they relate so closely to matters about which he was writing his friend that it seems more useful to depart from the normal chronological arrangement in this instance and to place them, as he himself did, with his own letter.

Sir,   London, Feb. 20, 1762.

I received your ingenious letter of the 12th of March last,[1] and thank you cordially for the account you give me of the new experiments you have lately made in Electricity. It is a subject that still affords me pleasure, though of late I have not much attended to it.

Your second experiment, in which you attempted, without success, to communicate positive electricity by vapour ascending from electrised water,[2] reminds me of one I formerly made, to try if negative electricity might be produced by evaporation only. I placed a large heated brass plate, containing four or five square feet, on an electric stand; a rod of metal, about four feet long, with a bullet at its end, extended from the plate horizontally. A light lock of cotton, suspended by a fine thread from the cieling, hung opposite to, and within an inch of the bullet. I then sprinkled the heated plate with water, which arose fast from it in vapour. If vapour should be disposed to carry off the electrical, as it does

9. The letter to Kinnersley is printed as Letter XXXVIII and the papers associated with it follow immediately as Letters XXXIX and XL. These documents also appear with the same numbers in the 1774 edition of *Exper. and Obser.,* pp. 405–35.

1. See above, IX, 282–93. Many of the matters BF discusses are in response to parts of Kinnersley's letter. Footnote references to the appropriate pages are given below.

2. Above, IX, 283.

the common fire from bodies, I expected the plate would, by losing some of its natural quantity, become negatively electrised. But I could not perceive, by any motion in the cotton, that it was at all affected; nor by any separation of small cork-balls suspended from the plate, could it be observed that the plate was in any manner electrified. Mr. Canton here has also found, that two tea-cups, set on electric stands, and filled, one with boiling, the other with cold water, and equally electrified, continued equally so, notwithstanding the plentiful evaporation from the hot water. Your experiment and his agreeing, show another remarkable difference between electric and common fire. For the latter quits most readily the body that contains it, where water, or any other fluid, is evaporating from the surface of that body, and escapes with the vapour. Hence the method long in use in the east, of cooling liquors, by wrapping the bottles round with a wet cloth, and exposing them to the wind. Dr. Cullen, of Edinburgh, has given some experiments of cooling by evaporation;[3] and I was present at one made by Dr. Hadley, then professor of chemistry at Cambridge,[4] when, by repeatedly wetting the ball of a thermometer with spirit, and quickening the evaporation by the blast of a bellows, the mercury fell from 65, the state of warmth in the common air, to 7, which is 22 degrees below freezing; and, accordingly, from some water mixed with the spirit, or from the breath of the assistants, or both, ice gathered in small spicula round the ball, to the thickness of near a quarter of an inch. To such a degree did the mercury lose the fire it before contained, which, as I imagine, took the opportunity of escaping, in company with the evaporating particles of the spirit, by adhering to those particles.

Your experiment of the Florence flask, and boiling water, is very curious.[5] I have repeated it, and found it to succeed as you describe it, in two flasks out of three. The third would not charge when filled with either hot or cold water. I repeated it, because I re-

3. BF had mentioned Dr. William Cullen's experiments on evaporation in a letter to Dr. John Lining, April 14, 1757; see above, VII, 184. Cullen's report is in the Edinburgh Philosophical Society's *Essays and Observations, Philosophical and Literary,* II (1755), 145–75.

4. In a letter to Lining, June 17, 1758, BF discussed in some detail Dr. John Hadley's experiments, which he had witnessed at Cambridge in May 1758; see above, VIII, 188–9, and below, pp. 203–4.

5. Above, IX, 283–4.

membered I had once attempted to make an electric bottle of a Florence flask, filled with cold water, but could not charge it at all; which I then imputed to some imperceptible cracks in the small, extremely thin bubbles, of which that glass is full, and I concluded none of that kind would do. But you have shewn me my mistake. Mr. Wilson had formerly acquainted us, that red hot glass would conduct electricity;[6] but that so small a degree of heat as that communicated by boiling water, would so open the pores of extremely thin glass, as to suffer the electric fluid freely to pass, was not before known. Some experiments similar to yours, have, however, been made here, before the receipt of your letter, of which I shall now give you an account.

I formerly had an opinion that a Leyden bottle, charg'd and then seal'd hermetically, might retain its electricity for ever; but having afterwards some suspicion that possibly that subtil fluid might, by slow imperceptible degrees, soak through the glass, and in time escape, I requested some of my friends, who had conveniences for doing it, to make trial, whether, after some months, the charge of a bottle so sealed would be sensibly diminished. Being at Birmingham, in September 1760, Mr. Bolton of that place[7] opened a bottle that had been charged, and its long tube neck hermetically sealed in the January preceding. On breaking off the end of the neck, and introducing a wire into it, we found it possessed of a considerable quantity of electricity, which was discharged by a snap and spark. This bottle had lain near seven months on a shelf, in a closet, in contact with bodies that would undoubtedly have carried off all its electricity, if it could have come readily through the glass. Yet as the quantity manifested by the discharge was not apparently so great as might have been expected from a bottle of that size well charged, some doubt remained whether part had escaped while the neck was sealing, or had since, by degrees, soaked through the glass. But an experiment of Mr. Canton's, in which such a bottle

6. *A Treatise on Electricity* (London, 1750), pp. 143–4.

7. Matthew Boulton (1728–1809), engineer, inherited in 1759 his father's silver-stamping and piercing plant at Birmingham and soon after BF's visit founded the important works at Soho. Subsequently he became associated with James Watt in developing the steam engine and provided the working capital that made Watt's great achievement possible. He had many scientific interests and was elected F.R.S. in 1785. *DNB.* On BF's visit to Birmingham in 1760, see above, IX, 231 n.

was kept under water a week, without having its electricity in the least impaired, seems to show, that when the glass is cold, though extremely thin, the electric fluid is well retained by it. As that ingenious and accurate experimenter made a discovery, like yours, of the effect of heat in rendering thin glass permeable by that fluid, it is but doing him justice to give you his account of it, in his own words, extracted from his letter to me, in which he communicated it, dated Oct. 31, 1760, *viz*.[8]

"Having procured some thin glass balls, of about an inch and a half in diameter, with stems, or tubes, of eight or nine inches in length, I electrified them, some positively on the inside, and others negatively, after the manner of charging the Leyden bottle, and sealed them hermetically. Soon after I applied the naked balls to my electrometer, and could not discover the least sign of their being electrical; but holding them before the fire, at the distance of six or eight inches, they became strongly electrical in a very short time, and more so when they were cooling. These balls will, every time they are heated, give the electrical fluid to, or take it from other bodies, according to the *plus* or *minus* state of it within them. Heating them frequently, I find will sensibly diminish their power; but keeping one of them under water a week, did not appear in the least degree to impair it. That which I kept under water, was charged on the 22d of September last, was several times heated before it was kept in water, and has been heated frequently since, and yet it still retains its virtue to a very considerable degree. The breaking two of my balls accidentally, gave me an opportunity of measuring their thickness, which I found to be between seven and eight parts in a thousand of an inch.

"A down feather, in a thin glass ball, hermetically sealed, will not be affected by the application of an excited tube, or the wire of a charged vial, unless the ball be considerably heated; and if a glass pane be heated till it begins to grow soft, and in that state be held between the wire of a charged vial, and the discharging wire, the course of the electrical fluid will not be through the glass, but on the surface, round by the edge of it."

By this last experiment of Mr. Canton's, it appears, that though by a moderate heat, thin glass becomes, in some degree, a con-

8. What follows here is the full text of Canton's letter printed above, IX, 240.

ductor of electricity, yet, when of the thickness of a common pane, it is not, though in a state near melting, so good a conductor as to pass the shock of a discharged bottle. There are other conductors which suffer the electric fluid to pass through them gradually, and yet will not conduct a shock. For instance, a quire of paper will conduct through its whole length, so as to electrify a person, who, standing on wax, presents the paper to an electrified prime conductor; but it will not conduct a shock even through its thickness only; hence the shock either fails, or passes by rending a hole in the paper. Thus a sieve will pass water gradually, but a stream from a fire engine would either be stopped by it, or tear a hole through it.

It should seem, that to make glass permeable to the electric fluid, the heat should be proportioned to the thickness. You found the heat of boiling water, which is but 210, sufficient to render the extreme thin glass in a Florence flask permeable even to a shock. Lord Charles Cavendish,[9] by a very ingenious experiment, has found the heat of 400 requisite to render thicker glass permeable to the common current.

"A glass tube,[1] of which the part CB was solid, had wire thrust in each end, reaching to B and C.

"A small wire was tied on at D, reaching to the floor, in order to carry off any electricity that might run along upon the tube.

"The bent part was placed in an iron pot, filled with iron filings; a thermometer was also put into the filings; a lamp was placed under the pot; and the whole was supported upon glass.

"The wire A being electrified by a machine, before the heat was

9. Charles Cavendish (c. 1693–1783), 3d son of the 2d Duke of Devonshire; M.P., 1725–41; F.R.S., 1727; awarded the Copley Medal, 1757, for his experiments on thermometers. He was a scientist of distinction but has been overshadowed by his son Henry Cavendish (1731–1810), later associated with BF on the Purfleet Committee of 1772. A. Wolf, *A History of Science, Technology, and Philosophy in the Eighteenth Century* (2d edit., 1961), pp. 225, 243–4, 313–15. The quotation from one of his papers BF gives here apparently appeared in print for the first time in 1769, when BF published this letter to Kinnersley. The only publication of an entire paper by Charles Cavendish appears to be one on thermometers in *Phil. Trans.*, L (1757), 300–10.

1. In *Exper. and Obser.*, 1769 edit., these words are followed by "(See *Plate* VI.)," obviously referring to the plate printed on the facing page and reproduced here on p. 43, although the plate in question is number "VII." The reference was corrected in the 1774 edition.

applied, the corks at E separated, at first upon the principle of the Leyden vial.

"But after the part CB of the tube was heated to 600, the corks continued to separate, though you discharged the electricity by touching the wire at E, the electrical machine continuing in motion.

"Upon letting the whole cool, the effect remained till the thermometer was sunk to 400."

It were to be wished, that this noble philosopher would communicate more of his experiments to the world, as he makes many, and with great accuracy.

You know I have always look'd upon and mentioned the equal repulsion in cases of positive and of negative electricity, as a phaenomenon difficult to be explained.[2] I have sometimes, too, been inclined, with you, to resolve all into attraction; but besides that attraction seems in itself as unintelligible as repulsion, there are some appearances of repulsion that I cannot so easily explain by attraction; this for one instance. When the pair of cork balls are suspended by flaxen threads, from the end of the prime conductor, if you bring a rubbed glass tube near the conductor, but without touching it, you see the balls separate, as being electrified positively; and yet you have communicated no electricity to the conductor, for, if you had, it would have remained there, after withdrawing the tube; but the closing of the balls immediately thereupon, shews that the conductor has no more left in it than its natural quantity. Then again approaching the conductor with the rubbed tube, if, while the balls are separated, you touch with a finger that end of the conductor to which they hang, they will come together again, as being, with that part of the conductor, brought to the same state with your finger, i.e. the natural state. But the other end of the conductor, near which the tube is held, is not in that state, but in the negative state, as appears on removing the tube; for then part of the natural quantity left at the end near the balls, leaving that end to supply what is wanting at the other, the whole conductor is found to be equally in the negative state. Does not this indicate that the electricity of the rubbed tube had repelled the

2. Kinnersley had written that he had begun to be doubtful of the "Doctrine of Repulsion in Electrised Bodies"; above, IX, 284. For an analysis of this discussion, see I. Bernard Cohen, *Franklin and Newton* (Phila., 1956), pp. 531–4.

PLATE VII.

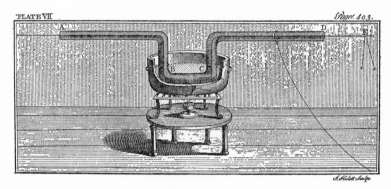

J. Hulett Sculp.

Lord Cavendish's Electrical Experiment

electric fluid, which was diffused in the conductor while in its natural state, and forced it to quit the end to which the tube was brought near, accumulating itself on the end to which the balls were suspended? I own I find it difficult to account for its quitting that end, on the approach of the rubbed tube, but on the supposition of repulsion; for, while the conductor was in the same state with the air, i.e. the natural state, it does not seem to me easy to suppose, that an attraction should suddenly take place between the air and the natural quantity of the electric fluid in the conductor, so as to draw it to, and accumulate it on the end opposite to that approached by the tube; since bodies, possessing only their natural quantity of that fluid, are not usually seen to attract each other, or to affect mutually the quantities of electricity each contains.

There are likewise appearances of repulsion in other parts of nature. Not to mention the violent force with which the particles of water, heated to a certain degree, separate from each other, or those of gunpowder, when touch'd with the smallest spark of fire, there is the seeming repulsion between the same poles of the magnet, a body containing a subtle moveable fluid, in many respects analagous to the electric fluid. If two magnets are so suspended by strings, as that their poles of the same denomination are opposite to each other, they will separate, and continue so; or if you lay a magnetic steel bar on a smooth table, and approach it with another parallel to it, the poles of both in the same position, the first will recede from the second, so as to avoid the contact, and may thus be push'd (or at least appear to be push'd) off the table. Can this be ascribed to the attraction of any surrounding body or matter drawing them asunder, or drawing the one away from the other? If not, and repulsion exists in nature, and in magnetism, why may it not exist in electricity? We should not, indeed, multiply causes in philosophy without necessity; and the greater simplicity of your hypothesis would recommend it to me, if I could see that all appearances might be solved by it. But I find, or think I find, the two causes more convenient than one of them alone. Thus I would solve the circular motion of your horizontal stick, supported on a pivot, with two pins at their ends, pointing contrary ways, and moving in the same direction when electrified, whether positively or negatively: When positively, the air opposite to the points being electrised positively, repels the points; when negatively, the air

opposite the points being also, by their means, electrised negatively, attraction takes place between the electricity in the air behind the heads of the pins, and the negative pins, and so they are,
in this case, drawn in the same direction that in the other they were
driven. You see I am willing to meet you half way, a complaisance
I have not met with in our brother Nollet, or any other hypothesis-
maker, and therefore may value myself a little upon it, especially
as they say I have some ability in defending even the wrong side
of a question, when I think fit to take it in hand.

What you give as an established law of the electric fluid, "That
quantities of different densities mutually attract each other, in order
to restore the equilibrium"[3] is, I think, not well founded, or else
not well express'd. Two large cork balls, suspended by silk strings,
and both well and equally electrified, separate to a great distance.
By bringing into contact with one of them, another ball of the same
size, suspended likewise by silk, you will take from it half its electricity. It will then, indeed, hang at a less distance from the other,
but the full and the half quantities will not appear to attract each
other, that is, the balls will not come together. Indeed, I do not
know any proof we have, that one quantity of electric fluid is attracted by another quantity of that fluid, whatever difference there
may be in their densities. And, supposing in nature, a mutual attraction between two parcels of any kind of matter, it would be strange
if this attraction should subsist strongly while those parcels were
unequal, and cease when more matter of the same kind was added
to the smallest parcel, so as to make it equal to the biggest. By all
the laws of attraction in matter, that we are acquainted with, the
attraction is stronger in proportion to the increase of the masses,
and never in proportion to the difference of the masses. I should
rather think the law would be, "That the electric fluid is attracted
strongly by all other matter that we know of, while the parts of that
fluid mutually repel each other." Hence its being equally diffused
(except in particular circumstances) throughout all other matter.
But this you jokingly call "electrical orthodoxy." It is so with some
at present, but not with all; and, perhaps, it may not always be
orthodoxy with any body. Opinions are continually varying, where
we cannot have mathematical evidence of the nature of things;

3. Above, IX, 284.

and they must vary. Nor is that variation without its use, since it occasions a more thorough discussion, whereby error is often dissipated, true knowledge is encreased, and its principles become better understood and more firmly established.

Air should have, as you observe, "its share of the common stock of electricity, as well as glass, and, perhaps, all other electrics *per se*."[4] But I suppose, that, like them, it does not easily part with what it has, or receive more, unless when mix'd with some non-electric, as moisture for instance, of which there is some in our driest air. This, however, is only a supposition; and your experiment of restoring electricity to a negatively electrised person, by extending his arm upwards into the air, with a needle between his fingers, on the point of which light may be seen in the night, is, indeed, a curious one. In this town the air is generally moister than with us, and here I have seen Mr. Canton electrify the air in one room positively, and in another, which communicated by a door, he has electrised the air negatively. The difference was easily discovered by his cork balls, as he passed out of one room into another. Pere Beccaria, too, has a pretty experiment, which shews that air may be electrised.[5] Suspending a pair of small light balls, by flaxen threads, to the end of his prime conductor, he turns his globe some time, electrising positively, the balls diverging and continuing separate all the time. Then he presents the point of a needle to his conductor, which gradually drawing off the electric fluid, the balls approach each other, and touch, before all is drawn from the conductor; opening again as more is drawn off, and separating nearly as wide as at first, when the conductor is reduced to the natural state. By this it appears, that when the balls came together, the air surrounding the balls was just as much electrised as the conductor at that time; and more than the conductor, when that was reduced to its natural state. For the balls, though in the natural state, will diverge, when the air that surrounds them is electrised *plus* or *minus,* as well as when that is in its natural state and they are electrised *plus* or *minus* themselves. I foresee that you will apply this experiment to the support of your hypothesis, and I think you may make a good deal of it.

4. *Ibid.*
5. For these experiments, described by Giambatista Beccaria in a letter to BF, Dec. 24, 1757, see above, VII, 307–11.

It was a curious enquiry of yours, Whether the electricity of the air, in clear dry weather, be of the same density at the height of two or three hundred yards, as near the surface of the earth; and I am glad you made the experiment.[6] Upon reflection, it should seem probable, that whether the general state of the atmosphere at any time be positive or negative, that part of it which is next the earth will be nearer the natural state, by having given to the earth in one case, or having received from it in the other. In electrising the air of a room, that which is nearest the walls, or floor, is least altered. There is only one small ambiguity in the experiment, which may be cleared by more trials; it arises from the supposition that bodies may be electrised positively by the friction of air blowing strongly on them, as it does on the kite and its string. If at some times the electricity appears to be negative, as that friction is the same, the effect must be from a negative state of the upper air.

I am much pleased with your electrical thermometer, and the experiments you have made with it.[7] I formerly satisfied myself by an experiment with my phial and syphon, that the elasticity of the air was not increased by the mere existence of an electric atmosphere within the phial; but I did not know, till you now inform me, that heat may be given to it by an electric explosion. The continuance of its rarefaction, for some time after the discharge of your glass jar and of your case of bottles, seem to make this clear. The other experiments on wet paper, wet thread, green grass, and green wood, are not so satisfactory; as possibly the reducing part of the moisture to vapour, by the electric fluid passing through it, might occasion some expansion which would be gradually reduced by the condensation of such vapour. The fine silver thread, the very small brass wire, and the strip of gilt paper, are also subject to a similar objection, as even metals, in such circumstances, are often partly reduced to smoke, particularly the gilding on paper.

But your subsequent beautiful experiment on the wire, which you made hot by the electric explosion, and in that state fired gunpowder with it, puts it out of all question, that heat is produced by our artificial electricity, and that the melting of metals in that way, is not by what I formerly called a cold fusion. A late instance here, of the melting a bell-wire, in a house struck by lightning,

6. Above, ix, 285.
7. Above, ix, 286–9.

and parts of the wire burning holes in the floor on which they fell, has proved the same with regard to the electricity of nature. I was too easily led into that error by accounts given, even in philosophical books, and from remote ages downwards, of melting money in purses, swords in scabbards, &c. without burning the inflammable matters that were so near those melted metals. But men are, in general, such careless observers, that a philosopher cannot be too much on his guard in crediting their relations of things extraordinary, and should never build an hypothesis on any thing but clear facts and experiments, or it will be in danger of soon falling, as this does, like a house of cards.

How many ways there are of kindling fire, or producing heat in bodies! By the sun's rays, by collision, by friction, by hammering, by putrefaction, by fermentation, by mixtures of fluids, by mixtures of solids with fluids, and by electricity. And yet the fire when produced, though in different bodies it may differ in circumstances, as in colour, vehemence, &c. yet in the same bodies is generally the same. Does not this seem to indicate that the fire existed in the body, though in a quiescent state, before it was by any of these means excited, disengaged, and brought forth to action and to view? May it not constitute part, and even a principal part, of the solid substance of bodies? If this should be the case, kindling fire in a body would be nothing more than developing this inflammable principle, and setting it at liberty to act in separating the parts of that body, which then exhibits the appearances of scorching, melting, burning, &c. When a man lights an hundred candles from the flame of one, without diminishing that flame, can it be properly said to have *communicated* all that fire? When a single spark from a flint, applied to a magazine of gunpowder, is immediately attended with this consequence, that the whole is in flame, exploding with immense violence, could all this fire exist first in the spark? We cannot conceive it. And thus we seem led to this supposition, that there is fire enough in all bodies to singe, melt, or burn them, whenever it is, by any means, set at liberty, so that it may exert itself upon them, or be disengaged from them. This liberty seems to be afforded it by the passage of electricity through them, which we know can and does, of itself, separate the parts even of water; and perhaps the immediate appearances of fire are only the effects of such separations? If so, there would be no need of supposing that

49

the electric fluid *heats itself* by the swiftness of its motion, or heats bodies by the resistance it meets with in passing through them. They would only be heated in proportion as such separation could be more easily made. Thus a melting heat cannot be given to a large wire in the flame of a candle, though it may to a small one; and this not because the large wire resists *less* that action of the flame which tends to separate its parts, but because it resists it *more* than the smaller wire; or because the force being divided among more parts, acts weaker on each.

This reminds me, however, of a little experiment I have frequently made, that shews, at one operation, the different effects of the same quantity of electric fluid passing through different quantities of metal. A strip of tinfoil, three inches long, a quarter of an inch wide at one end, and tapering all the way to a sharp point at the other, fixed between two pieces of glass, and having the electricity of a large glass jar sent through it will not be discomposed in the broadest part; towards the middle will appear melted in spots; where narrower, it will be quite melted; and about half an inch of it next the point will be reduced to smoke.

You were not mistaken in supposing that your account of the effect of the pointed rod, in securing Mr. West's house from damage by a stroke of lightning, would give me great pleasure.[8] I thank you for it most heartily, and for the pains you have taken in giving me so complete a description of its situation, form, and substance, with the draft of the melted point. There is one circumstance, *viz.* that the lightning was seen to diffuse itself from the foot of the rod over the wet pavement, which seems, I think, to indicate, that the earth under the pavement was very dry, and that the rod should have been sunk deeper, till it came to earth moister and therefore apter to receive and dissipate the electric fluid. And although, in this instance, a conductor formed of nail rods, not much above a quarter of an inch thick, served well to convey the lightning, yet some accounts I have seen from Carolina,[9] give reason to think, that larger may be sometimes necessary, at least for the security of the conductor itself, which, when too small, may be destroyed in executing its office, though it does, at the same time, preserve the house. Indeed, in the construction of an instrument so new,

8. Above, IX, 291–3.
9. For these accounts see the two extracts reprinted immediately below.

and of which we could have so little experience, it is rather lucky that we should at first be so near the truth as we seem to be, and commit so few errors.

There is another reason for sinking deeper the lower end of the rod, and also for turning it outwards under ground to some distance from the foundation; it is this, that water dripping from the eaves falls near the foundation, and sometimes soaks down there in greater quantities, so as to come near the end of the rod though the ground about it be drier. In such case, this water may be exploded, that is, blown into vapour, whereby a force is generated that may damage the foundation. Water reduced to vapour, is said to occupy 14,000 times its former space. I have sent a charge through a small glass tube, that has borne it well while empty, but when filled first with water, was shattered to pieces and driven all about the room: Finding no part of the water on the table, I suspected it to have been reduced to vapour; and was confirmed in that suspicion afterwards, when I had filled a like piece of tube with ink, and laid it on a sheet of clean paper, whereon, after the explosion, I could find neither any moisture nor any sully from the ink. This experiment of the explosion of water, which I believe was first made by that most ingenious electrician father Beccaria, may account for what we sometimes see in a tree struck by lightning, when part of it is reduced to fine splinters like a broom; the sap vessels being so many tubes containing a watry fluid, which when reduced to vapour, rends every tube length-ways. And perhaps it is this rarefaction of the fluids in animal bodies killed by lightning or electricity, that by separating its fibres, renders the flesh so tender, and apt so much sooner to putrify. I think too, that much of the damage done by lightning to stone and brick walls, may sometimes be owing to the explosion of water, found, during showers, running or lodging in the joints or small cavities or cracks that happen to be in the walls.

Here are some electricians that recommend knobs instead of points on the upper end of the rods, from a supposition that the points invite the stroke.[1] It is true that points draw electricity at

1. This is BF's first mention of a disagreement which developed into a major controversy among electrical scientists in Great Britain. It will be dealt with in considerable detail in connection with the so-called Purfleet Committee of 1772.

greater distances in the gradual silent way; but knobs will draw at the greatest distance a stroke. There is an experiment that will settle this. Take a crooked wire of the thickness of a quill, and of such a length as that one end of it being applied to the lower part of a charged bottle, the upper may be brought near the ball on the top of the wire that is in the bottle. Let one end of this wire be furnished with a knob, and the other be gradually tapered to a fine point. When the point is presented to discharge the bottle it must be brought much nearer before it will receive the stroke, than the knob requires to be. Points besides tend to repel the fragments of an electrised cloud, knobs draw them nearer. An experiment which I believe I have shewn you, of cotton fleece hanging from an electrised body, shows this clearly when a point or a knob is presented under it.

You seem to think highly of the importance of this discovery, as do many others on our side of the water.[2] Here it is very little regarded; so little, that though it is now seven or eight years since it was made publick, I have not heard of a single house as yet attempted to be secured by it.[3] It is true the mischiefs done by lightning are not so frequent here as with us, and those who calculate chances may perhaps find that not one death (or the destruction of one house) in a hundred thousand happens from that cause, and that therefore it is scarce worth while to be at any expence to guard against it. But in all countries there are particular situations of buildings more exposed than others to such accidents, and there are minds so strongly impressed with the apprehension of them, as to be very unhappy every time a little thunder is within their hearing; it may therefore be well to render this little piece of new knowledge as general and as well understood as possible, since to make us *safe* is not all its advantage, it is some to make us *easy*. And as the stroke it secures us from might have chanced perhaps but once in our lives, while it may relieve us a hundred times from those

2. The final paragraph of Kinnersley's letter (above, IX, 293) had extolled BF's "important Discovery" of the lightning rod: "May the Benefit thereof be diffused over the whole Globe. May it extend to the latest Posterity of Mankind; and make the Name of FRANKLIN like that of NEWTON, *immortal.*"

3. For Lord Marischal's interest in the lightning rod, however, see above, p. 17, and below, pp. 81, 82–3. It is not certain whether he intended to use it on his residence at Neuchâtel or on his family home, Keith Hall, in Scotland.

painful apprehensions, the latter may possibly on the whole contribute more to the happiness of mankind than the former.

Your kind wishes and congratulations are very obliging. I return them cordially; being with great regard and esteem, My dear Sir, Your affectionate friend, and most obedient humble servant, B.F.

Accounts from Carolina *(mention'd in the foregoing Letter)* of the effects of Lightning, on two of the Rods commonly affix'd to Houses there, for securing them against Lightning.

Charles-town, Nov. 1, 1760.

————It is some Years since Mr. Raven's Rod was struck by lightning.[4] I hear an account of it was published at the time, but I cannot find it. According to the best information I can now get, he had fix'd to the outside of his chimney a large iron Rod, several feet in length, reaching above the chimney; and to the top of this rod the points were fixed. From the lower end of this rod, a small brass wire was continued down to the top of another iron rod driven into the earth. On the ground-floor in the chimney stood a gun, leaning against the back wall, nearly opposite to where the brass wire came down on the outside. The lightning fell upon the points, did no damage to the rod they were fix'd to; but the brass wire, all down till it came opposite to the top of the gun-barrel, was destroyed.* There the lightning made a hole through the wall or back of the chimney, to get to the gun-barrel,† down which it seems to have pass'd, as, although it did not hurt the barrel, it damaged the butt of the stock, and blew up some bricks of the hearth. The brass wire below the hole in the wall remain'd good. No other damage,

*A proof that it was not of sufficient substance to conduct with safety to itself (tho' with safety *so far* to the wall) so large a quantity of the electric fluid.[5]

†A more substantial conductor.

4. In his letter to Hume mentioning this incident, BF referred to "the house of Mr. Raven, at John's Island, near Charlestown, South Carolina." Above, p. 19. The community of Johns Island is near the Stono River and about ten miles west of Charleston. A John Raven was a member in 1750 of the Charleston Library Company of which Dr. John Lining was president. Another John Raven, possibly a son, died in 1764, aged 38. *So. Car. Hist. and Geneal. Mag.*, XXIII (1922), 168; XXIX (1928), 240.

5. BF doubtless added this and the next note in printing this account in 1769.

as I can learn, was done to the house. I am told the same house had formerly been struck by lightning, and much damaged, before these rods were invented.————

Mr. William Maine's Account of the Effects of Lightning on his Rod, dated at Indian Land, in South Carolina, Aug. 28, 1760.[6]

————I had a set of electrical points, consisting of three prongs, of large brass wire tipt with silver, and perfectly sharp, each about seven inches long; these were riveted at equal distances into an iron nut about three quarters of an inch square, and opened at top equally to the distance of six or seven inches from point to point, in a regular triangle. This nut was screwed very tight on the top of an iron rod of above half an inch diameter, or the thickness of a common curtain rod, composed of several joints, annexed by hooks turned at the ends of each joint, and the whole fixed to the chimney of my house by iron staples. The points were elevated (a),[7] six or seven inches above the top of the chimney; and the lower joint sunk three feet in the earth, in a perpendicular direction.

Thus stood the points on Tuesday last about five in the evening, when the lightning broke with a violent explosion on the chimney, cut the rod square off just under the nutt, and I am persuaded, melted the points, nut, and top of the rod, entirely up; as after the most diligent search, nothing of either was found (b), and the top of the remaining rod was cased over with a congealed solder. The lightning ran down the rod, starting almost all the staples (c), and unhooking the joints, without affecting the rod (d), except on the inside of each hook where the joints were coupled, the surface of which was melted (e), and left as cased over with solder. No part of the chimney was damaged (f), only at the foundation (g), where it was shattered almost quite round, and several bricks were torn out (h). Considerable cavities were made in the earth quite round

6. William Maine (d. 1776) came to So. Car. from Ireland and in about 1756 purchased Jericho Plantation, about 22 miles west of Charleston. Here he planted mulberry trees as part of a silkworm project. *Transactions of the Huguenot Society of South Carolina*, no. 64 (1959), pp. 34–5. John R. Todd and Francis M. Hutson, *Prince William's Parish and Plantations* (Richmond, 1935), p. 215.

7. This and other italicised letters were apparently inserted by BF when he printed this account in order to provide reference points for his comments in the "Remarks" that follow.

the foundation, but most within eight or nine inches of the rod. It also shattered the bottom weather-board *(i)*, at one corner of the house, and made a large hole in the earth by the corner post. On the other side of the chimney, it ploughed up several furrows in the earth, some yards in length. It ran down the inside of the chimney *(k)*, carrying only soot with it; and filled the whole house with its flash *(l)*, smoke, and dust. It tore up the hearth in several places *(m)*, and broke some pieces of china in the beaufet *(n)*. A copper tea kettle standing in the chimney was beat together, as if some great weight had fallen upon it *(o)*; and three holes, each about half an inch diameter, melted through the bottom *(p)*. What seems to me most surprising is, that the hearth under the kettle was not hurt, yet the bottom of the kettle was drove inward, as if the lightning proceeded from under it upwards *(q)*, and the cover was thrown to the middle of the floor *(r)*. The fire dogs, an iron loggerhead, an Indian pot, an earthen cup, and a cat, were all in the chimney at the time unhurt, though great part of the hearth was torn up *(s)*. My wife's sister, two children, and a Negro wench, were all who happened to be in the house at the time: The first, and one child, sat within five feet of the chimney; and were so stunned, that they never saw the lightning nor heard the explosion; the wench, with the other child in her arms, sitting at a greater distance, was sensible of both; though every one was so stunn'd that they did not recover for some time; however it pleased God that no farther mischief ensued. The kitchen, at 90 feet distance, was full of Negroes, who were all sensible of the shock; and some of them tell me, that they felt the rod about a minute after, when it was so hot that they could not bear it in hand.

REMARKS.[8]

The foregoing very sensible and distinct account may afford a good deal of instruction relating to the nature and effects of lightning, and to the construction and use of this instrument for averting the mischiefs of it. Like other new instruments, this appears to have been at first in some respects imperfect; and we find that we are, in this as in others, to expect improvement from experience chiefly: But there seems to be nothing in the account, that should

8. BF probably wrote these remarks in 1769 specifically for inclusion in *Exper. and Obser.*

discourage us in the use of it; since at the same time that its imperfections are discovered, the means of removing them are pretty easily to be learnt from the circumstances of the account itself; and its utility upon the whole is manifest.

One intention of the pointed rod, is, to *prevent* a stroke of lightning. (*See pages* 126, 162.[9]) But to have a better chance of obtaining this end, the points should not be too near to the top of the chimney or highest part of the building to which they are affixed, but should be extended five or six feet above it; otherwise their operation in silently drawing off the fire (from such fragments of cloud as float in the air between the great body of cloud and the earth) will be prevented. For the experiment with the lock of cotton hanging below the electrified prime conductor, shews, that a finger under it, being a blunt body, extends the cotton, drawing its lower part downwards; when a needle with its point presented to the cotton, makes it fly up again to the prime conductor; and that this effect is strongest, when as much of the needle as possible appears above the end of the finger; grows weaker as the needle is shortened between the finger and thumb; and is reduced to nothing when only a short part below the point appears above the finger. Now it seems the points of Mr. Maine's rod were elevated only *(a) six or seven inches above the top of the chimney;* which, considering the bulk of the chimney and the house, was too small an elevation. For the great body of matter near them would hinder their being easily brought into a negative state by the repulsive power of the electrised cloud, in which negative state it is that they attract most strongly and copiously the electric fluid from other bodies, and convey it into the earth.

(b) Nothing of the points, &c. could be found. This is a common effect. (*See page* 163.[1]) Where the quantity of the electric fluid passing is too great for the conductor thro' which it passes, the metal is either melted, or reduced to smoke and dissipated; but where the conductor is sufficiently large, the fluid passes in it without hurting it. Thus these three wires were destroyed, while the rod to which they were fixed, being of greater substance, remained

9. This and other page references below are to the 1769 edition of *Exper. and Obser.* The two passages cited here are found in the present edition, v, 78; VI, 98–9.

1. Above, VI, 100.

unhurt; its end only, to which they were joined, being a little melted, some of the melted part of the lower ends of those wires uniting with it, and appearing on it like solder.

(c) (d) (e) As the several parts of the rod were connected only by the ends being bent round into hooks, the contact between hook and hook was much smaller than the rod; therefore the current through the metal being confin'd in those narrow passages, melted part of the metal, as appeared on examining the inside of each hook. Where metal is melted by lightning, some part of it is generally exploded; and these explosions in the joints appear to have been the cause of unhooking them; and, by that violent action, of starting also most of the staples. We learned from hence, that a rod in one continued piece is preferable to one composed of links or parts hooked together.

(f) No part of the chimney was damaged; because the lightning passed in the rod. And this instance agrees with others in shewing, that the second and principal intention of the rods is obtainable, viz. that of *conducting* the lightning. In all the instances yet known of the lightning's falling on any house guarded by rods, it has pitched down upon the point of the rod; and has not fallen upon any other part of the house. Had the lightning fallen on this chimney, unfurnished with a rod, it would probably have rent it from top to bottom, as we see, by the effects of the lightning on the points and rod, that its quantity was very great; and we know that many chimneys have been so demolished. But *no part of this was damaged, only (f) (g) (h) at the foundation, where it was shattered and several bricks torn out.* Here we learn the principal defect in fixing this rod. The lower joint being sunk but three feet into the earth, did not it seems go low enough to come at water, or a large body of earth so moist as to receive readily from its end the quantity it conducted. The electric fluid therefore thus accumulated near the lower end of the rod, quitted it at the surface of the earth, dividing in search of other passages. Part of it tore up the surface in furrows, and made holes in it: Part entered the bricks of the foundation, which being near the earth are generally moist, and, in exploding that moisture, shattered them. (*See page* 415.[2]) Part went through or under the foundation, and got under the hearth, blowing up great part of the bricks *(m) (s)*, and producing the

2. Above, p. 51.

other effects *(o) (p) (q) (r)*. The iron dogs, loggerhead and iron pot were not hurt, being of sufficient substance, and they probably protected the cat. The copper tea kettle being thin, suffered some damage. Perhaps, tho' found on a sound part of the hearth, it might at the time of the stroke have stood on the part blown up, which will account both for the bruising and melting.

That *it ran down the inside of the chimney (k)* I apprehend must be a mistake. Had it done so, I imagine it would have brought something more than soot with it; it would probably have ripp'd off the pargetting, and brought down fragments of plaister and bricks. The shake, from the explosion on the rod, was sufficient to shake down a good deal of loose soot. Lightning does not usually enter houses by the doors, windows, or chimneys, as open passages, in the manner that air enters them: Its nature is, to be attracted by substances, that are conductors of electricity; it penetrates and passes *in* them, and, if they are not good conductors, as are neither wood, brick, stone nor plaister, it is apt to rend them in its passage. It would not easily pass thro' the air from a cloud to a building, were it not for the aid afforded it in its passage by intervening fragments of clouds below the main body, or by the falling rain.

It is said that *the house was filled with its flash (1)*. Expressions like this are common in accounts of the effects of lightning, from which we are apt to understand that the lightning filled the house. Our language indeed seems to want a word to express the *light* of lightning as distinct from the lightning itself. When a tree on a hill is struck by it, the lightning of that stroke exists only in a narrow vein between the cloud and the tree, but its light fills a vast space many miles round; and people at the greatest distance from it are apt to say, "the lightning came into our rooms through our windows." As it is in itself extreamly bright, it cannot, when so near as to strike a house, fail illuminating highly every room in it through the windows; and this I suppose to have been the case at Mr. Maine's; and that, except in and near the hearth, from the causes abovementioned, it was not in any other part of the house; the *flash* meaning no more than *the light* of the lightning. It is for want of considering this difference, that people suppose there is a kind of lightning not attended with thunder. In fact there is probably a loud explosion accompanying every flash of lightning, and

58

at the same instant; but as sound travels slower than light, we often hear the sound some seconds of time after having seen the light; and as sound does not travel so far as light, we sometimes see the light at a distance too great to hear the sound.

(n) The *breaking some pieces of china in the beaufet,* may nevertheless seem to indicate that the lightning was there: But as there is no mention of its having hurt any part of the beaufet, or of the walls of the house, I should rather ascribe that effect to the concussion of the air, or shake of the house by the explosion.

Thus, to me it appears, that the house and its inhabitants were saved by the rod, though the rod itself was unjointed by the stroke; and that, if it had been made of one piece, and sunk deeper in the earth, or had entered the earth at a greater distance from the foundation, the mentioned small damages (except the melting of the points) would not have happened.

Joseph Browne to John Kelly[3]

ALS: American Philosophical Society; copy: Yale University Library

Febr. 22. 1762. Agreed, nem. con. at a meeting of the Heads of Houses that Mr. Franklin, whenever He shall please to visit the University, shall be offer'd the Compliment of the Degree of D.C.L. *Honoris causâ.*[4]   J BROWNE Vice Can.

Addressed: To | Dr. Kelly

3. Joseph Browne (*c.* 1700–1767), B.A., Oxon. (Queen's College), 1721; B.D., 1737; D.D., 1743; fellow, 1731; Sedleian professor of natural philosophy, 1741–67; provost of Queen's, 1756–67; vice chancellor, 1759–65. John Kelly (*c.* 1726–1772), B.A., Oxon. (Christ Church), 1747; B. Med., 1752; D. Med., 1756; Regius professor of medicine, 1759–72. *DNB;* Joseph Foster, *Alumni Oxonienses; The Members of the University of Oxford, 1715–1886* (London, 1887–88), I, 175; II, 784.

4. The degree was conferred on BF, April 30, 1762, and at the same time WF received an honorary M.A. degree; see below, pp. 76–8.

From [Samuel?] Mead[5]   AL: University of Pennsylvania Library

25th. Feby. 1762

Mr. Meads Compliments to Doctor Franklin and incloses him some account of the good Effects of Electricity, sent by a Curate of Doctor Douglass[6] in the Country, which Lord Bath wished he might see! It is to be published as I understand, and if Mr. Franklin has any thing to observe on it, Mr. Mead would be glad when it is returned to acquaint my Lord with it.

Doctor Franklin Craven Street.

Addressed: For / Doctor Franklin / in Craven Street.

From Thomas-François Dalibard[7]

ALS: American Philosophical Society

M. franklin
Monsieur,   A Paris ce   février 1762.

Je ne puis vous exprimer tout le plaisir que m'a causé La lettre que vous m'avez fait L'honneur de m'ecrire de Londres le 9. Décembre 1761. et qui m'a eté remise le 7. Janvier 1762. par M. Le Docteur Shippen.[8] La guerre avoit interrompu depuis plusieurs an-

5. Probably Samuel Mead (d. 1776), commissioner of the customs, 1742–76; F.R.S., 1738. His sister, the widow of James Gambier the elder, was perhaps the Craven St. neighbor with whom BF drank tea one day in the following May when Mrs. Stevenson failed to return home when he expected her. See below, p. 84.

6. Presumably John Douglas (1721–1807), D.D., 1758; vicar of Uppington and High Ercall, Shropshire; author of *Milton Vindicated from the Charge of Plagiarism* (London, 1751) and of *A Letter Addressed to Two Great Men* (London, 1760), of which BF wrote approvingly in the Canada Pamphlet; see above, IV, 335 n; IX, 52–3. Douglas was a protegé of the Earl of Bath; he lived in London and visited his livings only occasionally. *DNB.* The curate has not been identified and his paper on electricity has not been found.

7. The French scientist who translated BF's *Exper. and Obser.* and first carried out his proposed experiment to prove the identity of lightning and electricity; see above, IV, 302 n.

8. For BF's letter transmitting that part of Ebenezer Kinnersley's letter of March 12, 1761, which told of the stroke of lightning on William West's house in Philadelphia, see above, IX, 396 n. On young Dr. William Shippen, who carried BF's letter to France, see above, IX, 219 n. He was traveling in the capacity of physician attending Miss Louisa Poyntz, a victim of tubercu-

nées notre ancien commerce de lettres et j'en avois eté extrême-
ment mortifié. J'en ai eté d'autant plus sensible à la joye de recevoir
de vos nouvelles. J'ai tardé Longtems à vous répondre pour
plusieurs raisons. Je voulois m'informer s'il y avoit quelque décou-
verte nouvelle dans l'Electricité, pour vous les communiquer; L'on
m'a assuré qu'il n'y en avoit point qui pusse vous intéresser. Vous
serez peut être surpris que je ne le sçusse pas par moi même mais
je vous avouerai que depuis la dernière Edition de vos ouvrages[9]
j'ai presqu'entièrement renoncé aux Expériences Electriques. Voi-
cy Les raisons qui m'ont fait prendre cette résolution. 1° Les dif-
férentes commotions Electriques m'ont si fortement attaqué le
genre nerveux qu'il m'est resté un tremblement convulsif dans les
bras de façon que j'ai bien de la peine à porter un verre à ma
bouche; et si actuellement je touchois une seule étincelle Electrique
je serois 24. heures sans pouvoir signer mon nom. Une chose que
je remarque encore c'est qu'il m'est presqu'impossible de cachetter
une Lettre parceque L'Electricité de la Cire d'Espagne[1] se com-
muniquant à mon bras redouble mon tremblement. 2° J'ai beaucoup
d'autres occupations qui ne me permettent plus de suivre vos Expériences. 3° J'ai rencontré beaucoup d'opposition à vos principes
et le travail qu'il m'auroit fallu faire pour les détruire quoique je
l'eusse entrepris avec grande satisfaction m'en a dégoûté. 4° Je
n'ai plus les mêmes commodités que j'avois autrefois. Ainsi, Monsieur, je ne suis plus qu'admirateur des travaux des autres Physiciens; mais il y a icy d'autres Electriciens fort attachés à vos
principes. Je vous nommerai principalement M. Le Roy[2] de l'académie Royale des sciences qui depuis plusieurs années soutient
fortement votre systême d'Électricité contre son Confrere M.

losis and sister of Lady Spencer. Betsy C. Corner, *William Shippen, Jr.*
(Phila., 1951), p. 125 n; Whitfield J. Bell, Jr., "Philadelphia Medical Students
in Europe, 1750–1800," *PMHB*, LXVII (1943), 23.

9. The second edition of Dalibard's translation of *Exper. and Obser.*
appeared in 1756.

1. Sealing wax.

2. Jean-Baptiste LeRoy (1720–1800) had been elected to the French Academy of Sciences in 1751. He carried out important studies on positive and
negative electricity, thereby promoting BF's theories in opposition to those of
Nollet. He was also interested in problems of ventilation and the hygiene of
prisons and hospitals. He and BF began an extended correspondence later in
this decade and during BF's French years they became warm friends.

L'abbé Nollet et ses sectateurs. J'ai appris depuis peu qu'un de ces derniers nommé M. Dutour[3] avoit fait imprimer un recüeil d'Expériences par lequel il prétend deffendre le systême de M. L'abbé Nollet. Quoique son Livre ne soit point encore venu à ma connoissance je n'ai pas bon augure de son excellence. Voila tout ce que j'ai pu apprendre de nouveau sur L'Electricité.

Vous aurez sans doute vû à Londres Les lettres que M. L'abbé Nollet fit imprimer en 1753 en opposition aux votres.[4] Ainsi je ne vous parlerai point de ce mauvais Livre.

J'ai eté charmé de recevoir icy M. Le Docteur Shippen; quand il n'auroit pas le mérite personnel que je lui reconnois je lui aurois toujours fait le bon accüeil que je dois à un ami que vous m'avez adressé. Je lui ai donné La connoissance d'un de mes amis Docteur en médecine chez qui il a eté très bien reçu et qui est à portée de lui procurer tout ce qu'il peut desirer concernant sa profession. Je le menai il y a huit jours au jardin du Roy pour le presenter à M. de Buffon ancien ami de M. Collinson, mais il etoit absent parce qu'il etoit allé présenter au Roy le 8e et le 9e tome in 4° de son histoire naturelle.[5] C'est aussi Lui M. de Buffon qui a fait retarder ma réponse parcequ'il m'avoit prié d'y joindre une lettre pour M. Collinson à qui il vouloit demander quelques graines d'arbre dont il a besoin tant pour le jardin Royal des plantes que pour lui. Je suis allé le voir depuis trois jours et je l'ai trouvé in-

3. Etienne-François du Tour (or Dutour) de Salvert (1711-1789), physicist. Joseph Priestley's *History and Present State of Electricity* (London, 1767), pp. 454, [738], mentions du Tour's *Recherches sur les différens mouvements de la matière électrique* (Paris, 1760), calling its hypothesis difficult to understand but adding that "the author appears very much attached to it, and has no doubt of its accounting for all electrical appearances."

4. For Jean-Antoine Nollet's *Lettres sur l'électricité* (1753) attacking BF's theories, see above, IV, 423-8. In 1760 he published a new edition with a second volume continuing the controversy; see above, IX, 252 n.

5. On Georges-Louis Le Clerc, Comte du Buffon (1707-1788), naturalist, superintendent of the Jardin du Roi, 1739, and electrical experimenter, see above, III, 111 n. The eighth and ninth volumes of his *Histoire naturelle générale et particulière* were published in 1760 and 1761 respectively. Dalibard had sent BF copies of the first four volumes in 1755; above, VI, 98. Buffon and Peter Collinson, with mutual interests in botany, had corresponded for many years and in 1756 Collinson approved John Bartram's suggestion that the American should address his letters to the Englishman in Buffon's care in case they should be captured at sea by the French. Darlington, *Memorials*, pp. 199-200, 203.

commodé; il me dit qu'il n'avoit pu écrire à cause de son incommodité; mais il me chargea de Lui envoyer le mémoire des choses qu'il avoit à Lui demander. Je vous prie, Monsieur, de vouloir bien faire remettre à M. Collinson Le paquet cy joint. Je vous prie encore de vouloir bien écrire à notre ami M. Jean Bartram de Phyladelphie pour l'engager à recüeillir l'Eté prochain des graines ou semences de tous les arbres et arbustes que l'on trouve dan[s la] Pensylvanie et aux environs pour les envoye[r l'an] prochain à M. de Buffon [intenda]nt d[u jardin] des plantes à Paris. Il [*torn*⁶] Les espèces et quelles puissent [*torn*] état d'être semeés et de prod [*torn*].

J'ai fait imprimer dans nos [*torn*] observations de [*torn*] arrivé à Phila[delphie *torn*] West et je vo[*torn*] prouver l'esti[*torn*] de tout ce qu[*torn*] voulu étend[*torn*] n'en ai pa[*torn*].⁷

Vous m'avez mandé, Monsieur, que vous comptiez retourner en Amérique au printems prochain. Pourez vous vous déterminer à quitter l'Europe sans avoir fait un petit voyage en france pendant que vous en êtes si près? Pour moi je vous assure que je regarderois comme une des plus grande satisfaction de ma vie d'avoir L'honneur de vous recevoir à Paris et je ne suis pas le seul qui desireroit de vous y voire.⁸ Votre réputation vous y a précédé, votre nom y est peut être plus connu qu'à Londres et les Physiciens françois auroient le plus grand désir de rendre hommage à votre mérite. Tachez donc, je vous prie, de prendre sur vos affaires le tems de faire un voyage icy. Je me chargerai très volontiers de vous en aplanir les principales difficultés. J'imagine que la guerre est Le plus grand obstacle; mais j'espere venir à bout de le lever. Vous n'avez qu'à me faire savoir que vous avez envie de venir en france, j'obtiendrai du Ministère françois un passeport pour vous et pour

6. A ragged tear has caused the loss of nearly a quarter of the third and fourth pages of the letter sheet. On the third page, the loss is so extensive beyond this point, eleven lines from the bottom, that even conjectural restoration of the missing words is impossible.

7. This paragraph obviously referred to Dalibard's translation of the extract from Kinnersley's letter to BF, March 12, 1761, about the stroke of lightning which hit William West's house, and to the printing of the translation in Dubourg's *Gazette de médecine;* see above, IX, 391.

8. BF returned to America in the summer of 1762 without visiting France as Dalibard hoped. He did go there in 1767, however, and Dalibard and his wife entertained him. The remainder of this paragraph suggests the high esteem in which BF was already held in some French circles and foreshadows the enthusiasm which greeted his arrival as American commissioner late in 1776.

ceux qui vous accompagneront. Ayez, s'il vous plait, La bonté de me répondre sur ce sujet.

J'ai l'honneur d'être avec Les sentimens de [*torn*] attachement Les plus parfaits, [Monsieur,] Votre très humble et très [obéi] ssant serviteur   DALIBARD

[*torn*] La ruë Villedot à Paris

To Mary Stevenson

ALS: Yale University Library

Dear Polly   Monday morng. March 8. 62

Your good Mama has just been saying to me that she wonders what can possibly be the Reason she has not had a Line from you for so long a time. I have made no Complaint of that kind, being conscious that by not writing my self I have forfeited all Claim to such Favour;[9] tho' no Letters give me more Pleasure, and I often wish to hear from you, but Indolence grows upon me with Years, and Writing grows more and more irksome to me. Have you finish'd your Course of Philosophy?[1] No more Doubts, to be resolv'd; no more Questions to ask? If so, you may now be at full Leisure to improve your self in Cards. Adieu my dear Child, and believe me ever Your affectionate Friend   B FRANKLIN

Respects to Mrs. Tickel, &c.[2] Mama bids me tell you she is lately much afflicted and half a Cripple with the Rheumatism. I send you two or three French *Gazettes de Medecine* which I have just receiv'd from Paris, wherein is a Translation of the Extract of a Letter you copied out for me.[3] You will return them with my French Letters on Electricity[4] when you have perus'd them.

9. BF's last letter to Polly appears to have been that of Oct. 29, 1761; see above, IX, 377–8.

1. At Polly's suggestion she and BF had begun corresponding about moral and natural philosophy in the spring of 1760; see above, IX, 102.

2. BF probably intended greetings to Polly's two aunts at Wanstead, Mrs. Tickell and Mrs. Rooke, and her young friend Miss Pitt, often mentioned in earlier letters.

3. Ebenezer Kinnersley's letter of March 12, 1761; see above, IX, 282–93. On Dec. 9, 1761, BF sent an extract, reporting how a lightning rod had saved a Philadelphia merchant's house from destruction, to Thomas-François Dalibard, who translated it and published it in Barbeu Dubourg's *Gazette de médecine*, Feb. 6, 1762; see above, IX, 396.

4. Probably the second edition of Dalibard's translation of BF's *Exper. and*

From Mary Stevenson

ALS and draft: American Philosophical Society

Dear Sir   Wanstead March 10. 1762

I did not think you had been so keen a Satyrist.[5] I have not *finish'd my Course of Philosophy*, nor do I desire *to be at full Leisure to improve myself in Cards*. I confess you have just Reason to complain of me, and my Indolence merits your severe Rebuke. Your Letter fill'd me with Confusion, and I assure you it will be a Spur to my Industry. The Season is advancing that will admit of my rising early to have some Hours free from Interruption which I shall devote to the Improvement of my Mind. At present, tho' we live more retir'd, I have less Time to myself: Yet I have not been idle. I have read the Letters you favour'd me with,[6] and think I understand them. The Clearness of my Preceptor's Demonstration and Expression appear tho his Words are put into a foreign Language.

I was about to ask a Question I find you cannot answer—How it happens that the Surface of the Bottle[7] which contains less than it's natural Quantity of Electric Fire does not immediately replenish itself from the Hand that holds it, unless the Fire which has a Communication with the other Surface is applied to something that will receive it's superabundant Quantity.[8]

I was much pleas'd with your Conjectures upon Storms.[9] The Clouds being *positively* electrified and communicating their Fire

---

Obser.: *Expériences et observations sur l'électricité faites à Philadelphie en Amérique par M. Benjamin Franklin*... (2 vols., Paris, 1756).

5. See the document immediately above for many of the matters mentioned here.

6. The second edition of Dalibard's translation of BF's *Exper. and Obser.*, published in 1756.

7. The Leyden jar.

8. For BF's answer, see below, p. 67.

9. BF's letter to John Mitchell on thundergusts, April 29, 1749, above, III, 365–76. In the 1752 edition of *Expériences et observations sur l'électricité*, pp. 91–127, Dalibard printed this letter as it had appeared in the English original without indication of the person addressed. In his 1756 edition, however, it appeared, combined with part of another paper, as part of the first letter in the second volume (II, 1–41), and at the top of the first page he repeated the title of the whole work in a shortened form which included the names of Franklin and Collinson. At a quick glance, therefore, a reader might assume

to Eminences that came within their Sphere of Attraction, seem to me a full Explication of the Effects of Storms. But when the Clouds were prov'd to be *negative* I was at a Loss to account for the violent Descent of Rain, tho all the other Effects I could easily conceive to be the same in both Cases. To explain what I mean—"You say that the Particles of Water being electrified mutually repel, and fly from each other; but when they are reduced to their natural State, their Distance is contracted, they run into Cohesions, and descend in Drops." I did not consider that the Repulsion would be equal whether the Particles of Water were in a *positive* or a *negative* State. I am very ambitious of your Applause, and therefore carefully conceal my Defects; yet I would not erase what I had written, but proceeded in what I was about to say, tho' I discover'd my Stupidity while I was writing. I am oblig'd to you for the Papers you sent me. I receive a very high Joy when my dear Friend gains the Fame he deserves; and secretly join, with the warmest Sensibility, in all the Praises bestow'd upon him. I am Dear Sir your grateful and affectionate Servant   M STEVENSON

If you would chuse me to send your Books and Papers by the Post I will do it immediately upon the Receipt of a Letter from you; but I hope soon to have the Pleasure of bringing them to you.

I must beg you to entreat my dear Mother's Forgiveness of my long Silence which I intended to have made some amends for to day, but have not Time.

Endorsed: Miss Stevenson

To Thomas-François Dalibard

MS not found; translation of extract reprinted from *Gaʒette d'Epidaure, ou recueil de nouvelles de médecine*, III, no. XXXII (April 21, 1762), 256. (Bibliothèque Nationale)

[Londres 20 Mars 1762]

Je vous rends graces de la peine que vous avez bien voulu prendre pour la traduction et la publication de la Lettre de M. Kinnersley,

that this letter was addressed to Collinson. Barbeu Dubourg (*Oeuvres de M. Franklin*, I, 38–50), published in 1773, made this mistake in attribution. All American editors until I. Bernard Cohen (*Benjamin Franklin's Experiments*, 1941, pp. 200–11) repeated Dubourg's error.

à Paris.*¹ On m'a envoyé d'une autre de nos Colonies deux nouvelles rélations de maisons préservées par les mêmes moyens de tout dommage,² quoiqu'atteintes de la foudre; je prendrai la liberté de vous les envoyer avant de repartir pour l'Amérique. Votre fameuse expérience de Marly³ vous donne un droit incontestable pour être des premiers informé de toutes les nouvelles de cette espèce.

To Mary Stevenson

MS not found; reprinted from Stan. V. Henkels, Catalogue No. 1262 (July 1, 1920), pp. 15–16.⁴

My dear Friend,   London, March 22, 1762.

I must retract the Charge of Idleness in your Studies, when I find you have gone thro' the doubly difficult Task of reading so big a Book on an abstruse Subject and in a foreign Language.⁵ The Question you were about to ask is a very sensible one. The Hand that holds the Bottle receives and conducts away the electric Fluid that is driven out of the outside by the repulsive Power of that which is forc'd into the inside of the Bottle. As long as that Power remains in the same Situation, it must prevent the Return of what it had expell'd; tho' the Hand would readily supply the Quantity if it could be receiv'd.

Your good Mama bids me tell you, that she has made Enquiry and finds that the School for Lovers will not be acted till the Bene-

*Voyez notre Feuille Tom. III. no. vii, page 49 et suiv.

1. On Dalibard's translation and publication of a long extract from Kinnersley's letter to BF, March 12, 1761, see above, IX, 396 n. His paraphrase of the extract appeared in *Gazette de Médecine*, III, no. VII (Jan. 23, 1762), 49–53, and the actual translation in no. XI (Feb. 6, 1762), 82–6.
2. The two incidents of houses in So. Car., saved by lightning rods, recounted above, pp. 53–5.
3. Dalibard's great experiment, May 10, 1753, based on BF's suggestion, proving the identity of lightning and electricity; above, IV, 302–10.
4. The first two paragraphs were printed as Letter LIII in *Exper. and Obser.*, 1769 edit., pp. 460–1; 1774 edit., pp. 470–1.
5. Polly had been reading the second edition of Dalibard's translation of BF's *Exper. and Obser.* The question discussed in the next paragraph is one she had raised regarding a passage in it; see above, p. 65.

fits are over;[6] but when she hears that it is to be acted she will send you timely Notice. I need not add, that your and your Friends Company at Dinner that Day will be a great Pleasure to us all. But methinks 'tis a Pity, that when you are so desirous of studying in that School, it should not be open, and must we be depriv'd of the Happiness of seeing you till it is? Rather than that should be, I would almost venture to undertake reading you a few Lectures on the Subject myself.

If you are not to be in town in a few Days, I should be glad you would send the French Letters, on Electricity, as a Friend is desirous of perusing them.

My sincere Respects to Mrs. Tickell, Mrs. Rooke, Miss Pitt, etc. and believe me ever, my dear Polly, your affectionate Friend,

B. FRANKLIN.

From Peter Collinson

AL: American Philosophical Society

March 23: 1762

P. Collinsons Love and Respects to His Friend Franklin. Has sent some books and Catalogues for Library Company[7] and a piece for J. Bartram[8] to his Care.

Ball Account Delivered	13: 16: 5
No. 33 and 34 Modern History[9]	13: -
No. 27: 28: 29: 30 ball	14: 9: 5
4 plates inserts 2: 6	10 -
	£14: 19: 5

Endorsed: P Collinson: Acct Lib. Compa

6. *The School for Lovers,* a comedy in verse by William Whitehead (1715–1785), poet laureate, 1757–85, was first played at Drury Lane, Feb. 10, 1762, and its publication "this day" was announced in *London Chron.,* Feb. 13–16, 1762. An extended review in *Gent. Mag.,* XXXII (April 1762), 157–61, praised it for its "extremely well drawn, and sustained" characters, its "natural and spirited" dialogue, and its "chaste and elegant" sentiments. It was revived in 1775 and 1794. "William Whitehead," *DNB.*

7. For many years Collinson had been the purchasing agent for Lib. Co. Phila.

8. John Bartram, the eminent botanist, see above, II, 378 n. It is not clear what Collinson sent him.

9. For *An Universal History, from the Earliest Account of Time to the Present* and its complicated publication history, see above, III, 146 n.

To Deborah Franklin ALS: American Philosophical Society

My dear Child,   London, March 24. 1762
 I condole with you most sincerely on the Death of our good
Mother; being extreamly sensible of the Distress and Affliction it
must have thrown you into.[1] Your Comfort will be, that no Care
was wanting on your Part towards her, and that she had lived
as long as this Life could afford her any rational Enjoyment. 'Tis,
I am sure, a Satisfaction to me, that I cannot charge myself with
having ever fail'd in one Instance of Duty and Respect to her
during the many Years that she call'd me Son. The Circumstances attending her Death were indeed unhappy in some Respects; but something must bring us all to our End, and few of
us shall see her Length of Days.[2] My Love to Brother John
Read and Sister, and Cousin Debby, and young Cousin Johnny
Read, and let them all know, that I sympathise with them all affectionately.[3]
 This I write in haste, Mr. Beatty[4] having just call'd on me to
let me know that he is about to set out for Portsmouth, in order
to sail for America. I am finishing all Business here in order for
my Return, which will either be in the Virginia Fleet, or by the
Packet of May next, I am not yet determined which.[5] I pray God
grant us a happy Meeting.
 We are all well, and Billy presents his Duty. Mr. Strahan has

 1. On Dec. 7, 1761, Sarah White Read (F.3.2) "in a fit fell in the fire" and
was burned to death. She was buried the next day. Isaac Norris, Jr., Diary,
Rosenbach Foundation.
 2. She was about 86 at the time of her death.
 3. The in-laws BF mentions here are: DF's brother, John Read (E.1.2.5), a
wagonmaster under Gen. Edward Braddock (above, VI, 221 n), and his wife
Martha Coyle Read; DF's niece, Deborah Croker Dunlap (above, VIII, 305–6
n); and DF's nephew, John Kearsley Read (1746–1805), whom BF entered in
the Academy and College of Philadelphia in 1756, who later became a physician and mayor of Norfolk, Va., and who was a friend of John Paul Jones.
Francis J. Dallett, "Doctor Franklin's In-Laws," Penn. Geneal. Mag., XXI
(1960), 297–302; Montgomery, Hist. Univ. Pa., p. 548.
 4. For the Rev. Charles Beatty, who had been in England trying to raise
funds for poor Presbyterian ministers and their families, see above, IX, 30 n.
 5. The Va. fleet, the merchant ships for Va. under convoy, was scheduled
to sail from England on April 21, 1762. Pa. Gaz., May 13, 1762. BF did not
leave England until about August 23; see below, p. 149.

receiv'd your Letter;[6] and wonders he has not been able to persuade you to come over: Mrs. Stevenson desires her Compliments. She expected Sally would have answer'd her Daughter's Letter that went with the Gold Needle.[7] I have receiv'd yours by the last Pacquet, and one from our Friend Mr. Hughes.[8] I will try to write a Line to him, if I have Time.[9] If not please to tell him, I will do all I can to serve him in his Affair. Acquaint Mr Charles Norris, that I send him a Gardner in Bolitho.[1] The Particulars of your Letters I shall answer in the same Ship.[2] Tell Sally and Cousin Johnny that I receiv'd their Letters also.[3]

I can now only add, that I am as ever My dear Debby Your affectionate Husband   B FRANKLIN

From John Whitehurst[4]   Extract:[5] The Royal Society

Franklin, like other members of the Royal Society, sometimes served as a means of communication whereby nonmembers with news of

6. That of Jan. 24, 1762 (not found), in reply to one of Strahan's of October 1761, urging DF to come to England, Strahan to David Hall, Oct. 6, 1761, March 13, 1762, APS.

7. For mention of Polly Stevenson's letter to Sally Franklin, written in October 1761, see above, IX, 377.

8. DF's letter, probably written in January 1762, and John Hughes's letter have not been found; but on the latter, which probably related to his desire to buy some land in N.J. from the English heir of "one Dr. Barker," see below, pp. 156–8, 163.

9. No reply to Hughes has been found.

1. In "Account of Expences," p.[64] (not printed in full in Eddy, *PMHB*, LV, 100–32), is a list of BF's charges against Charles Norris, the final entry in which is "1762 Cash advanc'd a Quarter's Wages to Gardener £5." While in the receipted bill to Norris printed below (p. 139) this entry reads less specifically "Cash advanc'd to Gardner £5 0. 0.," it seems probable that BF had complied with a request from Norris to find and send him a competent English or Scottish gardener for his estate.

2. If BF wrote DF by Bolitho, his letter has not been found.

3. Not found.

4. John Whitehurst (1713–1788) of Derby, horologer and maker of philosophical instruments, whom BF may have first met on his journey to Scotland in 1759; see above, IX, 42 n. *DNB*.

5. In BF's hand, and headed "Extract of a Letter from Mr. Whitehurst of Darby, to Dr. Franklin, dated March 28. 1762."

curious phenomena or interesting discoveries might hope to have their reports transmitted to the Society to be read and printed. In this instance John Whitehurst passed on to Franklin a letter he had received from Rev. Samuel Evatt of Ashford[6] about an archaeological find in the nearby village of Wardlow. Evatt wrote that upon removing a large heap of stone near a turnpike road under construction in 1759, workmen had discovered a group of seventeen graves arranged for the most part in a semicircle. The bodies, of which some teeth and small bones remained, had apparently been laid on the surface of the ground on long flat stones. Two of them were surrounded by small stone walls and completely covered by other flat stones, but the remaining fifteen had only the heads and chests thus protected from the weight of the stone heap. Certain indications led Evatt to the conclusion that the graves dated from about the time of the Wars of the Roses. Franklin transmitted this account to Dr. Charles Morton, one of the secretaries of the Royal Society.[7] It was read May 13, 1762, and, illustrated by an engraving of the sketch Evatt had supplied, was printed in *Philosophical Transactions,* LII (1761–62), 544-6.[8]

[March 28. 1762]

A remarkable Piece of Antiquity has been discover'd in this County lately: As I imagine it is somewhat curious, I have taken the Liberty of sending you a Sketch with the Letter I receiv'd with it, from the Revd. Mr. Evatt at Ashford near Bakewell in this County.

Addressed: To / Dr Moreton

Endorsed: Read at R.S. 13 May 1762.

6. Not further identified.

7. Charles Morton (1716–1799), M.D., Leyden, 1748; practiced in Kendall and London; physician at the Middlesex and Foundling Hospitals; F.R.S., 1752; secretary, 1760–74; under-librarian of the British Museum, 1756; principal librarian, 1776. *DNB.*

8. *Phil. Trans.* incorrectly prints the date of reading as May 13, 1761. The endorsements on BF's note to Morton and on his copy of Evatt's letter both give the year clearly as 1762.

To [Thomas Holme][9]

MS not found; reprinted from John Bigelow, ed., *The Works of Benjamin Franklin* (Federal edition, N.Y. and London, 1904), XII, 281–3.

Rev'd Sir,   London, 30 March, 1762.

I am favored with yours of the 27th instant, enclosing a bank note of £20, which makes £70 now repaid by Overal.[1] I acquainted you in mine by last Saturday's post that I had reason to think the whole sum to be repaid would not be so great as I before computed it, and perhaps not exceed £79 or £80. It will be a pleasure to me to find it so, that I may have no occasion to have recourse to the law, which is so disagreeable a thing to me, that through the whole course of my life I have never entered an action against any man. But I own I was not a little provoked with these people, as I concluded they must certainly have known of the mortgage (and indeed the letters they have since produced show that they did, particularly the last you mentioned of December 28, 1756); and yet when I asked them if there was no mortgage or other incumbrance on the estate, the man said none that he knew or had ever heard of; and the woman added:

"And to be sure, if there had been any such thing in so long a time as we have received the rent, we must have heard of it." There was such an apparent simplicity in their manner, and they answered with such readiness and confidence, that I was perfectly satisfied; and therefore the more surprised and chagrined when I afterwards found how easily I had been imposed on. They likewise had instructed Mr. Winterbottom[2] to assure the purchaser

9. The printed version from which the text is taken is headed merely "To Rev. M——." The letter concerns the Philadelphia property BF had bought from James and Ann Overall of Wellingborough, July 11, 1761 (above, IX, 328–30), and on which he later found there was an undisclosed mortgage held by a Mr. Spofford (above, IX, 395 n). The addressee of this letter had been an intermediary in the resulting dispute and was apparently a clergyman acquainted with all the parties; he must have been the Rev. Mr. Thomas Holme, vicar of Wellingborough, whom BF had known since 1759; see above, VIII, 121 n, 224–5, 288–9, 302, 325.

1. None of the correspondence referred to in this paragraph has been found.

2. Abraham Winterbottom of Old Broad Street was apparently a lawyer commissioned by the Overalls to manage the sale of their property; see above.

APRIL 5, 1762

(as he did me) that the house had lately undergone a thorough repair, whereas Spofford in his letter had informed them "it will soon want a great deal of repair." I think with you that they are weak and foolish people; but there seems no small mixture of knavery with their folly. I likewise imagined, as you do, that they were but little accustomed to money, from some conversation between them when they were about to receive it. The man said he had been bred to a trade, but that he never liked to work at it. "Well, my dear," says she, "you know you will now have no occasion ever to work any more." They seemed to think it so great a sum that it could never be spent.[3]

I am very sensible, sir, that this must have been a disagreeable affair to you, and I am the more obliged. The very [*mutilated*] and generous manner in which you have executed it will ever demand my thankful acknowledgment, which I beg you to accept, and believe me, with the sincerest esteem and respect, sir, your most obedient and most humble servant,   B. FRANKLIN

From David Hall

Letterbook copy: American Philosophical Society

Sir,   Philada. April 5. 1762.

Yours of December 10.[4] by the Packet, I received, with your Opinion relating to my remitting you; and have, accordingly sent you the first Copy of a Bill of Exchange for Three Hundred Pounds Sterling (Exchange Seventy-seven and a Half) drawn by Messieurs Plumsted and Franks, on Sir James Colebrooke Baronet, Arnold Nesbitt, George Colebrooke, and Moses Franks, Esquires;[5] the Receipt of which you will please to acknowledge, and

---

IX, 329–30. In November 1762 WF employed him to collect a debt. WF to Strahan, November 1762, Yale Univ. Lib.

3. BF had paid the Overalls £350 on the signing of the papers.

4. See above, IX, 398–9.

5. William Plumsted (1708–1765) and David Franks (d. 1794) were partners in a Philadelphia mercantile firm. James Colebrooke (1722–1761), created baronet 1759, his brother George (1729–1809), Arnold Nesbitt (1721?–1779), and Moses Franks (d. 1789), brother of David, held profitable contracts for

advise of its being paid, when you have got the Money.[6] I am Sir Yours, &c.   D. HALL

Sent Via New-York, by Pitt Packet.[7]

To Thomas Birch[8]   AL: British Museum

Cravenstreet, Friday morng. [April 16, 1762][9]
Mr. Franklin's Compliments to Dr. Birch and returns Mr. Delaval's and Mr. Canton's Papers.[1] Mr. F. thought he had prevail'd with each of those Gentlemen to omit or change some Expressions that might tend to occasion a Dispute, but on farther Discourse finds that neither of them cordially approve the Alterations propos'd, tho' they might consent to them at the Instance of their Friends; so the Papers are return'd unalter'd;[2] and Mr. F. begs Pardon of

---

servicing the British forces in America. Namier and Brooke, *House of Commons*, II, 235–7; III, 194–5.

6. BF probably received this bill toward the end of June 1762 (see the next note) but did not record its receipt in his "account of Expences," as he almost invariably did with Hall's bills. He was probably too busy preparing to return home.

7. *London Chron.*, June 19–22, 1762, carried a report from Falmouth, June 17, of the arrival of the *Pitt* packet, Captain Goddard, after a voyage of thirty-six days from N.Y.

8. Secretary of the Royal Society.

9. The date is in another hand, similar to one found on several endorsements of papers in the Royal Society.

1. Edward Delaval's paper, entitled "An Account of several Experiments in Electricity: In a Letter to Mr. Benjamin Wilson, F.R.S.," was read before the Royal Society, Dec. 17, 1761, and printed in *Phil. Trans.*, LII, pt. I (1761), 353–6. John Canton's paper, "A Letter from John Canton, M.A. and F.R.S. to Benjamin Franklin, LL.D. and F.R.S. containing some Remarks on Mr. Delaval's Electrical Experiments," printed above, pp. 23–6, was read at the Society, Feb. 4, 1762, and was published in *Phil. Trans.*, LII, pt. II (1762), 457–61. These two electricians had disagreed about why changes in temperature caused changes in the conductivity of certain substances. Delaval argued that hot air on the surfaces of heated substances or their absorption of moisture had nothing to do with their conductivity; Canton held the contrary opinion; both men offered experiments to prove their contentions.

2. Though there is a trace of asperity in Delaval's paper, both his and Canton's performances seem remarkably temperate at this distance in time.

74

Dr. Birch for the Trouble his Officiousness has given him; and requests his Acceptance of a Book[3] herewith sent him.
The Pacquet was brought by a Friend of Mr. F.'s from France.
Addressed: To | Revd. Dr Birch

From R. Hippisley[4]   ALS: American Philosophical Society

Sir.   Apr. 19. 1762

Having completed an Analysis of Oratory, as more particularly mentioned in the enclosed proposals,[5] Upon a plan never attempted before in any language, I take the liberty to address You, as a friend to learning and an Encourager of arts and sciences.

You will view the drawing, now laid before you, as the first, and as it were a rude, sketch of the Design, since greatly improved by me both in the subject-matter and plan; that intended to be engraved, being in the hands of the Engraver, executing it after a design by Wale.[6]

If You will permit me to add YOUR name, as a subscriber, to those of many noble and other eminent persons, no less distinguished for their elegant taste in polite literature than for the dignity of their birth and rank, a list of which waits upon you with

3. Possibly the second edition of Dalibard's translation of *Exper. and Obser.* If so, the friend who brought the packet from France, mentioned in the next sentence, may have been young William Shippen; see above, IX, 396, and this volume, pp. 64–5 n.

4. The writer, not otherwise identified, was the author of *Bath and It's Environs, A Descriptive Poem, in Three Cantos* (Bath: printed by R. Cruttwell, for J. Almon ... London; and W. Frederick ... Bath. 1775). In the Yale Univ. Lib. copy of the poem is a short ALS dated Jan. 29, 1775, in the same hand and with an unmistakably identical signature, presenting the copy to "My Lord" and describing the writer as the author of the poem and "your unfortunate Annuitant." The Richard Hippisley, rector of Stow-on-the-Wold, Gloucestershire, listed in both the Oxford and Cambridge alumni records, died in 1764 and so could not have been the same man.

5. Neither the proposals, the drawing, nor the list of subscribers, both mentioned below, survive among BF's papers; the British Museum *Catalogue of Printed Books* lists no work on oratory by an author of this name.

6. Samuel Wale (d. 1786), painter and engraver, member of the Society of Artists and of the Royal Academy, made illustrations for various books and periodicals. *DNB.*

the ANALYSIS, and thereby contribute not only to the number but to the splendor of the names that adorn the subscription, I shall esteem the Compliment, as reflecting no small lustre upon the Work as well as honour upon the AUTHOR Who begs leave to write Himself Sir Your very obedient Servant   R HIPPISLEY[7]

Oxford University:
Record of Degree of Doctor of Civil Law

MS Register of Convocation, University Archives: Oxford University

The "Heads of Houses" at Oxford University had voted, Feb. 22, 1762, to confer on Franklin the honorary degree of Doctor of Civil Law "whenever He shall please to visit the University." Above, p. 59. The ceremony took place at a special Convocation on April 30, 1762. No copy of the diploma survives and the only official record is in the Register of Convocation printed below. "The very distinguished man," Benjamin Franklin, Esquire, is described as "agent of the Province of Pennsylvania to the Court of the Most Serene King, deputy general of the Post Office of North America, and of the postal service of all New England, and Fellow of the Royal Society." His son William, who received the Master of Arts degree at the same ceremony, is described as "learned in municipal law."

Preceded by the beadles (spelled "bedels" at Oxford) Franklin was escorted into the hall by Dr. William Seward, fellow of the College of St. John the Baptist.[8] Seward presented him to the vice-chancellor and

7. No reply to this letter has been found.

8. William Seward (1720–1789), matriculated at Trinity Coll., Oxford, 1738; fellow of St. John's Coll.; B.C.L., 1748; D.C.L., 1753. He was vicar of Charlbury, Oxford, until the time of his death. Joseph Foster, *Alumni Oxonienses; The Members of the University of Oxford, 1715–1886* (London, 1887–88), IV, 1275. In a communication to *The Nation*, LXXVI (June 23, 1903), describing this ceremony and printing a rather unsatisfactory translation of this record, a correspondent signing himself as "D" contended that by assigning Seward, a man of no distinction, to introduce BF, the university authorities deliberately slighted him, since Nowell, who introduced WF, was "one of the chief dignitaries of the University." In *ibid.*, LXXVII (Nov. 19, 1903), 403, James A. H. Murray of Oxford University ridiculed this interpretation. He pointed out that the regular procedure at Oxford had been, and still was, for candidates to be presented for the degree of Doctor of Civil Law by the Regius professor of Civil Law (in 1762 this would have been Robert Jenner) or in his absence or indisposition, by his deputy (in

proctors "with the prescribed graceful speech," and the vice-chancellor, by his own authority and that of the whole university, thereupon solemnly admitted Franklin to the degree. In like manner, Thomas Nowell, M.A., fellow of Oriel College and public orator,[9] presented "the very distinguished young man," William Franklin, and the vice-chancellor conferred upon him his degree.

No documentary evidence has been discovered to suggest whether the initiative for the granting of these degress came from within the university or from an outside, possibly political, source. It may be remarked, however, that at this time the only honorary degrees Oxford University was conferring were those of Doctor of Divinity, Doctor of Civil Law, and Master of Arts. Obviously, if Franklin was to be honored at all, the degree of Doctor of Civil Law was the most appropriate for a person of his attainments.

Termo Paschatis 1762 Convoc[atione]　　　[April 30, 1762]
Domino Doctore Browne Vice-Cancellario[1]

Die Ven[eris] Viz Tricesimo Die Mensis Aprilis Anno Dom. 1762 Causa Convocationis erat ut Ornatissimus Vir Benjaminus Franklin Armiger Provinciae Pensylvaniae Deputatus, ad Curiam Serenissimi Regis Legatus, Tabellariorum per Americam Septentrionalem Praefectus Generalis, et Veredariorum totius Novae Angliae Praefectus Generalis, necnon Regiae Societatis Socius (si ita Venerabili Coetui placeret) ad Gradum Doctoris in Jure Civili, et Gulielmus Franklin Armiger Juris Municipalis Consultus ad Gradum Magistri in Artibus admitterentur, necnon ut Literae ab Honoratissimo Cancellario ad Senatum datae legerentur et ut alia Negotia Academica peragerentur.

Causâ Convocationis sic indictâ proponente sigillatim Domino Vice-Cancellario placuit Venerabili Coetui ut praedictus Ornatissimus Vir Benjaminus Franklin Armiger ad Gradum Doctoris in

---

this case William Seward). All candidates for the Master of Arts degree had been, and still were, presented by the public orator. The relative personal distinction of the incumbents of these positions had nothing to do with the matter.

9. Thomas Nowell (1730?–1801), matriculated at Oriel Coll., Oxford, 1746; B.A., 1749–50; M.A., 1753; proctor, 1761; B.D., 1767; D.D., St. Mary Hall, 1764; principal, 1764–1801; public orator, 1760–76; Regius professor of modern history, 1771–1801. Foster, *Alumni Oxonienses*, III, 1031.

1. The vice-chancellor at this time was Joseph Browne; see above, p. 59 n.

Jure Civili, et Gulielmus Franklin Armiger ad Gradum Magistri in Artibus Honoris Causa admitterentur.

Spectatissimum Virum Benjaminum Franklin Armigerum praeeuntibus Bedellis in Domum Convocationis ingressum Dextrâque prehensum Dominus Doctor Seward Collegii Divi Joannis Baptistae Socius sub eleganti Orationis Formulâ Domino Vice-Cancellario et Procurantibus praesentabat ut ad Gradum Doctoris in Jure Civili Honoris Causa admitterentur: Quemque hoc modo praesentatum Dominus Vice-Cancellarius suâ et totius Universitatis Authoritate ad dictum Gradum Honoris Causâ solenniter admisit.

Ornatissimum Iuvenem Gulielmum Franklin Armigerum a Thoma Nowell A. M. Collegii Orielensis Socio et Publico Oratore similiter praesentatum Dominus Vice-Cancellarius ad Gradum Magistri in Artibus similiter admisit.[2]

2. Rev. William Smith, provost of the College of Philadelphia, had received the degree of Doctor of Divinity from Oxford in 1759, a month after St. Andrews had made BF a Doctor of Laws. At about that time Smith wrote a letter to Dr. Thomas Fry (1718–1772), president of St. John's College, Oxford, in order, as he afterwards put it, "to prevent his [Franklin's] having a Degree" there also. Later, perhaps while at Oxford in April 1762, BF learned of this letter, "which he took in great Dudgeon" according to Smith, and was apparently given a copy. At a subsequent meeting between BF and Smith at William Strahan's house this letter was read over "Paragraph by Paragraph." As Strahan reported the matter, Smith acknowledged "that it contained many Particulars in which he had been mislead by wrong Information, and that the whole was written with too much Rancor and Asperity; but that he would write to the Dr. contradicting what was false in it." Smith declined Strahan's suggestion of writing the retraction then and there but promised "in a Day or two" to show Strahan what he had written. He never did so. In February 1763, Smith was again at Oxford and, being questioned about the original letter to Dr. Fry and his promise to Strahan, "He denied the whole, and even treated the Question as a Calumny." In reporting this conversation to Strahan, John Kelly, Regius professor of medicine (above, p. 59 n), observed: "I make no other comment on this behaviour than in considering him [Smith] extremely unworthy of the Honour, he has received from our University." Smith to Richard Peters, Aug. 14, 1762, Albert F. Gegenheimer, *William Smith Educator and Churchman 1727–1803* (Phila., 1943), p. 150; Kelly to Strahan, Feb. 11, 1763; Strahan to Kelly, [Feb. 1763]. Strahan evidently sent copies of the last two to BF in a letter of Feb. 28, 1763 (not found, but see below, p. 271). They are now among the Franklin Papers, APS.

To Mary Stevenson   ALS: American Philosophical Society

                                        Cravenstreet May 10. 62
I received this Morning my dear Polley's kind Present of two
Tickets for the Latin Play at Hackney,[3] enclos'd in her agreable
little Letter of the 8th. for both which she will please to accept
my Thanks.[4] I am oblig'd also to Mrs. Tickell and to her for the
kind Invitation of Dining on the Day of the Play. But I think we
are engag'd for that Day to Dine at Hackney at Mr. Sylvanus
Bevan's,[5] who invited us sometime since desiring we would fix a
Day, and last Week we wrote him that we would wait on him
Saturday the 15th. Instant, if convenient to him. If he writes in
Answer, that he shall expect us on that Day, we must go; and
shall go from his House to see the Play. But if that Appointment
should not take Place, (which I shall know to day) then I believe
we shall not see the Play, but return the Tickets. I have not yet
communicated the Invitation to dine at Wanstead to the Person
you mention,[6] to whom I am sure it ought to be extreamly agreable, so can say nothing from him. Mama is well and sends her
Love, &c. My best Respects to Mrs. Tickell, and believe me ever
My dear Friend, Yours affectionately   B Franklin
Love to Mrs. Rooke and to Pittey.[7]

From David Hall   Letterbook copy: American Philosophical Society

Sir,   Philada. May 10. 1762.
   Inclosed you have the second Copy of the above mentioned
Bill,[8] which I hope will come safe to your Hands; and am Yours,
&c.   D. Hall
Mr. Franklin

   3. Hackney is a northeastern borough of London, the site of many fine
residences in the eighteenth century. What the Latin play was and whether
BF attended it is not known.
   4. Not found.
   5. Sylvanus Bevan, a wealthy London Quaker apothecary; above, VIII,
437 n.
   6. Probably WF.
   7. Polly's friend, Miss Pitt, whose first name never happens to be mentioned in any of the letters between BF and Polly.
   8. See above, p. 73.

MAY 10, 1762

Copy sent by the Patty, Captain Widdet from this Port to Bristol,[9] in which was inclosed the second Copy of the above Bill.

Third Copy of Do. sent by the Grace, Captain Kerr, to Bristol, Via New-York.[1]

From David Hume

ALS: American Philosophical Society

Dear Sir   Edinburgh 10 May 1762
I have a great many Thanks to give you for your Goodness in remembering my Request, and for the exact Description, which you sent me of your Method of preserving Houses from Thunder.[2] I communicated it to our philosophical Society, as you gave me Permission; and they desire me to tell you that they claim it as their own, and intend to enrich with it the first Collection, which they may publish.[3] The establish'd Rule of our Society is, that, after a paper is read to them, it is deliverd by them to some Member who is oblig'd, in a subsequent Meeting, to read some Paper of Remarks upon it. It was communicated to our Friend, Mr. Russel;[4] who is not very expeditious in finishing any Undertaking; and he did not read his Remarks, till the last Week, which is the Reason, why I have been so late in acknowleging your Favour. Mr. Russel's Remarks, besides the just Praises of your Invention, contain'd only two Proposals for improving it: One was, that in Houses, where the Rain Water is carry'd off the Roof by a lead Pipe, this metallic Body might be employd as a Conductor to the electric Fire, and save the Expence of a new Apparatus: Another was, that the Wire might be carry'd down to the Foundation of the House, and be thence convey'd below Ground to the requisite Distance, which woud better secure it against Accidents. I thought

9. *Pa. Gaʒ.*, May 20, 1762, reported the clearance of the *Patty*, Capt. J. Widdet; *London Chron.*, July 3–6, 1762, reported its arrival at Bristol.

1. *N.-Y. Mercury*, May 17, 1762, reported the clearance of the *New Grace*, Capt. Alexander Kerr.

2. See above, pp. 17–22, for BF's letter and many of the matters discussed here.

3. The "first Collection" of the Edinburgh Philosophical Society to appear after this letter was vol. III of *Essays and Observations, Physical and Literary*, published nine years later in 1771. BF's letter to Hume is on pp. 129–40.

4. See above, pp. 22–3, for James Russell and his remarks on BF's letter.

it proper to convey to you these two Ideas of so ingenious a Man, that you might adopt them, if they appear to you well founded.

I have sent off your Letter to Lord Mareschal,[5] who will consider himself as much beholden to you. His Lordship is at present very much employd in settling the Controversy about the Eternity of Hell-Torments, which has set the little Republic of Neuf-chatel in Combustion.[6] I have ventur'd to recommend to his Lordship the abridging these Torments as much as possible, and have usd the Freedom to employ your Name, as well as my own, in this Request: I have told him, that, as we have taken so much Pains to preserve him and his Subjects from the Fires of Heaven, they cannot do less than to guard us from the Fires of Hell. My Lord told me, when in England, that the King of Prussia could not at first be brought to regard this theological Controversy as a Matter of any Moment, but soon found from the Confusions, to which it gave rise, that these were not matters to be slighted. But surely, never was a Synod of Divines more ridiculous, than to be worrying one another, under the Arbitration of the King of Prussia and Lord Marischal, who will make an Object of Derision of every thing, that appears to these holy Men so deserving of Zeal, Passion, and Animosity.

I am very sorry, that you intend soon to leave our Hemisphere. America has sent us many good things, Gold, Silver, Sugar, Tobacco, Indigo &c.: But you are the first Philosopher, and indeed

5. See above, p. 17 n. Sparks (*Works*, VI, 243–5) printed this letter but omitted this entire paragraph without indication. Bigelow (*Works*, III, 189–90) and Smyth (*Writings*, IV, 153–5) obviously copied from Sparks, with the same omission, although Smyth had cited as his source the original MS in APS. The full letter, including this paragraph, was first printed in Raymond Klibansky and Ernest C. Mossner, *New Letters of David Hume* (Oxford, 1954), pp. 66–8.

6. Earl Marischal was governor of the principality of Neuchâtel, which had passed into the hands of Prussia in 1707. A dispute, provoked by the preaching of one liberal clergyman, broke out in 1758 over eternal punishment. When the other clergy tried to silence him, his supporters appealed to the government, thereby involving Frederick the Great and Earl Marischal, both freethinkers. They suspected the French of using the issue to take over the principality. In 1762 the clergy made good their point by dismissing their offending colleague and thereby effectively asserted their local rights. The controversy attracted wide attention. Edith E. Cuthell, *The Scottish Friend of Frederick the Great: The Last Earl Marischall* (London, 1915), II, *passim*.

the first Great Man of Letters for whom we are beholden to her: it is our own Fault, that we have not kept him: Whence it appears, that we do not agree with Solomon, that Wisdom is above Gold:[7] For we take care never to send back an ounce of the latter, which we once lay our Fingers upon.

I saw yesterday our Friend Sir Alexander Dick, who desird me to present his Compliments to you. We are all very unwilling to think of your settling in America, and that there is some Chance for our never seeing you again: But no-one regrets it more than does Dear Sir Your most affectionate humble Servant DAVID HUME

To David Hume

ALS: Royal Society of Edinburgh

Dear Sir,   London, May 19. 1762.

It is no small Pleasure to me to hear from you that my Paper on the means of preserving Buildings from Damage by Lightning, was acceptable to the Philosophical Society.[8] Mr. Russel's Proposals of Improvement are very sensible and just. A Leaden Spout or Pipe is undoubtedly a good Conductor so far as it goes. If the Conductor enters the Ground just at the Foundation, and from thence is carried horizontally to some Well, or to a distant Rod driven downright into the Earth; I would then propose that the Part under Ground should be Lead, as less liable to consume with Rust than Iron. Because if the Conductor near the Foot of the Wall should be wasted, the Lightning might act on the Moisture of the Earth, and by suddenly rarifying it occasion an Explosion that may damage the Foundation.[9] In the Experiment of discharging my large Case of Electrical Bottles thro' a Piece of small Glass Tube fill'd with Water, the suddenly rarify'd Water has exploded with a Force equal, I think, to that of so much Gunpowder; bursting the Tube into many Pieces, and driving them with Violence in all Directions

7. Several passages in Proverbs suggest this idea; the closest to Hume's thought is probably Prov. 16:16: "How much better is it to get wisdom than gold!"

8. For BF's letter to Hume on lightning rods, James Russell's remarks on it, and Hume's reply to BF, see above, pp. 17–23, 80–2.

9. In his letter to Kinnersley of Feb. 20, 1762, BF had already developed somewhat more fully the thoughts expressed in the passage which begins here; see above, pp. 50–1.

and to all Parts of the Room. The Shivering of Trees into small Splinters like a Broom, is probably owing to this Rarefaction of the Sap in the longitudinal Pores or capillary Pipes in the Substance of the Wood. And the Blowing-up of Bricks or Stones in a Hearth, Rending Stones out of a Foundation, and Splitting of Walls, is also probably an Effect sometimes of rarify'd Moisture in the Earth, under the Hearth, or in the Walls. We should therefore have a durable Conductor under Ground, or convey the Lightning to the Earth at some Distance.

It must afford Lord Mareschall a good deal of Diversion to preside in a Dispute so ridiculous as that you mention.[1] Judges in their Decisions often use Precedents. I have somewhere met with one that is what the Lawyers call *a Case in Point*. The Church People and the Puritans in a Country Town, had once a bitter Contention concerning the Erecting of a Maypole, which the former desir'd and the latter oppos'd. Each Party endeavour'd to strengthen itself by obtaining the Authority of the Mayor, directing or forbidding a Maypole. He heard their Altercation with great Patience, and then gravely determin'd thus; You that are for having no Maypole shall have no Maypole; and you that are for having a Maypole shall have a Maypole. Get about your Business and let me hear no more of this Quarrel.[2] So methinks Lord Mareschal might say; You that are for no more Damnation than is proportion'd to your Offences, have my Consent that it may be so: And you that are for being damn'd eternally, G–d eternally d—n you all, and let me hear no more of your Disputes.

Your Compliment of *Gold* and *Wisdom* is very obliging to me, but a little injurious to your Country. The various Value of every thing in every Part of this World, arises you know from the various Proportions of the Quantity to the Demand. We are told that Gold

1. On George Keith, Earl Marischal, and the theological controversy in which he became involved as governor of Neuchâtel, see above, pp. 17 n, 81 n.

2. As previously noted, Sparks omitted without indication Hume's paragraph on the controversy at Neuchâtel "about the Eternity of Hell-Torments." Here he relaxed enough to print BF's anecdote about the maypole, but he ended the paragraph at this point, primly and silently omitting BF's application of the story to the situation at Neuchâtel; *Works*, VII, 237–8. Bigelow (*Works*, III, 192) and Smyth (*Writings*, 156–7) followed Sparks, although Smyth had noted the location of the MS original.

and Silver in Solomon's Time were so plenty as to be of no more Value in his Country than the Stones in the Street.[3] You have here at present just such a Plenty of Wisdom. Your People are therefore not to be censur'd for desiring no more among them than they have; and if I have *any*, I should certainly carry it where from its Scarcity it may probably come to a better Market.

I nevertheless regret extreamly the leaving a Country in which I have receiv'd so much Friendship, and Friends whose Conversation has been so agreable and so improving to me; and that I am henceforth to reside at so great a Distance from them is no small Mortification, to My dear Friend, Yours most affectionately

B FRANKLIN

My respectful Compliments if you please to Sir Alexr. Dick, Lord Kaims, Mr. Alexander,[4] Mr. Russel, and any other enquiring Friends. I shall write to them before I leave the Island.

David Hume, Esqr.

Addressed: To / David Hume, Esqr / Edinburgh

To Mary Stevenson

ALS: American Philosophical Society

May 24. 62.

According to Promise I write on Monday to let my good Girl know how her Mama does; but so late in the Day that I fear I might as well have let it alone till Tuesday. She is not yet quite well, but so well as to be abroad ever since Morning. I went early into the City, Din'd there, and return'd hoping for the Pleasure of a Dish of Tea with her; when I learnt that she went out soon after me, and had not since been at home: So was forc'd to beg my Tea at Mrs. Gambier's.[5] This will look a little like a Complaint, but I don't intend it.

---

3. II Chron. 1:16: "And the king [Solomon] made silver and gold at Jerusalem as plenteous as stones." Both Hume and BF had been reared in the Calvinist tradition; both had shed the orthodoxy of their upbringing. Hume had used a scriptural allusion in his most recent letter, showing that he still knew his Bible; BF, not to be outdone, now responded in kind.

4. Probably Robert Alexander, Edinburgh merchant; see above, VIII, 444 n.

5. Probably one of Mrs. Stevenson's neighbors in Craven Street. Mrs.

Are you provided with a House? If not, look into Tomorrow's Daily Advertiser where you will find one to be let at Ealing, which I know and think I could recommend as to the Pleasantness of the Neighbourhood, Roads, &c. if the Description appears such as may make the rest agreable. I know there is a good deal of Garden, and abundance of Room in and about the House.[6]

I shall be glad to hear that you got well home, and found all well. Present my best Respects to Mrs. Tickell, Mrs. Rooke and to Pitty. I am, my dear Friend, Yours affectionately   B FRANKLIN

Addressed: To / [Miss Ste]venson / [at] Mrs Tickell's / [Wa]n-stead / Essex[7]

Endorsed: May 24-62

To John Pringle[8]   ALS: Princeton University Library[9]

For nearly twenty years Franklin had been interested in the possibility that a navigable waterway between the Atlantic and Pacific Oceans might be found somewhere north of Canada. He had read the pamphlets on the controversy between Arthur Dobbs and Christopher Middleton which followed Middleton's unsuccessful voyage of 1741-42, and he had included in *Poor Richard* for 1748 a long and vivid account of the conditions the members of that expedition had encountered while

Gambier may have been the mother of John and Samuel Gambier of the Bahamas, to whom BF sent two boxes of goods in 1759; see above, VIII, 424 n.

6. *The Daily Advertiser,* May 27, 1762, advertised a "neat convenient House" for lease at Great Ealing in Middlesex Co. The house contained three parlors, four bedrooms, four servants' rooms, stabling for four horses, and a "Garden wall'd and planted with the best Fruit-Trees, and full cropp'd."

7. Part of the address page has been torn off.

8. John Pringle (1707-1782), M.D., Leyden, 1730; practiced in Edinburgh where he was professor of pneumatics (metaphysics) and moral philosophy at the University, 1734-44; served with the British forces in Flanders and in the Jacobite rebellion, 1742-45; F.R.S., 1745, president, 1772-78; settled in London, 1748; physician-in-ordinary to the Queen, 1761; fellow of the Royal College of Physicians, 1763; created baronet, 1766; physician to the King, 1774. *DNB.* He became an intimate friend and traveling companion of BF, and through his professional connection with the royal family doubtless was in close contact with Lord Bute.

9. This letter was first printed, with an introduction by Bertha Solis-Cohen, "Benjamin Franklin Defends Northwest Passage Navigation," *Princeton University Library Chronicle,* XIX (1957-58), 15-33.

wintering over at Churchill River on the western side of Hudson Bay.[1] Later he had been one of the leading sponsors of two expeditions in which the *Argo*, commanded by Charles Swaine, had sailed from Philadelphia in 1753 and again in 1754, in unsuccessful search for the Northwest Passage.[2]

In spite of these and other failures, Franklin and many of his contemporaries continued to hope that a practicable route might be found. His optimism was somewhat strengthened by an account, printed in two installments in *The Monthly Miscellany: or, Memoirs for the Curious*, April and June 1708, purporting to be a letter from an "Admiral Bartholomew de Fonte, then Admiral of New Spain and Peru and now Prince of Chili."[3]

De Fonte (or Bartolomé de Fuentes, to give him the Spanish name some commentators ascribed to him) told how he had sailed with four ships up the west coast of the Americas from Peru in the spring of 1640. Detaching one vessel to determine whether Lower California was an island or a peninsula, de Fonte and his other ships continued on to 53 degrees north latitude, which would be in the vicinity of what is now called Hecate Strait, separating the Queen Charlotte Islands from the mainland of British Columbia. Here on June 14 he entered a river he called Los Reyes and sent Captain Pedro de Barnarda up a large tributary to the north. Barnarda found a body of water, Lake Valasco; there he left his ship and with three Indian pirogues traveled 140 leagues west and then 436 leagues east northeast to the 79th parallel (which if true would have placed him somewhere among the northern islands in the Arctic Ocean). He reported that there was no water communication with Davis Strait.

Meanwhile de Fonte continued generally northeastward in the tidal River Los Reyes "in a fair navigable Channel" to an Indian town Conosset on the southeast side of what he called Lake Belle. On the opposite side he found a river he named after his interpreter Parmentiers, through which he traveled in small boats, passing eight falls with a total drop of thirty-two feet into a lake 160 leagues long he called

1. See above, II, 410 and note; III, 245–8.

2. See above, IV, 380–4, 389, 413–14, 448–9, 466; V, 148, 331; VI, 89.

3. II (1708), 123–6, 183–6. The account is conveniently reprinted in Amer. Antiq. Soc. *Proc.*, new series, XLI (1931), 190–6, in an article by Henry R. Wagner, "Apocryphal Voyages to the Northwest Coast of America" (pp. 179–234), which establishes conclusively the spurious nature of the narrative. Eighteenth-century controversies growing out of the de Fonte letter are extensively treated in Glyndwr Williams, *The British Search for the Northwest Passage in the Eighteenth Century* ([London], 1962), *passim*, and most of the letter is reprinted, pp. 277–82.

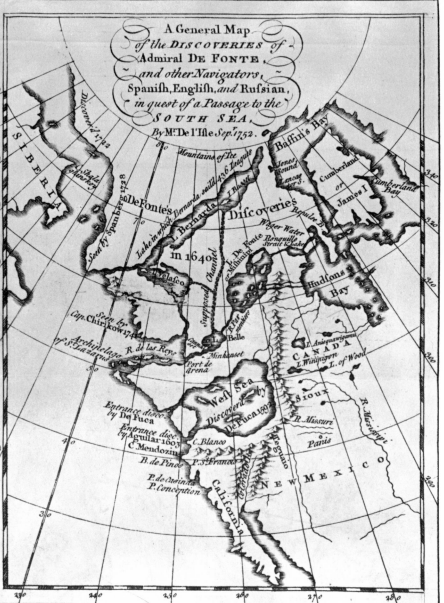

A General Map
of the DISCOVERIES of
Admiral DE FONTE
and other Navigators
Spanish, English, and Russian,
in quest of a Passage to the
SOUTH SEA.
By Mr De l'Isle Sep.r 1752.

SIBERIA

Discover'd 1792

Shalatshaness

Seen by Spanberg 1728

DeFonte's

Mountains of Ice

Lake in which Bernarda saild 436 Leagues

I. Barnet

L. Bernarda

Discoveries

in 1640

R. De Fonte or Minhimina

Velasco

Supposed Channel

Baffin's Bay

Jones Sound
Lancae ter S.

Cumberland
or
James I.

Cumberland
Bay

Bequire B.

Wager Water

Ronquillo
Strait & Lake

Hudsons
Bay

Seen by
Cap. Chirikow 1741

Archipelago
of S. Lazarus

R. de las Reys

Conqui
Sur

R. Par
meniar
Belle

Minhanset

Port de
Arena

L. Aniequawigamu

CANADA

L. Winnipigon

L. of Wood

Sioux

R. Missouri

R. Mississippi

West Sea
Discover'd by
De Fuca 1592

Entrance disco.
by De Fuca

Entrance disc.
by Aguilar 1603

C. Mendozin

B. de Pinos

P. de Cusinia
P. Conception

C. Blanco

P. S. Frances

California

R. Seguio

Panis

NEW MEXICO

Lake de Fonte. From this lake he passed into the Strait and Sea of Ronquillo (named for another of his captains), a distance of thirty-four leagues. The country hereabouts "grew very sensibly worse" in both temperature and fertility from what he had previously observed. On July 17 his party arrived at an Indian town which stood, presumably, on the northwestern or western shore of Hudson Bay.

The Indians told his interpreter of "a great Ship" nearby and upon investigation this proved to be a Boston vessel. De Fonte sailed to it and on July 30 met its owner, Major General Scimor (*sic*) Gibbons, and its navigator, Captain Shapley. After a courteous exchange of presents the Spaniards began their return trip, reaching their ships at Lake Belle on August 16. De Fonte restocked them with "good Salt Provisions," dropped down the River Los Reyes, was rejoined there by Captain Barnarda on September 3, and soon afterwards sailed for home, "having found that there was no Passage into the South Sea by that they call the North West Passage."

There were many, even in Franklin's time, who were skeptical of the authenticity of this account, but so little was then known of the true geography of the northwest parts of North America that no one could demonstrate conclusively the impossibility of such a water-borne exploration of the region as was here related. Today the account is recognized as a complete hoax; its author is generally believed to have been James Petiver, a botanist and entomologist of considerable standing, the editor and possibly also the owner of *The Monthly Miscellany* in which the de Fonte narrative appeared.[4]

Franklin, himself the author of several successful hoaxes, seems nevertheless to have been completely taken in. And he was not alone. Among others was the French geographer Joseph-Nicolas Delisle. Aided by Philippe Buache, he published in September 1752 a *Carte Générale des Découvertes De l'Amiral de Fonte Et autres Navigateurs Espagnols, Anglois et Russes, pour la recherche du Passage à la Mer du Sud*, which undertook to depict cartographically discoveries on both sides of the north Pacific, including the waterways through which

4. James Petiver (1663–1718) was an apothecary by trade "and seems to have had a good practice, though not one of a high order, since he advertised various quack nostrums." He published extensively in the fields of his scientific interest and was elected F.R.S. in 1695. *DNB*. For the most thorough analyses of the account and the sources of information available to its author, see the article by Wagner cited in the footnote immediately above and his *The Cartography of the Northwest Coast of America to the Year 1800* (Berkeley, Calif., 1937), pp. 158–62; and Percy G. Adams, "Benjamin Franklin's Defense of the De Fonte Hoax," *Princeton Univ. Lib. Chron.*, XXII (1960–61), 133–40.

de Fonte and his subordinate Barnarda reputedly had passed. Henry R. Wagner has called this map, with considerable justification, "one of the most astonishing examples of imaginary geography which has ever appeared."[5] *The Gentleman's Magazine* reproduced the map, somewhat simplified and with place names and inscriptions translated into English, in 1754.[6] Thomas Jefferys, the royal geographer, published in 1761 a translation of Gerhard F. Müller's *Voyages from Asia to America, For Completing the Discoveries of the North West Coast of America.* In it Jefferys included three new maps, one of which was a redrawing of that part of the Delisle map which showed de Fonte's reputed discoveries. It was a copy of this map which, as Franklin explained in the postscript below, he found "done to my Hand," and which he marked and sent to Pringle with this letter. In doing so he either failed to notice or purposely ignored several statements in the text in which Müller severely criticized Delisle and one in which he spoke scornfully of "the pretended discoveries of de Fonte."[7]

Apparently Franklin and his friend Pringle had recently talked at some length about the de Fonte account; the likelihood that Great Britain would soon acquire title to all of Canada would naturally have stimulated their interest in the geography of its northern parts. Pringle, presumably, had challenged the authenticity of de Fonte's narrative; Franklin had defended it. Then Pringle, perhaps at the urging of his fellow Scot the Earl of Bute, now at the head of the British government, had pressed Franklin for a full statement of his opinion and the reasons for it, before he should leave for America. The consequence was the letter that follows.

Dear Sir,   Cravenstreet, May 27. 1762

In Compliance with your Request, I sit down to give you my Reasons for believing as I do, that De Fonte's Voyage is genuine. You know I would have postpon'd this 'till my Return to Philadelphia, where my Papers might enable me to relate with more Precision the Facts that incline me to that Opinion;[8] but as you insist

5. Amer. Antiq. Soc. *Proc.*, new series, XLI (1931), 205. The justice of this characterization can be readily seen by comparing the accompanying reproduction of Jefferys' redrawing of a portion of it with any modern map of Canada, especially one showing clearly the high Rocky Mountains through which de Fonte allegedly sailed so easily.

6. XXIV (1754), facing p. 123.

7. Müller, *Voyages from Asia to America*, p. 74.

8. Probably the papers relating to the *Argo* expeditions, which he had promised Peter Collinson, June 26, 1755, that he would "some Day" send him; above, VI, 89.

on my doing it here before my Departure, you will excuse unavoidable Defects.

The only Account of this Voyage at present existing, as far as we know, is that publish'd by Pettiver, in a periodical Work call'd *Memoirs for the Curious,* for the Months of April and June 1708. It is there intitled, "A Letter from Admiral Bartholomew De Fonte, then Admiral of New Spain and Peru, and now Prince of Chili; giving an Account of the most material Transactions in a Journal of his from the Calo of Lima in Peru, on his Discoveries to find out if there was any Northwest Passage from the Atlantic Ocean into the South and Tartarian Sea." Whoever reads it there, will easily perceive it to be an Abridgment and a Translation, and bad in both respects. If a Fiction, it is plainly not an English one.[9] But it has none of the Features of Fiction. Entertainment does not appear to be aim'd at in it, nor does it seem calculated to promote any Scheme of a new Voyage for Discovery, as the Country is not describ'd to be wealthy, and the Passage for Ships from Sea to Sea is deny'd: 'Tis in short a mere dry Account of Facts, which, tho' all possible and probable, are none of them wonderful like the Incidents of a Novel.

That the Spaniards should now deny the Reality of this Voyage, is natural enough, jealous as they are of the maritime Power of their Neighbours, and apprehensive for their extensive Settlements on the Coasts of the South Sea. They deny it however but faintly. And they seem far from being convinc'd that there is no practicable Water Communication between the two Seas by the Northwest; as in a late Work of Miguel Venegas, a Spanish Mexican Jesuit, publish'd at Madrid in 1758, the making a strong Settlement and erecting Fortresses on the Northwest Coast of California is warmly recommended to secure the South Seas against the English, who may possibly come into those Seas thro' such Passage.[1]

9. In arriving at this conclusion BF overlooked, among other details, that the author dated several early English voyages in search of the Northwest Passage by their occurrence during the reigns of Elizabeth and James I and for others gave the specific regnal years in the reign of Charles I—hardly a method a non-English author would have used. Percy G. Adams has called attention to this discrepancy (*Princeton Univ. Lib. Chron.*, XXII, 137).

1. Miguel Venegas, *Noticia de la California* (3 vols., Madrid, 1757). It was edited by Andrés Marcos Burriel, who supplied appendices on geography. An

The Description given by De Fonte of his Passing thro' the Archipelago St. Lazarus, and of the River Los Reyes, is a natural One; the little Fall of Water out of Lake Belle into the River Los Reyes, till half Flood; and the Flood beginning to set gently into Lake Belle an hour and quarter before High Water, the Lake itself fresh, and the Water of Los Reyes fresh 20 Leagues distance from its Mouth, are all natural and consistent Circumstances: The Fish mention'd as found in Los Reyes and Lake Belle are proper to those Latitudes and to fresh Water; and when he comes to describe Lake De Fonte, which by its other Circumstances you find must be Salt Water, tho' he does not say it was so, yet the Fish he mentions are northern Saltwater Fish. The Description of the Birds, Beasts, Trees, Wild Fruit and Berries, are likewise all such as we know are proper to the Northern Parts of America. That the Country *grew sensibly worse* as they came farther Eastward tho' in nearly the same Latitude, is a singular Circumstance not likely to be observ'd in a Work of Invention; but from other Accounts of the Difference of Cold in the same Latitudes on the Eastern and Western Coasts of the same Continents must undoubtedly be Fact. In North America, on the Eastern Coast, from 50 Degrees Northward, all Vegetation is extreamly check'd by the Severity of the cold Northwest Winds, which blow three quarters of the Year, and make the Winters excessively hard. While the Western Coast of Europe in the same Latitudes, has plenty of strong Vegetation, large Growths of Timber, &c. and is comfortable for human Habitation. Again the Eastern Coast of the European and Asiatic Continent in those Northern Latitudes, viz. Kamschatka, &c. is exactly in the same Circumstances with the Eastern Coast of America; while the Western Coast of America, opposite to Kamschatka, is as happy in respect to Climate and Vegetation as the Western Coast of Europe. See the Observations of Mr. Steller the Russian Botanist, who was

---

English translation, *A Natural and Civil History of California* (2 vols., London, 1759) omitted two of the appendices, one of which was a thorough refutation of the de Fonte letter and the use made of it in the Delisle map of 1752. The recommendation of strong posts is in general reference to possible attempts of the English, Dutch, or others, who might want to break into the Oriental trade in the Pacific. English trans., II, 385. Williams (*British Search,* pp. 154–5) believes that the omission of the appendices was a deliberate suppression of evidence by the English editor.

employ'd in their late Discovery of America, Page 479, 480 of the Philosophical Transactions, Vol. LI. Part II. for the Year 1760.[2] He says, "The American Land is in a much better State, with regard to the Climate, than the farthermost Eastern Coast of Asia. The Mountains of Asia, are ruinous, cleft, and broken, cover'd with perpetual Snows; no Wood nor Herbs grow on the Coast, except in the Vallies, where is seen small brush Wood, and stiff Herbs. On the contrary, the Mountains of America on the opposite Coast, are covered on the Surface, not with Moss, but with fruitful Earth or Mould, and therefore are decked from the Foot to the very Top of them, with thick and very fine Trees. In America, even the Sea Shores at 60 Degrees Latitude, are woody; but in Kamschatka, at 51 Degrees Latitude, no Place set even with small Willows and Alder Trees is found nearer than 20 Versts from the Sea, birch Trees not nearer than 30 Versts, Pitch Trees 50 Versts; at 62 Degrees there is no Wood in Kamschatka." The above from Steller. Now we know the Eastern Coast of America in those Latitudes, viz. Labrador, Hudson's Bay and Greenland, to be in nearly the same bad State that he describes of Kamschatka. The Moravians who have a Mission in Greenland, carried from New York the Timber to build their Church and House, no Wood being found there. They carried also Earth for their Garden. Father Gabriel Marest, a Jesuit, who was some time at the Fort on Bourbon River, now called York River, in Hudson's Bay, Lat. 57. says, in his Letter printed in the Travels of the Jesuits, "the Soil is very barren; there is little Wood, and that very small; for about 30 or 40 Leagues about the Fort there are no Timber Trees; owing to the excessive Cold and almost continual Snows, &c."[3] P. Charlevoix says of the same Bay, "Rien

2. Georg Wilhelm Steller (1709–1746), German born and educated, went to Russia and in 1737 joined as botanist Capt. Vitus Bering's second expedition to Siberia, which established a settlement on Kamchatka and explored the shores of the Pacific. The paper in *Phil. Trans.* is headed in part "An Account of that Part of America which is nearest to the Land of Kamtchatka; extracted from the Description of Kamtchatka by Professor Krashennicoff [Krasheninnikov], printed at Petersburg, in two Volumes, 4to. in 1759." *Phil. Trans.*, LI, pt. II (1760), 477–97. BF's quotation of Steller's reported observations is very free, with many silent omissions.
3. Gabriel Demarest, in John Lockman, *Travels of the Jesuits* (2d edit., corrected, London, 1762), II, 497. In BF's quotation "and that very small" should read "and that very short."

n'est plus affreux que le Pays dont elle est environée; de quelque côté qu'on jette les yeux, on n'aperçoit que des Terres incultes et sauvages, et des Rochers escarpés, qui s'élevent jusqu'aux Nuës, qui sont entrecoupés, de Ravines profondes, et de Valées stériles, où le Soleil ne pénétre point, et que les neiges et les glaçons, qui ne fondent jamais, rendent inabordables."[4] Steller assures us from his own Observation, that the Western Coast is a fine Country. Therefore, any one passing thro' Lakes and Rivers from the Western to the Eastern Coast, as DeFonte says he did, must observe, if he took any Notice of the Country at all, that it *grew sensibly worse and worse*, the farther he went Eastward. In a Paper of mine long since wrote,[5] there is an Hypothesis that accounts for the almost constant blowing of N.W. Winds in those cold Countries, for the Coldness of those Winds, and the Tempering they receive in passing over a Sea, which I will not here repeat, as you have a Copy of that Paper.

The Late Russian Discoveries afford another probable Circumstance in favour of the Truth of DeFonte's Account. By his Description the Northern Part of America appears to be Land broken and divided by large Lakes communicating by Streights and Rivers; this State of the Country would afford an easy Communication to the People of the N.E. Coast of North America, who live by Whale Fishing, and have those singular kind of light Boats, made of Skins, and cover'd all but a Hole for one Person to sit in, which they close round their Bodies with a kind of Purse-Mouth, to prevent any Entrance of Water.[6] Now the Russians in crossing the Western Sea, met with People and Boats that answer this Description exactly, employ'd in the same Way, using the same kind of Instruments, and having the same Manners. They had moreover Iron Knives, which no Indians can make, and which these northern Indians buy of our Hudson's Bay Company, or of the Danes at Greenland. As these

4. Pierre-François Xavier de Charlevoix, *Histoire et description générale de la Nouvelle France* (4to edit., 3 vols., Paris, 1744), I, 473–4.

5. "Physical and Meteorological Observations, Conjectures and Suppositions," above, IV, 241; read at the Royal Society, Dec. 23, 1756, but not printed in *Phil. Trans.* until 1765.

6. On the retained draft of a letter BF wrote to George Whitefield, June 19, 1764 (APS), is a rough sketch, in view from above, of just such a boat as BF describes here, though rather too broad of beam for a typical Eskimo kayak. It bears no relation to the subject of the letter to Whitefield.

People live by the Produce of the Sea, and every Man has one of this kind of Boats, may we not suppose that they pass freely in those Boats thro' such Lakes and Passages, fishing in either Sea, as the differing Seasons occasion the Whales, &c. to appear in one or the other at different Times.

Again, by the Account of DeFonte's Passage out of Lake Belle which was fresh Water, into Lake DeFonte which appears to be Salt Water, thro' the River Parmentiers, it seems that this latter Salt Water communicating with the Eastern or Atlantic Sea, was lower in its Level than the Salt Water of the Western Sea; for, a little before High Water, he found that the Tide flow'd into Lake Belle on the Western Side; and there was only a small Fall out of it at other Times; whereas in coming out of that Lake on the Eastern Side in his Boats, he found a Descent of Water to Lake DeFonte by 8 several Falls or Rapides, which in the whole he computes might amount to about 32 feet perpendicular. It is not taken Notice of as a wonderful Thing that there should be any Difference of Level between the two Seas. No Attempt is made to account for such an Improbability. And one would think no Writer of a feign'd Voyage, who desir'd to have it receiv'd as true, would of Choice invent and insert a Circumstance so objectionable. The Facts seem to be simply related, without Attention to the consequential Difficulty. Now if it should be found from subsequent Considerations, that there ought to be a considerable Difference in the Level of the two Seas, the Improbability of such a Thing at the Time the Journal was written, affords another internal Evidence of the Truth of that Journal. And that Lake DeFonte was suppos'd by the Writer to communicate with the Atlantic, appears from this, that in the Strait Ronquillo leading out of that Lake, Admiral DeFonte, as he says, found a Ship from New England, trading with the Natives for Furs; of which Ship more hereafter. As to the Difference of Level in Seas, it is well known, that strong Winds have a considerable Effect on the Surface of the Sea; moving the Waters so as to raise them on some Coasts and depress them on others.[7] Occasional Winds produce these Effects

7. In his article previously cited, Percy G. Adams has pointed out that BF was "guilty of an error in science" in this discussion. BF could not know what more recent studies have shown, that the difference in mean level of the oceans is at most a matter of inches. In particular areas, of course, factors such as tides may create from time to time much greater differences in the

occasionally on the Coasts of Britain, Ireland, Holland, &c. Constant Winds in other Countries produce the same Effects more constantly. The Trade Wind blowing over the Atlantic Ocean constantly from the East, between the Tropics, carries a Current to the American Coast, and raises the Water there above its natural Level. From thence it flows off thro' the Gulf of Mexico, and all along the North American Coast to and beyond the Banks of Newfoundland in a strong Current, called by Seamen *the Gulph Stream*.[8] In those Northern Latitudes the Winds blowing almost constantly Northwest, as appears by the Voyages of Middleton, Ellis, and others, the Waters are mov'd away from the North American Coast towards the Coasts of Spain and Africa, whence they get again into the Power of the Trade Winds, and continue the Circulation. Thus the North West Winds keep the Level of the Sea lower in the North East Seas of America, as the Easterly Trade Winds accumulate it on the Coast between the Tropics. But if one could not assign the Cause of such Difference of Level in the same Ocean, the Fact must nevertheless be allow'd; since so long and so strong a Current as that of the *Gulph Stream*, thro' all the Latitudes of variable Winds, can only be accounted for, by its having a considerable Descent, and moving from Parts where the Water is higher, to Parts where it is lower. Now the very same Cause, viz. The almost constant Northwest Winds blowing in the Northern Region, which carry the Waters away from the North East Coast of America, bring them to and accumulate them on the N. West Coast. And by all Accounts of Voyages in those N. Western Seas, particularly that of Sir Francis Drake, that of Sebastian Viscaino in 1602, and the late Voyages of the Russians, the Northwest Wind is there a kind of Trade Wind, and blows violently. And if Winds may produce a Difference of Level in the same Ocean, they certainly may in different Oceans, where the free Communication is obstructed by a Continent or by Islands.

About the Year 1752, a Person who had been Clerk to the California, in a Voyage made by that Ship and the Dobbs to Hudson's Bay, in Search of a N. West Passage, apply'd to me to promote a

---

levels of nearby bodies of water, whether these belong to the same or different oceans.

8. This is the first mention of the Gulf Stream found in BF's writings, a phenomenon about which he was to write significantly in 1768, and the first chart of which he had prepared.

Subscription for another Attempt.[9] He put into my Hands, among other Pieces relating to the Probability of such a Passage, Mr. Dobbs's Account of this Letter of DeFonte's,[1] wherein I found Mention of his Meeting with a Ship from Boston in New-England, commanded by one Shapley, and own'd by Major General Gibbons of that Country, who was on board, trading with the Natives in those Parts. As this was a very remarkable Circumstance, and, if true, would show that the Lake DeFonte, and the Strait Ronquillo, where Shapley's Ship was found, communicated with the Atlantic in or near Hudson's Bay, there being no Probability that a Boston Ship would go down to the Straits of Magellan and up the Western Coast of America, a Voyage of more than 5000 Leagues, to trade with the Indians in those Northern Countries, when they could meet with the same kind of People and Trade so much nearer home in or about Hudson's Bay. I resolved to make Enquiry concerning it. DeFonte's

9. Charles Swaine; above, IV, 380–3. A note to that document (p. 381) explains that there has been disagreement among scholars and bibliographers as to the authorship of two books on Northwest exploration, which have been attributed variously to Charles Swaine and Theodore (Theodorus) Swaine Drage. Recently Percy G. Adams has published an article to prove that these apparently different men were in fact the same individual, who for unknown reasons sometimes went by one name, sometimes by the other. "The Case of Swaine Versus Drage An Eighteenth-Century Publishing Mystery Solved," Heinz S. Bluhm, ed., *Essays in History and Literature Presented by Fellows of the Newberry Library to Stanley Pargellis* (Chicago, 1965), pp. 157–68. While the present editors are unable to accept this conclusion without some reservations, they agree that Professor Adams has advanced strong evidence for the identity of Swaine and Drage.

1. In *An Account Of the Countries adjoining to Hudson's Bay, in the North-west Part of America* (London, 1744), Arthur Dobbs had reprinted, nearly in full, the de Fonte letter, pp. 123–8, followed by his own commentary on it, pp. 128–30. Almost certainly it was this version of the account that BF had read, rather than the original one in *The Monthly Miscellany*. Dobbs declared that it "has all the appearance of being authentick," and "it has throughout the Air of Truth." His interpretation of the geography implicit in the letter was substantially different from that Delisle offered in his map of 1752. Dobbs explained de Fonte's final comment about his expedition (quoted in the headnote above) by saying that de Fonte must have meant either that there "was no Passage into the South Sea" by Barnarda's route to the far north, or that there was no passage by his own route for ocean-going ships, though there obviously was one for small boats. This book was one of Dobbs's contributions to his controversy with Christopher Middleton.

Description of Capt. Shapley is, that he was the greatest Man in the Mechanical Parts of the Mathematics that he ever met with, having fine Charts and Journals which he purchas'd of him for 1000 Pieces of eight; and of Major Gibbons, that he was a fine Gentleman. I imagin'd that some Remembrance of such Persons and such a Trade from New England, if they ever existed, might still be found there. Accordingly I wrote to Mr. Prince, a great Antiquarian of that Country,[2] and then employ'd in writing a chronological Account of its first Settlement, and all the remarkable Events of its History, desiring he would enquire and inform me if there had been such a Person as Seimor Gibbons, Major General of the Massachusetts Bay in New England about the Year 1640. In Answer he acquainted me that about 10 Years before, DeFonte's Journal in Manuscript had been put into his Hands with the same Request, by Capt. Warren (afterwards Admiral Warren)[3] then Commander of the Station Ship at Boston; that he readily found in their old Records that a Major General Gibbons liv'd at that time in that Colony; but that his Christian Name was not Seimor but Edward.[4] As to Captain Shapley, not finding any Mention of him, he apply'd to a Deacon Marshal, then above 90 Years of Age, to know if he had ever heard of such a Person. Deacon Marshal told him, he remember'd that when he was a Boy, there was Much Talk among the Boys of a Capt.

2. Thomas Prince (1687–1758), learned Boston clergyman, author of *A Chronological History of New-England in the Form of Annals* (Boston, 1736–55), from which BF quotes below. Neither BF's letters nor Prince's replies have been found. The correspondence probably took place about 1752–53, when BF was concerned in preparations for the first *Argo* expedition.

3. Peter Warren (1703–1752) of the Royal Navy served in American waters, 1730–46; commanded the squadron that assisted at the capture of Louisbourg, 1745, and was thereupon promoted to rear admiral. He was created Knight of the Bath, 1747, for his victory over the French off Cape Finisterre and advanced to vice admiral. He married Susannah DeLancey of the prominent N.Y. family, 1731, and acquired large estates in the Mohawk Valley. *DAB; DNB;* and above, III, 119 n.

4. The writer of the de Fonte letter could have taken the name of Edward Gibbons either from Increase Mather's *An Essay for the Recording of Illustrious Providences* (Boston, 1684), or Cotton Mather's *Magnalia Christi Americana* (London, 1702), in both of which he appears. Cotton Mather's work had been published in London just six years before the de Fonte letter was first printed in the same city. Again the editors are indebted to Percy G. Adams for this suggestion; *Princeton Univ. Lib. Chron.*, XXII, 138.

Shapley, and of his great Learning, he having, as they exprest it, learnt as far as the Black Art: That he liv'd and dy'd at Charlestown (a Town near Boston) but more of him he could not remember. Mr. Prince then went to Charlestown, where he found some of the Descendants of Capt. Shapley, and his Will on the Records of the Town. He therefore gave Credit to the Voyage in general, but suppos'd a Mistake as to Major General Gibbons being himself on board the Ship with Capt. Shapley, his Name being *Edward* and not *Seimor;* but said, he possibly might have a Brother of the Name of Seimor, who might be with Shapley. I wrote again to Mr. Prince, that the Major's Christian Name being mention'd in the following plain Manner, "having given the brave Navigator Captain Shapley for his fine Charts and Journals, 1000 Pieces of eight, and the Owner of the Ship Seimor Gibbons a Quarter Cask of Peruan Wine," &c. where some Title is given to Shapley and the Major, tho' allow'd to be a Gentleman of Rank, call'd only by his plain Christian and Sur Name, as a Quaker would have call'd him and in a manner not agreeing with Spanish Politeness; I suspected that what was put down *Seimor* by the Copier of the Account, might in the Original be the Spanish Title of Compliment, Seignior, which they write Señor or Sennor; if Sennor, it was an easy Mistake, by supposing the first Stroke of the first (n) to be an (i), then the second Stroke of the first (n) join'd to the two Strokes of the second (n) would make the (m) and so turn Sennor into Seimor.[5] Mr. Prince however did not seem satisfied that the Major General could himself be with Shapley; but I have since met with the following Particulars relating to him. In the New England Chronology printed at Boston 1736, I find he liv'd near Charlestown in 1630. [Charlstown was the Residence of Shapley when at home, and this makes a Connection between them the more probable][6] The Words are, "About a Mile distant [from Charlestown] upon the River, runs a small Creek, which takes its Name from Mr. Edward Gibbons, who dwelt there for some Years

5. BF's explanation is ingenious but invalid, as he would have recognized had he been using the original printed text in *The Monthly Miscellany* of 1708 instead of the Dobbs reprint of 1744. As emphasized in the headnote above, the original printing gave the name as "Scimor Gibbons"; Dobbs changed the first part to "Seimor." It would have been much less plausible to suggest that "Scimor" was a corruption of "Sennor."

6. These brackets and those below both in the MS.

after, and became Major General."[7] And in a Book, call'd *Remarkable Providences,* by Increase Mather, printed at Boston in New-England, 1684, there is a Story of him thus introduc'd, page 14. "Remarkable was that Deliverance mention'd both by Mr. Janeway and Mr. Burton, wherein that gallant Commander Major Edward Gibbons of Boston in New England, and others, were concerned. The Substance of the Story is this. A New England Vessel going from Boston *to some other Parts of America,* was thro' the Continuance of contrary Winds, kept long at Sea, So that they were in very great Straits for want of Provision." After relating many Circumstances of their Distress, and their casting Lots that one might die to be eaten by the rest, and their going to Prayers before they would actually kill the destin'd Victim; the Relation concludes thus, "One of them espies a Ship, which put Life into all their Spirits. They bear up with their Vessel, man their Boat, and beg like perishing humble Supplicants to board them, which they are admitted. The Vessel proves a French Vessel, yea a French Pirate. Major Gibbons petitions them for a little Bread, and offers Ship and Cargo for it. But the Commander knows the Major; (from whom he had received some signal Kindnesses formerly at Boston) and replied readily and chearfully, Major Gibbons, not a Hair of you or your Company shall perish, if it lie in my Power to preserve you. And accordingly he relieveth them." There is no Date to this Account, but the Book professedly relates all Events of the kind that had happened to New England People since the Settlement of that Country, and speaks of this Account as taken from former Books:[8] Then we find in the Relation compar'd with DeFonte's Account, the following Circumstances of Character that agree, viz.

7. Prince's *Chronological History,* I, 241. The passage quoted refers to events in 1630.

8. In a note in *North American Review,* XLVIII (1839), 558–63, James Savage completely demolished the identification of the major general whom de Fonte said he met July 30, 1640, with Maj. Gen. Edward Gibbons of Boston. Massachusetts had no major general in 1640; the first of that rank was appointed in 1644 and Edward Gibbons attained it only in 1649. The voyage cited in *Remarkable Providences* took place in 1637 and was to Bermuda—a very different matter from one to the far north. As a selectman of Boston and representative in the General Court, Edward Gibbons' presence in Massachusetts is accounted for at various dates in 1640, including July 2 (July 12 new style), only eighteen days before de Fonte said he met him a great distance away.

Mather	DeFonte
1. Gallant Commander; one that when at home show'd Kindness to Strangers, and gain'd their Esteem.	1. A fine Gentleman, modest Gentleman, made me a Present of Provisions. I prest him to accept a Diamond Ring.
2. A Major, of Boston, in New England.	2. Major General of the largest Colony in New England.
3. Us'd sometimes to make Voyages to other Parts of America.	3. Was in the Ship with Shapley on the N.E. Coast of America.
4. The Ship and Cargo his own, he offer'd them for Provisions to the Frenchman.	4. Was Owner of Shapley's Ship.
5. His Name *Edward* Gibbons.	5. His Name *Seimor* Gibbons.

This only Difference I have already endeavour'd to account for; and if I have conjectured truly, this very Difference is a farther Proof that the Journal is really a Translation from the Spanish, and not, as some have supposed, an English Fiction. I will now only add; that from Manuscript Journals I have seen and read in Boston, and other Accounts, I know that some of those Seamen who had been employ'd in Discovering Hudson's Bay, settled afterwards in New England, and were engag'd in constant yearly trading Voyages from Boston thither, which continu'd down with some Interruptions from the French, till the Establishment of the Hudson's-Bay Company in the Reign of Charles the second. At home I have a Number of Letters and Papers that give farther and stronger Light in this Matter; they are bundled together with the Manuscript Journals of the two Voyages I promoted from Philadelphia, which proved indeed unsuccessful, but the Journals contain some valuable Information; and the Charts taken of the Coast, Harbours, and Islands of Labrador, for a considerable Extent, may be useful. As you have exprest some Curiosity in this Affair, I wish them in your Possession; and if any Accident should happen to me in my Return I desire my Executors may consider this Letter as an Authority for their sending them intire to you. With the greatest Esteem, I am, Dear Friend, Yours affectionately   B FRANKLIN

P.S. My Opinion upon the whole is this, That though there may probably be no practicable Passage for Ships, there is nevertheless

such a Passage for Boats as DeFonte found and has describ'd; and
That the Country upon that Passage is for the most part habitable,
and would produce all the Necessaries of Life.

I intended to sketch a little Map, expressing my Idea of De
Fonte's Voyage, as you desired. But I find one done to my Hand,
which I send you annexed.[9] I only think it places the Entrance of
Los Reyes too far South, which Entrance I conceive, by the Distance sailed, 866 Leagues from Cape Abel, ought to be near Lat.
60. and that it carries the Strait Ronquillo too far North, which I
imagine should enter Hudson's Bay between Lat. 60 and 62, where
I have made two crooked red Lines. The Bay North of Cape Elias
discover'd by the Russians, is perhaps the Entrance of the Archipelago St. Lazarus, describ'd by DeFonte, leading to Rio Los
Reyes.

Doctor Pringle

Endorsed: Dr Franklin, on the Voyage of Admiral B. deFonte. found
amongst the papers of the Earl of Bute 1762.[1]

Deborah Franklin: Account of Expenses

AD: American Philosophical Society

When Franklin was about to leave for England in 1757 his wife Deborah
started to keep her household accounts in a memorandum book he provided her. This record is described above, VII, 167-8. On September 1
(the year is not stated) she indicated her intention to stop entering her
expenses in detail, "as I am not abell to set down every penney." But

9. See the map facing p. 86. The "two crooked red Lines" BF added may
be seen running from the middle of the eastern shore of "L. De Fonte"
through the mountains to near the "H" of "Hudsons Bay."

1. The endorsement is written on a sheet of paper watermarked 1840 in
which the letter and map are enclosed. The whole was sold at auction in
London in 1932 as having been "the property of the late Rt. Honble. Lord
North." For the provenance, see Bertha Solis-Cohen, *Princeton Univ. Lib.
Chron.*, XIX, 23. Almost certainly Pringle had given the letter and map to the
Earl of Bute. On June 19, 1783, John Adams recorded in his diary that "Dr.
Franklin once gave to Lord Bute his Reasons in Writing for believing this a
genuine Voyage." L. H. Butterfield et al., eds., *Diary and Autobiography of
John Adams* (Cambridge, Mass., 1961), III, 140. Doubtless this statement
referred to the present letter.

in May 1762 she took a new though short-lived resolve, inspired perhaps by the expectation of her husband's speedy return, and she compiled on a separate sheet the brief record printed below. It is given here
in full to suggest Deborah's characteristic spelling and some of her
expenditures during Benjamin's long absence from home.

1762

May the
I begin agen to keep an a Counte of expenses

a breste of vele 2 pound of butter 14—1 x 2 Sallis 6			
in all[2]		8	1
eges one shilling pigons 2–6		3	6
for goodeys for my pappey 2 Jars	6	3	9
6 yards of Duch Hollond for pillowcases	1	13	8
for a homspon Coverlid	4	0	0
att a vendue a Cotton Coverlid and bolster	1	16	9
paid Mrs. Bullock for mending 2 pair of Jumps[3] and			
the things comes to	1	4	0
Sallit and greens	0	0	10
paid Bettey for washin 15 and to my maid	4	15	0
Salley a Blew necklis 7-6 a dram of Black silk	0	8	0
home spun threed	0	0	8
for a sate of window curtins Crimsin Chaney[4]	2	5	0
a Jet Necklase for my Selef	0	7	6
in market vell 7-6 butter 2 eges 1	0	10	6
Sope Candels Sallet	0	1	0
for worsted	0	8	9
the milk man	0	8	0
for the Liberrey for papey and Mr. Grase[5]	1	0	0
for Billey fier Companey	0	1	0
Shues for Salley	0	8	6

2. The last part of this first entry is nearly indecipherable but appears to
read as indicated here. "Sallis" may mean "Sally's," but if so the meaning is
far from clear.

3. An under (or undress) bodice, fitted to the bust and often used instead
of stays; usually referred to, as here, as "a pair of jumps." *OED.*

4. Probably DF meant a set of window curtains of crimson China silk.

5. Robert Grace, one of BF's oldest friends, was an original member of the
Junto and a member of the first board of directors of the Library Co.; see
above, I, 209 n; III, 330 n.

6 pound of brown Shuger 4	2 Bottels Beer	0	5	0
Limes a quortor of Hundred			3	9
a pound of Green tee		1	12	0
in Market		0	10	0
2 Dos. of oringes		0	9	0

To Mary Stevenson
ALS: Yale University Library

Dear Polly   London June 7. 1762

I received your Favour of the 27th. past,[6] and have since expected your intended philosophical Epistle. But you have not had
Leisure to write it!

Your good Mama is now perfectly well, as I think, excepting
now and then a few Rheumatic Complaints, which however seem
gradually diminishing.

I am glad to hear you are about to enjoy the Happiness of seeing
and being with your Friends at Bromley. My best Respects to the
good Doctor and Mrs. Hawkesworth; and say to the dear Ladies
that I kiss their Hands respectfully and affectionately.[7]

Our Ships for America do not sail so soon as I expected; it will
be yet 5 or 6 Weeks before we embark, and leave the old World
for the New. I fancy I feel a little like dying Saints, who in parting
with those they love in this World, are only comforted with the
Hope of more perfect Happiness in the next. I have in America
Connections of the most engaging kind, and happy as I have been
in the Friendships here contracted, *those* promise me greater and
more lasting Felicity. But God only knows whether those Promises shall be fullfilled.

Adieu, my dear good Girl, and believe me ever Your affectionate
Friend   B FRANKLIN

6. Not found.

7. For Dr. and Mrs. John Hawkesworth, who were at this time managing
a school for young ladies in Bromley, Kent, see above, IX, 265–6 n. The "dear
Ladies" were Polly's close friends Catherine and Dolly Blunt; see above, IX,
327 n.

From David Hall   Letterbook copy: American Philosophical Society

Sir,   Philada. June 9. 1762.
In my last to you, of the 10th ult.[8] was designed to have been inclosed the third Copy of a Bill of Exchange for Three Hundred Pounds Sterling, but, by Accident, find I neglected to do it: This serves, therefore, to cover the same, to let you know that Mrs. Franklin and Sally are well; and that I am, Sir, Yours, &c.
                                        D. HALL
Mr. Franklin
Sent Via Liverpool By the Hope, Capt. Dee[9]

From Mary Stevenson   Draft: American Philosophical Society

Dear Sir   Bromley June 11. 1762
Whether the Invitation you give me to write to you proceeds from the Pleasure you receive or desire to bestow I shall not enquire;[1] the first would gratify my Vanity most, but I am not less pleas'd with thinking you love to indulge me.

When I say I have not Leisure for my favourite Amusements I am as much surpriz'd as you can be, and I wonder how my Time passes away without any Employment that appears of Consequence. Day after Day I have intended to furnish my Mind with something that would serve for the Subject of a Letter to you; but Day succeeded to Day without the Acquisition, and I now sit down to write with very little in my Head tho much in my Heart.

I have taken the Liberty you gave me of transcribing your Letter on Fire,[2] which gives a clearer Explication of it's Effects than I ever met with, yet some Questions remain for me to ask. Whence is it that Fire is increased by the Impulsion of the Air, yet if that Impulsion is too strong it is extinguish'd? I have seen you blow out

8. See above, pp. 79–80.
9. *Pa. Gaz.*, June 17, 1762, reported the clearance of the *Hope*, Capt. J. Dee.
1. For BF's "Invitation" to Polly to write him a "philosophical Epistle" and for some of the other matters mentioned in this letter, see above, p. 102.
2. Almost certainly BF's letter to John Lining, April 14, 1757; see above, VII, 184–90.

the Flame of the Bougie,[3] and, by drawing it swiftly thro' the Air, immediately rekindle it. Another Thing appears to me very unaccountable. To prevent the firing of Wheels we make use very effectually of those Materials which soonest catch fire as Pitch, Grease &c. Though I have acknowledg'd this to be unaccountable I have attempted to discover the Cause, but I cannot satisfy myself. I remember you told me no Degree of Heat was ever produc'd in Fluids by Friction. The Grease then being between the Nave and the Axle-tree of the Wheel prevents their rubbing against each other. You will give me Pleasure whenever you will satisfy me more fully, which you may not have Leisure to do by Writing, but as I hope for the Pleasure of seeing you once more it may serve for our Conversation, in the mean time I shall be glad of any Word you will condescend to send me.[4]

May you my dear Saint enjoy all the Felicity you Promise yourself in the New World! and May it be long ere you are remov'd to that other World where only your Votary can hope to meet you!

Present my dutiful Affection to my dear Mother, and Thanks for her kind Letter which I will soon repay. Our amiable Host[5] left us last Tuesday. He intended waiting on you, and if he did would tell you I receiv'd your *elegant affectionate Letter*. Those were his Words when he return'd it to me, for my Vanity made me shew it. Every Testimony of your Regard is too high a Honour not be felt and made the Boast of Dear Sir your most grateful and affectionate humble Servant   M STEVENSON

To William Strahan

MS not found; reprinted from *The Atlantic Monthly*, LXI (1888), 34.

Saturday, June 14, [1762?][6]

Mr. Franklin's Compliments to Mr. Strahan, and out of pure Kindness to him offers him an Opportunity of exercising his Benevo-

3. A wax candle which took its name from the North African town whence it was first imported into Europe.
4. See below, pp. 105–8.
5. Dr. John Hawkesworth.
6. June 14 fell on Saturday in 1762 and in 1773. In accordance with editorial practice this letter is placed at the earlier of these dates.

lence as a Man and his Charity as a Christian. One Spencer,[7] formerly a Merchant of Figure and Credit in North America, being
by various Misfortunes reduced to Poverty, is here in great Distress, and would be made happy by any Employment that would
only enable him *to Eat,* which he looks as if he had not done for
some Time. He is well acquainted with Accompts, and writes a
very fair Hand, as Mr. S. may see by the enclosed Letter. His
Expectations that brought him over, which are touched on in that
Letter, are at an End. He is a very honest Man, but too much
dispirited to put himself forward. Cannot some *Smouting,*[8] in the
writing way, be got for him? or come [some?] little *Clerkship?*
which he would execute very faithfully. He is at Mr. Cooper's, at
the Hat and Feather, Snow Hill.[9] Mr. F. has done what he could
to serve him (to little purpose indeed) and now leaves him as a
Legacy to good Mr. Strahan.

To [Mary Stevenson][1]

Draft: Library of Congress; copy: American Philosophical Society

Cravenstreet, June 21. 1762

Did you ever see People at work with Spades and Pickaxes, dig-
ging a Cellar?

7. Probably George Spencer, who went bankrupt in England, migrated to
N. Y. in 1757, and was later jailed there for his debts, although he said he had
been persecuted for informing against illicit traders. In 1766–67 he was
ordained in England and licensed for N.J. by the Society for the Propagation
of the Gospel. He served parishes in Spotswood and Freehold, N. J., but was
recalled the same year as "disreputable" and moved to No. Car. William
Smith wrote the S. P. G. about his bad character, blaming BF for recommending his ordination. *Colden Paps.,* VI, 89–99; William S. Perry, *Papers relating
to the History of the Church in Pennsylvania, A.D. 1680–1778* (n.p., 1871), pp.
416, 421; Frederick L. Weis, "The Colonial Clergy of the Middle Colonies,"
Amer. Antiq. Soc. *Proc.,* LXVI (1956–57), 318.

8. Part-time, irregular, or odd-job work in a printing office. BF had used
the word once before in a letter to Strahan; see above, VII, 116.

9. Snow Hill was a circuitous, narrow, and steep highway connecting
Holborn Bridge and Newgate. It was cleared away when the Holborn Viaduct
was constructed in 1867, though parts are incorporated in the present Snow
Hill. Mr. Cooper and the Hat and Feather Tavern have not been further
identified.

1. So identified because the letter is clearly a response to hers of June 11

When they have loosen'd the Earth perhaps a foot deep, that loose Earth must be carried off, or they can go no deeper; it is in their way, and hinders the Operation of the Instruments.

When the first foot of loose Earth is removed, they can dig and loosen the Earth a foot deeper.

But if those who remove the Earth, should with it take away the Spades and Pickaxes; the Work will be equally obstructed as if they had left the loose Earth unremoved.

I imagine the Operation of Fire upon Fewel with the Assistance of Air may be in some degree similar to this. Fire penetrates Bodies, and separates their Parts. The Air receives and carries off the Parts separated, which if not carried off would impede the Action of the Fire. With this Assistance therefore of a moderate Current of Air, the Separation encreases; but too violent a Blast carries off the Fire itself; and thus any Fire may be blown out as a Candle by the Breath if the Blast be proportionable.

But if Air contributes inflammatory Matter as some have thought, then it should seem, that the more Air, the more the Flame would be augmented, which beyond certain Bounds does not agree with the Fact.

Some Substances take Fire, i.e. are kindled by the Application of Fire much sooner than others. This is in proportion as they are bad or good Conductors of Fire, and as their Parts cohere with less or more Strength. A bad Conductor of Fire not easily permitting it to penetrate and be absorb'd and its force divided among the whole Substance, its Operation is so much the Stronger on the Surface to which it is apply'd, and is in a small Depth of Surface strong enough to produce the Separation of Parts which we call Burning. Wax, Sulphur, all Oils and Fats and most vegetable Substances are bad Conductors of Fire. The Oil of a Lamp, burning at the Top may be scarce warm at the Bottom; a Candle or a Stick of Wood inflam'd at one End is cool at the other. Metals which are better Conductors are not so easily kindled, tho' when sufficient Fire is apply'd to them to separate their Parts they will

---

(above, pp. 103–4) and because of a note she added at the bottom of the copy made by her eleven-year-old son, Thomas Tickell Hewson, many years later: "Transcribed by T. T. Hewson from a rough copy of a letter written by Dr. Franklin, intended for me, but never finished, nor shewn to me till at Passy Dec. 1784. M.H."

all burn. But the Fire apply'd to their Surfaces enters more easily
is absorb'd and divided; and not enough left on the Surface to over-
come the Stronger Cohesion of their Parts. A close Contact with
Metals will for the same Reason prevent the burning of more inflammable Substances: A flaxen Thread bound close round an Iron
Poker, will not burn in the Flame of a Candle; for it must imbibe
a certain Quantity of Fire before it can burn, i.e. before its Parts
can separate; But the Poker as fast as the Fire arrives, takes
it from the Thread, conducts it away and divides it in its own
Substance.

Common Fire I conceive to be collected by Friction from the
common Mass of that Fluid, in the same manner as the electrical
Fluid is collected by Friction, which I have endeavoured to explain in some of my electrical Papers, and to avoid Length in this
Letter refer you to them. In Wheels the Particles of Grease and
Oil acting as so many little Rollers and Preventing Friction between the Wood and Wood, do thereby prevent the Collection
of Fire.

[Elsewhere on this page arranged in a column:[2]] Col Ludwell /
Call at John Hunts / Mrs French / Dr Russell / Wm Do [ditto]

2. BF probably compiled this list, through parts of which lines are drawn, to
remind himself of people he wanted to see before he left London. Col. Philip
Ludwell (above, VI, 532 n) was a Va. planter and official who moved to
London in 1760 and who commissioned the Mason Chamberlain portrait of
BF in July or August 1762. John Hunt (above, VII, 373 n) was a London
Quaker merchant who had been sent by the English Friends as an adviser to
the Pa. Quakers in 1756. Mrs. French was possibly the Katherine French
whose inadequately dated notes inviting BF for music, chess, and literary
discussions seem to belong to the period of 1765–71. Alexander Russell (1715?–
1768), M.D., F.R.S., was a distinguished physician and naturalist, a friend of
Fothergill and Collinson; *DNB*. His brother William, also F.R.S., was
secretary to the Levant Co. Elias Bland (above, III, 141 n) was another
London Quaker merchant; BF had lent him £300, July 12, 1759, which Bland
repaid about four weeks later; "Account of Expences," pp. 42, 45; *PMHB*,
LV (1931), 121; see also below, p. 139 n. There were two Browns living at
the Charterhouse as pensioners at this time: Thomas, admitted 1755, died
Nov. 12, 1762; and John Walker, admitted 1748, died Feb. 7, 1769; "The
Registers and Monumental Inscriptions of Charterhouse Chapel," *Registers*,
XVIII, *Publications*, Harleian Soc. Which was BF's friend is not known. Mr.
Colepeper has not been identified. Henry & Cave, the firm which published
Gent. Mag., consisted at this time of David Henry (1725?–1792) and Richard
Cave, a nephew of Edward Cave, the founder. John Bevis (above, IV, 392 n)

/ Elias Bland / Brown Charter house / Mr Colepeper / Henry & Cave / Dr Bevis / Mr Wilson Canon street / Newbery / Crosson / Mildred / Aufrere / Sargent / Neat & Neave / Collinson / Post Office / Baker Cards Exp[enses?] / Willock / Dr Reeves / Dr Hadley / Mr Edwards / Memo. Becket Tully Old Age / Ephemerides Motuum / Mr Allen and Miss Downes
[In another column:[3]] Bellows. / Toys for Children / New Things at Turners. / Tin men Pewterers Brasiers.

Skaining of Worsted into hard twisted Rolls[4]

---

was an astronomer who also participated in electrical experiments. "Mr. Wilson Canon Street" was apparently not Benjamin Wilson (above, IV, 391 n), the painter and electrician, who lived at this time in Great Queen Street. Newbery was probably John Newbery, publisher of Johnson, Goldsmith, and other writers (above, VI, 279 n). Crosson was probably the tradesman from whom BF and WF had bought stockings and other clothing; "Account of Expences," p. 39; *PMHB*, LV (1931), 118. Daniel Mildred was a member of the mercantile firm of Mildred & Roberts. George Aufrere and John Sargent composed the firm of Sargent Aufrere & Co., merchants, who handled payment of the bills drawn on BF by the trustees of the Pa. Loan Office. William Neate and Richard Neave comprised another London mercantile firm with which BF had occasional business relations for many years (above, IV, 115). Peter Collinson (above, III, 115–16 n), one of BF's oldest and closest friends, needs no further identification. A visit to the General Post Office before departure would be an obvious duty for the deputy joint postmaster general of America. Baker is unidentified. Robert Willock was a bookseller at Sir Isaac Newton's Head from 1735 or earlier to 1767. Dr. Thomas Reeves was a London physician who attended Peter Collinson in his last illness six years later. John Hadley (above, VIII, 108), was the professor of chemistry at Cambridge with whom BF had performed experiments on evaporation in June 1758. Mr. Edwards may have been George Edwards (1694–1773), F.R.S., a distinguished ornithologist. Thomas Becket was the publisher of BF's Canada Pamphlet; BF left orders with him for pamphlets to be sent to America (below, p. 393) and gave Strahan some copies of his own printing of Cicero's *Cato Major* ("Tully Old Age") to deliver to Becket for sale (below, p. 108). *Ephemerides motuum coelestium* was a common title for almanacs. Mr. T. Allen was the brother-in-law of Elizabeth Downes, the girl WF married September 4, 1762.

3. Like every good family man returning home after a long absence, BF was obviously planning to bring presents for relatives, close friends, and those friends' children.

4. On another part of the same page with the memoranda printed above BF wrote this caption and drew the sketch reproduced opposite. Whether he did this at about the same time that he drafted the letter or much later is not known.

Skaining of Worsted
into hard twisted Rolls

Should be a Post

Iron

Hollow high &
not ground

4 or 5 In.

7 Inches

Iron Pin with a Head

about 1/2 Inch Diam.

about 10 Inches long

Experiments on Amber

MS not found; reprinted from Benjamin Franklin, *Experiments and Observations on Electricity*, 1769 edition, pp. 425–7.[5]

Saturday, July 3, 1762.

To try, at the request of a friend,[6] whether amber finely powdered might be melted and run together again by means of the electric fluid, I took a piece of small glass tube about $2\frac{1}{2}$ inches long, the bore about $^{1}/_{12}$ of an inch diameter, the glass itself about the same thickness; I introduced into this tube some powder of amber, and with two pieces of wire nearly fitting the bore, one inserted at one end, the other at the other, I rammed the powder hard between them in the middle of the tube, where it stuck fast, and was in length about half an inch. Then leaving the wires in the tube, I made them part of the electric circuit, and discharged through them three rows of my case of bottles. The event was, that the glass was broke into very small pieces and those dispersed with violence in all directions. As I did not expect this, I had not, as in other experiments, laid thick paper over the glass to save my eyes, so several of the pieces struck my face smartly, and one of them cut my lip a little so as to make it bleed. I could find no part of the amber; but the table where the tube lay was stained very black in spots, such as might be made by a thick smoke forced on it by a blast, and the air was filled with a strong smell, somewhat like that from burnt gunpowder. Whence I imagined, that the amber was burnt, and had exploded as gunpowder would have done in the same circumstances.

That I might better see the effect on the amber, I made the next experiment in a tube formed of a card rolled up and bound strongly with packthread. Its bore was about $\frac{1}{2}$ of an inch diameter. I rammed powder of amber into this as I had done in the other, and as the quantity of amber was greater, I increased the quantity of electric fluid, by discharging through it at once 5 rows of my bot-

5. Letter XLI in both the 1769 edition and that of 1774, where it is printed on pp. 435–7. While this paper is called a "Letter," and has the date and initialed signature in the usual places, it carries no salutation or complimentary close, and no addressee is indicated.

6. Identified in Barbeu Dubourg, *Oeuvres de M. Franklin* (Paris, 1773), I, 243, as John Pringle, presumably on information supplied by BF.

tles. On opening the tube, I found that some of the powder had exploded, an impression was made on the tube though it was not burst, and most of the powder remaining was turned black, which I suppose might be by the smoke forced through it from the burnt part:[7] Some of it was hard; but as it powdered again when pressed by the fingers, I suppose that hardness not to arise from melting any parts in it, but merely from my ramming the powder when I charged the tube.   B.F.

James Hamilton to Jared Ingersoll[8]

Extract from a transcript: Massachusetts Historical Society[9]

Governor Hamilton of Pennsylvania and Jared Ingersoll had become friends while both were in England in 1758–59, and they corresponded occasionally thereafter. The letter from which an extract is printed below deals chiefly with the threatened settlement by the Connecticut

7. In some degree these experiments supported Ebenezer Kinnersley's with gunpowder and his conclusion that electricity "will, by its violent Motion and the Resistance it meets with, produce Heat in other Bodies, when passing thro' them, provided they be small enough"; above, IX, 290. BF highly praised Kinnersley's "beautiful experiment" and agreed that it disproved what he himself had previously called "a cold fusion"; above, p. 48.

8. Jared Ingersoll (1722–1781), lawyer and Conn. public official, B.A., Yale, 1742, began the practice of law in New Haven in 1744 and in 1751 became King's attorney for the county. He was the colony's agent in England, 1758–61, and again 1764–65. Appointed Stamp Act distributor for Conn., he was forced by a mob to resign. In 1768 he was named judge of one of the new British Vice Admiralty courts with headquarters in Philadelphia, to which city he moved in 1771. During the Revolution he was loyalist in sentiments but lived quietly in Philadelphia until forced to return to New Haven on parole in 1777. *DAB*; Lawrence H. Gipson, *Jared Ingersoll A Study of American Loyalism in Relation to British Colonial Government* (New Haven, 1920). BF may have met Ingersoll during one of his visits to New Haven; in any case they became good friends while they were both serving as colonial agents in England. On Jan. 23, 1761, BF lent Ingersoll as Conn. agent £2000 of the Pa. parliamentary grant then in his hands, Ingersoll providing security. His fellow agent repaid the loan, March 27, with £14 accrued interest. "Account of Expences," pp. 58, 59; *PMHB*, LV (1931), 190.

9. In the Parkman MSS. The ALS was formerly among the Ingersoll Papers in New Haven Colony Hist. Soc., but cannot now be found, nor is it included in the extensive selection from those MSS printed in New Haven Colony Hist. Soc. *Papers*, IX (New Haven, 1918).

Susquehannah Company on lands within the charter boundaries of Pennsylvania which agents of the company had bought from the Indians at Albany in 1754.[1] Near the end occurs a paragraph which so well illustrates the feelings of proprietary leaders in Pennsylvania towards Franklin and his English mission that it merits inclusion here as a summary statement of their attitude.

Philadelphia July 8th 1762

*   *   *   *   *   *   *

Your Friend Mr. Franklin, and mine if he pleases, (for it will much depend on himself) is dailey expected from England. I cannot find that his five years negotiation at a vast expence to the province, hath answered any other purpose with respect to the publick, than to get every point that was in controversy, determined against them. Yet what is this to Mr. Franklin? Hath it not afforded him a life of pleasure, and an opportunity of displaying his talents among the virtuosi of various kingdoms and nations? and lastly hath it not procured for himself the Degree of Doctor of Laws, and for the modest and beautiful Youth, his son, that of master of Arts, from one of our most famous universities?[2] Let me tell you, those are no small acquisitions to the public, and therefore well worth paying for.

*   *   *   *   *   *   *

Sargent Aufrere & Co. to Charles Norris

LS and duplicate: [3]Historical Society of Pennsylvania

I.N.

Mr. Charles Norris   9th July [1762]
Sir,

The foregoing is what we wrote yesterday, since which we are favoured with yours of the 18 May covering a bill value £2500

1. See above, v, 350 n, and map facing p. 224.

2. Obviously a reference to BF's and WF's honorary degrees from Oxford; above, pp. 76–8. More precisely, BF's "Degree of Doctor of Laws" was the one he had received from St. Andrews in 1759 (above, VIII, 277–80), while the Oxford degree was that of "Doctor of Civil Law."

3. The LS follows, on a single sheet, a letter of July 8, which is not printed here because it relates entirely to the parliamentary grant for 1760, in which BF was not concerned. The duplicate is on a sheet by itself and is marked "Copy."

113

to Reimburse us for the Bills we paid that were drawn on Mr. Franklin,[4] and by the Carolina Captn. Friend who proposes Clearing out for your Colony next week we shall send you an Exact state of that Account.[5] We have the pleasure of informing you that just now the Lords of the Treasury have agreed to Issue their Warrant for £190,000 to be divided amongst the Colonys agreable to the last years Division, and the remaining £10,000 to be divided hereafter as it may appear to be due.[6] When we receive these Warrants you shall be duely advised thereof by the first Conveyance and also when the Money is paid, which may probably be some months first. We must request when you draw any more Bills on us you will please to furnish us with a list thereof, expressing the Number, date, sum and to whom payable to prevent any mistake, which will very much Oblige Sir Your very humble Servants

SARGENT, AUFRERE & CO

10th. July 1762[7]

Addressed: To / Mr. Charles Norris / In / Philadelphia

Endorsed: recd: July 8. 9. 10. 1762 Messrs Sargent Aufrere & Compa:

4. The trustees' letter of May 18 not found; on the Assembly's order to the trustees to reimburse Sargent Aufrere, see above, pp. 12–13 n.

5. For this account, see below, pp. 134–5. On the voyage of the *Carolina*, Capt. James Friend, on which BF sailed home, see the document immediately below.

6. On Jan. 20, 1761, the House of Commons voted £200,000 to reimburse the colonies for their expenditures during the campaign of 1760. The Treasury released only £190,000, however, because Mass. and Conn. said that they had performed extraordinary services during the campaign and deserved a larger share than they had received from the earlier grants. Therefore £10,000 was reserved pending the determination of their claims. Pa. received £24,988 0s. 6d. (after all the fees and commissions were paid) from the grant for 1760, but it was later discovered that the province had been overpaid £10,947 and in 1764 the Assembly was obliged to divide this amount among the other colonies. 8 *Pa. Arch.*, VII, 5514, 5583; *Pa. Col. Recs.*, IX, 47–51; Sargent Aufrere to Charles Norris, July 30, 1762, Hist. Soc. Pa.

7. So dated at the end of the MS here printed, in the same hand as the signature, but no such dating appears in the duplicate. Probably the letter was dictated on the 9th and signed on the 10th. The double dating obviously caused some confusion when the letter reached Philadelphia, as is shown by the endorsement and by Isaac Norris' statement to the Assembly (see the document immediately below). No other letter from Sargent Aufrere dated July 10 has been found.

advising the reception of the Trustees Letters of May. 11th. 12th.[8] and 18th. and the Amo of Parliamentary Recd per

To Isaac Norris

MS not found; abstract reprinted from *Votes and Proceedings of the House of Representatives*, 1761–1762 (Philadelphia, 1762), p. 54.

[September 21, 1762]

Mr. Speaker brought in, and communicated to the House, two Letters of the Tenth of July last, one from Messieurs Sargent, Aufrere, and Company, Merchants, in London, to the Trustees of the General Loan-Office, concerning the Provincial Bills of Exchange;[9] the other from Benjamin Franklin, Esq; to the Speaker, which were severally read by Order; the latter acquainting him that Mr. Franklin had taken his Passage for Philadelphia, in Captain Friend, then near ready to sail;[1] that he had just received Copies of the last Year's printed Votes, of our Supply Bill refused by the Governor, and of his Messages[2]—that, as he had heard of no new Agent yet

8. In their letter of July 8 (mentioned in the first note above) Sargent Aufrere acknowledged receipt of the trustees' letters of May 11 and 12.

9. See the document immediately above for Sargent Aufrere's letter dated both July 9 and 10.

1. The *Carolina*, Capt. James Friend, was reported at Portsmouth on August 12, awaiting a convoy. *Pa. Gaz.*, Oct. 21, 1762. Although *London Chron.*, Aug. 24–26, 1762, reported that H.M.S. *Scarborough* had sailed from Portsmouth convoying the North American trade "last Friday," that is, August 20, this report seems to be in error; at least, the *Carolina*, with BF aboard, did not sail until the 23d at the earliest, as shown by his letter of that date to Strahan (below, p. 149). The convoy stopped for three days at Madeira and the *Carolina* reached Philadelphia only on November 1, after a voyage of ten weeks from Portsmouth. *Pa. Gaz.*, Nov. 4, 1762. BF wrote Strahan, December 7, in praise of the care Captain Stott of the *Scarborough* had given the convoy; see below, pp. 166–7.

2. In response to two letters from Pitt's successor, the Earl of Egremont, both written on Dec. 12, 1761, and to three from General Amherst, Feb. 9, 21, 22, 1762, requesting Pa. to raise men for the campaign of 1762, the Assembly voted on March 11 to raise one thousand effectives and on March 19 passed a bill granting £70,000 to levy, pay, and clothe them. This supply bill produced the usual wrangle with the governor; Hamilton sent two long messages to the House about it, March 23 and 25, the Assembly dropped the measure and adjourned on the 26th. The Assembly did, however, pass a bill for £23,500 at a special session in May, and Hamilton approved it on the

appointed, he should leave the Affairs of the Province in Charge with Mr. Jackson, of the Temple,[3] who is well acquainted with them, very able, and will appear for the Assembly, if there should be Occasion.

To Giambatista Beccaria[4]

MS not found; reprinted from Benjamin Franklin, *Experiments and Observations on Electricity*, 1769 edition, pp. 427–33.[5]

That glass or porcelain vessels, or even some earthenware bowls, would give off musical tones when gently struck had been known in various parts of the world for centuries before Franklin's time, and men in both Asia and Europe had learned to entertain themselves and each other by playing tunes on a series of such containers appropriately graded in size.[6] Perhaps it was a group of convivial gentlemen sitting

---

14th. 8 *Pa. Arch.*, VI, 5304–10, 5314–20, 5322, 5324–5, 5327–31, 5333–5, 5343, 5347.

3. BF's good friend and legal adviser, Richard Jackson (above, V, 148 n). The Assembly formally appointed Jackson agent on April 2, 1763. 8 *Pa. Arch.*, VI, 5425.

4. On Giambatista Beccaria (1716–1781) of the teaching order of Piarists, professor of experimental physics at Turin, see above, V, 395 n.

5. Printed as Letter XLII in both the 1769 edition and that of 1774, where it appears on pp. 437–43. This letter was translated into Italian by Baron Giuseppe Vernazza di Alba and published as a small pamphlet with the title *L'Armonica Lettera del signor Beniamino Franklin al padre Giambatista Beccaria regio professore di fisica nell' università di Torino dall' Inglese recata nell' Italiano* (Turino, 1769) (Yale Univ. Lib.). This copy and the ones at Liceo Musicale of Bologna and Lib. Co. Phila. do not have the name of the translator on the title page; that at APS and some others do. For a discussion of the bibliographical problems concerning the Italian printings, see Antonio Pace, *Benjamin Franklin and Italy* (Phila., 1958), pp. 414–15.

6. The most thorough treatment of the subject of this headnote is A. Hyatt King, "The Musical Glasses and Glass Harmonica," Royal Musical Assn. *Proc.*, 72d Session, 1945–46, pp. 97–122, which has provided much of the information summarized here. Other helpful writings include Antonio Pace, *Benjamin Franklin and Italy*, pp. 268–83; E. Power Biggs, "Benjamin Franklin and the Armonica," *Daedalus Proceedings of the American Academy of Arts and Sciences*, LXXXVI (1955–57), 231–41; O.G. Sonneck, *Suum Cuique Essays in Music* (N.Y., London, Boston, [1916]), pp. 59–73; Horace Ervin, "Notes on Franklin's Armonica and the Music Mozart Wrote for It," *Journal, Franklin Institute*, CCLXII (1956), 329–48.

about a table with their wine who made the later discovery that glasses could be made to sing by rubbing a moistened finger around their rims. Experimentation showed that not only the size and thickness of the glass, but also the amount of liquid it contained would determine the pitch of its musical tone.

By the 1730s, at least, this scientific toy had begun to be taken seriously, and references occasionally appeared to sets of tuned glasses which were used to provide music in churches or were played in combination with violins and basses. At this time the *Verrillon,* as it was called, seems always to have been used as a percussion instrument.

A decade later an Irishman, Richard Pockrich, or Puckridge, entered the scene—a strange and visionary person, who operated a brewery which failed, proposed vineyards in the Irish bogs, offered to build unsinkable boats for the navy, and undertook to raise geese on a large scale on unsuitable land. Well ahead of his time with the germ of one idea, at least, he suggested blood transfusions as a means of rejuvenating the aged. Twice he failed of election to Parliament. A man of real musical abilities, in about 1741 he turned his attention to the musical glasses and began to give concerts professionally in England and Ireland. At first he seems to have played the glasses by striking them with sticks, but towards the end of his career he developed great skill in the method of rubbing their rims with moistened fingers, giving their notes a sustained quality not possible by percussion.[7]

Pockrich's success inspired others. In 1746 the young German composer Christoph Willibald Gluck played a concerto at a benefit for himself in London.[8] Others learned the art, both men and women, professionals and amateurs. By 1761 the musical glasses had become very much the vogue in London and in November of that year one

7. Pockrich died in 1759 in a fire in his room at a coffeehouse near the Royal Exchange, London. *DNB; Grove's Dictionary of Music and Musicians* (5th edit., London, 1954), VI, 832. A young man who knew him at the start of his musical career is authority for a distressing incident before a concert scheduled in Dublin: "About three hours before the concert was to begin, the Captain [Pockrich] went to range and tune his glasses, when unfortunately stepping out for some water, a large unmannerly sow entered, and, oh! guess the rest!—threw down the whole machine, and covered the ground with glittering fragments; destroying not only the hopes of the publick, but ours of a present and future subsistence. When the Captain returned, and found his lofty castles in the air reduced to an heap of rubbish, he looked just like Mark Anthony, when he beholds the body of Julius Caesar on the earth, and says: Oh! Mighty Caesar, dost thou lie so low?" *The Real Story of John Carteret Pilkington. Written by Himself* (London, 1760), pp. 66–7.

8. *Grove's Dictionary,* III, 676.

of the most skillful performers, Miss Anne Ford, published a set of instructions.[9] One of the amateur players was Edward Hussey Delaval, classicist and scientist, whom Franklin had helped elect to the Royal Society in 1759.[1] As Franklin told Beccaria in the letter below, it was Delaval who in turn introduced Franklin to the musical glasses.

Franklin was obviously delighted, but he found inadequacies in the glasses as then employed. Filling each of a series of glasses with just the right amount of water to make it give off truly its assigned tone was a delicate and time-consuming job and one which had to be repeated before each performance. Enough glasses to provide a reasonable range, including all the semitones, occupied a considerable space on a table and could be awkward to play. Furthermore, it was difficult if not impossible to play more than two at once, one with each hand. Characteristically, then, Franklin set about to improve the musical glasses; the result was his invention, sometimes at first called the "glassychord," but which he himself named the "armonica," as he told Beccaria at the end of this letter.[2] Some of his contemporaries began to put an unnecessary "h" in front of the word and "harmonica" became the name by which his instrument was usually called, thereby misleading many people of later generations into the belief that Franklin invented the mouth organ.[3]

It is not entirely certain just when Franklin devised the armonica, had his first instrument made, and began to play it. The evidence is strong, however, that these events took place at least as early as 1761, and by January of the following year a protégée, Miss Marianne Davies,

9. *Public Advertiser*, Nov. 2, 1761; *Gent. Mag.*, XXXI (1761), 606. There is a copy in Harvard Coll. Lib. of *By Miss Ford. Instructions For Playing on the Musical Glasses: so that Any Person, who has the least Knowledge of Music, or a good Ear, may be able to perform in a few Days, if not in a few Hours.*

1. See above, VIII, 359–60.

2. The earliest known appearance of the name "armonica" is in an advertisement in *Jackson's Oxford Journal*, May 29, 1762, in which Charles James "of Purpool, near Gray's Inn, London," announced that he could supply the instrument and that he had been "employed in the management of the Glass Machines from the beginning, by the ingenious and well-known inventor." Quoted in A. Hyatt King, Royal Musical Assn. *Proc.*, 1945–46, p. 107. *London Chron.*, June 17–19, 1762, carried a similar advertisement by James in which he explained that the armonica "may be so constructed, as to be either a Portable Instrument, or Genteel Piece of Furniture."

3. The mouth organ, or "mouth harmonica," was invented in 1829 by the London firm of Wheatstone and was called by them the "Aeolina." *Grove's Dictionary*, V, 919.

was giving public performances.[4] He himself took great pleasure from playing his armonica; he carried one home with him when he sailed a few weeks after writing this letter to Beccaria, and always thereafter seems to have had one in his living quarters wherever he might be.[5] Later volumes of this edition will contain many references to his continued interest and delight in his musical invention.

4. On April 13, 1761, Thomas Penn wrote Governor Hamilton that BF was spending his time "in philosophical, and especially in electrical matters, ... and musical performances on glasses," but these words could refer to his preliminary efforts on water-tuned drinking glasses before he had fully worked out the idea of the armonica. Penn Papers, Hist. Soc. Pa. Clearer evidence is found in a diary entry of Dr. William Stukeley, May 22, 1761: "Visited Dr. Franklyn, the electric genius. He has made a dulcimer of wooden sticks, very sweet; another of glass bells, that warble like the sound of an organ." *The Family Memoirs of the Rev. William Stukeley, M.D. (Publications of the Surtees Society,* LXXX), III, 480. The term "glass bells" makes certain that BF was here using something quite different from drinking glasses, and "warble like the sound of an organ" shows that he was not striking them with sticks or small hammers. The instrument had certainly passed the experimental stage well before the end of the year. Mrs. Martha J. Lamb, ed., *Magazine of American History with Notes and Queries,* XIX (1888), 83, printed without indication of source the following: "London, Jan. 12, 1762. In the *Bristol Journal* we find advertised 'The celebrated *Glassy-Chord* invented by Mr. Franklin, of Philadelphia; who has greatly improved the Musical Glasses, and formed them into a compleat Instrument to accompany the Voice; capable of a thorough Bass, and never out of Tune. Miss Davies, from London, was to perform in the Month of January, several favourite Airs, English, Scotch and Italian, on the Glassychord (being the only one of the Kind that has yet been produced) accompanied occasionally with the Voice and German Flute.' " The identical note, without the London date line, appeared in *N.-Y. Mercury,* April 19, 1762, in a series of London news items, the one immediately above it being dated "London, January 28." The editors have been unable to find any copy of the *Bristol Journal* for the appropriate period or to determine from which London newspaper the item might have been taken. In the first of his advertisements mentioned in a previous note, Charles James declared that his instruments were "on the same principles and guided by the same hand as that played on by Miss Davies at Spring Gardens, London, at Bath and Bristol."

5. The earliest mention of BF's performance on the armonica after his return to Philadelphia is in a letter dated Dec. 3, 1762, from Mrs. Ann Graeme to her daughter Elizabeth, the girl WF had jilted (see above, VII, 177 n). Mrs. Graeme had called on the Franklins the day before (about a month after BF had arrived); although the situation necessarily involved considerable strain, "we appear'd to have a very easy afternoon," and at the caller's request BF gave her "a tune on the Harmonica." *PMHB,* XXXIX (1915), 270–1.

Just when and how Marianne Davies was introduced to the armonica is not known. The daughter of a musician, she was already familiar in English concert halls as a singer and a performer on the flute and harpsi-chord.[6] The statement has occasionally been made—quite incorrectly —that she was somehow related to Franklin; it has also been said— with greater probability of truth—that he provided her with her first armonica. But no evidence has been found to suggest the circumstances under which they first became acquainted, and no letters between them survive earlier than one from her of April 26, 1783. In that she referred repeatedly to her "strong feelings of Gratitude" to her "Benefactor," and proudly mentioned that she had "the Prerogative (thro' your goodness) of being the first public Performer on that Instrument."[7]

In any case, she began her public performances on the armonica early in 1762, playing at various places of entertainment in London and the provinces; later she visited Ireland and the Continent. Sometimes she varied her programs with vocal numbers or others on the flute or harpsichord, but she became identified as the leading performer on the armonica. Her parents and younger sister Cecilia seem to have accom-panied her on her Continental tours.[8] By 1767 Cecilia's voice had matured and she began to share importantly in the programs as a singer, learning to assimilate her tones admirably to those of the ar-monica. The performance of the Davies sisters attained great popularity, and Marianne Davies, more than anyone else, was responsible for the vogue the armonica came to enjoy, especially in the German states and in Vienna.

Perhaps the high point in the sisters' joint career came in Vienna on June 27, 1769. The occasion was the marriage of the Archduchess Amalia to Duke Ferdinand of Parma. In honor of the bridal couple the Italian librettist Pietro Metastasio,[9] then court poet, composed an ode in Italian which the popular composer Johann Adolf Hasse set to music

6. Sketches of both Marianne Davies (1744–1816?) and her sister Cecilia (c. 1750–1836) appear in *DNB* and *Grove's Dictionary,* II, 608–9. In her letters to BF the elder sister signed her name "Mary Ann." Cecilia made her career chiefly as a singer of Italian opera and was often called "L'Inglesina."

7. APS.

8. In the letter of April 26, 1783, cited above, she recalled some of the problems of traveling with an armonica: "Well I remember the difficulties and expence attending it and the perpetual fear of its being damaged at each Custom House &c. &c. Yet at that time I was happy in my poor Dear Father's continual care and attention. The Protection likewise of our dear Parents made Travelling then appear to me quite in another light" from what it would be after they were both dead.

9. His real name was Pietro Antonio Domenico Bonaventura Trapassi.

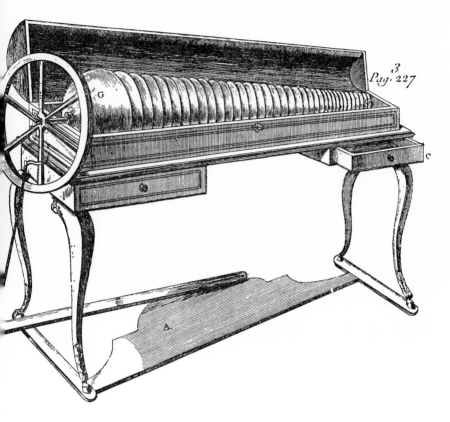

Pag. 227³

A. Pédale, ou planche mobile sur laquelle le pied est placé pour tourner la roue.

B. Roue, dont le contour est de plomb et les rais de fer.

C. Tiroir, pour y mettre l'éponge et de la craie en poudre.

G. Verres, dont le plus grand est la note G.

Franklin's Glass Armonica

for soprano with armonica accompaniment. The Davies sisters rendered this composition apparently to the great satisfaction and approval of the assembled guests. Marianne seems to have remembered her benefactor, for a copy of the words—though unfortunately not of the score—survives among the Franklin Papers.[1] For a good many years the armonica not only enjoyed great popularity with the public at large but also received the serious attention of distinguished musicians. Leopold Mozart, father of the great composer, wrote warmly of it to his wife in 1773, reporting that Friedrich Anton Mesmer, the proponent of "animal magnetism," had an instrument that he played unusually well and adding that "Wolfgang too has played upon it. How I should like to have one!"[2] Wolfgang Mozart, indeed, not only played the armonica experimentally as a youth but wrote for it later on, as did several other eighteenth-century composers. In 1791 Mozart heard a blind girl, Marianna Kirchgessner, perform in Vienna and was inspired to compose an Adagio for armonica solo (K. 356) and what E. Power Biggs has called "one of his most perfect and delightful works," a quintet, the Adagio and Rondo for armonica, flute, oboe, viola, and cello (K. 617).[3] In 1814 Beethoven wrote an armonica accompaniment to spoken words as part of the incidental music he composed for Friedrich Duncker's tragedy *Leonora Prohaska* (op. 202).[4]

1. "Poesia per l'occasione delle Nozze del Real Infante Duca di Parma con l'Arciduchessa d'Austria cantata in Vienna dalla Cecilia Davies detta L'Inglesina Sorella dell' eccelente Sonatrice del nuovo Istrumento di Musica Elettrica, chiamato L'Armonica Inventato dal Celebre Dottore Franklin." At the end of the poem appears: "Questa Cantata fù Scritta dal Abate Pietro Metastasio. e Messa in Musica da Giovanni Adolpho Hasse detto il Sassone." An endorsement reads: "Miss Davies Ode." APS. The words of the song are printed, with a shortened title and a few alterations, at the front of the 1769 Turin edition of BF's letter mentioned in the second footnote to this document. The reference in the title to the "Nuovo Istrumento di Musica Elettrica" is an interesting allusion to the inventor's fame as an electrical scientist.

2. Quoted by A. Hyatt King, Royal Musical Assn. *Proc.*, 1945–46, p. 109. In treating his patients Mesmer used the armonica as background music, and in 1779 BF and Mme. Brillon went to his house in Paris to hear him play.

3. E. Power Biggs, *Daedalus*, LXXXVI, 238, 257. The quintet has been recorded at least twice in recent years, with the armonica part played on the celesta or the harpsichord. The solo has also been recorded by Mr. Biggs, using the flute stops of the organ. For particulars on these records see Horace Ervin, *Journal, Franklin Institute*, CCLXII, 348. The solo is now often listed as K. 617a.

4. Alexander W. Thayer, *Ludwig van Beethovens Leben*, III (Leipzig, 1911), 459.

The armonica apparently gave forth a sustained, ringing tone, rather different in quality from the effect produced by tapping a glass with a stick or metal rod. Since Franklin's instrument included no device for damping the vibration and hence the tone, the playing of rapid passages acceptably must have been difficult. Various individuals in Europe or America attempted to improve the armonica. A trough filled with water was sometimes placed beneath the row of glasses so that as they turned their rims would remain constantly wet, simplifying the performer's task. Several people tried to convert the armonica into a keyboard instrument; one of these was Francis Hopkinson, Franklin's Philadelphia friend, who wrote Thomas Jefferson in 1786 that he was working on the scheme and had "little Doubt of Success." Jefferson replied that if Hopkinson's project worked out "It will be the greatest present which has been made to the musical world this century, not excepting the Piano forte."[5] Later Hopkinson reported substantial progress, but for all his optimism and Jefferson's enthusiasm, neither this nor any other attempt to turn the armonica into a satisfactory keyboard instrument proved really effective. No armonica of this sort seems to have survived, even in a museum.

Contemporary references generally describe the tones of Franklin's instrument by such adjectives as "ethereal," "sweet," "pathetic," or "melancholy," qualities which undoubtedly account for a good deal of its popularity during the first flush of romanticism in music.[6] Yet, as musical tastes began to change, the armonica lost much of its appeal. It was a difficult instrument to play really well, and was expensive—far more so than a simple set of glasses—and probably out of reach of many whose objective was mere diversion or the entertainment of patrons of pleasure gardens or music halls.[7] An inherent problem was the fragility of the glass: not only might one or more hemispheres

5. The correspondence of these men on the subject is printed in Julian P. Boyd et al., eds., *The Papers of Thomas Jefferson* (Princeton, 1950–), x, 78, 625–6; XI, 289. Jefferson reported on Hopkinson's experiments to Charles Burney, the English musician and writer on musical subjects, commenting that "However imperfect this instrument is for the general mass of musical compositions, yet for those of a certain character it is delicious." *Ibid.*, XI, 141.

6. Mr. E. Power Biggs, the distinguished organist, who has experimented with the instrument, commented to the editor in a letter of April 23, 1965: "The sound of a delicate flute stop, incidentally, rather resembles that of a glass armonica. Though it lacks, of course, the effect of coming from nowhere and the slow dying away into silence, which is a quite magical effect with the glasses."

7. In 1787 Jefferson, then in Paris, asked a friend in London to price an armonica of six octaves "if they ever comprehend as much." His friend replied

break when the instrument was moved about, but all too often a "note" could shatter through its own vibration when played.[8]

Most important, however, was the belief, which attained wide acceptance in the course of time, that the armonica was dangerous to the health of the performer. The cause, it seems, was partly physiological, partly psychological. The vibrations of the glasses, transferred through the fingers, were thought to have injured in time the entire nervous system of the player. This belief was a major reason for the many attempts to devise a satisfactory keyboard which would substitute mechanical "fingers" for those of the performer. Furthermore, the "pathetic" and "melancholy" tones of the instrument, if heard often and long enough, induced an unhappy state of mind which might result in what many people today would call a nervous breakdown. Leopold Mozart wrote, five years after his first enthusiastic letter about the armonica, that he had been listening to a famous oboist but that "this *nezza di voce* was too frequent for my taste and has the same melancholy effect on me as the tones of the armonica, for it produces almost the same kind of sound."[9] Whatever may have been the true medical reasons, the fact remains that Marianne Davies became ill and was confined to her room for more than a year; and Marianna Kirchgessner and at least one other professional performer had to give up playing because of nervous disorders. It may be remarked, on the other hand, that neither Franklin nor Mesmer, among other players, ever experienced nervous breakdowns; nor, oddly enough, did any of those who continued to perform publicly on the old-fashioned row of musical glasses on a table seem to have complained of the same harmful effects.

Nevertheless, for all these reasons, and perhaps for others not now recognized, the armonica gradually fell into neglect and in time passed completely out of use. Its final disappearance from the concert platform cannot be precisely dated, but it seems safe to say that public performances on Franklin's instrument, as distinct from the musical glasses, were rare after about 1825 or 1830. A few instruments survive

---

that he found they never exceeded three octaves and for one of that size he had been quoted a price of thirty guineas. *Ibid.*, XII, 235, 297.

8. In BF's later correspondence there are several references to broken glasses and to the difficulty of procuring good replacements. He seems to have taken a supply of "extras" of various sizes with him when he returned to America.

9. Quoted by A. Hyatt King, Royal Musical Assn. *Proc.*, 1945–46, p. 110. He also quotes (p. 113) a medico-musical writer in 1803, who declared that "Le timbre mélancholique de l'harmonica nous plonge dans un profond abattement, et relache tous les nerfs du corps, au point que l'homme le plus robuste ne sauroit l'entendre pendant une heure sans se trouver mal."

today in museums or collections of antique musical instruments or in private homes, but it is believed that none of them is fully playable. The armonica as Franklin gave it to the musical world of his time is now a curiosity of the past.[1]

Rev. Sir,   London, July 13, 1762.

I once promised myself the pleasure of seeing you at Turin, but as that is not now likely to happen, being just about returning to my native country, America, I sit down to take leave of you (among others of my European friends that I cannot see) by writing.

I thank you for the honourable mention you have so frequently made of me in your letters to Mr. Collinson and others, for the generous defence you undertook and executed with so much success, of my electrical opinions; and for the valuable present you have made me of your new work, from which I have received great information and pleasure.[2] I wish I could in return entertain you with any thing new of mine on that subject; but I have not lately pursued it. Nor do I know of any one here that is at present much engaged in it.

1. In anticipation of the 250th anniversary of BF's birth and the 200th of Mozart's, both of which occurred in 1956, the American Academy of Arts and Sciences sponsored the construction of an armonica. It was financed through the generosity of the Franklin Savings Bank of Boston; the Corning Glass Works blew the glass, and Herman Schlichter constructed a cabinet and keyboard mechanism. Numerous problems and difficulties appeared which suggested that some of the technical methods known to the eighteenth century may not have been as completely preserved as we today should like to believe; the experiment was not an unqualified success. At a meeting of the Academy, April 11, 1956, Mr. E. Power Biggs, organist, seven other instrumentalists, and Mr. Roland Hayes, tenor, presented a program of chamber music which included organ and instrumental numbers by Mozart, songs written by BF, the quartet for open strings he is believed to have composed, and the two compositions for armonica Mozart wrote after hearing Marianna Kirchgessner play. Mr. Biggs performed two eighteenth-century compositions for the musical glasses on a set of wine glasses and Mozart's Adagio for the Armonica (K. 356) on the experimental instrument. Then with other instrumentalists he played Mozart's Adagio and Rondo (K. 617), using the flute stop of the organ. The program of the concert is printed in *Daedalus*, LXXXVI (1955–57), 256–7.

2. In 1753 Beccaria had published *Dell' elettricismo artificiale, e naturale*, in which he had defended BF's electrical theories against those of Nollet, and in 1758 appeared his *Dell' elettricismo: lettere* of which he had sent BF a copy; see above, V, 395 n; VII, 315.

Perhaps, however, it may be agreeable to you, as you live in a musical country, to have an account of the new instrument lately added here to the great number that charming science was before possessed of: As it is an instrument that seems peculiarly adapted to Italian music, especially that of the soft and plaintive kind, I will endeavour to give you such a description of it, and of the manner of constructing it, that you, or any of your friends may be enabled to imitate it, if you incline so to do, without being at the expence and trouble of the many experiments I have made in endeavouring to bring it to its present perfection.

You have doubtless heard the sweet tone that is drawn from a drinking glass, by passing a wet finger round its brim. One Mr. Puckeridge, a gentleman from Ireland, was the first who thought of playing tunes, formed of these tones. He collected a number of glasses of different sizes, fixed them near each other on a table, and tuned them by putting into them water, more or less, as each note required. The tones were brought out by passing his fingers round their brims. He was unfortunately burnt here, with his instrument, in a fire which consumed the house he lived in. Mr. E. Delaval, a most ingenious member of our Royal Society, made one in imitation of it, with a better choice and form of glasses, which was the first I saw or heard. Being charmed with the sweetness of its tones, and the music he produced from it, I wished only to see the glasses disposed in a more convenient form, and brought together in a narrower compass, so as to admit of a greater number of tones, and all within reach of hand to a person sitting before the instrument, which I accomplished, after various intermediate trials, and less commodious forms, both of glasses and construction, in the following manner.

The glasses are blown as near as possible in the form of hemispheres, having each an open neck or socket in the middle.[3] The thickness of the glass near the brim about a tenth of an inch, or hardly quite so much, but thicker as it comes nearer the neck, which in the largest glasses

3. The accompanying illustration appears at this point in *Exper. and Obser.*, 1769 edit., p. 429. Presumably BF embellished the ALS he sent Becarria with a similar sketch.

is about an inch deep, and an inch and half wide within, these dimensions lessening as the glasses themselves diminish in size, except that the neck of the smallest ought not to be shorter than half an inch. The largest glass is nine inches diameter, and the smallest three inches. Between these there are twenty-three different sizes, differing from each other a quarter of an inch in diameter. To make a single instrument there should be at least six glasses blown of each size; and out of this number one may probably pick 37 glasses, (which are sufficient for 3 octaves with all the semitones) that will be each either the note one wants or a little sharper than that note, and all fitting so well into each other as to taper pretty regularly from the largest to the smallest. It is true there are not 37 sizes, but it often happens that two of the same size differ a note or half note in tone, by reason of a difference in thickness, and these may be placed one in the other without sensibly hurting the regularity of the taper form.

The glasses being chosen and every one marked with a diamond the note you intend it for, they are to be tuned by diminishing the thickness of those that are too sharp. This is done by grinding them round from the neck towards the brim, the breadth of one or two inches as may be required; often trying the glass by a well tuned harpsichord, comparing the tone drawn from the glass by your finger, with the note you want, as sounded by that string of the harpsichord. When you come near the matter, be careful to wipe the glass clean and dry before each trial, because the tone is something flatter when the glass is wet, than it will be when dry; and grinding a very little between each trial, you will thereby tune to great exactness. The more care is necessary in this, because if you go below your required tone, there is no sharpening it again but by grinding somewhat off the brim, which will afterwards require polishing, and thus encrease the trouble.

The glasses being thus tuned, you are to be provided with a case for them, and a spindle on which they are to be fixed. My case is about three feet long, eleven inches every way wide within at the biggest end, and five inches at the smallest end; for it tapers all the way, to adapt it better to the conical figure of the set of glasses. This case opens in the middle of its height, and the upper part turns up by hinges fixed behind. The spindle which is of hard iron, lies horizontally from end to end of the box within, exactly in the middle, and is made to turn on brass gudgeons at each end. It is round, an inch diameter at the thickest end, and tapering to a quarter of an inch at the smallest. A square shank comes from its thickest end through the box, on which shank a wheel is fixed by a screw. This wheel serves as a fly to make the motion equable, when the spindle, with the glasses, is turned by the foot like a spinning wheel. My wheel is of mahogany, 18 inches diameter, and pretty thick, so as to conceal near its circumference about 25 lb. of lead. An ivory pin is fixed in the face of this wheel and about 4 inches from the axis. Over the neck of this pin is put the loop of the string that comes up from the moveable step to give it motion. The case stands on a neat frame with four legs.

To fix the glasses on the spindle, a cork is first to be fitted in each neck pretty tight, and projecting a little without the neck, that the neck of one may not touch the inside of another when put together, for that would make a jarring. These corks are to be perforated with holes of different diameters, so as to suit that part of the spindle on which they are to be fixed. Then a glass is put on, by holding it stiffly between both hands, while another turns the spindle, it may be gradually brought to its place. But care must be taken that the hole be not too small, lest in forcing it up the neck should split; nor too large, lest the glass not being firmly fixed, should turn or move on the spindle, so as to touch and jar against its neighbouring glass. The glasses thus are placed one in another, the largest on the biggest end of the spindle which is to the left hand; the neck of this glass is towards the wheel, and the next goes into it in the same position, only about an inch of its brim appearing beyond the brim of the first; thus proceeding, every glass when fixed shows about an inch of its brim, (or three quarters of an inch, or half an inch, as they grow smaller) beyond the brim of the glass that contains it; and it is from these exposed parts of each glass that the tone is drawn, by laying a finger upon one of them as the spindle and glasses turn round.

My largest glass is G a little below the reach of a common voice, and my highest G, including three compleat octaves. To distinguish the glasses the more readily to the eye, I have painted the apparent parts of the glasses within side,[4] every semitone white,

4. That is, he painted the inside of that part of each glass which was exposed at the right of its left-hand neighbor.

and the other notes of the octave with the seven prismatic colours, *viz.* C, red; D, orange; E, yellow; F, green; G, blue; A, Indigo; B, purple; and C, red again; so that glasses of the same colour (the white excepted) are always octaves to each other.

This instrument is played upon, by sitting before the middle of the set of glasses as before the keys of a harpsichord, turning them with the foot, and wetting them now and then with a spunge and clean water. The fingers should first be a little soaked in water and quite free from all greasiness; a little fine chalk upon them is sometimes useful, to make them catch the glass and bring out the tone more readily. Both hands are used, by which means different parts are played together. Observe, that the tones are best drawn out when the glasses turn *from* the ends of the fingers, not when they turn *to* them.

The advantages of this instrument are, that its tones are incomparably sweet beyond those of any other; that they may be swelled and softened at pleasure by stronger or weaker pressures of the finger, and continued to any length; and that the instrument, being once well tuned, never again wants tuning.

In honour of your musical language, I have borrowed from it the name of this instrument, calling it the Armonica.

With great esteem and respect, I am, &c.

To [Oliver Neave][5]

MS not found; reprinted from Benjamin Franklin, *Experiments and Observations on Electricity* (London, 1769), pp. 435–7.[6]

Dear Sir,   July 20, 1762.

I have perused your paper on sound,[7] and would freely mention to you, as you desire it, every thing that appeared to me to

5. So identified by Barbeu Dubourg, *Oeuvres de M. Franklin* (Paris, 1773), II, 228–30, although in *Exper. and Obser.* the addressee is given simply as "a Friend." Virtually nothing is known of Neave, although he was probably a merchant connected with the London firm of Neate & Neave. BF's letter to him on swimming was published without date in *Exper. and Obser.*, 1769 edit., pp. 463–8.

6. Printed as Letter XLIV in *Exper. and Obser.*, 1769 edition, and in the 1774 edition, pp. 445–7.

7. Not found. While there are occasional statements about the nature and

need correction: But nothing of that kind occurs to me, unless it be, where you speak of the air as "the *best* medium for conveying sound." Perhaps this is speaking rather too positively, if there be, as I think there are, some other mediums that will convey it farther and more readily. It is a well-known experiment, that the scratching of a pin at one end of a long piece of timber, may be heard by an ear applied near the other end, though it could not be heard at the same distance through the air. And two stones being struck smartly together under water, the stroke may be heard at a greater distance by an ear also placed under water in the same river, than it can be heard through the air. I think I have heard it near a mile; how much farther it may be heard, I know not; but suppose a great deal farther, because the sound did not seem faint, as if at a distance, like distant sounds through air, but smart and strong, and as if present just at the ear. I wish you would repeat these experiments now you are upon the subject, and add your own observations. And if you were to repeat, with your naturally exact attention and observation, the common experiment of the bell in the exhausted receiver, possibly something new may occur to you, in considering,

1. Whether the experiment is not ambiguous; *i.e.* whether the gradual exhausting of the air, as it creates an increasing difference of pressure on the outside, may not occasion in the glass a difficulty of vibrating, that renders it less fit to communicate to the air without, the vibrations that strike it from within; and the diminution of the sound arise from this cause, rather than from the diminution of the air?

2. Whether as the particles of air themselves are at a distance from each other, there must not be some medium between them, proper for conveying sound, since otherwise it would stop at the first particle?

3. Whether the great difference we experience in hearing sounds

---

transmission of sound in BF's scientific writings, he seems never to have written a systematic paper on the subject. In *Poor Richard* for 1749 (above, III, 337) he had summarized the findings of three English scientists on the velocity of sound and some of their other observations, drawn from *Phil. Trans.*, XXVI (1708), 2, but neither there nor elsewhere had he shown any real interest in the means by which sound is transmitted.

at a distance, when the wind blows towards us from the sonorous body, or towards that from us, can be well accounted for by adding to or subtracting from the swiftness of sound, the degree of swiftness that is in the wind at the time? The latter is so small in proportion, that it seems as if it could scarce produce any sensible effect, and yet the difference is very great. Does not this give some hint, as if there might be a subtile fluid, the conductor of sound, which moves at different times in different directions over the surface of the earth, and whose motion may perhaps be much swifter than that of the air in our strongest winds; and that in passing through air, it may communicate that motion to the air which we call wind, though a motion in no degree so swift as its own?

4. It is somewhere related, that a pistol fired on the top of an exceeding high mountain, made a noise like thunder in the valleys below. Perhaps this fact is not exactly related: but if it is, would not one imagine from it, that the rarer the air, the greater sound might be produced in it from the same cause?

5. Those balls of fire which are sometimes seen passing over a country, computed by philosophers to be often 30 miles high at least, sometimes burst at that height; the air must be exceeding rare there, and yet the explosion produces a sound that is heard at that distance, and for 70 miles round on the surface of the earth, so violent too as to shake buildings, and give an apprehension of an earthquake. Does not this look as if a rare atmosphere, almost a vacuum, was no bad conductor of sound?

I have not made up my own mind on these points, and only mention them for your consideration, knowing that every subject is the better for your handling it. With the greatest esteem, I am, &c. B.F.

To William Strahan

MS not found; reprinted from John Bigelow, ed., *The Complete Works of Benjamin Franklin* (New York and London, 1887–88), III, 207–8.

Dear Sir: London, 20 July, 1762.
I received your very kind letter and invitation to Bath where I am sure I could spend some days very happily with you and Mrs.

Strahan, if my time would permit;[8] but the man-of-war, that is to be our convoy,[9] is under sailing orders for the 30th of this month so that 't is impossible for me to leave London till I leave it forever, having at least twenty days' work to do in the ten days that are only left me.

I shall send to the Angel Inn in Oxford a parcel directed to you, containing books I send as presents to some acquaintance there; which I beg you would cause to be delivered.[1] I shall write a line to one of them, as you desire. The parcel is to go by the Thursday's coach.

I hope for the pleasure of seeing you before I set out. Billy and Mrs. Stevenson join in respects and best wishes for you and Mrs. Strahan, with, dear Friend, Yours affectionately,   B. FRANKLIN.

P.S. I feel here like a thing out of its place, and useless because it is out of its place. How then can I any longer be happy in England? You have great powers of persuasion, and might easily prevail on me to do any thing; but not any longer to do nothing.[2] I must go home. Adieu.

8. On Aug. 10, 1762, Strahan wrote David Hall that he had returned to London on August 3 "after a three Weeks Tour, in which I visited Bristol Salisbury, and Oxford." He had also been at Bath where his wife had been receiving treatment for "a bilious Cholic" and had brought her back to London. Strahan to Hall, Aug. 10, 1762, APS.

9. H.M.S. *Scarborough*, Capt. Stott; see above, p. 115 n.

1. BF expected Strahan to deliver the parcel of books to Dr. John Kelly (above, p. 59 n), Regius professor of medicine, who had apparently been instrumental in procuring his honorary degree from Oxford; see below, p. 136. The only book identified as given to Oxford by BF was Richard Jackson's *An Historical Review of the Constitution and Government of Pensylvania* (above, VIII, 360–2), which is recorded as received by the Bodleian Library on Aug. 9, 1762. Howard P. Arnold, *Historic Side-lights* (N. Y., 1899), p. 100. The Angel Inn, often mentioned by visitors to Oxford, stood near the East Gate in the High Street, on the site of a medieval inn. It was destroyed in 1882–83. Charles E. Mallet, *A History of the University of Oxford*, III (London, 1927), 442.

2. On Strahan's sincere regret at BF's departure, see below, pp. 141–2.

Sargent Aufrere & Co. to the Trustees of the Loan Office: Account[3]   DS: Historical Society of Pennsylvania

The Trustees of the Loan Office of Philadelphia
to Sargent Aufrere & Co:

1762   Dr.

Feb: 26. To Cash per their draft No. 81 to Wm. Ball
           and Charges.[4]   £200 10 6
         To do Same Month [No]

		44 to Samuel Sargent.	300	– –
Mar:	4. To do	43 to Jo: Redman and Charges	300 10	3
	5. To do	93 to Peter Wickoff	200 14	6
	To do	63 to Jos: Swift	100 7	9
	To do	69 to do	100 10	3
	6. To do	66 to Geo: Robottom	150 10	3
	10. To do	24 to Abram Mitchell	100 10	3
	To do	36 to Peter Wickoff	100 10	3
	To do	4 to Isaac Paschall	100 10	3
	13. To do	70 to Jos: Swift	100 10	3
	15. To do	96 to Jno: Reynell	300 10	3
	23. To do	95 to Don: Williams	150 11	3
April	17. To do	125 to John Hughs	100 10	3
	28. To do	127 to Edward Milne	100 10	3

To Interest at 6 per Cent: on the several Sums ⎱
to August 11th: the time of your Bill falling due ⎰   60 5 10

July. 22. To Ballance in your favour   32 7 11
                                                    ―――――――
                                                    £2500 – –

NB. no Commission.

1762   per Contra   Cr:
July   9. By your Bill due August: 11th.[5]   £2500 – –

3. This account is the one Sargent Aufrere promised in their letter to the trustees, July 9, 1762, above, p. 114.

4. The bills listed here are those which BF's stock sales failed to cover and which Sargent Aufrere paid according to their agreement of Jan. 15, 1762. See above, p. 11.

5. For this bill, drawn by the trustees of the Loan Office, May 18, 1762, to reimburse Sargent Aufrere, see above, pp. 12–13 n.

£2400 0 0 Amount of Drafts paid By Messrs. S & A Co. drawn
      on BF Esqr.
  7 6 3 Amount of the Charges on said Drafts added together
———————
£2407 6 3
  60 5 10 Amount of Interest charged
———————
£2467 12 1
  32 7 11 Ballance overpaid by the Trustees
———————
£2500 0 0 Amount of Bill No. 212 drawn in favour of Messrs.
      S A & Co.

     London July 22d: 1762
     Errors Excepted.
     SARGENT AUFRERE & CO.

Charles Somerset Woodham to Samuel Soumain[6]

ALS: American Philosophical Society[7]

Dear Friend   Kingston Jamaica July 22. 62
 My long Silence has no doubt made you conclude, I had quite
forgot my old acquaintance, but the Motive of this cessation has
not been owing to disrespect, but rather Idleness, therefore hope
you will Excuse it; I some time ago Sent you a Power of Attorney
to recover Some plate of mine in the hands of Mr. Franklan but
you have never been kind enough to write me, if said plate is in
[his] Possession, shoud therefore Esteem it a Singular [Favour]
you would inform me how things are Situated, whether Mr.
Franklan if you have got the plate obliged you to pay what they
said was owing to 'em from Mr. Danills Estate, for that was the
reason they refused sending the plate to me if you have advanced

6. Woodham succeeded William Daniell (above, v, 355 n) in 1756 as
printer to the Jamaica Assembly, but served only one year. Frank Cundall,
A History of Printing in Jamaica from 1717 to 1834 (Kingston, 1935), pp. 10, 11.
Samuel Soumain (Soumien, Soumaine) (1718–1765?), one of BF's neighbors
while he lived at 325 Market Street, was a silversmith. He worked at Annapolis
and at Philadelphia for the remainder of his life. Stephen G. C. Ensko,
American Silversmiths and their Marks, III (N.Y., 1948), 123.
 7. The presence of this letter among BF's papers indicates that Soumain
gave it to him after BF's return from England.

the Money I hope you have made Mr. Franklan make Path to his Debt, otherwise I cannot charge it to Mr. Daniells Estate, to whom I am the administrator;[8] in Short advice me of your Proceedings, at same time Send an Account Current, that I may see what Ballance is due to you, and whatever it is, I will faithfully transmit it you, and give direction at same time, where I woud have you send my Plate. Mrs. Woodham joins in our best Respects to Self and Family   Remains me Your Sincere Friend

CHARLES SOMERSET WOODHAM

I am just come from England propose seeing it again next year Via Philadelphia.

Addressed: To | Mr. Samuel Soumain | Goldsmith | Philadelphia

Endorsed: Recd Octr 13-1762

To William Strahan

MS not found; reprinted from John Bigelow, ed., *The Complete Works of Benjamin Franklin* (New York and London, 1887–88), III, 208–9.

Dear Straney: London, 23 July, 1762.

As Dr. Hawkesworth[9] calls you, I send you inclosed a line to my good friend Dr. Kelley; which you will do me the favour to deliver with the parcel directed to him.[1] As it is vacation time I doubt whether any other acquaintance of mine may be in Oxford, or at least any on whose good nature I could so far presume; tho' according to the way of the world, having received a civility, gives one a kind of right to demand another; they took the trouble of show-

8. The plate had been given to BF as security for a debt owed by Daniell for paper. An undated entry in BF's Ledger D, p. 114 (described above, II, 232–4), explains the outcome: "Memo. Mr. Woodham, Successor of Mr. Daniel sent me a Box of Plate, which he redemanded when I was in England by his Power of Attorney to Mr. Soumaine who receiv'd the same, and paid the above Sum of £56 15s. od. by Part of the said Plate, viz. 126 oz. 2 dwt. at 9s. But with this Condition that if Mrs. Woodham chose to have the Plate again it should be delivered to her on her paying £56 7s. od."

9. For Dr. John Hawkesworth, see above, IX, 265–6 n.

1. BF's letter to Dr. John Kelly has not been found. On the books which BF sent him, see above, p. 133 n. Strahan was at this time on a three-weeks' tour which took him through Bristol, Salisbury, and Oxford.

ing me Oxford, and therefore I might request them to show it to any of my friends. None of the Oxford people are under any other obligation to me than that of having already oblig'd me, and being oblig'd to go on as they have begun. My best respects to Mrs. Strahan, and love to little Peggy.[2] They say we are to sail in a week or ten days. I expect to see you once more. I value myself much, on being able to resolve on doing the right thing, in opposition to your almost irresistible eloquence, secretly supported and backed by my own treacherous inclinations. Adieu, my dear friend. Yours affectionately,   B. FRANKLIN.

From James Short:[3] Bill and Receipt, with Notes on the Care of the Telescope DS and AD: Historical Society of Pennsylvania

1762 July 28th

Dr. Franklin Dr. to James Short
To three new Speculums to a 2 foot reflecting
Telescope and reparations of the Brass work &c; } £ 10. 10. –
    London 2d Aug. 1762 Received of Dr. Franklin the above Sum
      in full of all Demands JAS SHORT

[On the reverse side:]
Endorsed: Mr Short £10. 10. 0

Rules given by Mr. Short to keep the Telescope in Order[4]
1. Let the Speculums never be touch'd, or wip'd.
2. When the Tube in observing is left for any time open, let it be in a horizontal Position, that Dust may not settle either on the

2. Strahan's younger daughter, Margaret Penelope, was eleven at this time; she married John Spottiswoode on June 10, 1779. Her sons, Andrew and Robert, entered their uncle Andrew Strahan's printing business and inherited it in 1819. James A. Cochrane, *Dr. Johnson's Printer The Life of William Strahan* (Cambridge, Eng., 1964), pp. 156, 211–12.

3. James Short (1710–1768), F.R.S., whom BF described in 1758 as "a Friend of mine, and the great Optician here," was a distinguished astronomer and one of the most talented instrument makers of the day. *DNB;* and above, VII, 12 n; VIII, 158. The telescope for the repairs to which he billed BF here belonged to Lib. Co. Phila.

4. These rules are in BF's hand. Lib. Co. Phila. entered them on its minutes, Dec. 12, 1763, at the same time ordering repayment to BF for this and other expenditures he had made on its behalf.

great or small Speculums, which would on one or the other, if the Tube be either elevated or depress'd.

It is the Dust does the Mischief as it attracts the Moisture and both corrode.

To Peter Collinson

ALS: Pierpont Morgan Library

Wednesday, Augt 4. 1762

I did not receive my dear Friend's Letter of yesterday[5] till I came home late in the Evening. I have this Morning wrote the Directions you desired, and sent them to your Friend.[6] If you should hear that they are not quite clear in any particular, let me know that I may explain what is doubtful.

My Son presents his Respects. We intend our selves the Pleasure of Waiting on you to-morrow and taking a Dinner with you, if we do not hear that it will be an inconvenient Day for you. As the Ship is so near Sailing, I shall not have time to visit Mill Hill[7] and enjoy its Pleasures any more. I am, dear Friend, Yours affectionately   B FRANKLIN

5. Not found.

6. Collinson's friend may have been Henry Fox, first Baron Holland (1705–1774), paymaster general, 1757–65, and leader of the House of Commons, October 1762–April 1763, during which time he secured the votes, often through the "grossest bribery," to pass the peace treaty with France which concluded the Seven Years' War. *DNB*. Collinson frequently dined with Fox at Holland House and corresponded with him about a lightning rod which he had installed on his seaside home at Kingsgate, Kent, near the North Foreland. Therefore, if it was Fox to whom Franklin sent "Directions," they may have concerned the installation of a lightning rod. On Oct. 21, 1762, Collinson wrote Franklin that "Mr. Fox thinks himself extreemly obliged for your Letter," which may have covered the directions mentioned here. See below, p. 151; Norman G. Brett-James, *The Life of Peter Collinson F.R.S., F.S.A.* (London, [1926]), pp. 94–6.

7. Collinson's house near Hendon outside of London.

Statement of Account with Charles Norris

ADS: Franklin Institute, Philadelphia

Dr. Cha. Norris Esqr.[8]

1757			
Dec. 6.	Compleat Body of Gardening[9]		£ 1. 16. 0
1758		Do Husbandry	1. 15. 0
Sept. 15.		Do Gardening	1. 16. 0
	2	Do Husbandry	3. 10. 0
	2 Lisle's Observations on Husbandry		1. 0. 0
Nov. 1.	Charges on Shipping &c.		12. 9
1759			
Mar. 26.	Botanical Thermometer		18. –
30.	Parkinson's Herbal[1]		1. 0. 0
1762	Cash advanc'd to Gardner[2]		5. 0. 0
	Another Botanical Thermometer ⎱ omitted above ⎰		0: 18. 0

£18: 5:9

London, Aug. 5. 1762

Cr. by Cash receiv'd of Elias Bland[3] in full — 18. 5. 9

Errors excepted — per B FRANKLIN

Endorsed: Benja: Franklin Esqr His Sterling Account to Mr: Chas: Norris £18. 5. 9 Londo: Augt. 5th. 1762

8. This statement of account duplicates the entries on the last (unnumbered) page of "Account of Expences."

9. For this and the following four books, see above, VII, 176 n; VIII, 169.

1. John Parkinson, *Theatrum Botanicum: The Theater of Plants, or an Herball of large extent . . .* (London, 1640), as the title is recorded in Brit. Mus. Cat. *DNB* gives it as *Theatrum Botanicum: The Theater of Plantes, or An Universall and Complete Herball* (London, 1640).

2. On the gardener BF had apparently hired and sent to Philadelphia for Norris, see above, p. 70 n.

3. A London Quaker merchant who had lived in Philadelphia (above, III, 141 n). His name was on the list of people BF had recorded on his draft letter to Polly Stevenson, June 21, 1762 (above, pp. 107–8). Probably that entry was to remind BF to see Bland before leaving England because of some understanding that Bland would settle this account for Norris.

From Mary Stevenson

ALS: American Philosophical Society

Dear Sir   Wanstead Augt. 5. 1762

I was so unfortunate to lose the pleasure of seeing you yesterday in Cravenstreet, but I don't know whether I ought to say it
was unfortunate, for I only bring you distress. My Mother tells
me I made you unhappy by my Tears. Could you expect me to
part from you without shedding some? I am griev'd to think I
should cause you uneasiness, but you need not suffer any my
account, for my grief, will cease when I hear you are happily
arriv'd at Philadelphia, tho' while you are going I cannot help
being sorrowful. To know I have so valuable a Friend in the
World will always afford me great pleasure tho I cannot be with
him. Think on me, dear Sir, as one whom you have made happy,
and who will ever with a tender and grateful affection remain
Your oblig'd, devoted humble Servant   M STEVENSON

My Duty to my Mother.

Addressed: To | Dr Franklin | Cravenstreet | Strand

William Strahan to David Hall

ALS: American Philosophical Society (extract only printed here)

The extract printed below is not in any strict sense a part of the Franklin
Papers. It is included here, however, as a quite extraordinary tribute
to Franklin's personal qualities written by a British friend on the eve
of his departure from England. Franklin and Strahan had carried on a
business correspondence for fourteen years before they first saw each
other in the summer of 1757, but there are comparatively few letters
between them during the next five years when they were living in the
same city. There have been, consequently, few papers in this series to
show the way in which their personal acquaintance ripened into a deep
and lasting friendship. Something of what that friendship came to mean
to Strahan is revealed in this passage from his letter to his former journeyman, now Franklin's partner in Philadelphia. Even more significantly, perhaps, Strahan's words suggest something of the nature of
Franklin's gift for human relations and some of the reasons why he
achieved so warm a place in the hearts of many men and women from
different walks of life.

Dear Davie   London August 10. 1762.

* * * * * * *

This will be brought you by our worthy Friend Dr. Franklin, whose Face you should never again have seen on your Side the Water, had I been able to prevail on him to stay, or had my *Power* been in any measure equal to my *Inclination*. From the Acquaintance I have had of him, and the Intimacy with which he has been pleased to honour me for these five Years past, I have conceived, as you may easily imagine, the most cordial Esteem and Affection for him: For tho' his Talents and Abilities in almost every Branch of human Science are singularly great and Uncommon, and have added to the Pleasure and Knowledge of the greatest Geniuses of this Country, who all admire and love him, and lament his Departure; yet he knows as well how to condescend to those of inferior Capacity, how to level himself for the time to the Understandings of his Company, and to enter without Affectation into their Amusements and Chit-chat, that his whole Acquaintance here are his affectionate Friends. As for myself, I never found a Person in my whole Life more thoroughly to my Mind. As far as my Knowlege, or Experience, or Sentiments of every kind, could reach his more enlarged Sagacity and Conceptions, they exactly corresponded with his; or if I accidentally differed from him in any Particular, he quickly and with great Facility and Good-nature poured in such Light upon the Subject, as immediately convinced me I was wrong. It would much exceed the Bounds of a Letter to tell you in how many Views, and on how many Accounts, I esteem and love him, or how much and how universally he is esteemed by all who know him here. Suffice it to say, that I part with him with infinite Regret and Sorrow. I know not where to find his equal, nor can the Chasm his Departure leaves in my Social Enjoyments and Happiness ever be filled up. There is something in his leaving us even more cruel than a Separation by Death; it is like an *untimely Death,* where we part with a Friend to meet no more, *with a whole Heart,* as we say in Scotland. But I will still indulge myself in the Hope, however distant, that he may soon find it his Interest and Inclination to return to Britain, where he can be of great Use to his native Country—indeed wherever he is, he must be useful —or if that Happiness must forever be denied his friends on this

141

Side the Globe, that Peace, Prosperity, and every kind of Felicity may forever attend him and all his Connections; that he may long remain an honour to his Country and an Ornament to human Nature; and after he has lived to see his many useful, generous, and public spirited Schemes for the Good of the Society to which he belongs take full Effect and received the gratefull Acknowledgements of his Countrymen for all his Services, may he then, and not till then, in a good Old Age, take a final leave of all his Friends here, and enter into a State of more exalted and enlarged Knowledge, for which he seems by Nature to be so peculiarly fitted. Excuse my enlarging so much on this Subject; for I cannot tell you, after all, how much I feel on this melancholy Occasion, or how sensibly I am touched with parting from so amiable a Friend; a Separation so much the more bitter and agonizing, as it is likely to be *endless*.

* * * * * * *

I am with wonted Esteem and Affection, Dear Davie Most cordially Yours. WILL: STRAHAN

To Mary Stevenson ALS: Henry N. Haiken, New York City (1957)

My dear Polly Portsmouth,[4] Augt. 11. 1762
This is the best Paper I can get at this wretched Inn, but it will convey what is intrusted to it as faithfully as the finest. It will tell my Polly, how much her Friend is afflicted, that he must, perhaps never again, see one for whom he has so sincere an Affection, join'd to so perfect an Esteem; whom he once flatter'd himself might become his own in the tender Relation of a Child; but can now entertain such pleasing hopes no more;[5] Will it tell *how much* he is afflicted? No, it cannot.

4. *London Chron.*, Aug. 19–21, 1762, reported that "Last Week Benjamin Franklin, Esq; Postmaster-General of North America, set out from his house in Craven-Street, for Portsmouth, in order to embark for Philadelphia." The "Last Week" was that of August 8–14; BF must therefore have left London between the 8th and 10th to have been in Portsmouth in time to write Polly from there on the 11th.

5. That is, BF's wish that Polly might have married WF, whose marriage to Elizabeth Downes, Sept. 4, 1762, must by this time have certainly been arranged; see below, p. 146 n. There is no evidence that WF and Polly were ever

Adieu, my dearest Child: I will call you so; Why should I not call you so, since I love you with all the Tenderness, all the Fondness of a Father? Adieu. May the God of all Goodness shower down his choicest Blessings upon you, and make you infinitely Happier than that Event could have made you. Adieu. And wherever I am, believe me to be, with unalterable Affection, my dear Polly, Your sincere Friend   B FRANKLIN

From John Sargent[6]

Copy (incomplete), MS minutes: Trustees of the University of Pennsylvania

London 12 August 1763 [1762][7]

Dear Sir—   General Post Office

By our Friends here I am enabled to convey the enclosed Trifles to you, which are the best I could meet with at present and cost 5 Guineas each.[8]

You remember the Intention viz, for the two best Performances at the general Meeting or Publick Act of your College or Seminary.

The Subject of one to be, in a short English Discourse, or Essay "on the reciprocal Advantages arising from a perpetual Union between Great Britain and her American Colonies."

seriously interested in each other, and it is not known whether she or her mother was as yet aware that WF had fathered an illegitimate son (William Temple Franklin) during his English residence. There does seem to have been a degree of coolness toward him on the part of the Stevensons; in the correspondence between them and BF during the following years there are no greetings to or from him, no news about him, and no inquiries, however conventional, as to his health and welfare.

6. So identified in BF's statement presenting the letter to the Board of Trustees and in President Peters' reply, entered in the minutes of February 8 and April 12, 1763, respectively. On Sargent, see above, VII, 322 n.

7. The year date in the minutes is obviously an error.

8. Sargent sent these medals to BF "by the Channel of the Post Office." See the document immediately below. The Rev. William Smith, who was in England during 1762 raising money for the college, asked Sargent for a contribution. The merchant declined to "give any Thing that Way," but promised instead to give two gold medals annually "to some of the best Scholars, and had given his Directions about the Matter to Dr. Franklin." Smith was suspicious of Sargent's motives, thinking the plan "rather a Scheme for serving himself than us." Albert F. Gegenheimer, *William Smith* (Phila., 1943), pp. 153–4.

The other Prize, for some Classical Exercise, that you shall think best suited to your Plan of Education and the Abilities of your young people.

I submit to your Judgment whether the former shall be confined to your Students or left open to every one, whether of the Seminary or not. Yourself and Mr. Norris your Speaker and any third [*Here the copyist broke off, skipped the equivalent of about four lines, and continued the minutes of Feb. 8, 1763*].[9]

From Sargent Aufrere & Co. LS: American Philosophical Society

Dear sir   London 12th August 1762

We have just sent you by the Channel of the Post Office the two Gold Medal's which you will apply as a mark of our good Wishes for your College,[1] and now inclose a Letter of Credit which we hope you will never have occasion for, but if you should, we are persuaded the Name of B. M. da Costa[2] whatever Port you are

9. From the minutes that follow it would appear that Sargent went on to propose that Isaac Norris, BF, and some third person determine the subjects and conditions of the competition. But BF and Norris were disinclined to act because they felt that Sargent would not have proposed their names "if he had been acquainted with the Trustees or the Constitution of the Academy." Thereupon the trustees asked Richard Peters, their president, and BF to suggest a classical subject and to confer with Francis Alison, vice provost, and John Ewing, professor of natural philosophy, as to whether either of these subjects was suitable for the present degree candidates and whether "proper Orations" could be prepared in time for the next commencement. A later report indicated that the two faculty advisers thought the topic of perpetual Anglo-American union was "too high for the Present Candidates for Degrees," but that Roman education might be a suitable subject for the other competition. Peters wrote Sargent a letter of grateful thanks, April 6, 1763 (Minutes, April 12, 1763), but in the end, the competition for the two medals was not held until 1766, with an essay on union open to any holder of a degree from the college and one on a classical subject limited to the graduating seniors. The first medal was awarded to Dr. John Morgan (above, IX, 374 n), by then professor of medicine at the college, but the other prize was not awarded because the contestants, contrary to the rules set up, had revealed their identities beforehand. Montgomery, *Hist. Univ. Pa.*, pp. 365–71.

1. See the document immediately above.

2. Benjamin Mendez Da Costa (1704–1764) was an eminent London Jewish merchant and philanthropist, who yearly gave £3000 to the poor of all races

carried into will be respected and procure you all you wish. Whenever anything occurs in which we can either serve you or your Friends in Philadelphia, you may be assured of its being under taken by us with Zeal, punctuallity and the utmost Satisfaction, and that we are with the most sincere Regard Dear sir Your most faithfull and obedient Servants

SARGENT, AUFRERE & CO

Benjn. Franklin Esqr.

Addressed: To / Benjamin Franklin Esqr / at / Portsmouth / To be left at the Post / House till Call'd / for

To Sir Alexander Dick

ALS: Yale University Library

Dear Sir   Portsmouth, Augt. 16. 1762

I am now here just on the Point of departing for America. I cannot go without taking Leave of one from whom I received so many Civilities, so much real Kindness. Accept my sincerest Thanks, and do me the Justice to believe that wherever I am, I shall, while I live, retain a grateful Sense of your Favours. I cannot hope ever to see you in America; but possibly some Friends of yours may hereafter visit us. The least Line from you will make them welcome to me, and they may on your Account be assured of every Service in my Power. Be so good as to make my best Respects acceptable to your Lady and Children,[3] and permit me to subscribe myself, with the most perfect Esteem, Dear Friend, Yours affectionately   B FRANKLIN

Sir Alexr Dick

---

and creeds. Branches of his family, which came originally from either Spain or Portugal, were well established in practically every trading nation in Western Europe. *DNB; The Jewish Encyclopedia,* IV (1903), 289–91.

3. Sir Alexander's first wife, Janet, by whom he had two daughters, died on Dec. 26, 1760; on March 23, 1762, he married Miss Mary Butler by whom he had three sons. See above, VIII, 440 n.

To John Morgan[4]

ALS: Yale University Library

Dear Sir   Portsmouth, Augt. 16. 1762

I ought before now to have acknowledg'd the Receipt of a Letter from you after your Arrival in Scotland.[5] It gave me a good deal of Pleasure to hear you were well receiv'd there, and that you conceiv'd your being there would prove advantageous to you. I have not now your Letter before me, or should answer it more particularly. I am just departing for America, waiting here only for a Wind. I wish you a prosperous Completion of your Studies, and in due time a happy Return to your Native Country, where if I can be of the least Service to you, I shall be glad of the Occasion. Being, with much Esteem, Your affectionate Friend and humble Servant   B FRANKLIN

Present my Respects and best wishes to Mr. Russel, and Mr. McGowan when you see them.[6] My Son stays a little longer in England.[7]

Dr Morgan.

Addressed: To / Mr. John Morgan / Edinburgh

Endorsed: from B: Franklin Esqr Portsmouth Augst. 16. 1762.

4. For John Morgan, then a medical student at the University of Edinburgh, see above, IX, 374 n. Though Morgan had been apprenticed to Dr. John Redman in Philadelphia and had served as surgeon with provincial troops, BF's use of "Dr." with his name at the bottom of the page anticipated his M.D. degree by about a year.

5. Morgan's letter has not been found.

6. "Mr. Russel" was the surgeon apothecary James Russell, who was appointed professor of natural philosophy at the University of Edinburgh in 1764; see above, p. 22 n. Mr. McGowan has not been identified.

7. WF was staying in England for two reasons: to get married and to receive his commission as governor of New Jersey. On Sept. 4, 1762, he married Elizabeth Downes (d. 1777), a lady originally from the West Indies. The circumstances of his appointment to the N.J. governorship are far from clear. The Earl of Egremont notified the Board of Trade of the King's action on August 20, and a public announcement appeared in the Postscript of *London Chron.*, Aug. 24–26, 1762. The Privy Council approved the commission and instructions on September 1, the commission received the Great Seal on the 9th, and WF took the oaths the same day. 1 *N.J. Arch.*, IX, 368–72; *Board of Trade Journal*, 1759–63, pp. 287–8; *Acts Privy Coun., Col.*, IV, 548. BF's failure, in his last letters before sailing, even to hint that the appointment was under consideration suggests the secrecy surrounding the affair of which

To Lord Kames

ALS: Scottish Record Office

My dear Lord,   Portsmouth, Augt. 17. 1762

I am now waiting here only for a Wind to waft me to America, but cannot leave this happy Island and my Friends in it, without extream Regret, tho' I am going to a Country and a People that I love. I am going from the old World to the new; and I fancy I feel like those who are leaving this World for the next; Grief at the Parting; Fear of the Passage; Hope of the Future; these different Passions all affect their Minds at once; and these have tender'd me down exceedingly. It is usual for the Dying to beg Forgiveness of their surviving Friends if they have ever offended them. Can you, my Lord, forgive my long Silence, and my not acknowledging till now the Favour you did me in sending me your excellent

---

others complained: John Penn, for example, wrote William Alexander (Lord Stirling), Sept. 3, 1762, that "the whole of this business has been transacted in so private a manner, that not a tittle of it escaped until it was seen in the public papers; so that there was no opportunity of counteracting, or, indeed, doing one single thing that might put a stop to this shameful affair." William A. Duer, *The Life of William Alexander, Earl of Stirling,* N.J. Hist. Soc. *Colls.,* II (1847), 70. Thomas Penn's account, though hardly impartial, is the fullest that survives: "I cannot tell you," he wrote James Hamilton, March 11, 1763, "by whose Interest young Franklin was appointed, the Government was refused by Pownal, and less Interest was sufficient than to any place of two hundred Pounds a year here, it was done by the direction of Lord Bute and Dr. Pringle came from that Lord to the Secretary of State about it, whether he recommended him himself I cannot tell, he is Lord Butes Physician, and a Friend of Franklins—young Franklin sollicited less than a Month before to be Deputy Secretary of Carolina." Penn Papers, Hist. Soc. Pa. Some people in addition to the Penns were unhappy about the appointment, specifically because of the irregularity of wf's birth. Thomas Bridges, Richard Jackson's brother-in-law, wrote with some amusement to Jared Ingersoll, Sept. 30, 1762: "I hear there was some difficulty in his being Confirmed in his place, for in our Conscientious Age, many Scruples were raised on account of his *being Illegitimate,* which we were Strangers to till very lately." New Haven Col. Hist. Soc. *Papers,* IX, 278. And some forty years later John Adams could write in his autobiography: "Without the Supposition of some kind of Backstairs Intrigues it is difficult to account for that mortification of the pride, affront to the dignity and Insult to the Morals of America, the Elevation to the Government of New Jersey of a base born Brat." L. H. Butterfield et al., eds., *Diary and Autobiography of John Adams* (Cambridge, Mass., 1961), IV, 151.

Book?[8] Can you make some Allowance for a Fault in others which you have never experienc'd in your self; for the bad Habit of postponing from Day to Day what one every Day resolves to do tomorrow? A Habit that grows upon us with Years, and whose only Excuse is that we know not how to mend it. If you are dispos'd to favour me, you will also consider how much one's Mind is taken up and distracted by the many little Affairs one has to settle before the Undertaking such a Voyage after so long a Residence in a Country; and how little, in such a Situation, one's Mind is fitted for serious and attentive Reading, which with regard to the Elements of Criticism I intended before I should write. I can now only confess and endeavour to amend. In packing up my Books I have reserved yours to read on the Passage. I hope I shall therefore be able to write to you upon them soon after my Arrival:[9] At present I can only return my Thanks for them, and say, that the Parts I have read gave me both Pleasure and Instruction; that I am convinc'd of your Position, new as it was to me, that a good Taste in the Arts contributes to the Improvement of Morals; and that I have had the Satisfaction of hearing the Work universally commended by those who have read it.

And now, my dear Sir, accept my sincerest Thanks for the Kindness you have shewn me, and my best Wishes of Happiness to you and yours. Where-ever I am, I shall esteem the Friendship you honour me with, as one of the Felicities of my Life; I shall endeavour to cultivate it by a more punctual Correspondence; and I hope frequently to hear of your Welfare and Prosperity. Adieu, my dear Friend, and believe me ever Most affectionately yours   B FRANKLIN

My Son presents his Compliments. He stays in England a little longer.

Addressed: To / The right honourable Lord Kaims / at / Edinburgh

8. Kames's *Elements of Criticism,* which was apparently published in January 1762; see above, p. 27 n.

9. As he promised, BF read the *Elements of Criticism* on his passage to America, but did not write Kames about it until much later. He found "great Entertainment, much to admire, and nothing to reprove" in the book; he only wished that Kames "had explained more fully the Subject of Music." To Kames, June 2, 1765, Scottish Record Office.

[Edinburgh has been crossed out in another hand and Dunse[1] added.]
/ Free SAM POTTS[2]
Endorsed: Aug 17 1762

To William Strahan ALS: Pierpont Morgan Library

Dear Sir, Portsmouth, Monday, Augt. 23. 1762

I have been two Nights on board expecting to sail, but the Wind continuing contrary, am just now come on shore again, and have met with your kind Letter of the 20th.[3] I thank you even for the Reproofs it contains, tho' I have not altogether deserved them. I cannot, I assure you, quit even this disagreable Place without Regret, as it carries me still farther from those I love, and from the Opportunities of hearing of their Welfare. The Attraction of *Reason* is at present for the other Side of the Water, but that of *Inclination* will be for this side. You know which usually prevails. I shall probably make but this one Vibration and settle here for ever. Nothing will prevent it, if I can, as I hope I can, prevail with Mrs. F. to accompany me; especially if we have a Peace.[4] I will not tell you, that to be near and with you and yours, is any part of my Inducement: It would look like a Complement extorted from me by your Pretences to Insignificancy. Nor will I own that your Persuasions and Arguments have wrought this Change in my former Resolutions: tho' it is true that they have frequently intruded themselves into my Consideration whether I would or not. I trust, however, that we shall once more see each other and be happy again together, which God, etc.

1. Duns (or Dunse, a spelling in vogue 1740–82), one of the few considerable towns in Berwickshire, and probably the nearest post town to Lord Kames's estate at Kames.
2. Samuel Potts was the comptroller general of the General Post Office and apparently a brother of Henry Potts (above, IX, 179 n), the secretary to the Post Office.
3. Not found.
4. BF's thoughts about settling in England were apparently known to many of his friends; on Sept. 30, 1762, for example, Richard Jackson's brother-in-law, Thomas Bridges, wrote Jared Ingersoll of the report that "the Old Gentleman intends soon to bring over his *Lady* and Daughter to spend the remainder of their days in England." New Haven Colony Hist. Soc. *Papers,* IX (1918), 278.

My Love to Mrs. Strahan, and your amiable and valuable Children. Heaven bless you all, whatever becomes of Your much obliged and affectionate Friend   B FRANKLIN[5]

From John Winthrop

MS not found; reprinted from Benjamin Franklin, *Experiments and Observations on Electricity* (London, 1769), p. 434.[6]

Sir,   Cambridge, N.E. Sept. 29, 1762.

There is an observation relating to electricity in the atmosphere, which seemed new to me, though perhaps it will not to you: However, I will venture to mention it. I have some points on the top of my house, and the wire where it passes within-side the house is furnished with bells, according to your method, to give notice of the passage of the electric fluid.[7] In summer, these bells generally ring at the approach of a thunder cloud; but cease soon after it begins to rain. In winter, they sometimes, though not very often, ring while it is snowing; but never, that I remember, when it rains. But what was unexpected to me was, that, though the bells had not rung while it was snowing, yet the next day, after it had done snowing, and the weather was cleared up; while the snow was driven about by a high wind at W. or N.W. the bells rung for several hours (though with little intermissions) as briskly as ever I knew them, and I drew considerable sparks from the wire. This phaenomenon I never observed but twice; *viz.* on the 31st of January, 1760, and the 3d of March, 1762. I am, Sir, &c.

5. This was BF's last letter from England; his ship, the *Carolina*, Capt. James Friend, apparently sailed in convoy the same day, or possibly the next.

6. Printed as Letter XLIII in *Exper. and Obser.*, 1769 edition, and also in 1774 edition, p. 444.

7. In September 1753 BF wrote Collinson (above, v, 69) that a year earlier he had "erected an Iron Rod to draw the Lightning down into my House, in order to make some Experiments on it, with two Bells to give Notice when the Rod should be electrified." That letter was published in *Exper. and Obser.*, 1754 edit., and Winthrop probably read it there. For DF's uneasiness about the ringing of the bells in her house, see above, VIII, 94.

From Peter Collinson

ALS: American Philosophical Society

Londn: Octor 21: 1762

I impatienly expect the good News of my Dear Franklin's Safe Arrival.[8] Wee regret Your Abscence, but there is a Time the Dearest Friends must Part but Wee Cherish our Minds with the Hopes of Long enjoyeing your Correspondence and Shareing in the Discoveries, the Effects of your Fruitfull Genius, which can happyly Imploye it Self, to your own Benefit or that of the Publick.

Distance can not remove you from our Solicitation. Mr. Fox thinks himself extreemly obliged to you for your Letter. This draws on you a Simular request from His Intimate Friend Mr. Hamilton which I here Inclose.[9]

As you requested I insured for you £200 More.[1] I give you Joye on your Sons promotion. I wish his Government may Sett Easie[2] —for He has Two unruly Spirits, Sterling and Morris,[3] to contend with, but assisted with your Council He will Surmount them all.

I am with Sincere Esteem your Affectionate Friend

P COLLINSON

8. For BF's arrival at Philadelphia, Nov. 1, 1762, after a voyage of ten weeks from Portsmouth, see below, p. 153. The "good News" appeared in *London Chron.*, Dec. 30, 1762–Jan. 1, 1763.

9. On BF's letter, presumably about the erection of a lightning rod, to "Mr. Fox" (probably Henry Fox, first Baron Holland) see above, p. 138 n. Fox's "intimate Friend" was Charles Hamilton (1704–1786), the ninth son of the sixth Earl of Abercorn. Hamilton's seat, Painshill, near Cobham, Surrey, was a "famous show-place" and one of the "earliest examples of natural landscape gardening on a large scale." Collinson to BF, Aug. 23, 1763, APS; Wilmarth S. Lewis et al., eds., *The Yale Edition of Horace Walpole's Correspondence,* IX (New Haven, 1941), 71 n.

1. Apparently a reference to insurance bought to cover BF's belongings during his voyage to Philadelphia.

2. For WF's appointment as governor of N.J., see above, pp. 146–7 n.

3. "Sterling" was William Alexander (above, VI, 244 n), whose claims to the title of the sixth Earl of Stirling the House of Lords refused to recognize, but who adopted the title nevertheless and in America, at least, was generally called Lord Stirling. He served with distinction during the Revolutionary War and was appointed a major general by Congress on Feb. 19, 1777 . In 1775 he and WF conducted an acrimonious correspondence for which WF suspended him from the N. J. Council. Until that time, however, he and WF seem to have been on good terms. *DAB;* William A. Duer, *The Life of William Alexander, Earl of Stirling,* N.J. Hist. Soc. *Coll.,* II (1847), esp. pp.

Yesterday I had the pleasure of Breakfasting with your Son and takeing my Leave.[4] Think He has a Sensible and Agreeable Wife. I wish them much Comfort together

1762	Ben Franklin		Dr
March 21	To Ballance of Account[5]		£14: 19: 5
	To: 35th Vol. Mod. History[6] ⎱ taken		0: 6: 6
	To: 31 plate Inserts ⎰ with you		0: 2: 6
Augst: 13.	pd Insurance 15 guineas per Cent.		31: 10: –
21:	36 Vol Mod History		0: 6: 6
			£47: 4: 11

1762	Per Contra	Cr
Augt. 10:	By Net Draught	32: 9: 5

I am to Credit your account with return of Insurance when received.

I shall be Obliged to you for an Abstract of the Order of Councel for the Taxing Mr. Penns Land[7]

The Modern Histy are for the Lib. Com.[8]

80–1, 87, 109–11. After being supplanted as Governor of Pa. in 1756, Robert Hunter Morris (above, V, 527–8 n) returned to N. J. and resumed the office of chief justice to which his father had appointed him in 1739. Until his death in 1764, he and WF seem to have got along well.

4. The *Philadelphia Packet*, Capt. Richard Budden, left Portsmouth, where WF and his wife embarked, on November 20. The convoy under H.M.S. *Nightingale* ran into a violent storm in the Bay of Biscay and rescued the crew of a sinking ship, then most of the ships put back to Plymouth, where they remained until December 17. *London Chron.*, Dec. 2–4, 1762, carries a long account of this experience from a passenger on the *Philadelphia Packet*, possibly WF. The ship arrived in Delaware Bay during the first week of February 1763, but because of ice and contrary winds could not come up to Philadelphia immediately. The Franklins debarked, therefore, at Lewes, arrived at Philadelphia on February 19, and set out for N.J. on the 23d. *London Chron.*, Oct. 23–6, Dec. 21–23, 1762; *Pa. Gaz.*, Feb. 17, 24, 1763; WF to Strahan, November 1762, Yale Univ. Lib.; *PMHB*, XXXV (1911), 424.

5. See above, p. 68.

6. For the multivolume *An Universal History, from the Earliest Account of Time to the Present*, see above, III, 146 n. Lib. Co. Phila. apparently had a standing order for the 44 volumes of the octavo edition of the modern part.

7. See above, IX, 203–11.

8. Collinson had for many years been the purchasing agent for Lib. Co. Phila.

Addressed: To / Ben Franklin Esqr / in Philadelphia / These / per Capt Budden

To Jane Mecom

ALS: American Philosophical Society

Dear Sister,   Philada. Nov. 11. 1762.
I received your kind Letter of the 1st Instant.⁹ It was on that Day I had the great Happiness of finding my Family well at my own House after so long an Absence.¹ I am well except a little Touch of the Gout, which my Friends say is no Disease. Cousin Benja. has been to see me as you supposed, and yesterday he re-turn'd homewards.² My Love to Brother Mecom and your Chil-dren.³ Excuse the shortness of this, as my Time is much taken up at present. I am, my dear Sister, Your affectionate Brother

B FRANKLIN

Billy stays in England a little longer. My Wife can't write now but sends her Love.

Addressed: To / Mrs Jane Mecom / Boston / Free / B FRANKLIN

9. Not found.

1. For BF's voyage from England, see above, p. 115 n. *Pa. Gaz.*, Nov. 4, 1762, reported the arrival of the *Carolina* on the 1st, but did not mention BF by name. *London Chron.*, Dec. 30, 1762–Jan. 1, 1763, however, reported that on BF's arrival "he was waited on by all ranks of people, to congratulate him on his safe return to the province, his family and friends; from whom he received the highest marks of esteem and respect, and the fullest demonstra-tions of the high sense they entertained, as well of his upright and disinterested conduct, in the important trust committed to his care, by the Assembly of this Government, as of his steady attention to the interest of the colonies in general during his residence in Great Britain."

2. BF's nephew, Benjamin Mecom (C.17.3), had either recently given up his printing office in Boston, or was about to do so. He had apparently come to see BF to enlist his support for a new venture, the publication of a news-paper in N.Y. The paper, which Mecom called the *New-York Pacquet,* was a resounding failure; the first issue appeared on July 11, 1763, and apparently only six other issues followed. On Dec. 19, 1763, BF reported to Strahan that his nephew had "dropt his Paper." For Mecom's later publishing ventures, see above, IV, 355–6 n. See also BF to Strahan, Dec. 19, 1763, Pierpont Morgan Lib., and Clarence S. Brigham, *History and Bibliography of American News-papers 1690–1820* (Worcester, 1947), I, 677.

3. For Jane Mecom's husband and family, see above, I, lxi-lxii.

To Catharine Greene[4]   Copy: American Philosophical Society

My dear Friend.   Philada: Nov 25th. 1762.
I received your kind congratulations on my return,[5] and thank
you cordially. It gives me great pleasure to hear you are married
and live happily. You are a good Girl for complying with so essential a duty, and God will bless you. Make my compliments acceptable to your spouse; and fulfil your promise of writing to me; and
let me know everything that has happened to you and your friends
since my Departure, for I interest myself as much as ever in whatever relates to your Happiness. My best Respects to your Brother
and Sister Ward, and Compliments on his advancement to the Government of your Colony;[6] and believe me ever, My dear Caty Your
affectionate Friend and humble servant   B FRANKLIN.
My wife and Daughter join in presenting their Respects.

To Jane Mecom   ALS: American Philosophical Society

Dear Sister,   Philada. Nov. 25. 1762
I thank you for your obliging Letter of the 12th. Instant.[7] My
Wife says she will write to you largely by next Post, being at present
short of Time. As to the Promotion and Marriage you mention,[8] I
shall now only say that the Lady is of so amiable a Character,
that the latter gives me more Pleasure than the former,[9] tho' I

4. Catharine Ray, the sprightly young lady whom BF had met in Boston
in the autumn of 1754 (above, V, 502 n), had married her second cousin
William Greene, Jr., April 30, 1758, and was living in his family home at
Warwick, R.I. She had written BF in 1758, presumably telling of her im-
pending marriage; DF had forwarded the letter but it never reached him; see
above, VIII, 94.
5. Not found.
6. Her sister Anna was the wife of Samuel Ward (1725–1776), who was
elected governor of R.I. in 1762. BF had sent him some seeds of broom corn
in 1757; above, VII, 154–5.
7. Not found.
8. *Pa. Gaz.*, Nov. 25, 1762, carried a report from Boston, dated November
11, of WF's marriage to Elizabeth Downes and his appointment as governor of
N.J. BF had kept silent on both matters, even in his letter to his sister of November 11, apparently until he knew that both had been publicly announced.
9. It seems that WF had been courting Miss Downes for some time; Richard
Jackson's brother-in-law, Thomas Bridges, wrote Jared Ingersoll (who had

154

have no doubt but that he will make as good a Governor as Husband: for he has good Principles and good Dispositions, and I think is not deficient in good Understanding.[1] I am as ever Your affectionate Brother   B FRANKLIN

Our Love to Brother and your Children.

Addressed: To / Mrs Jane Mecom / Boston / Free / B FRANKLIN

To Jonathan Williams[2]

ALS: Mrs. George S. Maywood, Garden City, N.Y. (1955)

Loving Cousin   Philada. Nov. 25. 1762.

I thank you for your kind Congratulations on my Arrival and the Promotion of my Son.[3] I am in hopes I shall be able to see

known WF in England), Sept. 30, 1762, that soon after BF had sailed, "the Young Gentleman took unto him a Wife, I will not leave you to Guess who, for You cannot suppose it to be any other than his Old Flame in St. James's Street; we think the Lady has great luck on her side, to get a Smart Young fellow for her Husband, and the Honour of being a Governor's Lady." New Haven Col. Hist. Soc. *Papers,* IX (1918), 278. Strahan shared BF's pleasure in the marriage; writing to David Hall, Nov. 1, 1762, he declared that WF's "Lady is, in my mind, as good a Soul as breathes, and they are very happy in one another. She is indeed a Favourite with all who know her, give me leave therefore to recommend her to your particular Attention." APS.

1. Governor Hamilton did not share BF's opinion of WF's qualifications for a governorship. The appointment, he told Thomas Penn, Nov. 21, 1762, "occasioned a universal astonishment" in both Pa. and N.J., "as he is, perhaps, a Man of as bad a heart as I ever was acquainted with. He would certainly make wild work, without his Fathers experience and good Understanding to check and moderate his Passion." Penn Papers, Hist. Soc. Pa. Actually, neither BF's optimism nor Hamilton's pessimism was fully justified in the end. WF experienced the usual difficulties of any royal governor in reconciling his instructions with the Assembly's wishes, but he tried harder than some of his colleagues to get the home authorities to understand the reasons for colonial desires. He showed some skill in political maneuvering, and until the pre-Revolutionary crisis became acute, and he became an outspoken Loyalist, his administration was marked by considerable good will on both sides. For a survey of his governorship see Catherine Fennelly, "William Franklin of New Jersey," *William and Mary Quarterly,* 3d Series, VI (1949), 361–82.

2. Jonathan Williams (1719–1796), Boston merchant, was the husband of Grace Harris (C.5.3), daughter of BF's half sister Ann. BF seems to have relied on him to look after several of his Boston relatives; see above, VII, 191.

3. Williams' letter not found.

Boston the next Spring, and to have the Pleasure of finding you and my other Friends well.[4] I congratulate you on your having such a Number of Sons.[5] You remember the Blessing on him that has his Quiver full of them. My Love to your good Wife, and to the Children: Let me know how the eldest does, who had the Misfortune of losing his Sight.[6] I was acquainted with Mr. Stanley in London, who is an excellent Musician, and what is stranger, plays at Cards extreamly well and readily. I should be glad to know what you have done in my Affairs relating to Sister Douse:[7] and am, Your affectionate Uncle   B FRANKLIN

P.S. I thank you for your kind Invitation to your House, but doubt I should incommode you too much.[8]

Addressed: To / Mr Jonathan Williams / Mercht / Boston / Free / B FRANKLIN

Endorsed: Novr 25 1762   B Franklin. Novr 25 1762

From John Hughes[9]   ALS: American Philosophical Society

The lands which Hughes proposed to buy in this letter had a tangled history.[1] On Jan. 26, 1705, Col. Thomas Byerly[2] purchased from

4. BF visited Boston in the summer of 1763 on post-office business, arriving there on July 20 and leaving October 12. He was accompanied by his colleague John Foxcroft and by his daughter Sally. *Boston Evening-Post,* July 25, 1763; BF to James Bowdoin, Oct. 11, 1763, Mass. Hist. Soc.

5. Jonathan and Grace Williams had seven sons, of whom three lived to adulthood. See above, I, lvii-lviii.

6. Josiah Williams (C.5.3.1) went to London in 1770 to study with BF's friend, the blind musician John Stanley (above, IX, 320 n). Josiah died soon after returning to Boston in 1772.

7. BF's eldest half sister, Elizabeth Douse (C.1), died at Boston, Aug. 25, 1759. Since her estate owed BF £251 17s. 11 1/5d., her house on Unity Street, valued at £150, eventually came to BF in part payment. But because she had died intestate leaving no children, some time probably elapsed before title was formally transferred to BF. Williams may have been looking after BF's interests in the matter. Van Doren, *Franklin-Mecom,* pp. 78–9.

8. During BF's visit to Boston he lodged his daughter Sally at Williams' house so she could practice the harpsichord. See below, p. 292.

9. For John Hughes, friend and political ally of BF, see above, VI, 284 n; VIII, 90–1.

1. In preparing this note the editors have relied almost exclusively on

Robert Squibb, Jr., about 21,000 acres in present-day Hunterdon and Warren counties in western New Jersey and something less than 20,000 acres in other parts of the province. By his will, dated May 26, 1725, Byerly "conveyed his lands in trust to his executors, Joseph Murray and John Kinsey, with the instructions that one half or moiety was to be sold and the other was to go to Robert Barker of Gray's Inn, Middlesex, England." Barker's grandson, Robert,[3] eventually inherited the lands in western New Jersey, which had been reduced, however, to about 10,000 acres by sales to William Allen and Joseph Turner of Philadelphia and by a sale to satisfy a claim of George Clarke, lieutenant governor of New York, against Byerly's estate. Hughes's efforts to buy Barker's lands occasioned a considerable correspondence between Franklin and Richard Jackson, who tried to arrange the sale in England.[4] Far from being willing to sell, however, Barker began to take steps in 1764 to realize a profit from his estates by appointing an agent to collect rents from squatters. In 1790, after a prolonged legal battle about the validity of Barker's title, his agent, James Parker,[5] sold his lands to Philip Grandin for £4500 sterling.

Sir   Philada. Novembr 29th 1762.

The Best Information I can Give of the Land I want Your Assistance in purchasing is that one Byerley of London Somtime about the Year 1713 or 14 took up a Large Tract of Land in New Jersey on Delaware and Musonecunk Rivers[6] in partnership with One Barker of London a Brother in Law of his. And that many Year's Afterwards the said Byerley was in America and Dyed here I believe Insolvent however a writ of partition was Ishued by John Kinsey and Division made in the Tracts (as it was in 2 or 3 parcels).

Richard P. McCormick, "The West Jersey Estate of Sir Robert Barker," N.J. Hist. Soc. *Proc.*, LXIV (1946), 119–55.

2. Thomas Byerly (d. 1725) was receiver and collector of the revenues in N.Y. and a member of the Councils of N.Y. and N.J.

3. Robert Barker (1732?–1789), was an officer in the East India Company's military service, rising to become provincial commander-in-chief in Bengal, 1770–74; he was knighted, 1764; created baronet, 1781; M.P. for Wallingford, 1774–80; F.R.S., 1775. *DNB;* Namier and Brooke, *House of Commons*, II, 48–9.

4. See below, pp. 162–5, 243–4, 286, 297, 369, 413–14, and the next volume.

5. This James Parker (1725–1794) is not to be confused with BF's friend, the printer.

6. That is, the Musconetcong River. Byerly had his lands there surveyed by Edward Kempe, May 16, 1714. McCormick, "West Jersey Estate," pp. 121–2.

And Mr. Byerleys part Sold at publick Sale to Messrs. Allen and Turner for £3600 Currency which is about £2000 Sterling[7] which Sum I am willing to Give for the Other half altho, it is Much Injured by being all Settled, and Cut to pieces and Thousands of Cords of wood Sold off of it, besides the Greatest part of the best Land is very Much wore by Constant Tillage. I am also willing to pay Your friend Satisfactorily for his Trouble and if he Succeeds will Give 60 Guineas as a present.[8] I am Sir Yours   JON HUGHES

To Benjamin Franklin Esqr

Addressed: For / Benjamin Franklin Esqr

Endorsed: Philad Nov. 29th. 1762 from John Hughes To Benj Franklin Esqr

To John Pringle

MS not found; reprinted from Benjamin Franklin, *Experiments and Observations on Electricity* (London, 1769), pp. 438–40.[9]

Sir,   Philadelphia, Dec. 1, 1762.

During our passage to Madeira,[1] the weather being warm, and the cabbin windows constantly open for the benefit of the air, the candles at night flared and run very much, which was an inconvenience. At Madeira we got oil to burn, and with a common glass tumbler or beaker, slung in wire, and suspended to the cieling of the cabbin, and a little wire hoop for the wick, furnish'd with corks to float on the oil, I made an Italian lamp, that gave us very good light all over the table. The glass at bottom contained water to about one third of its height; another third was taken up with oil; the rest was left empty that the sides of the glass might protect the flame from the wind. There is nothing remarkable in all this;

---

7. Allen and Turner paid £5000, but it is not clear whether in local currency or sterling. *Ibid.*, p. 123.

8. It is not certain whether Hughes ever succeeded in acquiring N.J. lands from this effort. A Hugh Hughes advertised properties on the Musconetcong River for rent in 1768 (1 *N.J. Arch.*, XXVI, 319), but whether he was either John Hughes's son or brother of that name has not been established.

9. Letter XLV in the 1769 edition of *Exper. and Obser.* and also in the 1774 edition, where it is printed on pp. 448–50.

1. The convoy with which BF sailed to Philadelphia stopped at Madeira for three days.

158

but what follows is particular. At supper, looking on the lamp, I remarked that tho' the surface of the oil was perfectly tranquil, and duly preserved its position and distance with regard to the brim of the glass, the water under the oil was in great commotion, rising and falling in irregular waves, which continued during the whole evening. The lamp was kept burning as a watch light all night, till the oil was spent, and the water only remain'd. In the morning I observed, that though the motion of the ship continued the same; the water was now quiet, and its surface as tranquil as that of the oil had been the evening before. At night again, when oil was put upon it, the water resumed its irregular motions, rising in high waves almost to the surface of the oil, but without disturbing the smooth level of that surface. And this was repeated every day during the voyage.

Since my arrival in America, I have repeated the experiment frequently thus. I have put a pack-thread round a tumbler, with strings of the same, from each side, meeting above it in a knot at about a foot distance from the top of the tumbler. Then putting in as much water as would fill about one third part of the tumbler, I lifted it up by the knot, and swung it to and fro in the air; when the water appeared to keep its place in the tumbler as steadily as if it had been ice. But pouring gently in upon the water about as much oil, and then again swinging it in the air as before, the tranquility before possessed by the water, was transferred to the surface of the oil, and the water under it was agitated with the same commotions as at sea.[2]

I have shewn this experiment to a number of ingenious persons. Those who are but slightly acquainted with the principles of hydrostatics, &c. are apt to fancy immediately that they understand it, and readily attempt to explain it; but their explanations have been different, and to me not very intelligible. Others more deeply skill'd in those principles, seem to wonder at it, and promise to consider it.[3] And I think it is worth considering: For a new appearance, if

2. In a letter to William Brownrigg, Nov. 7, 1773 (Royal Soc.), BF recorded all he had "heard, and learnt, and done" about the interaction of oil and water, a matter which had interested him since boyhood when he had read Pliny's account of seamen stilling waves in a storm by pouring oil into the sea.

3. In May 1763 Pringle reported that he had read this letter to a group of friends and that everyone was "agog about this new property of fluids." See below, p. 269.

it cannot be explain'd by our old principles, may afford us new ones, of use perhaps in explaining some other obscure parts of natural knowledge. I am, &c.   B.F.

To Richard Jackson   ALS: American Philosophical Society

Dear Sir,   Philada. Dec. 2. 1762
    I arrived here well on the 1st. ultimo and had the Pleasure to find all false that Dr. Smith had reported about the Diminution of my Friends.[4] My House has been fill'd with a Succession of them from Morning to Night almost ever since I landed to congratulate me on my Return; and I never experienc'd greater Cordiality among them. The new Assembly had met and adjourn'd before my Arrival;[5] but expecting me, had omitted nominating a new Agent till they could have my Opinion and Advice as the Speaker tells me.[6] I was also unanimously chosen at the October Elections a Member for the City as heretofore; and am to take my Place in the House in the January Sitting, after which you may soon expect to hear from me on the Affair I mention'd to you.[7] I purpose writing to you more fully per Capt. Friend, who is to sail in a few Days.[8]

4. The Rev. William Smith had gone to England in March 1762 to raise money for the College of Philadelphia and apparently could not resist the temptation to spread rumors about BF's decline in popularity. Before Smith left London in May 1764 he had collected £7231 17s. 6d. Albert F. Gegenheimer, *William Smith* (Phila., 1943), pp. 72–3.
    5. The Assembly convened on Oct. 14, 1762, and on October 16 adjourned until January 10. 8 *Pa. Arch.*, VI, 5367–71.
    6. The Assembly appointed Jackson agent on April 2, 1763, *Ibid.*, p. 5425.
    7. BF appeared in the House and qualified on January 11; he had already been appointed the day before on a committee to notify the governor that the Assembly was in session. *Ibid.*, p. 5371. The "Affair" may have concerned either Jackson's appointment as agent or possibly land grants in the Ohio Valley which BF and some of his friends were interested in acquiring. See below, pp. 208–9.
    8. *Pa. Gaz.*, Dec. 9, 1762, reported the clearance of the *Carolina*, Capt. James Friend, for London. Friend was captured by the Spanish on Feb. 21 or 22, 1763, and carried into Bilboa, but since the capture was made after the peace treaties had been signed (Feb. 10, 1763), he was released. Jackson acknowledged the receipt of letters by the *Carolina* on April 4, 1763; see below, p. 241.

This goes per N York Packet,[9] and I have only time to add, that I am, with the greatest Esteem and Affection, Dear Sir, Your most obedient and most humble Servant   B FRANKLIN

My best Respects to your good Father and Sisters, and to Mr. Bridges.[1]

Addressed: To / Richard Jackson Esqr / Counsellor at Law / King's Bench Walks / Temple / London

Endorsed: Philad. Decr. 2d. 1762 B. Franklin Esqr

To William Strahan   ALS: American Philosophical Society

Dear Straney,   Philada. Dec. 2. 1762

As good Dr. Hawkesworth[2] calls you, to whom my best Respects. I got home well the 1st. of November, and had the Happiness to find my little Family perfectly well; and that Dr. Smith's Reports of the Diminution of my Friends were all false. My House has been full of a Succession of them from Morning to Night ever since my Arrival, congratulating me on my Return with the utmost Cordiality and Affection. My Fellow Citizens while I was on the Sea, had, at the annual Election, chosen me unanimously, as they had done every Year while I was in England, to be their Representative in Assembly; and would, they say, if I had not disappointed them by coming privately to Town before they heard of my Landing, have met me with 500 Horse. Excuse my Vanity in writ-

9. This letter missed the *Harriot* packet, which sailed from N.Y. on December 1. *Pa. Gaz.*, Dec. 9, 1762. Jackson, however, acknowledged receipt of the letter "by the Packet," so that it must have reached England in the *Earl of Halifax* packet, Capt. Bolderson, which sailed from N.Y., December 16. *N.-Y. Mercury*, Dec. 20, 1762.

1. Richard Jackson, Sr., of Weasenham, Norfolk, a London merchant; Elizabeth Jackson, who died unmarried in 1788, aged 67; Anne Jackson, who married first Thomas Bridges of Hedley, Surrey, and Binham Abbey, Norfolk (d. 1768), and second Admiral George Darby. She and her second husband both died in 1790. *DNB;* Namier and Brooke, *House of Commons,* II, 299, 569–72; *Gent. Mag.,* LVII (1787), 454; LX (1790), 282, 373, 473; G. A. Carthew, *The Hundred of Launditch . . . in the County of Norfolk,* III (Norwich, 1789), 445.

2. For Dr. John Hawkesworth, editor and essayist, see above, IX, 265–6 n. On BF's reception at home see also immediately above.

ing this to you, who know what has provok'd me to it. My Love
to good Mrs. Strahan, and your Children, particularly my little
Wife.[3] I shall write more fully per next Opportunity, having now
only time to add, that I am, with unchangeable Affection, my dear
Friend, Yours sincerely   B FRANKLIN

Mrs. Franklin and Sally desire their Compliments and Thanks to
you all for your Kindness to me while in England.

Addressed: To / Mr William Strahan / Printer / New Street
Square / Shoe Lane / London[4]

To Richard Jackson

ALS, duplicate LS, and (incomplete) draft:[5] American Philosophical
Society

Dear Sir,   Philada. Dec. 6. 1762
    I have already wrote to you via New York, but hear my Letter
did not reach the Pacquet; so this may come first to hand.[6] I arrived the 1st. of November, after a long but pleasant Passage, having in general fair Winds and good Weather; but being in a Convoy
could sail no faster than the slowest. I had the Happiness to find
my little Family well, and my Friends as hearty and more num-
berous than ever, notwithstanding Dr. Smith's Reports to the contrary. I had been unanimously chosen a Representative for the
City at the October Election; but the House had met and was ad-

3. Strahan's younger daughter, Margaret Penelope; see above, p. 137 n.
4. On the address page Strahan penciled some notes apparently recording
the votes of certain peers on unidentified measures in the House of Lords.
Before each of the names of Bute, Pomfret, and Talbot appears the letter "f"
(presumably standing for "for"), and before each of the names of Dartmouth,
Rockingham, Newcastle, Temple, and Littleton appears "a" (presumably
"against"). Below are totals: "Cont [for "Content"] 73 62"; and "NotC [for
"Not Content"] 39 38."
5. Part of the second leaf of the ALS is torn away; the missing words are
supplied in brackets from the duplicate and the draft. The duplicate appears
to be in Sarah Franklin's hand, but the signature and the postscripts are in
BF's. The second and third paragraphs of postscript appear only in the duplicate.
6. For the ship which carried BF's letter of Dec. 2, 1762, to Jackson and for
much of the material in this paragraph, see above, pp. 161–2.

journ'd before I arriv'd. They omitted the Nomination of an Agent, usual at the first Meeting, that they might, as the Speaker tells me, have my Advice in the Choice. They meet again in January, after which I shall write to you farther.

I would give you some Account of Madeira, where we stopt three Days, but that I suspect you know it better than I do. I shall only mention that it produces not only the Fruits of the hot Countries, as Oranges, Lemons, Plantains, Bananas, &c. but those of the cold also, as Apples, Pears and Peaches in great Perfection. The Mountains are excessively high, and rise suddenly from the Town, which affords the Inhabitants a singular Conveniency, that of getting soon out of its Heat after they have done their Business, and of ascending to what Climate or Degree of Coolness they are pleased to chuse, the Sides of the Mountains being fill'd with their Country Boxes at different Heights. They pretend to have ninety Thousand Souls on the Island, but I did not hear of any actual Numeration, and I suppose that the Account is exaggerated. They raise Wheat enough for their Consumption one Third Part of the Year; and I was told, that the Husbandry of Corn increases, and that of the Vine diminishes among them, from the Opinion of greater, more certain and more speedy Profit.

My Friend Mr. Hughes has given me the enclos'd Memorandum.[7] I apprehend the Barker mention'd was one Dr. Barker now deceas'd, a Man of Character for universal Knowledge, and a most agreable Companion. I heard when in London that he us'd to talk of Lands he had in America. By Enquiry of Mr. Barclay,[8] who purchas'd Byerly's Part for Mr. Allen, I understood that Barker's Heir is an Ensign in the East India Service. I should be glad if you could find Means to make this Purchase for Mr. Hughes.

My best Respects to your good Fa[ther and to your] Sisters and Brother Bridges. I hope [to have fre]quently the Pleasure of hearing that [you are] all well. Please to present my res[pectful Com]pliments also to the Speaker, and all the [good Brothers] of

---

7. See above, pp. 156–8, for John Hughes's proposal to buy lands in western N.J. from the heirs of "One Barker of London," and for identification of the grandson and heir.

8. Either David Barclay or his son of the same name (above, IX, 190–1 n), London merchants and bankers, who acted as business agents for William Allen.

that truly estimable Family;[9] al[so to Mr.] Blackbourn and Mr. Cooper[1] when you [see them.] You procur'd me such a numerous [Acquaintance] it would be endless to name them [particularly,] but I shall always retain a grateful [Sense of] your Friendship and their Civilities. With the greatest Esteem, I [am,] Dear Sir Your oblig'd and [most] obedient humble Servant   B FRANKLIN

P.S. Suffer me to remind you of the useful and necessary Piece you proposed to write, and to beg you would not defer it.[2]
I forwarded your Letters to Connecticut and Boston.

[The Memorandum[3] mention'd in the above Letter was concerning a Tract of Land in the Jerseys formerly belonging jointly to two Persons, Barker and Byerly, both living in England. Byerly's Part was purchas'd for Mr. Allen: Barker's remain'd unsold, and Mr. Hughes would purchase it of his Heirs if they can be found. In the Memorandum he nam'd a Sum he was willing to give for it, and another to you for your Trouble in purchasing, but he is out of town, and I have forgot those Sums, and have no Copy of the memorandum.

9. BF was probably sending greetings to the current speaker of the House of Commons, Sir John Cust (above, p. 32 n), and his brothers Peregrine (1723–1785) and Francis (1722–1791), both members of Parliament and Peregrine deputy chairman of the East India Co. The former speaker, Arthur Onslow (1691–1768), who retired from the chair in 1761, had only one brother, Richard, who had died in 1760. *DNB;* Namier and Brooke, *House of Commons,* II, 289–93; III, 226, 230.

1. "Mr. Blackbourn" may have been Francis Blackburne (1705–1787), a liberal clergyman, suspected of being a Unitarian, whose most important work, *The Confessional* (first published in 1766, though written several years earlier), attacked the requirement that clergymen of the Church of England subscribe to the Thirty-Nine Articles. *DNB;* Caroline Robbins, *The Eighteenth-Century Commonwealthman* (Cambridge, Mass., 1959), pp. 324–8. "Mr. Cooper" was probably Grey Cooper; see below, p. 185 n.

2. Jackson's "Piece" has not been identified. On April 4, 1763, he informed BF that his negotiations for a seat in Parliament had taken up most of his time and he had only completed a "Skeleton" of his work, but on Dec. 27, 1763, he reported that he had begun to print. On seeing Thomas Pownall's anonymous *The Administration of the Colonies* (1764), BF guessed that it might have been Jackson's piece.

3. This and the next paragraph are printed from the duplicate; they were not needed in the original ALS since BF had sent Hughes's memorandum with it.

164

[P.S. Since the above I have seen Mr. Hughes. The Sum he would give for the Land is £2000 Sterling. What he offer'd for your Trouble was 60 Guineas. Mr. H. thinks some others are now endeavouring to purchase, so requests you would make Enquiry as soon as possible.]

Addressed: To / Richard Jackson Esqr / Counsellor at Law / Temple / London / Per the Carolina / Capt. Friend

Endorsed: Philad. [?] Decr. 6 1762 Franklin Esqr[4]

To Peter Collinson

ALS: Pierpont Morgan Library

Dear Friend,   Philada. Dec. 7. 1762

I arrived here the first of last Month, and had the great Happiness, after so long Absence, to find my little Family well, and my Friends as cordial and more numerous than ever.

Mr. Bartram I suppose writes to you concerning the great Bones at the Ohio.[5] I have delivered to him and to the Library Company what you sent by me.[6]

4. Jackson's endorsement of the duplicate is almost identical.

5. On June 11 and July 25, 1762, Collinson wrote John Bartram that two Indian traders, George Croghan (above, V, 64 n) and Joseph Greenwood (above, IV, 318 n), had supplied him with a description of the bones and skeleton of the "Great Buffalo" which they found at a licking place near the Ohio River. They had also passed along some information about the "skeletons of six monstrous animals" which had turned up in the same vicinity. In response to a plea that he inquire about these "wonderful" bones, Bartram informed Collinson on Dec. 3, 1762, that he had already written him twice about them (neither letter has been found) and added that it was "a great pity, and shame to the learned curiosos, that have great estates, that they don't send some person that will take pains to measure every bone exactly, before they are broken and carried away, which they will soon be, by ignorant, careless people, for gain." William Darlington, ed., *Memorials of John Bartram and Humphrey Marshall* (Phila., 1849), pp. 238, 239, 243. See also George G. Simpson, "The Beginnings of Vertebrate Paleontology in North America," APS *Proc.*, LXXXVI (1942–43), 139–41.

6. BF apparently delivered volumes XXXV and XXXVI of *An Universal History, from the Earliest Account of Time to the Present* and "31 plate Inserts" to the Lib. Co.; see above, p. 152. It is not clear what he brought Bartram, although in his letter to Collinson of Dec. 3, 1762, Bartram acknowledged the receipt of "books and prints," among which appear to have been Benjamin Stillingfleet's *Miscellaneous Tracts relating to Natural History* (2d edit,

There is great Complaint here of the last Summer's Drought.[7] It has occasion'd a great Scarcity of Hay, and if the Winter proves hard the Creatures must greatly suffer. Apples too have generally fail'd this Year.

Accept my sincerest Thanks for all your Kindness to me and my Son while in England, and my best Wishes of Long Life Health and Happiness to you and yours.

With the greatest Esteem and Attachment I am, Dear Friend, Yours most affectionately   B FRANKLIN

Mr Collinson

Addressed: To / Peter Collinson, Esq / Gracechurch street / London / Per the Carolina / Capt. Friend

To William Strahan   ALS: Pierpont Morgan Library

Dear Friend,   Philada. Dec. 7. 1762

I wrote you some time since[8] to acquaint you with my Arrival, and the kind Reception I met with from my old and many new Friends, notwithstanding Dr. Smith's false Reports in London of my Interest, as declining here. I could not wish for a more hearty Welcome, and I never experienc'd greater Cordiality.

We had a long Passage, near ten Weeks from Portsmouth to this Place, but it was a pleasant one;[9] for we had ten Sail in Company and a Man of War to protect us.[1] It was the Scarborough, Capt. Stott, who took the greatest Care of his little Convoy that can be imagined, and brought us all safely to our several Ports. I wish

London, 1762), which included the author's *Calendar of Flora* and Johann Friedrich Gronovius' *Flora Virginica* (2d edit., Leyden, 1762).

7. On Aug. 15, 1762, Bartram wrote Collinson that the "extreme hot, dry weather still continueth, although we have once in two or three weeks a shower that wets the ground two or three inches deep; but yet the ground is one foot deep as dry as dust." Darlington, *Memorials*, p. 240.

8. Probably a reference to his short letter of December 2 (above, pp. 161–2), though there may have been an earlier and longer one, not found.

9. This paragraph, slightly modified and shortened, was printed in *London Chron.*, March 19–22, 1763, with the caption: "Extract of a Letter from Philadelphia, Dec. 7."

1. The next two sentences are written in the margin with a symbol at "Man of War" to show that BF intended them to be inserted here.

you would mention this to his Honour in your Paper. We had pleasant Weather and fair Winds, and frequently visited and dined from Ship to Ship; we call'd too at the delightful Island of Madeira, by way of half-way House, where we replenish'd our Stores, and took in many Refreshments. It was the time of their Vintage, and we hung the Cieling of the Cabin with Bunches of fine Grapes, which serv'd as a Disert at Dinner for some Weeks afterwards. The Reason of our being so long at Sea, was, that sailing with a Convoy, we could none of us go faster than the slowest, being oblig'd every day to shorten Sail or lay by till they came up; this was the only Inconvenience of our having Company, which was abundantly made up to us by the Sense of greater Safety, the mutual good Offices daily exchanged, and the other Pleasures of Society.

I have no Line from you yet, but I hope there is a Letter on its way to me.[2]

My Son is not arrived, and I begin to think he will spend the Winter with you.[3] Mr. Hall I suppose writes by this Ship.[4] I mention'd what you desir'd in your Letter to me at Portsmouth;[5] he informs me he has made some Remittances since I left England, and shall as fast as possible clear the Account. He blames himself for ordering so large a Cargo at once, and will keep more within Bounds hereafter.

Mr. Hall sends you I believe, for Sale, some Poetic Pieces of our young Geniuses;[6] it would encourage them greatly if their Per-

2. On March 28, 1763 (below, p. 235), BF acknowledged letters from Strahan dated October 20 and November 1, both brought by WF.

3. WF arrived at Philadelphia with his bride on Feb. 19, 1763; see above, p. 152 n.

4. On May 10, 1763, Strahan acknowledged receipt of a letter from Hall, Dec. 8, 1762, by the *Carolina*, Capt. Friend. APS.

5. Strahan's letter of Aug. 20, 1762, to BF has not been found, but its contents may be surmised from one to Hall of October 20. A bill of exchange for £500 Hall had sent Strahan had been temporarily refused by the payer, but had since been accepted for payment in November. Meanwhile, Strahan had found himself straitened "prodigiously" by heavy expenses including the marriage of a daughter. Nevertheless, he had procured and sent virtually everything Hall had ordered, the total charge amounting to over £1000. APS. Apparently Strahan had asked that BF tell Hall to go a little more lightly on his orders.

6. Hall sent Strahan 100 copies of *The Court of Fancy* by Thomas Godfrey (1736–1763), a poem described in *Pa. Gaz.*, Aug. 12, 1762 (the day of its publication) as written on "a Subject which none but an elevated and daring

formances could obtain any favourable Reception in England; I wish therefore you would take the proper Steps to get them recommended to the Notice of the Publick as far at least as you may find they deserve. I know that no one can do this better than your self.

You have doubtless long since done Rejoicing on the Conquest of the Havana.[7] It is indeed a Conquest of great Importance; but it has cost us dear, extreamly dear, when we consider the Havock made in our little brave Army by Sickness. I hope it will, in the Making of Peace, procure us some Advantages in Commerce or Possession that may in time countervail the heavy Loss we have sustained in that Enterprize.[8]

I must joyn with David in petitioning that you would write us all the Politicks; you have an Opportunity of hearing them all, and no one that is not quite in the Secret of Affairs can judge better of them. I hope the crazy Heads that have been so long raving about Scotchmen and Scotland, are by this time either broke or mended.[9]

Genius durst Attempt, with any Degree of Success." In considering the poem *The Monthly Review*, XXIX (1763), 226–7, agreed that Godfrey had genius but lamented that "he had not education to improve it." At various times during 1762 *Pa. Gaʒ.* printed or announced the publication of poems by Nathaniel Evans (1742–1767) and Francis Hopkinson (1737–1791); e.g., Evans' "Rural Ode," "Ode to a Friend," "Hymn to May," and "An Ode on the Late Glorious Successes of His Majesty's Arms," published in *Gent. Mag.*, XXXIII (1763), 251–2, and Hopkinson's "Science," and Hall may have sent a selection to Strahan as well. *Pa. Gaʒ.*, Feb. 11, March 11, 18, 25, June 3, Oct. 28, Nov. 18, 1762. Some of these poems were probably among the "Blossoms of American Verse" which BF sent to Caleb Whitefoord on Dec. 9, 1762. See below, p. 173.

7. A British expeditionary force, commanded by the Earl of Albemarle as lieutenant general, and with Rear Admiral Sir George Pocock in charge of the naval squadron, besieged Havana for about two months in the summer of 1762 and effected its surrender on August 13. Disease and hot weather, to which most of the British troops were not acclimated, caused far greater casualties than did enemy action. Gipson, *British Empire*, VIII, 262–8.

8. At the end of the war the British exchanged Havana for Florida.

9. James A. Cochrane remarks on Strahan's "ability to be present at all major debates [in Parliament] long before he became King's Printer with an ex officio right of attendance." *Dr. Johnson's Printer The Life of William Strahan* (Cambridge, Mass., 1964), p. 171. In this passage BF may have been referring to some particular individual, possibly John Wilkes, or to the hostility toward Scots prevalent at that time in all levels of English society. BF's sympathy for the Scots, indicated here, contrasts markedly with the

My dear Love to Mrs. Strahan, and bid her be well for all our sakes. Remember me affectionately to Rachey and my little Wife, and to your promising Sons, my young Friends Billy, George and Andrew.[1] God bless you and let me find you well and happy when I come again to England; happy England! My Respects to Mr. Johnson; I hope he has got the Armonica in order before this time, and that Rachey plays daily with more and more Boldness and Grace, to the absolute charming of all her Acquaintance.

In two Years at farthest I hope to settle all my Affairs in such a Manner, as that I *may* then conveniently remove to England, provided we can persuade the good Woman to cross the Seas.[2] That will be the great Difficulty: but you can help me a little in removing it.

Present my Compliments to all enquiring Friends, and believe me ever, My dear Friend, Yours most affectionately B FRANKLIN

Addressed: To / Mr Strahan / Printer / Newstreet, Shoe Lane / London / per Capt. Friend

---

feelings about Scottish army officers expressed in his letter to *London Chron.*, May 9, 1759; above, VIII, 352–5. In recent years BF had found some of his warmest British friends among the Scots, including Sir Alexander Dick, Lord Kames, David Hume, Dr. John Pringle, and Strahan himself.

1. Rachel Strahan (1742–1765) married Andrew Johnston, an apothecary in Bread Street, London, on March 9, 1761. My "little Wife" was Strahan's younger daughter, Margaret Penelope; see above, p. 137 n. Strahan's eldest son, William (1740–1781), entered the printing business with his father and was made a partner in 1767, but in 1771 he went into business for himself. George Strahan (1744–1824) was apprenticed to a bookseller but was averse to the business and matriculated at Oxford, Nov. 13, 1764, and graduated B.A., 1768; M.A., 1771; B.D. and D.D., 1807. In 1773 he was presented to the vicarage of Islington and later held other livings in Essex and Kent. George was befriended by Samuel Johnson, who wrote his will in Islington vicarage and also entrusted private papers to him. These were published in 1785 as *Prayers and Meditations*. Andrew Strahan (1750–1831) went into the family business and upon his father's death inherited his "private printing business as well as the share of the King's printer's patent, and proved to be as active and successful as his father had been." Between 1796 and 1820 he sat in Parlament for various constituencies. He was succeeded in the business in 1819 by his nephews, Robert and Andrew Spottiswoode, the sons of his sister Margaret Penelope and John Spottiswoode. For the Strahan family see *DNB* and James A. Cochrane, *Dr. Johnson's Printer*.

2. BF returned to England in 1764 to assist Richard Jackson in an effort to secure royal government for Pa. DF did not accompany him.

To John Fothergill

Draft: American Philosophical Society

On Nov. 8, 1762, William Shippen (above, IX, 219 n), who had recently arrived in Philadelphia from London, informed the treasurer and managers of the Pennsylvania Hospital that Dr. John Fothergill had sent by the *Carolina* (the ship which had brought Franklin home) a present of seven cases of materials for the study of anatomy. Three contained drawings by the Dutch medical artist Jan van Rymsdyck, described in the Hospital minutes as "Eighteen different curious Views of various parts of the Human Body in Crayons framed and glaized"; three other cases contained "Anatomical Castings"; the seventh contained a skeleton and a foetus. In advising James Pemberton of his intention to make the gift in a letter of April 7, 1762, Fothergill expressed the hope that the materials might be used by Shippen and John Morgan (above, IX, 374 n) as a basis for a "Course of Anatomical Lectures" and that they might be stored in "some Low Apartment of the Hospital" and be shown to the public for a fee. With the Hospital Managers' approval Shippen announced a series of lectures in *Pennsylvania Gazette*, Nov. 11, 1762, which were given the following winter. Shippen also became curator of Fothergill's collection, housed in the Hospital and shown to the public for a dollar.[3]

Dear Doctor,   Philada. Dec. 8. 1762

I arrived here the first of last Month, and had the Happiness after so long an Absence of finding my little Family well.

The Anatomical Drawings and Casts that you sent over, got safe and well to the Hospital, except the Breaking some of the Glasses, which the Managers have repair'd. I understand that no Letter from you came with them, which leaves the Managers at some Loss in Writing to you concerning them.

I congratulate you on the Taking of the Havanah. 'Tis an Important Conquest, but the amazing Mortality among our brave Troops from Sickness, has made it a very dear one.

My best Respects to your good Sister,[4] and believe me ever, Dear Friend, Yours affectionately   B FRANKLIN

3. Betsy C. Corner, *William Shippen, Jr.* (Phila., 1951), pp. 98–100; Thomas Morton and Frank Woodbury, *The History of the Pennsylvania Hospital 1751–1895* (Phila., 1895), pp. 356–8.

4. Ann Fothergill (d. 1802) moved into her brother's house in 1754 and served as his housekeeper and hostess. R. Hingston Fox, *Dr. John Fothergill and His Friends* (London, 1919), pp. 20–1.

To Edward Nairne[5]   Draft: American Philosophical Society

Mr. Nairne,   Philada. Dec. 8. 1762
I forget whether I paid you for the Magnet. Let me know.
If you can make a Thermometer agreable to the enclos'd Direc-
tions, please send it me.[6] Mrs. Stevenson where I lodg'd will pay
you.
My Respects to Mr. Canton[7] when you see him. I am &c.

To Caleb Whitefoord[8]

ALS: British Museum; draft: American Philosophical Society

Dear Sir,   Philada. Dec. 9. 1762[9]
I thank you for your kind Congratulations on my Son's Promotion and Marriage. If he makes a good Governor and a good

---

5. Edward Nairne (1726–1806), F.R.S., 1776, was an English electrician
and instrument maker. In 1774 he published a paper showing the superiority
of pointed lightning rods over rounded ones, thus supporting BF in his
controversy with Benjamin Wilson. BF bought various things from Nairne
during his first mission and on Sept. 6, 1765, during his second mission purchased an "Achromatic prospective Glass with two Eye Glasses in one
Slider that Magnifies Different," a set of "6 Inch Magnetts in Mahogany Case,"
and an "Electrical Machine with 6 Inch Globe in a plain box." *DNB;* "Account
of Expences," pp. 5, 41; *PMHB*, LV (1931), 104, 121; Nairne to BF, Sept. 6,
1765. APS.
   6. These directions have not been found, but they may relate to an "Electrical Air-thermometer" which Ebenezer Kinnersley "contrived" and described
to BF in a letter of March 12, 1761; see above, IX, 286–9.
   7. John Canton, the English electrical experimenter; see above, IV, 390 n.
   8. Caleb Whitefoord (1734–1810), wine merchant, was born in Edinburgh
and educated at the university there. His father intended him for the ministry,
but he objected and instead he was placed in the countinghouse of a London
wine merchant to learn the business. Then, after spending two years in
France, he formed a partnership with Thomas Brown at 8 Craven Street,
next door to Mrs. Margaret Stevenson. He apparently returned from a long
business trip to Portugal in 1757, shortly before BF took up lodgings with Mrs.
Stevenson. The two men became good friends, though their close proximity
during the years of BF's English missions made extended correspondence
unnecessary. In 1782 Lord Shelburne took advantage of their intimacy, sending
Whitefoord to France to arrange with BF for Richard Oswald's peace negotia-
(Footnote 9 appears on next page)

Husband (as I hope he will, for I know he has good Principles and good Dispositions) those Events will both of them give me continual Pleasure.

The Taking of the Havanah, on which I congratulate you, is a Conquest of the greatest Importance,[1] and will doubtless contribute a due Share of Weight in procuring us reasonable Terms of Peace; if John Bull does not get drunk with Victory, double his Fists, and bid all the World kiss his A—e; till he provokes them to drub him again into his Senses.[2] It has been however the dearest Conquest by far that we have purchas'd this War, when we consider the terrible Havock made by Sickness in that brave Army of Veterans, now almost totally ruined!

I thank you for the humorous and sensible Print you sent me, which afforded me and several of my Friends great Pleasure.[3]

---

tions and then appointing him secretary of the commission. He had a reputation as a wit, and contributed numerous light essays, poems, and epigrams to the London press, many taking the form of political persiflage. Samuel Johnson and Horace Walpole thought well of his writings, and he enjoyed the close friendship of the Earl of Bute and David Garrick. *DNB;* W. A. S. Hewins, ed., *The Whitefoord Papers* (Oxford, 1898).

9. The draft is dated December 7. Sparks (*Works,* VII, 242–4), Bigelow (*Works,* III, 215–18), and Smyth (*Writings,* IV, 183–4) all printed from the draft and used the earlier date.

1. See above, p. 168 n.

2. In the draft the words from "if John Bull" to "Senses" are heavily canceled. So far as they can still be read, they do not seem to be materially different from what appears in the ALS. Sparks and Bigelow omitted the passage, Smyth did not.

3. Whitefoord may have sent BF one of the last notable prints by William Hogarth (1697–1764), called "The Times" (plate I), which was issued Sept. 7, 1762. In a highly complex scene it depicts William Pitt with a bellows trying to keep the world in flames, Bute with fire fighters trying to quench the fire, and Newcastle supplying copies of John Wilkes's paper, the *North Briton,* to serve as fuel. The print led to a violent quarrel in which Wilkes and the satirist Charles Churchill wrote scathing attacks on Hogarth, and the artist retaliated with devastating caricatures of the writers. On Oct. 25, 1764, Hogarth became seriously ill; he was said to have just received "an agreeable letter" from BF and finished the rough draft of a reply when he was taken with a violent seizure and died within two hours. Unfortunately, neither BF's letter nor Hogarth's draft reply has been found. *DNB;* [J. Nichols], *Biographical Anecdotes of William Hogarth; with a Catalogue of His Works* (2d edit., London, 1782), pp. 68–80, 84, 300–4; Robert R. Rea, *The English Press in Politics 1760–1774* (Lincoln, Neb., [1963]), p. 31 and facing p. 86.

The Piece from your own Pencil is acknowledg'd to bear a strong and striking Likeness; but it is otherwise such a Picture of your Friend as Dr. Smith would have drawn, *black and all black*.[4] I think you will hardly understand this Remark, but your Neighbour, good Mrs. Stevenson, can explain it.[5]

Painting has yet scarce made her Appearance among us; but her Sister Art, Poetry, has some Votaries. I send you a few Blossoms of American Verse, the Lispings of our young Muses; which I hope your Motherly Critics will treat with some Indulgence.[6]

I shall never touch the sweet Strings of the British Harp[7] without remembring my British Friends, and particularly the kind Giver of the Instrument, who has my best Wishes of Happiness—for himself,—and for his Wife and his Children, against it shall please God to send him any.[8] I am, Dear Sir, with the sincerest Esteem Your most obedient and most humble Servant   B Franklin

My Compliments to Count Brown.[9] Will is not yet arriv'd. Perhaps he winters once more in your Happy Island!

Mr. Whitefoord

4. Apparently Whitefoord, who was an amateur artist of sorts, had sent a pencil caricature or sketch of BF; it has not survived. Charles C. Sellers, *Benjamin Franklin in Portraiture* (New Haven and London, 1963), pp. 60–1, 408–9. William Smith, in England at the time, had been spreading reports of BF's declining popularity at home. "Black and all black" seems to have been a favorite expression of Whitefoord's. See Hewins, ed., *Whitefoord Papers,* p. 142 n.

5. Mrs. Stevenson advised BF never again to receive Smith as a friend. See below, p. 234.

6. See above, pp. 167–8 n.

7. "Lyre" in the draft. Nothing further is known about this instrument, which seems to have been a parting gift from Whitefoord. It may be mentioned, however, that after BF's return to England his ledger account book contains an entry (p. 28) dated May 21, 1765: "pd Hintz[?] for Stringing Harp £1 18s. 6d."

8. Whitefoord did not marry until 1800, when he was 66; thereafter he had four children.

9. Whitefoord's partner, Thomas Brown, appears to have been nicknamed "The Count." Hewins, ed., *Whitefoord Papers,* pp. 144, 152.

To Elias Boudinot, Junior[1]

MS not found: reprinted from extract in American Art Association Sale Catalogue, Dec. 2, 3, 1926, Item no. 428.

[December 11, 1762]

I thank you for your kind congratulations on my return to my family and country. It gives me great pleasure to hear that you are married and well-settled and your brother and sister also.[2] ...
I hope your good father's indisposition will be of no long continuance. ...

[Mr. Boudenot]   [B. FRANKLIN]

To Jared Ingersoll   ALS: New Haven Colony Historical Society

Dear Sir   Philada. Dec. 11. 1762

I thank you for your kind Congratulations.[3] It gives me Pleasure to hear from an old Friend, it will give me much more to see him. I hope therefore nothing will prevent the Journey you propose for next Summer, and the Favour you intend me of a Visit.[4] I believe

1. Elias Boudinot, Jr. (1740–1821), son of BF's former neighbor (above, VII, 275 n), was born in Philadelphia but moved to Princeton, N.J., in about 1753, where his father became postmaster. After studying law with his brother-in-law, Richard Stockton, he opened an office in Elizabethtown in 1760. He married his teacher's sister, Hannah Stockton, April 21, 1762. When the Revolutionary crisis developed he became a relatively conservative supporter of the American cause; Congress appointed him commissary-general of prisoners, 1777; he served as a member of Congress, 1777–84, president, 1782; and secretary of foreign affairs, 1783–84. He was director of the U. S. Mint, 1795–1805, and devoted the rest of his life to writing on religious subjects, including his final work, *A Star in the West* (1816), an attempt to prove the identity of the American Indians with the ten lost tribes of Israel. He was a trustee of the College of New Jersey for forty-nine years. *DAB;* George A. Boyd, *Elias Boudinot Patriot and Statesman 1740-1821* (Princeton, 1952).

2. John Boudinot (b. 1734), a physician, married Catherine Van Norden, but the date is not known. The elder sister Annis (1736–1801) had married Richard Stockton about 1755; and a younger one, Mary (1742–1801), married Abner Hetfield, but again the date has not been found.

3. Not found.

4. Ingersoll's journey southward did not materialize. He became deeply involved in a struggle with Gov. Benning Wentworth of New Hampshire.

I must make a Journey early in the Spring, to Virginia, but purpose being back again before the hot Weather.⁵ You will be kind enough to let me know beforehand what time you expect to be here, that I may not be out of the way; for that would mortify me exceedingly.

I should be glad to know what it is that distinguishes Connecticut Religion from common Religion: Communicate, if you please, some of those particulars that you think will amuse me as a Virtuoso. When I travelled in Flanders I thought of your excessively strict Observation of Sunday; and that a Man could hardly travel on that day among you upon his lawful Occasions, without Hazard of Punishment;⁶ while where I was, every on[e] travell'd, if he pleas'd, or diverted himself any other way; and in the Afternoon both high and low went to the Play or the Opera, where there was plenty of Singing, Fiddling and Dancing. I look'd round for God's Judgments but saw no Signs of them. The Cities were well built and full of Inhabitants, the Markets fill'd with Plenty, the People well favour'd and well clothed; the Fields well till'd; the Cattle fat and strong; the Fences, Houses and Windows all in Repair; and *no Old Tenor*⁷ anywhere in the Country; which would almost make

---

who was also surveyor general of the woods in America, over a contract Ingersoll had negotiated to supply white pine masts for the Royal Navy, after floating them down the Connecticut River. Lawrence H. Gipson, *Jared Ingersoll* (New Haven, 1920), pp. 79–110.

5. BF set out for Va. about the middle of April 1763 and was back in Philadelphia by May 20.

6. A Conn. law of 1688, often reinforced and most recently in 1751, forbade the profanation of "the Sabboth by unnecessary travell or playeing thereon in the time of publique worshipe, or before or after," under penalty of a 5-shilling fine or sitting in the stocks for one hour. *Public Records of the Colony of Connecticut*, II, 88; X, 45–6. President Washington found himself handicapped by this law during his tour of 1789. John C. Fitzpatrick, ed., *The Diaries of George Washington 1748–1799* (Boston and N.Y., 1924), IV, 50. On BF's travels in Flanders in August–September 1761, see above, IX, 364–5.

7. Between 1710 and 1740 Conn. issued large quantities of bills of credit which underwent steady depreciation in terms of silver. In an effort to reform the currency, the General Assembly passed an act in May 1740 providing for a new issue under somewhat different terms. While these bills also depreciated, they did not do so as rapidly as those of the "old tenor" emissions. Accounts continued to be kept in "old tenor" values, but bills of the "new tenor" came in time to be worth three and a half times as much in business transactions. The situation was extremely complicated, and a

one suspect, that the Deity is not so angry at that Offence as a New England Justice.

I left our Friend Mr. Jackson well.[8] And I had the great Happiness of finding my little Family well when I came home; and my Friends as cordial and more numerous than ever. May every Prosperity attend you and yours. I am Dear Friend, Yours affectionately   B Franklin

Endorsed: Benj: Franklin Esqr, Letter Decembr. 11 1762.

To James Bowdoin

als: The Royal Archives, Windsor Castle;[9] transcript: Massachusetts Historical Society

Dear Sir,   Philada. Dec. 15. 1762

I have read with great Pleasure the College Poems you were so kind as to send me:[1] I think, and I hope it is not merely my

---

traveler in Conn. needed to be on his guard when dealing with the local currency. Henry Bronson, "A Historical Account of Connecticut Currency, Continental Money, and the Finances of the Revolution," New Haven Col. Hist. Soc. *Papers,* 1 (1865), esp. 29–70.

8. During Ingersoll's agency in England he and Richard Jackson had become warm friends.

9. We have to acknowledge the gracious permission of Her Majesty Queen Elizabeth II to make use of material from the Royal Archives, Windsor Castle.

1. The volume Harvard College issued commemorating the death of George II and the accession of George III: *Pietas et Gratulatio Collegii Cantabrigiensis Apud Novanglos* (Boston, 1761). In addition to a prose preface addressed to the King, it contained 31 poems: 3 in Greek, 16 in Latin, and 12 in English; while all were anonymous, attributions of some have been made to Gov. Francis Bernard, Rev. Samuel Cooper, John Winthrop, and James Bowdoin himself. Copies were sent to England and Jasper Mauduit, who with Richard Jackson personally presented one to the King, reported that the verses were much approved. (He did not say what his Majesty thought of them.) *The Monthly Review,* xxix (1763), 22–26, considered that many of the poems were indifferent performances, "but these, though they cannot so well be excused when they come from ancient and established Seats of Learning, may at least be connived at here; and what we could not endure from an illustrious University, we can easily pardon in an infant Seminary." *The Critical Review,* xvi (1763), 289–91, however, supported bf's "American Vanity" by concluding that "the verses from Harvard College seem already to bid fair for a rivalship with the productions of Cam and Isis." A later

176

American Vanity that makes me think, some of them exceed in Beauty and Elegance those produced by the Mother Universities of Oxford and Cambridge, on the same Occasion. In return, please to accept some Poetical Blossoms of our young Seminary.[2]

I rejoice at this Renewal of our Correspondence. If any thing new in the Philosophical Way has occur'd among you in my long Absence, be so good as to communicate it to Dear Sir, Your most obedient humble Servant   B FRANKLIN

J. Bowdoin Esqr.

Endorsed: Doct. Benja. Franklin's Letter Decr. 15. 1762 [*In another hand:*] acknowledgd the Rect. of the College Poems. wth. his compliments,

[*At the foot of the inside page:*] Boston. 19 Octr. 1860. Presented to H.R.H. The Prince of Wales with the best respects of Robt. C. Winthrop.[3]

To Joshua Babcock[4]   ALS: Yale University Library

Dear Sir,   Philada. Dec. 16. 1762.

I thank you most cordially for your kind Congratulations on my Arrival, which I have the more Pleasure in, as among my other

---

American critic was less charitable; Moses Coit Tyler called the volume: "This magnificent effusion of provincial gush and king-worship . . . this premeditated and ostentatious torrent of adulatory drivel." *History of American Literature* (London, 1879), II, 58–63. See also Justin Winsor, "Pietas et Gratulatio. An Inquiry into the Authorship of the Several Pieces," Harvard Univ. Lib., *Bulletin*, I (1879), 305–8; *Sibley's Harvard Graduates* under Cooper (1743) and Bowdoin (1745); the long note in Evans 8877; and 6 Mass. Hist. Soc. *Coll.*, IX, 15, 17.

2. See above, p. 167–8 n.

3. During his North American tour in 1860 the Prince of Wales (later Edward VII) visited Boston, October 17–19. Robert C. Winthrop, president of the Massachusetts Historical Society, was a former speaker of the U.S. House of Representatives and later a senator. The ALS presented to the Prince was at the time among the Bowdoin Papers, then owned by Winthrop but now by Mass. Hist. Soc. For the presentation see 1 Mass. Hist. Soc. *Proc.*, V (1860–62), 97–8.

4. On Joshua Babcock (1707–1783) of Westerly, R.I., physician, merchant, and public official, see above, VI, 174 n. BF often enjoyed his hospitality when passing through Westerly on journeys to or from Boston.

Friends, I find you and yours alive and well: I rejoice with you likewise in the safe Return of your two valuable Sons, to whom, on Account of their own Merit as well as the Obligations I am under to you, I wish it had been in my Power to have been any way serviceable.[5] Be so good as to assure them of my best Respects and Wishes, which also attend Mrs. Babcock and the other Branches of your good Family. I hope to have the Pleasure next Summer of seeing you all once more, in a Journey I purpose to Boston. I shall ever retain a grateful Remembrance of your Hospitality, and of the pleasing Hours I have pass'd in your Conversation and with your most agreable Family; and I long for a Repetition of that delightful Entertainment. Please to remember me affectionately to the good Samaritans;[6] and do me the Justice to believe me ever, with the sincerest Esteem and Respect, Dear Sir, Your most obliged and most obedient humble Servant

B FRANKLIN

Honble Joshua Babcock Esqr

Endorsed: Ben Franklin Esq Decr. 16. 1762 recd. 6 Jany 1763

To Ezra Stiles

ALS: Yale University Library

Dear Sir, Philada. Decr. 19. 1762

This Line is just to salute you, and acquaint you with my Return to America, Thanks to God, well and hearty. I hope you are so. With this you will receive a Thermometer which craves your Acceptance.[7] With the greatest Esteem, I am, Dear Sir, Your most obedient and most humble Servant B FRANKLIN

Revd Mr. Stiles

5. Two of Babcock's sons had called upon BF in London the year before; see above, IX, 397 n.

6. Probably Samuel and Anna Ward of Westerly and Rev. Nathaniel Eeles of Stonington, Conn., or "the charitable Misses Stanton," relatives of Mrs. Babcock, to whom he sent greetings through Catharine Ray in 1757. See above, VII, 143.

7. BF had promised to send Stiles a thermometer, May 23, 1757; above, VII, 217. On Feb. 20, 1765, Stiles asked BF to forward to a scientist in St. Petersburg a series of "Thermometrical Observations" at Newport in 1764, "which your beneficence has enabled me to make." APS. From the time he received this thermometer until his death in 1795 Stiles kept faithful records

To John Winthrop

MS not found; reprinted from American Autograph Shop, *American Clipper* (Merion Station, Pa.), December 1935, p. 171.[8]

Sir,   Philad. Dec. 23, 1762.

Mr. Short's Remarks were only in a Letter of his to me. I now send you the Original.[9] You will observe that the Perallax [Parallax] mentioned in this, differs from that I sent you; But this was in the Beginning of February, the other he gave me in August; and I suppose had been corrected by Accounts received in the mean time from more Observers.[1] I believe the Astronomers are still desirous that Provision should be made to observe the next Transit.

I thank you for your kind Congratulations; and for the College Poems which I hope my Son will have received before his Leaving of London. I send you in return some Poetical Blossoms of our young Seminary.[2]

Inclos'd is another Letter I receiv'd from a Friend while at Portsmouth, containing an Account of what was transacted at a late Board of Longitude.[3] When you have read it, please to return it.

With great Esteem, I am, Sir, Your most obedient humble Servant,   B. FRANKLIN

---

of the temperature, direction of the wind, and general condition of the weather, entering his observations several times a day. Edmund S. Morgan, *The Gentle Puritan A Life of Ezra Stiles, 1727–1795* (New Haven and London, 1962), pp. 134–6.

8. The description of this letter in *American Clipper* indicates that Winthrop used the blank pages of the ALS for the drafts of his reply to BF and a letter to James Short. Neither of those letters has been found in any form.

9. On James Short, F.R.S., instrument maker, see *DNB* and above, p. 137 n. His letter has not been found.

1. A brief report by Short on his observation of the transit of Venus, June 6, 1761, at Savile House, London, was read before the Royal Society, June 11, 1761. His longer paper, comparing observations made at many different points in Europe and at the Cape of Good Hope and determining the parallax of the sun from them, was read to the Society, Dec. 9, 1762. *Phil. Trans.*, LII (1761–62), 178–81, 611–28. The information he had given BF in August 1762, before BF's sailing, probably summarized the findings presented in the second of these papers.

2. On the Harvard "College Poems" and the Philadelphia "Poetical Blossoms," see above, pp. 176 n, and 167–8 n, respectively.

3. BF had been a member of the Council of the Royal Society which had

To Hughes and Co.: Directions for Making a Musical Machine

AD: The Assay Office, Birmingham, England

In an advertisement for the armonica[4] in the *London Chronicle,* June 17–19, 1762, addressed "To the Nobility, Gentry, &c., "Charles James of Purpool Lane, near Gray's Inn, called himself "The Maker [who] has been employed by the Gentleman who is the real Inventor, in the First ever made in England, and continues to be honoured with his Approbation." In 1770 Franklin confirmed this claim to the extent of saying that James was "the only Workman here acquainted with such Matters." He was, however, "a very negligent, dilatory Man," and was now unable to supply one of Franklin's friends because "at length he died suddenly."[5]

It is evident, however, that at some period Franklin employed another glassblower. Writing to Polly Stevenson, March 25, 1763, he expressed his regret that James had been "dilatory" in making an armonica for another person and then commented: "I was unlucky in both the Workmen that I permitted to undertake making those Instruments. The first was fanciful, and never could work to the purpose, because he was ever conceiving some new Improvement that answer'd no End: the other [James], I doubt, is absolutely idle. I have recommended a Number to him from hence, but must stop my hand."[6] The "fanciful" workman was probably the "Mr. Barnes" of the firm of Hughes and Co. at the "Cockpit Glasshouse" to which the following directions were addressed. The document is undated, but is placed here at the end of 1762 because that was the year in which Franklin first described his musical invention, and it seems helpful to print the two papers in the same volume.[7]

---

advised the Board of Longitude, July 3, 1761, on the equipment to be taken on the voyage to Jamaica to test John Harrison's chronometer; see above, VII, 208–10. At a session on Aug. 17, 1762, the Board of Longitude voted Harrison and his son £1500 for the successful test (*Gent. Mag.*, XXXII, 333); the first half of the grand prize offered by Parliament was not voted until 1764, and Harrison received the second half only in 1774. The friend from whom BF received news of the August 17 meeting might have been James Ferguson (above, VIII, 216 n), or one of BF's Royal Society friends such as John Ellicott (1706?–1772), clockmaker and general scientist.

4. See above, pp. 116–30.

5. To Michael Hillegas, March 17, 1770, *The Historical Magazine, and Notes and Queries,* III (1859), 213.

6. Below, p. 235.

7. In the journal account book BF kept during his second mission to Great Britain is an entry dated Dec. 23, 1765, which may relate to the blowing of

[1762]

Messrs. Hughes and Co. at the Cockpit Glasshouse, opposite St. Paul's.

A Set of musical Glasses, such as Mr. Franklin had, of the following Dimensions

6 of 2½ Inches diam.
6 of 3
6 of 3½
6 of 4
6 of 4½
6 of 5
6 of 5½   The Sides to be as near as may be upright.
6 of 6   The Necks of all an Inch deep; and in the
6 of 6½   smallest ¾ of an Inch Diameter; in the
6 of 7   largest an Inch and half Diameter; the
6 of 7½   others in Proportion.
6 of 8.

The Form of the Glasses

    The upright of the Sides to be in the smallest ¾ of an Inch, adding a ¼ of an Inch to every larger Size, so that the upright of the largest will be 3½ Inches.

    Mr. Barnes is desired to take Notice, that the Glasses are not to be made hollowing up, like those Mr. Franklin had last, but like those he had first with Bottoms nearly even.

    To fix them I us'd a Frame like the Figure in the Margin with an upright Iron Rod, on which was a Screw from End to End; The Rod turn'd on it's Point.

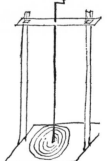

    The Bottom Board had a Number of concentric Circles.

    I had a Number of Brass female Screws, about an Inch long.

    One of these was to be cemented in the Neck of each Glass.

    On the Board I plac'd a round bit of Card a little bigger than the Neck of the Glass, then the female Screw upon that, then turn'd

glasses for an armonica by the Cockpit Glasshouse: "Profit and Loss my draft in favour of Barnes & Co. Glasses per Bill £20 0s."

the Glass down with its Edge upon the Circles, then put the Screw Rod thro' the Neck of the Glass and enter'd the female Screw, and drew it up with the Card till it came into the Neck of the Glass, the Card coming close to stop the Neck; then having center'd the Glass, I pour'd in the Cement. When cold, remov'd that Glass; and plac'd another. The Neck of the Glass should be a little warm'd, and the Cement not too hot.

When the Glasses were all furnish'd with Screws in their Necks; I put them on the Rod, a thin Piece of Cork between their Necks to screw them hard upon, and prevent Jarring and make each Screw water-tight.[8]

Endorsed: Mr. Franklins directions for making a Musical Machine Mr Franklins directions for Glasses Musical

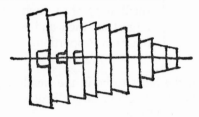

Notes on Reading an Account of Travel in China

AD: American Philosophical Society

These notes in Franklin's hand appear to have been memoranda jotted down during the reading of some unidentified account of travel in the Far East. The listing of the eclipses suggests that the date was not earlier than 1762, though Franklin's reading might well have taken place considerably later.

[1762?]

Painted Candles, of what are they made?
Vinegar of Liche, what is it?[9]
A Silversmith and his Apprentice earn 6s. 3d. in 22 Days. Their
    Provisions allow'd cost 3d. per Day.
Physicians Pay, for a Visit of 4 Miles, in a Chair receives One

8. In addition to the sketches on these pages, the MS contains one which is too indistinct to reproduce here or even to permit determination of its purpose.

9. Possibly a vinegar made from the fruit of the litchi *(Nephelium litchi)*, a tree of the soapberry family native to China and cultivated elsewhere in eastern and southern Asia and nearby islands.

Mace 4 Candrins. Note the 4 Candrins is for Chair hire. The
Mace is 7½d. Sterling 10 Candrins is a Mace
Oct. 17. 1762 between 5 and 6 PM. an Eclipse of the Sun[1]
Nov. 12. 1761 A total Eclipse of the Moon near Canton, between
6 and 10 aClock PM
Nov 2. 1762 An Eclipse of the Moon at 4 in the Morning
Fees paid on a Gift from the King of £200 amounted to £23 5s. 6d.

To Peter Franklin

MS not found; reprinted from extract in Benjamin Franklin, *Experiments
and Observations on Electricity* (London, 1769), pp. 441–3.[2]

[1762?–1764][3]

You may acquaint the gentleman that desired you to enquire my
opinion of the best method of securing a powder magazine from
lightning,[4] that I think they cannot do better than to erect a mast
not far from it, which may reach 15 or 20 feet above the top of it,
with a thick iron rod in one piece fastened to it, pointed at the
highest end, and reaching down through the earth till it comes to

1. The three eclipses noted here are also listed in *Poor Richard* for 1761
or 1762, with Philadelphia times very roughly corresponding to those given
here after allowing for the difference in longitude from Canton. There is a
short account of the eclipse of the moon at Canton, Nov. 12, 1761, in *Phil.
Trans.*, LXIV (1774), 43.

2. Printed as Letter XLVII in *Exper. and Obser.*, 1769 edit., and also in the
edition of 1774, pp. 451–3.

3. The date of this letter is uncertain, but because it is headed in *Exper.
and Obser.* as "To Mr. P. F. Newport," it must have been written before
Peter Franklin moved to Philadelphia. When BF and Sally returned from
Boston in November 1763, Peter seems to have accompanied them, or followed them soon after (below, p. 392), perhaps in order to arrange for the
assumption of the Philadelphia postmastership and to find a suitable house.
By the summer of 1764 he and his wife appear to have been well settled into
their new home, to which the Post Office was moved in October (BF to
Jane Mecom, July 10, 1764, APS; *Pa. Gaz.*, Oct. 17, 1764). Either in 1762 or
early in 1763 BF apparently also wrote John Pringle on the preservation of
gunpowder (below, p. 268). It seems probable, therefore, though there is no
positive evidence, that BF wrote the present letter after his return from
England; hence it is printed here.

4. The inquiry may refer to some proposal concerning the magazine at
Fort George, on Goat Island, off Newport, R.I., though there is no reference
to the matter in *R.I. Col. Recs.*

water. Iron is a cheap metal; but if it were dearer, as this is a pub-lick thing, the expence is insignificant; therefore I would have the rod at least an inch thick, to allow for its gradually wasting by rust; it will last as long as the mast, and may be renewed with it. The sharp point for five or six inches should be gilt.

But there is another circumstance of importance to the strength, goodness, and usefulness of the powder, which does not seem to have been enough attended to: I mean the keeping it perfectly dry. For want of a method of doing this, much is spoilt in damp magazines, and much so damaged as to become of little value. If instead of barrels it were kept in cases of bottles well cork'd; or in large tin canisters, with small covers shutting close by means of oil'd paper between, or covering the joining on the canister; or if in barrels, then the barrels lined with thin sheet lead; no moisture in either of these methods could possibly enter the powder, since glass and metals are both impervious to water.

By the latter of these means you see tea is brought dry and crisp from China to Europe, and thence to America, tho' it comes all the way by sea in the damp hold of a ship. And by this method, grain, meal, &c. if well dry'd before 'tis put up, may be kept for ages sound and good.

There is another thing very proper to line small barrels with; it is what they call tin-foil, or leaf-tin, being tin mill'd between rollers till it becomes as thin as paper, and more pliant, at the same time that its texture is extreamly close. It may be apply'd to the wood with common paste, made with boiling water thicken'd with flour; and, so laid on, will lie very close and stick well: But I should prefer a hard sticky varnish for that purpose, made of linseed oil much boil'd. The heads might be lined separately, the tin wrapping a little round their edges. The barrel while the lining is laid on, should have the end hoops slack, so that the staves standing at a little distance from each other, may admit the head into its groove. The tin-foil should be plyed into the groove. Then one head being put in, and that end hoop'd tight, the barrel would be fit to receive the powder, and when the other head is put in and the hoops drove up, the powder would be safe from moisture even if the barrel were kept under water. This tin-foil but about 18 pence sterling a pound, and is so extreamly thin, that I imagine a pound of it would line three or four powder barrels. I am &c.   B.F.

From [Grey] Cooper[5]

AL: American Philosophical Society

Saturday [1762?][6]

Mr. Cooper presents his Compliments to Mr. Franclin and begs he will give Mr. Cooper leave to bring Lady Abdy and Miss Baldwyn[7] to hear the glasses on Monday or Thursday Evening next (which is most convenient to Mr. Franclin) about seven oClock. The Ladies have heard Mr. Franclin perform once before which has only given them a greater desire to hear him again.

Addressed: To Mr. Franclin at the bottom of / Craven Street.

From [Keane] Fitz Gerald and [Charles] Morton[8]

AL: American Philosophical Society

Monday even [1759–1775?][9]

Mr. Fitzgerald and Dr. Morton's Compliments to Dr. Franklyn, and if it be agreable, purpose to wait upon Him on Friday even next, about 6 o'clock, with 2 Ladies.

5. Though the writer's first name does not appear, he was probably BF's good friend Grey Cooper (*c.*1726–1801), barrister of the Middle Temple, 1751; M.P., 1765–84, 1786–90; secretary to the Treasury, 1765–82; lord of the Treasury, 1783. In 1775 he assumed a baronetcy as heir to the eldest brother of his great-grandfather; while he was usually thereafter called Sir Grey Cooper, his claim was never confirmed. *DNB;* Namier and Brooke, *House of Commons,* II, 250–1.

6. Tentatively assigned to 1762, the year in which the first dated reference to BF's armonica appears in this edition.

7. Probably Catherine Abdy (d. 1790), wife of Sir Anthony Thomas Abdy, baronet (1720?–1775), barrister of Lincoln's Inn, 1744; bencher, 1758; K.C., 1765; M.P., 1763–75. Namier and Brooke, *House of Commons,* II, 1. Miss Baldwyn has not been identified.

8. The first of these men may have been Keane Fitz Gerald, or Fitzgerald, of Poland St., London, F.R.S., 1756, who contributed papers on such diverse subjects as improvements to and uses for the steam engine, improvements to the thermometer and barometer, and methods of "checking the too luxuriant Growth of Fruit-Trees"; *Phil. Trans.,* L (1757–58), 53–7, 370–4, 727–32; LI (1759–60), 823–33; LII (1761–62), 71–5, 146–54. The second of these men was almost certainly Dr. Charles Morton, physician and secretary of the Royal Society; see above, p. 71 n.

9. This note may have been written at almost any time between February 1759, when BF received his doctorate at St. Andrews, and August 1762, or

Addressed: To / Benjamn. Franklyn / Esqr. Dr. of Laws. / Craven Street

From Isaac Garrigues[1]   ALS: American Philosophical Society

New England Coffee House Threadneedle Street
Worthy Sir   Friday Afternoon one O Clock [1762?][2]
You will please to Excuse my thus addressing as I am personally an intire Stranger to you and I can find nobody at present that knows me or my Family.

You have been pleased once to do a great favour for my Mother with Respect to her finding her Father the late Mr. Ralph for which you have laid us all under a lasting Obligation to you. And as my Mother is still very anxious to know many particulars concerning his death she has laid her Commands upon me upon my Arrival here to Satisfy her as far as is my power with Respect to his leaving any Children or Will at his decease[3] and as you are

---

during his second mission to England. According to established practice, it should have been printed with similarly undated documents at the end of Volume VIII, but through an editorial error it was misfiled and overlooked until the present volume was in preparation. It must therefore be printed, with apologies, among other undated documents apparently belonging to 1762.

1. Isaac Garrigues (b. 1741), the son of Samuel and Mary Garrigues, was the Philadelphia-born grandson of James Ralph, the friend who had accompanied BF to England in 1724 and had remained there, deserting his American family and marrying again; see above, I, 58 n.

2. There would have been time for news of Ralph's death, Jan. 24, 1762, to have reached Philadelphia and for this grandson to have arrived in London with his mother's instructions before BF's departure in August. While it is possible that this letter belongs to the period of BF's second English mission, such a dating seems unlikely; Mrs. Garrigues would have had ample opportunity to get the information she wanted directly from BF during his stay in Philadelphia, 1762–64.

3. On Ralph's death and that of his English-born daughter, both during the first months of 1762, see above, IX, 404 n. On the evenings of April 5 and 6, 1762, BF attended an auction of Ralph's library and bought 55 titles (about 115 volumes), paying a total of £6 5s. He failed to get a collection of some 80 pamphlets, for which the agent of Lord Bute outbid him, running the price to more than £25 for the lot. John B. Shipley, "Franklin Attends a Book Auction," *PMHB*, LXXX (1956), 37–45.

the only Gentleman from America that knows any thing concerning her Father you will please to pardon my Troubling you at this time. I should be extremely thankful to you for an Answer either by writing or waiting upon you which may suit you best. And in the Interim I am Worthy Sir with the Greatest Respect your much Obliged and most Obedient Servant

ISAAC GARRIGUES

Addressed: To / Benjamin Frankling Esqr. / Craven Street / The Strand

Endorsed: Mr Isaac Garrigues

From Elizabeth Henmarsh:[4] Deed

Copy: Department of Records, Recorder of Deeds, City of Philadelphia

January 1, 1763

ABSTRACT: In consideration of £100, Elizabeth Henmarsh of Philadelphia, widow, grants and sells to Benjamin Franklin a lot of land in Philadelphia, 16 ft. wide, north and south, and 73 ft. deep, bounded east by Sixth Street, south and west by lands of Isaac Zane, and north by land granted by Zane to James Davis. This lot was part of a piece of land 132 ft. on High Street and 306 ft. on Sixth Street which William Penn granted by letters patent of the 7th day 4th month (June), 1684 to Thomas Holme, which later became legally vested in Elizabeth Henmarsh and others [the chain of title not being here recited].[5] On Nov. 14, 1742, these owners conveyed the whole piece to Isaac Zane, and on Feb. 24, 1743, Zane conveyed the lot here concerned back to Elizabeth Henmarsh. She also conveys to Franklin, if requested and at his charge, true copies of all deeds and other documents in her custody which relate to the property and she warrants to him a clear title. Signed by Elizabeth Henmarsh; witnessed by Fras. Hopkinson and

4. Elizabeth Henmarsh has not been identified. In the Franklin Memorandum Book, 1757–1776 (described above, VII, 167–8), however, BF recorded under date of Sept. 12, 1764, a series of payments for Mrs. Henmarsh's estate: a legacy of £20 "to her Sister Mary Moore," funeral expenses totaling £20, and expenses of her last illness amounting to £16 12s. 6d. It appears, therefore, that she died in 1764 and that BF acted as executor or administrator of her estate.

5. The tract granted by Penn to Thomas Holme was on the northwest corner of Sixth and High Streets. *PMHB*, LXXX (1956), 211.

Charles Thomson. Her receipt for £100 from Franklin is added, as is also Hopkinson's affidavit as witness, dated Feb. 23, 1789, before Mathw. Irwin. Recorded Feb. 23, 1789.[6]

Pennsylvania Assembly Committee: Report on the Laws

Printed in *Votes and Proceedings of the House of Representatives,* 1762–1763 (Philadelphia, 1763), p. 13.

Throughout Franklin's absence in England he had been re-elected to the Assembly from the city of Philadelphia every October. When the House met on Jan. 10, 1763, he appeared to take his place for the first time in about five and three-quarters years, and at once resumed an active part in its work. During this session, which lasted until March 4, he served on eleven committees of varying importance, most of them concerned with the drafting of bills.[7] One of the earliest of his committee assignments came on January 14 when he and two other members were directed to examine the laws and report "such as have been found defective or are near expiring, and require to be amended or revived." The committee submitted a written report five days later.[8]

[January 19, 1763]

In Obedience to the Order of the House, we have inspected the Laws of this Province, and find that the Act to prevent Abuses in the Indian Trade, with its Supplement, expires in the Month of April next. We apprehend it to be a salutary Law, and submit it to the Consideration of the House, whether it may not be proper

6. This deed does not specify just where on Sixth Street, within Penn's original grant to Holme, the lot lay which Mrs. Henmarsh sold to BF. In the deed of Jan. 14, 1812, however, by which the heirs of BF's daughter Sarah Bache divided his real estate among themselves, the Henmarsh lot is described as bounded south by Mulberry Court (the easterly end of what is now St. James Street). In this distribution the lot was assigned to Sarah Bache (D.3.8). Department of Records, Recorder of Deeds, City of Philadelphia, Book I C, 19, pp. 3, 12, 19. In both the deeds of 1763 and of 1812 the property is described merely as a "lot or piece of ground," with no mention of buildings on it, but BF received rent for a house here at least between 1775 and 1787. *PMHB*, LXXX (1956), 46–73.

7. For a listing of these committees and the duties with which they were charged, see BF's Record of Service in the Assembly, 1751–64, above, IV, 176.

8. *Votes,* 1762–63, pp. 9, 13. On BF's two fellow committee members, Samuel Rhoads and John Ross, see above, II, 406 n; VI, 384 n.

to continue it, with such Amendments as the Experience of the Commissioners, who have executed it, may enable them to suggest.[9]

That the Act directing the Choice of Inspectors for the Counties of Chester, Lancaster, &c. is expired.[1]

That the Act for regulating the nightly Watch, and enlightening the Streets of the City, with its Supplement, will expire at the End of the Sessions of Assembly next after the Fifteenth Day of September next.[2]

That the Act to regulate Waggoners, Carters, Draymen and Porters, in the City of Philadelphia, will expire the Sixth Day of April next.[3]

9. Gov. William Denny signed an act, April 8, 1758, "for Preventing Abuses in the Indian Trade," which put the trade under the control of commissioners named in the act. A supplementary law of April 17, 1759, increased the capital which the commissioners might borrow to carry on the trade. Immediately after the reading of the present report the Assembly ordered the commissioners to present a representation on the state of the Indian trade; they did so on January 28, and on February 8 the House appointed a committee of eight members, including BF, to prepare a bill. The committee reported the bill on the 12th and it passed the Assembly on the 23d, but Governor Hamilton would not agree on the method of raising the necessary funds, so the measure failed. The Friendly Association for Regaining and Preserving Peace with the Indians then intervened; a new committee of seven, including BF, was appointed at the next session, March 29, and on the following day it presented a revised bill avoiding taxation; Hamilton accepted it and it became law on April 2. *Votes*, 1762–63, pp. 14, 17, 22, 25, 27, 30, 32–5, 39–41; *Statutes at Large, Pa.*, V, 320–30, 396–400; VI, 283–93.

1. An act for appointing inspectors of elections in Chester, Lancaster, York, Cumberland, Berks, and Northampton Counties was approved March 11, 1752, and renewed in 1755 and 1759. The Assembly appointed a committee to bring in a new bill not including Chester Co. on January 20, and the resulting measure was enacted March 4, 1763. *Votes*, 1762–63, pp. 14, 16, 17, 18, 19, 22, 35–6; *Statutes at Large, Pa.*, V, 153–8, 195–6, 465–6; VI, 253–61.

2. This act was first passed on Feb. 9, 1751; it was revised and renewed for seven years on Sept. 15, 1756. A short bill for continuing it was enacted Sept. 30, 1763, during BF's absence in New England. *Votes*, 1762–63, pp. 54, 55, 57, 60, 64; *Statutes at Large, Pa.*, V, 111–28, 224–43; VI, 309–10.

3. First passed, March 14, 1761. A committee of five members, including BF, was appointed on Jan. 21, 1763, to bring in a new bill; it reported February 22, and the measure was enacted without conflict on March 4, 1763. *Votes*, 1762–63, pp. 14, 29, 30, 35–6; *Statutes at Large, Pa.*, VI, 65–9, 249–50.

JANUARY 19, 1763

That the Act for establishing Courts of Judicature, appears to
want some Alterations and Amendments.[4]

And your Committee are of Opinion, that if the several Acts
now in Force for the Relief of the Poor were reduced into one
general Law, with some Amendments, the same would be more
intelligible, more easily executed, and of greater Utility to the
Province.[5]

> *Submitted to the House, by*
> BENJAMIN FRANKLIN,
> SAMUEL RHOADS,
> JOHN ROSS.

To Catharine Greene   ALS: American Philosophical Society

Philada. Jany. 23. 1763

I received with great Pleasure my dear Friend's Favour of
December 20.[6] as it inform'd me that you and yours are all well.

Mrs. Franklin admits of your Apology for dropping the Correspondence with her, and allows your Reasons to be good;[7] but

---

4. On Sept. 29, 1759, Governor Denny approved a supplement to the act
of 1722, "for Establishing Courts of Judicature in This Province," which
granted Pa. judges tenure during good behavior, but this was disallowed by
the King in Council, Sept. 2, 1760 (above, IX, 205, 210). The act of 1759 had
also extended the terms of the Court of Quarter Sessions in Bucks and Chester
Counties. On Jan. 21, 1763, the Assembly appointed a committee of ten
members, including BF, to bring in two bills, one for regulating the courts of
judicature and the other for limiting the continuation of actions in the courts,
but neither bill became law. The first was presented January 26 (its terms are
not stated); it was debated on February 10 and 24 and then tabled, but an
unnamed member thereupon presented a bill confined to enlarging the time
for holding the Quarter Sessions in Bucks and Chester Counties, and this was
enacted on March 4. The committee presented a bill to limit the continuation
of actions on February 4 and this measure passed the Assembly, but the
governor rejected it on the ground that such matters should be left to the
discretion of the judges. *Votes,* 1762–63, pp. 14, 17, 21, 23, 24, 26, 31, 32, 36;
Statutes at Large, Pa., V, 462–5; VI, 273–4.

5. The Assembly appointed a committee of thirteen members, including
BF, for this purpose on January 21, but the committee made no report during
the life of this Assembly. *Votes,* 1762–63, p. 14.

6. Not found.

7. DF and Caty had corresponded in 1757, but Caty apparently stopped

hopes when you have more Leisure it may be renew'd. She joins with me in congratulating you on your present happy Situation. She bids me say, she supposes you proceeded regularly in your Arithmetic, and that, before you got into *Multiplication,* you learnt *Addition,* in which you must often have had Occasion to say, *One that I* CARRY, *and two, makes Three.*[8] And now I have writ this, she bids me scratch it out again. [But] I am loth to deface my Letter, so e'en let it [stand].

I thank you for your kind Invitation. I purpose a Journey into New England in the Spring or Summer coming.[9] I shall not fail to pay my Respects to you and Mr. Greene when I come your Way. Please to make my Compliments acceptable to him.

I have had a most agreable time of it in Europe; have in company with my Son, been in most Parts of England, Scotland, Flanders and Holland;[1] and generally have enjoy'd a good Share of Health. If you had ask'd the rest of your Questions, I could more easily have made this Letter longer. Let me have them in your next. I think I am not much alter'd; at least my Esteem and Regard for my Katy (if I may still be permitted to call her so) is the same, and I believe will be unalterable whilst I am &c.

B FRANKLIN

My best Respects to your good Brother and Sister Ward.[2] My Daughter presents her Compliments. My Son is not yet arriv'd.[3]

Mrs. Greene

---

writing, perhaps after her marriage to William Greene, Jr., on April 30, 1758; see above, VII, 277, and this volume, p. 154 n.

8. By this time Caty had two daughters: Phebe, born on March 20, 1760, and Celia, born on June 15, 1762. Her first son, Ray, was born on Feb. 2, 1765, and after him came Samuel Ward, June 24, 1771, and Anne, June 17, 1774. Louise B. Clarke, *The Greenes of Rhode Island* (N. Y., 1903), p. 175. In a letter of Oct. 16, 1755, BF had joked with Caty about "Addition," "Multiplication," and the "Rule of Three." See above, VI, 225.

9. For BF's summer journey to New England, see below, pp. 276–9. He visited the Greenes at Warwick, R. I., on his way to Boston in July and on his return to Philadelphia in October.

1. For BF's travels during his first mission to England, see above, VIII, 133–46, 430–1; IX, 231 n, 364–5.

2. Caty's sister Anna and her husband Samuel Ward; see above, p. 154 n.

3. WF arrived in Philadelphia on Feb. 19, 1763.

Pennsylvania Assembly Committee: Report on the Dock

Printed in *Votes and Proceedings of the House of Representatives*, 1762–1763 (Philadelphia, 1763), p. 23.

"A Remonstrance and Petition from divers Inhabitants" of Philadelphia was presented to the Assembly, Jan. 24, 1763, complaining, among other things, that the public dock or creek in the southern part of the city[4] was "in a great Measure useless, and in its present Condition a Recepticle for the Carcases of dead Dogs, and other Carrion, and Filth of various Kinds," and had become most offensive and injurious to health. The petitioners pointed out that the dock might be rendered navigable for small craft and useful for conveying firewood, building materials, and other necessaries if properly cleaned, walled, and provided with a plank bottom. Another petition read the next day asked for a law for cleansing the dock and keeping it open under proper regulations.[5] The Assembly considered these complaints, February 3, and appointed a committee of six members, including Franklin, to inquire into the condition of the dock, find whether there were any private claims on it, and determine what sites suitable for public landings might be available for purchase along the river front. The committee reported six days later.[6]

[February 9, 1763]

The Committee appointed to enquire into the State of the Dock, the private Claims thereon, and whether any suitable Lots for public Landings are to be purchased, beg Leave to report to the House,

That they have enquired into the State of the Dock, and find it very necessary for the public Utility that the same be cleansed, and properly walled; and that they cannot find that any Persons have any just and legal Claims to the said Dock, or the Streets laid out adjoining thereto; and that they apprehend convenient Lots for Landings for the City of Philadelphia, may be purchased at a reasonable Price, above and below the City, on the River Delaware.[7]

4. For the location of the dock and creek see the map of Philadelphia, above, II, facing p. 456.

5. Fifteen years earlier, in February 1748, BF had been on a committee of the Philadelphia City Council to consider what should be done about the dock and the swamp out of which the creek flowed. The committee had recommended extensive improvements, but nothing of lasting benefit had been done because of the expense involved. See above, III, 276–9.

6. *Votes*, 1762–63, pp. 15, 21, 23.

7. The six members of this committee had already been appointed, January

To Isaac Norris; Pennsylvania Assembly
Committee of Accounts: Report

I. Draft: American Philosophical Society. II. ALS: Historical Society
of Pennsylvania. III. Printed in *Votes and Proceedings of the House of
Representatives*, 1762–1763 (Philadelphia, 1763), pp. 28–9.

On Feb. 9, 1763, Franklin drafted a letter to serve as preface to a statement of his expenses as agent of the Assembly in England (Document
I). After considering the draft, however, he must have felt that it gave
the impression of extravagant living in London and was too personal in
tone, so on February 15 he composed another letter incorporating only
the first and part of the second paragraph of the previous draft and
saying nothing about his manner of life in England (Document II).
Isaac Norris laid "sundry Letters, Accounts, and other Papers" relating to Franklin's disbursements on behalf of the province before the
Assembly on February 16, together with other "Papers and Accounts,
for incidental Expences" from Robert Charles, the other agent, and
all these were referred to the Committee of Accounts.[8] The Committee's report of February 19 and the Assembly's resolutions are
printed as Document III.

I

Sir,   Philada. Feb. 9. 1763
It is now six Years, since, in Obedience to the Order of the
House, I undertook a Voyage to England, to take care of their
Affairs there.[9]

Fifteen Hundred Pounds of the Public Money was at different
Times put into my Hands,[1] and I was instructed to keep Accounts
of the Disbursements I sh[ould] make in the Publick Service.

28, to bring in a bill supplementary to the act of 1762 for paving the city
streets. The committee now incorporated in that measure clauses authorizing
the purchase of one convenient lot on the river "at or near each side of the
said city" as public landing places, directing the street commissioners to
clean, repair, and make navigable the dock, and requiring owners of lots on
the streets flanking it to wall in with stone at their own expense their sections
of its banks. This bill became law, March 4, 1763. Another act approved the
same day contained a clause to forbid throwing any "carcase, carrion or filth,"
or any dirt or rubbish into the dock under penalty of 40s. fine. *Votes*, 1762–63,
pp. 18, 24, 28, 29, 32, 35–36; *Statutes at Large, Pa.*, VI, 232, 238–40.

8. *Votes*, 1762–63, p. 27.

9. BF accepted appointment as agent, Feb. 3, 1757; he left Philadelphia,
April 4, and sailed from Sandy Hook, June 20; above, VII, 109–11, 174.

1. On April 1, 1757, the Assembly voted BF £1500 sterling "for transacting

But I soon found such Accounts were in many Instances impracticable. For example I took my Son with me, partly to assist me as a Clerk and otherways in the Publick Service, and partly to improve him by showing him the World. His Services were considerable but so intermix'd with private Services, as that I could not well attend it.[2] I made Journies, partly for Health,[3] and partly that I might, by Country Visits to Persons of Influence, have more convenient Opportunities of discoursing them on our publick Affairs[4] the Expence of which Journies was not easily proportioned and separated. And being myself honour'd with Visits from Persons of Quality and Distinction,[5] I was oblig'd (for the Credit of the [Province?]) to live in a Fashion and Expence, suitable to the Publick Character I sustain'd, and much above what I should have done if I had been considered merely as a private Person; and this Difference of Expence was not easy to distinguish, and charge in my Accounts. The long Sickness and frequent Relapses I had the first and part of the second Winter, occasioned by a Change of Climate, were many ways expensive to me, of which I could keep no Account if indeed I ought to have charg'd the Province with such Expences.[6] The Disbursement of the following Sums I have however Accounts and Receipts to avouch, viz.

II

Sir,   Philada. Feb. 15. 1763

It is now six Years, since, in obedience to the Order of the House, I undertook a Voyage to England, to transact their Affairs there.

the publick Affairs of this Province in Great-Britain." He received £750 sterling of this sum on April 3, and Isaac Norris remitted the rest to him at various times. *Votes*, 1756–57, p. 107; above, VII, 166–7; VIII, 405.

2. This sentence is inserted between lines, and there are a few indecipherable words in the margin which may have been a further revision.

3. At this point BF wrote "and Amusement" but later struck it out.

4. For BF's travels during his first mission to England, see above, VIII, 133–46, 430–1; IX, 231 n, 364–5.

5. At this point BF wrote "of both Houses" but later struck it out.

6. For BF's illness of "near Eight Weeks" during the late summer and fall of 1757, see above, VII, 271, 272–4. At this point in the draft BF first wrote, but then struck out: "but particularly in the Charge of a Chariot. And as I was instructed to take all Opportunities [*illegible*]." While in London, BF hired a coach from one T. Bowman for 12 guineas per month. "Account of Expences," pp. 5, 12, 13, 14, 17, 24, 25, 33, 40, 43, 48; *PMHB*, LV (1931), 103, 107, 109, 110, 111, 113, 116, 123, 225. See also, above, VII, 380.

Fifteen Hundred Pounds of the Public Money was at different Times put into my Hands, for which I ought to account. The following Articles are vouch'd by the Receipts inclos'd, viz.

1758 Jan. 26.	Paid Robert Charles Esqr. for the Province 26 Guineas[7]	27.	6. 0
April 20.	Paid Richard Partridge Esqr. for Ditto[8]	40.	0. 0
May 2.	Paid Do. for Do.[9]	30.	0. 0
Sept. 27.	Paid T Osborne for 3 Vols. Journals House of Commons.[1]	10.	10. 0
	And for Indexes to the whole	1.	1. 0
1759 Dec. 31.	Paid Accounts for Printing sundry Pieces in Defence of the Province[2]	213.	13. 0
1760. Dec. 2.	Paid the Solicitor's Bill[3]	470.	8. 8

£792. 18. 8

Deduct ¹/₆th of the Solicitor's Bill it being charg'd in the Trustees Account[4]   78. 8. 1

£714: 10: 7

7. BF recorded this payment in his "Account of Expences," p. 12; *PMHB*, LV (1931), 108.

8. BF noted that this payment was for employing Partridge "in feeing counsel and other expences on Smith's petition." "Account of Expences," p. 19; *PMHB*, LV (1931), 110. For William Smith's petition to the King in Council praying for relief from his allegedly unjust imprisonment by the Pa. Assembly in January 1758, see above, VIII, 28–51.

9. BF recorded this expenditure in his "Account of Expences," p. 15, but Eddy omitted it in printing the "Account" in *PMHB*, LV (1931), 97–133.

1. See above, VIII, 169.

2. See above, VIII, 453–4.

3. BF paid his solicitor Francis Eyre in three installments for the costs of the hearings before the Board of Trade and Privy Council on the 19 Pa. acts passed in 1758 and 1759; see above, IX, 125–31, 196–203. On Feb. 4, 1760, he paid Eyre £21, on March 7, £131 10s., and on December 2, £317 18s. 8d. "Account of Expences," pp. 52, 53; *PMHB*, LV (1931), 127 (Eddy omits 10s. which BF paid Eyre on March 7). For a description and summary of Eyre's bill see above, IX, 22–4.

4. Presumably the trustees of the Provincial Loan Office.

I made many other Disbursements for which I have no Receipts; such as for Postage of Letters and Pacquets, which were often very heavy, containing Bills and Duplicates, &c. under the Great Seal, brought by Post to London from the Out-Ports, which to compute moderately could not, I think, fall short of £15 per Annum. Also for customary New Year's Gifts, and Christmas Presents to Door-keepers and Clerks of the Publick Offices, Tavern Dinners for the Lawyers and our other Friends at Hearings, Coach Hire, &c. for which I know not what to reckon, having kept no Account of such things.

I therefore can make no Claim of Allowance for them.

The House will therefore please to consider the Remainder of the £1500 put into my Hands, so unaccounted for, as now in their Disposition; for as to any Compensation for my Time and Pains in their Service, though I am conscious of having done faithfully every thing in my Power for the Publick Good, according to the best of my Abilities, yet as the House, when they appointed me their Agent at first, and afterwards from Year to Year, did not vote any particular Sum as my Salary, I am therefore not warranted to charge any thing, but do now, with the same Confidence I have ever had in the Justice and Goodness of the House, chearfully submit the same to their present Discretion.

With the greatest Respect and Esteem, I am, Sir, Your most obedient and most humble Servant   B FRANKLIN

Isaac Norris Esqr

Endorsed: Benjamin Franklin Letter, dated in Philadelphia Febry. 15th. 1763

III

February 19, 1763.

In Obedience to the Order of the House, we have examined the Account of Benjamin Franklin, Esq; with the Vouchers to us produced in Support thereof, and do find the same Account to be just, and that he has expended, in the immediate Service of this Province, the Sum of Seven Hundred and Fourteen Pounds, Ten Shillings and Seven-pence, out of the Sum of Fifteen Hundred Pounds Sterling, to him remitted and paid, exclusive of any Allowance or Charge for his Support and Services for the Province. We have also examined the Account of Robert Charles, Esq; against this Province, and find the same is reasonable and just, except a Charge

196

of Sixty Pounds for his Share of Commissions on the Money received from the Crown by Benjamin Franklin, Esq; which we submit to the Consideration of the House.

JOSEPH FOX,	JOHN MORTON,
JOHN HUGHES,	WILLIAM ALLEN,
SAMUEL RHOADS,	JOHN ROSS,
JOHN WILKINSON,	JOHN MOOR,
ISAAC PEARSON.	

The House taking the foregoing Report of the Committee of Accounts into Consideration, and having spent some Time therein,
Resolved,
That the Sum of Five Hundred Pounds Sterling per Annum be allowed and given to Benjamin Franklin, Esq; late Agent for the Province of Pennsylvania at the Court of Great-Britain, during his Absence of Six Years from his Business and Connections, in the Service of the Public;[5] and that the Thanks of this House be also given to the said Gentleman, by Mr. Speaker, from the Chair, as well for the faithful Discharge of his Duty to this Province in particular, as for the many and important Services done America in general, during his Residence in Great-Britain.[6]
Resolved,
That the Account of Robert Charles, Esq; late Agent for this Province, be allowed, and discharged.

To Jane Mecom
ALS: American Philosophical Society

Dear Sister   Philada. Feb. 21. 1763
I have now the Pleasure of acquainting you that my Son and Daughter are safely arriv'd at my House, and both very well.

5. In a pamphlet written in December 1764 the Rev. William Smith stated that the Assembly settled on the sum of £500 sterling per annum because the colony of Va. had voted a like sum to one of its agents who had lately served in London. William Smith, *An Answer to Mr. Franklin's Remarks on a late Protest* (Phila., 1765). The bitter controversy between Franklin and the proprietary party in 1764 about the allegedly exorbitant costs of his mission to England (in which the compensation voted on this day was always cited) will be treated at length in the next volume.

6. Norris formally expressed the House's thanks on March 31, 1763; see below, p. 238.

197

They present their Duty to Brother Mecom and you. He sets out for his Government on Wednesday.[7]

I am greatly to blame for not sending the enclos'd sooner. It was wrote by your Sister[8] several Weeks since, and given to me to be forwarded. I thought it was done or rather did not think of it at all till this Morning, when I found it on my Desk cover'd with some Papers. Excuse me, if you can.

Tell me how you do, and where you live, and what you would advise me to concerning Lodging when I come to Boston.[9] As I think I shall stay two or three Months, I have half a Mind to keep House, that is, Bachelor's Hall, in that which was Sister Douse's.[1] Cannot one hire Furniture for a Quarter or Half a Year? In London one may very easily. I hope to see you in May or June.

My Love to all. I am as ever Your affectionate Brother

B FRANKLIN

To [Philip Ludwell][2]   Draft: American Philosophical Society

My dear Friend,   Philada. Feb. 22. 1763

I received your kind Congratulations on my Son's Promotion[3] with great Pleasure, and thank you cordially for your good

---

7. WF and his wife arrived at Philadelphia on Feb. 19, 1763, and he and BF left for N.J. on February 23.

8. DF; the enclosure has not been found.

9. At this time Jane apparently lived, and kept boarders, at a house in Hanover Street which had belonged to her father. Van Doren, *Franklin-Mecom*, pp. 7–8.

1. BF had acquired his half-sister Elizabeth Douse's house on Unity Street as part payment for debts owed him by her estate. He spent £148 4s. 8d. repairing the house so that it might be rented and then arranged to have the rent paid to his sister Jane. She moved into the house in 1784. *Ibid.*, pp. 21–2, 78–9.

2. I. Minis Hays believed that this letter was intended for John Pringle and William Strahan because a notation "This to Dr. Pringle and Mr. Strahan" appears in the margin opposite a canceled passage in the second paragraph about the effects of the peace (*Calendar of the Papers of Benjamin Franklin*, Phila., 1908, III, 454–5). It seems clear, however, that BF meant merely to transfer the passage to letters to those men, and it does in fact appear almost unchanged in his letter to Strahan of March 28 and more briefly in one of February 23 (see below, p. 236, and the letter immediately following this one).

Wishes concerning him. I have great Hopes of his doing well, as I know he has good Principles and good Dispositions.

I congratulate you on the glorious Peace we have made, the most advantageous to Great Britain, in my Opinion, of any our History has recorded.[4]

I must shortly make a Journey to your Country, which I should undertake with much greater Pleasure, if I could promise my self the Happiness of meeting there with my dear Friend, (but that is not to be expected, for I hear you are to continue this Year in England). I pray sincerely that every Blessing may attend you, wherever you are, and particularly that of Health. O that I could invent something to restore and establish yours![5] But we shall meet, I trust, in a better Country, and with better Constitutions, vigourous Health and everlasting Youth; and since t'will be an additional Pleasure so great in itself and so easily afforded us, I am persuaded we shall know one another. In the meantime believe me ever, my dearest Friend Yours most affectionately BF

No letter to Pringle of these months has been found. Reference in the third paragraph to an intended "Journey to your Country," from which the addressee was absent in England, shows that he must have been either a Virginian or a New Englander, since it was to those colonial areas that BF planned trips on post-office business in the near future. The compliments offered to "Miss Ludwell and the other young Ladies" in the canceled postscript, quoted in the final footnote below, establish that the addressee was Col. Philip Ludwell (above, VI, 532 n, and this volume, p. 107 n), who, with his daughters, had moved from Va. to London in 1760, where BF had come to know him well.

3. Not found.

4. The preliminary peace treaty was signed at Paris, Nov. 3, 1762, and the definitive treaty, Feb. 10, 1763. The canceled passage about the peace, referred to in the first note above, follows at this point.

5. At this point in the draft BF began a new paragraph with "My Son is now with me, and joins in best Wishes and," then crossed out these words and wrote: "PS. Please to make my Compliments and best Wishes acceptable to Miss Ludwell and the other young Ladies; and believe me ever, with the most perfect Esteem and Affection, my dear Friend." Then BF canceled this postscript, placed a caret after "yours!," and added in the margin the remainder of the letter as printed here.

To William Strahan ALS: Pierpont Morgan Library

Dear Straney, Philada. Feb. 23. 1763

I have only time to write one Line by this Conveyance, just to congratulate you on the glorious Peace you have made, the most advantageous for the British Nation in my Opinion, of any your Annals have recorded.[6] The Places you have left or restor'd to the French I look upon to be so much in our Power in Case of a future War, as to be so many Hostages or Pledges of their good Behaviour.[7] Love to Mrs. Strahan and your Children. Billy joins in every affectionate Sentiment,[8] with, Dear Friend, Yours affectionately B FRANKLIN

Addressed: To / Mr William Strahan / Printer / New Street, Shoe Lane / London

To Deborah Franklin ALS: American Philosophical Society

My dear Child Trenton, Feb. 24. 1763

We din'd at Bristol, and got here last Night in good time; the River was hard and firm, and we got well over.[9] Sir John Sinclair

6. The terms of the preliminary peace treaty, signed Nov. 3, 1762, had been summarized in *Pa. Gaz.*, Jan. 27, 1763. Grenada, the Grenadines, Tobago, Dominica, and St. Vincent in the West Indies were to become British; Martinique, Guadeloupe, Marie Galante, and St. Lucia were to be French. Havana was to be restored to Spain in return for the cession to Great Britain of St. Augustine and all of Florida. France was to retain the islands of Miquelon and St. Pierre in the Gulf of St. Lawrence and to have freedom to catch and cure fish (but no territorial rights) on a limited portion of the Newfoundland coast. Most important of all, France was to cede to Great Britain the whole of Canada and the region the French called Louisiana between the British colonies on the mainland and the Mississippi River, including the Ohio Valley, together with the right of navigation of the Mississippi.

7. This sentence essentially repeats a part of the canceled passage in the draft letter to Philip Ludwell immediately above.

8. WF and his wife had reached Philadelphia, February 19.

9. BF and WF left Philadelphia on Feb. 23, 1763, spending the night at Trenton and the next at New Brunswick. The Middlesex Troop of Horse and "several Gentlemen in Sleighs" met the new governor on the road and escorted him to Perth Amboy. The outgoing governor, Josiah Hardy, and the Council greeted him there, his commission was read in Council, where he took the "usual Oaths," and then his assumption of office "was published

William Franklin

came to us and very obligingly offer'd his Chariot and four for the rest of the Journey.[1] This Morning we set out for Brunswic.

The Thing I wanted to mention to you, but forgot, was; that in the Hurry of our Arrival from Chester I did not see Tabb when he went away with the Chaise, and so omitted to send my Respects and Thanks to good Mrs. Masters for her Favour in lending it; pray do this for me, and make my Apology.[2] And moreover give Tab as from the Governor, a couple of Dollars.

Billy presents his Duty to you and Love to his Sister. I know not whether he will have time to write to his Betsey.[3] My Love to her, and believe me ever Your affectionate Husband

B FRANKLIN

Addressed: To / Mrs Deborah Franklin / Philadelphia / per favour of / Mr Stevens.[4]

---

in the Court House, amidst a numerous Concourse of People; and the whole was conducted with as much Decency and good Decorum, as the severe Season would possibly admit of." BF and WF went back to New Brunswick on March 1 and the next day went on to Princeton. There the president and tutors of the College of N.J. presented an address, commending, among other things, his "Education under the Influence and Direction of the very eminent Doctor Franklin." On March 3 they arrived at Burlington, where WF was received "with the greatest Demonstrations of Joy"; the next day his commission was "opened and declared," and he dined with the City Corporation. On March 5 the Franklins returned to Philadelphia, "attended by the principal Gentlemen" of Burlington. 1 *N.J. Arch.*, XXIV, 146–54.

1. Sir John St. Clair (above, VI, 22 n), deputy quartermaster general under Braddock, had after the campaign of 1758 settled in N.J. on an estate near Elizabeth Town. In 1762 he eloped with Elizabeth Moland of Philadelphia and married her in Burlington, N.J.

2. After landing at Lewes, 150 miles from Philadelphia, on February 12, WF and his wife traveled "above 100 miles in an open one-horse-chair, as no other carriage was to be had, the weather extremely severe: We then met with a chariot which had been waiting for us some time, and before we reach'd Philadelphia a considerable number of gentlemen, with my father and sister, came out to meet us and escorte us into the city." WF to Strahan, April 25, 1763, *PMHB*, XXXV (1911), 424–5. "Tabb" was evidently a servant of Mrs. Mary Lawrence Masters, widow of BF's old friend and associate in many civic enterprises, William Masters (above, VI, 312 n). Masters had died, Nov. 24, 1760, and BF had been named one of his executors. Charles P. Keith, *The Provincial Councillors of Pennsylvania* (Phila., 1883), p. 453.

3. WF's wife Elizabeth had evidently remained in Philadelphia because of the inclement weather.

4. Not identified.

To Cadwallader Colden

ALS: New-York Historical Society; draft (incomplete): American Philosophical Society

Dear Sir,   Perth-Amboy, Feb. 26. 1763
Your Favour of the 14th. Instant,[5] I met on the Road in my Journey to this Place with my Son, who joins with me in Thanks for your good Wishes relating to his Administration here. I thank you also for your kind Endeavours in obtaining the Discharge of William Forrester,[6] who is accordingly discharged.

I condole with you most sincerely on the repeated grievous Breaches that have been made in your Family.[7] Loss of Friends and near and dear Relations, is one of the Taxes we pay for the Advantage of long Life, and a heavy Tax indeed it is!

The most remarkable Discovery that has been made within these three Years, is, that Quicksilver is in reality a melted Metal; with this new Character only, that of all others it requires the least Heat to melt it. The Academy of Sciences at Petersburgh, have found, that by dipping a mercurial Thermometer into repeated cooling Mixtures, and so taking from the Mercury the Heat that was in it, they have brought it down some hundred Degrees (the exact Number I cannot remember) below the Freezing Point, when the Mercury became solid, and would sink no lower; and then the Glass being broke, it came out in the Form of a silver Bullet, adhering to a Wire which was the slender part that had been in the Tube. Upon Tryal it was found malleable, and was hammer'd out to the Bigness of a Half Crown; but soon after, on receiving a small Degree of Warmth it return'd gradually to its fluid State again. This Experiment was repeated by several Members of that Academy two Winters successively, and an authentic Account of it transmitted to our Royal Society.[8]

5. Not found.
6. Not identified; possibly some Pennsylvanian in the N.Y. military service or a prisoner for debt or legal offense.
7. Colden's wife, Alice Chrystie (or Christy), died in March 1762; his youngest daughter, Catherine, born in 1733, died in June 1762. E. R. Purple, "Notes, Biographical and Genealogical, of the Colden Family," *N.Y. Gen. and Biog. Record*, IV (1873), 165, 170. Colden had recently passed his seventy-fifth birthday.
8. "An Account of artificial Cold produced at Petersburg: By Dr. Himsel.

I suppose you have seen, in the 2d Vol. of the new Philosophical
Essays of the Edinburgh Society, an Account of some Experiments
to produce Cold by Evaporation, made by Dr. Cullen, who mentions the like having been before made at Petersburg.[9] I think it
is but lately that our European Philosophers have known or acknowledg'd anything of such a Power in Nature. But I find it has
been long known in the East. Bernier, in the Account of his Travels
into India, wrote above 100 Years since,[1] mentions the Custom of
Travellers carrying their Water in Flasks covered with wet wool-
len Cloth, and hung to the Pomells of their Saddles, so as that the
Wind might act upon them in order to cool the Water. I have also
seen a kind of Jar for cooling Water, made of Potter's Earth, but
unglaz'd, and so porous that the Water gradually ouzed through to
the Surface, supplying Water just sufficient for a constant Evaporation. I try'd it, and found the Water within much cool'd in a few
Hours. This Jar was brought from Egypt. Mentioning this Matter
to Dr. Hadley, then Professor of Chemistry at Cambridge, he immediately made the following Experiment at which I was present:[2]
He dipt the Thermometer into a Quantity of the highly rectified
Spirit that goes by the Name of Ether, famous for its quick Evaporation. The Ether having stood in the same Room with the Thermometer, was therefore of the same degree of Warmth, and of
course there was no Alteration of Height in the Mercury while it
remain'd in the Ether. But as soon as the Thermometer was taken
out, and the Ether with which it was wet began to evaporate from
its Surface, the Mercury fell several Degrees. The Doctor repeated

In a Letter to Dr. De Castro, F.R.S. Translated from the French by James
Parsons, M.D. F.R.S.," *Phil. Trans.*, LI (1760), 670–6. In summarizing this
paper, *Gent. Mag.*, XXXI (1761), 402–4, pointed out that it was a double
translation, from Russian to French and then to English, and left some matters very obscure. In 1761 William Watson presented to the Royal Society
a further report on the Petersburg experiments, based on a Latin dissertation
of J. A. Braun of the Academy of Sciences. *Phil. Trans.*, LII (1761–62),
156–72.

9. William Cullen, "Essay on the Cold produced by Evaporating Fluids,"
Edinburgh Phil. Soc., *Essays and Observations, Philosophical and Literary*,
II (1755), 145–75.

1. François Bernier. For the edition of his work BF may have used and the
observations repeated here, see above, VIII, 109 n.

2. For earlier accounts of this experiment, see above, VIII, 108–9, and this
volume, p. 38.

the Wetting with a Feather, and I quicken'd the Evaporation by a Bellows, that the Repetitions of Wetting might succeed quicker; and the Event was, that the Mercury sunk from 65, the Temperament of the Air on that Day, down to 7, which was 25 Degrees below the Freezing Point; so that the Moisture of the Air and Breath of the Bystanders, collecting round the cold Ball of the Thermometer, froze there, and form'd a rough Ice all round, and near ¼ of an Inch thick. It seems by this, that a Man naked, and standing in the Wind, and repeatedly wet with Spirits might be frozen to death in a Summer's Day. I think none of our common Philosophical Principles will serve us in accounting for this. Perhaps yours may do it.

Professor Æpinus of Petersburgh, has publish'd a Work on Magnetism and Electricity, in which he endeavours to apply my Theory of the latter to the Explanation of certain Phenomena in the former.[3] He supposes Magnetism to be a particular Fluid equally diffus'd in all Iron, easily flowing and easily moving in soft Iron, so as to maintain or recover an Equilibrium. But in hard Iron, i.e. Steel, moving with more Difficulty. And that in making an Artificial Magnet of Steel, nothing is added, the Magnetism is only moved from one End towards the other, and not easily returning remains there, so that one end of it has more of it than its natural Quantity, the other less; or in other Words, one End has positive Magnetism, the other negative. I have while in England made many Experiments with Magnets, and own myself inclined to Æpinus's Opinion, tho' there are some Difficulties in his Doctrine that as yet I do not see how to solve. Shall I venture to mention moreover, a Suspicion I have, to wit, that Magnetism fills all Space, and that its general Direction is what we call North and South, except only where it is made to deviate by Nearness to particular Magnets, as this Globe of Earth, a Stone, or Steel Bar; and that a Being capable of Passing from one Heavenly Body to another, might be directed in his Course by a Compass, as well as a Mariner on our Ocean. I suspect too, that one Use of this Universal Magnetism may be, to keep the Axes of the Planets and other heavenly Bodies nearly in

3. Franz Ulrich Theodor Aepinus, *Tentamen theoriae electricitatis et magnetismi* (St. Petersburg, 1759). For a discussion of the relation of this work to BF's electrical theory, see I. Bernard Cohen, *Franklin and Newton* (Phila. 1956), pp. 537–43.

their respective Directions; tho' I at the same time see Difficulties in and Objections to this Opinion that are yet too hard for me.

While in England, after my chief Business was over, I amus'd myself, with contriving and bringing to a considerable Degree of Perfection, a new musical Instrument, which has afforded me and my Friends a great deal of Pleasure;[4] but the Description of it would make this Letter, already too long, much longer. I am, with great Regard and Sincerity, Dear Sir, Your most obedient and most humble Servant B FRANKLIN

My Compliments to your very ingenious Son, Mr. David Colden. I suppose he has seen Nollet's Letter in answer to a Piece of his publish'd with mine on Electricity.[5]

Honble Cadr. Colden Esqr

From John Mills[6] ALS: American Philosophical Society

Sir, London, March 2d. 1763.

Our worthy Friend, Mr. Small,[7] is so kind as to undertake to convey to you and to Dr. Eliot,[8] the first Volume of my Husbandry,[9] which is at length finished at the Press, where the second Volume is now half done. But I have, unfortunately, a most dilatory, as well slovenly Printer to deal with,[1] as you will perceive too plainly

4. See above, pp. 116–30.
5. For David Colden and his remarks on Nollet, published in BF's *Exper. and Obser.*, Part III (1754), see above, v, 135–44, 435. For the new edition of Nollet's book with a second volume containing a letter in which he replied to David Colden, see above, IX, 252 n.
6. John Mills (d. 1784?) was a British writer on agriculture whom BF helped to nominate for membership in the Royal Society in June 1765; see above, VIII, 357.
7. Alexander Small (above, IX, 110–11 n), an agricultural writer and the inventor of the chain plow.
8. For the Rev. Jared Eliot of Killingworth, Conn., the author of the well-known *Essays upon Field-Husbandry in New England*, see above, III, 147–8. Since Eliot died on April 22, 1763, BF sent Mills's work (mentioned in the note immediately below) to his son, Col. Aaron Eliot (1718–1785). Mills to BF, July 12, 1764, APS.
9. Mills's opus, *A New and Complete System of Husbandry* (5 vols., London, 1762–65), was reissued in 1767 as *A New System of Practical Husbandry*.
1. *The Critical Review*, XVIII (Aug., 1764), 87, lists the printer of the first

by his egregious and repeated blunders. I most heartily wish that
the Book was in a condition fitter, in every respect, to be offered
to you, both as to the Printer's performance and my own: but if
you will do me the honour of accepting it, such as it is, I shall
esteem it an obligation added to those which you have already
been pleased to confer on, Sir, Your most obedient, and most humble
Servant, JOHN MILLS.

[Addressed:] To / Dr. Franklin

Province of Pennsylvania: Account with Franklin; Isaac Norris: Certificate for Payment

I. DS: Historical Society of Pennsylvania. II. Printed form with MS
insertions in blanks: Historical Society of Pennsylvania

On March 4, 1763, the Pennsylvania Assembly's Committee of Accounts, which had approved Franklin's expenses on his English mission
on February 19 (see above, p. 195), laid "before the House a State of the
Account of Benjamin Franklin; Esq; with the Province," and they
having reported that the province owed Franklin £2214 10s. 7d., "a
Certificate was drawn for the said Balance and signed by Mr. Speaker
by Order of the House."[2] Document I printed below is a summary of
Franklin's account with the province, part of which appears to be in
Isaac Norris' hand. Document II is the certificate signed by Norris.

I
Province of Pennsylvania in Account with Benja. Franklin

Dr		Sterl.
1763. To Expences in Behalf of the Province as per Account rendered the Committee[3]		£714. 10. 7.
To a Compensation voted in Assembly for Six Years Service in Great Britain as Agent for the Province		3000 – –
		£3714. 10. 7.

volume of Mills's work as "Baldwin." This could have been either Henry
Baldwin (d. c.1766), the proprietor of the Britannia Printing Office, White-
friars, Fleet Street, printer of *Read's Weekly Journal* and *The Daily Chronicle*, or Richard Baldwin (d. 1777), or his son Richard Baldwin, Jr. (d. 1770).
H. R. Plomer, G. H. Bushnell, E. R. McC. Dix, *A Dictionary of the Printers
and Booksellers . . . 1726–1775* (Oxford, 1932), p. 14; John Nichols, *Literary
Anecdotes of the Eighteenth Century* (London, 1812), III, 716–17.

Cr   Sterl.

1757.   By Cash taken with him and remitted to   ⎫
          him while in England[4]   ⎬ £1500. − −
          Ballance due to B Franklin   ⎭ 2214. 10. 7.

                                          £3714. 10. 7

a Certificate for the Ballance drawn and signed in Assembly by Order of the House   March the 4th 1763   I Norris Speaker

Endorsed: I. N. March 4th. 1763 Benjn Franklin's Agent Acct Currt with the Province while in London from 1757. Examined[5] The ball. of £2214. 10. 7 Sterlg. is Entd. in Bills of Excha. account, March 16. 1763. per Votes 1766.

The other Article in Credit of the within accot. being £1500 Sterling: is charg'd the 14. June 1759.[6]

II

                       In Assembly, *Mar: 4th* 17 *63.*
THESE are to certify, That the Sum   *of two thousand two hundred and fourteen pounds ten Shillings and sevenpence Sterling*   is allowed to *Benjamin Franklin, Esquire* for his Service as *late Agent to the Province of Pennsylvania* and that the same ought to be paid[7] out of Money raised for discharging the public Debts. Signed by Order of the House,   Isaac Norris *Speaker*

[*In the margin:*] Sterlg. £2214. 10. 7 at 72½ per Cent

2. *Votes,* 1762–63, p. 34.
3. For this and the next item, see above, pp. 195, 197.
4. See above, VII, 166–7 n; VIII, 405.
5. The remainder of this endorsement is in an unidentified hand. The reference to £2214 10s. 7d., entered under March 16, 1763, in a report of a committee "appointed to audit and settle the Loan-Office and other Public Accounts," submitted to the Assembly on Sept. 18, 1766, precludes the possibility that either Norris could have written it, because Charles Norris died on Jan. 15, 1766, and Isaac died on July 13, 1766. 8 *Pa. Arch.* VII, 5906, 5911.
6. That is, the Assembly's payments of £1500 sterling to Franklin before he went to England and while he was there were entered June 14, 1759, as £2362 10s. Pa. currency, in the accounts of the commissioners appointed to disburse the £100,000 voted by the Assembly on April 22, 1758. 8 *Pa. Arch.,* VI, 5154.
7. The printed form reads at this point "paid out of such Money as may hereafter be raised." The words not reproduced here were struck out on the form.

Endorsed: March 9th 1763 Pay the Contents to Benjamin Franklin Esqr or Order   To the Trustees of the General Loan Office
                                                              JON HUGHES[8]
March 16th: 1763 Recd of Charles Norris[9] the Sum of Two thousand two hundred and fourteen pounds and ten Shillgs and Seven pence Sterling being the Trustees draft on Messrs. Sargent Aufrere & Co.[1] per   B FRANKLIN

To Richard Jackson   ALS: American Philosophical Society

Dear Sir,   Philada. March 8. 1763.
    The enclos'd is a Copy of my last.[2] The Preliminaries of Peace, on which I congratulate you, are since come to hand, and are universally approved of in these Parts.[3] While we retain our Superiority at Sea, and are suffer'd to grow numerous and strong in North America, I cannot but look on the Places left or restor'd to our Enemies on this Side the Ocean, as so many Pledges for their good Behaviour. Those Places will hereafter be so much in our Power, that the more valuable they are to the Possessors, the more cautious will they naturally be of giving us Offence. So that I think this Peace has all the Appearance of being a durable one.
    Since all the Country is now ceded to us on this Side the Missisipi, is not this a good time to think of new Colonies on that River, to secure our Territory and extend our Commerce; and to separate the Indians on this side from those on the other, by intervening Settlements of English, and by that means keep them more easily in order? What think you now of asking for a Slice of Territory, to be settled in some manner like that I once propos'd?[4] When I was

8. Hughes apparently signed this order in his capacity as a member of the Assembly's Committee to "settle and audit" the accounts of the trustees of the Loan Office. 8 *Pa., Arch.* VI, 5369.
    9. One of the trustees of the Loan Office.
    1. That is, the trustees paid BF by drawing a bill of exchange on Sargent Aufrere, who along with the Barclays had been appointed to manage the province's share of the parliamentary grants for 1759, 1760, and 1761. See above, IX, 358–9 n.
    2. Presumably the letter of Dec. 6, 1762, above, pp. 162–5.
    3. See above, p. 199 n.
    4. Probably a reference to BF's Plan for Settling Two Western Colonies, drafted in the autumn of 1754; above, V, 456–63.

about to leave England, I refer'd Mr. Sargent[5] to you for a Plan of that nature. Did he apply to you?

I find this City greatly increas'd in Building, and they say it is so in Numbers of Inhabitants. But to me the Streets seem thinner of People, owing perhaps to my being so long accustom'd to the bustling crowded Streets of London.

The Expence of Living is greatly advanc'd in my Absence; it is more than double in most Articles; and in some 'tis treble.[6] This is by some ascrib'd to the scarcity of Labourers and thence the Dearness of Labour; but I think the [Dearness] of Labour, as well as of other Things the Labour of which was long since perform'd, or in which Labour is not concern'd; such as Rent of old Houses, and Value of Lands, which are trebled in the last Six Years, is in great measure owing to the enormous Plenty of Money among us. The Crown, I am inform'd, has paid £800,000 Sterling in this Province only, for Provisions Carriages, and other Necessaries in the Service. Beside which, the Province has struck £5 or 600,000 great part of which is still current; and in New Jersey and New York, they have had proportionable Quantities. This is such an over Proportion of Money to the Demand for a Medium of Trade in these Countries, that it seems from Plenty to have lost much of its Value. Our Tradesmen are grown as idle, and as extravagant in their Demands when you would prevail on them to work, as so many Spaniards. But what with burning our Paper yearly, and paying our Debts to England with our Silver, we shall, 'tis to be hop'd, soon reduce the Quantity, and come again to our Senses. And this leads

5. John Sargent, of Sargent Aufrere & Co.

6. In WF's first letter to the Board of Trade after his arrival in N.J., dated May 10, 1763, he declared that "all the Necessaries of Life in this Country are encreas'd in Price near Three fold to what they were Seven Years ago." He hoped to persuade the Assembly to increase the salaries of governmental officers. 1 *N.J. Arch.*, IX, 384. The rise in wholesale commodity prices, considered apart from other elements, while considerable, does not appear to have been nearly so great as the Franklins reported for the entire "Expence of Living." With the monthly averages for the years 1741–45 taken as a base, the annual arithmetic indices of wholesale prices of twenty commodities were 112.5 in 1757 and 140.1 in 1762; the annual geometric indices for the same years were 110.9 and 134.6 respectively. Falling prices in the latter part of 1763 produced drops in the indices for that year of 2.6 in the arithmetic and 1.6 in the geometric. Anne Bezanson, Robert D. Gray, Miriam Hussey, *Prices in Colonial Pennsylvania* (Phila., 1935), pp. 306–7, 433.

me to an Observation, that your Commerce is now become so profitable, and naturally brings so much Gold and Silver into your Island, that if you had not now and then some expensive foreign War, to draw it off, your Country would, like ours, have a Plethora in its Veins, productive of the same Sloth, and the same feverish Extravagance.

Our Assembly met lately, but have yet appointed no Agent: They will I believe do it at their next Sitting, which is to be in three Weeks from this Time.[7] On settling my Accounts and considering my Services, they found themselves indebted to me £2214 10s. 7d. Sterling, which they order'd to be immediately paid me; together with the Thanks of the House by the Speaker for my Services.[8] This I mention to you, because I hear that Mr. T. Penn has insinuated to Mr. Collinson that I had embezzled the Publick Money, and made use of it in my private Affairs in England;[9] and possibly the same may have been intimated to you and others of my Friends.

I enclose an Estimation of the Numbers of Indians inhabiting near our present advanc'd Posts. It was made by a Person lately sent to visit those Posts.[1] He call'd the chief Men of each Nation together, assur'd them of the Good will of the English, and that they should be well supply'd with Goods for their Peltry; but bringing no Presents for them, they were disappointed and generally disgusted. I think he was sent per Order of General Amherst, who

7. See below, pp. 246–7.

8. See the documents immediately above; also below, p. 238.

9. This accusation foreshadowed the charges leveled against BF in the election campaign of 1764. No surviving letter from Collinson to BF alludes to such an insinuation by Penn.

1. On orders from Sir William Johnson, superintendent of Indian affairs, his deputy George Croghan had sent Thomas Hutchins (1730–1789) to visit the western Indians in areas previously under French domination. Hutchins had been an army officer during the war; as an engineer he had laid out Fort Pitt and another fort at Pensacola, Florida. In 1781 Congress appointed him geographer to the United States. *DAB.* He left Fort Pitt on his westward mission, April 4, 1762, visited the Indians at Detroit and at various other places in the Great Lakes region, and returned to Fort Pitt September 24. His report, a map he prepared, and his census of Indian fighting men are in *Johnson Papers,* x, 521–9, 544–6. See also *ibid.,* III, 605, 662; x, 543. His report mentions repeatedly the Indians' dissatisfaction that he had brought them no presents.

perhaps has no Allowance for such Presents, or judges them now unnecessary; but in my Opinion, we should let the Indians feel as little as possible, the Superiority we have acquir'd, and should treat them with as much Consideration, for some time at least, as we did while the French Power in America subsisted:[2] And as they never negotiate among themselves, or call any Meeting of another Nation or Tribe, without Presents, they ought not to have been omitted on this Occasion by us. The Indians think us so wealthy, and that we have such Plenty of every thing valuable to them, that if we omit so essential and so establish'd a Ceremony, it cannot be through Want, it must proceed from Contempt. I hope however, that this Mistake of ours, if it was one, will soon be rectified.

There are now some considerable little Towns on the Line of Communication between this Place and Fort Pitt; and the Town, under that Fort, has, they say, at least 200 Log Houses.[3] There is a Brewery, would you think it, near the Town, that lets for £100 a Year. Smiths, Carpenters, Taylors, Shoemakers, and most other common Trades are in the Town; and the Inhabitants, on some mistaken Intelligence of a Design among the Indians to attack the Place, form'd two good Companies of Militia. Their Fuel is chiefly Stone Coal, brought from just across the Monongahela, and sold in the Town at two pence a Bushel. I cannot call it Pittcoal, because it is not dug out of Pits, but broke off the Cliff into Boats in the River; the Vein 3 feet thick.[4] The Government, civil as well as military, is in the commanding Officer, Col. Bouquet,[5] whose Will

2. Johnson and Croghan, like others who understood the Indians and their expectations, were highly critical of "the General's Frugality in Lessening the Expence of Presents." *Johnson Papers*, III, 965; X, 597, 652.

3. Life in the village at Fort Pitt in 1762–63, "more sordid than elegant," is well described in Nicholas B. Wainwright, *George Croghan Wilderness Diplomat* (Chapel Hill, [1959]), pp. 192–4.

4. John Bartram, who visited Fort Pitt in September 1761, evidently reported to Peter Collinson on the coal he had seen there. Collinson replied prophetically: "When the country grows populous and the wood scarce and dear, coal may be of infinite service to supply that deficiency." William Darlington, ed., *Memorials of John Bartram and Humphry Marshall* (Phila., 1849), p. 237. James Kenny, a Quaker working at the trading store set up near the fort, mentions the "stone coal" several times in his journal, 1761–63, and describes the easy method of procuring it which BF reports here. *PMHB*, XXXVII (1913), pp. 6, 20, 22, 25, 46.

5. On Henry Bouquet, see above, VII, 63 n.

is the Law; and as he is a very good Man it is a very good Government. The People have Balls for Dancing, and Assemblies for Religious Worship, but as they cannot yet afford to maintain both a Clergyman and a Dancing-master, the Dancingmaster reads Prayers and one of Tristram Shandy's Sermons every Sunday.[6] A considerable Indian Trade is now carried on there, by the Publick Store of this Province, by Sir William Johnson's Agent (who claims I know not on what Foundation, some Right of governing the Indian Trade) and by private Traders, some of whom take Licences of Sir William's Agent.[7] The Province has likewise a Trading House at Fort Augusta on Susquehanah.

I am glad on many Accounts to hear you have at length got into Parliament.[8] I hope much Good to America from your Influence there.

I wish you sincerely every kind of Happiness, and among the rest that of a good Wife when you chuse it;[9] being as ever, with perfect Esteem, Dear Sir, Your most obedient and most humble Servant   B FRANKLIN

P.S. March 22.[1] Since writing the above, Messrs. William and Daniel Coxe, Descendants of Dr. Daniel Coxe, formerly Pro-

6. James Kenny states that in December 1761 the inhabitants had engaged a schoolmaster and that he, a Presbyterian, "Reads the Littany and Common Prayer on the first Days to a Congregation of different Principels." In the following July Colonel Bouquet "sat up the Common Prayer and Littiany to be read on the first Days the Week," a duty then performed by the commissary, John Ormsby. *PMHB*, XXXVII (1913), 29, 163. Kenny makes no mention in this connection of a dancing master or of sermons, Tristram Shandy's or any others. BF was referring to Laurence Sterne's *The Sermons of Mr. Yorick* (London, 1761).

7. The provincial commissioners of Indian affairs maintained a public store and trading house at Fort Pitt. At this time BF's nephew, Josiah Davenport (C.12.4), was in charge with James Kenny as assistant. Sir William Johnson and his deputy George Croghan had been licensing traders and fixing prices at Fort Pitt since 1759, regardless of the Pa. law governing the Indian trade. Wainwright, *George Croghan*, p. 182; *Johnson Papers*, III, 495, 527–8.

8. Jackson was elected M.P. for Weymouth and Melcombe Regis, Dorset, Dec. 1, 1762; Namier and Brooke, *House of Commons*, II, 669.

9. Jackson never married.

1. This letter and especially the two postscripts reflect the interest BF and many others in England and America were beginning to take in the West, either as prospective settlers or as speculators in the lands presumably opened

prietor of Carolana, have applied to me to recommend to them some proper Person in England to solicit their Claim to that Country, and obtain for them either a Renewal of the Grant, or a Grant of some other Territory in Lieu of it, or an equivalent Sum as a Compensation for the Expences of the Family in the Discovery and Attempts of Settlement in that Country, which were frustrated by the French, as you will see in the Journals and Papers transmitted to you. I have assur'd them that no one was more capable, or would be better dispos'd to serve them, than yourself; and I beg leave to recommend them and their Interests to you most cordially and warmly, as they are good Friends of mine, and Persons of Worth, Candour and Honour, on whose Proposals, Offers and Promises, relating to Shares in the Propriety recovered, you and your Friends, if dispos'd to engage in the Affair, may place the fullest Confidence. You know there was a

---

up by the elimination of French competition. In 1629 Charles I had granted to Sir Robert Heath a vast proprietorship named "Carolana" (not "Carolina") covering the whole North American continent between the 31st and 36th parallels. On the Atlantic coast the tract included virtually the whole of the present state of Georgia, all of South Carolina, and the part of North Carolina south of Albemarle Sound, together with the Bahama Islands. William L. Saunders, ed., *No. Car. Col. Recs.*, I (1886), 5–13. Heath took no effective steps to settle his domain and after his claims had passed through several hands they were acquired in 1696 by Dr. Daniel Coxe (1640–1730), court physician and promoter. *PMHB*, VII (1883), 317–37. In 1684–86 Coxe had already gained large interests in the tangled proprietary rights to East and West Jersey. He never moved to America, but his son Col. Daniel Coxe (1673–1739) did, and the colonel became in time one of the largest land-holders in N.J. and one of the leaders in the protracted quarrels over control of the colony's land. *DAB;* John E. Pomfret, *The New Jersey Proprietors and Their Lands* (Princeton, 1964). Colonel Coxe tried with only limited success to get the family's claims to Carolana recognized—at least those to the southern and western, unsettled portions—and in this effort, as BF explains in this postscript, Coxe's son William (d. 1801), of N.J. and Philadelphia, and his grandson Daniel (c. 1739–1826), William's nephew, followed him. In 1769 the Privy Council declared these claims invalid, because of the lapse of time and the active settlement of the Carolinas and Georgia by others since the original grant, but agreed to award the Coxe family 100,000 acres in Oneida Co. in upper N.Y. as compensation and in return for a formal surrender of all claims to Carolana. *Acts Privy Coun., Col.*, V, 140–2. Subsequent correspondence between BF and Jackson contains numerous references to this affair.

Scheme between Mr. Sargent, Sir Matthew Featherstone,[2] and myself, of obtaining a Grant in America, thro' some Interest of theirs, in which I told you I intended you to have what Share you thought proper. I know not how that Application goes on, or if it is like to succeed; but think it rather probable that it may fail, as Sir Matthew's Interest must have been much weakened by the Resignation of the Duke of Newcastle. In that case, if this Application of Messieurs Coxe should succeed, which, from its great Equity may I think be very reasonably expected, I would very willingly engage with you and those Gentlemen, and any others you may think proper to associate with you, and take a Fifth of the Half Messrs. Coxe offer in their Letter to you, upon the Terms there mentioned; and shall use all my Diligence and all my Interest in these Colonies to promote a speedy Settlement. As to the proper Constitution of Government to be obtain'd, and the Modes of Settling, &c. you and I have so often discours'd on these Topics, and understand one another's Sentiments so fully, that I need not mention anything concerning them, knowing, as I do, that you will endeavour to obtain all the suitable Powers, as far as the Crown in their present Sentiments can be prevail'd on to grant. I would only request you to offer a Share to my good Friend Dr. Pringle, as, if the Affair succeeds it may be advantageous to him whom I much desire to serve, and I have reason to think he has an Interest that may greatly facilitate the Application.[3]

I inclose you part of a New Jersey Magazine for 1758, by which you may see something of the common Opinion of a western Settlement at that time, when the French were suppos'd to retain Canada;[4] but now that Power is reduc'd, we may sup-

2. Sir Matthew Fetherstonhaugh, baronet (1714?–1774), F.R.S., 1752; M.P., 1755–74; son of a merchant of Newcastle-upon-Tyne. He inherited great wealth from an uncle in 1746 and in the next year purchased the estate of Uppark in Sussex. A large holder of stock in the East India Co. and the Bank of England, he was later associated with John Sargent, Samuel Wharton, BF, and others in the Vandalia land project. Politically he was a protégé of the Duke of Newcastle. Namier and Brooke, *House of Commons*, II, 422–3. There is no information on the scheme projected before BF left England.

3. BF probably had in mind Dr. John Pringle's friendship with the Earl of Bute, but Pringle declined joining in this scheme because he disliked financial speculation. See below, p. 416.

4. Among the Jackson Papers, APS, are pp. 343–50 of *The New American*

pose People are much more willing to go into those Countries. And in fact there appears every where an unaccountable *Penchant* in all our People to migrate westward.

March 29. Since the above I have receiv'd the two inclos'd Letters from Mr. Finley, President of the Jersey College,[5] by which you will see, the People begin already to think of moving. Messrs. Coxe have likewise had Applications made to them. I believe we must strike while the Iron is hot, and engage a Number of Settlers while you are transacting the Affair in England.[6] Mr. Lyon's Plan appears very crude, yet he tells me above a hundred Families have already declared there readiness to migrate on that Scheme.[7] BF.

Mr. Jackson

Addressed: To / Richard Jackson Esqr / Counsellor at Law / Inner Temple / London / Dicks / Coffe hous[8]

Endorsed: Philad Mar 8th 1763 B Franklin Esqr

Magazine, No. XIII for January 1759, undoubtedly the part BF sent. Most of the eight pages are occupied by "The Historical Chronicle, For January, 1758." The "1758" is an obvious typographical error for "1759" which was corrected later in the press run, as other copies show, but it explains BF's citation of the earlier date. On p. 349 is a news item marked in ink from "Perth-Amboy, Jan. 29" about a proposal to apply to the King and Parliament for a royal charter "to settle a new colony on the Ohio, by the name of PITTSYLVANIA." The article continues with warm approval of the scheme as a check to French power in America and with an expression of belief that it would attract about 10,000 families as settlers, including at least 1000 from N.J. "And what is still a greater encouragement, there is room enough for ten times the number to settle upon extraordinarily good land." The promoters of the plan are not identified.

5. See below, pp. 224–5, 231.

6. WF joined his father in enthusiastic support of the Coxe scheme. Writing to the Board of Trade, May 10, 1763, he declared: "And such is the Spirit of Migration now in America, that should the Descendant of Dr. Cox (who is a Gentleman of Character and Fortune in this Province) succeed in his Application for a Grant of Lands on the Missisipi, there will be little Occasion for any Inhabitants from the Mother Country, as there might by proper Management be at least 20,000 Persons procur'd to settle there from the Northern Colonies in less than five Years. The Places of these would be soon supply'd again by the great natural Encrease of the Inhabitants of this Country, and by the Accession of Foreigners." 1 *N.J. Arch.,* IX, 386.

7. See below, pp. 256–7.

8. The last three words in another hand.

From Mary Stevenson

ALS (mutilated):[9] American Philosophical Society

Dear Sir   Kensington March 11. 1763

It was with great pleasure I h[eard of] your safe and happy arrival at Philadelphia; and [hearti]ly congratulate you and the dear Partakers of y[our Socie]ty, but you must all forgive me if I repine [that] you are oblig'd to enjoy it at so great a d[istance] from me. My Mother receiv'd yours of [?   ] November and another a few days ago, of a la[ter date][1] in which you tell her you have sent som[e   ?   ]presents by Capt. Friend, and have written [to me at] large by him, but the Ship being taken [those] Letters are lost that would have afforded [us great] pleasure.[2] I need not tell you the grateful [?   ] your particular remembrance of her; sh[e was concerned?] rather too much over your other Correspo[ndents and] began to be a little jealous. She has filled s[everal] sheets of paper to send you, but her Letter [is not] quite finish'd,[3] therefore she bids me write [by this] opportunity. It will appear strange to you [that] I wanted to be bidden to do what I used to take so great delight in, when you are conscious I can have no reason for an alteration of sentiment. I have no alteration of sentiment towards you, my dear [Sir.] I still, and must ever, love you with filial tender[ness and] veneration; my indisposition to write is owing, [not] to the coldness of my heart, but the emptiness [of my] head, and I may add, the dejection of my spirits, [which] have not yet recover'd the shock of parting [from] my dear Pitt.[4] She has had bad weather since she [sail]'d, but I imagine she is now clear

---

9. An irregular strip has been torn from the edge of the sheet; missing words have been supplied conjecturally in brackets wherever possible.

1. Neither of these letters has been found.

2. For the capture of the *Carolina*, Capt. James Friend, see above, p. 160 n. An extract of BF's letter to William Strahan of Dec. 7, 1762, sent by the *Carolina*, was printed in *London Chron.*, March 19–22, 1763, which dates the arrival of the *Carolina's* letters in London. It is not clear, however, whether the Stevensons received the letter and presents sent by that ship.

3. Mrs. Stevenson apparently sent her letter to BF on April 14, 1763; see below, p. 297.

4. Polly's friend Miss Pitt has been mentioned frequently in letters to BF, but little is known about her except that she was about Polly's age and lived in Jamaica.

of our coast, [and I] hope her dangers and distresses are over. God grant [her a] safe and happy voyage! [If I h]ad more to say I should not have time to [write it] for I must send my Letter to my Mother [quick]ly. At all times, and upon all occasions, [believe me] to be Dear Sir Your grateful Friend and affectionate Servant   M STEVENSON

Addressed: To / Dr Franklin / at / Philadelphia

Anthony Todd[5] to Benjamin Franklin and John Foxcroft (I)

Copy: Yale University Library

Copy

Gentlemen   General Post Office the 12th. of March 1763

His Majesty's Post Master General[6] having been pleased, at the same time, They have thought fit to lay down the Correspondence with His Majesty's Islands in the West Indies, to Establish Four Packet Boats of 130 Tons each, with 18 Hands, in order to continue a Monthly Correspondence between Great Britain, and the Continent of America, in time of Peace; and until the same can be

5. Anthony Todd (1717–1798) began his career at the Post Office in 1732, was appointed a clerk in the Department's Foreign Office in 1738, was promoted to foreign secretary in 1752 (serving until 1787), and to secretary on Dec. 1, 1762, serving until his death, with the exception of one three-year interval (1765–68). As secretary he was "the executive and responsible officer" of the Post Office. He amassed a fortune from the perquisites of his various offices, the most lucrative being fees from packet expenditures, and in 1782 married his daughter to the son of the seventh Earl of Lauderdale. Todd also speculated in American lands, being associated with BF in the Grand Ohio or Walpole Company. The best account of Todd's career is in Kenneth Ellis, *The Post Office in the Eighteenth Century* (London, 1958), pp. 78–123. For John Foxcroft, BF's colleague as deputy postmaster general of North America, see above, IX, 378 n.

6. The postmasters general at this time were Robert Hampden-Trevor (see the document immediately below) and John Perceval, second Earl of Egmont (1711–1780), who was appointed on Nov. 27, 1762, and resigned on Sept. 10, 1763. Egmont's successor was Thomas Villiers (1709–1786), created Baron Hyde on June 3, 1756, and Earl of Clarendon on June 14, 1776. *DNB.* Although two men occupied the office jointly, Todd regularly referred to the "PostMaster General" in the singular.

provided, to employ the Four Vessells already in that Service;[7] I am Commanded to acquaint you thereof by this Mail, which is the first dispatched upon this new Plan, that you may immediately give Public Notice thereof,[8] and take every other Step to extend the benefit, which this Conveyance is intended to be of, to all His Majesty's Subjects, particularly the Trading part of them, in the American Colonies; a safe and regular Correspondence, being the Spirit and life of Commerce, and in general one of the greatest accomodations to Mankind.

I need not observe to you, that as the sole Conveyance of Letters by Land or Sea, to all His Majesty's Dominions, is the undoubted Privelege of His Majesty's Postmaster General, The Packet Boats are wholly under Their Direction, and are not to be put out of their Course of sailing on any Account, or to be employed in any Service foreign to their true Destination; In times of War it has indeed, now and then, been allowed for the Commander in Chief, to detain a Packet Boat, for the pressing Concerns of the State, upon his Signing a Certificate, and transmitting it to The Postmaster General, of the absolute necessity of so doing, on Account of His Majesty's urgent Service; which by the happy Restoration of Peace can be no longer alledged;[9] On this presumption it is The Postmaster General's Orders, that a Mail be now dispatched from hence, and from New York, precisely on the second Saturday of every Month throughout the Year, and the Packet Boat in turn on either side, to sail therewith directly, without waiting for the Arrival of another Mail or Packet.

By your being able to give Public Notice, of this regular Monthly Period of the Packet Boats being to sail from New York, which

7. Packet service between N.Y. and Falmouth was established by the Post Office in 1755–56 (see above, VI, 277 n). The four packets in service in 1763 were the *Duke of Cumberland*, Capt. Goodridge (Goodrich); the *Pitt*, Capt. Bridstock; the *Harriot*, Capt. Robinson; and the *Earl of Halifax*, Capt. Jefferies (Jeffery).

8. BF and Foxcroft wrote Todd on June 10, 1763, that they had advertised the new packet schedule and had "order'd the Advertisement to be constantly inserted for twelve Months to come in all the News Papers of America." See below, p. 280.

9. For BF's complaints about Lord Loudoun's detention of packets in 1757, which delayed BF's departure to England by two months, see *Autobiog.* (APS-Yale edit.), pp. 250–3.

can now be depended on, all persons throughout the extensive and flourishing Empire of America, may calculate, according to the course of the Inland Posts, at what time to Write, so that their Letters for Europe may arrive by the proper day at New York.

I am also to inform you, that this Establishment, now continued for the Benefit of His Majesty's Subjects, and more particularly of those of America, being undertaken at a great Expence to the Revenue of this Office; The Postmaster General is willing to make a fair Tryal of its utility, and would be sorry from the inconsiderable amount of the Postage it may produce, to be under the necessity of laying it down again; They therefore recommend it to you heartily, to exert your utmost attention and abilities, that the Inland Posts of America, may be so managed and improved as to come in Aid, and support of this Service; A Country of growing Wealth and Commerce, so speedily Multiplying its Inhabitants, cannot fail to keep pace in an increase of Correspondence; especially under your Management, who are so capable of improving a Work of This kind; and you cannot exert Yourselves on any Subject, that will do you more honour, or your Native Country greater Service, than in rendering the intercourse of Letters, every day more safe and expeditious to your fellow Subjects.

It will be a Satisfaction to The PostMaster General, if, for the future, in making up your Mail for this Office, you bind up the Letters from Each Government, or Province, in seperate Bundles, marking at the same time upon each Bundle, the exact Number of Letters contained therein, and the amount of the Inland Postage paid thereon.

The Accomptant General of this Office not having finished his Observations upon the last state of your Account,[1] I have for the present only to acquaint you, That you are hereafter to allow in your Account with Mr. Colden Deputy Postmaster of New York,[2] the Salary of £60 per Annum, Sterling, which he has hitherto been paid from This Office, as Agent for the Packet Boats, to commence from the 5th. of January last, whereof I have this day given him Notice, as also of every matter relating to the Packet

1. This account, covering approximately four years, ending in August 1761 (see the document immediately below), has not been found.
2. For Alexander Colden, see above, VI, 113 n.

Boat Service, having sent This Letter to him open for that purpose. I am Gentlemen Yours &c.   ANTH: TODD Secry.

To Benjamin Franklin and John Foxcroft Esqrs.
Deputy PostMaster General of America

Anthony Todd to Benjamin Franklin and John Foxcroft (II)

Copy: Yale University Library

Copy

Gentlemen   General Post Office the 12 of March 1763

The Accomptant General of this Office, having now finished his observations (for which I prepared you in my other Letter of this date)[3] upon the state of your Accounts, and His Majesty's Post-Master General having adopted the same; I am Commanded to observe to you, that your last Account for about Four Years ending with August 1761,[4] being sworn to in London in April last by Mr. Franklin, it is much to be lamented, that the Opportunity was then neglected, of entering into a full Examination of it, as well as into a clear detail of the American Posts in general; together with the Improvements lately made, or to be made, therein; as many useful Informations and Lights, might by That means, have been acquired much easier and better than by Writing.

The Sums on the Credit side of the said Account cannot be regularly traced, as they ought to be, because in the several Postmasters seperate Accounts delivered in therewith, are neither stated the respective Receipts, nor Balances of such several Postmasters.[5]

An Account ought to be made out Quarterly with each Postmaster, and Copies thereof transmitted hither.

Every Article of Money, mentioned to have been either paid, or remitted, should stand upon the general account also, To enable you to be more distinct hereafter, I inclose you some Forms which will explain Themselves,[6] and are modelled upon the Practice of

3. See the document immediately above. The accountant general of the Post Office at this time was Thomas Pitches (d. 1767).

4. This account has not been found.

5. For BF and Foxcroft's defense of the irregularities in the accounts of the American postmasters, see below, pp. 281–2.

6. These forms have not been found.

our Deputy PostMasters General for Scotland and Ireland; who even transmit hither the original Vouchers to all material Articles. Upon the Debtor side of your said Account there are two Sums of £32. 11s. and £59. 17s. for 31 and 57 days travelling Charges of Mr. Hunter;[7] which The PostMaster General altogether disapprove, and think them too exceptionable to pass without Notice. They observe on This Occasion that the Post Act[8] requires the Chief Office to be establish't and kept at New York; consequently the Deputy Postmaster General is understood to reside there; the absurdity is therefore the stronger that Mr. Hunter should not only have lived at a distance from his proper station, but that he should have brought a charge upon the Revenue, for passing to and from New York, where strictly speaking, he ought to have had his Residence; and now that Packet Boats are established a fresh, with a View to connect His Majesty's North American Dominions, even in time of Peace, with These Kingdoms; New York must still continue to be the Centre of That important Correspondence.

The PostMaster General having it, as you may perceive, much at heart to improve Correspondence, and the Revenue committed to Their Care; every Thought you may have to suggest for the Benefit of America in that respect, will be particularly attended to, and if you should be of Opinion, that an able Surveyor or two could give you further Informations, and assist in laying out post Roads, as well as in instructing, and supervising your several Deputies in the regular performance of their Duty; and informing proper cheque offices, upon particular parts of Roads, where Letters ought to Turn, or go across; I am inclined to think, They would not upon your Application, refuse you an assistant so material.[9]

For the mean time, The PostMaster General would have you, in order that They may form some Idea of the Improvements you

7. For William Hunter (d. 1761), Foxcroft's predecessor as joint deputy postmaster general of North America, see above, v, 18 n. For BF's defense of his expenditures, see below, p. 283. BF had asked Col. John Hunter for a state of William Hunter's accounts, Oct. 9, 1761; see above, IX, 363–4.

8. 9 Anne, c. 11 (1710), "An Act for establishing a General Post-Office for all Her Majesties Dominions." See above, IX, 303 n.

9. In answering this letter on June 10, 1763, BF and Foxcroft informed Todd that "an able Surveyor would be of great Use," but no such officer was appointed until 1772, when Hugh Finlay (see the document immediately below) was given the job.

have made, or intend making, send them one or more Maps of America, with the Post roads, Towns, Stations, and Distances, carefully marked throughout;[1] with a Table of all the Post Towns, Postmasters Names, and their Salaries, distinguishing how much for their Office Duty, and how much for Their Riding work, These Lights and helps are grown the more necessary to Them, as They have been given to understand, that amongs't the many National schemes of Improvement now on foot, great matters are expected of Them relating to the Posts in His Majesty's American Dominions.

I have only to add, that you are to remit immediately to The PostMaster General the Balance of your Account with this Office, in good Bills payable to Robert Trevor Esq.[2] Receiver General of the Revenue of the Post Office, taking care to distinguish such part thereof, as became due before the 25th of October 1760 being the day of His late Majesty's Demise; such part as has since accrued, must be accounted for to the aggregate Fund.

You are desired to bring your next Account down to the 5th. of April 1762;[3] and afterwards to make the same up Yearly.

It is taken for granted that no Governor of a Province, on pretence of His Majesty's Service, or any other person, have ever been allowed to send or receive Letters free of Postage. I am Gentlemen Yours &c.   ANTH: TODD Secry.

To Benjamin Franklin and John Foxcroft Esqrs.
Deputy PostMaster General of America

1. No maps of this description have been found in BF's papers.
2. In July 1762 a Robert Trevor was appointed receiver general of the Post Office, which position he held until his death on Oct. 21, 1785. In his obituary in *Gent. Mag.* he was identified as a brother of the second Viscount Hampden, whose father, Robert Hampden-Trevor (1706–1783), was postmaster general, 1759–65, and was created first Viscount Hampden in 1776. But since neither of the first viscount's sons was named Robert, the receiver general was probably a more distant relative. *DNB; Gent. Mag.,* xxxii (1762); lv (1785), 837.
3. This account has not been found.

Anthony Todd to Benjamin Franklin and
John Foxcroft (III)

Copy: Yale University Library

Copy

Gentlemen. General Post Office 12th March 1763.

Inclosed I send you, by Command of His Majesty's PostMaster General, the Copy of a Letter just received from General Murray Governor of Quebec;[4] as likewise the Copy of a Memorial inclosed therein from the British Merchants residing in That Government;[5] by which they plainly appear to labour under many difficulties for the want of a safe and Speedy Conveyance of Letters; also that they are detained, Lost, and opened on the Road, with great Prejudice to their Concerns.

The Postmaster General do therefore wish, as there appears by the said Memorial and other Informations they have received, to be already a Number of His Majesty's Subjects settled in Trade and Business at Quebec, that you might find it practicable to establish a regular Post between That Government and New York,[6] which it is presumed here, according to a Letter from Mr. Franklin to The PostMaster General in June 1762,[7] may be already set on foot, by way of Albany and Montreal.

Upon This Occasion I am commanded to put you again in Mind of Mr. Finlay,[8] whom The PostMaster General, by my Letter of the

4. James Murray (1719?–1794), the commander of the British left wing at the battle on the Plains of Abraham, was appointed governor of the town of Quebec on Oct. 27, 1760, and promoted to major general on July 10, 1762. After Canada was ceded to Britain in 1763, he was appointed governor of the new province of Quebec, serving until 1766. He became governor of Minorca in 1774 and commanded the garrison at Fort St. Philip, which surrendered to the French in February 1782 after gallantly resisting a siege of several months. *DNB*.

5. Neither Murray's letter nor the merchants' memorial has been found.

6. See below, p. 279, for Franklin and Foxcroft's efforts to establish postal service between N.Y. and Quebec.

7. Not found.

8. Hugh Finlay (c. 1731–1801), a Scot, emigrated to Canada soon after the French capitulation, becoming a merchant and justice of the peace in Quebec. Appointed postmaster by BF and Foxcroft, June 10, 1763 (below, p. 279), as ordered by the authorities in England, he took jurisdiction over the post offices at Montreal and Three Rivers as well as at Quebec. In 1765 he was appointed to the provincial Council and in 1772 he became the first surveyor

8th of January last,[9] proposed to you as a proper person to be Postmaster of Quebec, and who intends to sail from Glasgow about the 15 Instant, with a Recommendation from The PostMaster General, to the favour and protection of General Murray, you will therefore not fail to appoint the said Mr. Finlay immediately upon his arrival at Quebec. I am Gentlemen, &c.   ANTH: TODD Secry.[1]

Benj. Franklin and Jno. Foxcroft Esqrs.
Depy. Postmasrs. Genl. of No. America.

From Samuel Finley[2]   ALS: American Philosophical Society

Dear Sir,   Princeton. March. 17th. 1763
I received Your Favour of the 7th Instant,[3] with the Plan of Education in the College of Glasgow, inclosed,[4] for which I most

---

general of the American postal system. In this capacity he undertook a tour of inspection, 1773–74, which extended as far south as Savannah, Ga. His *Journal* of this trip (Frank H. Norton, ed., Brooklyn, 1867) is a valuable account of the postal service and of the colonial scene on the eve of the Revolution. When BF was dismissed from office in 1774, Finlay succeeded him as deputy postmaster general. After British recognition of American independence he held the office of deputy postmaster general of Canada until 1799. His services are described in William Smith, *The History of the Post Office in British North America 1639–1870* (Cambridge, Eng., 1920), pp. 42–95.

9. Not found.

1. Todd wrote Governor Murray on the same day, telling him of this letter to the deputy postmasters general and of the new packet service between N.Y. and England, and informing him that Finlay was about to sail for Quebec and was expected to become postmaster there. Copy: Yale Univ. Lib.

2. Samuel Finley (1715–1766) emigrated to Philadelphia in 1734 from County Armagh, Ireland. He studied at the famous "Log College," a seminary founded at Neshaminy, Pa., by William Tennent to train New Light Presbyterian ministers, and he was ordained in 1742. Finley took a leading part in the Great Awakening, preaching as far north as Conn. and publishing several polemical pamphlets. From 1744 to 1761 he was a minister at Nottingham, Pa., where he conducted a school which produced such men as Benjamin Rush and John Bayard. On May 31, 1761, he was unanimously elected president of the College of N.J. and served until his death. *DAB*.

3. Not found. The letter probably arose from discussions which BF had with Finley while he and WF were visiting the College of N.J. on March 2, 1763. See above, pp. 200–1 n.

4. The plan has not been found. BF spent several days in Glasgow in Sep-

224

heartily Thank you. I have taken a Coppy of it, and return it inclosed according to your Desire. I also delivered your Compliments, which were very acceptable.

I last night received a Letter, from a Gentleman,[5] desiring me to form a Scheme for a Settlement on the Mississipi, and communicate it to some of my Friends in London, who have Access to Men in Power. I quickly resolved, that I had not Sufficient Skill in Politics for such an Undertaking; and if I even had, yet I have no Leizure to bring it to maturity: but wishing some good Plan might be laid, and considering who cou'd prosecute the Matter most advantageously, I soon fixed on Doctor Franklin, and there did and do rest. A Settlement there seems to me necessary; and if so, the Plan shou'd be well concerted, and popular. If Monopolies and Proprietaryships are admitted, I am afraid it will hurt, if not defeat the Design. The People wou'd most willingly adventure under a Leader of their own Chusing at first, and had rather have the King himself their Proprietary than any other.

I have only Time for these half-spoken embrio-notions. If you think that forming Such a Scheme wou'd be at all to the Purpose, I doubt not you will think of one.

Please, Sir, to accept my Sincere Compliments, in which mrs. Finley[6] joins, and present the same to mrs. Franklin, and miss Sally. If his Excellency is yet with you, I wou'd, with all due Respect, beg his acceptance of the same. You will excuse my Hurry, and believe me to be, with cordial Respect, dear sir, Your most humble servant   SAML: FINLEY

Doctor Franklin

Endorsed: March 17th. 1763 Saml. Finley to B Franklin[7]

---

tember 1759, being admitted a burgess and guild brother on September 19, and may have acquired there either a published plan of education of the college or have taken notes which he passed on to Finley. See above, VIII, 430–1.

5. Unidentified.

6. Finley's second wife, whom he married in 1761, was Anne Clarkson, the daughter of Matthew Clarkson of N.Y. and the stepdaughter of the famous revivalist, Gilbert Tennent. *DAB.* Her sister Catherine was the wife of Samuel Hazard, whose scheme for a western settlement BF had criticized in 1755; above, VI, 87. Her brother, Matthew Clarkson, was associated with BF in 1765 in a project to acquire lands in Nova Scotia. *PMHB,* LI (1927), 273–4 n.

7. BF sent this letter to Richard Jackson, along with Finley's of March 21.

From John Whitehurst

ALS: American Philosophical Society

This letter from one of Franklin's English scientific friends, which touches briefly on a variety of matters, is perhaps less important in the history of science than the enclosure which follows it. In the postscript Whitehurst mentions that he is sending "a short sketch of a General Theory of the Earth." On June 27, 1763, Franklin acknowledged receiving both the letter and its enclosure.[8] When the Franklin Papers in the American Philosophical Society Library were arranged many years ago the letter and the sketch to which it refers became separated and the authorship of the enclosure was left undetermined.[9] This paper has now been identified, and it is here restored to its proper place immediately following the text of the letter it accompanied.

Fifteen years later, in 1778, Whitehurst published *An Inquiry into the Original State and Formation of the Earth*, a major treatise on which he is known to have been working for several years. Examination shows that this enclosure contains an outline or summary of the first chapter of the 1778 publication, following the same order of presentation and argument and often using the same phraseology. The sketch is much shorter and omits any reference to the illustrative diagrams and plates which are found in the book and discussed in its first chapter, but the basic ideas are the same in both.[1]

The manuscript of this "short sketch" is unusual. It begins as a letter with the salutation "Sir," but it carries no date line. It is written on a four-page sheet; the first two pages and part of the third are in Whitehurst's hand; then, after the first word of a new paragraph, for some unknown reason a distinctly different handwriting appears and continues to the end, about the middle of the fourth page. In the next to last line Whitehurst inserted four words his copyist had omitted, but he failed to add the complimentary close and signature which might be expected in a paper he had begun in letter form.

Although these peculiarities remain unexplained, this document and Franklin's acknowledgment of its receipt clearly establish that Whitehurst had begun work on his *magnum opus* at least fifteen years before he completed and published it.

8. See below, pp. 300, 302.

9. The letter is filed as I, 72, and the enclosure as XLIX, 48. I. Minis Hays, *Calendar of the Papers of Benjamin Franklin* (Phila., 1908), records them at I, 24 and 53, respectively, suggests no author for the sketch, and assigns it a rough dating of "[*circa* 1765?]."

1. Entire credit for the suggestion of comparing this apparently anonymous paper with Whitehurst's *Inquiry* to discover the possible writer belongs to Assistant Editor Helen C. Boatfield. L.W.L.

Dear Sir   Derby 18th Mar: 1763
It was a matter of great Joy to me, to see an Account in the public papers of your safe Arrival in North America; where I hope you found your family and friends all well.

I sincerely congratulate you Sir, on Mr. Franklins Appointment to the Government of New-Jersey, where I hope he and his Lady are safely arrived.

The bearer Mr. Tunicliff,[2] is a farmer of good Credit, from this neighbourhood. He has lived many years at Langley, a Vilage four Miles from hence. He visits North America with a Veiw of Purchasing two or three thousand Acres of uncultivated land, and bringing his family over to Settle there, having too great a Spirit to comply with the terms which farmers in general are now oblig'd to comply with at this time in England. Viz. of occup[y]ing lands at the Will of the Lord. And therefore is determined to take up his aboad in a Land of greater liberty, and to situate himself so, as to carry on some Trade with the Indians.

In the execution of this plan, I hope Sir, you will be so kind to give my friend and neighbour a little Advice. He is esteem'd an excellent Farmer, and very Active in business: hence, cannot fail of making a Valuable member of Society. I took the liberty of consulting the Governor[3] on this occation before he left England, in regard to the probability of suceeding in such a Scheme, and he gave great incouragement to undertake it.

Doctor Darwin[4] and Mr. Tissington[5] send Complements, are

2. John Tunnicliff of Langley Lodge near Derby came to Philadelphia in 1763 and had apparently returned to England by 1765. The following year he asked BF's assistance in acquiring a "good Plantation either in Pennsylvania or the Jerseys" and sent him a woodcock and a partridge. Whitehurst to BF, April 23, 1765; Tunnicliff to BF, Dec. 21, 1766, APS.

3. WF.

4. Erasmus Darwin (1731–1802), F.R.S., 1788, grandfather of the author of *On the Origin of Species*, graduated from Cambridge in 1754, went on to Edinburgh to study medicine, began practicing in Nottingham in September 1756, and moved to Lichfield in November of the same year. His practice was extremely successful, and he eventually earned about £1000 a year from it. Darwin was one of the founders of the Lunar Society of Birmingham, wrote on a number of medical and scientific topics, and was an inventor of some repute. He also wrote poetry, some of which was well received by the critics of the time. *DNB;* Robert Schofield, *The Lunar Society of Birmingham* (Oxford, 1963).

5. For Anthony Tissington, mineralogist, whom BF nominated to the Royal Society in 1766, see above, IX, 42 n.

both well. The Doctor I hope will be able to entertain you with some discoverys on Cold next winter.[6]

The Parliament has Mr. Harri[s]ons improvem[en]t of Measuring equal time at Sea under their Consideration, and I imagin will give him a hansom reward.[7] And the King has orderd this improvement to be made known to all his foreign Minesters. I suppose with some View of procuring a reward from those several Courts for Mr. Harrison, as well as making the discovery of General Use. This account Taylor White[8] gives me.

Ferments amongest the In's, and out's, I think subside apace. The King is determin'd to persevere in every legal step that can be taken for the general good and benefit of his Subjects. Should we live but one seven years, I expect to see a great reformation in the Management of Public affairs.

My Wife desires to joyne me in our most affectionate respects and I am Dear Sir, Your most obedient Humble Servant

J WHITEHURST

P.S. With this I [enclose?] you a short sketch of a General Theory of the Earth for your approbation.

Pray sir, do you, [keep] a journal of heat and cold. I imagin I cou'd derive some advantageous discoverys from general observations of this kind with respect to a more general theory of the earth. But Im afraid tis not to be brought about. If any thing of this sort is done amongst Your acquaintance in North America I should be extremely obligd to you for a Coppy and in return will send you an application of more observations in a general theory.[9]

Addressed: To / Benj: Franklin, Esqr / at / Philadelphia

6. No letter from Darwin to BF describing such discoveries has been found, nor does Darwin ever appear to have published anything about cold.

7. For John Harrison's invention of a chronometer which won a parliamentary prize of £20,000, see above, VII, 208–10.

8. Taylor White (1701–1772), a barrister with large practice on the northern circuit, judge of North Wales and of the County Palatine of Chester (1757–72); F.R.S., 1725; treasurer of the Foundling Hospital, 1745–72. R. H. Nichols and F. A. Wray, *The History of the Foundling Hospital* (London, 1935), pp. 312–13 *et passim; Gent. Mag.,* XLII (1772), 199; *London Chron.,* March 28–31, 1772.

9. BF told Whitehurst, June 27, 1763, of a Philadelphia friend (possibly John Bartram) who had kept such a journal for years and would send a copy. See below, p. 302. Dr. John Lining and Ezra Stiles were among BF's American

[Enclosure]

Sir

I here take the liberty of presenting you with a few hints, relative to a general theory, or natural history of the earth: principally calculated to prove that fossell shells were originally the offspring of the sea.

The period of time since the DEITY created the Constituent parts of the Earth, and brought them into Contact: appears too unlimited and Void of Natural evidence, to admit of a Philosophical solution. And therefore nothing can be deduced from the Antiquity of the Earth in aid of a General Theory.

But the figure of the earth being truly ascertain'd and proved beyond all contradiction to be an oblate spheroid; is a circumstance highly favorable for the establishment of a general theory: for from this fact alone, and its agreement with the general laws of Nature; many other essential truths are derived, as I presume, will appear, by the following Investigations, and will also plainly shew, that there is no other point or Datum from whence a general theory, or history of the Earth can truly flow.

Hence it was impossible, for men of the most extensive genius, to write a Consistant Theory, before our Great Philosopher[1] had reveald those Axoims to the World.

Prop. 1st.

According to the universal law of gravitation, the constituent particles of all bodys mutually Attract each other; and therefore produce in themselves a Common center of gravity, which governs and regulates the whole, so as to cause all such as are fluid and at rest to become Spherical.

Gravitation, being a fundamental law of Nature; by which all Matter is equally and Universally govern'd: And there being no other law, or principle in Nature, from whence bodys can become spherical: it is therefore manifest, that all Spherical bodys

---

friends who kept thermometric journals. The table of American temperatures Whitehurst used in his *Inquiry into the Original State and Formation of the Earth* is one from Md., taken from *Phil. Trans.*, LI, 58–82.

1. Sir Isaac Newton. This passage is considerably expanded in *Inquiry*, p. 2, and mentions Newton by name.

must have been in a state of fluidity and rest, tho' they are firm, and solid, in their present state.

Prop: 2d

The constituent particles of all bodys which turn round their own axis, acquire a Centrifugal force in proportion to their Velocities, and therefore as their distances are to each other, from their axis or center of Motion: so is their Velocities, and so is their Centrifugal force.

Hence,[2] it is manifest, that the equilibrium of Gravitation is destroy'd in all revolving bodies. And therefore such as turn their own Axis in a state of fluidity, must become Spheroidical, and in a certain Ratio, according to their Periodical rotations.

From whence I conclude that since there is no other law or principle in nature from whence bodies can become Spheroidical it therefore follows; that all Spheroidical bodies must have turn'd round their own Axis in a state of fluidity, tho they are firm and Solid in their present state.

Now since the Equatorial diameter of the Earth, exceeds her Polar, in a certain Ratio according to the period of her diurnal rotation it is therefore evident, that she turn'd round her own Axis in a state of fluidity, tho' she is firm and solid in her present state. And that the period of her rotation, has suffer'd no change or variation, from thence to the present period of time; but has agreeable to the Immutable laws of nature perfom'd equal rotations in equal times, thro' all Ages of the World to the present period.

This chain of evidence Sir, appears to give as full and clear a testimony of the Earths having been in a fluid state, as any Physical Solution can well be suppos'd to do. Hence I consider the Fluidity of the Earth[3] as a fact, and shall now inquire what effects that fluidity wou'd produce.[4]

2. The handwriting changes from Whitehurst's to that of an unknown person after this word.

3. "Fluidity of the Earth" is added above the line in Whitehurst's hand.

4. This paragraph is a very brief statement of what appears in considerably altered and expanded phraseology as the final two paragraphs of the introductory chapter of Whitehurst's *Inquiry*. Thus this paper covers precisely the same ground as the first chapter of the book. The second chapter opens a discussion of "The consequences necessarily arising" from the earth's "original state of fluidity."

From Samuel Finley

ALS: American Philosophical Society

Dear Sir, Princeton. March. 21. 1763

The Bearer, Mr: James Lyon,[5] who is well known in Philadelphia, desired me to introduce him to you by a Line. He waits on you for your Opinion of a Scheme for a Settlement on Mississipi, which he will Show you;[6] and for your Directions, and, if you Shall see Cause to approve any thing to that Purpose, your asistance. He is a young Gentleman of a very good moral Character, and well respected and beloved where he is known. I am perswaded your candid Opinion and Advice wou'd be of great Importance, and Service to him, as he depends much upon it, and is disposed to give it a just Weight.

This is a different application from the one I mentioned in my Letter the other Day, which I hope you received by the Post. The Complements presented in it I beg Leave humbly to renew, and am dear sir, Your most respectful and obedient

SAML. FINLEY

Endorsed: Mr President Finley's Letters. March 1763

To Mary Stevenson

ALS: Yale University Library

My dear Polley Philada. March 25. 1763

Your pleasing Favour of Nov. 11[7] is now before me. It found me as you suppos'd it would, happy with my American Friends and Family about me; and it made me more happy in showing me

---

5. James Lyon (1735–1794) graduated from the College of N.J. in 1759, when he composed the music for the class ode. In 1761 he published a hymnal, *Urania,* which went through a second edition in 1767, and on which his fame as a psalmodist chiefly rests. He was ordained by the Synod of New Brunswick in 1764 and in the following year went to Nova Scotia, where he and several groups of associates were granted 570,000 acres. He preached at Halifax and Onslow, before taking a church at Machias, Maine, in 1772. He remained at Machias for the rest of his life. *DAB.* W. O. Raymond, "Colonel Alexander McNutt and the Pre-Loyalist Settlements of Nova Scotia," Royal Society of Canada *Proc. and Trans.* 3d ser., v (1911), section II, 86–92.

6. Nothing is known of Lyon's scheme. In his letter to Richard Jackson of March 8, 1763, BF called it "very crude." See above, p. 215.

7. Not found.

that I am not yet forgotten by the dear Friends I left in England. And indeed why should I fear they will ever forget me, when I feel so strongly that I shall ever remember them!

I sympathise with you sincerely in your Grief at the Separation from your old Friend, Miss Pitt.[8] The Reflection that she is going to be more happy when she leaves you, might comfort you, if the Case was likely to be so circumstanc'd; but when the Country and Company she has been educated in, and those she is removing to, are compared, one cannot possibly expect it.

I sympathize with you no less in your Joys. But it is not merely on your Account that I rejoice at the Recovery of your dear Dolly's Health.[9] I love that dear good Girl myself, and I love her other Friends. I am therefore made happy by what must contribute so much to the Happiness of them all. Remember me to her, and to every one of that worthy and amiable Family most affectionately.

Remember me in the same manner to your and my good Doctor and Mrs. Hawkesworth.[1] You have lately, you tell me, had the Pleasure of spending three Days with them at Mr. Stanley's.[2] It was a sweet Society! (Remember me also to Mr. and Mrs. Stanley, and to Miss Arlond)[3]—I too, once partook of that same Pleasure, and can therefore feel what you must have felt. Of all the enviable Things England has, I envy it most its People. Why should that petty Island, which compar'd to America is but like a stepping Stone in a Brook, scarce enough of it above Water to keep one's Shoes dry; why, I say, should that little Island, enjoy in almost every Neighbourhood, more sensible, virtuous and elegant Minds, than we can collect in ranging 100 Leagues of our vast Forests. But, 'tis said, the Arts delight to travel Westward.[4] You have

8. See above, p. 216.
9. For Dorothea (Dolly) Blunt, see above, IX, 327 n.
1. For the Hawkesworths, see above, IX, 265–6 n.
2. For John Stanley, the blind organist and composer, see above, IX, 320 n.
3. Stanley's sister-in-law who served as his "musical eyes." She would play through once only any composition that was new to him, after which he could repeat it from memory. "John Stanley," *DNB*.
4. Probably an allusion to Bishop Berkeley's famous line, "Westward the Course of Empire takes its Way," from his "verses . . . on the Prospect of Planting Arts and Learning in America," written in 1726 but not published until 1752. *A Miscellany Containing Several Tracts on Various Subjects*

effectually defended us in this glorious War, and in time you will improve us. After the first Cares for the Necessaries of Life are over, we shall come to think of the Embellishments. Already some of our young Geniuses begin to lisp Attempts at Painting, Poetry and Musick.[5] We have a young Painter now studying at Rome:[6] Some Specimens of our Poetry I send you, which if Dr. Hawkesworth's fine Taste cannot approve, his good Heart will at least excuse. The Manuscript Piece is by a young Friend of mine, and was occasion'd by the Loss of one of his Friends, who lately made a Voyage to Antigua to settle some Affairs previous to an intended Marriage with an amiable young Lady here; but unfortunately died there.[7] I send it you, because the Author is a great Admirer of Mr. Stanley's musical Compositions, and has adapted this Piece to an Air in the 6th Concerto of that Gentleman, the sweetly solemn Movement of which he is quite in Raptures with. He has attempted to compose a Recitativo for it; but not being able to satisfy himself in the Bass, wishes I could get it supply'd. If Mr. Stanley would condescend to do that for him, thro' your Intercession, he would esteem it as one of the highest Honours, and it would make him excessively happy.[8] You will say that a Recitativo can be but a poor Specimen of our Music. 'Tis the best and all I have at present; but you may see better hereafter.

(London, 1752). BF used this phrase again in a letter to Charles Willson Peale, July 4, 1771, APS.

5. For some of the "Lispings of our young Muses" which BF sent Strahan and Caleb Whitefoord on Dec. 7 and 9, 1762, see above, pp. 167–8 n, 173.

6. Benjamin West (1728–1820), the first American painter to gain an international reputation, had sailed for Italy in 1760 aboard a flour ship. He was supported there for three years by William Allen and Gov. James Hamilton (above, III, 297 n). *DAB;* William Allen to David Barclay and Sons, Oct. 10, 1762, Lewis B. Walker, ed., *The Burd Papers* ([Pottsville, Pa.], 1897), pp. 51–2.

7. Probably Francis Hopkinson's "An Elegy. Sacred to the Memory of Josiah Martin, Esq; jun. who died in the Island of Antigua, in June 1762," printed in *Gent. Mag.,* XXXIII (Aug. 1763), 407. Alternatively, BF may have sent Hopkinson's "Disappointed Love. Recitative." Both appear in his *The Miscellaneous Essays and Occasional Writings* (Phila., 1792), III, "Poems," 70–2, 74–6.

8. Polly returned Hopkinson's piece, somewhat altered by Stanley "in the Recitativo in order to admit the Bass" to BF on Aug. 30, 1763 (below, p. 333), and BF acknowledged its receipt on March 14, 1764, remarking that the revised version gave "great Satisfaction."

I hope Mr. Ralph's[9] Affairs are mended since you wrote. I know he had some Expectations when I came away, from a Hand that could help him. He has Merit, and one would think ought not to be so unfortunate.

I do not wonder at the Behaviour you mention of Dr. Smith towards me, for I have long since known him thoroughly.[1] I made that Man my Enemy by doing him too much Kindness. Tis the honestest Way of acquiring an Enemy. And since 'tis convenient to have at least one Enemy, who by his Readiness to revile one on all Occasions may make one careful of one's Conduct, I shall keep him an Enemy for that purpose; and shall observe your good Mother's Advice, never again to receive him as a Friend. She once admir'd the benevolent Spirit breath'd in his Sermons.[2] She will now see the Justness of the Lines your Laureat Whitehead[3] addresses to his Poets, and which I now address to her,

> Full many a *peevish, envious, slanderous* Elf,
> Is,—in his Works,—Benevolence itself.
> For all Mankind—unknown—his Bosom heaves;
> He only injures those with whom he lives.
> Read then the Man:—does *Truth* his Actions guide,
> Exempt from *Petulance,* exempt from *Pride?*
> To social Duties does his Heart attend,
> As Son, as Father, Husband, Brother, *Friend?*
> *Do those who know him love him?*—If they do,
> You've *my* Permission: you may love him too.

9. Certainly not BF's old friend, James Ralph, who died on Jan. 24, 1762. BF might mean the Philadelphia merchant John Relfe (above, VII, 276 n), although there is no proof that he was in England at this time, or a James Ralph, who was a lieutenant in the 60th (Royal American) Regiment.

1. Perhaps a reference to the rumors Smith spread in England about the "Diminution" of BF's friends while he was abroad, or to Smith's efforts to prevent him from receiving an honorary degree from Oxford and the ensuing controversy, when Smith refused to retract a libelous letter which he had written to the officers of the university. See above, pp. 78 n, 160.

2. Mrs. Stevenson had probably read a collection of Smith's sermons, published in London in 1759, under the title of *Discourses on several public occasions during the war in America.* A second edition was published in 1762.

3. William Whitehead (1715–1785) was appointed poet laureate in 1757. The lines which BF quotes are from his *A Charge to the Poets,* published in 1762.

Nothing can please me more than to see your philosophical Improvements when you have Leisure to communicate them to me. I still owe you a long Letter on that Subject, which I shall pay.

I am vex'd with Mr. James that he has been so dilatory in Mr. Maddison's Armonica.[4] I was unlucky in both the Workmen that I permitted to undertake making those Instruments. The first was fanciful, and never could work to the purpose, because he was ever conceiving some new Improvement that answer'd no End:[5] the other, I doubt, is absolutely idle. I have recommended a Number to him from hence, but must stop my hand.

Adieu, my dear Polly, and believe me as ever, with the sincerest Esteem and Regard, Your truly affectionate Friend, and humble Servant   B FRANKLIN

My Love to Mrs. Tickell and Mrs. Rooke,[6] and to Pitty when you write to her. Mrs. Franklin and Sally desire to be affectionately remembr'd to you.

P.S. I find the printed Poetry I intended to enclose will be too bulky to send per the Packet: I shall send it by a Ship that goes shortly from hence.

Miss Stevenson

Endorsed: Phil Mar 25—63

To William Strahan

ALS: University of Pennsylvania Library

My dear Friend   Philada. March 28. 1763

I have received your Favours of Oct. 20 and Nov. 1[7] by my Son, who is safely arrived with my new Daughter. I thank you for your Friendly Congratulations on his Promotion. I am just

---

4. On Charles James, the armonica maker, see above, p. 180. Mr. Maddison may have been John Maddison (1702–1793), brother-in-law of Anthony Todd, secretary of the Post Office (above, p. 217 n), or some member of his family. Kenneth Ellis, *The Post Office in the Eighteenth Century* (London, 1958), p. 144 *et passim*.

5. Probably "Mr. Barnes" of Hughes and Co.; see above, pp. 180, 181.

6. Polly's aunts.

7. Neither letter found, but letters from Strahan to Hall of the same dates are in APS.

return'd from a Journey I made with him thro' his Government, and had the Pleasure of seeing him every where receiv'd with the utmost Respect and even Affection by all Ranks of People.[8] So that I have great Hopes of his being now comfortably settled.

As to myself, I mention'd to you in a former Letter, that I found my Friends here more numerous and as hearty as ever. It had been industriously reported, that I had lived very extravagantly in England, and wasted a considerable Sum of the Publick Money which I had received out of your Treasury for the Province; but the Assembly, when they came to examine my Accounts and allow me for my Services, found themselves Two Thousand two hundred and fourteen Pounds 10s. 7d. Sterling in my Debt; to the utter Confusion of the Propagators of that Falshood, and the Surprize of all they had made to believe it. The House accordingly order'd that Sum to be paid me, and that the Speaker should moreover present me with their Thanks for my Fidelity, &c. in transacting their Affairs.[9]

I congratulate you[1] on the glorious Peace your Ministry have made, the most advantageous to Britain, in my Opinion, of any your Annals have recorded. As to the Places left or restor'd to France, I conceive our Strength will now soon increase to so great a degree in North America, that in any future War we may with ease reduce them all; and therefore I look on them as so many Hostages or Pledges of good Behaviour from that perfidious Nation.[2] Your Pamphlets and Papers therefore that are wrote against

8. Writing to Strahan, April 25, 1763, WF reported on his arrival: "My father gave us an affectionate welcome and accompany'd me to Amboy when I went to take possession of my Government." WF's reception by the former governor "was extremely genteel, and that from all ranks of people in New Jersey was equal to my most sanguine wishes." *PMHB*, XXXV (1911), 425.

9. See above, pp. 195–7, 206–7; and below, p. 238.

1. This paragraph repeats, with only a few minor changes, the one in BF's draft letter to Philip Ludwell, Feb. 22, 1763, part of which he canceled with the notation "This to Dr. Pringle and Mr. Strahan," as explained above, p. 198 n.

2. In a letter to BF, July 14, 1778, APS, five months after the American alliance with France, Strahan wrote: "Suffer me only to lament, as I dare say you do, the wide Difference between the present Times, and those in which (in your Letter to me of March 28. 1763. now lying before me) you wrote as follows:". He then quoted this paragraph through the words "that perfidious

the Peace with some Plausibility, give one Pleasure, as I hope the French will read them, and be persuaded they have made an excellent Bargain.

I rejoice with you and Mrs. Strahan, on Rachey's safe Delivery, and wish you much Happiness in your Grand Daughter.[3] My little Family is now altogether, and join in every good Wish for you and yours. Remember me affectionately to every one of them, and particularly to my Peggy.[4]

I do not forget any of your Reasons for my Return to England. The Hint you add in your last, is good and wise; it could not have been wiser or better if you had drank ever so much Madeira. It is however, impossible for me to execute that Resolution this ensuing Summer, having many Affairs first to arrange; but I trust I shall see you before you look much older.[5]

In the mean time, be happy; and make me happy by often letting me hear that you are so. I shall ever be, with the utmost Esteem and Affection, My dear Friend, Yours most sincerely

B FRANKLIN

Nation," and went on to quote BF's report, earlier in this letter, of the "utmost Respect and even Affection" with which the people of N.J. had greeted WF's arrival as governor. Exclaiming "What a Reverse of Fortune!" he repeated the news he had recently heard that WF was now "imprisoned in a Common Jail, and that his Wife had died last July at New York of a broken Heart." Without knowing what had "brought upon him this severe Treatment," Strahan commented that "whatever his Demerits may be in the Opinion of the reigning Powers in America, the Son of Dr. Franklin ought not to receive such Usage from them."

3. Rachel Strahan Johnston's first child was born Oct. 17, 1762. Strahan to Hall, Oct. 20, 1762, APS.

4. Strahan's younger daughter.

5. In his letter of April 25, 1763, WF told Strahan: "My mother is so averse to going to sea, that I believe my father will never be induc'd to see England again. He is now building a house to live in himself." *PMHB*, xxxv (1911), 426. The earliest recorded mention of BF's building project was less than three weeks before WF wrote. Under date of April 6, 1763, BF entered in his accounts a notation that he had "Advanc'd to Mr. [Robert] Smith the Carpenter £96 towards my House." Memorandum Book, 1757–1776, p. 13. Prior to this time the Franklins had always lived in rented quarters. The fact that he had now decided to construct his own house in Philadelphia suggests strongly that in the spring of 1763 he had no real expectation of moving permanently to England with his family, whatever he might write to friends he had left there.

I wrote to you per Capt. Friend soon after my Arrival and since via Bristol.[6]

Mr. Strahan

[*Addressed:*] To / Mr William Strahan / Printer / in Newstreet, Shoe Lane / London / via N York / per Pacquet

Pennsylvania Assembly:
Thanks to Franklin, and His Reply

Printed in *Votes and Proceedings of the House of Representatives,* 1762–1763 (Philadelphia, 1763), p. 40.

[March 31, 1763]

Pursuant to a Resolve of the Nineteenth of last Month,[7] that the Thanks of this House be given to Benjamin Franklin, Esq; for his many Services not only to the Province of Pennsylvania, but to America in general, during his late Agency at the Court of Great-Britain, the same were this Day accordingly given in Form from the Chair. To which Mr. Franklin, respectfully addressing himself to the Speaker, made Answer, "That he was thankful to the House for the very handsome and generous Allowance they had been pleased to make him for his Services; but that the Approbation of this House was, in his Estimation, far above every other Kind of Recompence."

Account with the Estate of James Franklin, Junior[8]

ADS: American Philosophical Society

Philada. April 4. 1763.

Dr Mr James Franklin Decd.   Dr to B Franklin,   Sterling Mo.
1758. Feb. 23.   For a Parcel of Printing Letters, for which he gave his Bond } 94. 0. 5[9]

6. A reference to his letter of December 7 and probably to that of February 23; see above, pp. 166–9, 200.

7. Above, p. 197.

8. James Franklin (c. 11.4), son of BF's brother James. After the death of

Int. on Do. to Aug. 12. 1762 being 4.Y. 5.M. 20.D. }	25. 4. 1¾
	119: 4: 6¾
Recd. Augt. 12. 1762 100 Dollars at 4s. 7d. Sterlg.[1] }	22. 18. 4
	96: 6. 2¾
Intr. on £96. 6s. 2¾d. to Octr. 22. 1762 being 2 Mo. 10 Days }	1. 1. 0
	£97: 7: 2¾
Recd. Oct. 22. per Capt. All, 174 Dollars at 4s. 7d. }	39. 17. 6
	57: 9: 8¾
Intr. on £57. 9s. 8¾d. to Mar. 31. 1763. being 5 Mo. 9 Days }	1. 8. 9¼
	58: 18. 6
Recd. Mar. 31. 1763, 46 Dollars at 4s. 7d.[2] }	10. 5. 10
	48: 12: 8

the boy's father BF had educated him and trained him as a printer. James had then joined his mother in the family printing business at Newport, R.I. He died on April 21, 1762. See above, II, 261–3, 388; V, 440–1.

9. The basis for charging this particular amount is not clear. BF had recorded in his accounts that the type, procured from Caslon, cost £87 2s. 9d.; insurance premium, advanced by Collinson, amounted to £16 17s. 6d.; miscellaneous charges were 16s. 9d., so the total should have been £104 17s. "Account of Expences," pp. 15, 30, 33; *PMHB*, LV (1931), 108, 113.

1. This payment and the one below dated October 22 are recorded thus in BF's Memorandum Book, 1757–1776, p. 11: "Nov. 5 [1762] Recd. from Mr. Parker of Woodbridge 274 Dollars, being part of James Franklin's Bond to me for £94. 0s. 5d. Sterling, left to be receiv'd by Mr. Parker £102 15s. 0d. [Pa. currency]."

2. Under date of April 11, 1763, BF recorded: "Recd. from Sister Ann Franklin 46 Dollars, thro' the Hands of Mr. Holt, which is credited on the Back of James Franklin's Bond, as paid to Mr. Holt the 31st March. £17 5s. 6d. [less] 5s. Carriage [net] 17. 0s. 6d. £17 0s. 0d. [sic]." Memorandum Book, 1757–1776, p. 13.

1759	Mar. 1.	For a Parcel of Stationary cost[3]	95. 5. 3

By Agreement with J.F. whatever Money I laid out for him in England he was to give his Bond and pay Intr. for, from the Time of my Disbursement. He accordingly gave his Bond for the Printing Letters, and should have done it for the Stationary, but omitted it. The Interest however ought to be paid me, as I had no Profit on the Goods; and it being 4 Years and 1 } 22. 17. 2

Mo. to April 1. 1763 is And I consign'd a Trunk of Books to him, to sell for me, on which he was to have 20 per Ct. Commissions, but never sent me any Account.[4] Value } 36. 14. 3

£203: 9: 4

This Note £15. 1s. 1d. Pensa. Currency is Sterling at 4s. 7d. per Dollar[5] } 9. 14. –

£213: 3: 4

Errors excepted   Sterling
B FRANKLIN

3. Recorded under date of March 26, 1759, as "3 Cases of Stationary Shipt him this day, on board the Sherborne Capt. Calif, amounting, (with Shipping Charges and Insurance) to £95 5s. 3d." "Account of Expences," p. 37; *PMHB,* LV (1931), 116.

4. Recorded under date of May 19, 1758, with the value in "Boston Lawful Money" noted as £48 19s. od., and that in sterling as given here. "Account of Expences," p. 32; *PMHB,* LV (1931), p. 111.

5. Nothing has been found in BF's accounts or correspondence to explain this entry.

Ja Franklin[6]

Dr	Cr
32. 14. 6	6. 18. 9
4 6 3	13. 2. 6
7. 17. 6	20. 1. 3
1. 19. 0	
– 3 –	
4. 3. 4	
8. 12. 6	
3. 7. 6	
9. 15. –	
73 18: 7	

From Richard Jackson

ALS: American Philosophical Society

Dear Sir   4 Apl 1763
I received your favour by the Packet, as well as those by the
Carolina,[7] I had before the Pleasure to hear of your safe Arrival
from Mr. Strahan,[8] which was the more acceptable, because the
time that had elapsed since your sailing was rather too long and
gave your friends room for Apprehensions. I have before wished
you Joy on Mr. Franklin's Promotion, I doubt not, it will give as
much pleasure to the Province of New Jersey as to him and your
friends; I saw him a Day or two before he left London, and acquainted him with my Situation, as to a seat in Parliament. I was
then pretty secure, but I shall never be sanguine again as long as
I live, though I was not disappointed on this Occasion, in fact I

6. The figures entered below, on an otherwise blank page of the account,
apparently relate to additional debits and credits of James Franklin's estate,
but they have not been identified. In Memorandum Book, 1757–1776, p. 17,
are two entries of June 1763, recording the receipt of 35 dollars and 70 dollars,
respectively, from "Brother Peter" (C. 9), the first and probably both of which
Peter had received from James's executors. The known exchange rates,
however, prevent these from being identified with the credit entries below.

7. BF's short letter of December 2, by the packet, and longer one of December 6, by the Carolina, which had been captured but released. See above, pp.
160–1, 162–5, and accompanying notes.

8. London Chron., Dec. 30, 1762–Jan. 1, 1763, reported BF's arrival at
Philadelphia.

was chose for Weymouth the Week in which the Parliament met in Nov. and have made as Prudent a Use of my Seat since that Time as I have been able.[9] A Seat in P., in this Kingdom is (you know) usually built on Negotiations, and these Negotiations, (in the Course of which I met with some Trouble) took up most of my last Summer, so that, I could complete but the Skeleton of my work.[1] I think however the more difficult part is finished, perhaps I might have said so, if I had only begun it. I shall certainly compleat it this Summer, though I do not mean to publish it as compleat as I make it. It will be necessary it should not be too long.

The Speaker has frequently inquired after you,[2] in a very particular Manner, he did so when I dined with him yesterday, expressly great pleasure in hearing of your safe Arrival and insisted on my remembering to send his Compliments.

I can yet get no satisfactory Information about Mr. Barker or his family, I wish I had some Circumstances concerning his Business.[3]

I think I collect from Charles, who you see is now Comptroller at the Post Office, that his Discontent conceived against the Assembly of Pensylvania, was upon their Refusal to abide by his and the Opinion at the Council upon the Supply Bill.[4]

I met Mr. Penn yesterday who was very civil to me.

Though nothing could give me more pleasure than to hear of

9. Namier and Brooke, *House of Commons*, II, 669, gives the date of Jackson's election for Weymouth and Melcombe Regis as Dec. 1, 1762. He succeeded John Olmius, Baron Waltham, who had died on October 5. Namier quotes Charles James Fox as writing Lord Bute, November 17: "Lady Waltham does not intend her son [to succeed his father], but one Mr. Jackson." From what Jackson wrote BF immediately below, he had apparently negotiated unsuccessfully for a different seat during the previous summer.

1. What "work" Jackson was preparing is not known. It probably dealt with colonial affairs, but he apparently never completed and published it. See above, p. 164 n.

2. Probably the current speaker, Sir John Cust, not his predecessor, Arthur Onslow; see above, pp. 32 n, 164 n.

3. On behalf of John Hughes, BF had asked Jackson to locate a Robert Barker and buy for Hughes his lands in western N.J.; see above, pp. 156–8, 163, 164.

4. Robert Charles, former Pa. agent, was now comptroller of the Inland Office of the Post Office. On the reasons for his resignation of the agency see above, IX, 332 n.

your safe Arrival and Health I had less pleasure in hearing of the Joy universally expressed at Philadelphia on the Occasion; in truth this was nothing but what I well knew before would be the Case, notwithstanding Dr. Smiths Opinion or Intelligence.

I was the better pleased with your Account of Madeira, because the Day I received your Letter, was the 2d of our sitting on a Committee to inquire into its State, in order with other facts to lay a foundation for extending the Indulgence already given to Rice (in Europe to the S[outh] of Cape Finisterre) thither.[5] Mr. Gordon a Gentleman who resided there many years[6] assured us, that he had seen the Numbers returned as Communicants from every Parish, by the respective Priests, into the Bishops Chamber, and that they amounted to 76000, these are all of both Sexes above 8 years. He was seemingly very cautious as well as exact in all his Evidence, and no ways interested, and if not mistaken makes the Number more than the greater mentioned to you. However I always suspect exaggeration as you do.[7]

Upon running over your Letter again, I suppose Mr. Hughes hears nothing more of Barker, than you mention to me, if the

5. By an act of 3–4 Anne, c. 5 (1704), Parliament placed rice on the list of "enumerated commodities," thereby forbidding its export from the colonies to any place in Europe except England. By acts of 1730 and 1735 this rule was relaxed to permit the export of rice from South Carolina and Georgia to any European port south of Cape Finisterre (that is, to Spain, Portugal, and the Mediterranean). 3 Geo. II, c. 28; 8 Geo. II, c. 19. Charles M. Andrews, *The Colonial Period of American History,* IV (New Haven, 1938), 95–8. On March 4 and 10, 1763, the House of Commons referred to a committee two petitions for liberty to extend the permitted area to include Madeira and other islands off the African coast. The committee reported favorably, but after several postponements and some debate Parliament was prorogued before any action took place. *Journals of the House of Commons* (Reprint of 1803), XXIX, 526–7, 541–2, 555, 568, 605–6, 613, 617, 621, 623, 625, 666.

6. His Christian name was James (*ibid.,* p. 605), but he is not further identified.

7. The House of Commons committee report said that Gordon placed the population of Madeira at 100,000 (*ibid.,* p. 605), but did not give his figures for the number of communicants. BF told Jackson (above, p. 163) that "They pretend to have ninety Thousand Souls on the Island, but I did not hear of any actual Numeration, and I suppose that the Account is exaggerated." Presumably the inclusion of adult noncommunicants and children under eight would account for the difference between the two reports of Gordon's testimony and for Jackson's comparison of it with BF's figure.

Heir has been or is now in the East India Service, I shall easily procure intelligence of him, at the India House but if he actually was in the East Indies some years ago, it is I fear 2 to 1, he is since Dead. I will the first Day I go into the City, inquire at the India House. They have the Name of every Man in India.

I had from Mr. Moore the Clerk of Assembly,[8] through the hands of Messrs. Sargent & Aufrere, a Manifest of Forces employed by your Province in 1760 and 1761.[9] It came not to me

8. Charles Moore (1724–1801). When WF resigned as clerk of the Assembly, Feb. 18, 1757, the House appointed Thomas Moore (1724–1799) in his place, but he found the office "too much interfering with his other Engagements in Business" and resigned the following March 2, whereupon his twin brother Charles was appointed. *Votes*, 1756–57, pp. 93, 97. Thomas and Charles were younger brothers of Samuel Preston Moore, provincial treasurer (above, IV, 259 n); Samuel Preston and Charles married sisters, Hannah and Milcah Martha Hill, and, making the family bond even closer, their wives were already their first cousins. Charles had graduated in medicine at Edinburgh in 1752 and practiced in Montgomery Co., Pa. Charles P. Keith, *The Provincial Councillors of Pennsylvania* (Phila., 1883), p. 74.

9. When the officials of the British Treasury were preparing in June 1762 to distribute the parliamentary grant for repayment of colonial expenses in the campaign of 1760, they had as yet received no exact return from General Amherst as to the number of troops each colony had raised in that year—the basis always used for such distributions. Some of the agents contended that their colonies had provided more men in proportion than in 1759; others held that the proportions had been essentially the same as before. At a meeting on June 25, 1762, the spokesmen for the colonies agreed that, rather than wait for full information from Amherst, they should receive the same proportionate shares as they had the year before; if, when Amherst's return arrived, it should show that any colony had received too much, then the excess would be deducted from the grant for the 1761 campaign and distributed among the colonies which had been underpaid for 1760. Amherst's return eventually did show that Conn. and Pa. had been overpaid for 1760 (though his figure for Pa. troops was lower than what the colony though it should have been) and that in consequence Pa. owed £10,947 sterling to other colonies. Unfortunately, Amherst said Pa. had contributed no troops for 1761, hence it was entitled to no part of the parliamentary grant for that year. Because the Barclays and Sargent Aufrere had transmitted to the colony nearly all its share of the grant for 1760, they could not now make good on their prior commitment. It was agreed among the agents in London, May 19, 1763, that responsibility for the £10,947 owed by Pa. to other colonies should be transferred to Philadelphia and the Assembly be advised to appropriate and distribute that amount, according to an agreed proportion, among the six colonies entitled to larger shares for 1760. The Pa. Assembly accepted this

:ill some Months after it reached London being misdirected, yet oon enough, because I fear it will be of no Use, as the Lords of the Treasury have resolved not to depart from the Generals Returns who has allowed the Province 1350 in 1760, but none in the last year. I know not the reason for this, unless he is pleased to suppose that the 265 men employed in 1761 were for the Provincial Defence only; yet they were under his Command. Perhaps it is a Mistake. I shall write by the Packet to Mr. Moore, and as the Money will not be probably distributed a great While, there will be time for the General, upon Application made to him to set this Right. I am Dear Sir with the sincerest Respects and Esteem your most Obedient faithfull humble Servant

RD JACKSON

From Peter Collinson
ALS: American Philosophical Society

Lond Aprill 6. 1763

I can only now express the great satisfaction I have and that of Our Family to Hear by your Kind Letter of the 7 Decemr[1] of your Safe Arrival. I have One more Wish and that Is, to Hear of your Son and Daughter. All your Friends are Well in particular Yours Sincerely P COLLINSON

Mr. Canton[2] desires his Compliments. hopes for a Letter

Addressed: To / Benn Franklin Esqr / in / [Philadelphia][3] Boston

---

arrangement, though there were several delays, and the necessary act became law March 23, 1764. *Pa. Col. Recs.,* IX, 47–52, 115, 160; 8 *Pa. Arch.,* VI, 5441; VII, 5505–6, 5509, 5511–12, 5514, 5572, 5583; 1 *Pa. Arch.,* IV, 121, 130, 149–51, 159, 169; *Statutes at Large, Pa.,* VI, 329–31.

1. See above, pp. 165–6.
2. For John Canton, the English electrical experimenter, see above, IV, 390 n.
3. Crossed out and "Boston" substituted in another hand.

From Joseph Greenwood[4]　　　ALS: Harvard College Library

Dear Sir　　　　　　　　　Philadelphia 6th of April 1763
　As I knowing of you to be a gentle-man that can doe a great deal to help a poor man to his Wrights and as I am much reduced and have a large family have made bold to Beg the Assistance of soe good a Gentleman to see me rightified who has it not in my own power without applying for your Assistance in geting of me Justice don against Collo. John Armstrong who has taken an Improvement from me in the last purchase of Lands[5] which I hope Mr. Franklin will take into Consideration and help me to my Wright as I am not able to help myself and have a Large family to maintain by my Labour which is but small as I never was brought up to it untill nesessity brought me to it for an honest lively hood and I shall in Duty Bound to pray for your wellfare. I am Sir your most Obedient humble Servant
　　　　　　　　　　　　　　　　　JOSEPH GREENWOOD
Addressed: To / Benjn. Franklin / Esqr
Endorsed: Patterson's[6] Complaint vs Col: Armstrong

To Richard Jackson　　　ALS: American Philosophical Society

Dear Sir,　　　　　　　　　Philada. April 11. 1763.
　I am now to acquaint you that the Assembly of this Province have unanimously made Choice of you as their sole Agent, and

4. For Greenwood, an Indian trader who made maps of the areas he traversed and who sent Peter Collinson a description of the bones and skeleton of a "Great Buffalo" which he had seen in the vicinity of the Ohio River, see above, IV, 318 n, 334, 342; and this volume, p. 165 n. In 1762 Collinson described him as "well known" to BF (it is not clear how the acquaintance came about) and hence the plea for assistance in the present letter. Collinson to John Bartram, July 25, 1762, Darlington, *Memorials,* p. 239.

5. John Armstrong (above, VII, 104 n), victor over the Indians at Kittanning in 1756, surveyed and laid out the town of Carlisle. When his house burned in 1763, many land records were destroyed and great difficulties in adjusting land claims ensued. Greenwood probably conceived himself ill-used in the adjustment of claims and asked BF to intercede on his behalf.

6. Neither his identity nor his relationship to the Greenwood case is known.

have united the two Salaries of £100, which they formerly paid to Mr. Partridge and Mr. Charles, by voting £200 Sterling as your Salary.[7] I hope this Appointment will not be disagreable to you, as I think I had your Permission to name you on the Occasion. If you accept, you will keep and exhibit yearly an Account of any Disbursements you find necessary to make for the Province, which will be paid besides the Salary.

Being myself appointed one of the Committee of Correspondence, I shall shortly send you the Minutes of the late Session, and from time to time whatever may be necessary to inform you of our Affairs. And I hope to receive from you early Notice of such Proceedings at home, as it may be useful for our Assembly to be acquainted with.

Be so good as to present my respectful Compliments to your Speaker,[8] whom I honour greatly, and to his worthy Brothers, whose Friendship and many Civilities I bear strongly in Memory. Please to remember me also very affectionately to your good Brother and Sister Bridges,[9] and any others of your Family that may do me the Honour to enquire after me. My Son is in his Government, where he seems to have a Prospect of being very comfortably settled. I know he intends to write you as soon as

7. The Assembly resolved, April 2, 1763: "That Richard Jackson, Esq; of the Inner Temple, be, and he hereby is appointed, Agent for the Province of Pennsylvania, to solicit the Affairs thereof at the Court of Great-Britain for the ensuing Year; and that the said Gentleman be allowed for his Services as aforesaid the Sum of Two Hundred Pounds Sterling per Annum." *Votes,* 1762–63, pp. 41–2. At the same time the Assembly ordered that this resolve, under the great seal, be transmitted to Jackson and that BF be added to the Committee of Correspondence. Governor Hamilton refused to apply the seal, probably because he had been allowed no part in the appointment, and Thomas Penn commended his refusal, adding that Jackson "told me he did not know he might accept it if he liked their manner of desiring it, but he must have one he liked under him, for that he had an affluent fortune and did not want it, he is now a Member of Parliament and Secretary to the Chancellor of the Exchequer." Julian P. Boyd, ed., *The Susquehannah Company Papers,* II (Wilkes-Barré, Pa., 1930), 257. Apparently Jackson asked for some change in the wording of his appointment (below, pp. 341, 404), but what he wanted is not known; in any case, he continued to serve as Pa. agent until 1770, when he was appointed counsel to the Board of Trade and felt obliged to resign his colonial agencies.

8. Sir John Cust.

9. Thomas and Ann Bridges, Jackson's brother-in-law and sister.

his Hurry is a little over. I am, with the sincerest Esteem: Dear Sir, Your most obedient and most humble Servant B FRANKLIN

Account of the Number of Churches form'd in the 4 Governments of New England, as they stood at different Periods[1]—viz

Anno 1637	—	16 Churches
1643	—	34 Do
1650	—	40 Do
1680	—	80 Do
1696	—	130 Do
1760	—	530 Do

An amazing Increase within the Memory of Man, 400 upon 130!
R. Jackson Esqr
Endorsed: Philad April 11th 1763 B Franklin Esqr

To John Ellicott[2]   ALS: The London Hospital

Dear Sir   Philada. April 13. 1763
I yesterday receiv'd your Favour of Jany. 8.[3] and as it would be a particular Pleasure to me to be any way serviceable to your Hospital,[4] I shall cause the Enquiry you desire to be carefully made at New York; and to that end I write to a Friend there by this Post:[5]

1. With one exception, BF procured the figures below from Ezra Stiles, *A Discourse on the Christian Union* (Boston, 1761), pp. 102, 112–17, 129–39. The exception was the figure for 1680, and he inserted this information between the lines in the letter, showing that it was a later addition; its source has not been identified. On Stiles's *Discourse,* see below, pp. 266–7.

2. John Ellicott (1706?–1772) F.R.S., 1738, succeeded his father in the clockmaking business and became clockmaker to George III. He contributed several papers to *Phil. Trans.* on his specialty and on other subjects, including electricity (above, III, 472 n, 473 n; IV, 10). He was one of several scientists in the London area who made observations of the transit of Venus in 1761. *DNB.*

3. Not found.

4. The London Hospital was founded in 1740 as the London Infirmary in Prescot Street, Goodman's Fields, but moved in 1752 to its present location in Whitechapel Road, where it has continued to serve the teeming population of the East End. Major additions during later years had made it by early in the twentieth century the largest hospital in Great Britain. Ellicott was apparently a contributor and possibly a member of its Board of Governors.

5. It would appear from what is said here and what BF wrote Ellicott, June

248

But as the Father of Capt. Holland is said in the Will to have been of James River, which is in Virginia, and there is likewise a York Town upon York River which is not far from James River in Virginia, I apprehend that may be the York intended, and not New York properly so named, and that at York in Virginia one may possibly hear something of Eliz. Holland if she is still in being or ever lived there. I am just about to take a Journey into Virginia on the Business of my Office, and shall go thro' York town, where I shall make strict Enquiry, and as soon as possible let you know the Result.

The Mention of the London Hospital puts me in mind of a Favour I once ask'd of you, which was, to procure me a Copy of the Song that was sung by Mr. Beard[6] on the Subject of Charity when I had the Pleasure of Dining with the Governors and other Contributors at your Invitation. I am concern'd in the Management of the Pennsylvania Hospital erected in this City, and think that Song on proper Occasions might be useful to us here. I would not suffer it to be printed, nor give any Copy of it. But perhaps you cannot easily procure it, and I should be sorry to give you much Trouble about it.[7]

I am sorry I cannot give you an agreable Account of the Performance of the Watch. The new Spring unfortunately broke soon after I left England. Since my coming here, the old one is put in again; but I have not yet accurately adjusted the Watch so as to bring it to keep time as well as it us'd to do in London.

My Compliments to Mr. Hazard,[8] and the rest of the Gentle-

23, 1764, that the will of a Capt. William Holland (in some way connected with the London Hospital) had made a bequest to his sister Elizabeth, thought to have been living in New York. Their father appears to have been described as "of James River." BF's inquiries for these people, actively pursued for more than a year, produced no certain results. He was still interested in the search as late as 1772.

6. Probably John Beard (1716?–1791), actor and singer. He first appeared as an actor in 1737 at Drury Lane, in Charles Coffey's ballad opera "The Devil to Pay," but perhaps his most popular performances in later years were in the part of Macheath in Gay's "Beggars' Opera" at Covent Garden. Handel composed major tenor parts expressly for Beard in "The Messiah" and other oratorios. *DNB*.

7. No copy of this song has been identified among BF's papers.

8. Possibly the Richard Hazard (d. 1784), who was elected F.R.S. in 1752. *Gent. Mag.*, LIV (1784), 719.

men at the George and Vulture.[9] I shall always remember with Pleasure the agreable Hours I pass'd in that chearful, sensible and intelligent Society. The Monday scarce comes round but I think of you and am present with you *in Spirit;* and shall take it kindly, if, when you are not crouded, you would order a Chair for me, and only caution one another not to tread upon my Toes.

My best Respects to Mrs. Ellicot and to your Son, and Daughters.[1] With sincere Esteem and Regard, I am, Sir, Your most obedient humble Servant   B FRANKLIN

Addressed: To / Mr Ellicot / Watchmaker / Royal Exchange / London / Per the Pitt / Packet

Endorsed: Dr Franklin Philadelphia Apr 13 1763

To Jonathan Williams

MS not found; reprinted from [Jared Sparks, ed.], *A Collection of the Familiar Letters and Miscellaneous Papers of Benjamin Franklin* (Boston, 1833), pp. 80–1.

Loving Kinsman,   Philadelphia, 13 April, 1763.

You may remember, that about ten years since, when I was at Boston, you and my brother sent directions here to attach on Grant's right to some land here, by virtue of a mortgage given him by one Pitt.[2] Nothing effectual could be done in at that time, there being

9. An inn and tavern just off George Yard, between Cornhill and Lombard Streets, familiar to readers of *Pickwick Papers* as the place where Mr. Pickwick "suspended" himself during the period of *Bardell* v. *Pickwick*. B.W. Matz, *The Inns and Taverns of "Pickwick"* (London, 1921), pp. 139–53. The Monday Club, which met weekly at the George and Vulture, consisted chiefly of "affluent merchants and tradesmen who cultivated scientific and charitable interests." Several were members of the Royal Society or the Society of Arts, or both. For a brief description and partial list of members, see Verner W. Crane, "The Club of Honest Whigs: Friends of Science and Liberty," 3 *William and Mary Quart.*, XXIII (1966), 213–15.

1. At his death Ellicott left two sons, Edward and John, and three unmarried daughters, Deborah, Mary, and Elizabeth. The son here mentioned was probably Edward (d. 1791), who became his father's partner in 1769, succeeded to the business, and was similarly appointed clockmaker to George III.

2. While in Boston in July 1753, BF had sent WF a power of attorney from BF's brother John (C.8) and his nephew by marriage, Jonathan Williams (C.5.3), enabling WF to place an attachment on their behalf on a second

prior mortgage undischarged. That prior mortgage is now near xpiring, and Grant's will take place. Pitt's widow is desirous of eing enabled to sell the place, which cannot be done, without aying off Grant's mortgage. Therefore, if your old demand against rant still subsists, you may empower me in any manner you think roper to recover it.

Is Grant living? Or, if dead, are there any of his representatives mong you? Inquire. Because here is a person desirous of pur- hasing, who, perhaps, may inquire them out, and get a discharge om them, before your claim is brought forward, unless the attach- ient formerly made in your behalf is still good, which I am in- lined to think may be.

I am going in a few days to Virginia, but expect to be back in iree or four weeks. However, send what you have to say on iis subject to my son, at Burlington, who was formerly em- owered by you, and he will take the steps necessary, if I should ot be returned.³ I am your loving uncle,   B. FRANKLIN.

'o Anthony Todd   ALS: Yale University Library

:opy⁴

ir   Philada. April 14. 1763

By the Harriot Packet, which arrived last Saturday at New ork, I received your Favours of Dec. 7. and January 8.⁵ and ongratulate you cordially on your Appointment to the Secretary's ffice, in which I wish you all Happiness.⁶

---

iortgage held by Joseph Grant of Boston on property in Walnut St., Phila- elphia, belonging to one Pitts and his wife, the former Molly Yeldhall. The urpose of the attachment was to give Franklin and Williams a claim on rant's mortgage prior to claims of others of Grant's creditors. The property ad been entailed by Molly's father, so no foreclosure on the mortgages could e effected until her son came of age, "9 or 10 Years" from the time BF wrote. bove, v, 15–16.

3. No response from Williams to BF or WF has been found; perhaps BF ttled the matter with his nephew personally when in Boston during the llowing summer.

4. So labeled, but entirely in BF's hand.

5. Neither letter has been found.

6. Todd was appointed secretary of the Post Office on Dec. 1, 1762; see oove, p. 217 n.

I am just setting out on a Journey to Virginia,[7] to settle Accounts with the Executors of my late Colleague Mr. Hunter,[8] and recover the Money due from them to the General Post-Office Mr. Foxcroft and myself then purpose a Journey to New England thro' the whole present Extent of the Post Road,[9] in order to examine every where into the State and Conduct of the Offices see what new Regulations are necessary and what Improvements the Revenue is capable of in the several Parts of the Country and before the next Winter we hope to render a satisfactory Account of our Proceedings to his Majesty's Post-master General

You may possibly remember that a little before I left England a Complaint of the Merchants of Quebec concerning the Difficulty and Uncertainty of Correspondence there, was communicated to the Postmaster General by Governor Murray.[1] When it was consider'd at the Board, I propos'd dispatching a special Messenger from New York with all the Canada Letters, immediately after the Arrival of every Packet, till it should be found convenient to establish a regular Post. This being approv'd of, I sent Orders accordingly to Mr. Colden,[2] directing him withal to apply to General Amherst[3] for Orders to the Commanding Officers at the several Military Posts on the Route, to assist and forward the Messenger as he was to go thro' a wild unsettled Country. On my Arrival here I wrote to Mr. Colden to know what had been done in the Affair and receiv'd the Answer and Papers which I enclose.[4] You will observe that both in Governor Murray's and Genl. Gage's Letters

7. BF appears to have left Philadelphia about April 17 or 18 and returned by May 17, 1763.

8. For William Hunter, joint deputy postmaster general of North America 1753–61, see above, V, 18 n. The executors were Benjamin Waller of Williamsburg and Thomas Everard of York Co. Memorandum Book, 1757–1776, p. 17

9. BF and Foxcroft left Philadelphia shortly after June 6, 1763, and arrived in Boston on July 20; they remained in New England for nearly three months See below, pp. 277–9.

1. For a complaint of the British merchants at Quebec on the same subject perhaps the same one mentioned here, see above, p. 233.

2. Alexander Colden, N.Y. postmaster; above, VI, 113 n.

3. Jeffery Amherst, at this time the British commander-in-chief in North America; above, VIII, 328 n.

4. Neither BF's letter nor Colden's answer and the papers he enclosed have been found.

5. Neither letter has been found. For Gen. James Murray, at this time the

Mention is made of the high Charge of Postage; which being setled by the Act of Parliament[6] in Proportion to Distances, we apprehend it not in our Power here to abate. I cannot on the whole but
be of Opinion with General Amherst, that while the Commander
in chief continues to send Expresses with the Officers Letters whenever a Packet arrives, and permits those Expresses to carry the
Merchants Letters, a Post is not so necessary: But whenever that
Practice is discontinued, I should think it adviseable to establish
a Post, tho' the Expence should for some time exceed the Produce
of the Letters; as the Facility and Regularity of Correspondence
increases Commerce, and of course increases Correspondence and
multiplies the Number of Letters; so that being carried on steadily
for some Time, the Posts would become profitable to the Office.
This I submit however to our Masters, and shall be glad to receive
their Orders thereupon, which I will punctually obey. In the meantime, the Appointment of a Postmaster at Quebeck, to receive and
deliver the Letters that may come there by Expresses or by Sea,
and to forward such as are sent abroad, will be very proper; and
as soon as I meet Mr. Foxcroft, which I hope will be in a few
Days, we shall pay due regard to what you write concerning Mr.
Hugh Finlay,[7] every the least Intimation of the Pleasure of the
Postmaster General, being a Law to us.

If the Packets are under absolute Orders to sail regularly, and
not to be either detain'd beyond their Time, or hurried away
before their Time, by the Commander in chief at New York, I
am of Opinion they will answer much better than they did in
time of War. At present the Merchants here have very little
Dependance on them. The Method of late has been to keep the
Packet that is in Port, till the Arrival of another, and then dispatch the first immediately. This is better than it has been, when
sometimes three Packets have been all in Port detain'd together,
and so long, that the fourth was daily expected. But yet any

---

governor of Quebec, see above, p. 223 n. Thomas Gage (1721–1787), who was
governor of Mass. and commander-in-chief of British forces in America at
the outbreak of the Revolutionary War, was at this time lieutenant governor
of Montreal. *DNB*.

6. 9 Anne, c. 11 (1710), An Act for Establishing a General Post-Office for
all Her Majesties Dominions.

7. See above, pp. 223–4 n.

Detention of a Packet after the 20 Days from her Arrival make
the Conveyance looked upon as uncertain; and those who woul
write for Insurance or send Orders for Goods, cannot depen
upon it. And the sudden Dispatch after the Arrival of anothe
Packet gives no Opportunity to the Merchants of Philadelphi
and Boston, two principal Trading Towns on this Continent, t
answer the Letters receiv'd by the second Packet, till she, afte
the like Detention, shall be permitted to sail. This has occasione
the Packets to be so little used by the trading People for th
Conveyance of their Letters. It is said the present Post, by whic
I now write, may possibly reach the Pitt Packet, and I have en
courag'd others to write; but it is very uncertain, as it depends o
the General's Pleasure.

After our Return from our intended Tour, we shall be able t
offer our Sentiments more particularly on the Points you men
tion, "the rendering Correspondence in the vast Empire c
North America of the greatest Use to his Majesty's Subjects, an
at the same time to improve the Revenue of it." I can now onl
desire you to present my humble Duty to my Lord Egmont an
Mr. Hampden,[8] and assure them of my most faithful and diliger
Service in the Execution of the Office they are so good as to con
tinue me in; and that you would do me the Justice to believe me
with sincerest Esteem and Regard, Sir, Your most obedient an
most humble Servant   B FRANKLI

Anth: Todd, Esquire

To Richard Jackson   ALS: American Philosophical Socie

Dear Sir,   Philada. April 17. 1763
    I wrote you a long Letter of the 8th and 29th of March o
various Subjects, too long to copy unless it should be lost. But a
Messrs. Coxe are sending Copies of their Request and Power t
you, I must repeat so much of my Letter as related thereto.
    [Here Franklin copied *verbatim* the long paragraph whic
    formed the largest part of the postscript dated March 22 to hi
    letter begun on March 8; see above, pp. 212-14. It is not re
    peated here.]

8. The joint holders of the office of postmaster general.

Thus far out of preceeding Letters. I have now only to add on this Head, that there are already several Schemes on foot among the People in different Parts of this and the neighbouring Provinces for Removal Westward, and great Numbers show a strong Disposition to go and settle on the Ohio or Missisipi, but they want Heads to form regular Plans of proceeding. I am convinc'd that a new Colony, that should be plac'd within Coxe's Bounds, on the Rivers that discharge themselves into the Bay of Mexico, between Cape Florida and the Missisipi would have a more rapid Progress in Population than any heretofore planted.[9]

Follows a Copy of my Letter of the 11th Instant sent via New York, viz

[Here Franklin copied *verbatim* the whole of his letter of April 11, including date line, salutation, and signature, but omitting the postscript about the growth in numbers of New England churches; see above, pp. 246-8. It is not repeated here.]

April 17. I am just setting out for Virginia, on Post Office Business. As I shall be on the Edge of North Carolina, I may have an Opportunity of learning something of their Land Affairs. I hope to be back in about 4 Weeks. Yours ut supra   BF.

P.S. In a former Letter I mention'd one Mr. Lyon's Scheme for a new Colony, as being very crude.[1] Another is just now put into

9. The original Heath grant of Carolana, to which the Coxe family laid claim, extended from the 31st to the 36th parallel, so the settlement BF had in mind could technically have been anywhere in the present states of Alabama and Mississippi except in their southern extensions to the Gulf of Mexico below the 31st parallel. Because the exact location of the parallel in that region was not understood, however, he might have contemplated a settlement almost anywhere north of the Gulf between the Apalachicola and Chattahoochee rivers on the east and the Mississippi on the west. Other people had ideas about this region. Following a Board of Trade recommendation of June 8, the King issued the proclamation of Oct. 7, 1763, which, among other things, established the royal province of West Florida, to occupy precisely that part of the Gulf Coast lying between those rivers and south of the 31st parallel. A supplementary commission to the first royal governor, George Johnstone, issued in the spring of 1764, extended the northern boundary of West Florida to a line drawn due east from the confluence of the Yazoo and Mississippi rivers, thereby nearly tripling the area of the province. These actions of the Crown put an effective stop to any scheme for a separate colony based on the Carolana grant. *Acts Privy Coun., Col.,* IV, 668; Cecil Johnson, *British West Florida 1763–1783* (New Haven, 1943), pp. 3–7.

1. See above, p. 215, and the document immediately below.

my Hands, that has in it many things quite absurd.[2] I send it you enclos'd. I know not who is the Mover at Bottom. These Things serve to show the present Disposition of the People.

Richd Jackson Esqr

Endorsed: Philad Apr 1763 B Franklin Esqr

From James Lyon[3]   ALS: American Philosophical Society

Sir,   Brunswick N. Jersey Apr. 1763
    As the least suspicion of a Letter from you to me might, possibly, dispose a curious Person to intercept it, permit me to inform you, That I have not yet been so happy as to recieve a Line from your Hand.
    I need not remind you, Sir, of the Necessity of putting our Scheme into Execution immediately, if ever:[4] And shall only tell you, that, without any Care or Pains of mine, for I have been entirely inactive since I had the Honor and Pleasure of conversing with you, the Number of Adventurers is vastly encreased. Daily Applications are made by Persons of Influence, who are ready to risque their all in such an Enterprize. Two Gentlemen in particular, of considerable Importance, one of which is worth £6000 or £7000 at least, came to me last Week to enquire if there was any

2. Lieut. Thomas Webb (*c*.1724–1796), British army officer and Methodist preacher, calling himself "one of the Proposalists," announced in *Pa. Gaz.*, April 21, 1763, a scheme for a colony on the Ohio to be named "New Wales." Emigrating families to the number of 4000 were to have 300 acres each and "Gentleman Proprietors" might buy tracts ranging from one to ten thousand acres at £50 per thousand, the proceeds to be used in buying the land and in furnishing stock, tools, and provisions. Webb assured the public that this colony would be "so advantageously situated, with respect to the easy Navigation to the West-Indies, that the Inhabitants will be able to transport their Commodities in a few Days." One week later *Pa. Gaz.* carried Webb's announcement withdrawing his proposal, since "it has been judged necessary I should desist entirely in the Prosecution thereof, until His Majesty's Pleasure is known concerning the Lands in Question." See below, p. 286.

3. See above, p. 231, for President Finley's introduction of his former student to BF. Lyon presumably wrote this letter a few weeks after his conference with BF in Philadelphia.

4. Lyon's scheme for a settlement on the Mississippi, referred to above, pp. 215, 231.

Probability of Success, and express'd great Desires to view the Country this Summer. Should the Scheme be so fortunate as to meet with your Approbation and Encouragement, I have some Thoughts of going with these Men to the Ohio, as soon as possible, while others are employed in raising the Settlers.[5] We impatiently wait to know your Sentiments and Advice, for by *these Laws* we shall govern ourselves; and be assured, we shall make use of the most proper Measures to express our sincerest Gratitude.[6] I am, Sir, your most humble obedient and obliged Servant.

JAMES LYON

P.S. Col. Bouquet's Sentiments will also be very acceptable.

Dr. B. Franklin.

Endorsed:[7] Brunswick N Jersey Apr. 1763 from Jas Lyon to To Benj. Franklin

Accounts between Benjamin Franklin and the Estate of James Parker   Three MS accounts: American Philosophical Society

Between Franklin and his fellow printer James Parker there existed not only a warm personal friendship but a business relationship of many years' standing and an official connection through Parker's position as comptroller of the American postal system. Each man faithfully executed commissions for the other and made or received payments for his friend whenever convenience dictated. Inevitably their accounts with each other became somewhat complicated, particularly when Parker paid to Deborah Franklin in Philadelphia money due to her husband in England, or when, as occasionally happened, post-office and personal funds became mixed.

Parker died on July 2, 1770, and it became necessary for his widow and executrix, Mary Parker, to settle all the outstanding claims and obligations of his estate. To this end she prepared and sent to William Franklin early in 1772 a statement of Franklin's account with the estate

5. From BF's comments to Jackson, cited in the note immediately above, it is unlikely that he would give Lyon his "Approbation and Encouragement." No reply to this letter has been found.

6. The fact that Lyon went to Nova Scotia in 1765 suggests that he did not pursue for long his scheme for western settlement. Pontiac's Uprising and the Proclamation of 1763 checked plans for the west.

7. In Richard Jackson's hand.

as it appeared on her husband's books. Governor Franklin sent a copy to his father in London with an explanatory letter in February 1772.[8] What is believed to be this copy, apparently in William Franklin's hand, survives with Mrs. Parker's original among the Franklin Papers in the American Philosophical Society Library.[9] It differs from Mrs. Parker's statement only in that someone, perhaps Benjamin Franklin himself, later added notations to show which figures represented Pennsylvania currency and which that of New York.

Meanwhile Franklin in London had sent his son a record of the account as it stood in his books on April 20, 1771, and William reported the next February that he had given it to the Parkers' daughter for her mother. While this paper has not been located, its contents are known in full from a restatement of the account with two added entries down to Jan. 14, 1772, prepared for Franklin in 1774, by his grandnephew Jonathan Williams, Jr., who was in London and was working on his relative's account books.[1]

Mrs. Parker's account, in its two nearly identical versions, and Franklin's are companion pieces and should be considered together. They are dealt with here because the earliest entry in the Parker account is dated April 1763. Apparently, during Franklin's stay with Parker in Woodbridge, N.J., in early June of that year they had adjusted and settled their accounts up to within a few weeks and Parker then started a completely fresh record in his books with a belated entry of one relatively small charge against Franklin.[2] It seems unnecessary to print

8. WF to BF, Feb. 28, 1772, APS.

9. These two documents and the Franklin account of 1774 mentioned in the next paragraph are in Franklin Papers, LXVII, 12, 28b, 29, and are recorded in the Hays *Calendar*, III, 558. On the blank pages of Mrs. Parker's original account are the draft of an advertisement for a runaway Negro boy, a receipt for money paid to another man, and some financial calculations, all apparently written during Parker's lifetime and having nothing to do with BF's affairs. The copy of this account presumably made by WF is endorsed "Copy of J. Parker's Acct. with B. Franklin Esqr." BF's statement has no endorsement.

1. BF to WF, Sept. 7, 1774, APS.

2. For BF's visit, see below, p. 277. This account does not have the opening entry, customary in such cases, of a balance due from one man to the other based on previous transactions. Almost certainly Parker was at that time in debt to BF for an amount substantially more than he could have paid over in ready cash. It seems probable, therefore, that BF proposed, and Parker agreed, that Parker would execute a bond for the amount he then owed (giving BF greater security than a mere book debt), and that they would start a new book account from scratch. If so, the bond Parker executed Nov. 15, 1763 (below, pp. 374–5), for an indebtedness of £178 18s., N.Y. currency, would represent the carrying out of this agreement.

these documents in full, though they should be described in sufficient detail to make clear their general contents and the nature of the two men's financial transactions with and for each other.

The entries in the two accounts are wholly different from each other because they are taken from separate ledgers and relate to different transactions. The Parker account shows expenditures he made in America chargeable to Franklin, money he had paid over to Deborah Franklin, and, contrariwise, money or goods he had received in America for which he gave Franklin credit. Franklin's account lists his payments in England for Parker and drafts by Parker that he had honored, and on the other hand drafts his friend had sent him in payment of debts, or money Franklin had received for Parker or his estate. In each statement the charges against the other man greatly exceed the credits to him, for neither one recorded the other's expenditures on the opposite side of the ocean. Mrs. Parker's account shows that her husband had twice struck a trial balance and that in the final unbalanced figures Franklin's debits exceeded his credits by £159 9s. 3½d., New York currency. Franklin's statement, on the other hand, shows that Parker's estate was indebted in the net amount of £263 3s. 10d. sterling.

The Parker record shows that in 1764 he had expended a total of £38 15s. 6d. on behalf of Franklin's unstable nephew, Benjamin Mecom, who was then transferring his printing activities from New York to New Haven, and that Parker had recovered and credited to Franklin £28 10s. by selling Mecom's stock at auction. On eight separate occasions between April 10, 1765, and April 16, 1770, while Franklin was in England, Parker made payments to Deborah totaling £125 8s. to reduce his indebtedness to her husband. He also bought shoes for Sally Franklin, a yard of "Paris net" and two ounces of thread for her mother, as well as "2 pots of Lobsters" and "1 barrell beets." Most of his other entries in this column related to payments Parker made to other men for Franklin. Among the few credits to Franklin perhaps the most surprisingly extravagant one was for receiving, apparently from Deborah, "a Piece of Silk for my Daughter" costing £17 10s.

Franklin's account listed his payments during his second English mission for books, type, stationery, and newspapers sent to Parker and for cash provided to honor two drafts on himself that Parker had drawn. The only credits listed were for one draft in his favor Parker had sent and a final payment on Parker's post-office salary received after the comptroller's death. All the entries in Franklin's account are taken directly from his ledger of Dec. 10, 1764, to July 8, 1775, to be described more fully in the next volume of this series.[3]

3. One entry in the ledger inexplicably has no counterpart in the account

The Parker-Franklin account was a troublesome one, both before and after Parker's death, and later volumes will contain many references to it. Settlement proved to be a complicated and unsatisfactory business, and there were understandable complaints by participants on both sides that the records were inadequate. When Franklin's amended account reached America during the last months of 1774, the matter had already dragged out for more than four years. By then the times were difficult: Franklin in England was preoccupied with his efforts to negotiate a satisfactory compromise of the disputes between the colonies and the mother country; his son William, the governor of New Jersey, was much involved in the problems caused by colonial unrest; and Deborah Franklin was failing in health and died before the end of December. Just how the accounts were finally adjusted and closed—if indeed they ever were—is unknown. The editors have found no document of any sort later than Franklin's amended account described here which even alludes to the affair.[4]

To William Strahan

ALS: Henry E. Huntington Library and Art Gallery

Dear Sir,   Virginia, May 9. 1763

I have been from Philadelphia about 3 Weeks on a Journey hither upon the Business of the Post Office,[5] but am now returning home, where I hope to find some Letters from you, as I hear that two Pacquets are arrived at New York since I came out. I

---

as BF transmitted it: a debt against the Parker estate, January 1772, of £3 7s. 9d., sterling, "To sundry accts." This account is notably deficient in crediting to Parker any of his five payments to DF for which she endorsed receipts on one or another of the three bonds he had executed as security for some of his debts to BF. Whether she had properly recorded all such payments and whether all those she did record should have been credited to the bonds rather than to unsecured book debts became points at issue in the later discussions of the whole affair. For the first of these bonds see the note immediately above.

4. Any attempt in 1966 to determine from these accounts and all other surviving papers what the final net indebtedness of the Parker estate to BF may have been is frustrated by uncertainty as to what rates of interest, if any, were chargeable on unsettled balances of both sides and what dates should be used for converting to a single monetary system the figures given variously in N.Y. currency, Pa. currency, and sterling, the rates of exchange among which fluctuated considerably.

5. For this trip, see above, p. 252 n.

have answer'd the Letters receiv'd from you by my Son,[6] and have little to add. I congratulate you sincerely on the signing of the Definitive Treaty, which if agreable to the Preliminaries, gives us a Peace the most advantageous as well as glorious, that was ever before obtain'd by Britain.[7] Throughout this Continent I find it universally approved and applauded; and am glad to find the same Sentiments prevailing in your Parliament, and the un-bias'd Part of the Nation. Grumblers there will always be among you, where Power and Places are worth striving for, and those who cannot obtain them are angry with all that stand in their way. Such would have clamour'd against a Ministry not their particular Friends, even if instead of Canada and Louisiana they had obtain'd a Cession of the Kingdom of Heaven. But Time will clear all Things, and a very few Years will convince those who at present are misled by Party Writers, that this Peace is solidly good, and that the Nation is greatly oblig'd to the wise Counsels that have made it.

My affectionate Regards to Mrs. Strahan and your Children; and believe me ever, My dear Friend, Yours sincerely

B FRANKLIN

Please to put Mr. Becket in mind to send me the French Work on the Arts as it comes out. Also any new Pieces that are thought good.[8]

Have you put the Cato Majors into his Hands?[9]

Mr. Strahan

6. Those of Oct. 20 and Nov. 1, 1762 (not found); see above, p. 235.

7. For BF's enthusiastic comments on the peace in earlier letters to Strahan, see above, pp. 200, 236. The definitive treaty was signed at Paris, February 10.

8. Thomas Becket of Tully's Head in the Strand had published BF's Canada Pamphlet, and while in England BF had engaged him to send books to Lib. Co. Phila.; see above, IX, 274. The "French Work on the Arts" was the multivolume *Descriptions des arts et sciences* (Paris, 1761–88). BF bequeathed his folio edition to the American Academy of Arts and Sciences in Boston and his quarto edition to Lib. Co. Phila.

9. BF had sent Strahan 300 copies of his 1744 edition of James Logan's translation of Cicero's *Cato Major;* see above, II, 404. Strahan remembered in 1782 that he had turned them over to someone; he thought it was Becket, but Becket had become bankrupt "some time ago" and Strahan did not know what had become of any copies remaining unsold. Strahan to BF, May 27, 1782, APS.

To Jane Mecom

ALS: American Philosphical Society

Dear Sister   Philada. May 20. 1763

I am just return'd from Virginia, and find your Favour of April 11.[1] I purpose setting out with my Colleague Mr. Foxcroft for New England, the Beginning of next Month, and hope soon for the Pleasure of seeing you;[2] but have no Expectation of bringing my Dame to undertake such a Journey; and have not yet ask'd her Opinion of Sally's going. My Love to Brother and your Children. I am, Your affectionate Brother

B FRANKLIN

Addressed: To | Mrs Jane Mecom | Boston | Free | B FRANKLIN

From W Hick[3]

ALS: American Philosophical Society

Dear Sir   Lancashire Furnace 23d. May 1763.

It gives us great pleasure to hear of your good Health, but are no less Mortified than you in not having the pleasure to see you, and do assure you that Mrs. Hick was so afraid of being out of the way when you call'd, that I could not prevail with her to go abroad for this three weeks past: but has now given up all thoughts of seeing you, for this year at least. I thank God we still continue

1. Not found.

2. BF, Foxcroft, and Sally Franklin arrived in Boston on July 20, 1763.

3. Probably the (William?) Hick whom William Allen employed about 1764 to manage his forge at the Union Iron Works in Hunterdon Co., N.J., on the recommendation of the London merchant Capel Hanbury (above, VI, 223 n). For the three previous years Hick had worked for the Principio Co., managing its Lancashire Furnace near the Patapsco River in Baltimore Co., Md. Allen was dissatisfied with him, writing Dec. 15, 1765, that he was "entirely unacquainted" with a forge, however experienced he might be with a furnace, and that he was "tho' a young man, weakly, and troubled with the Gout and Rheumatism, and from bodily Infirmities not able to go through the active Life that Business requires." Lewis B. Walker, ed., *The Burd Papers* ([Pottsville, Pa.], 1897), p. 69; *PMHB*, XI (1887), 196. BF may have met Hick at the Lancashire Furnace on his journey to Va. in April 1763 and, from what Hick says in the first paragraph, he may have expected BF to call again on his return trip. BF recorded in his Memorandum Book, 1757–1776, p. 17, having received, June 14, 1764, "from Mr. Hick £10 5s. in full of 6 Silver Spoons sent him sometime since."

to enjoy a good State of Health and are always glad to hear the same from our Friends.

I observe a proposal in the Pennsylvania Gazette of the 21th April to settle the Ohio,[4] and should be glad of your Opinion as to an Adventure in making a Purchase there, a Young Man who lives in our Company's Employ whose time (he Engag'd for) is nearly expir'd has an Inclination to go there and become a Proprietor, especially if he thought there was any probability of Iron Lead or Copper Mines. If it is your Opinion there is, as I make no doubt but you are Acquainted with that Country by Information from those that have been there: Three of us propose taking up five Thousand Acres, not in one Body but as Three Proprietors, which is one Mr. Phillips, Mr. Smith and myself;[5] how far such a Scheme may Answer I can't pretend to say, but if you give us Encouragement Intend to send Mr. Smith to the Ohio, as he is a Regular Miner, brought up in Mr. Tysington's employ,[6] and at present lives with me: He is really a very Ingenious Young Man and a good Mechannic. Should you approve of our Undertaking, your Advice how to Proceed will greatly oblige us.

I must beg you will be so obliging as to give me Directions for putting up the Iron Rod, Mrs. Hick is much more uneasy at the Smart Thunder we have had, then in case it was put up, and is very anxious to have it up.[7]

4. Lieutenant Webb's proposal; see above, p. 256 n. Webb had already rescinded it more than three weeks before Hick wrote.

5. Presumably Phillips was the Francis Phillips (d. 1769), manager of the Kingsbury Furnace of the Principio Co., near the Lancashire Furnace. A few months before his death he was put in charge of the company's Lancashire Furnace and North East Forge. Henry Whitely, "The Principio Company," *PMHB*, XI (1887), 196, 289. Nothing is known about Smith (apparently the young man whose time was soon to expire) beyond what Hick says in this letter.

6. On Anthony Tissington, mineralogist of Derbyshire, see above, IX, 42 n.

7. Apparently the erection of one of BF's lightning rods would quiet Mrs. Hick's fears. William Allen spoke rather scornfully of her in the letter quoted in the first note to this letter: "He has a Wife quite unfit for Iron Works, as she appears to be a fine Lady and expects to live with a Delicacy not common in these parts of the World, especially at Iron Works, either in England or here—The Mistress of such a Family as ours ought not to wear Silks, nor spend much of her time in decking her person, or dressing her head, but rather by Care endeavour all she can to promote Oeconomy and Frugality." *Burd*

Mrs. Hick Joins me in Compliments to you Mrs. Franklin and Miss Franklin. And am Dear Sir Your very Humble Servant

W HICK

Addressed: To / Benjn. Franklin Esqr. / In / Philadelphia

Endorsed: Lanc Furnace May 23d 1763 from Mr. Hick to B Franklin Esqr[8]

May 23d 1763 Mr Hick about Ohio

To Ezra Stiles   ALS: Yale University Library

Dear Sir,   Philada. May 29. 1763

I have now before me your Favours of Jany. 31. and March 1. the Receipt of which I ought sooner to have acknowledged.[9] Your kind Congratulations on my Arrival and the Advancement of my Son, are extremely obliging.

I think I have read somewhere that Fahrenheit's o was what he understood to be the greatest Cold of Siberia, Greenland, or any inhabited Country.[1] So he graduated from thence upwards, and found the Degree of Cold in Water just freezing happened to be the 32d of his Scale. Had the Divisions of his first Scale been larger or smaller, the freezing Point would have fallen on a different Degree, and that would have been a Matter of little Importance; but it was of Use to make all his subsequent Scales alike.

I doubt with you, that Observations have not been made with sufficient Accuracy, to ascertain the Truth of the common Opinion, that the Winters in America are grown milder; and yet I cannot but think that in time they may be so. Snow lying on the Earth must contribute to cool and keep cold the Wind blowing over it.

Papers, pp. 69–71. It was doubtless at her request that Hick got BF to send the silver spoons.

8. This much of the endorsement is in Richard Jackson's hand. BF probably sent him this letter as further evidence of the great interest in western settlement.

9. Neither of Stiles's letters has been found. They probably acknowledged the receipt of a thermometer which BF had brought from London and sent Stiles on Dec. 19, 1762 (see above, p. 178), and from the tenor of the next paragraph they probably contained queries about thermometers and heat.

1. Fahrenheit's thermometer had been in use since about 1720.

When a Country is clear'd of Woods, the Sun acts more strongly on the Face of the Earth. It warms the Earth more before Snows fall, and small Snows may often be soon melted by that Warmth. It melts great Snows sooner than they could be melted if they were shaded by the Trees. And when the Snows are gone, the Air moving over the Earth is not so much chilled; &c. But whether enough of the Country is yet cleared to produce any sensible Effect, may yet be a Question: And I think it would require a regular and steady Course of Observations on a Number of Winters in the different Parts of the Country you mention, to obtain full Satisfaction on the Point.

While I was at Cambridge in England, I assisted at an Experiment made by Dr. Hadley, then Professor of Chemistry there, at my Request, to find what Degree of Cold might be produced by Evaporation.[2] The Thermometer was plung'd into a Vessel of that highly rectified Spirit the Vitriolic Ether; which as it had long stood in the Room with the Thermometer, and consequently was of the same Temperament, did not in the least alter the Height of the Mercury; but the Moment the Thermometer was taken out, and the Ether with which the Ball was wet began to evaporate from its Surface, the Mercury fell several Degrees: The Doctor repeated the Wettings, while the Evaporation was quicken'd by blowing on the Ball with a Bellows, till the Mercury fell from 65, at which it stood before the Experiment began, to 7. that is, 25 Degrees below the Freezing Point. And accordingly the Moisture condens'd, by the Coldness of the Ball, upon its Surface, froze there, and form'd by Degrees a rough Coat of Ice all round it, of near ¼ Inch thick. So it should seem, that a naked Man standing in the Wind and repeatedly wet with strong Spirit, might be frozen to Death on a Summers Day.

The Russian Philosophers[3] have found that in extream Cold, Mercury itself becomes solid, and is malleable like other Metals. Hence it seems that in the State we have it, it is really a melted Metal, only it is a Metal that melts with less Heat than other

2. BF's account of this experiment is substantially the same as that which he had given Cadwallader Colden on Feb. 26, 1763; see above, pp. 203–4.
3. The material in this paragraph is repeated (in a condensed form) from BF's letter to Colden cited immediately above. It should be consulted for notes on the persons mentioned here.

Metals. Æpinus, a Member of the Academy of Sciences at Peters-burg, has lately published a Latin Work in 4to. entituled, Tentamen Theoriae Electricitatis et Magnetismi; wherein he applies my Principles of Electricity to the Explanation of the various Pheno-mena of Magnetism, and I think with considerable Success.

The Dispute you mention, between the French and Italian Philosophers still subsists.[4] You will not wonder at my supposing the latter have greatly the Advantage.

What relates to the Doctorate, I will communicate to you when I next have the Pleasure of seeing you, which I now hope soon to enjoy, as I am actually preparing to visit once more my native Country.[5]

You would do the Picture[6] too much Honour if you had it to place where you propose. I should however send you one if I had it; but the Painter thinking the Plate ill-done, it was sup-press'd. A few only came here, and none are to be had.

I have lately been favour'd with a Sight of your excellent Discourse on the Christian Union.[7] As I have some ingenious Friends in Britain to whom I am sure it would be acceptable, I purpose to distribute a few among them. In the Copy you sent to Professor Williamson,[8] I see you have made several manuscript

4. That is, the dispute between Nollet and Beccaria about the validity of BF's electrical theories which has been discussed in earlier volumes of this series. BF, of course, sided with his defender Beccaria.

5. BF stopped in Newport on his way to Boston in the first part of July 1763. Stiles recorded a conversation with him about weather and the popula-tion of Pa. on July 8, and on July 12 made a memorandum of the honors which BF had received including the doctorates from St. Andrews and Oxford. Franklin B. Dexter, ed., *Extracts from the Itineraries . . . of Ezra Stiles* (New Haven, 1916), p. 187; below, pp. 309–11.

6. Probably James McArdell's mezzotint, engraved in 1761, from Benjamin Wilson's 1759 portrait of BF. See above, IX, frontispiece, and the illustration note.

7. BF had cited statistics on the increase of New England churches from Stiles's *Discourse* in a letter to Richard Jackson of April 11, 1763; see above, p. 248.

8. Hugh Williamson (1735–1819) graduated from the College of Phila-delphia in 1757, then studied theology in Conn. without receiving ordination, and returned to his alma mater in 1761 as professor of mathematics, serving until 1764. A strong partisan of proprietary government, he wrote several anti-Franklin pamphlets in the election campaign of 1764, including the scurrilous *What is Sauce for a Goose Is Also Sauce for a Gander*. In the same

Notes.[9] I could wish the same Advantage to the Copies I purpose to send. May I beg the Favour of you to give it to twelve of them for which I will pay your Bookseller's Order. With great Esteem and Respect, I am, Dear Sir, Your most obedient and most humble Servant   B FRANKLIN
Verte

P.S. June 2. I send you enclos'd a little Piece [of] Æpinus's,[1] which has some relation to Points we have touch'd in our Letters. When you have perus'd it, you may forward it to Mr. Winthrop,[2] who can return [it] to me when I am in Boston.

Revd Mr Stiles

[*Note in margin by Stiles:*] I had requested of Dr. Franklin a Copy of his Diploma for the Doctorate of L.L.D. from the University of Oxford.

From John Pringle

AL (incomplete and mutilated): [3]American Philosophical Society

[May? 1763][4]

[*Torn*] would take the liberty of recommending [*torn*], who had been put in by Lord Bute, and [*torn: we*]ll qualified for his office.[5]

---

year he went to Europe and eventually received an M.D. from the University of Utrecht. He was elected to the APS in 1768. During the Revolution he was surgeon general of the North Carolina troops, and he represented that state in the Constitutional Convention of 1787 and in the first two Congresses of the new government. In 1793 he retired to N.Y., where he lived for the rest of his life and wrote scientific treatises. *DAB.*

9. Stiles's MS notes are in a copy of the *Discourse* in the Yale Univ. Lib.

1. Perhaps the *Tentamen* mentioned above, but more probably his *Cogitationes de distributione caloris per tellurem* (St. Petersburg, 1761).

2. Professor John Winthrop of Harvard.

3. An entire four-page folio is missing, with the resulting loss of approximately the first two-thirds of the text of the letter. The surviving second folio has a large piece torn from the upper inside corner.

4. So dated in I. Minis Hays, *Calendar of the Papers of Benjamin Franklin* (Phila., 1908), I, 25. Internal evidence and the note by Lawrence Reade on the address page support this approximate dating, although Pringle might have written the letter early in June.

5. Pringle appears to be describing an interview with the 2d Earl of Shelburne (1737–1805), who had been appointed president of the Board of Trade,

His Lordship then [*torn*] heard the young gentleman had ene-
[*torn*]ying that, I took an opportunity of telling [*torn:* ima]gined
it came about. Lord Shelburne made no promises, but [*torn*] hear
me with some indulgence.

This being the state of that affair, I am perswaded that if you
were determined before to return to England, you will now see a
good reason for hastening your departure; because your being
present yourself, may be a considerable weight in the scale, in
case matters should come near to a ballance.

I have forgot whether I wrote to you in answer to the last letter
I received from you before you sailed.[6] If I did not, I acknowledge
the favour now. Into Lord Bute's hands I put your proposal
about the preservation of gun-powder, and also mentioned your
thoughts about securing the health of our garrison at Senegal:[7] for
both which communications he desires me to return you thanks.
Neither did I omit letting Lady Bute know both yours and your
son's intentions to search the coast for shells;[8] but that Lady,
deeper in that study than either you or I, told me, that your seas
afforded none of any value, but was obliged to you for the trouble
you undertook. She then said that people in her way were fond
of those shells only in which the fish were found alive; for that
if they were dead shells found upon the beach, they lost a certain

---

April 23, 1763. What remains of the paragraph suggests that Pringle had
asked Shelburne's support for continuing WF in the N.J. governorship. Lord
Bute, who was probably responsible for WF's appointment, had resigned from
office on April 8.

6. The last surviving letter to Pringle before BF sailed was that of May 27,
1762, about the purported De Fonte search for the Northwest Passage; above,
pp. 85–100. It would seem from the sentences that follow here that BF wrote
another letter before sailing, now lost, concerned with the preservation of
gunpowder, the health of the garrison at Senegal, and shells for Lady Bute.
It is possible, however, that in this first sentence of the paragraph Pringle was
referring to the De Fonte letter and that what follows relates to a lost letter
written after BF reached Philadelphia.

7. In the spring of 1758 the British had captured the French posts at Senegal,
Goree, and the Gambia, and had established a garrison at the former French
Fort Louis at Senegal. Gipson, *British Empire*, VIII, 174–7.

8. Mary, Countess of Bute (1718–1794), was the daughter of the famous
Lady Mary Wortley Montagu. She married the third Earl of Bute in 1736,
and in 1761 was created in her own right Baroness Mountstuart of Wortley.
She was evidently a discriminating conchologist.

glow of colour on the inside, for which they were as much estimable as for the colours without. Her Ladyship said further, that if you favoured her with any shells, she wished to have none larger than her two fists, so as that she could put [*torn*] otherwise, by being exposed to the air [*torn*] colours.

I have never heard more of your pa[per? *torn*] told me to whom I was to apply for it.[9] I ha[ve? *torn*] name: so I beg of you to put me again upon [*torn*] that sketch of yours. I shall grudge losing the sligh[*torn*]

Our friends continue to meet at my house on the Sunday evenings.[1] I suspect they would not be so punctual, if they did not hope for your return; for having that in their view they could not with any face leave me now, and come back with you. Be that as it will, you are always mentioned by them with the greatest affection and esteem. I read to them your letter, and they begged me to remember to you in the warmest manner. (I believe I have said this before.) We are all agog about this new property of fluids.[2]

You remember our conditions of correspondence, and therefore My dear Doctor and good friend, sans ceremonie, adieu

[Here the author skipped the equivalent of three lines]

P.S. I mentioned your account of the paper currency to Lord Shelburne, and as he seemed desirous to see it, I am to send it to him.[3]

Dr. Watson has lately published an account of a cure he performed on a girl in the orphan hospital by means of electricity after the common remedies had failed.[4] The distemper was a

9. It is impossible to determine what Pringle was referring to here.

1. What group of mutual friends met regularly at Pringle's house on Sunday evenings is not known.

2. The effect of oil on water, as described in BF's letter to Pringle of Dec. 1, 1762, above, pp. 158–60.

3. Before leaving England BF may have given Pringle a copy of his 1729 pamphlet, *A Modest Enquiry into the Nature and Necessity of a Paper-Currency* (above, I, 139–57), but the reference could also be to some "account of the paper currency" by BF of which no copy, or even draft, is known to survive. It is perhaps worth noting that in writing his *Modest Enquiry* BF had relied extensively on a treatise by Sir William Petty, Lord Shelburne's great-grandfather.

4. William Watson's account of this case, dated Feb. 9, 1763, and read at

tetanas viz. an obstinate cramp of the muscles of the neck attended with several bad symptoms.

[*Torn*] you give of Lord Bacon's writings [*torn*] read him with attention, which gave me [*torn*]

Addressed: To / Doctor Benjamin Franklin / Conjunct Postmaster of North America / at / Philadelphia

[*In another hand:*] New York the 28 July 1763 Received under Cover and forwarded by Sir Your most Obedient Servant

LAWR: READE[5]

Endorsed: Dr. Pringle

To Anthony Todd
ALS: Yale University Library

Copy[6]

Sir,
Philada. June 1. 1763

In my last of April 14.[7] I acquainted you that I was then just setting out for Virginia, in order to settle Accounts with Mr. Hunter's Executors who reside there, and to obtain the Ballance I conceiv'd due to the General Post-Office from his Estate of more than £400 Sterling, out of which they would have deducted a Demand of £372. 12s. 8d., which I finally satisfied them was not well-founded, and they paid me the whole Ballance, which I accordingly now remit in Bills to Mr. Trevor, compleating the Ballance of our Account to the Time of Mr. Hunter's Death. In Virginia I met my new Colleague Mr. Foxcroft, and we had many Consultations concerning the Virginia Offices, which were formerly a Burthen and Charge, and but lately during Mr. Hunter's Time were brought to bear simply their own Expence; but having made several Changes in the Management, and directed some Alteration in

the Royal Society the next day, is printed, with a postscript of March 27, in *Phil. Trans.*, LIII (1763), 10–26.

5. A N.Y. merchant, who died in 1773 while on a visit to England. N.-Y. Hist. Soc. *Coll.*, 1899, pp. 243–5.

6. So labeled, but the letter is entirely in BF's hand.

7. See above, pp. 251–4. Notes to that letter and to the three letters from Todd to BF and Foxcroft of March 12, 1763, above, pp. 217–20, 220–2, 223–4, should be consulted for persons and events mentioned here.

the Stages, we have reason to believe they will now be profitable. Mr. Foxcroft is come up with me to this Place, and we are now proceeding in our intended Tour to inspect and regulate all the Offices in our Department, without which it will be impossible for us to render the regular Accounts required of us. Since our Arrival here we have received your three Favours of March 12. which we shall answer as fully as at present we can in a joint Letter from New York per the Packet;[8] and for the rest must refer to the Letters we purpose writing after our Return. In the mean time, with sincere Esteem, I am, Sir Your most obedient humble Servant

B FRANKLIN

Antho. Todd, Esquire

To William Strahan   ALS: Yale University Library

Dear Friend,   Philada. June 2. 1763

I have just received your Favour of Feb. 28.[9] being but lately returned home from Virginia. Dr. Kelly in his Letter, appears the same sensible, worthy, friendly Man I ever found him; and Smith, as usual, just his Reverse.[1] I have done with him: For I believe no body here will prevail with me to give him another Meeting. I communicated your Postscript to B Mecom, and receiv'd the enclos'd from him.[2] I begin to fear things are going wrong with him; I shall be at New York in a few Days, and will endeavour to secure you as far as it may be in his Power, and will write you from thence.[3] My Love to good Mrs. Strahan and to your Children. I hope to live to see George a Bishop.[4] Sally is

8. See below, pp. 279–84.

9. Not found.

1. With his letter of February 28, Strahan had apparently enclosed a copy of Dr. John Kelly's letter to him of Feb. 11, 1763, concerning William Smith's refusal to honor a promise, made at a meeting with BF at Strahan's house in 1762, to retract a letter he had written to Oxford in 1759 attacking BF. Smith's purpose had been "to prevent his [BF's] having a Degree at Oxford." See above, p. 78 n.

2. Not found.

3. See above, p. 153 n, for Mecom's move to N.Y. and his failure there.

4. For the Strahan children, see above, p. 169 n. In his letter of February 28 Strahan had apparently told BF that his son George intended to quit the book-selling business and go to Oxford with hopes of entering the ministry. In his

now with her Brother in the Jerseys. Mrs. Franklin joins with me in best Wishes, &c. I am, Dear Sir, Your most obedient and most humble Servant   B FRANKLIN

I fear my Letters to you per Capt. Friend never came to hand, as I hear he is taken. It was the Ship I came over in, the Carolina.[5] I wrote pretty fully to you and Mrs. Stephenson, but kept no Copies.

Addressed: To | Mr William Strahan | Printer | London | Snow James & Mary | Capt. Sparkes[6]

Endorsed: Mr. Franklin

To Catharine Greene

ALS: Mary A. Benjamin, New York City (1962); copy: American Philosophical Society

Dear Katy   Philada. June 6. 1763
    On my Return from Virginia lately, I found your agreable Favour of April 24.[7] by which I had the Pleasure of learning that you and Mr. Greene and your little ones were well.[8] Your Invitation is extreamly obliging, and certainly I could not have forgiven myself if I had pass'd thro' New England without calling to see you, and enjoying the Pleasure of finding you in the happy Situation I us'd to wish for you and advise you to. You desire to know the time I expect to be your way. In so long a Journey one cannot be exact to a Day or a Week. I can only tell you, that I purpose setting out tomorrow; and having Business to do, and Friends to see in several Places, I suppose it may be near the End of the Month

---

letter of Feb. 11, 1763, cited above, Dr. John Kelly told Strahan of meeting George, "a very amiable young Gentleman," who was then studying at Abingdon, preparatory to entering Oxford.

5. The *Carolina,* though captured by the Spanish in February, reached London about the first of April; see above, p. 160 n. BF's letters to Strahan of Dec. 2 and 7, 1762, went by the *Carolina.*

6. *Pa. Gaz.,* June 9, 1763, reported the clearance of the *James and Mary,* Capt. J. Sparks.

7. Not found.

8. For Caty's husband and family, see above, pp. 154 n, 191 n.

before I reach your Government.[9] My Thanks to Mr. Green and you for your kind Congratulations on my Son's Promotion and Marriage. All Happiness attend you both, in which good Wish my Wife joins, and my Children would join if they were here, but they are all in the Jerseys. I am, as ever, dear Katy, with the sincerest Esteem Your affectionate Friend and humble Servant

B FRANKLIN

My Respects to your late Governor and his Lady, your good Sister.[1] Ask him whether he does not find, (as General Shirley told me, when supers[ed]ed by Lord Loudon that he found) *a low Seat the easiest.*[2]

To Richard Jackson
ALS: American Philosophical Society

Dear Sir,   Philada. June 6. 1763
Supposing the Catalogue of our American Ores and Minerals collected by the late Mr. Hazard,[3] might afford you some Amusement, I send my Letter to Mr. Tissington open to you,[4] and give you the Trouble of forwarding it to him when you have perus'd it.

The Bearer of this is Mr. James Logan Son of my Learned Friend of that Name.[5] I beg Leave to recommend him to your Civilities, as a young Gentleman of Fortune and Character.

The Indians on the Ohio have broke out again, scalp'd a Number of People, and seiz'd some Horse Loads of Goods.[6] I do not hear

9. BF visited the Greenes at Warwick, R.I., on his way to Boston in the early part of July; see above, p. 278 n.

1. Caty's sister Anna married Samuel Ward, who had been governor of R.I., 1762–63; see above, p. 154 n.

2. BF repeated this anecdote in his *Autobiog.* (APS-Yale edit.), p. 254.

3. Samuel Hazard (1714–1758), who published in 1755 a scheme for a western settlement; above, VI, 87 n. His mineralogical collection, purchased for Lib. Co. Phila. after his death, is described and the catalogue mentioned in *The Charter, Laws, and Catalogue of Books, of the Library Company of Philadelphia* (Phila., 1764), pp. 25–6.

4. Not found.

5. James Logan the younger (1728–1803) was fellow trustee with BF of the Loganian Library.

6. The first published news of the Indian uprising, commonly called Pontiac's Uprising, was in an extract from a letter from Fort Pitt, May 31, printed in *Pa. Gaz.*, June 9, 1763. The writer reported that Col. William

of any Offence given them, and suppose it occasion'd by the mere Relish they acquir'd in the last War for Plunder.

I am just setting out for New York, and purpose writing to you from thence. I am, with perfect Esteem and Respect Dear Sir, Your most obedient and most humble Servant   B FRANKLIN

Richard Jackson Esqr

Endorsed: B Franklin 6 June 1763

From Peter Collinson

ALS: American Philosophical Society

Londn. June 8: 1763

The Going away of Ships are So uncertain, and I am So Frequent out of Town—I write this Letter to my Dear Friend premature because I do not Inclose a receipt for the Box which I expect to do in my Next if I am not out of Town when the Ship Sails.

The Box comes by Capt. Friend in the Carolina.[7] In it is Books and Catologues for Lib: Company,[8] Some for J: Bartram and the Hist. Florida for your Self.[9] If you have it by no Other Hand I am perswaded it will be Acceptable.

Clapham (above, VI, 383 n) and his family had been murdered at their settlement twenty-five miles away; eleven men had been attacked at Beaver Creek (northwest of Fort Pitt), eight or nine of them had been killed, and twenty-five pack horses captured; "St. Dusky" (Sandusky, Ohio) was cut off; and the fort at Detroit had been invested. This news must have reached Philadelphia several days before it was published, because Colonel Bouquet, then in the city, reported it to General Amherst, who received it in N.Y. on June 6. Pontiac's Indians began their depredations in the vicinity of Detroit on May 7 and he launched his attack on the fort there on the 9th, thereby effectively starting the war. Howard H. Peckham, *Pontiac and the Indian Uprising* (2d edit., Chicago, 1961), pp. 130–44, 166, 171, 176. BF, like Amherst and others, at first failed to recognize the significance of the news from Fort Pitt.

7. *Pa. Gaz.*, Sept. 22, 1763, recorded the entry at Philadelphia of the *Carolina*, Capt. James Friend.

8. Collinson, who had been purchasing books for Lib. Co. Phila. since 1732 (above, I, 248 n), apparently sent volumes XXXVII and XXXVIII of *An Universal History, from the Earliest Account of Time to the Present,* for which there seems to have been a standing order (see above, p. 152 n); and George Edwards' *A Natural History of Uncommon Birds* ... (4 vols., London, 1743–51) and the same author's *Gleanings of Natural History, containing Figures of Quadrupeds, Birds, Insects, and Plants &c.* (3 vols., London, 1758–64).

9. This may have been William Roberts' *An Account of the First Discovery*

As I have no Account with the Lib: Com. I make you Debtor for their Books So please to be reimbursed by them.

I had the pleasure of yours of 1obr [December]: 7[1]—and felicitate you on the Comforts that both I and you Enjoye in our Family Connections. These are Joyes better felt, than Expressed. I am Sincerely Yours 　　　　　　　　　　　P COLLINSON

More in my Next

1763 　　　　　　　Ben Franklin 　　　Dr.
Aprill

16	To No 37 and 38 of Modn. Histy	– 13: –
	To Histy of Florida 2 v	– 6: –
	To Edwards Hist of Bird and [Binding?]: VII Vol	2: 5: –
	Box	– 1: –
		3: 5: –

　　　　　　Shiping Charges
　　　　　　Don't yett know

The Box is Directed For You and Committed to the Care of Danl. Mildred[2] to Ship with his Goods.

Lett not the Lib: Com bind up the Colour'd Prints of Insects for I Expect 2 or 3 More Plates.[3]

Mr. Canton[4] thinks you have forgot Him.

From the New York News Paper I See a New Colony called New Wales is going to be Setled on the Ohio.

In the Advertizement Mention is made that a Work will Shortly be published relating to this Expedition. When it comes out pray send it Mee.[5]

Addressed: To / Benn: Franklin Esqr / in / Philadelphia

---

and Natural History of Florida (London, 1763), although a letter from Capt. Thomas Robinson with which the book concludes is dated June 22, 1763. Collinson could, however, have acquired an advance copy.

　1. See above, pp. 166–9.

　2. A London Quaker merchant.

　3. These prints may have been intended for Edwards' *Gleanings of Natural History*.

　4. John Canton, the English electrical experimenter; see above, IV, 390 n.

　5. For Lieut. Thomas Webb's proposed colony of New Wales, see above, p. 256 n. Webb's advertisement, which was printed in the *Pa. Gaz.*, April 21, 1763, was reprinted, with alterations, in *London Chron.*, June 9–11, 1763, and *Gent. Mag.*, XXXIII (June, 1763), 287–8.

Benjamin Franklin and John Foxcroft to Anthony Todd

LS: Yale University Library; draft (incomplete): 6American Philosophical Society

This letter marks the first stage of the inspection trip Franklin and Foxcroft took through New Jersey, New York, and New England between June 7 and November 5, 1763. Lasting just two days less than five months, this was the longest time Franklin was ever away from home on post-office business. Accompanied most of the time by Sarah ("Sally") Franklin, who celebrated her twentieth birthday while in Boston, the deputy postmasters general traveled as far north as Portsmouth, New Hampshire, inspecting the offices along the way and transacting other business. Characteristically, however, Franklin seized every opportunity to visit with friends en route and during the long stay in Boston. Not the least of his satisfactions must have come from the chance to show his daughter the New England in which he had been born, but which she had never seen before, and in turn to present her for the first time to his relatives and acquaintances in Boston, Rhode Island, and Connecticut.

Two accidents marred the journey for him. On some rough road along the western shore of Narragansett Bay he fell from his "chair" (presumably the chaise in which they were riding) and injured his shoulder, forcing him to stay for recuperation considerably longer than he had planned in the home of William and Catharine Greene at Cowesett, near East Greenwich. He had another fall, injuring his shoulder again, during his trip between Boston and Portsmouth, forcing a postponement of the return journey to Philadelphia. In spite of these misfortunes, the tour seems to have been one of the most enjoyable of his many travels through the colonies.

It may be useful to provide here a chronology of the trip, as detailed as possible, both because references to places and dates in the letters that follow are occasionally rather confusing, and because later writers have sometimes placed him during the journey in communities he did not visit or have ascribed to him activities he would never have had time to perform within the days he spent along the route.[7]

6. The surviving single page of the draft contains only the concluding two and a half paragraphs of the letter. It is entirely in BF's hand.

7. For example, in a recent article Joseph B. Stephens firmly places BF in Litchfield, Conn., during July 1763. He paints a delightfully detailed picture of the postmaster general driving from Woodbury to Litchfield along the New Haven-Litchfield Turnpike in his chaise, with daughter Sally by his side counting the revolutions of the wheel to determine where each milestone

June 7: BF and Foxcroft leave Philadelphia for the north.[8]

June 9?-14: At Woodbridge with James Parker, controller of the Post Office.

June 14: BF and Foxcroft leave Woodbridge, go to Elizabeth Town, are joined by the Franklin "children," and attend a dinner given by the Corporation for WF; reach New York before dark.

June 15: BF and Foxcroft wait on Governor Monckton and General Amherst; dine with Lord Stirling; BF attends Archibald Kennedy's funeral in evening.

June 16: BF and Foxcroft dine with General Amherst.

June 19: Sally is in Amboy with WF and wife; will go to New York in a few days.

July 1?: BF, Foxcroft, and Sally embark on packet for Newport, R.I., traveling by water because of the "hott weather," instead of through Connecticut as first planned.[9]

---

should go, and BF pounding in a stake at each mile for the information of the workmen, who "lumbered along far behind" with a wagonload of prepared stones. "Connecticut's Famous L and M's," *Yankee,* June 1964, pp. 86–7, 162–3. But Litchfield had no post office at this time to require the presence of the deputy postmaster general on his inspection trip; Woodbury did not lie on the New Haven-Litchfield Turnpike; that turnpike was not even authorized by the General Assembly until six years after BF's death; and in July 1763 BF, Foxcroft, and Sally traveled from N.Y. to Newport by water, without setting foot anywhere in Conn. There are also local traditions in Conn. towns along the route of the old "Post Road" (now essentially U.S. Route 1) that BF personally erected, or at least supervised the workmen in erecting, milestones along that road either on the journey to Boston in July 1763 or on the return in October. The voyage by water on the eastward trip and the rate of travel on the westward one make these traditions, pleasant as they are, hopelessly unhistorical. In fact, there is no evidence that BF ever had anything to do with the erection of milestones anywhere, at any time; such aids to travelers were a local responsibility and had no connection with the colonial postal service in BF and Foxcroft's charge. On BF's alleged visit to Quebec during these months see a later note to this letter.

8. Sally probably accompanied her father as far as Woodbridge, N.J., then joined WF and his wife at Perth Amboy, where WF had gone for the meeting of the N.J. Assembly, and went with them on an expedition to see the Passaic Falls. When BF and Foxcroft left for N.Y. on the 14th she remained temporarily in N.J.

9. The date of sailing is uncertain. BF told DF on Thursday, June 16, that the packet for R.I. "sails next Friday Week," by which he might have meant either June 24 or July 1. He was still in N.Y. on June 28, and a note in *N.-Y. Mercury,* June 27, that the *Providence* packet, Capt. Jeremiah Lippitt, had "Cleared for Departure" for R.I. would be consistent with a sailing four days

July 8: In Newport (arrival date not certain), BF visits with Ezra Stiles, July 8 and 11.[1]

July 13?-18: After leaving Newport (date of departure not certain), party goes to Cowesett, near East Greenwich, R.I., to visit William and Catharine Greene; somewhere en route BF suffers fall and injures shoulder; they remain at Greene home until he is able to travel.[2]

July 18-19: At Providence, the Greenes having accompanied them part way.

July 19-20: At Wrentham, Mass., for the night.

July 20: Arrive at Boston.[3] BF probably stays with Jane Mecom, and Sally with Jonathan Williams. Foxcroft's lodgings are not known.

July 20-October 12: With Boston as headquarters, BF and Foxcroft transact post-office business; sometime between August 12 and September 5, they travel to Portsmouth, N.H., and back. On this trip a second fall, dislocating BF's shoulder, causes delay in return journey to Philadelphia.

October 12: Leave Boston; visit Nathaniel Ames, almanac maker, at Dedham; probably spend night there.[4]

October 14-15: Spend night with the Greenes at Cowesett.

October 15-18: Spend from Saturday evening to Tuesday afternoon at Newport.

October 19-21: At Westerly, R.I., with Joshua Babcock and family.

October 21-25: At New London, Conn., "among our Friends."[5]

---

later. Why they traveled to Newport by water is explained in an undated letter from Joseph Chew of New London to Jared Ingersoll of New Haven in the Ingersoll Papers, New Haven Col. Hist. Soc. *Papers*, IX (New Haven, 1918), 285. Chew had expected that both he and Ingersoll would see BF during the trip through Conn. *Ibid.*, p. 283.

1. On these dates Stiles recorded conversations with BF. Franklin B. Dexter, ed., *Extracts from the Itineraries and other Miscellanies of Ezra Stiles, D.D., LL.D. 1755–1794* (New Haven, 1916), p. 187; see below, p. 309.

2. Chew reported to Ingersoll, Aug. 10, 1763, that Col. Eliphalet Dyer had "met with Mr. Franklin at Greenwich, where the Latter was confined with a hurt occasioned by a Fall from his Chair." New Haven Col. Hist. Soc. *Papers*, IX, 286.

3. William G. Roelker, ed., *Benjamin Franklin and Catharine Ray Greene Their Correspondence 1755–1790* (Phila., 1949), p. 36.

4. An entry in Ames's diary under this date reads: "Mr. Benj. Franklin here." At a later time he added at the same point: "famous Dr. Franklin." Sam Briggs, ed., *The Essays, Humor, and Poems of Nathaniel Ames, Father and Son* (Cleveland, 1891), p. 31.

5. The quotations here and in following entries are from BF's letters to Jane Mecom, November 7, and to DF, October 31. In a letter to Joshua

October 27-28: At New Haven from Thursday morning to Friday afternoon.

October 31: Arrive in New York about 11 A.M., after a "very pleasant Journey, and without the least ill Accident."

November 1: Spend one day and night at Woodbridge with James Parker.

November 4: With WF at Burlington, he having met them "20 Miles on the Road."

November 5: Arrive at Philadelphia "on Saturday Night."

Copy[6]
Sir   New Jersey[7] June 10th. 1763
    Your three Letters of March 12th. are now before us.[8]
    As soon as we have settled the Business of the Office here, we shall proceed to New York, where we Expect to be in a few Days, and shall, agreable to the pleasure of the Post-Master General, signify'd to us by you,[9] use our best Endeavours to Establish a Regular Post between that place and Canada, which we hope may be effected during 8 Months of the Year, if not for the whole. We have not yet heard of the Arrival of Mr. Finlay at Quebec, but have made out a Commission, appointing him Postmaster there.[1]
    We observe in the Memorial of the Merchants by you transmitted to us, a Complaint that "an excessive high and exorbitant Postage has been of late exacted from them." If this is meant of the postage mark'd on their Letters by Mr. Colden Postmaster of New York, when he sent a Post there two or three Times last Summer; we can at present only say, that we suppose he govern'd himself by the Act of Parliament; but we shall enquire into that matter, and if he has made any Mistakes they shall be rectified.[2]

Babcock, Nov. 10, 1763, BF makes clear that the Babcocks accompanied the Franklin party westward until within one day of New York City.

6. So labeled; the text of the copy is in a clerical hand, but the complimentary close is in BF's and the signatures are in the hands of BF and Foxcroft respectively.

7. BF's letters of this date to Jackson, Polly Stevenson, and Strahan (below) show that he and Foxcroft were at Woodbridge, N.J., on June 10.

8. See above, pp. 217-24. Nearly everything in the present letter is in response to one or another of those three. Cross references below will distinguish them simply as Letter I, II, or III, without repetition of page numbers.

9. Letter III.

1. Finlay's commission not found, but see the document immediately below.

2. The act of 1710 established the rates for postage in the colonies primarily

We hope the Continuance of the Packets will in a short time be as advantageous to the office, as it must be to the Commerce of Britain and the Colonies.[3] Nothing in our Power shall be wanting to second the laudable Views with which that Continuance is order'd. It is already advertis'd, and we have order'd the Advertisement to be constantly inserted for twelve Months to come in all News Papers of America.[4] The regular and punctual Dispatch of the Mails will greatly recommend the Use of the Packets to the Merchants; and we doubt not but the good Effect of that Regularity will soon appear in the great Increase of Letters. If some Method could be fallen upon effectually to oblige the Masters of Ships to deliver all their Letters into the Office, it would raise a great Sum in Aid and Support of the Packets. A Clause inserted in some Act of Parliament relating to the Revenue requiring an Oath of every Captain, to be taken at the Custom House when he enters, that he had sent his Letters to the Office; and making it penal to break Bulk till that was done; might possibly have a very good Effect. Or perhaps a Clause obliging all Coffee Houses where Bags are put up, to bring such Bags of Letters to the Post Office before they are sent away; to be seald and directed to the Post Office of the Port to which the Ship is bound; and allow the Coffee House a

according to the distance covered. At these rates a single-sheet letter carried between N.Y. and Montreal would cost two shillings, one between N.Y. and Quebec, three. A parliamentary act of 1765 (5 Geo. III, c. 25, sec. ii) reduced these rates to one shilling and one shilling fourpence respectively. The postal system of Canada under the French and the beginnings of the Canadian system under British authority are described, with one important error, in William Smith, *A History of the Post Office in British North America 1639–1870* (Cambridge, Eng., 1920), pp. 37–57. On p. 42 Smith states that after the terms of the peace treaty of 1763 were known BF "came to Quebec to arrange for the establishment of a postal service between Quebec, Three Rivers, and Montreal, and for a regular exchange of mails between those places and New York. At Quebec he met with Hugh Finlay." BF took no such trip in 1763 or 1764, and the only time he was ever in Canada was in 1776 when he was one of the commissioners sent by Congress to try to persuade the French inhabitants to support the Revolutionary cause. So far as is known, he and Finlay never met personally.

3. Letter 1.

4. There appear to be no formal advertisements of the new packet service in the newspapers the editors have examined, although there are occasional notices in *N.-Y. Mercury* by Alexander Colden, the local postmaster, of the prospective sailing of a packet.

half penny per Letter, for their Trouble in Collecting them; might be of use. All Opening of Ship Bags, at Coffeehouses or elsewhere by Persons not authorized from the Post Office, and distributing the Letters gratis to the Persons they are directed to, or others, should likewise be forbidden.[5]

These Things we suggest, as what occur to us at present; the Post master-General will judge how far such Provisions would be useful, or whether if they might be useful, it would be practicable to obtain them.

We have directed Mr. Colden, in making up the Mail for England, to bind up the Letters from each Government or Province in separate Bundles, marking at the same time upon each Bundle the exact Number of Letters contained therein, and the amount of the inland Postage paid thereon, agreable to your Directions;[6] and have acquainted him, that he will be allow'd by us, in his future Accounts the Salary of £60 Sterling per Annum as Agent for the Packet Boats.

With regard to what you mention concerning the Account exhibited by Mr. Franklin in April 1762,[7] we would observe, that the Receipts and Ballances of the several Postmasters could not then be stated, as few of them had been regular in sending in their Quarterly Accounts, tho' always directed so to do; and this Point has been found very difficult to obtain. The Advantage of the Office to a postmaster in these Countries has been in many Places so inconsiderable, that the Office is not sought after as in England, but we were glad to find an honest careful Man who would at our Request undertake it, to oblige us and his Neighbours. Such Persons would remit us Money from time to time as it arose in their Hands, and when it suited with their Leisure draw out and send us their Accounts but if rigidly required to do it at certain Periods, would decline the Service, and desire us to provide some other

5. The act of 1765 (5 Geo. III, c. 25, sec. iii) forbade any ship to make entry or break bulk upon arriving at a port with postal service in the British dominions until the captain, passengers, and others aboard had delivered to the postal authorities all letters (with certain limited exceptions) which they carried. The penalty was a fine of £20, but the act did not require an oath such as BF and Foxcroft suggested, nor did it in any way mention the coffee houses. The new law was obviously difficult to enforce.

6. Letter I.

7. Letter II.

Person to undertake it. We were therefore under some Necessity of tolerating these Omissions, and content ourselves with obtaining a Settlement when we could. As Correspondence is lately much encreased, more of the Offices become valuable; and as People increase in the Towns, it is more easy to find suitable Officers. In these Cases, we can insist more absolutely on a Regularity in the Execution of the Office; and shall do it; but as in this growing Country there is a Continual Necessity of erecting new Offices in Young Places, the same Difficulty will for a Time continue in such Places, and we do not see how it can be avoided. Every Direction, however, contained in your Letters concerning our future Accounts, shall be complied with as far as in our Power.

Undoubtedly an able Surveyor would be of great Use to us,[8] and prevent the Necessity we are under of making frequent and long Journeys in Person, to see things with our own Eyes, regulate what is amiss, and direct the necessary Improvements; and if on the general Settlement of Accounts we are now making with every Office, we find, as we hope we shall, that the income will be sufficient to defray the additional Expence of such an Officer, we shall not hesitate a Moment to apply for one, especially as you have intimated to us your Opinion that an Assistance so material would not be refused to us, on our Application.[9] And when it is considered, that we have hitherto been without such Assistance, perhaps the Article of travelling Charges in our Accounts will not be thought quite so exceptionable, especially as they amount to much less than the constant Salary of such an Officer. If we reside in New York, to be sure no Journey can be necessary to settle Affairs there; but then it may be necessary from New York to other Places where we now reside, which would be equally distant and expensive. It would be equally agreable to us to live in New York,[1] but there is no House there belonging to the General Post-Office in which we might reside and keep the Office. Perhaps the Postmaster-Gen-

8. Letter II.
9. The office of surveyor was not created until 1772, when Hugh Finlay was appointed.
1. Letter II. It seems doubtful that either the Philadelphian or the Virginian deputy postmaster general meant this statement wholeheartedly. The financial cost to the Post Office suggested in their following comment probably made them feel quite safe in declaring their willingness to move to N.Y.

:ral may be willing to allow us to rent a suitable House there till the Produce of the Office will bear the Expence of Building one, which we suppose will in time be thought proper and necessary, f the Packets are continued.

With regard to the Articles of £32 11s. od. and £59 17s. od. 'or 31 and 57 Days travelling Charges of the late Mr. Hunter,[2] we send you an Original Letter of his to Mr. Franklin[3] explaining the Necessity of undertaking those Journeys, and showing hat the Affairs of the Office required his presence in many Places on the Road as well as at New York, particularly at Annapolis in Maryland.

In the first Journey he made with Mr. Franklin in 1754 he got a severe Fever that left him under an obstinate Disorder in his Bowels which reduced him extremely,[4] baffled all the Skill of our American Physicians, and obliged him to go to England, to recover his Health if possible by change of Air and better Advice. He was near three Years in England, at great Expence, and almost continually harrass'd by that Disorder, before he obtain'd a Cure and was able to return. He therefore, as you will see by his Letter, undertook these new Journeys with extreme Reluctance: and his Apprehensions seem not to have been groundless, for in the last of them, he got a severe Cold which fell upon his Lungs, and put an End to his valuable Life.[5] We think when those Circumstances are known and considered, it will not be required of us to insist with the Executors on their refunding that Money; but we shall wait farther Directions, which it will be our Duty to obey.

We shall set about the Maps of America as soon as we return from our present Journey, and send them with all the particulars required, as well as Tables of all the Post Towns, Postmasters Names, Salaries &ct.[6] and in every thing else, shall endeavour punctually to comply with every Order, and every Intimation of he Pleasure, of the Postmaster-General; and exert our utmost Abilities for the Improvement of this part of the Revenue.

Several Governors of Provinces have refused Payment of

2. Letter II.
3. Not found.
4. See above, v, 333 n, 395, 438, 440, 492.
5. See above, ix, 363.
6. Letter II.

Postage,[7] of which Mr. Franklin acquainted the Board when he was in London, but some of them have since paid their Accounts, and we have now Hopes of obtaining Payment from them all. We are, with great Regard, Sir Your most obedient humble Servants   B FRANKLIN

J. FOXCROFT

Benjamin Franklin and John Foxcroft: Certificate of Hugh Finlay's Appointment as Postmaster

Printed form with MS insertions in blanks: Maine Historical Society

In consequence of the royal proclamation George III issued four months after his accession, which is summarized in the preamble below,[8] Franklin and Foxcroft prepared and had printed this form of certificate to protect their local postmasters from any interruptions in the performance of their duties. The certificate was, of course, not itself the postmaster's commission,[9] but rather an additional document intended to satisfy the civil or military authorities that he was properly entitled to the specified exemptions and privileges.

[Seal]   [June 10, 1763]

BENJAMIN FRANKLIN, and JOHN FOXCROFT, Esquires, joint Post-Masters-General of all his Majesty's Provinces and Dominions on the Continent of North-America.

To all Governors, Mayors of Corporations, Justices of the Peace; and to all other his Majesty's Officers and Ministers, Ecclesiastical, Civil, or Military, within the said Provinces and Dominions, Greeting.

WHEREAS His Majesty, by his Royal Letters Patents under the Great Seal of Great-Britain, bearing Date the 28th Day of February, 1761, and in the First Year of His Majesty's Reign; to the End the Deputies, Agents, and other Officers, employed in the Service of His Majesty's Revenue of the Post-Office might not be

7. Letter II.
8. The editors have not succeeded in locating in print the full text of this proclamation.
9. For an example of the standard commission to a colonial postmaster, see above, V, 451–2.

284

impeded or hindered in their respective Duties, was thereby pleased to declare his Royal Will and Pleasure, That no such Deputies, Agents, and other Officers, shall be compell'd or compellable to serve on any Jury or Inquest, or to appear or serve at any Assize or Session, or to bear any public Office or Employment, either Ecclesiastical, Civil, or Military.

These are to certify, That the Bearer hereof *Hugh Finlay Esquire is appointed by us to be Postmaster of Quebec*[1] which Employment requires at all Times his Personal Attendance, and that His Majesty's Revenue in the Post-Office (great Part of which is now subjected to the Payment of the public Debts), may suffer very much by his being obliged to serve in the Train'd-Bands, or any other public Office, Ecclesiastical, Civil, or Military: For Notification whereof, We have Signed and caused the Seal of our Office to be hereunto affixed, this *Tenth* Day of *June* in the *Third* Year of his Majesty's Reign. B FRANKLIN

J. FOXCROFT

To Richard Jackson ALS: American Philosophical Society

Dear Sir, Woodbridge, New Jerse June 10. 1763

I have your Favours of Mar. 10. and April 4.[2] Your being in Parliament gives me great Pleasure;[3] it will afford you many Opportunities of patronizing effectually the important Interests of your America. I rejoice to hear your Work is finished: and feel already the Obligations we shall all be under to you for it.[4] You mention a Proposal to charge us here with the Maintenance of 0,000 Men.[5] I shall only say, it is not worth your while. All we

1. See the document immediately above.

2. Jackson's letter of March 10 not found; for that of April 4, see above, p. 241–5.

3. See above, pp. 241–2.

4. In the letter cited above Jackson said that he had found time to "complete but the Skeleton of my work." BF was clearly too optimistic, for Jackson seems never to have completed and published this unidentified "work."

5. This proposal must have been mentioned in Jackson's letter of March 10. *London Chron.*, March 5–8, 1763, reported that 10,000 men would be in America, to be paid for the first year by Great Britain and afterwards by the colonies. The next issue (March 8–10) listed the regiments stationed in America, amounting to 10,001 (*sic*) effective men.

can spare from mere Living, goes to you for Superfluities. The more you oblige us to pay here, the less you can receive there. thank you for your Congratulations on my Son's Promotion. The People seem much pleas'd with him, and the Assembly have added £200 to the old Salary of £1000.[6] I forget whether I mention'd to you, that Mr. Symmer, a Gentleman that lives in Moun Street, near Berkely Square, could give you some Information concerning Dr. Barker, Father of the Heir to the Land Mr Hughes desires to purchase.[7] In preceding Letters I mention'd to you the great Eagerness of the People to remove westward; send you enclos'd two Letters I happen to have with me that show something of it.[8] One is from a Projector, who has a Number of Adventurers engag'd. Ensign Webb's crude Scheme is suppress'd by Order of Gen. Amherst; but even that, had a great Number of Subscribers.[9] The Indians however ought to be previously and prudently prepar'd for such Things, or they canno succeed. The Delawares have broke out again, and kill'd 14 o 15 People about the Ohio;[1] if this is in consequence of any general Discontent in that Nation concerning their Lands, as I apprehend it is; we shall have more Trouble before they are quelled. I am here on a Journey to New England, to regulate and improve the Post Offices. If you or any Friend of yours can have a convenient Opportunity of speaking a few kind Things of me to my new Master Lord Egmont,[2] who does not know me, it may be o

6. WF reported to the Board of Trade, June 27, 1763, that he had persuade the N.J. Assembly to increase his and some other officers' salaries. "The Augmentation its true is small, and no ways adequate to the increas'd Expenc of Living in America: But it was all I could at that time obtain." I *N.J.Arch* IX, 389.

7. Probably Robert Symmer (d. 1763), F.R.S., an electrical experimenter see above, IV, 276–7 n. On Barker and the N.J. land that John Hughes wante to buy, see above, pp. 156–8, 163–4.

8. The letters from James Lyon and W. Hick, above, pp. 256–7, 262– the originals are endorsed in Jackson's hand.

9. See above, p. 256 n.

1. See above, pp. 273–4 n.

2. John Perceval, 2d Earl of Egmont (1711–1770), M.P. for various Englis constituencies, 1741–62, succeeded his father in the Irish peerage, 1748, an was created Baron Lovel and Holland in the peerage of the United Kingdom May 7, 1762, and thereupon moved to the House of Lords. He was joint post master general from Nov. 27, 1762, to Sept. 10, 1763, when he was advance

Service to me, and I shall be greatly obliged. I am, Dear Friend,
Yours most affectionately   B FRANKLIN

I wrote you before of your being chosen our Agent with £200
Sterling Salary.³ I hope it will not be disagreable to you.

R Jackson Esq

Endorsed: Woodbridge N. Jersey 10 June 1763 B Franklin Esqr

To Mary Stevenson   ALS: Dartmouth College Library

Woodbridge, New Jersey, June 10. 1763

I wrote to my dear Friend's good Mama to day,⁴ and said I
should hardly have time to write to you; but finding a spare
half Hour, I will indulge myself in the Pleasure of spending it
with you. I have just receiv'd your most agreable Epistle of
March 11.⁵ The Ease, the Smoothness, the Purity of Diction, and
Delicacy of Sentiment, that always appear in your Letters, never
fail to delight me; but the tender filial Regard you constantly
express for your old Friend is particularly engaging. Continue
then to make him happy from time to time with that sweet Intercourse, and take in Return all he can give you, his sincerest
Wishes for you of every kind of Felicity.

I hope that by the Time this reaches you, an Account will arrive
of your dear Pittey's safe landing in America among her Friends.
Your Dolly too, I hope, has perfectly recover'd her Health, and
then nothing will remain to give you Uneasiness or Anxiety.
Heaven bless you, and believe me ever, my dear Child, Your
affectionate Friend and humble Servant   B FRANKLIN

---

to first lord of the Admiralty. He resigned that position in August 1766.
Egmont was a successful pamphleteer, an able debater, and an ardent genealo-
gist. *DNB;* Namier and Brooke, *House of Commons,* III, 266–8.

3. See above, pp. 246–7.
4. Not found.
5. See above, pp. 216–17.

To William Strahan

ALS: Yale University Library

Dear Straney   Woodbridge New Jersey June 10. 1763.

I am here in my Way to New England, where I expect to be till towards the End of Summer. I have writ to you lately and have nothing to add.[6] 'Tis against my Conscience to put you to the Charge of a Shilling for a Letter that has nothing in it to any Purpose, but as I have wrote to some of your Acquaintance by this Opportunity,[7] I was afraid you would not forgive me if I did not write also to you. This is what People get by not being always as good-natured as they should be. I am glad however that you have this Fault; for a Man without Faults is a hateful Creature, he puts all his Friends out of Countenance: but I love you exceedingly.

I am glad to hear that Friend was dismiss'd and got safe with his Ship to England;[8] for I think I wrote you a long Letter by him, and fear'd it was lost; tho' I have forgot what was in it, and perhaps it was not very material, but now you have it. Tell me whether George is to be a Church or Presbyterian Parson?[9] I know you are a Presbyterian yourself, but then I think you have more Sense than to stick him into a Priesthood that admits of no Promotion. If he was a dull Lad it might not be amiss, but George has Parts, and ought to aim at a Mitre. God bless you and Farewell. If I write much more, I must use a Cover, which will double the Postage. So I prudently cut short (thank me for it) with, Dear Straney, Your affectionate Friend and humble Servant

B FRANKLIN

Addressed: To | Mr William Strahan | Printer | Newstreet Square | Shoe Lane | London

6. See above, pp. 271–2.

7. See the letters immediately above to Richard Jackson and Polly Stevenson.

8. For the capture of the *Carolina,* Captain Friend, by the Spanish and her release, see above, p. 160 n. BF's letters to Strahan of Dec. 2 and 7, 1762, had gone by the *Carolina.*

9. For the plans of George Strahan (1744–1824) to become a clergyman, see above, p. 271 n. As BF facetiously recommended here, he entered the Anglican ministry, but he never became a bishop. He was vicar of St. Mary's, Islington, 1773–84, and thereafter was rector of a succession of parishes in Essex and Kent, and was appointed a prebendary of Rochester in 1805. Joseph Foster, *Alumni Oxonienses . . . 1715–1886,* IV (Oxford, 1888), 1363.

From Anthony Armbruster[1]

MS letter:[2] American Philosophical Society

Honour'd Sir.   Philadelphia June 13th. 1763

It is the greatest necessity that urges me to give You this trouble; as I have not been favoured with an answer of the first, sent by Mrs. Franklin,[3] made me think it is unwarranted, but flatter myself You'l excuse both.

As you are on a Journey and not expected to be back for some Weeks, and as the circumstance will not allow to wait till then, and am at the loss how to get relief: I should take as an inestimable Favour, if you would send orders to procure me the sum you gave me some hopes of, before the commencing of [your] Journey.[4]

I do assure you the distress is very great and if you do not rescue me, I shall be a great sufferer in my business: but I expect your generous disposition will prevent it. This inestimable favour shall during my life be acknowledged from Honoured Sir Your very humble and Obedient Servant   ANTHONY ARMBRUSTER

Addressed: To | Benjamin Franklin Esqr. | General Postmaster of North-America | In | Boston

1. For BF's assistance to Anthony (Anton) Armbruster in 1755 in starting the *Philadelphische Zeitung,* a German newspaper with very limited success, see above, V, 421–2 n.
2. Entirely in a clerical hand.
3. Not found.
4. On Nov. 26, 1763, after his return from New England, BF recorded that he had "Lent Anthony Armbruster on a Mortgage of his Printing Materials £50." Armbruster repaid £26 10s. on March 29, 1764, and on October 31 of that year, just before leaving for England BF recorded: "I have this Day sold to Anthony Armbruster the Dutch Printing Office with the English Letters therein, at 14d. per lb. and to give him a Year's Credit, on his Bond with Interest. The Dutch Cases he is to have into the Bargain." Memorandum Book, 1757–1776, pp. 14, 16, 18. Armbruster's total debt amounted to £88 5s., for which he gave BF his bond in double that amount. The principal and interest remained unpaid a year later, so on Oct. 29, 1765, Armbruster signed a chattel mortgage assigning to BF his German and English type and other printing materials in case the debt remained unpaid by Oct. 31, 1766. Apparently he never succeeded in meeting his obligation and the mortgage is now in APS, uncanceled. On Nov. 12, 1785, and April 26, 1786, Armbruster, then living in poverty at Germantown, wrote begging letters to BF in which he recounted his imprisonment for a debt of £17 and the seizure and disposal of his printing equipment. APS.

To Deborah Franklin   ALS: American Philosophical Society

My dear Child,   New York, June 16. 1763
    We left Woodbridge on Tuesday Morning and went to Eliz.
Town, where I found our Children[5] return'd from the Falls and
very well: The Corporation were to have a Dinner that day at
the Point for their Entertainment, and prevail'd on us to stay.
There was all the principal People and a great many Ladies:[6]
after Dinner we set out and got here before dark. We waited on
the Governor[7] and on General Amherst yesterday; din'd with
Lord Sterling;[8] went in the Evening to my old Friend Mr. Kennedy's Funeral,[9] and are to dine with the General to day. Mr.
Hughes[1] and Daughter are well, and Betsey Holt.[2] I have not yet
seen B. Mecom, but shall to day.[3] I am very well.
    I purpose to take Sally at all Events, and write for her to day,
to be ready to go in the Packet that sails next Friday Week.[4] If

5. WF and his wife and Sally Franklin, who appears to have been at Woodbridge with the Parkers.
    6. *N.-Y. Mercury,* June 20, 1763, and *London Chron.,* Aug. 2–4, 1763,
printed an account of the reception given WF and his wife by the Corporation
of Elizabeth Town, June 10, 1763, and also the texts of the speeches which
WF and the Corporation exchanged on that occasion.
    7. The governor of N.Y. at this time was Gen. Robert Monckton (1726–
1782), who had made a distinguished record during the recent war: at Fort
Beauséjour in 1755 (above, VI, 448), on the Plains of Abraham, 1759, where
he was wounded, and at Martinique, 1762; above, IX, 252 n. He was lieutenant
governor of Nova Scotia, 1755–61, before coming to N.Y., of which he was
governor until 1763, when he returned permanently to England. *DAB; DNB.*
    8. For William Alexander, "Lord Stirling," see above, p. 151 n.
    9. For Archibald Kennedy, a prominent N.Y. official, land speculator, and
author of several pamphlets on colonial affairs, see above, IV, 117 n.
    1. Probably Hugh Hughes (*c.* 1727–1802), brother of BF's friend John
Hughes. A tanner by trade, Hughes was plagued by business failures and was
forced to keep a school to support a large family. An ardent Son of Liberty,
he served during the Revolutionary War as deputy quartermaster general
for the Continental Army and quartermaster general for N.Y. 1 *N.J. Arch.,*
XXIV, 646 n; *PMHB,* XXXV (1911), 442.
    2. Perhaps the former Elizabeth Hunter, wife of the N.Y. printer John
Holt (see above, V, 441 n), or a daughter or niece.
    3. BF's nephew, Benjamin Mecom, was in N.Y. trying to found a news-
paper; see above, p. 153 n.
    4. BF went to Newport, the first stop on his trip to Boston, by water to
avoid the "hott weather" prevailing along the east coast. Joseph Chew to Jared

there is no other suitable Company, Mr. Parker[5] will go with her and take care of her.

I am glad you sent some Wax Candle with the Things to Boston; I am now so us'd to it, I cannot well do without it.

You spent your Sunday very well, but I think you should go oftner to Church.

I approve of your opening all my English Letters, as it must give you Pleasure to see that People who knew me there so long and so intimately, retain so sincere a Regard for me.

My Love to Mr. Rhoads[6] when you see him, and desire he would send me an Invoice of such Locks, Hinges and the like as cannot be had at Philadelphia, and will be necessary for my House, that I may send for them. Let me know from time to time how it goes on.

Mr. Foxcroft and Mr. Parker join in Compliments to you and Cousin Lizzey.[7] Mr. F. prays his Mama to forgive him and he will be a better Boy.[8] I am, my dear Debby, Your affectionate Husband   B FRANKLIN

From Anthony Todd
Copy: Yale University Library

Copy

Sir   General Post Office June the 18th. 1763

I had the pleasure to receive your Letter of the 14th. of April,[9] on Wednesday the 8th. Instant, and the same day laid it before His Majesty's PostMaster General,[1] who were extremely well satisfied and promise Themselves great Information from your Correspondence.

They are very glad to find that before you had received my

Ingersoll, undated, New Haven Colony Hist. Soc. *Papers*, IX (1918), 285–6.

5. For James Parker, printer to N.Y. and N.J. and to Yale College, see above, II, 341 n.

6. For Samuel Rhoads, the carpenter and builder who was supervising the construction of BF's new house at 318 Market St., see above, II, 406 n.

7. Not identified.

8. It is impossible to do more than speculate as to the peccadillo for which Foxcroft prayed DF's forgiveness.

9. See above, pp. 251–4.

1. The postmasters general at this time were Robert Hampden-Trevor and John Perceval, 2d Earl of Egmont; see above, p. 217 n.

Letters to you of the 12th. of March,[2] your own sentiments were the same with Theirs upon almost every point, which makes it unnecessary to add more for the present.

The Harriot Packet has been detained a Week that the Merchants might have Time to answer the Letters which were brought by her,[3] but it is to be hoped this will seldom happen, and that when the Boats are once properly established, a regular Course of sailing may be depended on the second Saturday of every Month from both sides. I am Sir Yours &c.   ANTH: TODD Secry
To Benj: Franklin Esqr.

To Jane Mecom   ALS: American Philosophical Society

Dear Sister,   New York, June 19. 1763
We are thus far on our Way to Boston, and hope to be there in about three Weeks.[4] I purpose to lodge at your House if you can conveniently receive me. Sally is now with her Brother at Amboy, and will be here in a few Days.[5] If I can well do it, I shall bring her with me; and if you cannot accommodate us both, one of us may lodge at Cousin Williams's;[6] on second Thoughts, it will be best that she should be there, as there is a Harpsichord, and I would not have her lose her Practice; and then I shall be more with my dear Sister. I have seen Cousins Benny and Johny[7] here, and they are both well, and the Children; I purpose to go again this Afternoon, to see Betsey,[8] who was not at home when I was there. My Love to Brother, &c. I am, Dear Jenny, Your ever loving Brother   B FRANKLIN
Addressed: To / Mrs Jane Mecom / Boston / Free / B FRANKLIN

2. See above, pp. 217–20, 220–2, 223–4.

3. *London Chron.*, June 7–9, 1763, reported the *Harriot* packet, Capt. Robinson, at Falmouth on June 4. The packet sailed from there on June 22 and arrived in N.Y. on August 7. *N.-Y. Mercury*, Aug. 8, 1763.

4. BF, his daughter Sally, and his colleague John Foxcroft arrived in Boston on July 20, 1763.

5. Sally had reached N.Y. by June 28; see below, pp. 305–6.

6. BF's nephew by marriage, Jonathan Williams, Sr.

7. Jane Mecom's sons, Benjamin (C.17.3) and John (C.17.7); John was working in N.Y. at this time as a goldsmith.

8. Benjamin Mecom's wife, Elizabeth.

From David Hall

ALS: American Philosophical Society

Dear Sir,   Philada. June 23. 1763.

I recd. yours Yesterday,[9] and observe what you say relating to what is inserted in the York Papers. That relating to Lord Bute shall be published next Week, if we have Room; the other the North Briton, if you had not mentioned it, should not have been inserted.[1]

Yesterday very bad Accounts came to hand relating to the Indians; but as our Governor, his Council, and Provincial Commissioners, it seems, were not pleased with our publishing what we did the two last Weeks, we resolved to say nothing about them this, until something more certain should be known of their Proceedings; but the Advices now received come so well confirmed, that there is not the least Reason to doubt that the Indians design us all the Mischief in their Power.[2] The Substance of what is come is as follows.

Colonel Armstrong writes Mr. Hoopes,[3] that an Indian, who he knows well, and is married to a white Woman, is come to Shippensburgh from Potowmack, and says, he has been made acquainted with the Indians Intentions: That a great many Tribes

9. Not found.

1. *Pa. Gaz.*, June 30, 1763, printed a vindication of "the late Minister," Lord Bute, which had first appeared in April in a London pamphlet, *A Letter from a Gentleman in Town to his Friend in the Country*. Hall did not reprint, as *N.-Y. Mercury*, June 20, 1763, had done, John Wilkes's violent attack on the King's speech to Parliament in *North Briton*, No. 45, which called the speech "The most abandoned Instance of Ministerial Effrontery ever attempted to be imposed on Mankind."

2. Issues of *Pa. Gaz.* for June 9 and 16, 1763, had carried reports of Indian attacks from Forts Pitt, Bedford, and Ligonier; the issue of June 23 carried none, but that of June 30 resumed the reports of depredations and of the flight of western settlers from their homes. At meetings of the Council, June 20 and 23, Governor Hamilton presented several letters from the west and on the advice of the Council issued writs for a special meeting of the Assembly. The minutes contain no reference to the *Pa. Gaz.* publication of the bad news from the frontier. *Pa. Col. Recs.*, IX, 30–1.

3. Col. John Armstrong (above, VII, 104 n), and Adam Hoops (or Hoopes), commissary of provisions (above, VI, 444 n). Part of what follows in this paragraph is a direct quotation from an extract of this letter, which Hall printed as from Carlisle, June 20, in *Pa. Gaz.*, June 30, 1763. The other accounts here are all taken from letters quoted or summarized in the same issue.

are joined in the Affair: That they are to carry the War to as great an Extent as they can: That they are to attack the Inhabitants in the Season of the Harvest: That they design to burn and destroy all Kinds of Provisions; and are determined to make no Prisoners, but to kill all that fall into their Hands. This Account, the Colonel says he had from several People who had seen the Indian. He adds, that the People are leaving their Places fast, and that the Distress and Confusion the Country is in, is more easy to imagine than express.

Fort Bedford, June 18. 1763.
"The Scene of Indian Cruelty is at length opined. A Dog came into the Garrison wounded, upon which a Party went out immediately, and about 13 Miles from hence found his Master killed and scalped. With him a great many must have shared his Fate, as the Woods are full of Indian Tracts [Tracks]. Just come in a Man and his Wife, about eight Miles from this Place, who being in an adjacent Field to their House, heard a Gun go off, upon which a Cry insued, and then six Guns more were fired, when they set off for the Fort. About an Hour ago, the House was seen in Flames, and no Doubt the People are all murdered that were in the House."

At Shippensburgh they are in great Confusion, expecting to be attacked, where they have neither Arms nor Ammunition. In the Path Valley[4] they expected the Indians every Moment. The Accounts from Carlisle and Shippensburgh the 20th. Pittsburgh is certainly invested, and the Communication cut off, as there are no Accounts from thence since the Second of this Month. Wish I may soon have better News to send you. Hope you will return as soon as possible, as your Advice may be of Use, in this Time of Calamity. Our Governor and Commissioners have ordered 120 Men to be raised forthwith for the Garrison at Augusta. Shall be glad to hear from you by every opportunity. Our Compliments to Miss Sally and Mr. Foxcroft. I am, in Haste, Yours, &c.   D. HALL

Addressed: To / Benjamin Franklin Esq; / at / New-York

Endorsed: Philad June 23d 1763 from Mr. Hall to Ben: Franklin Esqr

4. In Cumberland (now Franklin) Co., east of the Tuscarora Mountain ridge. The West Branch of Conococheague Creek flows through it.

To [Jonathan Williams][5]

ALS: Yale University Library

Dear Kinsman   New York, June 26. 1763

Inclos'd is a Receipt for some things of mine sent to your Care.[6] I am thus far on my Journey to Boston, and hope now to have soon the Pleasure of seeing you. My Love to your Wife and Children. Tell my Cousin to have his Harpsichord in good Order, for I love Music and shall be pleas'd to hear him.[7] My Daughter too, that comes with me, plays a little, and will be glad of his Instructions.[8] I am, Your affectionate Kinsman

B FRANKLIN

To Richard Jackson

ALS: American Philosophical Society

Dear Sir,   New York, June 27. 1763

Since my Arrival here, News is brought from all Quarters of the Indians having suddenly and pretty generally commenc'd Hostilities, without having first made any Complaint, or alledging any Reason.[9]

I find the General[1] is of Opinion, that it is the Effect of a large Belt sent last Year among them by the French Commander in the Ilinois Country, which was stopt sometime in one of their Towns, but afterwards carried round thro' the Nations: and he thinks, it will cease when those French come to know that a Peace is concluded between England and France. But others here say, the Indians are disgusted that so little Notice has lately been taken of them, and are particularly offended that Rum is prohibited, and Powder dealt among them so sparingly. They have received no

5. The address page is missing, but Jonathan Williams, BF's nephew by marriage, is the only Boston relative whom the contents of this letter would fit.

6. See above, p. 291, for the wax candles and other things DF had sent to Boston for her husband.

7. The blind Josiah Williams (C.5.3.1), Jonathan's elder son, was the musician of the family.

8. On the harpsichord BF had sent from England for Sally, see above, IX, 395 n.

9. See above, pp. 273–4 n, for the beginnings of the Indian uprising.

1. Gen. Jeffery Amherst, the British commander-in-chief in North America.

Presents: And the Plan of preventing War among them, and bringing them to live by Agriculture, they resent as an Attempt to make Women of them, as they phrase it: It being the Business of Women only to cultivate the Ground: their Men are all Warriors.[2]

Perhaps these Causes have jointly contributed to produce the Effect. I think too, that we stoop'd too much in begging the last Peace of them;[3] which has made them vain and insolent; and that we should never mention Peace to them again, till we have given them some severe Blows, and made them feel some ill Consequences of breaking with us. The Papers will tell you most of our News.[4] The inclos'd Letter has some Particulars not yet publish'd.[5]

Your Favour by Mr. Tunnicliff reach'd me here.[6] I have recommended him for a Purchase of Land to Lord Stirling,[7] who has great Tracts in the Jerseys out of the Indians way, and says he should like such a Man for a Neighbour, being himself employ'd at present in making great Improvements near Baskinridge where he purposes Building a Seat. I have recommended him also to Mr. Hughes,[8] who is well acquainted with Country Affairs, and

2. Howard H. Peckham places the blame for the uprising chiefly on Amherst's shortsighted policy of refusing to supply the western Indians with presents, ammunition, and rum, although he does not discount French intrigue and the encroachment of settlers on Indian lands. *Pontiac and the Indian Uprising* (Chicago, 1961), esp. pp. 101–7.

3. BF is probably referring to the Indian treaty at Lancaster, Pa., in August 1762, at which the Indians requested the removal of troops from Fort Augusta and the regulation of traders there and at which Governor Hamilton tried unsuccessfully to obtain the Indians' permission to build a trading post at the head of the Susquehanna River. *Johnson Papers*, III, 873–5.

4. *N.-Y. Mercury*, June 27, 1763, carried an account of Pontiac's unsuccessful attempt to take Detroit by a ruse, his subsequent attacks on outlying settlers, and his failure to take the fort by a direct assault. The June 20 issue carried accounts of Indian depredations on settlers and traders around Fort Pitt.

5. According to Carl Van Doren, David Hall's letter to BF of June 23, 1763, above, pp. 293–4. *Letters and Papers of Benjamin Franklin and Richard Jackson 1753–1785* (Phila., 1947), p. 106.

6. For John Tunnicliff, an Englishman who had come to America to buy lands, see above, p. 227 n. He probably carried Jackson's letter to BF of April 4, 1763; see above, pp. 241–5.

7. For William Alexander, "Lord Stirling," see above, p. 151 n.

8. BF's good friend, John Hughes.

capable of giving him the best Advice. When I return to Pensilvania, which I hope will be about the Beginning of September, I shall readily afford him such Assistance as may be in my Power.

I have wrote to you lately, and little now occurs to add. I see in the Account of our Success at the Manillas, on which I congratulate you, one Barker mention'd as an Officer. It is probably the same we have been enquiring after.[9] I hear our Assembly is to meet on Occasion of these Indian Disturbances, before the time to which they stood adjourn'd.[1] With the greatest Esteem, I am, Dear Sir, Your most obedient humble Servant   B FRANKLIN

P.S. This Renewal of Indian War in the Northern Parts, would incline our People much more to a southern Settlement. I long to hear your Sentiments of the Coxes Affair.[2]

The Indians engag'd its said are the Outaways and Chippaways with some Seneca's and Delawares.[3]

R Jackson Esqr

Endorsed: New York June 27 1763 B Franklin Esqr

To Mary Stevenson   ALS: American Philosophical Society

Dear Polley,   New York, June 27. 1763

I received here your kind little Letter of April 14. with your good Mama's Favour of the same Date.[4] I write this Line chiefly to acknowledge it, having wrote to you lately, and little now to

9. *N.-Y. Mercury,* June 13, 1763, carried an account of the British siege and capture of Manila, Oct. 6, 1762. Maj. Robert Barker, from whom John Hughes, with BF's assistance, was trying to buy land in N.J. (see above, pp. 157–8), was commended in the account for his "most excellent skill" in commanding the British artillery during the battle.

1. On April 2, 1763, the Pa. Assembly adjourned until September 12, but reconvened at Amherst's request on July 4. 8 *Pa. Arch.,* VI, 5425.

2. See above, pp. 212–14.

3. Pontiac is generally agreed to have been an Ottawa, although one of his parents may have been a Chippewa or a Miami. He was supported by his own tribe and by the Chippewa, Potawatomie, Huron, Delaware, Shawnee, Mingo, and Seneca. Peckham, *Pontiac and the Indian Uprising,* pp. 15–16, 96–107 *passim.*

4. Neither letter has been found.

add. I congratulate you on your Dolly's Recovery,[5] which you mention as nearly compleated, assuring you that I do, as you suppose, participate your Pleasure. Tell her that the old American loves her; and all that agreable Family that he remembers and honours them. I am glad you are pleas'd with your new Neighbours; those you left you us'd to like, and as Wanstead is in itself a more pleasant Place than Kensington, you must have suffer'd greatly by the Exchange if those you found there were disagreable.[6] I am asham'd to send a Letter so far with so little in it; In some future Letter I will endeavour to make Amends. My respectful Compliments to your good Aunts; I am, as ever, my dear Friend, Yours affectionately   B FRANKLIN

Endorsed: New York June 27—63

To John Waring[7]   ALS: American Philosophical Society

Reverend and dear Sir,   New York, June 27. 1763

Being here on my Journey to New-England, I received your Favour of April 5.[8] You will easily conceive that after an Absence of near Six Years from my Family and Affairs, my Attention must be much engross'd on my Arrival by many Things that requir'd it; not to mention a Multiplicity of Visits, &c. that devour abundance of Time, I enquir'd however of Mr. Sturgeon[9] concerning the Negro School tho' I could not visit it, and had the Satisfaction to hear it was full and went on in general well, tho' he had met with some Difficulties during the late Dissensions in the Church; but they were pretty well over.[1] He gave me the en-

5. Polly's friend, Dolly Blunt.

6. Polly's missing letter of April 14 apparently reported that the aunts with whom she lived, Mrs. Tickell and Mrs. Rooke, had moved from Wanstead to Kensington.

7. On the Reverend John Waring, secretary of the Associates of Dr. Bray, see above, VII, 98 n.

8. Not found.

9. William Sturgeon, one of the assistant ministers of the united churches of Christ Church and St. Peter's, Philadelphia, and catechist of the school for Negro children supported there by the Bray Associates. See above, VII, 252 n.

1. In the winter of 1762–63 the Society for the Propagation of the Gospel, which paid a small part of Sturgeon's salary, was told that he was neglecting

clos'd List of the Scholars. As soon as I return to Philadelphia, which I hope to do by the Beginning of September, I shall inspect the School very particularly, and afford every Assistance in my Power to Mr. Sturgeon, in promoting the laudable Views of the Associates, to whom please to present my best Respects. Since my Arrival in America, I made a Journey too to Williamsburgh, near 350 Miles, which took me 5 Weeks; on Business of the Post Office. I there had a long Conversation with Mr. Nicholus[2] concerning the School in that Place, of which I need not give you any Account, as you have receiv'd his Letter which he told me he had written to you. He appears a very sensible and a very conscientious Man, and will do his best in the Affair, but is sometimes a little diffident as to the final Success, in making sincere good Christians of the Scholars; their Continuance at the School being short. I think to visit the School here, which Mr. Auchmuty[3] tells me is in a good way. And as I expect to be at Newport in Rhodeisland next Week, I shall speak to Mr. Brown concerning the Letters you have wrote him, and promote a School there if

---

his duties as catechist. A local committee, consisting of the rector, Rev. Richard Peters, and four vestrymen, investigated and on April 23, 1763, completely exonerated him. Nevertheless, soon after receiving this report, the S.P.G. dismissed Sturgeon from its service. The criticism may have come originally from Rev. William Smith, then in London, who was not friendly to Sturgeon, or as the accused minister believed, from John Ross, a former Christ Church vestryman who was a member of the S.P.G. and had become leader of a movement as the result of which numerous communicants withdrew and founded St. Paul's Church with Rev. William McClanachan as its minister. Later the S.P.G. relented and Sturgeon continued in service until his retirement in 1766. William S. Perry, ed., *Papers Relating to the History of the Church in Pennsylvania, A.D. 1680–1778* (privately printed, 1871), pp. 332,355–6; Benjamin Dorr, *A Historical Account of Christ Church, Philadelphia* (N.Y., Phila., 1841), pp. 137–8; Edgar L. Pennington, "The Work of the Bray Associates in Pennsylvania," *PMHB*, LVIII (1934), 7–9.

2. William Hunter and Commissary Thomas Dawson had been in charge of the Negro school in Williamsburg (above, IX, 21 n), but both had died and Robert Carter Nicholas (1728–1780), a leading lawyer and treasurer of Va., and Rev. William Yates took over as trustees. Edgar L. Pennington, "Thomas Bray's Associates and Their Work among the Negroes," Amer. Antiq. Soc. *Proc.*, new series, XL (1938), 355–6.

3. Rev. Samuel Auchmuty, assistant rector of Trinity Church, and catechist of the Negro school in N.Y. See above, IX, 21 n. On his work for the school see Amer. Antiq. Soc. *Proc.*, new series, XL, 390–3.

practicable.[4] I thank you for your kind Congratulations on the Marriage and Proferment of my Son, and am with great Esteem, and Respect, Reverend Sir, Your most obedient humble Servant

B FRANKLIN

P.S. At my Return I shall pay my Subscription as you desire to Mr. Sturgeon.

Mr. Waring

Addressed: To / The Revd Mr Waring / at Mr Burd's a Bookseller / in Ava Mary Lane, near St. / Paul's / London

Endorsed: Dr. Franklin June 27. 1763

To John Whitehurst

LS:[5] Yale University Library

Dear Sir   New York, June 27. 1763
Being here on a Journey to New-England, I received your Favour of March 18 with great Pleasure as it inform'd me of your and Mrs. Whitehurst's Welfare.[6]

As I was not at home to receive Mr. Tunnicliff and afford him personnally my Advice and Assistance, all I could do was to recommend him to some able and intelligent Friends there, who I am sure will be glad to serve him;[7] and when I return, which I hope will be in about two Months I shall chearfully render him every Service in my Power.

---

4. In 1760 Rev. Thomas Pollen, rector of Trinity Church, Newport, had been asked to take charge of Negro education at Newport, but in that year he severed his connection with the church and Rev. Marmaduke Browne (*c.*1731–1771) took his place as rector. Browne wrote the S.P.G., Jan. 9, 1763, that he had started a school for fifteen Negro boys and fifteen girls. Wilkins Updike, *A History of the Episcopal Church in Narragansett Rhode Island* (2d edit., enlarged and corrected by Daniel Goodwin, Boston, 1907), I, 617; II, 325; III, 85–6; Amer. Antiq. Soc. *Proc.*, new series, XL, 398–400.

5. The body of the letter is in an unidentified hand; "Mr. Whitehurst" and the signature are in BF's.

6. For Whitehurst's letter and some of the matters to which BF replies and people he mentions here, see above, pp. 226–30.

7. John Tunnicliff, the bearer of Whitehurst's letter, wanted to buy land and settle in America. BF put him in touch with William Alexander, Lord Stirling, in N.J., and with John Hughes in Pa. See above, pp. 296–7.

I thank you for your kind Congratulations on my Son's Marriage and Promotion. He and his Wife are safely arrived and settled. He is here at present with me, and desires his Respects to you.

My Compliments to Mr. Tissington and tell him a Silver Mine is discover'd here which they say is as rich as Potosi.[8] Gen. Monckton[9] carries over Specimens of the Ore.

Unluckily it lies under Water in the River. How it is to be work'd I know not, But as it is near the Shore perhaps it extends under the Bank into the Land and may there be wrought to Advantage. I have lately sent him, Mr. Tissington, a Catalogue of Ores, and Minerals found in these Parts.[1] Remember me respectfully to Dr. Darwin. I shall be glad to see his Thoughts on Cold when he thinks fit to favour me with them.[2] I am sure they will be ingenious and instructive.

8. On Philipse Manor, Westchester Co., N.Y. "Royal mines," as those of the precious metals were called, were vested in the Crown but were usually leased to the landowners or other interested parties on condition of paying a "royalty" of one-twentieth of all gold and silver produced. In 1761 five men formed a partnership to prospect for such ores in N.Y., Conn., and N.J. and applied the next year for a 99-year grant of any mines they might discover. The Privy Council referred the application to the Board of Trade and that body asked the governor of N.Y. for an opinion. In 1764 Frederick Philipse, last lord of the manor, who had heard of this application, petitioned the King that any mines on his land be excepted from the grant to this partnership and be leased to him instead, and that, "if the mine already discovered there" should prove to extend under the Hudson River, as he thought it did, he be allowed to exercise all rights to it "as if the mine were wholly within the manor." The Board of Trade decided to take no action until the parties concerned should apply again. Philipse's petition came up again in 1771 and on the Board of Trade's advice the Privy Council instructed the governor to grant him a lease of his mine. In 1774, however, Gov. William Tryon reported that the Philipse mine yielded only a small quantity of silver and should more properly be considered a richer sort of lead mine. Thus faded the dream of a new Potosi in Westchester Co. 1 *N.J. Arch.*, IX, 318–21; *Acts Privy Coun., Col.*, IV, 549–50; V, 298–9; *Board of Trade Journal*, 1759–63, pp. 302–3; 1764–67, p. 92; 1768–75, pp. 231, 233, 246, 249; *N.Y. Col. Docs.*, VII, 449.

9. Robert Monckton, governor of N.Y., sailed for England the day after BF wrote this letter. Cadwallader Colden to the Board of Trade, July 8, 1763, N.-Y. Hist. Soc. *Coll.*, 1876, p. 217.

1. See above, p. 273.

2. Whitehurst had told BF that he hoped Darwin would "be able to entertain you with some discoverys on Cold next winter," but no publications on this subject by Darwin have been located.

Your new Theory of the Earth is very Sensible, and in most particulars quite Satisfactory.[3] I cannot now give you my Sentiments fully upon it, this Ship just Sailing; but shall write you at large from Boston, where I expect to be some time.

I am glad to hear Mr. Harrison is like to obtain some handsome Encouragement.[4] I have heard that Mr. Graham, (the famous Graham of your Trade)[5] should say, Harrison deserv'd the Reward if it were only for his Improvements in Clockmaking: The Error of his Watch in the Voyage between Portsmouth and Portroyal in Jamaica, was it seems but 23 seconds of Time! A surprizing Exactness, if it holds. I never kept a Journal of the Weather but one Year. But have a Friend at Philadelphia who has kept it several Years, and I will get him to send you a Copy of it when I return.[6]

I am ashamed to read here the Clamour of your political Scriblers against the Peace.[7] Never did England make a Peace more truly and substantially advantageous to herself, as a few Years will evince to everybody; for here in America she has laid a broad and strong Foundation on which to erect the most beneficial and certain Commerce, with the Greatness and Stability of her Empire. The Glory of Britain was never higher than at present, and I think you never had a better Prince: Why then is he not universally rever'd and belov'd? I can give but one Answer. The

3. See above, pp. 229–30. The letter BF promised to write from Boston has not been found.

4. On John Harrison's invention of the chronometer and the voyage to Jamaica to test it, see above, VII, 208–10, and esp. p. 209 n.

5. George Graham (1673–1751), clockmaker and "mechanician." Among other important inventions, he created the mercurial pendulum which compensated for the expansion of a steel pendulum by the differing expansion of mercury in a jar connected with it, and the "dead-beat escapement," an important improvement of its predecessors. He also made several major scientific instruments and pieces of apparatus. DNB.

6. Which "Friend at Philadelphia" BF had in mind is not certain; it may have been John Bartram, Ebenezer Kinnersley, or Isaac Norris.

7. The most prominent of the "political Scriblers" at this time was, of course, John Wilkes. They attacked the Treaty of Paris not so much, perhaps, because they sincerely objected to its terms, but because its champion was the personally unpopular Earl of Bute, who had little political experience and less skill in the art of politics. News of his resignation as first lord of the Treasury, April 8, had reached N.Y. and Philadelphia by the middle of June.

King of the Universe, good as he is, is not cordially belov'd and faithfully serv'd by all his Subjects. I wish I could say that half Mankind, as much as they are oblig'd to him for his continual Favours, were among the truly loyal. Tis a shame that the very Goodness of a Prince, should be an Encouragement to Affronts. An Answer now occurs to me, for that Question of Robinson Crusoe's Man Friday, which I once thought unanswerable, *Why God no kill the Devil?*[8] It is to be found in the Scottish Proverb; *Ye'd do little for God an the Deel were Dead.*

I believe I desired you in a former Letter[9] to deliver the Thermometer you was to make for me, well pack'd, to Mrs. Stevenson, who will pay you for it. The Derby China was so well pack'd that not even the thinnest part of the Foliage was Damag'd, It is much admired here.[1] I am, with Sincerest Esteem, Dear Sir, Your most obedient humble Servant   B FRANKLIN

Mr. Whitehurst.

Endorsed: Dr Franklin 27 June 1763 to Mr Whitehurst [*Note following endorsement:*] (Indorsement by Dr. Hutton, whose daughter gave me the letter.[2])

To William Strahan   ALS: Pierpont Morgan Library

Dear Friend,   New York, June 28. 1763

You will hear before this reaches you, that the Indians have renew'd their Hostilities.[3] They have not as usual made any pre-

8. "*But,* says he again, *if God much strong, much might as the Devil, why God no kill the Devil, so make him no more do wicked?*" Daniel Defoe, *The Life and Strange Surprizing Adventures of Robinson Crusoe of York. Mariner.* (London, 1719), p. 259.

9. Not found.

1. When BF had ordered a set of Derby china sent to America is uncertain. The "English China" he sent to DF in February 1758 (above, VII, 381) had gone before he had done any traveling from London and presumably before he had met Whitehurst. Perhaps he ordered it when he was in Derbyshire in August 1759 (above, VII, 431).

2. Charles Hutton (1737–1823), mathematician, F.R.S., 1774; LL.D., Edinburgh, 1779. *DNB.* He edited Whitehurst's works (1792) with a memoir and so probably had his surviving papers. The writer of this note has not been identified.

3. For notes on matters in this paragraph, which summarizes what BF

vious Complaint, and various Conjectures are therefore made of the Cause. Some think it is merely to secure their Hunting Countries, which they apprehend we mean to take from them by Force and turn them into Plantations, tho' this Apprehension is without Ground. Others, that too little Notice of them has been taken since the Reduction of Canada, no Presents made them as before. Others, that they are offended at the Prohibition of selling them Rum and Powder; but I do not find this Prohibition has been general, and as to Powder that enough has been allow'd them all for their Hunting. Others, that they acquir'd a Relish for Plunder in the late War, and would again enjoy the Sweets of it. Others that it is the Effect of a large Belt sent among them by the French Commander in the Ilinois Country, before he heard of the Peace, to excite them to renew the War, and assure them of Supplies and Assistance. Others think all these Causes may have operated together. The Nations chiefly concern'd are said to be the Outawas and Chippewas who live West and North of the Lakes, and the Delawares on the Ohio; but some other Nations who have not yet appear'd are suspected privily to encourage them. It is however a War that I think cannot last long, tho' for the present very mischievous to the poor Settlers on the Frontiers.

I expected when I left England, to have learnt in your Letters the true State of Things from time to time among you; but you are silent, and I am in the dark. I hear that Faction and Sedition are becoming universal among you, which I can scarcely believe tho' I see in your public Papers a Licentiousness that amazes me.[4] I hear of Ins and Outs and Ups and Downs, and know neither why nor wherefore. Think, my dear Friend, how much Satisfaction 'tis in your Power to give me, with the Loss only of half an Hour in a Month that you would otherwise spend at Cribbidge. I left our Friend David[5] and his Family well. I hope this will find you so. I am here on my Journey to New England, whence I hope to return in about 2 Months. Sally goes with me. Billy and

wrote Richard Jackson on June 27 about the Uprising of Pontiac, see above, pp. 295–6. The paragraph was printed in *London Chron.*, Aug. 11–13, 1763, under the heading of "Extract of a Letter from New-York, June 28."

4. The worst offense was the attack on the King's speech in John Wilkes's *North Briton*, no. 45, which was reprinted in *N.-Y. Mercury*, June 20, 1763.

5. David Hall.

his Wife, came over here last Night from the Jerseys to spend a few Days with their Friends at New York, so that we are all together at present, except my Wife, and all join in best Wishes for you and good Mrs. Strahan and your Children. I wrote to you by the last Packet,[6] and can now only add, that I am, with sincerest Esteem and Affection, Dear Sir, Your most obedient humble Servant

B FRANKLIN

Mr. Strahan

Endorsed: Britannia, Tillet   Philadelphia Packett Budden[7]

From Peter Collinson

ALS: American Philosophical Society

Lond June 28. 1763

I received my Dear Friends Obligeing Letter[8] with another Inclosed to our Friend Hamilton[9] which I forwarded to Him. Doubt not but will proof Satisfactory. This Serves to convey Advice of a Box of Books for Thy Self, Lib: Com. and J. Bartram perticulars as under.[1] From His Affectionate Friend

P COLLINSON

The Box is Directed for Thee and comes by the Carolina Capt. Friend. Hope to Inclose the Capts. Receipt. I have made Thee Debtor for the whole as I keep no Account with the Lib: Comy.

6. BF's letter to Strahan of June 10 apparently went by the *Duke of Cumberland* packet, Capt. Goodridge, which sailed from N.Y. on June 13. *Pa. Gaz.*, June 16, 1763.

7. The reason for these endorsements is unknown. There is no newspaper record of the departure of either of these vessels from N.Y. or Philadelphia or of its arrival in England during the time this letter was in transit. Strahan mentioned, August 18, that he had received the letter "last Friday," August 12. BF probably sent it by the ship *Edward*, Captain Davis, which sailed from N.Y. on June 28 carrying Gov. Robert Monckton. *N.-Y. Mercury*, June 27, July 4, 1763.

8. Either BF's letter of Dec. 7, 1762 (above, pp. 165–6) or one of a later date, not found.

9. Charles Hamilton; see above, p. 151 n. BF's letter to him was probably about the erection of lightning rods; see *ibid.*

1. The remainder of this letter is essentially repeated from Collinson's letter to BF of June 8, 1763 (above, p. 275); see it for the appropriate notes.

for	No. 37 and 38 of Mod History 6. 6	–: 13: –
Lib: Com	Edwards VII Vol Birds and binding	2: 5: –
	and many Catalogues	–: –: –
for YourSelf	History Florida I thought this might be	6: –
	Entertaining to you	

Box	1: –
	3: 5.
primage &c	4 –
	3: 9:

N:B. Mr Edwards has left off publishing. If the Lib: Com. have a Mind to Compleat their Sett, if any is wanting Lett them Send in Time. He has published seven Volumes of Birds and animals &c.

I wrote much to the Above purpose by Last Packet. I have seen nothing of your proprietor for a long while.

Addressed: To / Benn: Franklin Esqr / in / Philadelphia

From [Alexander Small][2]

AL (incomplete): American Philosophical Society

Dear Sir   London July 5th 1763

I do not know whether any of our Burnet Seed,[3] has yet been sent to your great World; and therefore to make sure of it, I send you Six pounds. It is a Native of England, but has hitherto passed unnoticed. The attention now paid it is intirely owing to one Roque a Gardener near Chelsea, a most curious Mortal.[4] I

2. Identified by comparing the handwriting with that in other later letters from Small. For Alexander Small, see above, IX, 110–11 n.

3. Burnet is the popular name given to plants of the rose family which belong to the genera *Sanguisorba* and *Poterium,* native to temperate and southern parts of Europe. Great or Common Burnet *(Sanguisorba officinalis)* is common in meadows and Lesser or Salad Burnet *(Poterium Sanguisorba)* in chalk areas. The name pimpernel was formerly applied to both. *OED;* L. H. Bailey, ed., *Cyclopedia of American Agriculture,* II (N.Y., 1907), 306.

4. Bartholomew Rocque (d. 1767) was a gardener and nurseryman of Walham Green, London. He published *Some Hints Relative to Burnet and Timothy* in London in 1764 and *A Treatise on Cultivating Lucern, Burnet, and Timothy Grass* in 1765. G. E. Fussell, *More Old English Farm Books* (London, 1950), pp. 44–5; *Gent. Mag.,* XXXV (1765), 148; *London Chron.,* Aug. 14, 1764; *Annual Register,* VIII (1765), 141–6.

truely think the World will be greatly indebted to him for the discovery. I never saw land bear so great a Burden of any grass as I have seen of this. It has a singular good quality for Northern Situations, viz. that its leaves are not destroyed by the Frost, of which we have had a remarkable Instance this Year, when the severest Winter which we have had since the Year 1740, did not in the least injure it. This promises to be of an Inconceivable advantage to Sheep and Lambs, which in the Spring seldom have any Succulent Plant to feed upon. The following [is] nearly the Culture of it which Mr. Roque recommends. It may be sown in Spring, tho' he prefers August, because the Drought during its first weak state in the Summer is apt to criple or destroy it; whereas in the Autumn, Rains are more frequent, and the Nights longer and moister: He allows ten or 12 pounds to the Acre. After it is grown up, it must be kept clear of Weeds and thinned where too thick. If sown in Spring, it may be cut in July and again in September; but not later, because it acquires strength in the Winter, and keeps the ground warm, when a good Cover is left. If sown in August it will bear but little cutting that Season. The Weeds must be kept carefully under next Spring, the Burnet thinned where too thick, or transplanted where too thin, so that the Plants may stand in rich ground at the distance of nine Inches from one another, and of Six in poor land. The Seed will be ripe in the latter end of June; but if intended only for Hay, it may be cut Sooner. In either Case it will yield a good 2d Crop, and leave an abundant Winter Crop. It will so cover the Earth next Spring that it effectually destroys all Weeds, and will ever after bear being cut thrice every Year. Horses are extremely fond of it; and it seems by what Roque has observed, to be a kind of Panacea for them, having performed some great Cures. This being only the 3d Year that he has cultivated it with Attention, you may beleive experiments have not yet made us fully acquainted with its Virtues.

Considering the low State of Mind to which the good Mr. Eliot was brought, I cannot say but I rather rejoiced to hear of his Death.[5] His Ralations will, I hope, have the Satisfaction of

5. Rev. Jared Eliot, the New England clergyman, physician, and agronomist (above, III, 147–8 n), died April 22, 1763. The Society of Arts had recently conferred on him a gold medal for his production of iron from sea sand. He

receiving his letter; which gave him and them so much uneasiness, inclosed in my last to you. Had he been in his pris-
tine State, this new grass would have afforded him pleasure in
cultivating it.

When mentioning new plants, I can only inform You that the
Marquiss of Turbilly[6] has sent the Society[7] a very small quantity
of the Seed of an uncommonly good Cabbage which grows in
Anjou. Of that small quantity I could only procure a few Seeds.
Some of them are Sown and have come up. As soon as any Seed
is saved, You shall have some, with an Account of the Plant.
Thus it is I endeavour to decoy you into a Correspondence,
which turns so much to my Pleasure and no small fame.

In Course of Posts, I should have had an Answer to mine relating to Mr. Mure's thought of the Hemp Machine.[8] Lest it may
have miscarried, I shall here repeat it as well as my Memory can
recollect a Subject I have ceased thinking of for sometime. Mr.
Stevens[9] the Ironmonger is much of Opinion it will Answer, as
indeed is every one to whom I have mentioned it. Mr. Mure took
the Hint from the Sugar Mills. His Proposal is that when the
Hemp is thoroughly dry, (perhaps laid for sometime in an Oven
or in a Kiln) it shall be pressed between two Cylinders, a little
fluted, so as not only to crush the bun or reed, but also break it

was also known in England for his development of timothy grass. The letters
referred to in this paragraph have not been found. That to Eliot may have
been one of March 1763 covering John Mills's gift of his *A New and Complete
System of Husbandry;* see above, p. 205.

6. Louis-François-Henri de Menon, Marquis de Turbilly (1712–1776), was
a French agriculturalist who resigned from the army in 1737 and devoted his
life to reclaiming the lands around his native Villiers-Charlemagne in Anjou,
introducing a grazing industry, and "amena dans ce petit territoire l'abondance
et la richesse." His *Mémoire sur les défrichements* (Paris, 1760) was translated
into English in 1762 as *A Discourse on the Cultivation of Waste and Barren
Lands.* His cabbage is described in *Annual Register,* VIII (1765), 99–100.

7. The Society of Arts, of which both BF and Small were members.

8. Mr. Mure was probably William Mure (1718–1776), M.P., Renfrewshire,
1742–61; baron of the Scottish Exchequer, 1761–1776; and lord rector of the
University of Glasgow, 1764–65. He was manager of Lord Bute's estates and
an "established authority" on agricultural improvements. *DNB;* Namier and
Brooke, *House of Commons,* III, 181–2. Small's letter to BF about Mure's hemp
machine has not been found, nor has BF's reply, if he wrote one.

9. Not identified.

in Pieces, so that it may be the more easily separated from the Hemp. Mr. Stevens thinks that these Cylinders should be of Iron, and is of opinion they may be cast small enough for this purpose. We did propose that he should have made a Pair, to be sent over, but recollected that as you have founderies, you may cast them, and thereby lessen the Expence of Carriage, &c. If you think Mr. Stevens will do it better, having the Idea of it clearer in his head, which can at the same time have Mr. Mure's Joined with it, we shall set [*remainder missing.*]

Ezra Stiles: List of Franklin's Honors

AD: Yale University Library

During his stay at Newport in July Franklin had an opportunity to renew acquaintance with his old friend Ezra Stiles, now minister of the Congregational Church there, and to engage in conversations with him. On July 11 Franklin showed Stiles some of the papers which reflected the recognition accorded him, in America and abroad, for his scientific achievements. Almost certainly Franklin had brought these documents with him from Philadelphia at Stiles's request. Stiles copied these papers into a volume of miscellaneous extracts now among the Stiles MSS in the Yale University Library, pp. 97-108. He headed them: "July 12, 1763. Copies of Papers taken by the Leave of Dr. Benjamin Franklin of Philadelphia in Newport July 11, 1763." Eleven documents follow.[1]

1. In the order of their appearance in the Stiles volume these documents are: 1. Diploma from the University of St. Andrews, Feb. 12, 1759 (above, VIII, 277–80); 2. Freedom of the city of Edinburgh, Sept. 5, 1759 (above, VIII, 434–5); 3. Freedom of the city of Glasgow, Sept. 19, 1759 (above, VIII, 436); 4. Joseph Browne's note to John Kelly, Feb. 22, 1762, containing the vote of the Oxford "Heads of Houses" to confer the doctorate on BF (above, this vol., p. 59); 5. Freedom of the burgh of St. Andrews, Oct. 2, 1759 (above, VIII, 439); 6. Diploma from the College of William and Mary, April 2, 1756 (above, VI, 430–1); 7. Extract of a letter from Giambatista Beccaria to Peter Collinson, 1756 (see a later note to the present document); 8. Extract of a letter from the Count de Saluce (Saluzzo) to Henry Baker, Sept. 17, 1760 (see a later note to the present document); 9. "Compliments from Father Beccaria of Turin" (above, VII, 315); 10. The "Series of Dr. Franklin's Honors &c." printed herewith; 11. Extract of Peter Collinson's letter to BF, May 27, 1756?, on the unanimity of BF's election to the Royal Society (above, VI, 449). Later Stiles copied nos. 1–7 above and the text of BF's Yale M.A. diploma into a volume of Yale College Records (Yale Univ. Lib.).

Ten of them are copies of diplomas, citations, or extracts of letters, most of which have been previously printed in this edition. The next to last, however, is the summary of Franklin's "Honors" which Stiles compiled on this occasion and which is printed here.

Series of Dr. Franklin's Honors &c.

1706.   Born in Boston N England[2]
1746.   Immersed in Electrical Experiments[3]
1752.   Received a Compliment from the King of France[4]
1753.   Complimented with the Degree of A.M. in Harvard College.[5]
1753.   Do. in Yale College—and an Oration[6]
1756. Apr. 2.   Do. Wm and Mary College[7]
   Id. June   Father Beccarias Letter to P. Collinson[8]

2. Stiles had recorded this fact at the end of one of the documents listed in the preceding note. Whether this son of Connecticut regarded the place of BF's birth as one of his "Honors" is problematical.

3. For the beginning of BF's electrical experiments, see above, III, 110–11, 114–15, *Autobiog.* (APS-Yale), pp. 240–1.

4. Above, IV, 315–16, 466–7.

5. July 25, 1753; above, V, 16–17. It may be observed that at this time Stiles (almost certainly on information from BF) correctly placed the Harvard honorary degree ahead of the Yale one, although years later BF twice stated that Yale had been the first to honor him. *Autobiog.* (APS-Yale), p. 209; BF to Stiles, March 4, 1790, Yale Univ. Lib.

6. The degrees, Sept. 12? 1753; above, V, 58. Stiles's Latin oration, Feb. 5, 1755; above, V, 493–500. Stiles did not copy either the Harvard or Yale diploma or his Yale oration in honor of BF into this volume of miscellaneous extracts.

7. Above, VI, 430–1. In copying this diploma Stiles stated that "this was the first Degree conferred in Virginia College."

8. This letter, dated the Ides of June (June 13), 1756, which Stiles had copied in its Latin original a few pages earlier, may be summarized as follows: I have received the second Paris edition of BF's experiments with Dalibard's notes. I see that on p. 308 BF has courteously and fully given his opinion of me, even while disagreeing on the subject of whirlwinds (above, VI, 98), and he has my gratitude. I shall also be most grateful to him and to you if I may receive from you, as my deputy, whatever he writes. If you have any others of his papers I beg you to send them to me (see below, p. 340). Be assured that I want nothing more eagerly than to make progress and shall acknowledge the source of that progress. I have ready some selected specimens relative to the history of fossils to send to Dr. Parsons (above, VI, 85 n) but see no way to send them. Give my greetings to him, and to BF when you write and let

1757	Elected F.R.S.[9]
1759. Feb. 12.	Degree of J.U.D. from the University of St. Andrew[1]
1762 Feb. 22.	Degree of J.C.D. voted him at Oxford and conferred the Summer following[2]
1759 Sept. 5	Freedom of the City of Edinburgh[3]
Sept. 19	Do. City of Glasgow[4]
Oct. 2	Do. City of St. Andrew[5]
1760	Letter of Count de Saluce at Turin[6]

me know how I may oblige you. Consider me deeply indebted to you and take care of your health.

9. Above, VI, 375–6.

1. Above, VIII, 277–80. In the Latin of the diploma, St. Andrews created BF "Utriusque Juris Doctorem," that is, "Doctor of Both Laws," civil and canon, a title which Stiles indicated by the initials "J.U.D." The less specific title of "Legum Doctor" was the more familiar usage, especially in England and America, indicated by "LL.D.," the initials normally affixed to BF's name after he received this degree. In copying this diploma Stiles noted that St. Andrews was "the oldest University in Scotland."

2. Above, pp. 59, 76–8. Oxford conferred the degree of Doctor of Civil Laws on BF, April 30, 1762.

3. Above, VIII, 434–5.

4. Above, VIII, 436.

5. Above, VIII, 439.

6. Count Guiseppe Angelo Saluzzo was one of the founders of the Academy of Sciences at Turin. Antonio Pace, *Benjamin Franklin and Italy* (Phila., 1958), pp. 63, 65–6, 87–8. Stiles copied into his volume of extracts part of Saluzzo's letter of Sept. 17, 1760, to Henry Baker, a founder of the Society of Arts (above, VI, 449 n), in both the original French and in an English translation. The latter reads: "It is reported here that the Theory upon Electricity, of which Mr. Benjamin Franklin has laid the Foundation, to the Admiration of true and celebrated Philosophers, is at present refuted or rather rejected by modern Electricians. Mr. the Abbe Nollet has printed two Volumes of Words and Invectives to oppose that ingenious Doctrine. This Frenchman often has Recours to very futile Resources. Our celebrated Father Beccaria laughs at his Works and continues to unfold with surprising Success this so interesting Branch of Natural Philosophy."

Benjamin Franklin and John Foxcroft: Receipts to
Thomas Vernon[7]   ADS: Redwood Library and Athenaeum, Newport

[July 12, 16, 1763]
Receiv'd July 12. 1763. of Mr. Vernon, One Hundred and Fifteen
Pounds four Shillings and Sixpence on Account of the Post-Office,
per us   B FRANKLIN
                                                              JOHN FOXCROFT

Recd July 16th. 1763 of Mr. Vernon One hundred and Thirty nine
Pounds three Shillings on account of this post office. For B:
Franklin and Self   JOHN FOXCROFT[8]

To William Greene   ALS: American Philosophical Society

Dear Sir   Providence July 19. 1763
   From the very hospitable and kind Treatment we met with at
your House I must think it will be agreable to you to hear that
your Guests got well in before the Rain.[9] We hope you and Mrs.
Green were likewise safe at home before Night, and found all well.
We all join in the most cordial Thanks and best Wishes, and shall
be glad on every Occasion to hear of the Welfare of you and yours.
   I beg you would present our Compliments to your good Neigh-
bour Capt. Fry,[1] and tell him we shall always retain a grateful
Remembrance of his Civilities.
   The Soreness in my Breast seems to diminish hourly. Rest and
Temperance I ascribe it to chiefly, tho' the Bleeding, &c. had
doubtless some Share in the Effect. We purpose setting out to go

7. For Vernon, postmaster at Newport, R.I., 1754–75, see above, v, 451 n.
For BF's stay in Newport on his way to Boston, see above, p. 278.
   8. Foxcroft may have remained in Newport, not accompanying BF and his
daughter to Cowesett, R.I., to visit William and Caty Greene, or he may have
joined the Franklins and signed this receipt in the way he did because of BF's
injured shoulder; see above, ibid.
   9. For BF's visit with William and Catharine Greene at Cowesett, R.I.,
July 13?–18, 1763, which was unfortunately marred by a fall which injured
his shoulder, see above, ibid.
   1. Capt. Thomas Fry (1691–1782) was the husband of William Greene's
aunt Mary. Louise B. Clarke, The Greenes of Rhode Island (N.Y., 1903),
pp. 113–14.

to Wrentham this Afternoon, in order to make an easy Day's Journey into Boston to morrow. Present our Respects to Mrs. Ray,[2] and believe me, with much Esteem, Dear Sir, Your obliged, and most obedient humble Servant   B FRANKLIN

From [Henry] Jackson   Copy: Rutgers University Library

This extract of a letter and the accompanying remarks survive only in a copy headed "In a Letter from London to B. Franklin Esqr. which he sent me," found among extensive manuscript notes on agriculture written, 1746–71, by Charles Read of Burlington, N.J.,[3] and interleaved in a copy of John Worlidge, *Systema Agriculturae* (3d edit., London, 1681). The writer of the letter and remarks must have been Henry Jackson, a London chemist who, in addition to earlier writings on bread and tar water, published in 1765 *An Essay on British Isinglass*. What may have occasioned his correspondence with Franklin is not known, nor the reason why Franklin gave this paper to Read.

Eastsmithfield Londn. July 29 1763
A Method of Making Glue from Sturgeon &c.[4]

The Skin and Cartilages must be freed as much as possible from the other parts of the Fish and particularly from what are fat and

2. Deborah Greene Ray was Catharine Greene's mother and a first cousin of William Greene's father. She died, Dec. 11, 1763. *Ibid.,* p. 101.

3. Charles Read (1715–1774), the third in a succession of five fathers and sons of the same name, was born in Philadelphia and established himself as a court clerk in Burlington, N.J., 1739, where he was soon also appointed customs collector of the port. He engaged extensively in land speculation, mercantile enterprise, and agricultural experimentation. He was the owner of the farm which writers and editors for many years ascribed to BF and which led many to credit BF with far greater activity in practical agriculture than the facts warrant (see above, III, 436). Read was deputy secretary of N.J., 1744–7; assemblyman, 1751–60; speaker, 1751–54; councilor, 1761–73; justice of the Supreme Court, 1749–53, 1762–73, and chief justice briefly in 1764. In 1773 he retired with impaired fortunes to the West Indies and died in No. Car. the next year. Carl R. Woodward, *Ploughs and Politicks Charles Read of New Jersey And His Notes on Agriculture 1715–1774* (New Brunswick, 1941).

4. In contrast to the method described here, the manufacture of fish glue in the twentieth century relies heavily on the use of a variety of chemicals at various stages of the process. See George F. White, *Fish Isinglass and Glue* Appendix IV to the Report of the U.S. Commissioner of Fisheries for 1917. Bureau of Fisheries Document No. 852. Washington, 1917).

unctuous, let them be washed clean and then boiled gently in a Sufficient Quantity of Water till they are disolved as much as possible or till little remains except some very gross Parts, The Liquor must be skimm'd pretty often, during the Coction and when it begins to grow thick, must be kept continually stirring to prevent burning; after wich the Decoction must be strained thro a fine wicker basket, permitted to settle an hour or 2 and then the clear Liquor must be evaporated in a proper Vessel till it is very thick, when it must be pourd into proper Moulds of Wood or Tin to stiffin, after wich it must be taken out and laid upon Netts stretchd in Frames, to dry till it becomes hard enough for Use.

Remarks

Copper Vessells for making Glues are most commodious. They must be of two kinds, One to boil the Subject in and the Other to evaporate the superfluous Moisture; The first may be constructed like a Brewers Copper fixed in Brick work with a Door, Grate, &c. After the Usual Method; The Other must be a double Vessel, or Water Bath, the outward Vessel of which, must be likewise set in Brick Work or the evaporating Vessel may be adapted to the Boiling Vessel wich thus may Answer two Purposes, first to boil the Subject in and afterwards receive the other Vessel to evaporate the Liquor, but where Dispatch in Busness is required it will be found to most advantage to have them seperate, that one may be boiling while the Other is evaporating; the double Vessel must therefore be very large in Diamiter and so shallow that altho it be large enough for its Companion to contain all the Decoction yet need not be more than 2 feet Deep or thereabouts; The two Vessels may be Set contiguous to each other with diffirent Flews in the same Chimney; The Companion to this shallow Pan must be adapted in such manner that it must be suspended within the Other by a broad Rim of Copper rivetted to its sides 6 Inches below [its] Edge or upper Rim, which Rim must rest upon the Edge or Top of the fixed Copper, the inward vesel must be less in Diamitir to the other, so as to leave 3 inches Space between the sides of the Two Vessels, every where around when the inner Vessel is suspended and 4 Inches Space from the bottom; At the Distance of every Foot in the Rim may be cut vent Holes, about Three Inches Long and two Inches Wide to let out the Steam of the boiling water in the outward Vessel; That Part of the inward Vessel above the Rim may be 6 or 8 inches that it may contain the more Matter to be evaporated, and be more readily taken out occasionally.

After the Glutinous Subjects have been disolved [*word missing*] slow continued boiling with repeated Quantities of water in the boiling Vessel; The Decoctions must be strained, permitted to sub-side in wooden Casks or tubs drawn off pretty Clear and put into the evaporating-vessel, previously suspended in the Other already filled 2 thirds with Water; The Fire must then be kept up, so as to keep the water round the inner vesel in a continued boiling State which water must be supply'd Occasionally as it wastes and the Decoction stir'd frequently till all the superfluous Moisture is evaporated and the Magma⁵ becomes just thin enough to pour into the moulds very slightly greased to prevent its sticking; In this state it must dry till it is stiff enough to lay upon Netts to be further dried for use; The Tin Pans need only to be made of a Sheet of tin, 6 or 8 inches Square, with the Edges turned up equal to the intended Thickness of the Glue Cake. The Nett Frames for drying resemble a little Hutt, They may be about eight Feet long as many high and Four wide, fixed about 6 inches distance from each other and one over another from the Ground to the Eaves of the Roof, wich Roof is weather boarded, the Hutt with its Roof must be built first, and the Frame with the Netts fastned within it afterwards; Thus the Netts will be open on all sides to the Air except the Top wich Defends them from Rain, the great Dificulty in making Glue is to prevent its burning which is effectualy done by this Method as the Decotion can receive no greater heat than [the] boiling water; The evaporating Pan is made broad and Shallow because all evaporations is in proportion to Surface exposed to the Air, Common Glue is generally of a brown Colour being generally a little burnt and full of heterogene particles, but Glue made after this Process will be the most perfect that can Possibly be made and will when finished appear tranparant and of a grenish Hue, it is the strongest that can be made and grows so hard between Timber as to resist moisture incredibly. Size is only Glue left in the Consist[ency] between Jelly and Glue, and Jellys are only thin

5. A crude mixture of mineral or organic matters in the state of a thin paste.

Size, Papins Machine⁶ will disolve Animal Substance more readily, but is Inapplicable in a large way. Iron or Copper Ladles will be nessesasary to lade out the Glue; I know of nothing more worth describing but what will naturally occur to the Practitioner.

H JACKSON

To Catharine Greene   ALS: American Philosophical Society

Dear Friend,   Boston, Augt. 1. 1763

I ought to acquaint you that I feel myself growing daily firmer and freeer from the Effects of my Fall;⁷ and hope a few Days more will make me quite forget it. I shall however never forget the Kindness I met with at your House on that Occasion.

Make my Compliments acceptable to your Mr. Greene, and let him know that I acknowledge the Receipt of his obliging Letter⁸ and thank him for it. It gave me great Pleasure to hear you got home before the Rain.

My Compliments too to Mr. Merchant⁹ and Miss Ward¹ if they are still with you; and kiss the Babies for me.² Sally says, *and for me too:* She adds her best Respects to Mr. Greene and you, and that she could have spent a Week with you with great Pleasure, if I had not hurried her away.

6. In about 1680 the French physicist Denis Papin (1647–1714) invented a "steam digester, or engine for softening bones" under high pressure, which he described in a pamphlet *La Manière d'amolir des os et de faire couire toutes sortes de viandes en fort peu de temps, et à peu de frais* (Paris, 1682).

7. For BF's fall while traveling in R.I. and for his recuperation at the Greenes, see above, p. 278.

8. Not found.

9. Henry Marchant (1741–1796), A.M., College of Philadelphia, 1762, was related by his father's second marriage to the Wards, who were in turn related to the Greenes. Marchant traveled with BF on his Scottish tour in 1771 (keeping an extensive journal) and was one of the leaders of the Revolutionary movement in R.I., serving in the Continental Congress, 1777–9. He then led the fight for the adoption of the Constitution in R.I. Washington appointed him judge of the U.S. District Court, July 2, 1790, in which position he served until his death. *DAB*.

1. Probably one of the three unmarried sisters of Caty Greene's brother-in-law Samuel Ward (above, v, 504 n): Hannah, Elizabeth, or Margaret.

2. Caty's daughters, Phebe and Celia; see above, p. 191 n.

My Brother is return'd to Rhodeisland.[3] Sister Mecom thanks
ou for your kind remembrance of her, and presents her Respects.
With perfect Esteem and Regard, I am, Dear Katy (I can't
et alter my Stile to Madam) Your affectionate Friend

B FRANKLIN

Irs Cath. Greene

To [Benjamin Waller][4]

ALS: Mrs. Daniel Buckley, Broadaxe, Pennsylvania (1955)

ir   Boston, Augt. 1. 1763

I receiv'd yesterday your Favour of June 25.[5] relating to the
on of my dear Friend Mr. Hunter. I am sensible that the Care of
he Education of young Persons, is attended with Trouble, and
ke other old Men I begin in most things to consult my Ease: But
shall with Pleasure undertake the Charge you propose to me, if
be, as I suppose it is, agreable to his other Friends; for I loved
is Father truly, and think it a Duty to perform the Request of a
riend deceas'd, who living would I am sure have thought little
f any Trouble in obliging me.[6] Mr. Foxcroft tells me, that your

3. Peter Franklin (C.9) of Newport apparently accompanied BF to Boston.
4. Benjamin Waller (1716–1786) of Williamsburg, Va., landholder, lawyer,
nd public official. *Va. Mag. of Hist. and Biog.*, LIX (1951), 352, 458–60. In
he will of William Hunter, BF's colleague in the colonial deputy postmaster-
hip, he and BF were named among Hunter's friends. As one of Hunter's
xecutors and because of this friendship Waller had assumed responsibility
or arranging the education of Hunter's natural son William.
5. Not found.
6. BF entered Billy Hunter in the Academy of Philadelphia in 1764. Mont-
omery, *Hist. Univ. Pa.*, p. 541. In Memorandum Book, 1757–1776, p. 16,
nder the year 1764 an entry reads: "Memo. On Thursday the 22d of this
nstant March, Billy Hunter came to board and live with me. Paid for his
ntrance at Schools £1. Enquir'd the Price paid by such Boarders of Mrs.
innersley who tells me it is 35 per Annum including Washing and Mending
–but thinks it too little." Immediately following is an incomplete entry
ecording BF's purchase of a hat for the boy. On p. 29, under date of Oct. 21,
776 (just before BF sailed for France), is the following: "Memorandum, That
mong Mrs. Franklins Papers I find an Account paid by her to Cottringer,
aylor, for Clothes for Billy Hunter amo[unting] to £25 5s. 7¾d. Query, Is
here not besides this, a considerable Sum due for his Board, Education, and
ther Expences." Two letters from Billy Hunter to DF, Feb. 12, 1768, and

317

Son is likewise of a mild tractable Temper and Disposition; and a
they will be Company for each other, and when I have under
taken the Care of one the Care of a second will be but little addi
tional Trouble, I do not pretend to lay you under any Obligatio
in consenting to receive them both.[7] I shall be happy in being use
ful to them. As soon as I return to Philadelphia, which I purpos
some time next Month I will procure and send you an Estimat
of Expence of their Maintenance and Education and advise th
time of sending them.

I shall give an Order to Mr. Foxcroft to receive at his Retur
the further Payment [you] mention,[8] and am, with great Esteem
Sir Your most obedient Servant   B FRANKLI

To Richard Jackson

ALS: American Philosophical Societ

Dear Sir,   Boston, Augt. 8. 1763.
Being here on the Business of the Post-Office, I have receive
your obliging Favour of May 19.[9] which I shall answer by th
next Pacquet. At present I have only time to introduce to you Col
Dyer,[1] the Bearer of this Letter, a Gentleman of Character an

Aug. 4, 1769 (APS), after his return to Williamsburg, ask her to send hir
certain schoolbooks so that he may continue his studies.

7. Waller apparently declined BF's invitation. The only one of his sons ol
enough to be sent away to school was John (b. 1753); there is no record c
his entry in the Academy of Philadelphia or of his boarding with BF.

8. It is not certain whether this payment was on account of the indebtednes
of William Hunter's estate to the Post Office or its indebtedness to BF per
sonally. In June 1764 BF recorded in Memorandum Book, 1757–1776, pp. 17
18, two payments by Hunter's executors of £79 17s. 3d. and £60 2s. 9d. i
sterling bills, "which with £200 Sterling he paid [at] my Order [to] M
Foxcroft is in full of my Account against Mr. Hunters Estate except th
Article of Papers."

9. Not found.

1. Eliphalet Dyer (1721–1807), B. A., Yale, 1740, was a prominent Conr
politician and jurist, who served in both the General Assembly, 1747–62, an
the Council, 1762–84, as an associate justice of the Superior Court, 1766–8
and as chief justice, 1789–93. An ardent patriot, Dyer was a delegate to th
Stamp Act Congress and to the First and later Continental Congresses. H
helped to organize the Conn. Susquehannah Co. (founded at Windhan
July 18, 1753) and actively promoted its interest for many years. In 1763 h
went to England as the Company's agent to procure a royal charter for th

Reputation in your Colony of Connecticut. He goes to England to lay the Affair of their Purchase on Sasquehanah before his Majesty, the Settlement of that Purchase being oppos'd by Mr. Penn.[2] I have taken the Liberty to recommend him to you as the Person in all England most capable of advising and serving him in his Solicitation. As to the Sentiments of our People on that Settlement, I can assure you, that there is scarce a Man in Pensilvania who does not wish it to go on, provided it be with the free Consent of the Indians;[3] as it would, when once establish'd be a good Barrier for our N. West Frontier in case of a future Indian War; and the intended Settlers are a kind of People whose Neighbourhood we should like. I am even at a loss to guess on what Principle the Proprietor opposes it; since if the Land is not within his Grant, or the prior Grant of Connecticut is valid, he has no right to intermeddle; and if it finally appears to be within his Grant, and that of Connecticut does not extend to it, the Settlers must become his Tenants. With the greatest Esteem, I am, Dear Sir, Your most obedient humble Servant   B FRANKLIN

R. Jackson Esqr.

Endorsed: Boston Augst 8th 1763 B Franklin Esqr

lands which it claimed in northeastern Pa., but owing to the opposition of Thomas Penn and Sir William Johnson he was unsuccessful. *DAB;* George C. Groce, Jr., "Eliphalet Dyer: Connecticut Revolutionist," in Richard B. Morris, ed., *The Era of the American Revolution* (N.Y., 1939), pp. 290–304. For the Susquehannah Co. purchase at Albany, 1754, see map, above, v, 225.

2. Upon the recommendation of the Board of Trade, Jan. 14, 1763, the British government through Gen. Jeffery Amherst ordered Conn. emigration to northeast Pa. halted until the dispute between Thomas Penn and the Susquehannah Co. over the legality of the settlement could be decided by the King in Council. The Susquehannah Co. officially complied, though it did not stop continued emigration by small groups and individuals, and at the same time it sent Dyer on the mission mentioned in the previous note. Julian P. Boyd, ed., *The Susquehannah Company Papers* (4 vols., Wilkes-Barré, Pa., 1930), II, xxxiii–xlii, 191–3.

3. Writing to Jared Ingersoll on Aug. 10, 1763, Joseph Chew of New London attributed rather different sentiments to BF; if Conn. "Expected a Government and to obtain a Charter, we should be disappointed," BF is alleged to have said, "that our Claiming all the Lands to the West Seas was Idle and Ridiculous, that no Person could pretend to think it consistant with common sense to have a Government 60 miles wide, and 3000 miles long, and many things of the kind." *Ibid.* p. 265; New Haven Col. Hist. Soc. *Papers,* IX (1918), 286–7.

To William Strahan
ALS: Yale University Library

Dear Friend,   Boston, Augt. 8. 1763

I have received here your Favour of May 3. and Postscript of May 10.[4] and thank you cordially for the Sketch you give me of the present State of your political Affairs. If the stupid brutal Opposition your good King and his Measures have lately met with should as you fear become general,[5] surely you would not wish me to come and live among such People; you would rather remove hither, where we have no Savages but those we expect to be such. But I think your Madmen will ere long come to their Senses; and when I come I shall find you generally wise and happy. That I have not the Propensity to sitting Still that you apprehend, let my present Journey witness for me, in which I have already travelled eleven hundred and forty Miles on this Continent since April and shall make Six hundred and forty Miles more before I see home.[6] No Friend can wish me more in England than I do my self. But before I go, every thing I am concern'd in must be so settled here as to make another Return to America unnecessary. My Love to every one of your dear Family, of whose Welfare I always rejoice to hear: being with the greatest Esteem and Affection, Dear Sir, Yours sincerely

B FRANKLIN

Addressed: To / Mr. William Strahan / Printer / London

4. Strahan's letter of May 3 and 10 with its political "Sketch" has not been found, but judging from a letter which he wrote to David Hall on May 10 it probably expressed his growing disillusionment with the King and Lord Bute and his contempt for John Wilkes, a "contemptible, nay infamous" person. Strahan to Hall, May 10, 1763, APS.

5. A reference to the furor caused by the arrest of and legal proceedings against Wilkes.

6. For BF's trips on post-office business to Va. in the spring of 1763 and to New England in the summer and early fall of the year, see above, pp. 252 n, 276–9. In the margin the figures 1140 and 640 are added together to produce the sum of 1780. Perhaps this is Strahan's calculation of the total mileage of BF's journeys.

320

To Peter Templeman[7]

ALS: Royal Society of Arts

Sir   Boston, Augt. 12. 1763

In my Journey from Philadelphia hither, I have had the Pleasure of meeting with sundry Persons in different Places, who are attempting the Produce of Silk from the Encouragement offered by the Society: And am persuaded that in time you will see very considerable Effects of that Encouragement.[8]

The Produce of Potash, cheap enough to be exported with Profit to Britain, which had almost been despaired of here, and the Attempt nearly laid aside, is now revived by Mr. Willard of this Country, who, animated by the Society's Offers, has persever'd in prosecuting the Design, and at length has found a more easy, certain, and much less expensive Process than what was heretofore known and used here, and which is said to produce a more perfect Commodity.[9] He sends home by this Ship 23

7. For Peter Templeman, secretary of the Society of Arts, see above, IX, 322 n.

8. In 1755 and 1756 the Society of Arts offered premiums for the cultivation of mulberry trees in Georgia and the Carolinas, but in the two following years it changed its premiums to awards for silk produced, not only in Georgia and the Carolinas, but in Conn. and Pa. as well. In 1759 the Society added a premium for each pound of raw silk imported into England, and although this offer lapsed after three years, the Society's premiums for silk produced in America continued until 1767. All told, the Society paid £1,370 in silk premiums, most of which went to Georgia. One of the "sundry" silk producers whom BF undoubtedly met on his trip to Boston was Ezra Stiles, who had about 3000 worms which were beginning to cocoon in July just when BF visited the future president of Yale at Newport. Robert Dossie, *Memoirs of Agriculture and other Oeconomical Arts*, 1 (London, 1768), 24–6, 233–9; Brooke Hindle, *The Pursuit of Science in Revolutionary America 1735–1789* (Chapel Hill, 1956), pp. 200–204; Edmund S. Morgan, *The Gentle Puritan A Life of Ezra Stiles 1727–1795* (New Haven, 1962), pp. 147–51.

9. The production of potash in the colonies had first been encouraged by Parliament, which in 1755 granted £3,000 to one Thomas Stephens, who had invented a method of economical production, on the condition that he go to America and supervise the erection of potash works there. The Board of Trade showed great interest in his survey and reports from the colonies. In 1758, when it became apparent that Stephens had failed, the Society of Arts offered premiums for potash imported from America into Great Britain and continued these premiums, although frequently changing their amounts and the conditions under which they were awarded, for several years afterwards. Dossie, *Memoirs of Agriculture*, 1, 247–60; Hindle, *The Pursuit of*

Tons, hoping that the Society have continued their Premiums on that Article for the Year 1763. He is very frank and candid in communicating his Method, and willing it should be made public for the general Good. I would therefore recommend to the Society a particular Examination of the Qualities of this Potash; and if it is found excellent, as I am told it is, that Mr. Willard may receive some Mark of the Society's Favour, tho' the Premiums offer'd for 1762, should happen not to be continued.

With sincerest Wishes of Prosperity to the Society, and Success to their most laudable Endeavours for the Publick Prosperity, I am, Sir, Your most obedient and most humble Servant

B FRANKLIN

Dr. Templeman

Anthony Todd to Benjamin Franklin and John Foxcroft

Copy: Yale University Library

Gentlemen   General Post Office August the 13th 1763
   I am glad to acquaint you that the Postmaster General are very well satisfied with Mr. Franklin's Letter of the 1st. and your joint Letter of the 10th. of June.[1]

The several proposed Regulations and Improvements which you mention, have met with Their entire approbation, and They wait your own Time for making the ample Report you mention at the End of this Summer season when you have finished your surveys,[2] so that for the present, I am required to say little more than acknowledge the Receipt of the two Bills for Four Hundred and Ninety four Pounds, four Shillings, and eight pence, being the Balance to Mr. Hunters Death, which Remittances for the future, you will send to The Postmaster General and make them payable only to Mr. Trevor.

Science, p. 208; *Board of Trade Journal,* 1754–58, pp. 3–5, 12–14, 18–20, 109, 271, 297, 306, 313, 319. Mr. Willard, the successful potash producer, was possibly Samuel Willard of Conn. who had been granted a potash monopoly by the colony's General Assembly in 1741. *Conn. Col. Recs.,* VIII, 395–6.

1. For these letters, see above, pp. 270–1, 279–84. Many of the matters mentioned in the present letter are discussed in them.
2. The "ample Report," if made, has not been found.

With regard to the articles of £32 11s. and £59 17s. for the said Mr. Hunters travelling Charges, they are both allowed of, for the reasons you alledge,[3] and herewith I return his Letter to Mr. Franklin upon that Subject in April 1760.

The hopes you express that the Continuance of the Packets, which must of Course be advantageous to the Commerce between Great Britain and North America will in a short Time be to the Benefit of this Office also, is very satisfactory and if a favourable opportunity should offer in the Course of the next Sessions of Parliament to obtain the Clause you so heartily recommend, to oblige the Masters of all Ships, to deliver their Letters into the Post Offices of the respective ports they arrive at, which at present appear to be too much exposed to the Curiosity of private persons, who often destroy or delay them, you may be assured that so material a point, towards rendering the Correspondence of His Majesty's Subjects more safe and expeditious, as well as a Benefit to this Office, will be carefully attended to.[4]

When you may be able to make it appear, that the Revenue intrusted to your Management, is become so flourishing, as clearly to admit of it, I should be glad to move The Postmaster-General on your behalf, to Rent a Convenient House in New York, or even to build a Commodious Chief Office there.[5]

That your most sanguine Views may meet with no cheque from hence, The Postmaster General have added a fifth Boat,[6] to maintain with greater certainty, the monthly Correspondence between Falmouth, and New York, which you will do well to make known throughout the several provinces.

I am glad to find that some Governors, who once refused have

3. See above, pp. 221, 283.

4. Apparently Todd later discovered that the Act for Establishing a Post Office in North America, 9 Anne c. 11 (1710), contained a partial remedy for the situation about which BF and Foxcroft had complained, for in the spring of 1764 he sent orders to BF (which were published in *Pa. Gaz.*, July 26, 1764) citing sections of the act which prohibited meddling with the mails by private persons and warned that all offenders would henceforth be "proceeded against and punished with the utmost Severity."

5. In either 1771 or 1772 Foxcroft was allowed £100 for house rental in N.Y. Ruth Butler, *Doctor Franklin Postmaster General* (Garden City, N. Y., 1928), p. 137.

6. Probably the *Lord Hyde* packet.

at length paid the postage due to this Office. For the Time to come, you are to consider it as a positive Injunction from His Majesty's Postmaster General, not to suffer any Letter or Packet whatsoever, though upon the Governments immediate Service to pass free, The Postmaster General having by the Act of the 9th. of Queen Anne no such dispensing Power. I am Gentlemen Yours &c.   ANTH: TODD Secry

Copy

To Benj: Franklin and John Foxcroft Esqrs:
Deputy Postmaster General of America

From William Strahan   ALS: Historical Society of Pennsylvania

Dear Sir   Bath August 18. 1763.
I had the favour of yours of June 28th[7] from New York last Friday. Next Morning I set out for Salisbury, where I had a little Business, and yesterday came from thence to this place, where my Wife has been these Six Weeks for her health, and I thank God not without Effect, for I found her greatly recruited. Here I propose to stay a few days, and leave her some Weeks longer, as the Waters agree so well with her. In the mean time, as there are two Ships to sail next Week for Philadelphia I take the first Opportunity of writing to you, and telling you all the News that at present occurs to me, that you may receive all the Satisfaction that is in my power to give you.
    You have seen, in general, by the public papers, what a Cry is raised against the peace, and how unpopular it has rendered Lord Bute.[8] I wish I cou'd say, that making this peace was Lord B's only fault, for I agree with you in thinking it a very good one. But I am sorry to tell you, that my Countryman has shewn himself altogether unequal to his high Station. Never did a Ministry, in our Memory, discover so much Weakness. They seem to have

7. See above, pp. 303–5. BF had chided Strahan for failing to inform him of the "why and wherefore" of British politics and begged his friend to take time out from cribbage to write in detail. In this letter Strahan makes his "Amends."
    8. Bute's most intemperate newspaper critic was, of course, John Wilkes.

WILLIAM STRAHAN ESQ.ᴿ

William Strahan. Mezzotint by John Jones after Sir Joshua Reynolds

neither Spirit, Courage, Sense, nor Activity, and are a Rope of Sand. Of Course the essential Interests of the Nation are neglected. Lord Bute, with even an enthusiastic Desire to promote the Glory and Prosperity of this Country, can never more take the Lead. He continues to see no body, and seems vastly pleased that he has shaken off that Burden to which his Shoulders was so unequal.[9] But that he had any Intention of giving up, to my Certain Knowledge is not true, tho' it was given out by his Friends: And the last Speech he made in the House of Peers, which I heard, demonstrated beyond all doubt, that he had then no Thoughts of Resigning. But that Speech appears since to have proceeded from Pride, and not from true Strength of Mind, in which he is, it seems, remarkably deficient, being subject to a very great Inequality of Spirits. From all this you may easily conceive, we are in a very unaccountable and untoward Situation. Here is a Young, virtuous, *British* King, who can have no Interest separate from that of his People, and who, tho' not possessed of any striking Talents, or any great Degree of Sagacity, yet having much Good Nature, and a Disposition to please, rendered, in the beginning of his Reign, singularly unpopular; and a Minister, hating Corruption, abhorring Hypocrisy, and having the Prosperity of his Country really at heart, the Object of universal Disgust. If you ask me how this comes about? The Reason is obvious. The Number of Places, and of Candidates for them, are very unequal. Of Course, it requires great knowledge of Men in the Minister of this Country, to balance Parties, and keep things quiet. Of this Knowledge Lord Bute is totally destitute, and was his temper suitable, which it is not, it is too late for him to learn. This Ignorance of the world, with a Timidity altogether inexcusable, has encouraged the Opposition to go lengths hitherto unprecedented. You see with what a high hand Mr. Pitt carries it with his Constituents, for presuming to differ from him their

9. Bute resigned as first lord of the Treasury on April 8, 1763. George Grenville replaced him and with Lords Halifax and Egremont as secretaries of state formed a "Triumvirate" which governed until Egremont's death on Aug. 21, 1763. The Duke of Bedford then replaced Egremont in the "Triumvirate," but as lord president of the Council, not as a secretary of state. Strahan's appraisal of Bute coincides closely with that of the late Sir Lewis Namier. *England in the Age of the American Revolution* (2d edit., London, 1961), pp. 131-4.

Representative, in regard to the Peace. Did you ever before hear of such an Instance of Arrogance? And what are we to expect, think you, if we again come under the Dominion of this imperious Tribune of the People.[1] His Clodius Wilkes, the most profligate of Men, is in high Spirits since the Trial of the Messengers, which I was not present at.[2] I expected no pleasure from that Transaction, having no desire to be a Witness of that Incendiary's temporary Triumph. In this Light only I considered it, for as to the liberty of the Press, I never thought it in any Danger, but from it's too great Licentiousness. The Judge acted throughout the whole of these Trials, with a Partiality which I little expected from one of his Ability and Integrity. He is carried away with the Popularity this behaviour brings him; but I am much mistaken if he will not some time hence, be ashamed of the Part he has taken on this Occasion. The Damages given by the Jury were enormous, and seem intended to mark in the strongest Manner their Contempt of the Government.

The Opening of next Session of Parliament will certainly be attended with much Confusion and Embarrasment, and during the Convulsion, the Power will devolve into some other hands; probably into Mr. Pitts, if some other Leader, whom we do not now dream of, does not start up.[3] But I believe you will agree with me

1. In May 1763 the corporation of Bath sent William Pitt and other representatives of the town an address to the King, congratulating him on the "adequate and advantageous" peace just concluded with France. Pitt "could not consent to present a document conceived in terms which contradicted his publicly avowed opinions; and he not only refused, but imparted peculiar bitterness to the dispute which ensued by allowing it to be clearly seen that he intended to retire from the representation of the town." Albert von Ruville, *William Pitt Earl of Chatham* (3 vols., London, 1907), III, 114.

2. On July 6 and 7, 1763, Chief Justice of the Court of Common Pleas Charles Pratt heard the suits of printers William Huckell and James Lindsay against the King's messengers who had arrested them by virtue of the notorious general warrants signed by Lord Halifax on April 26, 1763. Juries found for the printers, awarding Huckell £300 and costs and Lindsay £200 and costs. The government settled out of court with twelve other printers arrested at the same time, paying them the same damages that Lindsay had received. See Robert R. Rhea, *The English Press in Politics* (Lincoln, Neb., 1963), pp. 59–62.

3. The opening of Parliament was convulsed, as Strahan predicted, by a motion to expel the member from Aylesbury, John Wilkes. After Egremont's death, Aug. 21, 1763, Pitt conferred with George III and Bute about forming

in thinking it extremely dangerous to the Interest of this Country, to have Mr. Pitt, or any one Person, trusted with so unbounded a Sway, as coming in in this manner must necessarily give him; more especially Pitt, of whose honesty I entertain no good Opinion, and whom I strongly suspect to be a secret Abettor and Fomentor of the present unreasonable Discontents, and of that Contempt with which the King and his Government hath of late been treated. The Opposition are very busy gathering their Strength together and are really formidable, On Behalf of the Ministry, if it may be called one, which is entirely without form, nothing is going forward. They seem to console themselves with the Distance of the danger, and I suppose do not mean to stand their ground. In this Situation, are you not under some Apprehensions for the King, unless some able and honest Men step forth, in the critical moment, and rescue him from the Jaws of Faction? In my mind the danger is greater than most People seem to apprehend; and I wish from my heart something may interpose to divert the Storm. Unhappily for us, as well as for himself, his Majesty discovers no Talents that give us Room to hope he will ever make a shining Figure, or be able long to preserve his own Independency, amidst contending Factions, and 'tis a great Pity; for nobody can possibly mean better. To give you a Trait by the bye, of the Sagacity of Lord Bute in regard to him. T'other day, I was at Mr. Adams's the Architect, when he shewed me his Dedication to the King to be prefacd to his Ruins of *Dioclesian's Palace,* in which he praises his Majesty for his Knowledge in the art of drawing.[4] To this I objected as a Fact very im-

---

a new ministry, but the negotiations collapsed because the Great Commoner's demands were too high. Richard Pares, *King George III and the Politicians* (Oxford, 1959), p. 106. This "extraordinary negotiation" and the precarious political balance during the remainder of the year are well covered in *Annual Register,* 1763, pp. 38–42.

4. Robert Adam (1728–1792), the celebrated Scottish architect who designed many of the most imposing neoclassical buildings of his day and who was appointed architect to the King and Queen in 1762, published in 1764 a volume of engravings after drawings which he had made during an Italian tour ten years earlier called *Ruins of the Palace of the Emperor Diocletian at Spalatro in Dalmatia.* The dedication to the King read: "Your Majesty's early Application to the Study of this Art [drawing], the extensive Knowledge you have acquired of its Principles, encourages every Lover of his Profession to hope that he shall find in George the Third, not only a powerful Patron, but a skilful Judge." John Swarbrick, *Robert Adam and his Brothers* (London,

proper to tell the World, since a Prince ought certainly to be better employ'd, than in such trifling Amusements. But I was told both the King and Lord Bute had already seen it, and highly approved of it, as expressive of just praise without Flattery. Such are the Effects of a Prince being educated, under a Man who is himself ignorant of the World. Lord Bute's Brother Mr. Stewart Mackenzie[5] is Viceroy of Scotland, and is at present there: He too is a weak timid Man, and is suffering the Affairs of [the] Kingdom to run into the greatest Confusion, which the late Duke of Argyle used to manage with the greatest facility. John Home[6] is made Conservator of the Scots' Privileges in Holland, a Sinecure of £300 a Year, which gives universal Disgust, as that place was always in use to be bestowed on some eminent Merchants. Lord Bute's Resignation has thoroughly disconcerted his Friends there, and inspired his Enemys every where with fresh Courage and can you believe it, he is more unpopular in Scotland than here. Before I have done with John Home, I wou'd just observe how very strange and singular it is, for so inconsiderable a man (and a Worthy Man too) to have had it in his power to do so much Mischief. From this Man did Lord Bute take his Opinion too frequently of Men and things. I say, from this Man, as ignorant of the World, and the ways of Business, as a new born Infant. Dr. Robertson[7] was in Town lately. He is made Historiographer to the King, with a Salary of £200 a Year for Life. He is to quit his Church (not his Principality) and as soon as he has finished his History of Charles the Vth, is to set about writing the History of England, for doing

---

[1915]), p. 152. On Adam see also John Fleming, *Robert Adam and His Circle in Edinburgh & Rome* (London, 1962).

5. James Stuart Mackenzie (1719?–1800), Bute's younger brother, assumed the name upon inheriting his grandfather's estates. He was an M.P., 1742–80; envoy to Turin, 1758–61; lord privy seal for Scotland, 1763–65; and dispenser of Scottish patronage under his brother. Namier and Brooke, *House of Commons*, III, 503–7.

6. For John Home, Presbyterian minister and author of the tragedy *Douglass*, see above, IX, 4 n.

7. For William Robertson, the famous Scottish historian, see above, IX, 220 n. Robertson's *History of the Reign of Charles V*, which Strahan published, did not appear until 1769; his projected History of England was apparently never finished. His "principality," as Strahan calls it, was his office of principal of the University of Edinburgh.

which he is to be assisted with all the Public Records and every other help that can be procured, at the public Expence. This makes Robertsons Fortune and he deserves it, for he has much true Merit, both as a Man and a Writer.

Major General Beckwith[8] (who is married, you know, to a Daughter of Dr. Wisharts[9]) is now here, and tells me the Hereditary Prince,[1] who is to have our Princess Augusta, is by far the most accomplished Gentleman of his Years, he ever saw. Beckwith is very sensible and seems to know the State of Affairs on the Continent extremely well. He tells me the King of Prussia (in whose Service you know he is) is in every Shape in a better Plight, than at the Commencement of the War, that his Army is 200,000 Strong, that his Finnances are in excellent Order, and that his own Subjects have suffered very little, his Army having all along consisted chiefly of Forreigners. He gave me a long Detail of the excellent Oeconomy of his Government, shewed me with what care he collected his Revenues by appropriating such a District, for the payment of such a Number of Troops &c., which is done almost [*torn; about eight lines missing entirely*][2] to the [*torn*] *Life,* which was usually [*torn*] Remonstrance against

8. John Beckwith (d. 1787) commanded the 20th Regiment at the battle of Minden during the Seven Years' War and during the same war also commanded Frederick the Great's "British Legion," being promoted to major general in the Prussian service in the spring of 1763. He offered to serve in the American army in 1779; his daughter Sally emigrated to Philadelphia in 1782 with letters of introduction to the Baches from Strahan and BF. Beckwith's son, George, a British army officer, played an important role in talks with Alexander Hamilton preceding the negotiation of Jay's Treaty. *DNB* (under "George Beckwith"); *London Chron.,* May 21, 1763.

9. Beckwith married Janet, daughter of Dr. George Wishart (d. 1785), an esteemed minister at Edinburgh. Charles Rogers, *Life of George Wishart the Scottish Martyr* (London, 1876), p. 97; *Scots Mag.,* XLVII (1785), 312.

1. The hereditary prince, Charles-William Ferdinand of Brunswick-Wolffenbüttel, son and heir of the reigning Duke of Brunswick and nephew of Prince Ferdinand, commander of the allied forces in Germany during the Seven Years' War, married the Princess Augusta, sister of George III, on Jan. 16, 1764. *London Chron.,* Jan. 14–17, 17–19, 1764, carried an account of the wedding and of the military career of the bridegroom.

2. At this point almost a third of the page has been torn away. Nearly half of the text of the mutilated section is completely lost; the first words or parts of words of each of the last ten lines survive, as indicated, but it is virtually impossible to glean any connected meaning from them.

pas[sage *torn*] the Chancellor put the Seal [*torn*] the first thing Lord North³ [*torn*] of the Chancellor for so doing [*torn*].

Thus are our [*torn*] method is not speedily [*torn*] the Liberty and Happiness of [*torn*] force of all our Foreign En [*torn*] as well as men, to possess no Happiness without Alloy. By the Bye, has not our Constitution undergone some unperceived Alteration, when a Minister cannot keep his ground, even with a Majority of three to one, in the House of Commons? Does this arise from the great Increase of Power and Property without Doors, or from what other Cause?

I wrote to the Governor and Mr. Hall, just before I left London.⁴ Remember me most kindly to them both, and be so good as shew this to Mr. Hall, as he likes Politics, and tell him I have just now received his Letter of July 6th, by the Mary and Elizabeth Hardie, inclosing a Bill of loading for Two Thousand Dollars, which I shall answer by the next Ship. All his former letters I have already acknowledged the Receipt of.

I hope I have now made some Amends for my late Silence, as I have told you every thing I can recollect. Not an hour have I spent on Cribbige, since you left us, nor shall it cost me one till you return, which I hope you still *seriously* think of. If the Arguments I have formerly adduced have no Weight, I am sorry for it, for I think they are strong and unanswerable. I not only wish your own health, ease, and happiness, but that of all you are concerned in. I see with Particular Pleasure how well received your Son is in his Government the Continuance of which I am satisfied he has Sagacity enough, with your assistance, to deserve and Se-

3. This could have been Frederick North, Lord North (1732–1792) of American Revolutionary fame (later Earl of Guilford), at this time M.P. for Banbury and one of the lords of the Treasury; or Charles Compton, Earl of Northampton (1737–1763), ambassador to Venice, May 1761 to June 1763, who died in France the following October 18; or most probably Hugh Percy (Smithson), Earl of Northumberland (1715–1786; see above, IX, 365 n), who was appointed lord lieutenant of Ireland in April 1763 (*London Chron.*, April 12–14, 1763). If the last suggestion is correct, Strahan's passage may describe some controversy related to the sealing of the earl's patent of appointment. The lord chancellor at this time was Robert Henley, Lord Henley, Baron of Grange (1708–1772), who was created Earl of Northington in 1764. *DNB;* Namier and Brooke, *House of Commons*, II, 605.

4. Strahan left London for Salisbury on August 13; no letter of approximately that date to either WF or David Hall has been found.

cure.[5] My Wife Joins me in most affectionate Compliments to you and Mrs. Fr: Mr. and Mrs. Hall and all Friends. I am my Dear Sir with unalterable Esteem Your most Obedient Servant

WILL: STRAHAN

P:S: A new Indian War, is really terrible, but I hope proper measures will be taken, most effectually to extinguish it, and to prevent such dissagreable Interruptions, to the Encrease and prosperity of our Colonies for the future.[6]

From Peter Collinson   ALS: American Philosophical Society

My Dear Friend   Londn: 23d: Augst 1763

I am Just come from an Entertainment given your New Governor[7] per our Society[8] a Respect shown to all Governors where our Friends are Setled. Your Proprietor Thos. was there and Great Civilities pass'd on all Sides, I believe exact the Same Deputation that attended your Son who I hope is now well Setled in his Government and Sees Clearly the Coast he is to Steer. Pray when you write give my respects to Him and His Lady with my best Wishes.

Proprietor Thos. Took Mee Asside. Sayes He—I hear Mr. Franklins comeing Over to Solicit a revival of Doctor Coxs Grant for Lands on the Missisipi.[9] Do you know any thing of It, No not I, He Seemed uneasie about It.

5. On June 27, 1763, WF wrote Strahan that his first meeting with the N.J. Assembly had passed very amicably and that the Assembly had increased his salary £200 per annum "which is a point no Governor could ever obtain from them before." WF sent Strahan a copy of his introductory speech and the Assembly's answer with a request that Strahan publish them in the *London Chron.* He did so in the Aug. 4–6, 1763, issue. WF to Strahan, June 27, 1763, Charles H. Hart, ed., "Letters from William Franklin to William Strahan," *PMHB,* XXXV (1911), 427–9.

6. Both WF in his letter of June 27 and BF in his letter of June 28 had informed Strahan of the outbreak of the Uprising of Pontiac.

7. Thomas Penn's nephew John Penn (above, IV, 458 n) was commissioned lieutenant governor of Pa., June 18, 1763, to succeed James Hamilton. His sailing was noted in *London Chron.,* Sept. 13–15, 1763; he arrived in Philadelphia toward the end of October and read his commission before the Pa. Council, October 31. *Pa. Col. Recs.,* IX, 71–2; *Pa. Gaz.,* Nov. 3, 1763.

8. Presumably the Society of Friends.

9. For BF's interest in the Coxe grant of "Carolana," see above, pp. 212–14. Penn's information was, of course, false.

On the 21st: Wee lost Lord Agrement.[1] I wish Wee may be So happy in a New appointment of an able unbiassed Man of Weight to conciliate all parties. He has fairly Bilked Champion Welks non est inventis [*sic*][2] the Suits at an End.

Wee are concerned at the new rupture of the Indians,[3] French Emessaries may have had Some Share in it but I am afraid it is more owing to our Neglect and Misconduct.

There is Orders and In[s]tructions gone Over by the last Pacquets. I heartyly Wish they may prove Effectual to Bring about an Accomodation.

Your Friutefull Able Genius I hope will Exert it Self on this Weighty Occation. I Shall be pleased to Hear the Carolina is come Safe with the Books for thee and Library Company and J. Bartram.[4] Our Friend Mr. Canton[5] is conce[r]ned that he is forgott. Mr Clark Chaplain to our Ambassador Earl of Bristol has published a Modern History of Spain in 4to which I believe you would Like.[6] In Hast I am my Dear Friend Sincerely Yours

P COLLINSON

If I may Judge from aperances your New Governor dos not Seem to have Strikeing abilities then He'l be the Easier govern'd per his unkle.

1. Charles Wyndham (1710–1763), 2d Earl of Egremont, secretary of state for the Southern Department in the ministry which he, Grenville, and Lord Halifax directed, died on Aug. 21, 1763. Egremont had sanctioned the use of general warrants for which Wilkes had brought suit against him and threatened to challenge him to a duel. His death, however, "bilked" Wilkes of satisfaction either in court or on the field of honor. On Aug. 29, 1763, Wilkes wrote his supporter, the poet Charles Churchill: "What a scoundrell trick has Lord Egremont played me? I had form'd a fond wish to send him to the Devil, but he is gone without my passport." George Nobbe, *The North Briton* (N.Y., 1939), p. 238.

2. Non est inventus: the return made by a sheriff when a defendant is not to be found in his jurisdiction.

3. The Indian uprising led by Pontiac.

4. For the *Carolina's* arrival in Philadelphia, Sept. 22, 1763, and for the books she carried, see above, p. 274 n.

5. John Canton, the English electrical experimenter; see above, IV, 390 n.

6. Edward Clarke (1730–1786), clergyman, traveler, and author, was chaplain to George William Hervey, 2d Earl of Bristol (1721–1775), during the latter part of the earl's service as ambassador to Spain, 1758–61. Clarke's *Letters Concerning the State of Spain . . . Written at Madrid during the Years 1760 and 1761* (London, 1763) is replete with details and statistics.

Our Friend Hamilton gives a great Many Thanks and His Humble Service for your In[s]tructions.[7] He Hopes you will be tempted over by many Considerations and flatters himself with the pleasure of your Company at Pains Hill.

Addressed: To | Benn: Franklin Esqr | Philadelphia

From Mary Stevenson   Draft: American Philosophical Society

My dear Sir   Kensington August 30. 1763
I have two Letters to thank you for since I wrote to you from Bromley,[8] which tho short gave me pleasure as they assured me of your Welfare and the continuance of your Regard for your Polly.
I now have the pleasure of returning your Friend's Musick with the desir'd supplement.[9] Mr. Stanley begg'd I would present his best Respects to you, and tell you how much he rejoiced at having it in his power to do anything for you; he was oblig'd he says to make some alteration in the Recitativo in order to admit the Bass. He and his Family were much pleas'd with your Remembrance of them, and desir'd me to present their best Respects to you. My Aunt[1] and I have lately spent a week with them upon the For[?]t;[2] they have been with us in return, and left us this morning.
I thank you my dear Sir for the part you take in my cares. I had as you hop'd heard of my Friend's arrival at Jamaica,[3] and I

7. For Charles Hamilton of Painshill, see above, p. 151 n. The instructions which BF sent him almost certainly dealt with the erecting of lightning rods.

8. For BF's letters, see above, pp. 287, 297–8. Polly's letter from Bromley may have been that of March 11 or April 14, neither of which have been found.

9. The music returned was a score for one of Francis Hopkinson's poems, which the author himself had tried unsuccessfully to adapt to an air from the 6th Concerto of the blind British composer, John Stanley (IX, 320 n). Hopkinson had been unable to write the bass part, so BF asked his friend Stanley to do it and the composer cheerfully complied. See above, p. 233.

1. Either Mrs. Tickell or Mrs. Rooke, the elderly aunts with whom Polly lived; more probably Mrs. Tickell in view of Mrs. Rooke's lameness, mentioned in a later paragraph.

2. Two or three letters are illegibly overwritten; the word may be "Forest."

3. Polly is referring to Miss Pitt, or "Pitty" as she and BF frequently called her. For Polly's concern over her ocean voyage, see above, pp. 216–17.

am now in daily expectation of a more circumstantial account of her from one who saw her there. My Dolly's[4] Health is much mended, but she has had some severe attacks of her Disorder since I was with her at Bromley. Mrs. Blunt has brought another Son.[5]

My poor Aunt Rooke is still lame, and two days ago we were much alarm'd by her having the Gout in her stomach, but, thank, God that is remov'd. She thanks you for the tender mention you make of her.[6]

You make many happy by the hopes you give us of your Return to England. I long for you to fix the time, but I fear your Friends in America will hold you fast. All I wish for is to have those I love near me, could I but have you and my Pitt in England I should be happy. I like visiting *Acquaintance* at Kensington better than that at Wanstead, and all who are called *Friends* will come a few miles to see us, therefore I am pleas'd with our change of habitation.[7]

You see all are ready to follow you that can, the poor Girl who is the Bearer of this is excessively happy in accepting your invitation, and I hope good Success will attend her.[8] Accept my Thanks for your Kindness.

My Mother often tells me when Things don't go quite right that she wishes she had gone to Philadelphia, I don't think you blame me for preventing her, for the advantages of such a Voyage are precarious, and if you would second me I think her circumstances might be made easy. I want you who are Master of Dem-

4. Dorothea Blunt, see above, IX, 327 n.
5. Lydia Towne Blunt, wife of Dolly's younger brother Harry, gave birth to a son Henry in 1760, a daughter Lydia in 1761, and a second son Charles, referred to here, who died on Sept. 30, 1763. *Burke's Peerage and Baronetage,* (London, 1937), 314.
6. In his letter to Polly of March 25 (above, p. 235), BF had sent his love to Mrs. Rooke.
7. For BF's remarks on Polly's change of residence, see above, p. 298.
8. The "poor Girl" who carried this letter was probably her mother's servant Ann Hardy (called "Nancy" or "Nanny"), who spent a few years in Philadelphia, then returned to England and married a "worthless Fellow" named Elliot. DF to BF, Jan. 8, 1765; BF to DF, June 10, 1770, APS. BF's accounts during his second English mission record drafts in her favor sent to his bankers.

onstration to convince her that I shall be happier in seeing her enjoy a comfortable Income than I could be by even a large addition to my Fortune at her Death.[9]

I should be unfashionable if I did not wish for you here but I have a nearer concern than most; all *esteem* you, it is only the favour'd few that can love you as I do.

From Samuel Engs[1]   ALS: American Philosophical Society

Norfolk in Virginia 3rd Septemr. 1763

My Presuming, Sir, to Address a Gentleman of your distinguished Merit, will I doubt not be excused, from Your Well-Known principles of Humanity and Benevolence.

You may possibly recollect having (some Years past) been in my Company both, at the House of my Worthy Partner Mr. Collins of Rhode Island, and at His Brother's Mr. Ward; when you was pleased, on your Continental Tour to Honor the Town of Newport with a Visit.[2]

I am lately arrived at this place from England, having been strongly solicited to settle in this Colony; but tis so disagreable, on many accounts, particularly, the Unhealthiness of the Climate, that I have altered my resolution, and have almost fixed an intention of Setting down at Your City, but that will in a great measure depend on your Auspicious Approbation of my Plan, as it will be of a different Province to what I have formerly acted in, tho, such a one as I think not in the least Inadequate to my Capacity, and in which I imagine I could give intire Satisfaction.

On my Arrival at Newport from England (about 8 Years past) I heard with no Small regret Mr. Collins's information that the

9. Polly left about half a page blank in the draft before adding the next short paragraph.

1. Almost nothing is known of Engs beyond what he says about himself in this letter. His family may have originally been from New England, since the name Engs appears occasionally in Boston and Rhode Island records, and Engs himself was once mentioned as the partner of the Newport merchant Henry Collins (above, VII, 237 n).

2. Probably a reference to BF's visit to Newport in January 1755; see above, V, 475 n. Collins' brother, Mr. Ward, was actually his half brother, Richard Ward (1689–1763), father of Samuel Ward, governor of R.I., 1762, 1765–7.

very Agreable Mr. Kinnersly had just left the Town,[3] if that Gentleman is now at Philadelphia please with my respectful Compliments, to inform him that I hope to be Gratified with those pleasing and instructive scenes *there*, which my absence unhappily debarred me from When he was at *Newport*.

Permit me, Sir, to Say that I have frequently exulted, as your Countryman, and Townsman, on the expansion of that Fame you have so justly acquired; and the many Honors you have received in Consequence of Your ingenious and sagacious Electrical Experiments; as well as many other useful Improvements, and Signal Services, whereby you have not only been Singularly beneficial to the little Common-Wealth of which you are a Member, but have also become extensively Serviceable to [the] Greater Community of Mankind in General, and by that means an Honor to Human Nature.

May I now Sir, after this introduction, presume to inform you, that having occasion for a Trifle of Cash, to enable me to prosecute my Journey to Philadelphia, I have ventured to draw on you for £5 12s. 6d. Currency in favor of Mr. James Balfour.[4] I have Several Acquaintance at your City that I cou'd have drawn on with much more propriety, but as they are not known here, I have used a freedom I should not Otherwise have done, but You may depend on being Paid as soon as I get to Philadelphia which I expect to be nearly as soon as this reaches You.

I have the honor to salute You with the Greatest deference and am sir Your most devoted servant   SAML. ENGS

Sir   Annapolis in Maryland Septr. 16th. 1763.

I have obtained a passage per Water as far as this Town, from whence I shall pursue my journey to Philadelphia per Land. Inclosed I transmit you a draft on Mr. Sisson of Rhode Island[5] for the sum I have presum'd to value on you for, which you may either

---

3. Ebenezer Kinnersley, BF's chief electrical collaborator in Philadelphia; see above, IV, 192 n. Unless Kinnersley made an unrecorded visit to Newport in about 1755, Engs appears to have been about three years off in his memory of this incident. Kinnersley's only known series of lectures on electricity in Newport occurred during the early months of 1752.

4. For Balfour, a merchant and planter of Elizabeth City Co., Va., see above, VI, 428 n.

5. Sisson has not been further identified.

forward for payment or I will reimburse you at Philadelphia, which I submit to your option; and hope the Freedom I have used will not be Unacceptable to you, I am with the highest Consideration sir, Your most Obedient Servant   SAML ENGS
Benjamin Franklin Esqr.

To Joshua Babcock[6]   ALS: Yale University Library

Boston, Sept. 5. 1763

Returning hither from Portsmouth,[7] I find your agreeable Favour of Augt. 19.[8] containing your kind Invitation to Westerly, where I am sure I could pass some Days with great Pleasure; but doubt whether it will be in my Power.[9]

I perceive the Artifice of your Eloquence, which in some degree saves me from being carried away by its Force. You promise me the Communication of some new Philosophical Discovery. Then you pique my Pride, by challenging me at Drafts, and insinuate that I have not the Courage to meet you. Then you work upon my Fears, by your Prophecies and Auguries, threatening me with Mischief and Misfortune if I travel any other Road. All this is very good in its place; but you omit an Argument that weighs much more with me, the Happiness I should enjoy in your Conversation, and in the true, ancient, cordial Hospitality, with which you and good Mrs. Babcock always entertain your Friends. I can only wish that the more powerful Calls of Business and Duty, did not too forcibly draw me another way.

My sincere Respects and best Wishes, will however attend you and yours, while I am, Dear Doctor Your most obedient and most humble Servant   B FRANKLIN

My compliments to my young Friend the Colonel;[1] hope his Farming succeeds to his wish.

6. For Babcock, an important R.I. politician, who became chief justice of the colony and a major general of its militia in 1776, see above, VI, 174 n.

7. For BF's trip to Portsmouth, N.H., on which he dislocated his shoulder, see above, p. 278.

8. Not found.

9. BF did visit Babcock on his return trip to Philadelphia and spent a couple of days, October 19–21, with him; see below, pp. 362, 367.

1. Babcock's eldest son, Henry; see above, IX, 397 n.

Addressed: To / The honble Joshua Babcock Esqr / Westerly / Rh. Island Governmt / Free B FRANKLIN
Towe [?] 7th of Sept 1763 / Fo[rwarded?] by yr Honours hum[ble] / Servant / JOHN CASE [?]²

Endorsed: Benj Franklin Esq 5 Septr: 1763 of his not returning this Way.

To Catharine Greene   ALS: American Philosophical Society

Dear Friend,   Boston, Sept. 5. 1763
     On my returning hither from Portsmouth,³ I find your obliging Favour of the 18th past,⁴ for which I thank you.
     I am almost asham'd to tell you that I have had another Fall, and put my Shoulder out.⁵ It is well reduc'd again, but is still affected with constant tho' not very acute Pain. I am not yet able to travel rough Roads, and must lie by a While, as I can neither hold Reins, nor Whip with my right hand till it grows stronger.
     Do you think after this, that even your kindest Invitations and Mr. Green's, can prevail with me to venture my self again on such Roads? and yet it would be a great Pleasure to me to see you and yours once more.⁶
     Sally and my Sister Mecom thank you for your Remembrance of them, and present their affectionate Regards.

2. Part of the page where this memorandum is written and where BF's seal had been affixed has been cut away destroying some of the writing. Case has not been identified.

3. See above, p. 278.

4. Not found.

5. This was BF's second fall during his New England journey. The first, suffered in R.I., delayed his departure from the Greenes' house only briefly; the second, which occurred on the Portsmouth trip, was more serious and held him in Boston until October 12. Though the handwriting of this letter and the one immediately above shows that he had recovered enough to use a pen quite normally, however painfully, the effects of these accidents were long lasting. Almost a year and a half later he wrote that dressing and undressing still hurt him a little and that he usually had help, though he could do it alone. To DF, Feb. 9, 1765, APS.

6. BF visited the Greenes in October on his way to Philadelphia; see below, pp. 362, 368.

338

My best Respects to good Mr. Greene, Mrs. Ray,[7] and Love to your little ones. I am glad to hear they are well, and that your Celia[8] goes alone. I am, Dear Friend, Yours affectionately

B FRANKLIN

From Peter Collinson

ALS: American Philosophical Society

Londn Sepr 9: 1763

I reced both Yours from Boston[9]—it is a Pleasure to hear from the Man I Love.

I Submit the Inclosed to your perusal.[1] Your Free remarks on them will be acceptable. I that Live so remote am not so good a Judge of the Reasonabl[n]ess and practibility of Them.

They were drawn up at the breaking out of the Cherokee Warr[2] and presented to those at the Helm.

Its possible Some Hints (if attended to) might have been Drawn from Them and prevented these Cruel Recent Depredations.[3]

I am in perfect Health to hear the Like from you and yours will be a Peculiar Satisfaction to your Affectionate Friend

P COLLINSON

7. Caty's mother, who died in December 1763.

8. Caty's younger daughter, who had apparently just begun to walk; see above, p. 191 n.

9. Neither letter has been found.

1. Probably Collinson's "Two Proposals for establishing a lasting Peace and Friendship with the Indians in North America," dated Sept. 17, 1763, and printed in that month's issue of *Gent. Mag.*, XXXIII (1763), 419–20. The premise underlying Collinson's proposals was the customary Quaker one that Indian troubles in North America were caused by mistreatment of the redmen by the whites, land fraud being singled out as the most persistent form of injustice practiced against the Indians. Collinson's remedies were the appointment of surveyors in each colony whose job it would be to "ride the boundaries" and see that squatters on Indian lands were removed, forcibly if necessary, and the appointment of "advocates" from the Council in each province "to be impowered by the Assembly to act speedily and finally, in settling all complaints from the Indians." He would also have had the sale of rum to the Indians made a felony.

2. For the "Cherokee War" along the frontiers of So. Car., 1759–61, see above, IX, 30 n.

3. That is, depredations by Pontiac and his followers; see above, p. 273 n.

To Morrow I go to the Society.[4] If I see Canton[5] will show him the Letter. The Bad News is Just Arrived of our Defeat which Gives much Concern.[6]

Addressed: To / Benn: Franklin Esqr / in / Philadelphia
Endorsed: Mr Collinson Sept. 9. 1763

From James Bowdoin[7] ALS: American Philosophical Society

Dear Sir   Roxbury 20 Septr. 1763

I am much obliged for yesterday's Communications.[8] You'll permit me to adopt a request of Father Beccaria. "Si alia habeas [Scripta praesertim Franklini] quae a me desiderari posse putes (quid autem esse potest Franklinianarum Rerum quod non planè deperearm?) quaeque verecundè peti abs me posse arbitrere, ut mittas etiam atque etiam efflagito."[9]

I congratulate you upon the Honors confer'd upon you. Honors so well placed reflect a Lustre on the Bestowers. I am with much esteem Sir, Your most Obedient Servant   JAMES BOWDOIN

I now return the Papers you favoured me with yesterday.

Dr. Franklin

Addressed: Dr. Franklin.

4. Probably the Royal Society.

5. John Canton, the English electrical experimenter; see above, IV, 390 n.

6. Apparently a reference to a defeat inflicted by Pontiac, but it is difficult to tell which one. *London Chron.*, Sept. 15–17, 1763, prints letters about the fighting around Detroit and Collinson may be referring to the discouraging news in general.

7. On Bowdoin, BF's scientific correspondent, see above, IV, 69 n.

8. Not found, but from what follows probably a list of BF's honors and copies of his citations; see above, pp. 309–11.

9. A quotation from a letter by Giambatista Beccaria (above, V, 395 n) to Peter Collinson, June 13, 1756. Freely translated the quotation reads: "If you have any others [especially writings of Franklin] which you think I might desire (but what can there be of Franklin's papers which I should not be delighted with) I over and over earnestly beg that you send what you think I can reasonably ask." The bracketed words are Bowdoin's insertion. Ezra Stiles kept a copy of this letter among his papers (Yale Univ. Lib.) and another copy exists in the Yale College Records along with other documents relating to BF's honors. It is printed in full in Antonio Pace, *Benjamin Franklin in Italy* (Phila., 1958), p. 381.

To [John Ellicott][1]

ALS: Yale University Library

Dear Sir   Boston, Sept. 22. 1763.

In coming thro' New York to this Place, I made a second Enquiry after Mrs. Holland, and was assur'd there was not nor had been in that Place any such Person. As I return I shall notwithstanding cause an Advertisement to be printed in the Newspapers, if possible by that means to gain Intelligence of her. I will likewise cause another to be printed in the Virginia Gazette, having some Suspicion, that the York may be Yorktown in Virginia, which is not far from James River. I will then send home the Papers, that the Steps taken may be seen; with an authenticated Account of the Enquiry and every thing I can learn by it: My best Respects to the Club;[2] and please to acquaint Mr. Peyton that I have receiv'd his Letter, and shall observe the Contents.[3] I am Sir, with great Esteem Your most obedient Servant

                                                              B FRANKLIN

To Richard Jackson

ALS: American Philosophical Society

Dear Sir,   Boston, Sept. 22. 1763

As I write in pain with a lately dislocated Arm, I can do little more than acknowledge the Receipt of you several Favours of Apr. 7. May 19. and June 18.[4] all which I shall answer more fully when I get home, where I hope to be in about three Weeks; at the Meeting of our new Assembly; when I shall procure the Change you desire to be made in the Vote of Agency.[5] I must have express'd my self with strange Obscurity in my Letters relating

1. So identified because of the reference to Elizabeth Holland, for whom BF had been searching at Ellicott's request for several months. For this futile search, see above, pp. 248–9.

2. The Monday Club, which met at the George and Vulture Tavern; see above, p. 250 n.

3. Mr. Peyton has not been identified, and his letter has not been found.

4. No letters from Jackson of these dates have been found, but the first date may be BF's error for April 4; see above, pp. 241–5.

5. What change Jackson wanted is not known. For the wording of the Assembly resolution of April 2, 1763, appointing him agent, see above, p. 247 n.

to Coxe's Affair, or you read it with too little Attention.[6] I certainly never meant to propose taking a Share at that Price, and run the Risque of Success in the Application. The Proposal of Messrs. Coxe was, that in case the Grant was confirm'd, or a Territory equivalent obtain'd in lieu of it, we should have one half for £5000. If the Application does not succeed, we have nothing to pay as we are to receive nothing.[7]

The present Indian War, made upon our Western Posts and Settlements by the Chippaways and Ottawaws, French Indians, with whom we never before the Conquest of Canada had any Correspondence, was undoubtedly stirr'd up by the French Commandant in the Ilinois Country, who sent Belts among them last Fall, before the Peace.[8] They prevail'd on the Delawares to join them, who are grown fond of Plunder since the last War. But I think when the Indians see us in Possession of the Ilinois Posts, still occupied by the French, and of all the other Posts ceded to us by France; this War will cease. I hope however that they will be well chastis'd, particularly the Delawares, before we talk of Peace to them. Or they will be continually breaking with us.

I cannot not add but that I am, with the greatest Esteem, Dear Sir Your most obedient humble Servant   B FRANKLIN

Addressed: To / Richard Jackson Esqr / Member of Parliamt. for Weymouth / Inner Temple / London

Endorsed: Boston Sept. 22d, 1763 B Franklin Esqr.

6. For "Coxe's Affair" and BF's suggestion that Jackson and he take a part in this land speculation, see his letters of March 8, 22, and April 17, 1763, and the accompanying notes, above, pp. 212–15, 254–6.

7. Jackson replied explaining that the confusion arose, not from BF's letter, but from one by the Coxes; see below, pp. 370–1.

8. For BF's previous reports and comments on the Indian uprising, see above, pp. 295–7, 303–4. The most complete and balanced account of the entire contest is Howard H. Peckham, *Pontiac and the Indian Uprising* (2d edit., Chicago, 1961).

To William Strahan

ALS: Henry E. Huntington Library and Art Gallery

Dear Friend   Boston, Sept. 22. 1763

I write in pain with an Arm lately dislocated, so can only acknowledge the Receipt of your Favours of May 3. and 10.[9] And thank you for the Intelligence they contain concerning your publick Affairs. I am now 400 Miles from home, but hope to be there again in about 3 Weeks.[1] The Indian War upon our Western Settlements, was undoubtedly stirr'd up by the French on the Missisipi, before they had heard of the Peace between the two Nations; and will probably cease when we are in Possession of what is there ceded to us. My Respects to Mrs. Strahan and Love to your Children. I am, Dear Friend, very affectionately Yours

B Franklin

From Griffith Jones[2]

ALS: American Philosophical Society

Bolt Court Fleet Street

Sir   London, October 6, 1763

Though I presume Mr. Cumming's Letter,[3] which you receive at the same time with this, informs you of the Motive which induced the Friends of the Bearer to send him to Philadelphia; yet as being the Father of the Boy,[4] I thought it necessary for your

9. On August 8 BF acknowledged Strahan's "Favour of May 3. and Postscript of May 10" (above, p. 320) and thanked him for its "Sketch" of political affairs. No letter of either date has been found.

1. Chiefly because of his injury, it was more than six weeks before BF reached Philadelphia.

2. Griffith Jones (1722–1786), printer, journalist, and writer, trained as a printer under William Bowyer and then set up in business in Bolt Court, off Fleet Street. He was associated with Samuel Johnson in the *Literary Magazine* and with Tobias Smollett and Oliver Goldsmith in the *British Magazine*. During his career he was also editor of the *London Chronicle, Daily Advertiser,* and *Public Ledger*. In addition to writing various translations from the French and original pieces in English, he collaborated with his brother Giles in a series of popular books for children known as "Lilliputian Histories." *DNB.*

3. See the document immediately below, which should be read in conjunction with this letter.

4. Lewis (later spelled Louis) Jones (b. 1748) was the eldest son in a family of three boys and one girl. He was educated at St. Paul's School. *DNB* (under "Griffith Jones").

Satisfaction, briefly to relate to you my Reasons for taking this Step; and likewise to give you some Account of the Abilities of the Lad. He has from his Infancy been brought up in the Principles and Practice of Religion; but having had from the very Beginning of his Apprenticeship too much Liberty to go out after the Business of the Day was over (an Indulgence of a very pernicious Nature for Youth in this vice-abounding Metropolis) he began to contract an Acquaintance with Boys of the like Age and Situation with himself, and to go with them to Places of Entertainment; which I luckily heard of, just at the Commencement of their Connexion; and fearing that he might run into Irregularities and Extravagancies not suitable to his Age and Station, I consulted Mr. Cumming, with whose Friendship I am honoured, who advised the sending him abroad, and pointed out the Method I have been so free as to take of assigning him over to you for the Remainder of his Time. To this his Master, who is my particular Friend, at my Request, consented: And I should think myself extremely happy, if you, Sir, a Gentleman, of whom Mr. Cumming has given the most amiable Character, and which is confirmed by the universal Voice, will be so good as to accept him; and I hope he will prove an useful, diligent, and faithful Servant to you. As to his Abilities; he is now capable of earning his Bread, having serving two Years of his Time, and can work well. He has learnt Latin and a little Greek; can speak French fluently, and translate it as well as most of his Years. His Behaviour so far as I have ever seen or heard is orderly and obliging. But as Boys of his Age have seldom Resolution to withstand Temptation, I should esteem it as a great Favour, if you would give Instructions to the Person whom you shall think proper to place him under, that he may [be] kept closely to work, and not suffer'd to ramble out after the Hours of Business; but employ himself at Leisure Times in improving himself in French, Latin, &c. The Assignment is made according to the Custom of London, but if you think it not obligatory in Philadelphia, you are at Liberty to bind him in what Manner you think proper.[5] Not to trespass longer on your Time or

5. The subsequent career of Lewis Jones shows a regrettable failure to avoid those "Irregularities and Extravagancies" his father wanted him to escape by going to America. BF assigned the balance of the boy's apprenticeship to his friend and fellow printer James Parker in Woodbridge, N.J. After

Patience; permit me to conclude with assuring you, that if I can transact any Kind of Business for you here, I shall think myself highly honoured by receiving your Commands, and am with the most profound Respect, Sir Your most Obedient Humble Servant

G. JONES

Addressed: To / Dr Benjam Franklin, / Philadelphia

Endorsed: Mr Cumming and Griffith Jones

From Thomas Cumming[6]   ALS: American Philosophical Society

London 7th. Oct. 1763.

Dear and much esteemed Friend

It was a happy Opportunity I had, in Capt. Stout's return to Philadelphia;[7] as, unless it had been for that, I should not have

---

Jones had completed his time he went to work for a N.Y. printer, Hugh Gaine. A year later, Jan. 11, 1769, he married Mary Bennett (Gideon J. Tucker, *Names of Persons for whom Marriage Licenses were issued by the Secretary of the Province of New York, previous to 1784,* Albany, 1860, p. 208), a girl Parker described as "among the poorer sort." Soon Jones was caught using a counterfeit theater ticket to attend a play in N.Y. He accused Parker's son of giving him the ticket, but Parker easily proved that it had been printed in Gaine's shop. A little later Jones was arrested and indicted on three counts of uttering counterfeit N.J. bills of credit—a hanging offense. Parker generously came to his aid as a character witness, apparently using the BF connection in his testimony, and Jones was acquitted. With Parker's financial help he went off to Charleston, So. Car., but later returned to N.Y., where he continued to scrape out an existence for his wife, six children, and himself as a journeyman printer. In 1786 he wrote BF that he then had "the conducting and management" of *The New-York Morning Post* while its owner, William Morton, languished in jail for publishing "an obscene pamphlet called *The Philosophical Theresa.*" Jones asked BF to help him find "a more eligible situation," but there is no evidence that BF did anything more for him. Parker to BF, April 23, 24, 25, May 10, 1770, 2 Mass. Hist. Soc. *Proc.,* XVI (1902), 225–7; Jones to BF, Feb. 12, 1786, APS.

6. Thomas Cumming (d. 1774), a "sensible Quaker" merchant of London, of whose apparently checkered career only occasional parts can be put together from scattered sources. He appears to have been of Scottish birth (see his mention of David Hall in this letter), was once a printer in Cork, Ireland, and about 1750–51 was a merchant in N.Y. *Pa. Gaẓ.* June 6, 1765; *Johnson Papers,* I, 289. It was probably during this American stay that he visited Philadelphia, meeting BF and his family, Israel Pemberton, and others, and

(*Footnote 7 appears on page 346*)

been so fully convinced, of thy Readiness, to pay Regard to my Recommendations. I acknowledge myself thy Debtor; but alas, I must rely on thy Goodness, to accept of that Acknowledgment, instead of Value received! Even that Request encreases my Debt; not only so, but from thy Benevolence, which is inseparably con- nected with thy very Name; every where, I am emboldened, to contract a fresh Debt, which, in itself, will amount, almost, to as much as all my former put together! In short,

I was lately applied to, by a very particular Acquaintance of mine, Griffith Jones Printer in Fleet Street[8] (who served an Apprenticeship to—Boyer whom thou knowst, I think) for my Advice, how and where abroad, to send his Son to? The Letter my Friend sends herewith, and the Indentures, &c. save me the Trouble, and thee, of adding more on that Head.

Neither thou nor any one else, who know us both, and that I have the Happiness of knowing thee, will be surprized, that thou shouldst be the first that should occur to me, and that in an Instant, on such an Occasion; even, had the Lad been mine own and only Child.

The great Distance betwixt us, will plead my Excuse, for thus precipipately throwing a Load on thy Shoulders. The Exigence of the Case required it.

traveled to Va., where he made friends and acquired later business associates. By 1754, established in London, he made a trading voyage to the east coast of Africa, secured an agreement for trade from a native ruler, and after his return to England proposed to Pitt an expedition which led to the capture of the French Fort Louis at Senegal, 1758, and the establishment of a British colony there. Cumming accompanied the expedition. John Almon, *A Review of Mr. Pitt's Administration* (3d edit., 1763), pp. 83–5; Kate Hotblack, *Chatham's Colonial Policy* (London, 1917), pp. 32–35; Gipson, *British Empire*, VIII, 174–7. Although promised a monopoly of trade with the Gum Coast, he never received it, but was awarded instead a pension of £500 annually for thirty-one years. He seems to have spent the rest of his life in London, where he had already formed an acquaintance with Dr. Samuel Johnson and where he established a useful connection with Lord Shelburne. During 1763–67 the Mississippi Co. of Va. employed Cumming as their London agent to press their petition for lands on the Ohio. Clarence E. Carter, "Documents relating to the Mississippi Land Company," *Amer. Hist. Rev.*, XVI (1910–11), 311–17.

7. Probably Joseph Stout (d. 1773), a merchant-ship captain of Philadelphia who also served as a lieutenant in the Royal Navy. *PMHB*, V (1881), 88.

8. For Griffith Jones, his son Lewis, and the subject matter of the first half of this letter, see the document immediately above.

It will, I make no Doubt, appear to thee, that, at least, his (the Boy's Passage) should have been paid by his Father, here. The Father expected no other; but I frankly own, I advised the Step taken. My Reasons for doing so were these: First, it would lessen the Expence of Grief and Cash to the Parents, at parting with their beloved Son: And in Truth, it would be Cruelty not to do it, by any just Means. Secondly, I know, that a Lad of his Capacity, Qualifications and Experience in his Business, is well worth so much Money to any Master, who will take him for the Term of Years he has to serve. Thirdly, and above all, because it would convince the Boy, that he was more obliged to be obedient, diligent, &c. as a bought, than as merely, a bound, Apprentice.[9] I therefore hope, for these Reasons, thou wilt, at least, think I meant justly and well, with Respect to all Parties. But if thou should'st be of a different Opinion, I must request, that thou wilt advance the Money, and send an Order upon me for it, and it shall be duely honoured.

Although the Boy is assigned over to thee, yet I well know, that thou wilt be no more over him, than thou art over thy other Boys at the College, and every Inhabitant of the City, who may be all looked upon as thy Children: My worthy Friend and Countryman David Hall, I hope will be immediately over him.[1] Better, I have assured his Brother Jones, he could not wish his Son, than under him. Be that as it may, the Boy is thrown by my Means under thy sole Care, and disposal. I cannot but hope, through thee, he may turn out an useful Citizen of Philadelphia, a Credit to thee, an Honour and Blessing to his Parents, and above all (and which must follow) that his Life will redound to

9. A colonial master who paid the ship's captain for young Jones's transportation, as was the regular procedure with an indentured servant arriving in America, would theoretically have an even stronger claim on the lad's loyalty and obedience than the mere assignment of his apprenticeship papers would give. Whether BF relished the advantages of this somewhat expensive arrangement may be questioned.

1. Whether Cumming had known Hall before the latter came to America in 1744 or had met him in Philadelphia at the same time he met the Franklins is uncertain. The mention of Griffith Jones as Hall's "Brother" in the next sentence indicates merely that they were fellow printers. As stated in the note on Lewis Jones to the document immediately above, BF assigned his apprenticeship not to Hall but to James Parker.

his own Interest and Happiness here and hereafter. If he make:
as good, as ingenious and as amiable a Man as his Father, I coulc
wish for no better from a Son, had I one of mine own.

I did not forget thy Commission, concerning my 2d. bes•
Friend, the Earl of Shelburne.[2] I shewed him thy Letter.[3] Bu•
his Brother has been all this Summer in Paris, and is not yet returned.[4] There to my Eye-Sight, at least, last June, he out shines

2. William (Fitzmaurice) Petty, 2d Earl of Shelburne, 2d Baron Wycombe
and (1784) Marquess of Lansdowne (1737–1805), was the elder son of John
Fitzmaurice, who took the name of Petty upon succeeding to an uncle'•
estates in 1751 and was created Earl of Shelburne (in the Irish peerage), 1753
and Baron Wycombe (in the peerage of Great Britain), 1760. The son matriculated at Christ Church, Oxford, 1755, but left to enter the army, 1757, served
with distinction on the Continent, and was promoted to colonel and aide-de-
camp to the King, 1760. Elected M.P. for Chipping Wycombe, 1760, he never
sat in the Commons because, after his father's death in 1761, he entered the
Lords as Baron Wycombe. He was generally called, however, by his Irish title
of Lord Shelburne. Politically independent at first, he acted nevertheless as a
negotiator between Bute and Fox. Upon Grenville's accession to power in April
1763 he became president of the Board of Trade, but resigned Sept. 2, 1763,
when a scheme in which he was involved failed to bring Pitt into office in place
of Grenville. Soon thereafter he attached himself firmly to the Pitt faction; he
became secretary of state for the Southern Department in 1766, with complete
charge of colonial affairs until Hillsborough was given the new office of secretary for the colonies in January 1768. Shelburne stoutly opposed most of his
fellow ministers' policy of colonial coercion and resigned when Chatham did
the following October. In opposition during the next fourteen years, he was
outspoken in sympathy for the American point of view, but repeatedly declared
his objection to granting independence. Nevertheless, when he became secretary of state under Rockingham in March 1782, he took charge of the peace
negotiations which led to recognition of that independence. On Rockingham's
death in July 1782 he became head of the government, but resigned, February
1783, and never again held political office. Generally regarded in America as a
warm friend, he was bitterly hated and distrusted by fellow politicians in
Great Britain. *DNB;* Namier and Brooke, *House of Commons,* III, 271–2.

3. Not found.

4. Thomas Fitzmaurice (1742–1793) did not change his surname to Petty
as his father and brother did. He was educated at Eton, 1755–58; Glasgow,
1759; and matriculated at St. Mary's Hall, Oxford, 1761; Middle Temple,
1762; called to the bar, 1768. He served as M.P. for Calne, 1762–74, and for
Chipping Wycombe, 1774–80, but ill health, impaired finances, and care of
his Irish properties interfered with his attendance, and he withdrew from political affairs in 1780. Thereafter he became, not very successfully, a linen bleacher
and merchant. He married, 1777, Lady Mary O'Brien, only surviving child

ll that Showy City, in Splendid Equipages, &c. &c. &c. Lord Shelburne was very glad (as every body is) to hear of thy Welfare, and more so in being remembered by thee.[5] He told me, he had intended, on his being appointed first Lord of Trade, to have wrote to thee, for any Information, relating to the publick Good of thy Province, or the British Interest in general in America; and as he was then exceedingly busy with the Duties of his Office desired I would write to thee what his Request was, and that he should be greatly obliged to thee to favour him from Time to Time with thy Hints and Advice. But, the Turbulence, of an unreasonable, all-aspiring, routted Faction, occasioned, amongst other Changes, that of his chusing to resign![6] In short, he had a principal Hand in the K's sending for that Man, who, when he came, wanted, proposed, no less, than to be K. himself de facto![7] But, my Situation is such, that they may write News of that Sort, for me, who please.

Notwithstanding L.S. has resigned, as he has been at a Board, as he still is as much the King's Favourite as ever, as he may, soon too, again be replaced, or accept of some other high Employment, as he always must have great Interest every where, and as he desired thee to write to him, I think it would not be amiss, that thou shouldst, without taking Notice of my not writing till after his Resignation. He does not know, but that I wrote before; and therefore must expect thou wilt. Pray don't slight him, because out. (for he was not outted.)

---

nd heir of the Countess of Orkney. She inherited her mother's title in 1790. C.E.C[okayne], *The Complete Peerage* (under Orkney), x (London, 1945), 110; Namier and Brooke, *House of Commons*, II, 430. Letters of 1770 and 1787 to be printed in this edition show that BF and Fitzmaurice, together with Dr. Hawkesworth, John Stanley, and others, came to form a circle of friends who combined jolly companionship with philosophical interests and experimentation.

5. This sentence and what follows suggest a prior personal acquaintance between Shelburne and BF, but there seems to be no firm evidence that their direct contacts began until BF's second English mission. Compare the tentative reconstruction of a mutilated passage in a letter from Pringle of the previous spring, above, pp. 267–8 n.

6. For Shelburne's resignation, Sept. 2, 1763, see the biographical note above.

7. William Pitt.

I can see the tender Father in every Thing thou dos't and say'st, of the King's Representative in the N. Jerseys. Thence thy Wish and mine not according in Respect to his Translation.⁸ As a Friend to extensive Utility in general, and as a Well-wisher to him and his immediate Family in particular, I continue still of the same Opinion. To him, when thou first see'st, or writest I must beg, after thy best (and most deservedly best) and well beloved Bedfellow (if she has not forgot having seen me) to be most affectionately remembered. Pray how does thy only (and once, amiable Child of a) Daughter do? I dare say she is marriageable. Is she tied? If so, and with all Consents, she must be happy. Art thou Grand Papa?

Having almost finished, and fully tired myself, it is Time I should thank thee for thy kind mentioning my Name to my Virginia Friends (many of whom I love most dearly) and for thy Intententions [sic] of shewing Civilities to honest, meritorious Capt. Stout. Had he had Friends here, equal to his Desert, he must have been now high in the List of Post Captains! Pray is my very old Acquaintance David James Dove yet living?⁹ If he be, and in your Province, I shall be obliged to thee, if thou wilt remember me to him also. I was the happy or unhappy (he knows best) Means, of his ever crossing over the Atlantick. I could almost ask after my quondam Friend Israel Pemberton but, I fancy he would not thank me if he knew it.¹

Last Week I told my Friends Smith and Wright, Bankers, that I intended writing to thee soon.² They present their Respects

8. Just why Cumming had reservations about WF's "Translation" to the governorship of N.J. is uncertain.

9. For David James Dove (c.1696–1769), see above, IV, 223 n. In 1763 he was just opening a school in Germantown, and in the following year he was one of the scurrilous attackers of BF.

1. For Israel Pemberton, Jr. (1715–1779), wealthy Quaker merchant, see above, V, 424 n. The reason for his disapproval of Cumming is not explained. Perhaps the strict Friend in Philadelphia objected to Cumming's participation in the military expedition to capture Senegal.

2. A London banking firm consisting of Thomas Smith, John Wright, and Henry Gray. While BF and they had apparently been on friendly terms during his first English mission, his first business dealings with them of which a record survives were in February 1764 (Memorandum Book, 1757–1776, p. 15, APS); the connection became much more extensive during his second English mission.

and expected to have heard from thee. They are a Couple of sensible, expert, careful young Men, are encreasing their Business daily, and promise, I think, of being soon among the first of their Profession. I am, my invaluable Friend, Thine, in all Sincerity, and Affection. THOMAS CUMMING.

P.S. Lord Shelburne sends his Compliments to thee.

To James Bowdoin

ALS:[3] Massachusetts Historical Society

Dear Sir   Oct. 11. 63

We found we could not get quite ready to set out to-day, so have adjourn'd our Departure till to-morrow. As Company, (I know not how many) talk of going part of the Way with us,[4] I think it will be inconvenient to breakfast with you as proposed. We shall therefore only stop at your Door to take Leave. Herewith you have the Receipt you desired. When you write to Canton and Nairne, enclose your Letter to me, and I will write with it and forward it per the Packet.[5] Mr. Winthrop has Æpinus, and I think a Piece also of the same Author, on the Distribution of Heat.[6] When he has done with them he will deliver them to

3. The letter occupies the first page of the sheet; Bowdoin's first endorsement stands alone on the second. The recipe, in BF's hand, is on the third page; the address and Bowdoin's second endorsement are on the fouth.

4. It is not known who accompanied BF, Foxcroft, and Sally nor how far the Boston friends traveled with them.

5. John Canton, English electrical experimenter (above, IV, 390 n), and Edward Nairne, English instrument maker (above, this volume, p. 171 n). Bowdoin wanted "a Pedistal of a new Construction for his reflecting Telescope" and a micrometer fixed to the instrument. On Jan. 18, 1764, he wrote BF enclosing a letter he had written Canton, who was to make the arrangements with Nairne. BF forwarded Bowdoin's letter to Canton and on March 14, 1764, wrote Canton sending along Bowdoin's letter of January 18 to himself. Bowdoin had shipped the telescope directly to London. Nairne undertook to make the pedestal but reported that the attachment of the micrometer was impractical. Bowdoin to BF, Jan. 18, 1764, Mass. Hist. Soc.; BF to Canton, March 14, 1764, Royal Soc.; Canton to BF, June 29, 1764, APS.

6. For the Russian electrician, Franz Ulrich Theodor Aepinus, see above, VIII, 393 n. The books of his which BF lent Winthrop were evidently *Tentamen theoriae electricitatis et magnetismi* (above, p. 204 n) and *Cognitationes de distributione caloris per tellurem* (above, p. 267 n). Winthrop returned them

you. I am, Dear Sir, with great Esteem Your most obedient humble Servant,   B FRANKLIN

Endorsed: Dr. Franklin's Letter Oct. 11. 1763. taking leave.

To make Milk Punch

Take 6 quarts of Brandy, and the Rinds of 44 Lemons pared very thin; Steep the Rinds in the Brandy 24 Hours; then strain it off. Put to it 4 Quarts of Water, 4 large Nutmegs grated, 2 quarts of Lemon Juice, 2 pound of double refined Sugar. When the Sugar is dissolv'd, boil 3 Quarts of Milk and put to the rest hot as you take it off the Fire, and stir it about. Let it stand two Hours; then run it thro' a Jelly-bag till it is clear; then bottle it off.

Addressed: To / James Bowdoin Esq / Roxbury

Endorsed: Dr. Franklin's rect. to make milk punch.

To Joshua Babcock   ALS: West Chester (Pa.) State Teachers College

Dear Sir   Newport, Tuesday Oct. 18. 1763
    I hop'd to have had the Pleasure of being with you before this time, but various Remora's[7] have detain'd us in various Places. We are to set out this day, so as to lodge at Cases'[8] to night, and purpose to take a Bed under your hospitable Roof the Night, if not cast away among the dangerous Rocks of your Coast.[9] My best Respects to Mrs. Babcock, &c. I am, Dear Friend, Yours affectionately   B FRANKLIN

Addressed: To / Doctor Babcock / Westerly / Free / B FRANKLIN

---

through Ezra Stiles in Newport and BF acknowledged their receipt. Bowdoin to BF, July 2, 1764, Mass. Hist. Soc.; BF to Winthrop, July 10, 1764, Harvard Coll. Lib.

    7. Delays, obstacles; the term derives from "any of several fishes belonging to *Echeneis, Remora*" which attach themselves to larger fish or vessels by means of a suctorial disc on the head. The ancients believed that remora could check and even stop ships.

    8. Probably an inn along the shore road in southern Rhode Island which they were to traverse after crossing to the mainland from Newport.

    9. The Franklins arrived safely at the Babcock home on Wednesday, October 19, and stayed there until the 21st, when they and the Babcocks set out in company for New London and New Haven.

From Francis Bernard[1]   Letterbook copy: Harvard College Library

Sir   Boston Octo. 30. 1763
As you was so kind as to tell Mrs. Bernard[2] that you would
take care of my Son[3] if he came in your way, I am encouraged
to trouble you with particulars concerning him. By a letter
dated Octo.9 We learn he is at Bellhaven:[4] and as his Mony must
be all spent, and he is not provided with any Papers of credit, I
apprehend he may be necessarily detained there. I must therefore
desire you will procure him credit and assistance to return to
Philadelphia; and that you will procure him a passage by Sea
from Philadelphia to Boston. If that cant be conveniently had, I
must desire that you would return him home by way of New

1. Francis Bernard (1712–1779) was appointed governor of N.J. in 1758
through the influence of his wife's cousin Lord Barrington and served there
until 1760, when he became governor of Mass. Bernard's nine years in the
Bay Colony were stormy and they culminated in his removal by the British
government after the Mass. Assembly had preferred charges against him,
charges which were later adjudged "groundless, vexatious, and scandalous."
Created a baronet on April 5, 1769, he spent the remainder of his life in
retirement in England, after resigning the sinecure post of commissioner of
customs in Ireland in 1774. *DAB.*
2. The governor's wife was the former Amelia Offley of Norton Hall,
Derbyshire, niece of John Shute, first Viscount Barrington, and cousin of
William Wildman, second Viscount Barrington (1717–1793), secretary at
war, 1755–61, 1765–78; chancellor of the exchequer, 1761–2; and postmaster
general, 1782. Namier and Brooke, *House of Commons,* II, 55–9.
3. Bernard's eldest son, Francis (1743–1770), was a highly promising
scholar at Westminster, 1757, when in traditional celebration of an award to
him his fellow students tossed him in a blanket. Unfortunately, he fell on his
head and sustained a serious injury. He matriculated at Christ Church,
Oxford, 1761, and received his B.A., 1764 (Foster, *Alumni Oxoniensis, 1752–
1886,* I, 100), but suffered permanently in health and apparently in capacity for
responsible action. He seems to have been visiting his family in America
while still enrolled at Oxford when the difficulties referred to in this and later
letters arose. After graduation he returned to Boston and died there more
than a year after his father had gone back to England but before his mother
and other children had sailed. Mrs. Napier Higgins, *The Bernards of Abington
and Nether Winchendon A Family History* (London, 1903–04), I, 209, 218–19;
II, 69–71, 225, 226.
4. What is now named Alexandria, Va., was once called Belhaven, though
for some time either name seems to have been used. The present Belhaven
is a small community about two miles south of the center of Alexandria.

York. I should be glad that he may be concerned as little as possible in the expenditure and conduct of his journeys, that Delays and Deviations may be avoided as much as can be. Mrs. Child[5] in third Street Philadelphia has directions from him. All charges will be thankfully paid. I am &c   FRA B.

I have inclosed a Letter for him which you will be so good as to forward.

Benjm Franklin Esqr.

To Deborah Franklin   ALS: American Philosophical Society

My dear Child   New York, Oct. 31. 176[3]
    We arriv'd here safe [*torn*] this Morning about 11 aClock, [after a] very pleasant Journey,[6] and without [the] least ill Accident. Thanks to God. We purpose to proceed homeward tomorrow, if the Weather, &c. is suitable. I have receiv'd here a Number of Letters from you for which I thank you.[7] We must stay a Day at Woodbridge and then shall go forward so as to be at Burlington on Friday at Dinner, where if you can conveniently meet us, it will make all our Joys compleat. If not, we shall hope to be with you at home on Saturday. As Cousin Lissey[8] has left you, I hardly know how you can leave the House, so do not advise, but leave you to your own Judgment. Sally presents her Duty, and Mr. Foxcroft his Compliments. I am Your affectionate Husband
                                                        B FRANKLIN
Addressed: To | Mrs Franklin | at | Philadelphia | Free

From Jonathan Williams: Account

                                    AD: American Philosophical Society

For several years Jonathan Williams, Senior, husband of Franklin's niece, the former Grace Harris (C.5.3), had represented Franklin in

5. Not identified.
6. For BF's trip from Boston to N.Y. and for the last leg of the journey home, see above, pp. 278–9, and below, p. 362.
7. None of DF's letters have been found.
8. Not identified.

business matters at Boston and had acted for him in looking after their less fortunate relatives in that area. Franklin in turn seems to have performed various financial services for Williams in Philadelphia or during his travels. Before Franklin left Boston in October 1763 the two men settled their accounts and found that there was a balance in favor of Franklin amounting to a little over £12 Massachusetts "lawful money." Williams did not try to pay this debt at the time but, as was customary, he opened a new record of their running account showing this balance as a credit to Franklin.

On Dec. 24, 1774, Williams transcribed his account onto a single sheet, which he then sent to Franklin in England. Williams' son, Jonathan Junior (C.5.3.2), who was in England with Franklin, took his father's account, compared it with the entries in Franklin's books, and prepared a revised balance sheet. Besides making additional entries in both parts of the record, he consolidated into a single entry about 45 separate items in his father's statement, mostly for small sums, which related to expenditures during the last eleven years for maintenance and repairs of the house formerly belonging to Franklin's eldest sister Elizabeth Douse. This property in Unity Street, Boston, had passed to Franklin after her death,[9] and on Nov. 28, 1763 (below, p. 384), he instructed Williams to have it put in repair, rent it out, and pay the rents received to Jane Mecom to help her in providing care for her insane son, Peter Franklin Mecom (C.17.6).

On Feb. 29, 1776, Jonathan Williams, Senior, prepared a new account at Franklin's request covering essentially the same period as the two earlier versions. In a letter of transmission, March 1, 1776, he told Franklin that his son's version, of which he had received a copy, contained "some omissions," but the two items he cited specifically as having been overlooked do in fact appear in Jonathan Junior's account. The father admitted that he was handicapped in preparing his new account because "Some of my Old books and papers were Consumed Last may in my warehouses."

All three of these versions survive in the American Philosophical Society Library, but the account prepared by Jonathan Williams, Junior, is chosen for printing here because it appears to be the most reliable and systematic and in general the most fully intelligible. By using both red and black ink and a special symbol of his own devising, the young man showed which entries appeared only on his father's first account (reproduced here in roman type), which appeared in both his father's account and Franklin's books (reproduced in italics), and which only in Franklin's books (in italics and with asterisks after the

9. See above, v, 66–7.

figures[1]). As Jonathan Junior explained in his memorandum at the end, he had detected "some little Difference in sums which are here put right," so that the records do not agree in all particulars; but with two exceptions mentioned in notes below, a careful comparison of the documents shows that other differences are indeed trivial and do not merit detailed notice here.

This account is given in full since it illustrates, as no summarized description could, some of the ways in which members of this closely knit, though physically scattered, family worked together for the welfare of the others.

[October 1763]

No. 1

State of the Accot: between Doctor B Franklin and
Jona: Williams Senr: as it should properly stand

Dr.	Sterling	Lawfull Mony
To Sundry Expences in repairing and keeping in repair a House at the North End of Boston, the Rent of which was appropriated to the Use of Mrs. Jane Mecom from Novr: 15th: 1763 to the last charge Augt: 10th: 1774 Particulars as per Acct:	110. 8. 6	£147. 4. 8
1764 Mar: 9 To Cash paid your Order to Mrs. Mecom[2]	3. 15. –	5. – –
1766 Feby 1 To Ditto paid Mrs. Mecom by the desire of Mrs. Franklin[3]	1. 16. –	2. 8. –

1. In Jonathan Junior's MS account the debit and credit entries are in parallel columns on a wide sheet of paper. Because of typographical limitations, the account is printed here with the credit entries following the debits.

2. BF's "order" not found.

3. Jane Mecom's daughter Sarah Flagg died June 12, 1764, followed within a few months by two of Sarah's daughters and on Sept. 11, 1765, by Jane's husband Edward Mecom. As she wrote her sister-in-law DF, Sept. 28, 1765,

1768 Sept 10	To a Box of Crown Soap bot: of Mrs. Eliza: Franklin[4]	3. 1. –	4. 1. 4
	To Cash paid for 2 Gowns of New Engd Manu- facture for Mrs. Franklin	2. 1. 9	2. 15. 8
	To Ballance of Rent due from James Reilly who proved unable to Pay it and at last was Oblig'd to quit the House by a Writ of Ejectment.[5] This Rent was regularly paid to Mrs. Mecom	13. 16. 4	18. 8. 5
1769 *Mar 12*	*To a Prise Ticket in State* *Lottery*[6]	20. – –	26. 13. 4
1771 *July*	*To a Ditto*	20. – –	26. 13. 4

"Nothing but troble can you hear from me." On Feb. 27, 1766, she wrote DF again acknowledging a letter (not found) in which DF had compassionately suggested that Jonathan Williams be asked to give Jane some money, charging it to BF's account. Jane sent the letter to Williams; "he came Emediatly Himself and ofered me Eaght Dolars," which she accepted in order to buy some needed clothing. Van Doren, *Franklin-Mecom*, pp. 83–5, 88–9.

4. On the Franklin family's specialty, the manufacture of crown soap, see above, I, 348 n. Elizabeth Franklin was the widow of BF's brother John (C.8).

5. Jonathan Junior overlooked an entry in his father's account dated June 8, 1765: "To Benj. Kent for Removing a Tenent 15s." The lawyer was Benjamin Kent (1708–1788), distinguished Boston attorney, an acquaintance and later correspondent of BF.

6. As the credit side of this account shows and as the correspondence between the two men explains, BF bought two state lottery tickets in England for Williams in 1769 and again in 1770. In each instance one of the tickets won a £20 prize and the other was blank. BF to Williams, Oct. 4, 1769; June 6, 1770; March 5, 1771; Williams to BF, Nov. 16, 1770; Jan. 19, 1771; Oct. 17, 1773 (all APS); BF to Williams, July 7, 1773 (Pierpont Morgan Lib.). Because of a mix-up in reporting the results, Jonathan Senior's account gives himself credit for only one of the prizes. His son's account shows both transactions, but he failed to use his special symbol after one of these entries of a prize to indicate that it does not appear in his father's account. Jonathan Senior's statement of Feb. 29, 1776, shows the matter correctly.

1772	To a Bill of Exchange		
June	Drawn by Symmes on Gardoque[7]	100. – –	133. 6. 8
	two Dutch Bills neated	162. 11. 6	216. 15. 4
	One Ditto Ditto	92. 4. –	122. 18. 8
	One Ditto Wheatly	100. – –	133. 6. 8
Decr	To 1 Ditto Sheppard on King[8]	27. – –	36. – –
1773 Apr	To 1 Ditto drawn by T Russell	48. 15. –	65. – –

Note this Bill was for £50. but bought under Par and being remitted on Acco. of Mrs. Mecom is charg'd only as it cost, the Profit belonging to her. It is Part of the m[one]y recd of Hall and was sent home to purchase Millinary Goods for Mrs. M.[9]

7. This and the next three entries are dated June 1772 in all three versions of the account, but correspondence between Williams and BF shows that Williams sent the bills at various times between July 8 and Sept. 18, 1771, not 1772.

8. The December 1772 date for this bill is correct, as shown in correspondence between the two men.

9. Williams sent this bill of exchange to BF with his letter of Feb. 15, 1773 (APS), and BF reported its receipt and his purchases for Jane Mecom, June 4, 1773 (Lib. Cong.). She wanted to sell the goods to eke out her income. Hall was Samuel Hall, printer, who had married Sarah(?) (C.11.3), daughter of BF's brother James. He had gone into partnership with his mother-in-law in Newport about 1762, and transferred the printing business to Salem in 1768. He had owed BF a considerable sum of money for at least seven years without paying anything on principal or interest when in 1772 BF lost patience and asked Williams to prosecute Hall on his bond. Williams engaged John Adams to bring the action (see the last debit entry in this account) and, under pressure, Hall, or some of his friends, paid at least part of what was due. Franklin directed Williams to turn the money over to Jane Mecom for her own use. Several later entries in this account refer to Hall's payments. Van Doren, *Franklin-Mecom*, pp. 16, 133, 138; Williams to BF, Sept. 19, 1771 (APS); BF to Williams, Jan. 13, 1772 (APS); March 9, 1773 (Lib. Cong.).

May 3	To Cash paid Neice on her Marriage[1] £50. - -			
	Paid Mrs. Mecom	68. 6. 8		
Novr	Ditto paid Ditto	47. 8. 8		
1774 July	Ditto paid Ditto	16. 19. 6		
	L M[one]y 182. 14. 10		137. 1. 1½	182. 14. 2
	These Sums and Russells Bill were on Acco: of what was recd: and to be recd: of Hall			
Aug 10	To Cash paid John Adams Charges for a suit against Hall		3. 15. 4½	5. - 6
		£864.[2] 5. 7		1128. 7. 5
	Ballce: due Dr. F	15. 4. 1		20. 5. 5¾
	carried to Aud[it] No 2[3]	£861. 9. 8		1148. 12. 10¾

	Cr.	Sterling	Lawfull Mony
1763 Octr.	By Ballance of Old Accot.	£9. 2. 11½	12. 3. 11½
1764 June 12	By Cash of John Head	3. 12. -	4. 16. -
Feby. 27	By an Order in favr. Robbins	28. 19. 2¼	38. 4. 3
" 28	By Cash Recd. of Govr. Bernard[4]	24. 1. 1½	32. 1. 6

1. When BF learned that Jane Mecom's daughter Jane (C.17.9) was planning to marry Peter Collas, he wrote Williams, Nov. 3, 1772 (Lib. Cong.), that he wanted £50 laid out "in Bedding or such other Furniture as my Sister shall think proper, to be given the new-married Couple towards Housekeeping, with my best Wishes." The wedding took place March 23, 1773.

2. Jonathan Junior transposed two digits in this sum; it should read £846, not £864.

3. No such account has been found.

4. This and the next entry represent Gov. Francis Bernard's repayments of expenditures BF made in returning the governor's son to Boston from Va.

Aprl 10	By Ditto of Ditto	7.	11.	2¼	10.	1.	7¼
Augt. 1	By John Gooches Order	3.	12.	–	4.	16.	–
	By Over Charge in Braizers Bill in Sum for Repairs &c.	–	4.	1½	–	5.	6
1769 *July*	*By 2 Lottery Ticketts*	29.	5.	–	39.	–	–
1770 *July*	*By 2 Ditto*	28.	13.	–	38.	4.	–
1771 *July*	*By Cash advanced J Williams Junr*[5]	308.	16.	10½	411.	15.	10½
1772 *Jany*	*By Ditto Paid to James Warren*	83.	3.	9½	110.	18.	4
	By Ditto advanced to Josiah Williams 118 Guineas	123.	18.	–	165.	4.	–

1773

Jany 1	By Cash Recd. of Hall	133. 6. 8			
Novr.30	By Ditto of do.	47. 8. 8			
June	By Ditto of do.	11. – –			
July	By Ditto of do.	7. – –			
Aug	By Ditto of do.	4. – –			
	L M[one]y	202. 15. 4			

	152. 1. 6	202. 15. 4
Mrs. M. is paid	£ 65. – –	
	182. 14. 10	
	£247. 14. 10	

On Acct. of Halls Bond
but the above
is all Yet received

See above, pp. 353–4, below, pp. 373, 390, and several letters to appear in the next volume.

5. In the latter part of 1770 Williams' sons Josiah (C.5.3.1) and Jonathan Junior (C.5.3.2) went to England. Josiah was determined to study music, and BF arranged for him to work under his friend, the blind John Stanley (above, IX, 320 n). Jonathan was inclined toward business; BF gave him the task of putting his financial records in order and later wrote highly approving of the results and of the youth's assiduity. This contact was the beginning of a long personal relationship between BF and the younger Jonathan.

The following Sums are
    Omitted in
    J Williams Accot:

1772
May   *Paid Mr. Stanly teaching*
      Josiah Williams
      Music   *£31. 10. −**
June *Paid Ditto's Taylor* *19. 16. 11**
     6 Bottles of Elastic
     Gum   *1. 16. −**

1773
March *Paid for Behmens*
      Works[6]   *5. 12. −**
                 58. 14. 11   *78. 6. 7*

Memo:
   The Articles in red Ink
are in JW's Accot: and
not in D F. Books.
   Those in black Ink, are
in Doctr. Fs Books and
JW's Accot: too, except
some little Difference in
sums which are here put
right.[7]
   Those in Black Ink with
this mark*[8] are in D. Fs
Books and not in JW's
Acct.   £861. 9. 8   1148. 12. 10¾

Endorsed: Dr Franklins Aud[it] with Jona Williams Senr No 1
[*and in pencil:*] 1763 74 Drew up for F by Jno Wms Jr

6. Jakob Boehme (1575–1624), a German mystic, whose name was often
spelled Boehmen in English, believed that material powers are substantially
one with moral forces. Jonathan Senior became a devotee and in his later
years his preoccupation with Boehme's theories and with experiments using
poisonous drugs injured his business and his health to the dismay of his
relatives.

7. In the MS the heading, the memorandum, and the totals at the bottoms
of the columns are in black ink, as are the entries taken from BF's books, but
only the entries are printed above in italics.

8. In the MS the symbol is an X or plus sign imposed on a circle. For typo-

To Jane Mecom   ALS: American Philosophical Society

Dear Sister   Philada. Nov. 7. 1763
    We stopt one Day at Mrs. Green's, and We got to Newport the
Saturday Evening after we left you,[9] staid there till Tuesday Afternoon, got to Dr. Babcock's on Wednesday, staid there till Friday
then went to New London, where we staid among our Friends
till Tuesday, then set out for Newhaven, where we arriv'd on
Thursday Morning,[1] set out from thence on Friday Afternoon, and
got to New York on Monday following, and after staying one Day
there, one at Woodbridge with Mr. Parker, and one at Burlington
with Billy who met us 20 Miles on the Road, we got safe home on
Saturday Night the 5th. Instant, having had a most pleasant Journey without the least ill Accident, and found all well: Thanks to
God.
    Sally joins in Love to all Friends, and will write if she is not
too much interrupted by visiting Friends. I am Your affectionate
Brother   B FRANKLIN

Provincial Commissioners: Orders for Payment

                           DS: Historical Society of Pennsylvania

On Oct. 22, 1763, two weeks before Franklin returned to Philadelphia,
Governor Hamilton approved an Assembly bill appropriating £24,000
"for the defense and protection of this province" in the emergency
created by the Indian uprising. In order to avoid controversies such as
had plagued previous supply bills and had prevented the passage of a
much needed measure at the end of the last Assembly's session in
September, the new act imposed no additional taxation, called for no
fresh emission of bills of credit, and introduced no unacceptable new
details of any sort. Half of the £24,000 was to come from available
bills of credit received in connection with the transfer to the colony
of its share of parliamentary grants; the remaining £12,000 was to be

---

graphical convenience an asterisk has been substituted above wherever this
symbol appears.

    9. For BF's trip from Boston to Philadelphia, see above, pp. 278–9.
    1. The travelers' host in New London may have been Joseph Chew, the
postmaster. BF had a number of friends in New Haven; possibly Jared Ingersoll, whom he had known well in London, entertained the party.

made up from the unexpended balances of three other, smaller funds previously established for various purposes.[2]

Following the practice of other supply acts since the beginning of the war with France, the act of 1763 named seven provincial commissioners—two councilors and five assemblymen—who, "with the consent and approbation of the governor or commander in chief of the province for the time being and not otherwise," were to order and direct the expenditure of the £24,000 appropriated. Franklin was one of the commissioners appointed.[3] Thus, three days after reaching home from his long trip to New England, he found himself at a meeting of the provincial commissioners engaged in a task with which he had become thoroughly familiar during the busy months of 1756: considering and passing on applications for funds required for a military emergency.

The procedure followed seems to have remained essentially unchanged: any four or more of the commissioners might sign an order to pay a specified sum to the person who had furnished supplies or services or was about to incur expenses for provincial defense. The payee then presented the order at the General Loan Office, received the money, and receipted the order. This document then became part of the records of the Loan Office.[4]

During the remaining weeks of 1763 the provincial commissioners issued fifteen orders, of which Franklin signed ten. Following the practice of earlier volumes these orders are listed below, showing the date, the name of the payee, a summary of the purpose, and the amount of each.[5] The orders which BF failed to sign are indicated by an asterisk (*) following the date. Orders issued after the beginning of 1764 will be similarly listed in the next volume.

Date	Payee	Purpose	Amount
			£ s. d.
November			
8	Robert Levers	Victualling troops	320 0 0
12*	Asher Clayton	Recruiting Capt. Nicholas Haasacre's Co.	150 0 0

2. *Statutes at Large, Pa.*, VI, 311–19, 546–7; *Votes*, 1763–64, pp. 6, 7, 8, 9.

3. The other commissioners were: Lynford Lardner (above, III, 12) and Thomas Cadwalader (above, I, 209 n) of the council; Joseph Fox (above, VI, 284 n), John Hughes (above, VI, 284 n), Joseph Galloway (above, VII, 29 n), and John Baynton (above, VII, 37 n), from the Assembly. All these men had served previously as commissioners.

4. For an extended account of the workings of the system and reproduction of a pay order, see above, VI, 392–4.

5. See above, VI, 395–6, 438–40; VII, 3–5, 25–8.

Date	Payee	Purpose	Amount		
14	Maj. Asher Clayton	Recruiting advance for Northampton Co.	50	0	0
14*	John Jennings	For bringing Moravian Indians to Phila- delphia[6]	107	18	2
16*	Joseph Fox	To support Moravian Indians at Province Island	100	0	0
16*	Timothy Horsfield	Indian expenses and expresses	78	14	5
28*	Dorcas Buchanan, Widow	Billeting soldiers	16	4	2
29	John Bissell	47 tomahawks for new forces	5	5	9
29	William Coleman	Pay as assistant judge	100	0	0
29	Robert Levers	Provisions for troops in Northampton and Berks Cos.	400	0	0
29	Phillip Shilling	Powder horns for troops in North- ampton Co.	3	2	6
29	Jeremiah Warder	Wampum, bar lead, and duffels for new troops	50	1	0
December					
7	Robert Erwin	Expence servant Benj. Roads enlisting in King's service	11	13	4
7	Joseph Shippen	Pay as Clerk to the Council. ordered Sept. 30, 1763	22	17	6
12*	Robert Callender	Provisions for provin- cial troops	3,352	10	0

6. The next volume will contain many references to these Indians and the strenuous efforts of BF and others to protect them from massacre by enraged whites.

From John Sargent[7]

ALS: American Philosophical Society

Dear Sir   Londo. 8 Novr 1763

I have not had the Pleasure of a Line from you since that of the 8th Augt. from Boston,[8] which I had answerd, soon after it came, by the last Packet, if I had not been prevented by my Family's being in some Confusion by my Son's being brought home ill from Eton.[9] Thank God all that now is happily over, and We are all well again.

And on coming to Town to day I find Capt. Marshall on the point of taking away his Bagg.[1] Which just affords me a few minutes to assure You of my constant Regard, and attention to every Thing that can be of the least Use to you.

It is old News to You to tell You Lord Egmont is preferrd to a higher Employ and Lord Hyde Joynt Post master General in his place.[2] Had the former continued I had taken Measures to have done what You wished.[3] I do not know whether the same may be necessary with Regard to his Successour, but as an honourable Mention can do no hurt, and I expect a Friend in Town this Winter who is intimate with Lord Hyde, I shall get Him to do that Justice to Your Character which I wish every one to do, and you may be sure of; where ever I have any Connection and that I am happy in doing it.

Every Thing is in Confusion with Us here. Party never ran so high and it is a Great Prejudice to the Publick Concern.

God knows how it will end! The Scene opens in Parliament next Week. Both Sides are confident of Success. The Ministry will undoubtedly carry their Point in Parliament Regarding Wilkes.

---

7. For John Sargent of Sargent Aufrere & Co., see above, VII, 322 n; IX, 359 n.

8. Not found.

9. Both of Sargent's sons, George Arnold and John, were at Eton at this time.

1. The brig *Hope*, Capt. A. Marshall, arrived in Philadelphia on Feb. 12, 1764, after a voyage of eleven weeks from London. *Pa. Jour.*, Feb. 16, 1764.

2. Lord Egmont (see above, p. 286 n), appointed joint postmaster general on Nov. 27, 1762, was advanced to first lord of the Admiralty on Sept. 10, 1763. For his successor Thomas Villiers, Baron Hyde, see above, p. 217 n.

3. BF had evidently asked Sargent to recommend him to Lord Egmont; as he had also asked Richard Jackson to do, June 10, 1763; see above, p. 286.

But it is much questioned whether They will in Westminster Hall; which may bring Them into great Embarassements.[4]

And between You and I it is not clear how They stand among Themselves, Not much united it is said, but by common Danger, and most amazingly unpopular!

So much for a Sketch of the Times!

I next present You with a more pleasing one, namely that of Your account on which You will please to note, We will allow You 5 per Cent Interest for the Money in our hands, and it shall not lye without advantage to You.[5]

I hope Your Son is well and happy in his Government. Pray present all our Compliments both to Him, and his Lady.

His Prudence and Situation equally keep Him out of the Way of Party Byasses. By which I dare say He will remain undisturbed. I shall have an Attention to Things, and should I hear or learn any Thing material to his Conduct, I will write Him.[6]

My Wife The Collonel[7] Mrs. Deane, and all the old Sett at Mayplace wish You Health and Happiness.

Mr. Jackson tells me He hath written to You and Mr. Coxe fully on our Project.[8] I can add nothing to his Exactness.

Believe me ever Dear Sir Yours most affectionately J SARGENT.

4. At the opening of Parliament, Nov. 15, 1763, the ministry with Lord North as its manager induced the House of Commons to vote, 273 to 111, that the *North Briton*, no. 45, was "a false, scandalous, and seditious libel." On the same day the notorious *Essay on Woman,* which Wilkes had printed on his private press, was read in the House of Lords and adjudged "a most scandalous, obscene, and impious libel." These steps laid the groundwork for Wilkes's expulsion from the House of Commons on Jan. 19, 1764. His trial for libel in the Court of King's Bench, Feb. 21, 1764, resulted in his conviction *in absentia* (he had fled to Paris on Dec. 24, 1763) and his outlawry on Nov. 1, 1764. Robert Rea, *The English Press in Politics, 1760–1774* (Lincoln, Neb., 1963), chap. 5.

5. In BF's Memorandum Book, 1757–1776 (above, VII, 167–8), there is an entry, undated but immediately following one of Feb. 11, 1764, recording the receipt of a letter from Sargent (almost certainly this one), stating that BF had £1654 5s. 11d. on deposit with Sargent Aufrere.

6. It would appear from this and other letters that WF's friends in England feared for his governorship, now that Lord Bute, during whose ministry he had been appointed, was out of office and highly unpopular.

7. For Col. William Deane, see above, VII, 321 n.

8. See below, pp. 369–70.

To Joshua Babcock

ALS: Yale University Library

Dear Friend   Philada. Nov. 10. 1763

Your Goodnature will be pleas'd to hear that your Guests went on well after they left you. We got early into New York the next Morning;[9] staid there one Day, had a Pleasant Passage over the Bay the next Morning; spent some time with Friends in different Places of the Jerseys, and got safe and well home on Saturday Evening, where we had the additional Happiness of finding all well. Sally joins in grateful Remembrance of your many Civilities and Kindnesses to us, at your House and on the Road; and in best Wishes of every Felicity to you and yours. Our Respects to good Mrs. Babcock, the Colonel and your other Children.[1] By next Post you will hear from Mr. Foxcroft and me;[2] he presents his Compliments. I am, with sincerest Esteem and Affection, Dear Sir Your most obedient humble Servant   B FRANKLIN

Addressed: To / Joshua Babcock Esqr / Westerly / Rhodeisland / Free / B FRANKLIN

Endorsed: B. Franklin of 10 Novr. 63 of his Arrival at Philadelphia

To Catharine Greene

ALS: American Philosophical Society

Dear Katy   [November 10, 1763][3]

I should ask Mr. Greene's Permission now to call you so, which I hope he will give me, making Allowance for the Strength of

9. This statement, in conjunction with BF's letter to Jane Mecom, November 7 (above, p. 362), makes clear that Babcock, and probably his wife, had accompanied the Franklin party from Westerly to New London and New Haven and then for another day's journey before they separated on October 30, one night away from New York City.

1. For Babcock's children, see above, IX, 397 n.

2. Not found; the communication probably related to Babcock's appointment as postmaster at Westerly, presumably discussed during the visit at his home.

3. William G. Roelker, ed., *Benjamin Franklin and Catharine Ray Greene Their Correspondence 1755–1790* (Phila., 1949), pp. 40–1, gives this date with only the year in brackets. The upper corner of the sheet is now too badly torn to leave any part of the date line decipherable. Roelker may have been

old Habits. This is to acquaint you and him that your Guests, after a very pleasant Journey, got well home on the 5th. Instant, without the least ill Accident, and had the additional Happiness of finding their Friends all well. Mr. Green's Goodnature and yours, will be pleas'd to hear this, and therefore I take the first Opportunity of writing it. Sally joins me in Thanks to you both, for all your kindness to us, and in best Wishes of Prosperity to you and yours. Please to acquaint Mr. Rufus Green[4] that I shall write to him per next Post. I am, Dear Friend Yours affectionately

B FRANKLIN

Addressed: To / Mrs Katharine Greene / at Greenwich / Rhode-island

From Richard Jackson

ALS: American Philosophical Society

Dear Sir   London. 12th Novr. 1763

It gives me great Concern to hear of your Misfortune.[5] I have the Consolation however to understand that the Case when taken in Time, is seldom attended with any lasting Inconvenience and I have hopes the Cure is perfectly effected when I write this. I can assure you with great Truth there is not a Man upon Earth in whose Welfare I interest myself more, and I have the Pleasure of finding my Sentiments on this Subject those of almost all Mankind.

Your Letter informing me of your Misfortune came yesterday, by Mr. Irving[6] whose Company I had the pleasure of having at

able to read the month and day when he printed the letter; certainly the substance of this and the letters to Jane Mecom and Joshua Babcock written early in November, printed above, shows that the date as here given is at least approximately correct.

4. Rufus Greene (1712–1784), merchant and iron manufacturer of East Greenwich, R.I., was a distant cousin of both the Greenes, and an uncle of Gen. Nathaniel Greene of Revolutionary War fame. Perhaps BF intended to appoint Rufus Greene to some position in the Post Office. *Ibid.*, p. 40.

5. BF's "dislocated Arm," mentioned in his letter to Jackson of Sept. 22, 1763; see above, p. 341.

6. Probably one of the Boston Ervings, either John (d. 1786), reputed to be the richest merchant in the town, or one of his sons, John (1727–1816), William (1734–1791), George (1735–1806), or James (b. 1736). The last named was in England in 1759.

Dinner the same Day. I must confess I have always believed that the Proposal made by Messrs. Coxes was to be understood as you understand it,[7] that we should become Purchasers in case the Grant should be confirmed or a Territory equivalent obtained, and that both the Risk of Success, and the Costs of Obtaining were to be theirs. In fact I have acted on this Plan for though I am desirous to close with the Offer, and find Mr. Sargent[8] so too, I have drawn £50 of the Credit Messrs. Coxe gave me on Messrs. Sargent &c. to pay the Disbursements at the Record Offices and Council where I have not yet presented a Memorial, not only because I have been disappointed in all my Searches (except that for the Grant to Sir Robert,[9] and in some Lights I have obtained at the Board of Trade) tis because the Notions, that our settling backward has been the Occasion of the present Indian War, are infinitly too prevalent, though I flatter myself now declining. When I judge proper actually to present the Memorial, (which I have drawn *by* me,) I shall Employ Mr. Life[1] as Sollicitor. As the Draught now stands, I have stated the Grant of K. William to Dr. Coxe because it is a Fact of the Utmost Importance, but I must new Model the Draught, if we have no Proof of its ever having existed.[2] At present, after a Search made by myself as well as the proper Officers for many Hours several Successive Days among the Inrollments of Grants the Warrants for making out the Grants, which are in the same Office the Alphabets Bundles of Warrants and Memorandums, at the Signet and Privy Seal

7. For the part BF proposed that he and Jackson play in the efforts of William and Daniel Coxe to get royal confirmation and exploit the family's title to "Carolana," see above, pp. 212–14, 254–5, 341–2.

8. John Sargent of Sargent Aufrere & Co.

9. Charles I's original grant of "Carolana" to Sir Robert Heath in 1629; see above, p. 213 n.

1. Thomas Life of Basinghall St., Cripplegate, London, was a lawyer whom BF employed occasionally—in attempting, for example, to prove Springett Penn's title to the proprietorship of Pa. In 1760 Life was appointed co-agent (with Jackson) for Conn. and in 1773–74 he was BF's solicitor in the matters growing out of the "Hutchinson letters" affair and the petition of the Mass. House of Representatives to have the governor removed from office. *Mass. Hist. Soc. Proc.*, LVI (1922–23), 104–17.

2. Dr. Daniel Coxe (1640–1730) bought the Heath grant from private individuals in 1696. Apparently his descendants had led Jackson to believe that he had acquired the grant through a royal patent.

Offices, I can find no Trace of it or of any Order or Direction for making it out, nor do I yet find at the Council Office or the Plantation Office any Proof of Application for such a Grant. I have but one chance left, the Bundles of Warrants are kept at the Rolls Chappel and without Order, being of little Use, almost every Grant being inrolled; many years are confounded together.[3] I saw all the Bundles indorsed 11 W3 picked out of a Heap covered with Dust, and then examined through each Bundle, but, a Bundle might escape me in the heap and I will examine the Heap again, and perhaps go through 10th and 12th of W3. Of this Search I should have some Hopes, but that I am in a great Measure deprived of them by the Searches made at the Signet and Privy Seal Offices. I send you Mr. Rookes[4] Certificate, he is record keeper at the Rolls and a very Diligent carefull Officer.

Having finished this Subject I will tell you the Occasion of my Doubt (for it was but Doubt) upon Messrs. Coxes Proposal. It did not arise from any Obscurity in your Letter,[5] you referred me only to Messrs. Coxes; they write.

We engage to dispose of a Moiety &c. and go on "If this offer of ours be agreable you will be so good as to signify your Approbation to *us directly* and it shall be confirmed accordingly to Dr. F. as you may direct, but if not we pray the favour of you to proceed for our own particular Account and Use for which purpose we inclose you a Credit on the Messrs. Sargent &c."

In the Offer there are no eventual words, and from the adding to it, I inferred the Expence was to be ours if we accepted the

3. Documents such as royal land grants bore the great seal. The procedure was complicated, involving the preparation of a succession of documents whereby each office concerned authorized the next to act. These preliminary texts of the ultimate patent may sometimes, but not always, be found among the records of the Signet Office and the Privy Seal Office. The final authorizing warrant, the writ of privy seal, was enrolled in the patent rolls at the Rolls Chapel in Chancery Lane, but these suffered greatly from neglect. For a full account of the procedure see Charles M. Andrews, *Guide to the Materials for American History, to 1783, in the Public Record Office of Great Britain,* 1 (Washington, 1912), 268–73.

4. Henry Rooke was clerk of the records in the Rolls Chapel from before 1762 to 1775.

5. See above, pp. 213–14, 341–2.

Offer and not Messrs. Coxes and did not know therefore but that the Purchase Money was intended to become due at the same time, because you observe if we accepted the Proposal, I was to proceed for *the Joint Account and Use* and Messrs. Coxes particular &c.

I am pressed in Time, I am just come to Town, I have a good deal of Law Business, and the Parliament meets on Tuesday, Mr. Wilkess Business will come on the first Day and the House of Commons will probably express a good deal of Resentment at the Use he has made of their Privilege.[6] The Session is likely to be attended with great Heats and Animosities, but then Appearances often deceive one. I fear something relating to America will be done very much against my Opinion, but I shall endeavour to prevent it by all the means in my Power both in the House and out of the House. I shall write you more on this Subject next Week.[7] At present I shall only say that though I wish the duty on foreign Molasses was but 1*d*. I shall not oppose a Duty of 2*d*. a Gallon.[8] I have proposed 1*d*. ½ because it seems by the best lights I can get the nearest the Measure,[9] I judge right not as Agent for the Province of Pennsylvania, but as a Member of the British House of Commons. As such too I shall be against all Inland Duties[1] laid by the Parliament of Britain on the Colonies, because I see a very dangerous Tendency of such Duties to the Ruin of both, but it will be to no purpose that I should oppose all Duties, for £200000 a year will infallibly be raised by Parlia-

6. For the outcome of "Mr. Wilkes's Business" in the House of Commons, see above, p. 366 n.

7. If such a letter was written, it has not been found.

8. In the spring of 1763 Charles Townshend, then president of the Board of Trade, proposed that the duty on foreign molasses imported into the American continental colonies, fixed at 6*d*. per gallon by the Molasses Act of 1733, should be lowered to 2*d*. per gallon. The idea of increasing the revenue raised in the colonies by lowering the molasses duty to a realistic figure (finally set at 3*d*.) and by vigorously enforcing it was embodied in the Sugar Act, passed April 5, 1764.

9. "It was well known that the cost of smuggling molasses was about 1½*d*. a gallon, the price for which collectors generally agreed to look the other way." Edmund S. and Helen M. Morgan, *The Stamp Act Crisis* (Chapel Hill, 1953), p. 26.

1. A reference to an unidentified proposal to lay what would soon be called "internal taxes" in America.

ment on the Plantations.[2] I wish I could contrive that a large share might fall on the West Indians. For the rest I can only say at present that it will be a great Point carried to exclude all Revenue Officers from hence, but Customhouse Officers, they are become Constitutional in North America.[3] The Province of Pennsylvania, is excluded from all Share of the Money granted by Parliament for the Service of 1761.[4] I think this hard and did all I could to serve them, but the General had excluded them in his Return made, of which I have many times wrote to you and Mr. Moore,[5] and wished that Applications might have been made to the General to amend this: I have discovered that the Generals Opinion was that the Service of their Troops was provincial only. The Lords of the Treasury have long since come to a Resolution which they now invariably adhere to, to hear no Evidence against the Generals Return. I fear this is not the only Ill Office the General has done the Province, I am now employed in removing some ill Impressions received from him. I must do Mr. Penn the Justice to say I had my Intelligence from him, and that he has joined with me on this Occasion. I am Dear Sir with the greatest Truth and Esteem Affectionately yours   RD. JACKSON

My father Sisters and Mr. Bridges[6] all beg their Compliments to you and the Governor of N J.

Endorsed: Mr Jackson to Dec. 10. 1764

---

2. The ministry had resolved to keep 10,000 troops in America and it was estimated that approximately £200,000 per year would be needed to pay them. *Ibid.*, p. 22.

3. Jackson probably meant that, because there had been British customs officers in the colonies since the seventeenth century, they should by now be regarded as "Constitutional," but that the placement of any other British revenue officers in the colonies should be prevented if possible.

4. Parliament reduced the total colonial grant for the campaign of 1761 from the previous £200,000 to £133,333. On the basis of Amherst's return, Pa., Md., and So. Car. received nothing. Gipson, *British Empire*, x, 47–8.

5. Charles Moore, clerk of the Pa. Assembly.

6. Jackson's brother-in-law.

From [Levi Andrew] Levy[7]

AL: American Philosophical Society

12 Novembr. [1763?]

Mr. Levys compliments to Mr. Frankling will be obliged to him if he can Answer the inclosed requisitions or any part of them.

Addressed: To / Doctor Frankling

From Francis Bernard

Letterbook copy: Harvard College Library

Sir   Castle William Novr. 14. 1763

A fortnight ago I took the Liberty to trouble you with a request that you would procure for My Son at Alexandria credit to return to Philadelphia, and a passage from thence to Boston.[8] I have just now received a Letter from him at Alexandria at Mr. Sebastian,[9] a Tavern Keeper there. Altho' I hope, before this Comes to your hand, that my Son will be considerably advanced in his return home; yet that nothing may be wanted to accelerate it, I have thought fit to trouble you with the enclosed.[1] If he is passed Philadelphia when you receive it, you will please to burn it. I am Sir   F B

Benjm. Franklin Esqr.

7. The mention in this brief note of "requisitions" suggests strongly a reference to BF's activities (with the other provincial commissioners) in providing supplies for the frontier. The only November after he had become a "Doctor" in which he was thus active was November 1763 (above, pp. 362–4). If this inference is correct, the writer might have been either Isaac or Samson Levy (1722–1781), both Philadelphia merchants, or more probably Levi Andrew Levy (fl. 1750–1790) of Lancaster, an Indian trader, land speculator, and storekeeper, the partner and son-in-law of Joseph Simon of Lancaster.

8. See above, pp. 353–4.

9. Not identified.

1. Not found.

From James Parker: Bond[2]

Printed form with MS insertions in blanks: American Philosophical Society

KNOW all Men, by these Presents, That *I, James Parker of Woodbridge in the County of Middlesex and Province of New Jersey Printer,* am Held and firmly bound unto *Benjamin Franklin, Esqr. of the City of Philadelphia* in the Sum of *Three Hundred and fifty Seven Pounds, Sixteen Shillings and one penny,* Lawful Money of *New York* to be paid to the said *Benjamin Franklin his* certain Attorney, Executors, Administrators or Assigns: To which Payment well and truly to be made, *I bind my self, my* Heirs, Executors and Administrators, firmly by these Presents. Sealed with *my* Seal, Dated the *Fifteenth* Day of *November* in the Year of our Lord One Thousand Seven Hundred and *Sixty three* and in the *Fourth* Year of the Reign of our Soverein Lord *George the Third* by the Grace of God, King of Great-Britain, &c.

THE Condition of this Obligation is such, That if the Above-bounden *James Parker his* Heirs, Executors, Administrators, or any of them, shall and do well and truly pay, or cause to be paid unto the above-named *Benjamin Franklin, or his* certain Attorney, Executors, Administrators or Assigns, the just and full Sum of *One hundred and Seventy eight Pounds, eighteen Shillings,* Lawful Money aforesaid, on the *Fourth Day of June next, which will be in the year of our Lord One Thousand Seven Hundred and Sixty four,* without any Fraud or further Delay, then the above Obligation to be void, or else to be and remain in full Force and Virtue.

Sealed and Delivered in   JAMES PARKER [Seal]
   the Presence of us
   WM. SELLERS
   THOMAS TILLYER

2. The execution of this bond probably resulted from an adjustment and settlement of the accounts between Parker and BF in June 1763; see above, p. 258 n. The major item causing Parker's net indebtedness to BF at that time seems to have been an "Invoice of Stationary Insurance and Charges £103 15s. 2d." sterling that BF had paid in London for Parker, Feb. 1, 1760; "Account of Expences," p. 51; *PMHB,* LV (1931), 126. The bond was for double the amount of the debt (plus a penny), shown in the second paragraph to have been £178 18s., N.Y. currency.

Philadelphia: Printed by B. Franklin, and D. Hall.

Endorsed: Nov. 15 1763 Bond J Parker £178. 18. o New York Money[3]

Desember the 10 1766 Reseved of of James Parker Cash 24-19
D FRANKLIN

Aprill the 18 1770 Reseved of J Parker in Cash 20-0.0[4]
D FRANKLIN

Directors of the Library Company of Philadelphia to John Penn and Reply

MS Minute Book, Library Company of Philadelphia; also printed in *The Pennsylvania Gazette,* November 24, 1763, and *The Pennsylvania Journal,* November 24, 1763.

John Penn (above, IV, 458 n), son of Richard Penn, who owned a quarter interest in the proprietorship of Pennsylvania, and nephew of the principal proprietor Thomas Penn, arrived in Philadelphia, Sunday, Oct. 30, 1763, aboard the *Philadelphia Packet,* Capt. Richard Budden, to replace James Hamilton as lieutenant governor of the colony.[5] Many of the religious and civic organizations of Pennsylvania rushed to present addresses to the new governor and the Library Company was was no exception. On Nov. 14, 1763, Franklin, Thomas Cadwalader (above, I, 209 n), and Samuel Rhoads (above, II, 406 n) were appointed a committee to prepare an address, which they submitted to the directors on November 17.[6] The directors approved it and on November 21 ordered the secretary to sign it. They then waited on Penn, who received the address and made a suitable reply.

3. This much of the endorsement is in BF's hand; the remainder is in DF's.

4. Two similar bonds from Parker to BF survive in APS, one dated Aug. 1, 1765, for a debt of £65 12s. sterling, the other dated May 15, 1767, for £166 10s., "Current Money of Great Britain," on both of which DF endorsed receipts for partial payment. After Parker's death, July 2, 1770, the determination of the outstanding obligation on these three bonds caused friction between the families and a somewhat angry letter to BF from Parker's daughter, Jenny Bedford, Feb. 2, 1773, APS.

5. *Pa. Journal,* Nov. 3, 1763. Penn read his commission, dated June 18, 1763, to the Pa. Council on Oct. 31, 1763. *Pa. Col. Recs.,* IX, 71–2.

6. Lib. Co. Minutes, Nov. 14, 17, 1763.

[November 21, 1763]
To the Honourable John Penn Esqr. Lieutenant Governor of the Province of Pennsylvania and Counties of New Castle, Kent and Sussex upon Delaware.

The Address of the Directors of the Library Company of Philadelphia.

May it please your Honour!

We the Directors of the Library Company of Philadelphia beg leave to present our cordial Congratulations to your Honour on your Appointment to this Government, and on your safe Arrival here.

It gives us particular Pleasure to see amongst us, in the Station of Governor, a Descendant of that Family which has always favoured our Institution and promoted it by their frequent and generous Benefactions.[7]

The Encouragements it met with in it's Infancy have had good Effects. Many other Libraries, after our Example and on our Plan, have been erected in this and the neighbouring Provinces; whereby usefull Knowledge has been more generally diffused in these remote Corners of the World.

We therefore, flatter ourselves that it will continue to enjoy the Favour of our Honourable Proprietaries, and meet with your Honour's Countenance and Protection during your Administration; in which we sincerely wish you all Happiness.

Signed by Order of the Board

November 21st. 1763   FRANCIS HOPKINSON,[8] Secry.

To which the Governor was pleased to make the following Answer

Gentlemen!

I thank you for your congratulatory Address on my Appointment to this Government, and am extremely rejoiced at the Prosperity of the Library under your Direction. You may depend that I shall not fail to give it my Countenance; and I make not the least Doubt but the Proprietors will continue to favour so useful an Institution.

7. For the Penn family's gifts of land and scientific apparatus to the Lib. Co., see above, II, 207–10, 312; III, 141, 156, 164; IV, 3 n.

8. See above, pp. 167–8 n.

From Mary Stevenson   ALS: American Philosophical Society

Dear Sir   Kensington Novr. 25th. 1763

I take the opportunity of writing by a Gentleman whom I wish
to recommend to your Notice. His Name is Lyth,[9] he is a Clergyman going to settle in Virginia, where he has the promise of a
Living, and I hope he will meet with the Success I believe he
deserves. The little I have seen of him has prejudic'd me in his
favour, but I do not recommend him upon so slight authority,
his being the intimate Friend of a truly worthy Man of his own
profession encourages me to think he will be an equal Ornament
to it.

I wrote to you a few days ago at my Mother's request,[1] who
was made very uneasy by your supposing it possible for her to
become indifferent; but she tells me there was no opportunity of
sending my Letter, therefore I [will] give you the substance of it
in this. You have [an] apparent tho' not a real Cause to be offended
with her, for you had great reason to expect to hear from her by
Capt. Friend,[2] and she desires me to tell you she went to his
House and prevail'd with him to take the Goods on board you
commission'd her to buy,[3] and the day before he was to sail she
sent a large packet of Letters to him for you by the Waterman

9. John Lyth of Newton Pickering, Yorkshire, B.A., Cambridge, 1756,
was paid the King's bounty of £20 on Dec. 8, 1763, to defray the expenses
of his voyage to America. He received a license from the Bishop of London,
Oct. 10, 1765, to preach in So. Car. in 1767. He apparently
served as a chaplain in the Va. militia in 1777. Gerald Fothergill, *A List of
Emigrant Ministers to America 1690–1811* (London, 1904), p. 41; Frederick
L. Weis, *The Colonial Clergy of Virginia, North Carolina, and South Carolina*
(Boston, 1955), p. 32; *Va. Mag. of Hist. and Biog.*, X (1903), 297.

1. Probably a reference to her letter of Nov. 16, 1763, not found but acknowledged in BF's letter of March 14, 1764, APS.

2. Capt. James Friend's ship, the *Carolina*, left Deal, outward bound, on
July 5 and arrived in Philadelphia on Sept. 20, 1763. *London Chron.*, July
5–7, 1763; *Pa. Gaz.*, Sept. 22, 1763.

3. In his Memorandum Book, 1757–1776 (see above, VII, 167–8), BF made
a notation on April 11, 1763, of sending Mrs. Stevenson two orders, totaling
£50 sterling, on his London bankers, Henton Brown & Son. It is not known
what he instructed her to buy with this money, but on Dec. 8, 1763, he
noted sending her an order for £60 sterling "to pay for Candlesticks" and
"a Suit of Clothes and 6 pair of Shoes."

you used to employ. In that packet was a Letter of mine, to which was added a postscript by Dr. Hawkesworth, at whose House I then was; a long Letter from my Mother, which she wrote sometime before, and, because she had not leisure to write at that time, she sent you a Letter of mine to her to let you see the reason she did not accept your Invitation; there was likewise a Letter from Mr. Small, and I believe some others.[4] I hope you will receive the packet, but, if not, you will now retract the Charge you have laid against those who never can forget you. My Mother presents her Thanks for the Candles you were so kind to send her. They could not be legally imported, but Mr. Small gives her hopes that she shall get them smuggled. What will you say to that?[5]

I hope you are recover'd from the bad Effects of the Accident you met with.[6] Many must suffer when you feel pain.

My poor Aunt Rooke continues lame; she has lately been very ill, but is, thank God! recover'd.[7] My Mother's Health is but indifferent, and she won't take as much care of herself as she ought to do: I wish you were in England, for you have an influence over her. I have heard of my Friend Pitt's safe arrival in her Native Country.[8]

4. No letters have been found from Polly and her mother which can be certainly identified as among those in the packet described here as carried by Captain Friend; but see below, pp. 427–9. Alexander Small's letter of July 5, 1763 (above, pp. 306–9), might have just reached this ship in time.

5. Acts of 1709 and 1710 had laid substantial duties on the importation of candles into Great Britain. Charges of frauds and abuses led Parliament in 1750 to forbid their importation except in containers holding at least 224 lbs. of candles, the containers to be stowed openly in the ship's hold. 23 Geo. III, c. 21, sect. 27. Apparently BF had sent a small package of candles—perhaps made from spermaceti—as a gift to Mrs. Stevenson. No letter of his has been found commenting on this proposal, but writing to Polly, Sept. 2, 1769 (APS), he explained her mother's tolerance of smuggling as based on an honest resentment of "the Waste of those Taxes in Pensions, Salaries, Perquisites, Contracts and other Emoluments for the Benefit of People she does not love, and who do not deserve such Advantages, because—I suppose because they are not of her Party."

6. For BF's two falls and injuries to his shoulder during his trip to New England, see above, pp. 276, 278, 338.

7. Mrs. Rooke had been suffering from "Gout in her stomach"; see above, p. 334.

8. Polly's friend, Miss Pitt, had sailed for Jamaica early in 1763.

My best Respects attend Mrs. and Miss Franklin. I am with the truest Esteem and Gratitude Dear Sir Your faithful and affectionate Servant   M STEVENSON

From Henton Brown[9]   ALS: American Philosophical Society

Benj: Franklin Esqr   London Nov 26 1763
Esteemed Friend
    I embrace this opportunity per the extra packett to acknowledge the receipt of the several letters[1] and to transmitt a State of the account as it now Stands with us[2]—that drawn payable to Stevenson £25—has not yet appeared.[3] I understand Richard Jackson Esqr. here is appointed Agent to the province of Pensilvania.[4] I shall be greatly obliged if thou will be so good to recommend us to him to be bankers to the province as we were to the late Richd. Partridge deceased[5]—we are so to him for the province of Connecticut but have not Spoke to him on that of Pensilvania thinking it would be better taken and come with more weight by a recommendation from thee which we shall esteem as a favour.[6] We have had very indefferent times. The failures at Holland and Hamburgh S. Touchett and others here[7] have all contributed to

    9. For Brown, senior partner in Henton Brown & Son, BF's banker during his first mission to England, see above, IX, 218–19 n.
    1. None of these have been found.
    2. This account is printed at the end of the present letter.
    3. A mistake by the Browns; see the account. The "Stevenson £25" here appears to have been inserted in a space left blank when the letter was first written.
    4. For Jackson's appointment, April 2, 1763, see above, p. 247 n.
    5. Richard Partridge, formerly the agent of Pa., died on March 6, 1763.
    6. Whether by inadvertence or by design, BF appears not to have recommended Henton Brown & Son to Jackson.
    7. Gent. Mag., XXXIII (Aug. 1763), 411, reported the failure of 31 mercantile houses at Amsterdam and 14 at Hamburg. Samuel Touchet (c.1705–1773), M.P., Shaftesbury, 1761–68, was an important though apparently somewhat unscrupulous London merchant, who became a leading government contractor and financier. A friend and adviser of Charles Townshend, he recommended the duties which Townshend imposed upon America in 1767. Touchet stopped payment on Oct. 21, 1763, owing about £300,000. His failure and those in Holland and Hamburg were caused, though in some cases rather indirectly,

the fall of the Stocks 10 and 12 per Cent and some more which has Scattered distress in various Shapes and been very extensive, to which may be added the unsettled State of the ministry—the Court has [a] great majority as appeared in the house upon the question relative to Wilkes North Brittain No. 45 which was 309 to 110.[8] He has had a duel with Sam Martin late of the treasury was wounded with a shot in the belly but it is said he is like to recover[9]—the above paper is voted to be burnt by the hands of the Common Hangman and it is thought the authour above will be expelled but no farther proceedings will be against him untill he is able to attend the house.[1]

I am very respectfully for self and Son thy Obliged Friend

HENTON BROWN

———

by the failure of the Amsterdam banking house of Neufville on July 25, 1763. Namier and Brooke, *House of Commons*, III, 533–6.

8. The vote in the House of Commons, Nov. 15, 1763, on whether John Wilkes's *North Briton* No. 45 was libelous was 273 in the affirmative, 111 in the negative. An earlier vote on a technicality also went against Wilkes 300 to 111. Robert Rea, *The English Press in Politics 1760–1774* (Lincoln, 1963), pp. 73–4.

9. Samuel Martin (1714–1788), M.P., Camelford, 1747–68, Hastings, 1768–74; secretary of the Treasury, Nov. 1756–April 1757, April 1758–April 1763, was "one of the men closest to Bute" and was apparently attacked by Wilkes for this reason. In *North Briton* No. 37 Wilkes called Martin "a very apt tool of ministerial persecution" and in No. 40 "the most treacherous, base, selfish, mean, abject, low-lived and dirty fellow that ever wriggled himself into secretaryship." Martin in the parliamentary debate of Nov. 15, 1763, repaid Wilkes in his own coin, calling him "a cowardly, malignant, and scandalous Scoundrel," and the next day challenged him to a duel which was fought within hours and in which Wilkes received a painful wound in the side. Namier and Brooke, *House of Commons*, III, 114–16; George Nobbe, *The North Briton* (N.Y., 1939), pp. 174, 186, 245–50.

1. For Wilkes's expulsion from the House of Commons, see above, p. 366 n.

2. In the MS the debit and credit columns are placed in parallel horizontally on the paper, but for typographical convenience they are printed here in sequence. All entries through the £35,868: 18 8 total in the debit column and all through the 58. 19: 9 balance in the credit column were in the account as sent to BF by Henton Brown. The remainder of each column, including the words "Balla: due to B F" in the credit column, is in BF's hand, indicating his additions and revisions.

[Enclosure]

Benjamin Franklin Esqr with Henton Brown & Son[2]

Dr

	To Sundries per acct furnish'd[3]	£35780.	12		
Ap 26. To	Stevenson[4]	20			
June 14	do	30			
23	Allison[5]	2.	10.	4	
Aug 2	Strahan	25	–	–	
31	Hall	8.	3.	10	
Oct 11	Beale	2.	12.	6	
		£35,868:	18	8	
	Stevenson[6]	60.	0.	0	
	WF's Ballance[7]	20.	17.	0	
	Error Steevens on Grant of July 1. 1763 that Bill being sent to Mrs. Stevenson[8]	20.	0.	0	
	Geo. Dillwyn[9]	7.	3.	4	
	Becket[1]	12.	0.	0	
		£35,988:	19:	0	
	T Collinson[2]	31.	15.	3	
	P. Collinson	2.	7.	6	
		36:023:	1:	9	
	May 1. Stevenson	20.	0.	0	

3. Included in this large sum and the comparable sum in the credit column are almost certainly Pa.'s share of the parliamentary grant for 1758 (see above, IX, 241–2) and the funds which Isaac Norris sent BF during his first mission for the purpose of buying stock (see above, VIII, 147–8).

4. For this and the following order, see a note to the document immediately above.

5. In his Memorandum Book, 1757–1776 (above, VII, 167–8), BF noted, April 13, 1763, that he had drawn on the Browns for £2 10s. 4d. sterling "in favour of Mr. M. Allison of Falmouth being Balla. of his Acct for News Papers sent to our Printing Office."

6. See a note to the document immediately above.

7. In his Memorandum Book BF recorded, March 29, 1764, sending the Browns a bill for £20 17s. sterling to cover a balance due them for WF.

(Remaining footnotes for this table on next page)

Cr

By Sundries per acct furnished		£35757.	18. 5
Grant		20	
Sargent[3]		150	

		35927:	18: 5
		35868.	18. 8

Balla: due to B F.		58:	19: 9

Query { more the Order for Stevenson mention'd in this Letter suppos'd to be a Mistake for that of Strahan £25 which being included in the £35,780: 12. o should be carried to my Credit } ... 25. 0. 0

	Also Sturgeon on Waring[4]	7.	18. 0
July 1. 1763	Stevens on Grant	20.	0. –
Jan. 1. 1764	Do on Do	20.	0

		£131:	17: 9
Mar 17. 1764	Two Bills[5]	29.	0. 0
Apr. 11	one Do[6]	45.	0 0
May 5	one Do	49.	4. [5]

---

8. BF frequently sent bills to England drawn by Mrs. Mary Stevens (or Steevens) on Sir Alexander Grant; see, for example, above, VII, 368 n. On Dec. 8, 1763, he entered a query in his Memorandum Book "whether I sent to her [Mrs. Stevenson] or Messers. Brown, the last Bill on Sir Alexander Grant drawn July 1. 1763. by Mrs. Stevens here." This bill and the one for £20 entered below may have comprised the £40 Mrs. Stevenson mentioned in her undated letter, below, p. 427.

9. Recorded in Memorandum Book, May 17, 1764.

1. On Aug. 10, 1764, the bookseller Thomas Becket (above, IX, 274 n) acknowledged receiving a letter from BF of June 17, 1764, enclosing a bill for £12.

2. These bills in favor of Thomas and Peter Collinson are not entered in BF's Memorandum Book nor referred to in surviving correspondence.

3. On March 24, 1763, BF recorded sending the Browns a bill for £150 sterling, drawn by the trustees of the Pa. Loan Office on Sargent Aufrere.

4. Recorded in Memorandum Book, Feb. 11, 1764.

5. Recorded March 29, 1764.

6. This and the next bill were recorded May 1, 1764. The 5d., missing from the end of the MS, is supplied from the Memorandum Book entry.

To George Whitefield[7] ALS: Morristown National Historical Park

Dear Sir   Philada. Nov. 28. 1763
   Inclos'd is a Packet I receiv'd under my Cover from Boston, which I thought to have deliver'd into your Hands, but am told you do not return hither from Princetown, as was expected, and are gone forward to N York, which mortifies me not a little, that I should so long omit waiting on you here, as to be at length finally depriv'd of the Pleasure of seeing you.[8]
   Wherever you are, you have the sincere Esteem and best Wishes of Dear Sir, Your affectionate Friend and most obedient Servant   B FRANKLIN

To the Revd. G Whitefield

Endorsed: Franklin Answer'd   F

To Jonathan Williams

Photostat: Historical Society of Pennsylvania

Loving Kinsman,   Philada. Nov. 28. 1763
   I receiv'd yours acquainting me that the Chair is shipt.[9] It is not yet come to hand, but the Armonica is arrived safe, not a

---

7. For George Whitefield, the famous evangelist, see above, II, 241 n. Whitefield landed in Va. toward the end of August 1763 for what was destined to be his last visit to America. He reached Philadelphia on September 20 receiving a warm welcome there even from the previously hostile Anglican clergy. He visited Princeton about November 14, and after "four sweet seasons" of preaching at the college and two at Elizabeth Town, N.J., went to N.Y. and then on to New England, where he stayed until June 1764. He then went to Ga., stopping at Philadelphia on the way, and returned there in May 1765, just before he sailed to England from N.Y., June 9, 1765. *Pa. Gaz.*, Sept. 15, 22, 1763; Luke Tyerman, *The Life of the Rev. George Whitefield* (London, 1876–77), II, 467–86. William S. Perry, *Papers Relating to the History of the Church in Pennsylvania* (privately printed, 1871), pp. 354–5, 360; *PMHB*, XVIII (1894), 37–8.

8. Whitefield's departure from Philadelphia must have taken place a little more than a week after BF's return from New England.

9. When BF and his party traveled to New England in the summer of 1763, they used a "Kittareen [kittereen] Chair," a West Indian term for a kind of one-horse carriage. He may have left the chair in Boston (perhaps for repairs) and had it shipped after him, or he may have commissioned Williams to buy

Glass hurt.[1] I am much obliged by your Care of my little Affairs. The House, when repair'd, I would have you let to as good a Tenant and for as good a Rent as you can well get: and let me have the Account of Repairs, that it may be adjusted as soon as possible.[2]

My Wife and Daughter join in Love to you and yours, with Your affectionate Uncle   B FRANKLIN

Mr. Foxcroft's Compliments I am desired by him to add.

It is farther my Desire and Direction, that the Rent of the House be applied to assist my Sister Mecom in the Maintanance of her unhappy Son, and I request you to pay it to her for that purpose as it arises.   B FRANKLIN

Addressed: To | Mr. Jonathan Williams | Mercht | Boston | Free | B FRANKLIN

Endorsed: Dr Franklin Novr 28 1763 F

To Sir Alexander Dick   ALS: New York Public Library

Dear Sir   Philada. Dec. 11. 1763

I take the Opportunity of a Ship from this Place to Leith,[3] once more to pay my Respects to my good Friend from this Side the Water, and to assure him that neither Time nor Distance have in the least weakened the Impression on my Mind, stampt there

---

a new one and send it to him. See BF's Memorandum Book, 1757–1776 (above, VII, 167–8), entry of May 29, 1763, and William G. Roelker, ed., *Benjamin Franklin and Catharine Ray Greene Their Correspondence 1755–1790* (Philadelphia, 1949), p. 35.

1. BF had brought an armonica home with him in 1762; see above, p. 119 n. Either he sent this one to Boston (probably by water) before his journey to New England in the summer of 1763 so that he could play it for his friends there, or had ordered another one sent from England directly to Boston, and Williams had now sent it to Philadelphia.

2. See above, p. 356, for Williams' account of the expenses incurred in repairing the house formerly belonging to BF's sister Elizabeth Douse and for the rent which it produced for the support of Jane Mecom's insane son, Peter.

3. *Pa. Gaz.*, Dec. 8, 1763, reported that the ship *Boyd*, Captain Dunlap, was outward bound for Leith and on the 15th that it had cleared.

by his Kindness to me and my Son, while we were in Scotland.[4] When I saw him last, we talk'd over the pleasant Hours we spent at Prestonfield, and he desired me, whenever I should write, to join with mine his best Respects to you and to Lady Dick, your amiable Daughter and the rest of your domestic Circle.[5] He is very happy in his Government as well as in his Marriage.

My Daughter has been endeavouring to collect some of the Music of this Country Production, to send Miss Dick, in Return for her most acceptable Present of Scotch Songs.[6] But Music is a new Art with us. She has only obtain'd a few Airs adapted by a young Gentleman of our Acquaintance to some old Songs,[7] which she now desires me to enclose, and to repeat her Thanks for the Scotch Music, with which we are all much delighted. She sings the Songs to her Harpsichord, and I play some of the softest Tunes on my Armonica, with which Entertainment our People here are quite charmed, and conceive the Scottish Tunes to be the finest in the World. And indeed, there is so much simple Beauty in many of them, that it is my Opinion they will never die, but in all Ages find a Number of Admirers among those whose Taste is not debauch'd by Art.[8]

I expected before this Time some of yours and Dr. Hope's botanical Orders to execute, which I shall do with great Pleasure whenever they come to hand.[9]

Be pleased to present my Respects to our Friends the Russels, when you see them; to the two Doctors Monro, Dr. Cullen, Dr.

4. On the visit of BF and WF to Sir Alexander and Lady Dick at Prestonfield, Oct. 6–12, 1759, see above, VIII, 431, 440–1, 442–4.

5. Janet, Lady Dick, whom BF had known in Scotland, had died Dec. 26, 1760. Sir Alexander had married Mary Butler of Pembrokeshire, March 23, 1762. The elder daughter, to whom BF refers here and in the next paragraph, was named Janet for her mother and was about fourteen at the time BF was writing.

6. If the "Scotch Songs" were not MS copies, as seems possible, Janet Dick's gift to Sally may have been one of several collections published by Robert Bremner (d. 1789). DNB.

7. Probably Francis Hopkinson. See above, p. 233, and George E. Hastings, The Life and Works of Francis Hopkinson (Chicago, [1926]), pp. 70–4.

8. Franklin explained his particular enjoyment of Scottish tunes in a letter to Lord Kames, June 2, 1765, Scottish Record Office. His preference for simple music appears in several letters of later date.

9. See above, p. 16.

Clark, Mr. M'Gawen, and any others who may do me the Honour to enquire after me,[1] not forgetting Pythagoras, who, from his Temperance I conclude is still living and well.[2] I send him the Picture of a Brother Philosopher in this Country.[3] And withal I send you a Piece of our American Husbandry, which will show you something of the State of Agriculture among us; and a Book of our Poetry too, which from so remote a Country may probably be esteem'd some Curiosity if it has no other Merit.[4]

    With the sincerest Esteem and Affection, I am, Dear Sir, Your most obedient humble Servant   B FRANKLIN

Sir Alexr Dick

Library Company of Philadelphia: Rules for the Librarian

MS Minute Book, Library Company of Philadelphia; also printed in *The Charter, Laws, and Catalogue of Books, of the Library Company of Philadelphia* (Philadelphia, 1764), pp. 19–21.

On Nov. 14, 1763, the directors of the Library Company appointed a committee consisting of Franklin, Francis Alison, Samuel Rhoads, and Charles Thomson to prepare a set of rules for the conduct of the librarian. The committee reported at the meeting of the Board of Directors on Dec. 12, 1763. The librarian at this time was one John

    1. The persons mentioned are: James Russell (d. 1773), apothecary surgeon (above, p. 22 n); Alexander Monro, primus (1697–1767), professor of anatomy at Edinburgh (*DNB*), and Alexander Monro, secundus (1733–1817), his father's associate at Edinburgh (see above, IX, 230 n); William Cullen (1710–1790), professor of chemistry at Edinburgh (above, VII, 184 n); George Clark, later author of a paper on shallow plowing in *Essays and Observations, Physical and Literary* of the Philosophical Society of Edinburgh, III (1771), 56–67. "Mr. M'Gawen" is not identified beyond the fact that in a letter to WF, Jan. 30, 1772 (APS), BF mentioned "Mr. McGowen" as one of their "old Acquaintance" whom he had again met at Edinburgh in the autumn of 1771.
    2. For John Williamson of Moffat, called "Pythagoras" by the Dick family, see above, VIII, 445 n.
    3. Possibly a picture of Benjamin Lay, Pa. eccentric, painted by William Williams and engraved by Henry Dawkins; see above, II, 357 n; VIII, 92.
    4. The first of these books was probably Jared Eliot's *Essays upon Field-Husbandry in New-England* in either the Boston or N.Y. enlarged edition of 1761. The second book may have been one of the "Poetic Pieces of our young Geniuses" or "Blossoms of American Verse," as BF had called them to Strahan and Whiteford a year earlier; see above, pp. 167, 173.

Edwards, who served for only a few months and was succeeded, Feb. 13, 1764, by Francis Hopkinson, the company's secretary.[5]

[December 12, 1763]

The Committee appointed for that Purpose produced to the Board a Sett of Rules to be observed by the Librarian; which were approved of, and are as follows.

"RULES, made by the Directors, in Pursuance of a Law of the Company, to be observed in the Library, relating to the lending of Books &ca.

"1st. The Librarian is to give Attendance on Saturdays from 4 o'Clock till 8 in the Afternoon at the Library in Order to lend out and receive in the Books; and shall keep a Book Columnwise, in which shall be noted the Title of the Book lent, the Name of the Borrower, the Time for which the Book is lent, the Sum for which the Note was given, the Day when the Book should be returned and the Forfeitures weekly arising for all Defaults.

"2dly. Each Borrower, being a Member of the Company shall give a Promissary Note to the Librarian for the Sum set in the written Catalogue against the Book he borrows, conditioned for returning the same Book within the Time mentioned in the said Catalogue; at the Expiration of which Time, if the Borrower inclines to keep the Book longer, he must renew his Note.

"3dly. A Borrower, not being a Member, shall sign a Note and deposite with the Librarian the Sum against the Book in the Catalogue, as a Security for his returning the Book as aforesaid; and shall pay 8*d*. per Week for Folios, 6*d*. for Quartos and 4*d*. for others for the Use of the Library; to be applyed towards repairing of Bindings, encreases of the Books &c.

"4thly. Every Borrower who keeps a Book beyond the Time limited in his Note; may return it on any of the four next succeeding Attendance Days paying One Shilling for every Week's Neglect. Which not being done, the Note or Deposite Money is to [be] deemed forfeit.

"5thly. If a Borrower, who has forfeited his Note or Money deposited, shall afterwards return the Book three fourths of the Sum mentioned in his Note shall be remitted; he paying the

5. *Catalogue of the Books Belonging to the Library Company of Philadelphia* (Phila., 1835), I, xxxvi.

weekly Fine; and, if not a Member, both the Fine and weekly Hire of the Book as above.

"6thly. Books returned are to be delivered into the Hands of the Librarian to be examined whether damag'd or not.

"7thly. No Borrower from whom any Penalty or Forfeiture is due, or who hath damag'd any Book shall be permitted to borrow another Book, till Satisfaction be made.

"8thly. No Borrower may lend a Book to any Person out of his House.

"9thly. When a Member of the Company applies for a Book that happens to be lent out, the Librarian (if desired) is to take a Memorandum of the Application, and the first Borrower shall not be allowed to renew his Note; but must return the Book at the Time agreed on; that the new Applier may have it.

"10thly. The Librarian may lend to one Person at one Time 2 Volumes in Octavo, 3 in Duodecimo, and four Pamphlets, provided they have been in the Library at least Twelve Months.

"11thly. Every Saturday Evening, before the Library is shut up, the Librarian shall examine his Book of Entries and make out a List of the Forfeitures which have arisen that Week; in a Book to be kept for that Purpose; and on the Second Monday in every Month he shall from that List deliver a Copy to the Secretary of all the Forfeitures incurred the preceeding Month to be laid before the Directors at their usual Meetings."

To Ezra Stiles ALS: Universitätsbibliothek Leipzig, Sammlung Kestner

In the spring of 1763 Ezra Stiles began to experiment with the raising of silkworms at his home in Newport, R.I. When Franklin visited him in early July the minister's 3,000 worms were just beginning to cocoon, and he had just finished the strenuous task of gathering up to five bushels of mulberry leaves each day from his own and neighbors' trees to satisfy their voracious appetites.[6] No doubt Stiles regaled his visitor with accounts of his experience and asked for any information Franklin could supply on various stages of the production of silk.

6. For an account of Stiles's experiments with the production of silk, see Edmund S. Morgan, *The Gentle Puritan A Life of Ezra Stiles, 1727–1795* (New Haven and London, 1962), pp. 147–51.

This letter represents Franklin's effort to help his friend. The editors have been unable to identify the prints he sent or the Chinese pictures from which they were derived. Whether they proved helpful to Stiles is unknown; in any case, as late as the following June Franklin had not heard whether Stiles had even received the prints.[7]

Dear Sir   Philada. Dec. 12. 1763

According to my Promise I send you herewith the Prints copied from Chinese Pictures concerning the Produce of Silk. I fancy the Translator of the Chinese Titles, has sometimes guess'd and mistaken the Design of the Print, in his Account of what is represented in it. But of this you will better judge than I can. I have some Accounts of the Silk in Italy which I will, the first Leisure I have, transcribe and send you. I am with great Esteem, Dear Sir, Your most obedient humble Servant   B Franklin

ps. Did I leave with you Æpinus's Discourse on the Distribution of Heat over the Earth? If not, I have forgot what I have done with it.[8]

Addressed: To | The Revd Mr Stiles | Newport | Rhodeisland | per favour of | Capt Durfey. | with a Parcel[9]

Endorsed: Recd. 27 Dec 1763 Doctor Franklin

From Francis Bernard[1]   Letterbook copy: Harvard College Library

Sir   Boston Decr. 13. 1763

The Surveyor General[2] having this day acquainted me that he shall to morrow send an express to Philadelphia, I take this

7. BF to Stiles, June 19, 1764, Yale Univ. Lib.

8. See above, p. 351 n. In his letter of June 19, 1764, cited immediately above, BF acknowledged the return of this work.

9. *Pa. Gaz.*, Dec. 8, 1763, reported that sloop *Ranger*, Capt. E. Durfee, was entered outward for R.I., and on the 22d reported its clearance.

1. On the subject matter of most of this letter, see above, pp. 353–4.

2. John Temple (1732–1798), was born in Boston in a family related to the Grenvilles and Pitts in England. He married a daughter of James Bowdoin (above, IV, 69 n). He was surveyor general of the customs for the Northern District, 1761–67; one of the commissioners of the customs, 1767–74; lieutenant governor of New Hampshire, 1761–74; and the first British consul general in the U.S., 1785–98. He succeeded to the Temple baronetcy in 1786.

oppurtunity to add to the trouble I have before given you on Account of my Son. By the last Post I received a letter dated Alexandria Novr. 16; by which I find he had not then been made acquainted with any orders of yours in his favor, which is well accounted for by his adding that there were then two mails due from Philadelphia.

As the Bearer of this (Mr. Wyer[3]) is well known to me, and will go to Philadelphia to return hither immediately if my Son shall not be forwarded to me, when this Messenger arrives, I should like to have him return with him, as Wyer is quite a Master of the road, and can, I suppose, furnish him with a horse from Stage to Stage, and will take due care of him. If He should not be arrived at Philadelphia when Wyer comes, I would have Wyer (with your Approbation, as the expediency will depend upon Circumstances) go on to Alexandria, for which Journey I must be alone answerable to him: but this will depend upon the Necessity of his returning from Philadelphia immediately; of which I am not now a Judge. So that upon the whole I must beg the favour of you to order evry thing as you shall think for the best. As I think it greatly against probability that my Son will return with Wyer, as I suppose the Much greater chance will be that he is set out before, I shall not provide Wyer with Money, relying upon your goodness, if there should be occasion to furnish him with what shall be Necessary, which will be thankfully re-paid whenever you shall order it.

Least my Son should suffer in your opinion by his extravaga-tion, which you may Perceive has not been agreable to me, I will give you my real thoughts of him. He is an uncommon schollar being master of the Latin Greek and Hebrew Languages to a greater perfection than I believe allmost any of his age is of all the three. His present Misfortune is that having been worked too much (by Himself) in litteral learning, he now runs riot at the entrance of Science, altho' abundant curiosity is among his chief faults. He is therefore impelled by a precipitate desire of hurrying into the Study of Life and manners, altho' in my Opinion by no

His involvement with BF in the affair of the Hutchinson letters in 1772 and the somewhat equivocal part he played during the American Revolution will bring him more extended notice in later volumes.

3. Probably an employee of the customs service.

means qualifyed for it as yet: whereas I think it necessary that he should pass thro' the medium of Science, before he begins to read men. This is at present or rather is to be an interesting dispute between us, which must be soon determined by his returning or not to Christ Church at Oxford of which he is a Student, an appointment equivalent to that of a fellow of another Colledge.[4]

I informed you, when at Boston of my thoughts of Sending a Son of mine to the Colledge at Philadelphia;[5] and desired that you would furnish me with advice concerning lodging of him and other management. He is a very good Classick Scholar for his age, which is under 14, and will be above the common pitch by next Summer, as he now remains at School beyond the usuall time of the class he is in, all of which, besides himself, according to usage, went to College last Summer. I should not choose to Spend more of his time than 3 years in Academical Exercises, which I think you told me was all that was required at Pensylvania. I should be glad to have your thought upon this Subject at your own time. I am &c.

Benjm. Franklin Esqr.

4. In a letter of March 31, 1764, to his patron and relative by marriage, Lord Barrington, Governor Bernard gave a somewhat longer and more candid appraisal of his son, stressing the youth's instability and "boundless Curiosity." Illustrating the latter characteristic, the father commented: "I dare say He had rather be appointed Secretary to an Embassy to China, than have a place of five times the Value at home." Edward Channing and Archibald C. Coolidge, eds., *The Barrington-Bernard Correspondence and Illustrative Matter 1760–1770* (Cambridge, Mass., 1912), pp. 73–5.

5. This was Thomas Bernard (1750–1818), the governor's third son. Instead of attending the College of Philadelphia, he went to Harvard, receiving his A.B. in 1767. He was called to the bar from the Middle Temple in 1780, specialized for some years in conveyancing, and then retired to devote himself to philanthropic enterprises. He was treasurer of the Foundling Hospital, 1795–1806; a founder of the Royal Institution, Piccadilly, 1800; chancellor of the diocese of Durham, 1801; and helped to establish, among other institutions, a school for training teachers at Bishop Aukland in 1808. Two years later he inherited from his next older brother the baronetcy which had been conferred on their father in 1769. *DNB*.

From Frederick Shinkle: Bill and Receipt

ADS: Historical Society of Pennsylvania

Mr. Benjamin Franklin Esqr.
  To Frederick Shinkle⁶

1762

January 8	To 1 pr. Breeches for Dunlaps⁷ Negroe	£1.	7. –

1763

May. 13	To 1 pr. Breeches for Negroe	1.	7. –
	To Washing and altering 2 pr. Breeches	–	7. 6
	To 1 [*illegible*] Wool	–	2. –
	To 2 pr. Gloves at 7s. 6d.	–	15. –

£3. 18. 6

Dec. 13. 1763 Recd the within in full of all Accounts per me⁸

FREDERICK SHINKLE

Endorsed: F. Shinkle old Acct

To Jane Mecom

ALS: American Philosophical Society

Dear Sister   Philada. Dec. 15. 1763

I thank you for your kind Congratulations on my safe Return. Brother Peter is with me, and very well, except being touch'd a little in his Head with something of *the Doctor,* of which I hope to cure him.⁹ For my own Part, I find myself at present quite clear of Pain, and so have at length left off the cold Bath; there is however still some Weakness in my Shoulder, though much stronger

---

6. Shinkle seems to have been a Philadelphia tailor or leatherworker who specialized in breeches and gloves for Negroes. Several similar bills of later dates survive.

7. Probably William Dunlap (see above, V, 199 n; VII, 158), postmaster at Philadelphia.

8. This much of the receipt, and the endorsement, are in BF's hand.

9. Peter Franklin (C.9) may have traveled to Philadelphia with BF and Sally, or come from Newport by himself soon afterwards. He was appointed postmaster of Philadelphia sometime in 1764, probably in October. Later letters from DF to BF report that Peter was in poor health but, fancying his own medical knowledge, treated himself repeatedly though unsuccessfully. He died July 1, 1766.

than when I left Boston, and Mending.[1] I am otherwise very happy in being at home, where I am allow'd to know when I have eat enough and drank enough, am warm enough, and sit in a Place that I like, &c. and no body pretends to know what I feel better than I do myself.[2] Don't imagine that I am a whit the less sensible of the Kindness I experienc'd among my Friends in New England, I am very thankful for it, and shall always retain a grateful Remembrance of it. Remember me affectionately to all that enquire after Dear Sister, Your loving Brother B FRANKLIN

My Compliments to good Mrs. Bowles.[3] Sally writes.

To Thomas Becket[4]   ALS: Columbia University Library

Sir   Philada. Dec. 17. 1763

I have received yours of Sept. 12. with the Pamphlets, as mentioned.[5] I have before acknowledged yours of June 24, which came duly to hand with the Books &c. I approve of your continuing Les Arts et Metieres.[6]

The Directors of the Library Company thought the Books you sent them rather higher charg'd than usual;[7] they had therefore,

1. For the injury to BF's shoulder incurred on a trip between Boston and Portsmouth, see above, p. 338.

2. Apparently Jane Mecom and others in Boston had been somewhat over-solicitous for her brother's comfort and well-being while he was in Boston.

3. Grace Davenport Bowls (or Bowles) was the stepdaughter of Sarah Franklin Davenport (C.12), BF and Jane Mecom's sister. Mrs. Bowls was the daughter of James Davenport's first wife, Grace Tileston, and the widow of Samuel Bowls (or Bowles), an apothecary of Dorchester, Mass.

4. On this London bookseller, see above, IX, 274 n.

5. None of the letters mentioned in this paragraph have been found.

6. *Descriptions des Arts et Métiers* were issued at Paris by the Académie Royale des Sciences, 1761–88, as separate numbers and constituted "an effort to present a scientific picture of all the industrial processes employed in France in the eighteenth century." For an account of this series and a listing of its contents, see Arthur H. Cole and George B. Watts, *The Handicrafts of France as Recorded in Descriptions des Arts et Métiers 1761–1788* (Publication No. 8 of the Kress Library of Business and Economics, Cambridge, Mass., [1954]). In his last will BF bequeathed his folio set to APS and his quarto edition to Lib. Co. Phila.

7. For a large shipment of books Becket had sent to Lib. Co. Phila. in 1761 with the price of each, see above, IX, 274–7.

before I came home, fallen on another Method of being supply'd; which on your Account gave me some Concern, as they are constant Buyers, and good Pay.

On the other Side is List of a few Books, which I request you to send me per next Ships. I was glad to learn by your last, that my Friend Mr. Strahan was in good Health, as I had no Line from him. I am Your humble Servant

B FRANKLIN

Philosophic Transactions[8] Part 1st. of Vol. 49.
——and Part 2d of Vol. 50.
Ditto Vols. 52, and 53. and 54 if published. All in blue Covers only, unbound.
Debates in the House of Commons by Anchitel Gray Esqr.[9]
Mallet's Works.[1]
Astronomical Tables and Precepts for calculating Eclipses, new and Full Moons, &c. to A.D. 7800 by James Ferguson[2]
Concise Account of the Rise of the Society of Arts. Hooper 1s.[3]
Essay on Oeconomy—Richardson[4]

8. These volumes of *Phil. Trans.* were: XLIX, Part I, for 1755 (published in 1756); L, Part II, for 1758 (published in 1759); LII, Part I, for 1761 (published in 1762), and Part II, for 1762 (published in 1763) paged continuously; LIII, for 1763, and LIV, for 1764, were not published until 1764 and 1765 respectively.

9. Anchitel Grey (d. 1702), *Some Account of Debates of the House of Commons, from the Year 1667 to the Year 1694* (10 vols., London, 1763), was favorably reviewed in *Gent. Mag.*, XXXIII (May 1763), 238–9.

1. David Mallet (1705–1763), a Scottish intellectual and freethinker. *The Works of David Mallet* (new edit., 3 vols., London, 1759).

2. Published in London, 1763. For BF's acquaintance with Ferguson, and for his magic squares, magic circle, and diagram of a three-wheel clock that Ferguson published, see above, IV, 392–401; VIII, 216–19.

3. Derek Hudson and Kenneth W. Luckhurst, *The Royal Society of Arts, 1754–1954* (London, 1954), p. 384, gives the author and title of this book as Thomas Mortimer, *A Concise Account of the Rise, Progress, and Present State of the Society* . . . . The author was probably Thomas Mortimer (1730–1810), a writer on economics. *DNB.* The publisher was Samuel Hooper (d. 1793).

4. The author was Edward Watkinson. The publisher was either Samuel Richardson or his nephew William. This popular essay on thrift (not on economics) went through many editions and printings in England and the colonies.

Fielding's Universal Mentor.[5]
2 Prints of the Earl of Bute; best.[6]

With the above let me have my Account that I may send you a
Bill to discharge it.   BF.

Addressed: To / Mr T. Becket / Bookseller / Strand / London
Endorsed: Philadelphia Decbr 13. 1763 Mr franklin Ansd 27 June

To John Waring[7]   ALS: American Philosophical Society

Reverend and dear Sir,   Philada. Dec. 17. 1763
Being but just return'd home from a Tour thro' the northern
Colonies, that has employ'd the whole Summer, my Time at
present is so taken up that I cannot now write fully in answer to
the Letters I have receiv'd from you,[8] but purpose to do it shortly.
This is chiefly to acquaint you, that I have visited the Negro
School here in Company with the Revd. Mr. Sturgeon[9] and some
others; and had the Children thoroughly examin'd. They appear'd
all to have made considerable Progress in Reading for the Time
they had respectively been in the School, and most of them
answer'd readily and well the Questions of the Catechism; they
behav'd very orderly, showd a proper Respect and ready Obedience to the Mistress, and seem'd very attentive to, and a good
deal affected by, a serious Exhortation with which Mr. Sturgeon

5. Sir John Fielding, *The Universal Mentor* (London, 1762).
6. In transferring this order to William Strahan, Sept. 1, 1764 (Pierpont
Morgan Lib.), BF specified that the prints of Lord Bute were to be "by Ryland,
if good 2 of them." This was William Wynne Ryland (1732–1783). Soon
after the accession of George III he had been commissioned to engrave Allan
Ramsay's full-length portraits of the King and of Bute. *DNB.*
7. For the Rev. John Waring, secretary of the Associates of the Late Dr.
Bray, see above, VII, 98 n; and for the activity of this organization in promoting Negro education in the colonies and BF's connection with it, see
above, VII, 100–1, 252–3, 256, 377–9; VIII, 425; IX, 12–13, 20–1, 174; and
this volume, pp. 298–300.
8. Not found.
9. On William Sturgeon, Philadelphia clergyman and catechist of the
Negro school there, see above, VII, 252 n; and on the criticism of his work,
from which he was exonerated, see this volume, pp. 298–9 n.

concluded our Visit. I was on the whole much pleas'd, and from what I then saw, have conceiv'd a higher Opinion of the natural Capacities of the black Race, than I had ever before entertained. Their Apprehension seems as quick, their Memory as strong, and their Docility in every Respect equal to that of white Children.[1] You will wonder perhaps that I should ever doubt it, and I will not undertake to justify all my Prejudices, nor to account for them. I immediately advanc'd the two Guineas you mention'd, for the Mistress,[2] and Mr. Sturgeon will therefore draw on you for £7 18s. only, which makes up the half Year's Salary of Ten Pounds.[3] Be pleased to present my best Respects to the Associates, and believe me, with sincere Esteem Dear Sir, Your most obedient Servant   B FRANKLIN

Addressed: To / The Reverend Mr Waring / to be left at Mr Burd's a / Bookseller in Ave Mary Lane / London

Endorsed: Dr. Franklin Philadelphia Decr. 17: 1763 read March: 1: 1764[4]

1. This is one of the earliest, if not the very first, of all statements by distinguished Americans of a belief, based on personal observation, that Negro children's intellectual capacity fully equals that of white children. On March 20, 1774 (APS), BF wrote the Marquis de Condorcet that the Negroes were "not deficient in natural Understanding, but they have not the Advantage of Education."

2. Elizabeth Harrison, wife of Richard Harrison, master of the free school in the Academy, had been appointed mistress of the Negro school, May 1, 1761. A new mistress, Mrs. Ayres, was put in charge in November 1764. *PMHB*, LXIII (1939), 288 and note.

3. In the previous June BF had told Waring that he would pay his annual subscription of two guineas to Sturgeon. His Memorandum Book, 1757–1776, p. 14, shows under date of Nov. 26, 1763, that he had paid over this subscription (£3 8s. Pa. currency) and had also taken Sturgeon's bill for £7 18s. sterling drawn on Waring, giving £13 17s. Pa. currency for it. He sent this bill to Henton Brown in London for collection.

4. The Bray Associates Minute Book, pp. 200–1, records the reading of this letter and summarizes its contents.

[Keziah Folger Coffin?]: Genealogy of the Folger Family

AD: Historical Society of Pennsylvania

Franklin's interest in his family background and connections extended throughout his life. In 1739 he had sought and received from his father information about the family name and his paternal line;[5] in England he had visited Ecton, Banbury, and Birmingham and had looked up the records of his ancestors, met as many as possible of his and his wife's living relatives, and laboriously prepared a genealogical chart of the Franklin family.[6] The one branch which he had not carefully investigated was that of his mother's relatives, the Folger family of the island of Nantucket.

The opportunity apparently came to him during his and Sally's summer and early autumn stay in Boston, 1763, when he seems to have met one of his Nantucket relatives also visiting there, Mrs. Keziah Folger Coffin, a first cousin once removed.[7] In that part of his papers which Franklin left to his grandson William Temple Franklin at his death and are now at the Historical Society of Pennsylvania,[8] are two ill-spelled, unsigned sheets containing genealogical information about the Nantucket Folgers, which date from late in 1763. The handwriting looks very much like surviving samples of Keziah Coffin's, and it seems probable that when Franklin met her he asked that when she reached home she would write out and send him this information.[9] The dating, "10 mo.," in Quaker fashion (Quakers predominated in Nantucket at this time), might mean October or December, but in 1763 the more usual meaning was December.

Nantucket the 10mo. the 18d. 1763
John Foulger the Ancestor of our Family Came out of the City of Norwich in the County of Norfolk. He married Miriba Gibs in

5. Above, II, 229–32.
6. Above, VIII, 114–21, 133–46.
7. Keziah Coffin (B.1.4.2.2.2) was related to BF through both her mother Abigail Folger (B.1.7.7), BF's first cousin, and her father Daniel Folger (B.1.4.2.2), BF's first cousin once removed. She played a conspicuous part in island affairs during the American Revolution and was accused of being a Tory informer. On the probable meeting of BF and Sally with her in Boston in 1763, see Van Doren, *Franklin-Mecom*, p. 96.
8. Above, I, xxii.
9. Many, but not all, of the persons mentioned below are included in the selective genealogy and chart of the Folger family printed above, I, liii–lvi, lxx–lxxi.

DECEMBER 18, 1763

Great Britain and Brought Hir and His Son Petor and one Daughter
to new england. The Daughter married to a Paine on Longisland
and there is a numerous of Spring from Hir but for Perticlars, I
know nothing.[1] Peter married with Mary Morrils a young woman
that Came from England with Hew Petors,[2] and had two Sons,
John and Eleazer and Seven Daughters namely Johanna married
a Coleman Darcas married a Pratt, Barsheba married a Pope,
Patiance married Harker, Bethiah married Barnard, Exsperiance
married to a Swain, Abiah married Franklin. Bethiah Dyed without Issue.[3] The Rest have Children and Grand Children to the
forth Generation. John Had Six Sons and Eleazer Had three that
all had Children so that there is a Great number of the name heare
and until last year there was never one of the name that lived
of this Island and than Shubil Foulger and his Son Beniamin
Remooved to Cape Sables.[4]

It is unsertain in what year John Foulger Came out of England

1. The editors have made no attempt to trace the Paine family of Long
Island. So far as is known, BF never made any contact with its members.

2. Hugh Peter (often spelled Peters; 1598–1660), dissenting clergyman,
came to Mass. in 1635, and was minister at Salem, 1636–41. Sent to England,
1641, as one of the colony's agents, he served as a chaplain with the Parliamentary army and was a leading clergyman during the Interregnum. Upon
the Restoration he was arrested, tried, and executed at Charing Cross. *DAB;*
Raymond P. Stearns, *The Strenuous Puritan: Hugh Peter, 1598–1660* (Urbana,
1954). Mary Morrils came to America as his bond servant.

3. Bethia Folger (B.1.2) married John Barnard of Nantucket in February
1668; both were drowned a year and a half later.

4. That is, all the descendants of John Foulgier in the male lines continued
to live on Nantucket until 1762. Then English settlement in the Cape Sable
region of Nova Scotia, which drew away numerous families from Cape Cod,
Martha's Vineyard, and Nantucket, brought the first defections among the
male Folgers. Before these men left there appear to have been about 27 or
28 males surnamed Folger living on Nantucket, sons and grandsons of John
and Eleazer Folger. Probably about as many daughters and granddaughters
of these two lived there and an uncounted number of men and women in the
same generations but with other surnames, descended from those of Peter
Folger's daughters who had married Nantucket men. If to all of these are
added the adults and children of later generations living there in 1762, it is
probable that there were between 150 and 200 persons among the 3500 residents of Nantucket whom BF could have called his relatives, provided he
could have identified them all.

398

or of what Age he or His Son was.[5] As for the Lettor that I mentioned to thee it is not to be found.

[On a separate sheet in the same hand:]
John Foulger married to Mirriba Gibs in old England. By hir he had one Sone named Peter and one Daughter that married a Pain on Long Island. Peter married Mary Morrils and Settled on the Island of Nantucket.[6] By hir he Had two Sons and Six Daughter the Sons nams John and Eleazer. Of Johns Children in the male Line there is Six named with ther Sons under neath[7]

Jethro[8] who has 2 Sons Trustrum and Jethro
Jonathan has Reubin and Jonathan
Nathaniel Has Paul
Shubil[9] has Seth and Shubil
Richard[1] has David Solamon and Elisha
Zaccheus[2] has John James and Zaccheus

Eleazers Childrin is[3]
Peter had 1 Son Daniel[4]
Eleazer[5] had Urian and Elipah Charles Stephen Fredrak and Peleg. They have many Daughters and are very numerous
Nathan Had Abisha and Timothy and Peter and Berzilla

5. John Foulgier (c.1593–1660), progenitor of the American Folger family, arrived in Boston on the *Abigail* with his wife, son, and daughter, Oct. 6, 1635. He moved to Martha's Vineyard about 1648. His son Peter was born in Norwich in 1617.

6. There are several MS genealogies of the Folger family in the Nantucket Hist. Soc. and Nantucket Atheneum and one has been printed in *New-Eng. Hist. and Gen. Reg.*, XVI (1862), 269–78. While they do not agree with each other in all particulars, they show that the present listing of the sons, grandsons, and great-grandsons in the male lines of BF's grandfather Peter is not entirely accurate or complete. For example, Peter's two sons are listed in the wrong order in the next sentence: Eleazer (1648–1716) was older than John (1659–1732) by eleven years, but is given here as if he were the younger.

7. The order of birth of John Folger's sons should be: Jethro, Nathaniel, Jonathan, Richard, Shubael, and Zaccheus. These men, and the sons of Eleazer in the second column, were all BF's first cousins.

8. Jethro (B.1.7.1) had four sons, not two, but Jedidiah had died in 1757 and John had probably also died before this list was compiled.

9. The genealogies list three sons of Shubael (B.1.7.6), not two: Seth (d. 1807), Benjamin (1731–1819), and Shubael (1737–1774). The statement in the first sheet of this report that "Shubil and his Son Benjamin Remooved

(Remainder of footnotes for this genealogy on next page)

To Peter Collinson

ALS: Yale University Library

Dear Friend, Philada. Dec. 19. 1763

I am but lately return'd from my Tour of these Northern Colonies, having been from the Southernmost Part of Virginia to the easternmost Part of New England.[6] I think I wrote you from Boston that I had by a Fall dislocated my right Arm at the Shoulder Joint;[7] it is now pretty well recovered, tho' not quite so strong as before. Your obliging Favours of June 8, and 28; and of Augt. 23. came all duly to hand, and the Books are deliver'd to the Library Company.[8] At the next Meeting of the Directors, I will show them what you mention concerning the compleating their Set of Edwards, and binding the colour'd Prints of Insects.[9] The Proposal of a Colony to be called New Wales, was made without Authority, and by weak Heads, and is accordingly come to nothing.[1] I am glad what I wrote proves acceptable to your

---

to Cape Sables" and the omission of Benjamin from this listing leave somewhat unclear which members of this branch of the family were the emigrants to Nova Scotia.

1. Richard (B.1.7.5) had four sons, not three, though the eldest, Sylvanus (b. 1728), probably died young.

2. Zaccheus (B.1.7.8) had six sons, not three, including Nathaniel, Andrew, and Reuben, of whom Nathaniel lived until 1777.

3. Eleazer (B.1.4) had five sons not three, in the following order: Eleazer, Peter, Daniel, Elisha, and Nathan, but Daniel and Elisha died young.

4. Daniel was Keziah Folger Coffin's father; he had married his first cousin once removed, Abigail, youngest daughter of John Folger, whose sons (but not daughters) are listed in the first column.

5. Eleazer (B.1.4.1) had seven sons, not six, in the following order: Gideon, Urian, Elipaz, Charles, Frederick, Stephen, and Peleg. The eldest, Gideon, died unmarried. The names of the "many" daughters (all by his second wife, the former Mary Marshall) were Deborah, Bethiah, Ruth, Margaret, Sophia, and Mary.

6. For these trips, April–May and June–November, see above, pp. 252, 276–9.

7. BF's letter has not been found. For his fall (he actually fell twice), see above, pp. 278, 338.

8. See above, pp. 274–5, 305–6, 331–3.

9. See above, pp. 275, 306.

1. For Lieut. Thomas Webb's scheme for New Wales, see above, p. 256 n.

Friend Hamilton.[2] The new Governor arriv'd before my Return;[3] I waited on him to pay my Respects, and have since met him often in various Places at Dinners,[4] and among the Commissioners for carrying on the War, of which I am one.[5] He is civil, and I endeavour to fail in no Point of Respect; so I think we shall have no personal Difference, at least I will give no Occasion. For though I cordially dislike and despise the Uncle, for demeaning himself so far as to back bite and abuse me to Friends and to Strangers, as you well know he does, I shall keep that Account open with him only,[6] and some time or other we may have a Settlement; if that never happens, I can forgive the Debt. I have heretofore done him Service, and I have done him Honour; and I never did him Injury, unless he Deems it one, that I supported and carried a just Cause against him in favour of his Province. He may sleep in Peace at present. I am not coming over as he has heard, to solicit any thing about Dr. Coxe's Grant:[7] Though I own I love England and my Friends there so well, that middling Reasons[8] for my Making such a Voyage, would be apt to seem very good ones.

We just now learn that the Indians over the Lakes, being informed by a Belt from the Ilinois French Governor that Peace was concluded between the English and French, that he must surrender that Country, and could no longer supply or support them, have humbly sued for Peace to the Commanding Officer at Fort Detroit, who has referr'd them to the General, and in the

2. Charles Hamilton of Painshill, Surrey; above, pp. 151 n, 333.

3. John Penn arrived in Philadelphia, Oct. 30, and BF reached home from New England, Nov. 5, 1763.

4. One dinner at which BF must have met Penn was that given on November 21 by the merchants of the city to the new governor, his predecessor James Hamilton, the Council, and the provincial commissioners. *Pa. Gaz.*, Nov. 24, 1763.

5. See above, pp. 362–3.

6. Opposite this line in the MS Collinson wrote "on Corn Linnen," but the editors have been unable to find any dictionary or other authority to explain this term or its application to the passage in BF's letter.

7. Collinson had written, August 23 (above, p. 331), that Thomas Penn had told him of hearing of BF's intention to come to England "to Solicit a revival of Doctor Coxs Grant for Lands on the Missisipi." For BF's interest in the Coxe grant, see above, pp. 212–14.

8. BF also used this phrase in a letter to Strahan the same day; see below.

meantime granted them a Cessation of Arms.[9] This we expect will soon occasion a like Application from the other Tribes. I only fear they have not yet smarted enough to make them careful how they break with us again.

Pray assure Mr. Canton, that I respect him greatly, and purpose shortly to write him a very long Letter.[1] My having so much to say to him, is one Reason of my not having set about it before, tho' I own it is a bad one.

With sincerest Esteem, I am, my dear Friend Yours affectionately   B FRANKLIN

Addressed: To / Peter Collinson Esqr / Gracious Street / London / per Capt / Budden.[2]

Endorsed: answered Feby 3 per King Prussia[3]

To Jared Ingersoll   ALS: Yale University Library

Dear Sir,   Philada. Dec. 19. 1763.

Mr. Holt,[4] late of your Town, Postmaster, having fallen in Debt to the Office £320 18s. 9d. lawful Money, which seems not likely to be otherwise obtained, this is to request and impower you to endeavour the Recovery of that Sum, by attaching what you can find of his Estate in your Government. I hear he has

9. *Pa. Gaz.*, Dec. 22, 1763, printed an extract of a letter from Detroit, dated November 1, reporting that a "French Officer, from the Illinois, has brought a Belt and Letter to the Savages, with an Account of Peace between England and France, which neither the Savages nor French have believed till now." The same issue of the paper also carried an extract of a letter from Fort Pitt, dated December 1, reporting that the "Overlake Indians" had sued for peace to Major Gladwin, the British commander at Detroit, who had granted them a suspension of arms and had referred them to Gen. Jeffery Amherst.

1. BF apparently did not write Canton until March 14, 1764.

2. *Pa. Gaz.*, Dec. 22, 1763, reported the clearance of the *Philadelphia Packet*, Capt. Richard Budden.

3. Collinson's reply has not been found. *London Chron.*, Feb. 14–16, 1764, carried a report from Deal, February 14, that the *King of Prussia* had arrived there outward bound for Philadelphia.

4. For John Holt, James Parker's partner in newspaper publishing in New Haven and N.Y. and Parker's deputy as postmaster of New Haven, 1755–60, see above, V, 441 n.

lately made a considerable Purchase there.[5] Mr. Green[6] can inform you. There may possibly be other Attachments,[7] but the above Debt being due to the Crown I apprehend is by Law entitled to Preference in Payment. The Post-Office Money is Part of the Revenue; of which Mr. John Foxcroft and myself as Deputy Post-masters General of America are authoris'd Collectors. The Action will therefore be in the King's Name, as I suppose; but this I leave to your better Judgment. I enclose a Thirty Shilling Bill by way of Fee;[8] and desire a Line from you with Directions if any formal Power of Attorney is necessary from us, and what Proofs are to be sent of the Account.[9] My Daughter joins in best Respects to you and Mrs. Ingersol, with Dear Sir, Your most obedient humble Servant   B FRANKLIN

Endorsed: Mr Franklin Letter 19 Decembr 1763.

To Richard Jackson

ALS: American Philosophical Society

Dear Sir   Philada. Dec. 19. 1763

I must not let these Ships go without a Line to you,[1] tho' I have but little to say. I have been from home all Summer, and am but

5. In 1759 Holt bought a house and a printing office in New Haven for £400. Beverly McAnear, "James Parker versus John Holt," N.J. Hist. Soc. *Proc.*, LIX (April, 1941), 82.

6. Thomas Green (1735–1812) became manager of Parker and Holt's *Connecticut Gazette* (New Haven) in 1760 upon Holt's departure to N.Y. In 1764 Green moved to Hartford and established *The Connecticut Courant;* he moved back to New Haven in 1767 and founded *The Connecticut Journal; and New-Haven Post-Boy. DAB.*

7. BF had probably heard from James Parker of Holt's business debts and delinquencies, as well as his post-office debts, all of which figure largely in Parker's letters to BF from November 1764 on.

8. In the margin: "32s. York Money."

9. Ingersoll brought suit against Holt, but it is not clear how or indeed when the case was settled. "Auditors, or Referrees" were appointed to look into the merits of the dispute, but they apparently had not reached a final determination as late as 1767. James Parker to BF, Jan. 4, 1766, APS; Parker to Ingersoll, Feb. 19, 1767, New Haven Colony Hist. Soc. *Papers*, IX (1918), 397–99, 400–1.

1. BF sent this letter by the *Philadelphia Packet*, Capt. Richard Budden, clearance of which was reported in *Pa. Gaz.*, Dec. 22, 1763.

lately return'd, so know but little of our province Affairs; I suppose Mr. Moore[2] or some of the Committee of Correspondence have communicated to you what was necessary. The present Assembly at their first Meeting renew'd their Choice of you.[3] My Return in time to word it to your Mind, was prevented by an Accident, the Dislocation of my Shoulder, which disabled me from travelling some Weeks.[4] I have now pretty well recovered the Use of it, tho' not its full Strength.

I have made no Engagement with Messrs. Coxe but wish them Success,[5] and wonder no Traces can be found of the Grant from K. William. If they had succeeded, I did encline to take a 10th. on the Terms they offer'd, imagining I could have been of Use in procuring Settlers; but begin to think myself too old to engage in new Projects that require Time to become advantageous; and since much time is like to be spent before even a Beginning can be made believe I shall decline it, unless your engaging in it should induce me to continue.

We have Advices this Day, via Fort Pitt,[6] that the Governor of the Ilinois Country has at length sent a Belt to the Ottawaws and Chippewaes, acquainting them that a Peace is made between England and France, by the Terms of which he is obliged to deliver up his Forts and all the Territory to the English, and can no longer supply or support them; on which they have apply'd to Major Gladman,[7] who commands at Detroit and beg'd for Peace in the most abject Terms. He has refer'd them to the General, as to a final Peace, but granted them a Cessation of Arms, which they gladly accepted; and the Garrison has taken the Opportunity of getting considerable Supplies from the Country round, which were wanted. It is thought this will draw on like Applications

2. Charles Moore, clerk of the Pa. Assembly.

3. The Assembly renewed Jackson's appointment as Pa. agent on Oct. 15, 1763, the first meeting of its fall session at which business was transacted. *Votes,* 1763–64, p. 4.

4. What change Jackson wanted in the wording of his appointment is not known. See above, p. 341, for BF's promise to procure a change.

5. For BF and Jackson's interest in the efforts of "Messrs. Coxe" to get an old land grant confirmed, see above, pp. 212–14, 254, 297, 341–2, 369–71.

6. See above, p. 402 n, for the "Advices," printed in *Pa. Gaz.,* Dec. 22, 1763, about the conclusion of Pontiac's Uprising.

7. Major Henry Gladwin, the British commander at Detroit.

from the Delawares, Shawnese, and Seneca's. I only fear we shall conclude a new Peace before those Villains have been made to smart sufficiently for their perfidious Breach of the last; and thereby make them less apprehensive of breaking with us again hereafter. And yet perhaps 'tis best to conclude the War as soon as possible; for tho' it may be that these Colonies, if they were united in their Measures, and would exert their united Strength, could fill the Indian Country with so many and such strong Parties, as to ruin them in one Summer, and forever deter[8] them from future Attempts against us. Yet we see and know that such Union is impracticable. The General's Requisition is not comply'd with in any of the Colonies, because (they say) *he did not make it of all;* and where it was made, *it was not in due Proportion,* &c.[9] Thus, tho' strong, we are in Effect weak; and shall remain so, till you take some Measures at home to unite us.

Our Assembly met to day. I am, as far as I see, upon good Terms, personally, with our new Governor;[1] what Disputes may arise during the Session, I know not; but fear a Money Bill will revive the old ones.[2]

I am, dear Sir, Your most obedient humble Servant

B FRANKLIN

R. Jackson, Esqr.

Endorsed: Philada. Decr. 19th. 1763 Benjn. Franklin Esqr

8. "and disable" struck through.

9. On Nov. 5, 1763, Gen. Jeffery Amherst wrote Gov. James Hamilton (the general did not know that John Penn had succeeded Hamilton) requesting Pa. to raise 1000 men "to act against the Delawares, Shawanese, and other Tribes" who had joined Pontiac, and to have the men ready to take the field by March 1, 1764. Somewhat earlier Amherst had applied to N.Y. and N.J. to raise men "for carrying on offensive Operations by way of Lake Erie." The Assemblies of these two colonies refused to comply because, they complained, New England had not been required to contribute men. The Pa. Assembly, however, called into special session by Penn on Dec. 19, 1763, voted on December 22 to comply with the requisition. *Votes,* 1763–64, pp. 12–14, 15.

1. For more on BF's initial reaction to John Penn, see above, p. 401.

2. BF was right. On Jan. 6, 1764, the House voted £50,000 to support the 1000 men it had resolved to raise on Dec. 22, 1763, but by the time Penn finally consented to pass a supply bill on May 30, 1764 (the sum of money granted had in the meantime been raised to £55,000), relations between him and the Assembly had become so embittered that the Assembly had sent a

To William Strahan

ALS: Pierpont Morgan Library

Dear Straney   Philada. Dec. 19. 1763.

I have before me your Favours of July 16,[3] and Augt. 18.[4] which is the latest. It vexes me excessively to see that Parker and Mecom are so much in Arrear with you. What is due from Parker is safe, and will be paid, I think with Interest; for he is a Man as honest as he is industrious and frugal, and has withal some Estate: his Backwardness has been owing to his bad Partners only, of whom he is now nearly quit.[5] But as to Mecom, he seems so dejected and spiritless, that I fear little will be got of him. He has dropt his Paper, on which he built his last Hopes. I doubt I shall lose £200 by him myself, but am taking Steps to save what I can for you; of which more fully in my next.[6]

Now I am return'd from my long Journeys which have consum'd the whole Summer, I shall apply myself to such a Settlement of all my Affairs, as will enable me to do what your Friendship so warmly urges. I have a great Opinion of your Wisdom (Madeira apart;) and am apt enough to think that what you seem so clear in, and are so earnest about, must be right. Tho' I own, that I sometimes suspect, my Love to England and my Friends

---

petition to England praying the king to give the province a royal government. The conflict between Penn and the Assembly and the movement for royal government in the province will be covered extensively in the next volume.

3. Not found. On the same day Strahan wrote to David Hall that "Messrs. Parker and Mecom are both shamefully behind with me (not to mention Read) as Dr. Franklin will tell you to whom I have writ by this Conveyance to settle with them, if possible." APS.

4. Above, pp. 324–31.

5. On Feb. 1, 1765, some weeks after he had arrived in England on his second mission, BF paid Strahan £163 13s. 7d., sterling, for the "Balance due him from Mr. Parker" (Franklin-Parker Accounts, above, pp. 257–60), and "on Advice thereof" Parker paid DF £100 sterling and executed a bond to BF, Aug. 1, 1765, for the balance (APS). Parker's tangled relations with his partners have been exhaustively described by Beverly McAnear in "James Parker versus William Weyman" and "James Parker versus John Holt," N.J. Hist. Soc. *Proc.*, LIX (Jan., April, 1941), 1–23, 77–95.

6. For the failure of Benjamin Mecom's *New-York Pacquet*, see above, p. 153 n. Mecom went to New Haven in 1764, rented a printing office from Parker, and revived Parker's *Connecticut Gazette*, but this venture, too, failed in 1768.

there seduces me a little, and makes *my own* middling Reasons for going over; appear very good ones. We shall see in a little Time how Things will turn out.

Blessings on your Heart for the Feast of Politicks you gave me in your last.[7] I could by no other means have obtain'd so clear a View of the present State of your public Affairs as by your Letter. Most of your Observations appear to me extreamly judicious, strikingly clear and true. I only differ from you in some of the melancholly Apprehensions you express concerning Consequences; and to comfort you (at the same time flattering my own Vanity,) let me remind you, that I have sometimes been in the right in such Cases, when you happen'd to be in the wrong; as I can prove upon you out of this very Letter of yours. Call to mind your former Fears for the King of Prussia, and remember my telling you that the Man's Abilities were more than equal to all the Force of his Enemies, and that he would finally extricate himself, and triumph. This, by the Account you give me from Major Beckwith,[8] is fully verified. You now fear for our virtuous young King, that the Faction forming will overpower him, and render his Reign uncomfortable. On the contrary, I am of Opinion, that his Virtue, and the Consciousness of his sincere Intentions to make his People happy, will give him Firmness and Steadiness in his Measures, and in the Support of the honest Friends he has chosen to serve him; and when that Firmness is fully perceiv'd, Faction will dissolve and be dissipated like a Morning Fog before the rising Sun, leaving the rest of the Day clear, with a Sky serene and cloudless. Such, after a few of the first Years, will be the future Course of his Majesty's Reign, which I predict will be happy and truly glorious. Your Fears for the Nation too, appear to me as little founded. A new War I cannot yet see Reason to apprehend. The Peace I think will long continue, and your Nation be as happy as they deserve to be, that is, as happy as their moderate Share of Virtue will allow them to be: Happier than that, no outward Circumstances can make a Nation any more than a private Man. And as to their Quantity of Virtue, I think it bids fair for Increasing; if the old Saying be true, as it certainly is,

7. Strahan's letter of August 18, mentioned above.
8. Above, p. 329. BF failed to call Beckwith by his correct title; he had been promoted to major general in the spring of 1763.

Ad Exemplum Regis, &c.
My Love to Mrs. Strahan and your Children in which my Wife
and Daughter join with Your ever affectionate Friend

B FRANKLIN

[*Written in:*] First under London P.S. Extract of a Letter from
Philadelphia dated Decr. 19.[9]

P.S.[1] The western Indians about Fort Detroit now sue for Peace,[2]
having lost a great Number of their best Warriors in their vain
Attempt to reduce that Fortress; and being at length assur'd by a
Belt from the French Commander in the Ilinois Country, that a
Peace is concluded between England and France, that he must
evacuate the Country and deliver up his Forts, and can no longer
supply or support them. It is thought this will draw on a general
Peace. I am only afraid it will be concluded before these Bar-
barians[3] have sufficiently smarted for their perfidious breaking
the last.

The Governor of Detroit, Major Gladwin, has granted them a
Cessation of Arms, till the General's Pleasure is known.
Mr Strahan

To Richard Jackson   ALS: American Philosophical Society

Dear Sir   Philada. Dec. 24. 1763
Since my last of the 19th Inst. which went per Budden,[4] our
Assembly have voted a Compliance with General Amherst's Requisition of 1000 Men from this Province, to act offensively in
the Spring against the Indians.[5] This is the more remarkable, as

9. This insertion is in what looks like Strahan's hand and is almost certainly
a direction to the printer of *London Chron.* The passage which follows here
was printed on the last page of the issue of Jan. 28–31, 1764, as the first item
in the "Postscript" section, and was headed "Extract of a Letter from Philadelphia, Dec. 19."

1. Crossed out in the MS, probably by Strahan.
2. See above, p. 402 n.
3. BF had written "the Villains"; the change was probably made by Strahan.
4. See above, pp. 402–5.
5. For Amherst's requisition and for the Assembly's vote to comply with
it, see above, p. 405 n.

this Province us'd to be reckon'd backward in such Measures, and New York and the Jersies, have just set us but an indifferent Example; Maryland was not call'd upon, the Reason I know not; and what Virginia will do is yet uncertain: We are therefore the first, as far as we know, that have comply'd fully and heartily as soon as requir'd. I doubt not but you will take care to mention this in our Favour where proper; and let us be prais'd a little by way of Encouragement to be good Boys for the future.

I enclose some of our latest Papers.[6] I suppose Peace with the Indians will be talk'd of among you, and some Orders sent over as to the Terms. When the last Peace was made, the Indians invited our Merchants to send Goods into their Country, promising all Safety and Protection to the Traders and their Effects.[7] In full Reliance on those Promises, great Quantities of Goods were accordingly sent among them; when they perfidiously broke the Peace, without making the least Complaint of any Injury receiv'd, or demanding Satisfaction for any pretended to be receiv'd, seiz'd the Goods and massacred the Traders in cold Blood.[8] It will appear reasonable to all, that if a Peace is granted to them, they ought to make all the Restitution and Satisfaction in their Power: But the Goods are consum'd, and they have no Money. And yet, if they are allow'd to enjoy the whole Benefit of their Villany, without suffering any Inconvenience, they will more readily repeat it the first Opportunity. It is therefore my Opinion, that they should always on such Occasions be obliged to give up some Part of their Territory most convenient for our Settlement, which might be apply'd to the Indemnification of the Merchants.[9]

6. One of these was almost certainly the December 22 issue of *Pa. Gaz.*, which carried extracts of letters from Forts Pitt and Detroit, mentioning the Indians' desire for peace.

7. By "the last Peace" BF may have meant one made at a "huge good-will assembly" held at Fort Pitt in August 1759 by George Croghan, attended by about 1000 Indians; or one at a conference held by Croghan at Detroit in the late fall of 1760; or one at a larger conference held at the same place by Croghan and Sir William Johnson in September 1761. See Howard H. Peckham, *Pontiac and the Indian Uprising* (Chicago, 1961), pp. 56, 66, 78–9.

8. For the beginnings of and causes of the Pontiac Uprising, see above, pp. 273–4 n, 295–6.

9. On Dec. 7, 1763, and again on the 12th, a group of merchants engaged in the Indian trade who had suffered at the hands of the natives during the French and Indian War and during the Pontiac Uprising met at the Indian

Or, where that can't be done, given to some other Nation of Indians who have been faithful to us, and may want it. I am, with sincere Esteem, Dear Sir, Your most obedient humble Servant

B FRANKLIN

Richd. Jackson Esqr.

Endorsed: 24 Decr 1763 Benjn Franklin Esqr

From Francis Bernard   Letterbook copy: Harvard College Library

Sir   Boston, Dec 27. 1763

I have this day received a letter from my Son dated Alexandria Nov 27. in which he takes no notice of Any letter or orders from me. When I observe that your letter of Nov. 10.[1] acknowledges the receipt of mine of mine of Oct 30,[2] and expresses that you shall by that post write to some friend of yours to forward my Son to Philadelphia, I must conclude that your letters upon this occasion have miscarried. Whatever have been the cause of this disappointment, I must still renew my request to you as to get my Son from Alexandria to Philadelphia and forward him by the best means to Boston. He is at Mr. Johnsons in Alexandria.[3] I

Queen Tavern in Philadelphia and appointed George Croghan and Moses Franks their agents to lay a memorial before the Board of Trade praying for compensation for their losses. The merchants, later known as the "Suffering Traders," envisaged monetary compensation "from the French Prises," but Croghan after spending several fruitless months in London began to suggest that his associates work for a land grant instead—precisely the idea BF is suggesting here. This idea was accepted and in 1766 the "Suffering Traders" became the Illinois Company, later the Vandalia Company, and finally the Walpole Company. The extremely complicated evolution of the "Suffering Traders" into a series of land companies and BF's affiliations with them will occupy considerable space in subsequent volumes. *The Papers of Sir William Johnson,* IV (Albany, 1925), 264–66, 267–71.

1. Not found.
2. See above, pp. 353–4.
3. George Johnston (d. 1766), an able lawyer whose estate of "Belvale" was near Alexandria. A burgess of Fairfax Co., 1758–66, he seconded Patrick Henry's resolutions against the Stamp Act in the Va. House of Burgesses, 1765. John C. Fitzpatrick, ed., *The Diaries of George Washington 1748–1799* (Boston and N.Y., 1925), I, 119 n. BF's Memorandum Book, 1757–1776, p. 16, records, March 29, 1764: "Paid to Mr. G. Johnston's Order £12 12s. od.

wrote to you (13 inst.⁴) upon this Subject by Wyer an express
sent to Philadelphia by the surveyor general. I am &c.

B. Franklin.

From Richard Jackson

ALS: American Philosophical Society

Dear Sir   Temple December 27, 1763

I write to you by every Packet, but having heard that a Vessel
sails for Philadelphia to morrow am desirous of troubling you
with a few Lines which I hope will be in Time. I have had but
one letter from you a great While,⁵ but though this would be
Matter of Chagrin to me at all Times, the Occasion of my Loss
gives me much more concern, I flatter myself however your Cure
is now perfectly effected, I assure you with great Truth I am
capable of no greater pleasure; than it would give me to hear you
are perfectly recovered and free from any inconvenient Consequences. When I have the satisfaction of knowing this myself, I
shall give pleasure to a 1000d People here by telling it to them.

I did not forget to name you in the Manner you deserve to
Lord Egmont,⁶ but affairs here never were so mutable. Lord
Egmont is 1st Lord of the Admiralty and Lord Hide in the former
Place,⁷ I do not at all know this Lord, but shall take care he shall

---

for Mr. Bernard, and desired him [Bernard] to pay the same for me to Mr.
Williams, Boston. [*Added later:*] It was paid accordingly."

4. See above, pp. 389–91.

5. Probably BF's letter of Sept. 22, 1763 (see above, pp. 341–2), in which
he mentioned his "dislocated Arm," to which Jackson refers here.

6. In his letter of June 10, 1763 (above, p. 286), BF had asked Jackson to
speak "a few kind Things of me to my new Master Lord Egmont," joint
postmaster general. Egmont had received the more important position of first
lord of the Admiralty on September 10, holding that office until 1766.

7. Thomas Villiers, 1st Baron Hyde of Hindon (1709–1786), had occupied
diplomatic posts in Poland, Saxony, Austria, and Prussia, 1737–48, and was
M.P. for Tamworth, 1747–56, vacating his seat upon his elevation to the
peerage. He had served as one of the lords of the Admiralty, 1748–56. Sworn
of the Privy Council, Sept. 2, 1763, he succeeded Egmont as postmaster
general ten days later, holding his position until July 1765 and again from
December 1783 to his death. He was chancellor of the Duchy of Lancaster,
1771–82 and 1783–86. He was created Earl of Clarendon, 1776. *DNB;* Namier
and Brooke, *House of Commons,* III, 587–8.

be acquainted with your Merit. It is now said Lord Egmont and Lord Sandwich are to change Places, that is the latter to return to his Place.[8] I wish Lord Egmont was in Lord Halifax's Place, who has now the Superior Administration of American Affairs, perhaps few so unfit for it.[9] This Mutability of Offices is no proof of an unstable Ministry, it seems more established than ever, I need not inform you that Mr. Grenville is at the head of it,[1] and I

8. Jackson meant that Lord Egmont, now first lord of the Admiralty, and Lord Sandwich, secretary of state for the Northern Department, were to exchange ministries, but this event did not take place. John Montagu, 4th Earl of Sandwich (1718–1792), served in the Admiralty, 1744–51, becoming first lord in 1748. He was secretary of state for the Northern Department, August 1763 to July 1765. During this time he incurred great obloquy and the nickname "Jemmy Twitcher" (from *The Beggar's Opera*) by turning on his former crony John Wilkes and denouncing the latter's *Essay on Woman* in the House of Lords. He was joint postmaster general (with another boon companion, Lord Le Despenser), 1768–71, and again first lord of the Admiralty, 1771–82. Scandals relating to his private life, and corruption, mismanagement, and neglect in the Navy during this later Admiralty service made him the object of bitter and violent invective, perhaps not entirely deserved. *DNB;* George Martelli, *Jemmy Twitcher A Life of the Fourth Earl of Sandwich, 1718–1792* (London, 1962); G. R. Barnes and J. H. Owen, eds., *The Sandwich Papers* (4 vols., London, 1932–38); Frank Spencer, ed., *The Fourth Earl of Sandwich Diplomatic Correspondence 1763–1765* (Manchester, 1961).

9. George Montagu Dunk, 2d Earl of Halifax (above, VIII, 67 n, IX, 71 n), was secretary of state for the Southern Department and hence the minister directly in charge of colonial affairs.

1. George Grenville (1712–1770), brother of Lord Temple and brother-in-law of William Pitt and of Lord Egremont, was educated at Eton; Christ Church, Cambridge; and the Inner Temple. M.P. for Buckingham, 1741–1770, he developed unusual skill as a "Parliament-man." He was a lord of the Admiralty, 1744–47; lord of the Treasury, 1747–54; treasurer of the Navy for three periods between 1754 and 1762; secretary of state for the Northern Department, May–October 1762; then first lord of the Admiralty until April 1763. When Bute resigned, Grenville, Halifax, and Egremont (later succeeded by Bedford) assumed control of the administration with Grenville as first lord of the Treasury and chancellor of the Exchequer. Though his name is usually associated in American history with the Stamp Act, responsibility for that measure was divided among several leaders. George III thoroughly disliked him, personally and officially, and on July 10, 1765, succeeded in dismissing him and the ministry he headed. During the rest of his life Grenville was in opposition to the administrations that followed his. *DNB;* Namier and Brooke, *House of Commons,* II, 537–44.

412

have a good Deal of Access to him, and have too received a very considerable Mark of his good will and Esteem, and what is generally too deemed a Mark of his Confidence;[2] but I suspend my opinion on the Subject; when I know more I will write fuller on this Subject, at present American Affairs are in a Critical Situation. I have taken great pains and made the Utmost Use of my Access to Men of Rank and Weight and hope I have not thrown my Pains away. Some Men whose Judgment I esteem equal if not superior to any of the Nation, seem to think as I wish they should. In the mean time I publish nothing for obvious Reasons, though I have begun to print.[3] There are many things, while I have the honour to be in favour with Administration, that will [be] more serviceable in private than Publick, but which if I find I cannot do the Service to the Colonies (and my Mother Country too, for I consider their Interests as inseperable as far [as] I go) I wish, in the station I am in, may as well be made publick as not.

You rightly conjecture, Major Barker at Manilla is the Gentleman whom you seek after,[4] I made the same guess, and have been a good deal since employed in inquiring whether, he was returning to England, or was to continue in the Companys Service there and in the latter Case, how I could treat with him. From the best Information I could get I expect him in England in February or March. I find others have the same View. Mr. Sherwood[5] told me he had such a Commission.

I wish I could give you more satisfaction, on Messrs. Coxes Application, but I fear the whole will prove very Uphill work.[6] It is not however my fault I assure you, I have taken a great deal of Pains, and will yet engage them in as little Expence as I can

2. The connection between Jackson and Grenville is somewhat obscure, but Jackson seems to have served the chancellor of the Exchequer in some sort of secretarial capacity. Carl Van Doren, *Letters and Papers of Benjamin Franklin and Richard Jackson 1753–1785* (Phila., 1947), pp. 23, 190.

3. Nothing that Jackson had "begun to print" at this time has been identified; he may have been referring to some anonymous contribution to a newspaper.

4. See above, pp. 156–8, 163, 297.

5. Joseph Sherwood (d. 1773), a Quaker lawyer of Austin Friars, London, agent for R.I., 1759–73, and for N.J., 1760–66.

6. See above, pp. 212–14, 369–71.

make sufficient. The Indian War, the Strength this adds however groundlessly to many inveterate Prejudices, the length of time this Claim has been deserted, and what is worst a Report of the Attorney and Sollicitor General, the last my friend deGrey and Dr. Hay Kings Advocate[7] against Lord Cardigans Claim of St. Vincent and S[ant]a Lucia though the Duke of Montagus Desertion was only because forced by France.[8] I dare say I need not assure you that I do not magnify difficulties, either to make those Gentlemen give up their Claim or augment any merit of mine, I have some Reliance on Materials at the Board of Trade, that I have a promise of an Access to.

I write Mr. Galloway by the same Ship, this goes in, but in great haste in answer to one of his. I flatter myself the Province stands justifyed in the Eyes of Administration against any Complaint of G[eneral] Amherst.[9] Mr. Allen has much contributed

---

7. On William de Grey, now solicitor general, who with Jackson had served as counsel for BF and Charles at the hearings on the Pa. acts in 1760, see above, VII, 61 n; IX, 23 n. On George Hay, a specialist in civil and canon law, see above, VIII, 5 n.

8 George Montagu (formerly Brudenell), at this time 4th Earl of Cardigan and later Duke of Montagu (1712–1790), claimed the islands through a grant by George I to his wife's father, the 2d Duke of Montagu, in 1722. An attempt by that duke to establish an English settlement had been frustrated by the French, who asserted prior rights, and Montagu's deputy governor and settlers had been driven off. In 1761 Cardigan and his wife petitioned for the recognition of their rights or a compensating grant elsewhere if the islands were to go to France by the prospective peace treaty. Following an adverse report by the law officers, Dec. 24, 1763, the Privy Council formally declared the grant of 1722 void in March 1764. *DNB* (under George Montagu, and John Montagu, 2d Duke of Montagu); *Acts Privy Coun., Col.,* IV, 618–19; *Board of Trade Journal,* 1759–63, pp. 401, 424; *Calendar of Home Office Papers,* 1760–65, pp. 54, 320, 322, 332.

9. On Oct. 19, 1763, Halifax wrote Governor Penn expressing the King's "Surprise and Displeasure" at the discovery, upon reading Amherst's dispatches, that the Pa. Assembly had "inflexibly persisted, in refusing or neglecting to pay any Regard to the pressing Instances" in which Amherst had urged measures of defense against the Indians. Upon reading this letter, Jan. 9, 1764, the House appointed a committee to review the general's letters to the governors of Pa. since news of the uprising had reached him in June. The committee reported at length, March 3, quoting Amherst's letters, stating what the colony had done in response, and vigorously denying any neglect. *Votes,* 1763–64, pp. 23–4, 53–7. Jackson's letter to BF of Nov. 12, 1763 (above, p.

to this,[1] to whom I have opined my Sentiments fully on the *General* Interests of America, especially those that may be affected by expected Measures in Parliament. I am much pleased with Mr. Allen.

A Revenue to be raised in America for the Support of British Troops is not now to [be] argued against: it would answer no Purpose to do so. I only contend that it should be built on a foundation consistent with the Constitutions of the Colonies, and on the Principles of Relation between the Mother Countries and her Colonies; it is not disputed that the M[othe]r Country is Mistress of the Trade of its Colonys, this Right has always been challenged and exercised, by England and all other Countries, the M C [Mother Country] may prohibit foreign Trade, it may therefore tax it. And the Colonys have a Compensation, in Protection but I dread internal Taxes.

I beg you will make my Compliments to Mr. Galloway. I shall always esteem myself much honoured as well as instructed by his Correspondence, and shall never think his Letters too frequent or too long, though great Variety of Business, and hurry of Spirits may shorten or obscure mine.

I agree perfectly with you in your sentiments about a Plethora of Money,[2] the Advantages of Commerce are derived from the Industry it inforced and the Money it gains should be impounded, that which passes into Circulation often does great Mischief, and casualy that impounded as all impounded things will sometimes do when they break down their Banks. Every Body speaks in favour of Col. Bouquet but those whose Business it should chiefly be to do

---

372), had also referred to the "ill Impressions" Amherst's dispatches had created.

1. Chief Justice William Allen (above, III, 296–7 n) had sailed for England, April 27, 1763, with his two daughters; he returned in August 1764. *Pa. Gaz.*, April 28, 1763; Aug. 16, 1764.

2. In his letter of March 8, 1763, BF had complained to Jackson of the great increase in prices in Pa. during his absence in England and attributed the rise chiefly "to the enormous Plenty of Money among us." The Crown had spent £800,000 sterling, he said, "for Provisions Carriages and other Necessaries in the Service" in Pa. alone, and the province had emitted between £500,000 and £600,000 in bills of credit, most of them still outstanding. The situation in N.J. and N.Y. was similar. See above, p. 209.

so, I do not mean but that some of them do so too.[3] It would have given me immense Pleasure to have seen Pittsburgh in its Prosperity in time of Peace, yet I do not despair, the Indian War is calamitous and the sufferers are to be pittied, yet I comfort myself with viewing the State of England after all the Ravages committed by the Danes.

I thank you for your good wishes as to my Marriage.[4] I assure you I have been chiefly prevented from Marrying by a Resolution I have taken to enjoy a full Political Independence, this I am sure I shall do while I remain single, I think I shall do so now even though I should marry, unless I should have 10 Children but that Number or any Near it is a strong Temptation in this Corrupted Country. I am too apt, besides to think all Conditions of Life like a Merchants Ledger ballanced at bottom though they differ at first sight in length, Value or other Circumstances, to be very entent about changing those I chance to be in. I am Dear Sir with the most unfeigned Esteem your most Obedient Affectionate humble Servant

R JACKSON

I inclose a List of Acts sent to me by Mr. Wilmott Agent for the Proprietors,[5] which I sent a Duplicate of by the last Packet to you and intended but omitted sending this to Mr. Galloway.

Dr. Pringle altogether declines any Concern in our Schemes,[6] only because he says he makes it a Rule to prevent Views of Profit from intruding on the Quiet necessary a Life of Literary Pursuit and Speculation.

3. In the same letter BF had praised the military and civil government at Pittsburgh under Col. Henry Bouquet, and Jackson was probably hitting at Amherst here for not sufficiently commending the colonel.

4. In the concluding sentence of the first part of the same letter BF had wished his bachelor friend "every kind of Happiness, and among the rest that of a good Wife, when you chuse it." Jackson never did marry.

5. The Pa. acts of which Henry Wilmot had sent a list were those passed on March 4 and April 2, 1763, referred by the Privy Council to the Board of Trade on December 9 and 15, and allowed to remain in force through lapse of time. *Statutes at Large, Pa.*, VI, 230–93; *Acts Privy Coun., Col.*, IV, 809; *Board of Trade Journal*, 1759–63, p. 425.

6. BF had suggested that Dr. John Pringle be allowed to take a share, along with Jackson and BF, in their prospective speculation in the Coxe land project; see above, p. 214.

Benjamin Franklin and John Foxcroft: Tables of Rates of Postage
Broadside: New Jersey Historical Society

Franklin and Foxcroft prepared this broadside for prominent display in every American post office. While it is undated, its use of the rate structure prescribed by the parliamentary act of 1710[7] indicates that it must have been drawn up before word of the new act of 1765[8] reached the colonies, and it seems probable that the two deputy postmasters general worked it out during one of their long periods together in 1763.

Most of this large sheet is given over to a table showing the rates for a single-sheet letter between any two of the forty-one post offices on the main route from Falmouth (the present Portland, Me.) to Norfolk, Va. It is constructed in somewhat the same form as that in which tables of mileages often appear on modern automobile road maps: a large right-angled triangle composed of boxes arranged in vertical columns and horizontal rows. Along the hypotenuse of the triangle are listed the names of the post offices in geographical order, each connecting with both a column and a row, and in the boxes are numbers representing pennyweights and grains of silver. These range from 1:8 (1 pennyweight, 8 grains) to 11.

To determine the rate between any two post offices along this route, the postal patron was to run his eye down the vertical column of boxes headed by the name of the more northerly of the two offices till it met the horizontal row of the more southerly office. The figure in the box at the intersection of the column and row indicated the number of pennyweights and grains of silver that a single-sheet letter would cost if sent in either direction between these towns. The cost in sterling money could then be figured at the rate of 3d. per pennyweight. The broadside gives no directions for converting the sterling cost into local currency, probably because the rates differed from colony to colony and from one date to another.

Two similar but smaller triangles of boxes provided information of the same sort for the route between New York City and Quebec and the inland route from New York to Boston via Hartford and Spring-

7. 9 Anne, c. 11, sect. 6. This section prescribed the rates, in considerable detail, between London and various places in Europe, London and the British West Indies, London and N.Y., and between the principal post offices then established in British North America. It also authorized the postmasters general to prescribe rates for American offices to be established in the future.

8. 5 George III, c. 25.

field. Below these tables the deputy postmasters general gave instructions for the use of the tables and supplementary information.

While it seems unnecessary to reproduce these tables in full, the explanatory text at the bottom as prepared by Franklin and Foxcroft is reprinted below, and some of the significant information derived from the tables themselves is summarized here.

The three tables list a total of 48 colonial post offices in operation in or about 1763. What was regarded as the principal office in each colony or geographical section was set in capitals and small capitals as indicated below. In order as shown on the tables the post offices were:

"Falmouth, in Casco-Bay,"; "Portsmouth, in New-Hampshire."

"In Massachusetts-Bay Government": Newbury, Ipswich, Salem, Marblehead, BOSTON.

"In Rhode-Island Government": Providence, Greenwich, Tower-hill,[9] NEWPORT, Westerly.

"In Connecticut Government": New-London, Guildford (Guilford), New-Haven, Stratford, Norwalk, Stanford (Stamford).

NEW YORK

"In New Jersey": Elizabeth-Town, Woodbridge and Perth-Amboy (combined), New-Brunswick, Prince-Town, Trenton, Bristol and Burlington (combined).

"In Pennsylvania": PHILADELPHIA, Newcastle and Wilmington (combined).

"In Maryland": Susquehanna, Joppa, Patapsco, ANNAPOLIS, Marlborough.

"In Virginia": Alexandria, Fredericksburg, Port-Royal, Hob's Hole (Tappahannock), Urbanna, WILLIAMSBURG, York, Hampton, Norfolk.

On the New York-Quebec route: Albany, Montreal, QUEBEC.

On the New York-Boston inland route: (New-Haven), Middletown, Hartford, Springfield, Worcester.

The lowest rate shown on any of the three tables was one pennyweight, eight grains (equal to 4*d*. sterling), which was charged as postage between any two offices not more than sixty miles apart.[1] The highest charge shown was 11 pennyweight (equal to 2*s*. 9*d*. sterling) for a letter between Falmouth and any office south of Alexandria, or

9. The landing place on the west side of Narragansett Bay for vessels to and from Newport.

1. While the act of 1770 established this rate for postage of single letters between New York City and places within sixty miles, it also specifically set the rate between New York and Perth Amboy at 6*d*. This table gave the rate as 4*d*., as it should have been in the act.

between any other office north of Boston and one beyond Williams-burg. A few representative rates, converted into sterling, were: Boston –New York, 1s.; Boston–Philadelphia, 1s. 9d.; Boston–Williams-burg, 2s. 6d.; New York–Philadelphia, 9d.; New York–Annapolis, 1s.; New York–Williamsburg, 1s. 3d.; Philadelphia–Annapolis, 9d.; Philadelphia–Williamsburg, 1s.; Annapolis–Williamsburg, 1s.

[1763]

TABLES of the Port of all Single LETTERS, carried by Post in North-America, as establish'd by Act of Parliament in the Ninth Year of the Reign of Her late Majesty Queen ANNE, Entitled, *An Act for Establishing a* General Post-Office, *for all Her Majesty's Dominions.*

Rated in *Penny-weights* and *Grains* of Silver, at Three-Pence *Sterling* for each *Penny-weight.*

[*Here follow the tables described in the headnote.*]

EXPLANATION.

These TABLES shew the Rate of a Single Letter, from any one Post-Office to another, *viz.* by the Figure, or Figures, set down at the Angle of Meeting, or in the Square which points to both Places.

EXAMPLE.

To know the Postage of a Letter from New-York, to Williamsburg: Look in the Table for New-York, and thence carry your Eye strait down until it comes opposite to Williamsburg, and in that Point of Meeting you'll find [5] which is Five Penny-weight of Silver, for the Port of a Single Letter between those Two Offices.

I. The Rates set down in these Tables must be doubled for all Double Letters, and trebled for all Treble Letters, and for every Ounce Weight Four times as much must be charged as is here set down.

II. All Ship-Letters and Packets must be charged, over and above the Rates set down in these Tables, with 16 Grains Weight of Silver, for such as are received from on Board; and with 8 Grains Weight, for such as are directed on Board any Ship or Vessel: And the whole Postage of these last Sort, must be paid down at the Post-Office where such Letters and Packets are delivered in.

III. For all extraordinary Posts and Expresses sent along the Post Road, and for all Expresses sent from any Stage to any Place out of the Post Road, there must be charged and paid One Penny-weight of Silver for every Mile such Express shall be sent.

Note, *In the above Tables, the several Places are ranged as they lye in the Course or present Route of the Post.*

B. FRANKLIN.
J. FOXCROFT.

Woodbridge: *Printed by James Parker, by Order of the Post-Master General: Note, These Tables are to be pasted on a Board, and hung up in open View, in the most convenient Place in each respective Post-Office.*

A Scheme for a Western Settlement

Draft (fragment): American Philosophical Society

This draft of a memoir in Franklin's hand survives only in the lower two-thirds of one leaf, written on both sides. The mention of the writer's presence "in Connecticut in August last" indicates that it was written during the last four months of 1763 or the first seven months of 1764. Actually, Franklin was not in Connecticut during August 1763, having gone from New York to Newport by water on his way to Boston, but in July he did meet and discuss the Susquehannah Company's affairs with its agent, Eliphalet Dyer, in Greenwich, R.I., while recuperating at the Greenes' house after the first of his two traveling accidents.[2] On his return trip in October he passed through Connecticut and undoubtedly discussed the company with Joseph Chew, postmaster at New London and a lukewarm member of the company. Franklin's memory was not always exact on such details of time and place.

On the basis of Connecticut's sea-to-sea charter of 1662 and the Susquehannah Company's land purchase at Albany in 1754,[3] the company was actively promoting settlement in the Wyoming region of Pennsylvania in 1762 and 1763. Vigorous opposition developed in several quarters: the Penns and their local officials, the Delaware and Iroquois Indians, Sir William Johnson, and the British government.[4]

2. See above, pp. 278 n, 318–19 n.
3. See above, v, 350 n, and map p. 225.
4. For a discussion of the company's activities during these years and the opposition to it and for related documents, see Julian P. Boyd, ed., *The Susquehannah Company Papers,* II (Wilkes-Barré, 1930), introduction and pp. 119–284; *Johnson Papers,* IV, 106, 118–19.

Dyer went to England in the late summer of 1763 on an ill-timed and fruitless mission to secure a royal charter for the company. Precisely what Franklin thought of the whole project is not clear and there are somewhat conflicting contemporary statements of his views. The company's claims and some of its plans must have seemed to him unrealistic, and its dealings with the Indians highly questionable; on the other hand, he may have been privately pleased that it was causing trouble to Thomas Penn, and his long-standing interest in western settlement may have aroused his sympathy for the company's major objectives.

Too little of this document survives to establish its immediate occasion or the full nature of the scheme he had in mind. From what does remain it seems possible that he thought that if the Susquehannah Company could secure royal sanction, if its proposed settlement did not encroach on lands justly claimed for any other colony, and if others than Connecticut residents were allowed to take shares in the enterprise, the company should be encouraged. Then (and only then) it could serve as the basis for an organized western settlement in which he and others equally interested might profitably invest.

[1763–1764]
[First part missing]
That every Contributor of *[blank]* Dollars, shall be entitled to a Quantity of Land equal to a Settler, for every such Sum of *[blank]* Dollars contributed and paid to the Company's Treasurer; and a Contributor for *[blank]* Shares to have an additional Share gratis. That Settlers may likewise be Contributors, and have Right to Land in both Capacities.

That Settlers and Contributors from all the Colonies shall be freely received into the Company, without Distinction, except a small Distinction in favour of the People of Connecticut, who shall have their Shares *[blank]* Dollars cheaper, in consideration of their Right to the Soil by Charter as aforesaid.

That the better to preserve the Good will of all the neighbouring Colonies to this intended new Settlement the Company will not attempt to settle on any Lands or interfere with any Grant now held by other Colonies, tho' subsequent to that of Connecticut.

[About five lines missing]
might be there allotted them, and Encouragement to Settle, &c.

The Assembly not doubting their Right to the Soil but apprehending some Inconveniencies might attend their maintaining a Jurisdiction in a Country divided from them by an intervening Province, took Time to consider till the October Session.[5]

Since the Assembly rose, the Number of the Petitioners are greatly increased; and when B.F. the Writer of this Memoir was in Connecticut in August last he was assured that not less than 1000 Families would be ready to move on the Grant of a Settlement. And being apply'd to for his Advice and Assistance in furthering and promoting such Settlement by some of the principal Persons of that Government, he heartily engag'd therein, as judging it might not only be a means of extending the [remainder missing].

Nathaniel Evans:[6] Verses Addressed to Benjamin Franklin

Printed in *The London Chronicle*, August 31–September 3, 1765; also printed (with modifications) in Nathaniel Evans, *Poems on Several Occasions, with Some Other Compositions* (Philadelphia, 1772), pp. 108–9.[7]

Precisely when Evans composed these verses cannot be established, but there seems to be no reason to disregard the statement in the sub-

5. While the Susquehannah Co. was politically strong in Conn., the governor and Assembly were careful at this time to keep the record clear that the company's project was a private venture and not directly or indirectly an activity of the colonial government. The printed records of the Assembly's May session of 1763 contain no references to the company's affairs. On Jan. 27, 1763, the British secretary of state, Lord Egremont, wrote Gov. Thomas Fitch expressing the King's displeasure at Conn. people's activity in the Susquehanna region and directing him to use "every legal Authority" and his "utmost Influence to prevent the prosecution of any such Settlement" until the issues were settled in England and fresh troubles with the Indians could be averted. Fitch transmitted these orders to the company and at a meeting on May 18, 1763, it voted that no member was to settle on the lands in question until the case could be laid before the King and his pleasure learned. Settlers already there were not withdrawn, however, nor did emigration to Wyoming wholly stop. Boyd, *Susquehannah Co. Papers*, II, xxxiii–xxxiv, 194–6, 218; *The Fitch Papers Correspondence and Documents during Thomas Fitch's Governorship of the Colony of Connecticut 1754–1766*, II (Hartford, 1920), 224–5, 232, 244–5, 246.

6. Nathaniel Evans (1742–1767), son of a Philadelphia merchant, Edward Evans, was a student at the Academy of Philadelphia for about six years before being apprenticed at a countinghouse. Finding the mercantile life uncongenial,

heading of the *London Chronicle* printing in 1765 that he wrote them in 1763. Franklin is known to have played his armonica for at least one visitor to his Philadelphia home even before the end of 1762;[8] friends' reports of his new instrument undoubtedly spread rapidly through the little city and many acquaintances must have found opportunity to hear it during the months before he set off on his travels to Virginia and New England or after his return in early November. That the *Chronicle* printed the verses in the late summer of 1765 while Evans was in London for ordination suggests strongly that he had brought them with him and either actively sought their publication or acquiesced when someone else, possibly William Strahan, asked him to make them available for the *Chronicle*.

When William Smith included them in the 1772 volume of Evans' poems, five years after the young man's death, the verses had undergone considerable change. Instead of the 48 lines in the 1765 printing, there were now only 30, and several of them differed in varying degrees from their earlier form.[9] In his preface to the book Smith stated with regard to the poems: "Many of them are *fragments,* and unfinished; and but few of them were revised by himself, with a view of their being pub-

---

he returned after his apprenticeship to the College of Philadelphia and on May 30, 1765, "on account of his great merit and promising genius," the trustees awarded him the M.A. degree on recommendation of the provost and faculty, although he had never taken the B.A. degree. He then went to England and received ordination from the Bishop of London. In December 1765 he returned to America and, under the auspices of the Society for the Propagation of the Gospel, assumed his charge as an Anglican missionary in Gloucester Co., N.J. Less than two years later he died of tuberculosis. A fellow passenger on his return voyage from England had been Elizabeth Graeme, WF's former sweetheart (above, VII, 177 n), and with her Evans conducted a poetical correspondence during his remaining years. To her and to his former teacher, William Smith, he left his poems, and in 1772 Smith published them, together with one of Evans' sermons. *DAB;* Edgar L. Pennington, *Nathaniel Evans A Poet of Colonial America* (Ocala, Fla., 1935). Along with Thomas Godfrey and Francis Hopkinson, Evans was probably one of the "young Muses" of Philadelphia, some of whose verses David Hall and BF had sent to Strahan and Whitefoord in December 1762; see above, pp. 167-8, 173.

7. The list of subscribers printed in the 1772 volume indicates that DF subscribed to one copy and WF to three.

8. A month after BF reached Philadelphia, Mrs. Ann Graeme, Elizabeth's mother, wrote her daughter that she had called at the Franklin home and had heard BF play. To Elizabeth Graeme, Dec. 3, 1762, *PMHB,* XXXIX (1915), 270-1.

9. The 1772 version also divided the whole into five stanzas of six, six, four, six, and eight lines respectively.

lished. Some corrections have, therefore, been made, where there appeared anything materially faulty in respect to Grammar, the exactness of the rhymes, &c. But in these the Publisher has been sparing, and has taken care that the Author's sense should in no case be deviated from."

In the light of this statement it is impossible to determine which of the changes in this piece Evans himself made and which Smith or his collaborator Elizabeth Graeme decided upon before sending the book to the printer. The 1765 version is reprinted here and the 1772 changes are all indicated in the notes.

To Benjamin Franklin, esq; ll.d. f.r.s.

Occasioned by hearing him play on the Armonica. Written in Philadelphia, 1763.[1]

Long had we, lost in grateful wonder, view'd[2]
Each gen'rous act thy patriot soul pursu'd;
Our little State resounds thy just applause,
And pleas'd from thee new fame and honour draws.[3]
Envy is now, by merit overthrown,
Oblig'd in thee superior worth to own.
The Muse to sacred virtue ever bound,
Beams the bright ray her glorious sons around;
And sure in thee those virtues are combin'd,[4]
That form the true pre-eminence of mind.[5]
How were we fixt with rapture and surprize,
When first you told the wonders of the skies!
By simple laws deducing truths sublime,
Before, deep-bosom'd in the womb of time.
With admiration struck, we did survey[6]
The lambent lightnings innocently play,

1. In the 1772 version "F.R.S." after bf's name and "Written in Philadelphia, 1763" are omitted.
2. In the 1772 version the first line reads: "In grateful wonder lost, long had we view'd."
3. The 1772 version omits the next four lines.
4. In the 1772 version this line reads: "In thee those various virtues are combin'd."
5. The 1772 version omits the next four lines.
6. In the 1772 version this line reads: "What wonder struck us when we did survey."

And the red thunder from th' ethereal round[7]
Burst the black clouds and harmless smite the ground,
As down thy ROD was seen the dreaded fire,
In a swift flame to vanish and expire:
Blest use of art! apply'd to serve mankind,
The noble province of the sapient mind![8]
This, this be wisdom's, this the sage's claim,
To trace the godhead thro' this wondrous frame;
For this the soul's grand faculties were giv'n,[9]
To search the chain connecting man with heav'n.
But not alone those weightier thoughts controul[1]
Thy comprehensive far-pervading soul;
The softer studies thy regard command,
And rise with fair refinement from thy hand.
Aided by thee, URANIA's heavenly art
With finer raptures charms th' extatic[2] heart;
Th' ARMONICA[3] shall join the sacred choir,
Fresh transports kindle, and new joys inspire.
Hark! the soft warblings, rolling[4] smooth and clear,
Strike with celestial ravishment the ear,
Conveying inward, as they sweetly roll,
A tide of melting music to the soul.
And sure if aught of mortal-moving strain,
Can touch with joy the high angelic train,

7. In the 1772 version this couplet and the next are transposed and revised. They now read: "And down thy rods beheld the dreaded fire / In a swift flame descend—and then expire; / While the red thunders, roaring loud around, / Burst the black clouds, and harmless smite the ground." After "rods" is an asterisk and Smith added a footnote: "Alluding to his noble discovery of the use of Pointed Rods of metal for saving houses from damage by lightning."

8. The 1772 version omits the next two lines.

9. In the 1772 version this couplet reads: "For this the soul's best faculties were giv'n, / To trace great nature's laws from earth to heav'n!"

1. For this and the next couplet the 1772 version substitutes a single one: "Yet not these themes alone thy thoughts command, / Each softer *science* owns thy fostering hand."

2. The 1772 version substitutes "feeling" for "extatic."

3. The 1772 version spells ARMONICA with an "H."

4. The 1772 version substitutes "sounding" for "rolling."

'Tis such a pure transcendent sound divine[5]
As breathes this heart-enchanting frame of thine.[6]
Shall not the Muse her slender tribute pay?
Her's is no venal, but the grateful lay;
Apollo bids it, where such virtues shine,
And pours a graceful sweetness thro' each line;
Her country too, responsive to the sound,
Swells the full note, and tells it all around.

From Peter Franklin

AL (incomplete): American Philosophical Society

Dear Brother   [1763?][7]
    These Comes to Inform you that I got Home well In three Days
after my Departure From you; I Have not met aney Good Oper-
tunity to Send for that money, Desire youd Imbrace the first Good
One that you Have.
    I would Beg one Favour that youd go to the Post Office and En-
qur whether there was a Letter for me, In the Time in that Time
that I was In Boston For my wife gave one to mr. Cambel[8] to Put
In the male and He Says He did, and whether Theye Ever thay Re-
turne Letter to the Place thay Come from after thay Ben there But
a week.

    5. In the 1772 version this couplet reads: " 'Tis this enchanting instrument
of thine, / Which speaks in accents more than half divine!"
    6. The 1772 version omits the remaining six lines.
    7. Peter Franklin (C.9) was in Boston with BF in the summer of 1763; on
Aug. 1, 1763, BF wrote Catharine Greene that his brother had returned to
Newport. See above, p. 317. Peter's mention in this note of having been in
Boston with BF strongly suggests that it was written in late July or in August
1763. But since Peter also visited BF in Philadelphia in December 1763 (see
above, p. 392), this note may instead have been written after his return from
that trip. Following editorial practice when dating within a year is uncertain,
it is placed at the end of the year.
    8. Not identified.

From Margaret Stevenson ALS: American Philosophical Society

This is the earliest surviving letter to Franklin from his London land-lady. The handwriting and spelling explain why she said in a later letter that "writing to me is an oddieus taske," and why relatively few letters from her exist. Comparing her letters and Deborah Franklin's on the one hand with those of their daughters on the other suggests that a considerable advance in female education may have taken place within a single generation in both English and American cities. The editors have done what they could to clarify many of her words but confess to uncertainty in some instances.

[1763?][9]

[*First part missing*] I hop you wont send for Morr but Come whar the light is,[1] doe my Dear Sir Bring your Beter half and your Dear girle and let her shine in this Country you cant doute. I doe not I am Shur She has Merits and her name is Franklin.

I have write to your Poor Pensioner[2] and exprist your Love in the kin[dest] Maner I am capeable. I expecit to have a letter of [theirs?] for you, I sent a Frank to Inclows it to me that I may forward It to you—as to the afair of Moneys.

[Dear] Sir you shall see I have of yours, Cash remaining in my hands and if I hade not your bills or orders shall be excusid. I have not sint In your forty Pound yeat to Messrs. Brown[3] Nor has Fin-low[4] cald to be Paid but I will goe to him as soon as I am able, for

9. This letter obviously falls in the period between Franklin's two English missions, but it is impossible to date it precisely. Mention here of Mrs. Steven-son's housemaid Naney (or Nancy) suggests that it was written before Aug. 30, 1763, for on that date Polly referred to the "poor girl" who was going to America (above, p. 334), and later references suggest that she was a former servant of Mrs. Stevenson. On Nov. 25, 1763, Polly told BF that "sometime before" her mother had written him "a long Letter" (above, p. 378), and this may be it. Hence it is printed here.

1. Perhaps Mrs. Stevenson is alluding to some candles which BF sent her and which Polly mentioned in her letter of Nov. 25, 1763; see above, p. 378.

2. Perhaps BF's first cousin, Anne Farrow (A.5.2.3.3) or her daughter, Hannah Farrow Walker (A.5.2.3.3.1).

3. For these orders on Henton Brown & Son which BF sent Mrs. Stevenson and for some of the articles which he commissioned her to buy, see above, pp. 377 n, 379. The editors have not discovered an order for £40 in her favor, although two orders of £20 each are recorded in BF's accounts with Henton Brown, Nov. 26, 1763. See above, p. 381.

4. Not identified.

I am verey ounwell, according to your Frass [*Phrase*]: but my Mood
of Exprission is, I am verey Bade. My Disorder is in my head; for
six weeks Past; I have a Constant Slow Pain and Hissing noass
[*noise*] in my head, that warrs [*worries*] me extreemley, I am shur
you wod not know your old Landlady. Mr. Small[5] adveiss [*advises*]
me to have the Opinion off the Docters. But Mr. Mead[6] says they
will draw a Bill of health own me, so I belive I shall take the Barke
and call in Dr. Pations [*Patience*] if he can atend me. I hop he will,
for I have woorket hard in Reaparing my Furniture, got Cold in and
at the same time my House was Painting for I assur you my Pations
has not binn much wasted at Fifteen too know verey littell Cribbag
and when I have plad not with out Sucksis Mrs. Gambirr[7] says with
her youshal [*usual*] Quicknsse it is to much; yeas Madam noe Madam.

Now I shall ask if you will send amrca [*American*] Lodgers to my
House if thay Love you thay shall Be well treeted, I have not want-
ed for Lodgers Nor good wons. As soon as my House was ready Sir
Jams was threetin [*thirteen*] Weeks at 2 gienes [*guineas*] and ½ per
week and only the furst Floor; and affter he Left me, a Gentle Man
of Kent and his 2 Neiss [*Nieces*] 3 Men Servant a Housekeeper and
Cook and my Naney [*or* Nancy?][8] is hous Maid. I dine with Mr.
Brockman &ct. whin I Pleas I have a litell Bead [*Bed*] in the Back
pallor and five gieneas per week: but the Season will Be soon over.
I have this day dined with them Drank your health and Eate a Tarte
maid of the Cranberris, which Pleasd Much. Thay dede not know
of it tell the Sarvant seat it one the Table. Pray Sir thank your Dear
good Woman for them and her kind letter not in the common Mood
of thanks, but what truly flows from a gratful harit, I hope one day
to tell Mrs. Franklin I Love her Dearly and truly.

My Letter or reather my writing Opliges [*apologizes*], for my neglecting to Corrspond with my Best freinds.

5. Probably BF's friend, Alexander Small, see above, IX, 110 n.
6. Probably Samuel Mead, see above, p. 60 n.
7. Mrs. Gambier was either Mrs. James Gambier, Samuel Mead's sister and
the mother of John and Samuel Gambier, public officials in the Bahamas to
whom BF sent goods in 1759, or the wife of John or Samuel. See above, VIII,
424 n, and this volume, pp. 60 n, 84–5 n.
8. For Mrs. Stevenson's servant, Ann Hardy, who spent several years in
America, see above, p. 334 n. It seems impossible to determine here or in
other letters whether the fourth letter in the name is intended as "e" or "c".
Both "Naney" (or "Nancy") and "Nancy" are nicknames for "Ann."

Pray Sir how Pritly you can flater. You tell me I need Escusse for not writing at all[.] well: I have an excuss, that my head akes and i will Excuss you if you will Excuss the Length of this and so litel you can make of it, and all that [I] desire is to be able to writte for you to read that I am Dear Sir Your Sincer Friend and Moste obliged humble Servant   MARGT STEVENSON

Timothy Folger: Petition to Sir Jeffery Amherst[9]

Draft: American Philosophical Society

The end of the war with France aroused great interest in possible new settlements not only in the West but also in the region to the northeast, particularly in Nova Scotia and the Island of St. John in the Gulf of St. Lawrence, now Prince Edward Island. It was natural that these maritime lands should seem especially attractive to the people of southeastern New England—Cape Cod, Martha's Vineyard, and Nantucket—for from new homes there they might be able to continue and expand the fishing and whaling activities in which they had long been engaged.

On May 1, 1764, Franklin wrote to Richard Jackson explaining the petition he had drafted for his relative Timothy Folger of Nantucket: "The Nantucket Whalers, who are mostly my Relations, wanted a Settlement there [the Island of St. John], their own Island being too full. At their Request I drew a Petition for them last Year, to General Amherst; but he had no Power to settle them any where. They are desirous of being somewhere in or near the Bay of St. Lawrence, where the Whale—as well as other—Fishing is excellent."[1]

"Last Year" dates this petition in 1763 and it is quite likely that Franklin drew it during his stay in Boston in the summer and fall. While there he probably met Keziah Folger Coffin[2] and perhaps also Timothy Folger, two of his Nantucket cousins. This draft of the petition, in Franklin's hand, remains among his papers.[3]

9. Timothy Folger (B.1.4.6.1.3), BF's first cousin twice removed, was a ship's captain of Nantucket Island and later BF's informant on the Gulf Stream. Amherst, the British commander-in-chief in North America during the latter years of the Seven Years' War (above, VIII, 328 n), returned to England in November 1763.

1. APS.

2. See above, p. 397 n.

3. Neither the *Board of Trade Journal* nor the *Acts Privy Coun., Col.*, mentions this petition.

To his Excellency Sir Jeffery Amherst, General of all his
   Majesty's Forces in America.

The Memorial and Petition of Timothy Folger of the Island of
   Nantucket in Behalf of himself and many others Inhabitants of
   the said Island,

Humbly Sheweth,
   That the chief Occupation of the Inhabitants of the said Island,
hath ever been the Cod and Whale Fishery in which they now employ above One hundred Sail of Vessels.
   That since the Reduction of Canada by his Majesty's Arms under
the Conduct of your Excellency, they have entred the great
Gulph of St. Laurence with their Whaling Vessels, and have met
with extraordinary Success there in that Fishery.
   That they could carry on the same with still greater Advantage
to themselves and to the Publick if they had some Settlement in or
near the said Gulph, which they might make a Home for themselves
and Families, and where the Land would be capable of producing
Corn and feeding Cattle for their better Subsistence. That some of
them did the last Summer look into several Harbours and Places
round the said Gulph of St. Laurence to see if any could be found
suitable for that purpose; and have reported, that the Island of St.
Johns, (which was early in the War reduced by your Excellency,
and the French Inhabitants removed) is extreamly well situated to
carry on the said Fishery, and has all the other Requisites for a comfortable Settlement.
   A considerable Number therefore of the Inhabitants of Nantucket, induc'd by these Conveniences, as well as for that they are
over populous and greatly straitned for Room in the Island they at
present inhabit, would remove to the said Island of St. Johns, if
they might be permitted so to do, and could obtain a Grant of Lands
there for their Settlement.
   And as many of them are desirous of making a Beginning there
the ensuing Summer, they humbly pray your Excellency to grant
them such Permission; and that you would also appoint Lands for
them on the said Island, to be held on such Terms and under such
Government as his Majesty in his Wisdom shall hereafter direct,
which Terms they have no doubt will be good and encouraging;

and that your Excellency would moreover in your Goodness recommend this Settlement to his Majesty that it may as soon as possible obtain the Royal Countenance and Protection.
And your Petitioners, as in Duty bound, shall ever pray, &c.

TIMO. FOLGER in Behalf
of the People of Nantucket

Endorsed: Petition of T. Folger to Gen Amherst

Index

Abdy, Catherine: identified, 185 n; to hear BF play armonica, 185
Academy of Philadelphia. *See* College of Philadelphia
Academy of Sciences, St. Petersburg, experiments with mercury at, 202
Adam, Robert: biographical note, 327 n; dedicates book to King, 327–8
Adams, John: on BF belief in de Fonte, 100 n; on WF appointment, 147 n; brings debt action for Williams, 358 n, 359
Aepinus, Franz Ulrich Theodor: writes on magnetism and electricity, 204–5, 266; books of, lent to Stiles, 267, 389; books of, lent to Winthrop, 267, 351
Agency: hostility toward BF's, 113; Jackson succeeds BF in, 115–16, 116 n, 246–7, 287; Assembly awaits BF advice on, 160; BF's 2d, in England, 169 n; BF's expense account, 195; salary to BF for, 196, 197; W. Smith on expenses of, 197 n; accounts settled, 206–8, 210, 236; no appointment yet made, 210; waste of money, disproved, 236; Jackson asks change in terms of, 341; as client of Brown, 379; Jackson reappointed to, 404; Jackson's serviceability to, 413
Air: effect of temperature on conductivity, 24–5; experiments in electrifying, 47–8; effect of, on fire, 103–4, 106; as conductor of sound, 131–2; electricity in, tested with bells, 150
Albany, N.Y.: to be on Quebec–N.Y. post road, 223; post office in, 418
Albemarle, Earl of, victorious at Havana, 168 n
Alexander, Robert: greetings to, 84; mentioned, 29
Alexander, William. *See* Stirling, Lord
Alexandria, Va.: Bernard, Jr., in, 353, 373, 390, 410; post office in, 418
Alison, Francis: to help choose topics for competition, 144 n; on Lib. Co. committee, 386
Allen, T., identified, 108 n
Allen, William: consulted about American affairs, 15; buys N.J. land, 157, 158, 163; signs report, 197; patron of B.

West, 233 n; dissatisfied with the Hicks, 263 n
Allison, M., in Brown account, 381
Amalia, Archduchess, armonica played at wedding of, 120–1
Amber: heat and conductivity in, 24; experiments with, 26, 111–12
America: climate in, 91–2, 264–5; arts and poetry in, 232–3; Britain to maintain troops in, 285
Ames, Nathaniel, BF visits, 278
Amherst, Sir Jeffery: requisitions for troops, 115 n, 405, 408; neglects to send Indian presents, 210–11; fails to return data on forces, 245; on postal service for Quebec, 253; hears of Pontiac uprising, 274 n; BF and Foxcroft visit, 277, 290; stops Webb settlement scheme, 286; explains Indian uprising, 295; responsibility for Indian troubles, 296 n; orders Conn. emigration halted, 319 n; excludes Pa. from 1761 return, 372; and Indian peace, 402 n, 404, 408; Pa. justified on complaints against, 414; fishery petition to, 429–31
Analysis of Oratory, BF patronage sought for, 75–6
Angel Inn, Oxford, BF to send books to, 133
Annapolis, Md., post office in, 418
Argo (ship), BF sponsors voyage of, 86
Argyle, Duke of, successful administrator, 328
Arlond, Miss, greetings to, 232
Armbrüster, Anthony (Anton): asks loan from BF, 289; letter from, 289
Armonica: general history of, 116–26; confusion about name, 118; great popularity of, 123; compositions for, 123; quality of music of, 124; efforts to improve, 124; decline in popularity of, 124; limitations and problems of, 124–5; as menace to health, 125; gradual disuse of, 125–6; played at BF-Mozart anniversary, 126 n; BF describes, 127–30; method of playing, 130; repaired for Rachel Johnston, 169; directions for making, 180–2; Hughes & Co. and James manufacture, 180; BF asked to

433

453

Rhode Island, post offices in, 418
Rice, change in law on exportation of, 243
Richardson, Samuel or William, publishes Watkinson book, 394
Roads, Benjamin, servant of, enlists, 364
Robbins, ——, order in favor of, 359
Roberts, William, *Hist. of Florida* sent to BF, 274
Robertson, William: historiographer to King, 328; histories by, 328
Robinson, Capt., commands *Harriot*, 218 n, 292 n
Robinson Crusoe, BF cites, 303
Robottom, George, bill of exchange in favor of, 134
Rockingham, Charles Watson-Wentworth, 2d Marquis of, vote in Lords recorded, 162 n
Rocque, Bartholomew: identified, 306 n; develops burnet, 306–7
Ronquillo, Strait and Sea of, purportedly in Canada, 87, 93, 95
Rooke, Mrs.: greetings to, 64, 68, 79, 85, 235, 298; health of, 334, 378
Rooke, Henry, identified, 370 n
Ross, John: signs committee report, 190, 197; and Sturgeon affair, 299 n
Rotation, laws of, 230
Royal Society: BF to show Canton paper to, 26; Winthrop recommended for membership in, 30; BF communicates letter to, 71; papers read to, 71 n, 74 n, 179 n; committee advises on chronometer test, 179–80 n; mercury experiments reported to, 202; BF election to, 311; Collinson to attend meeting, 340
Rum: Indians complain of lack of, 295, 304; sale of, to Indians, 339 n
Russell, Alexander, identified, 107 n
Russell, James: identified, 22 n; on BF's lightning-rod instructions, 22–3; expert on chimneys, 28; greetings to, 84, 146, 385
Russell, T., bill drawn by, 358, 359
Russell, William, identified, 107
Russians, travel descriptions by, 90–1, 94
Rutt, G., stock sold to, 34
Rymsdyck, Jan van, medical drawings by, sent to Pa. Hosp., 170

Sabbath observance, in Conn. compared with Flanders, 175–6
Sable, Cape, Folgers move to, 398
St. Andrews, University of, BF degree from, 113 n, 311
St. Clair, Sir John, lends chariot for BF, 200–1

St. John, Island of: petition for grant on, 429–31; suitable for fishing industry, 430
St. Lawrence, Gulf of, fishing success in, 430
St. Lazarus Archipelago, purportedly off Canada, 90
St. Petersburg: Stiles sends thermometer paper to, 178 n; mercury experiments at, 202
St. Pierre, to be French, 200 n
St. Vincent: to be British, 200 n; Montagu claims to, 414
Salem, Mass., post office in, 418
Salisbury, Eng., Strahan visits, 324
Saluzzo (Saluce), Count Giuseppe Angelo, on BF-Nollet controversy, 311
Sandusky, Ohio, Indians cut off at, 274 n
Sandwich, John Montagu, 4th Earl: biographical note, 412 n; in Ministry shuffle, 412
Santa Lucia: to be French, 200 n; Montagu claims to, 414
Sargent, George Arnold, at Eton, 365
Sargent, John: identified, 3 n; donates medals for Academy, 143–4; and colonizing plan, 209, 214, 366; letters from, 143–4, 365–6
Sargent, John, Jr., at Eton, 365
Sargent, Samuel, bill of exchange in favor of, 134
Sargent Aufrere & Co.: will cover drafts, 3–5, 11, 12–13, 35; BF gratitude to, 11–12; BF asks immediate reimbursement to, 12–13; discharge overdrawn bills, 33; have received 1759 parliamentary grant, 32–3; Trustees reimburse, 113–14; account with Pa. Loan Office, 134–5; send BF letter of credit, 144–5; agency draft on, 208; manifest sent to, 244; and Coxe grant, 369; in Brown account, 382; letters from, 3–4, 7–8, 11, 32–3, 113–15, 144–5; letters to 4–5, 9–10, 11–12; mentioned, 108 n
Savage, James, on identity of Gibbons, 98 n
Scarborough, H.M.S., convoys *Carolina*, 115 n, 166
School for Lovers, BF and Stevensons to attend, 67–8
Scotland: BF on hostility towards, 168; BF recalls travels in, 191; contrasting administrations of, 328
Scots Magazine, The, describes *Elements of Criticism*, 27 n
Sea level, differences in, 93
Seal of Pa., refused for Jackson appointment, 247 n
Seals, royal, order of authority, 370 n